LR Perfection

A Complete Guide to Perfecting the Logical Reasoning Section for the Intermediate/Advanced LSAT Student

DRAGON
TEST

To my students, may you conquer life as you conquered the LSAT, through introspection and devotion.

Table of Contents

1. Knowledge, Habits, and Patterns

The Problem

Getting this book means you are probably struggling with LR. Perhaps there are a few types of questions that you have trouble with, perhaps you have read all the books you can find on the market and have gone through hundreds of LR questions but saw no significant improvement. Whether you are getting five questions wrong per LR section or just two or three, that has been the case for a while now. You tried doing more questions, found more resources, asked questions online, looked at explanations to specific questions, or even spoke to a tutor, but you are nowhere close to that elusive 100% accuracy rate.

But not all hope is lost! Like the Logic Games section, LR is an entirely learnable section. With self-reflection and drilling, there's no reason why we cannot consistently attain a perfect score on this section. For the majority of students, the reason we struggle so much with LR is due to our approach.

How most students study for LR, and why it's not the most effective

Most of us, me included, followed a traditional approach to studying for the Logic Reasoning section. I started by reading the available prep books on the market, did the questions at the end of each chapter, and started doing LR sections.

During the early phase, I saw fairly decent improvements. After initial practice, I got my error rate down to approximately -5 to -3 per section. But then, I plateaued. I would do section after section of questions, make mistakes, study my errors, go to online LSAT forums, look at the questions I got wrong or didn't understand, and kept on grinding.

But my error rate stayed around -3. The wrong questions piled up. I was frustrated and even wrote out all my mistakes into one giant word document. My notes were close to a hundred pages long, complete with the stimulus, answer choices, and explanations in my own words.

But still, my accuracy rate was not improving. Occasionally, on a really good section, I would get a -1, but most times, I made two to three mistakes. Like many advanced students, I was doing well in the Logic Games, and I wondered if it was ever possible to attain a perfect score in LR as I had in LG.

I returned to the prep books I bought, reread them, and took more notes. I printed my notes out so I could refer back to them even as I practiced. But I was still stuck, still making mistakes, still getting frustrated.

It was then that I had a realization. The LR prep books I bought taught me the basics of tackling different LR questions. The rules and theory they imparted sufficed for simpler questions, but on the more difficult questions, they were not enough. Questions got more difficult as you progressed through a section, and I kept making mistakes in the Q15 to Q25 range. Even when I slowed down or referred back to the books and my notes, I was still not understanding the stimulus or getting stuck between two answer choices and kept on picking the wrong one.

My Journey

So I knew there was a knowledge gap between the test prep materials and what I needed to get a perfect score on LR. This knowledge was not readily available on the market, and I had to compile it myself. I began to look at each flaw question and compared them to lists of logical fallacies. I read up on philosophy and studied formal and informal logic. Eventually, I was at a point where I had more than enough tools in my arsenal to attack the LR section.

Too much knowledge can also be a curse: focus on habits

But my confidence was short-lived. A new problem arose. On an actual timed PT, I had only a minute or two to tackle each question. I didn't have enough time to slow down, dissect each stimulus, and apply all the knowledge I had gathered. My thinking was hazy, and I had to rely on intuition. I went through the questions mechanically, selecting answers because they appeared right. If you had asked me why I picked answer choice A over B, I couldn't have given you a coherent, legitimate answer. I was able to think things through untimed, but under time constraints, it was as if I was a completely different person.

You see, the LSAT is such a fast-paced test that you really won't have enough time to do an in-depth examination of each individual question. With the added stress of exam day and the grueling crucible of multiple sections one after the other, your mind will most likely be in a haze during the entire test. You may or may not have enough time to go back and double-check your answers, and you will most definitely miss certain aspects of questions during the exam itself. As a result, whether during a timed PT or the actual exam itself, you will be falling back on your involuntary habits. Learning from your mistakes and building up that knowledge base is helpful when you slow down and review your answer choices, but that doesn't mean anything if we cannot apply all that knowledge on the actual test itself. The actual test is a test of habits, and perfection is still far away unless we can fundamentally rewire our test-taking habits.

But how can we change our involuntary habits through practice? I reviewed the questions I got wrong, and it appeared that I was able to understand this specific question. But if a similar question appeared three months from now and I only had a minute left, how do I make sure that I won't make the same mistake?

I began to look for ways to upgrade my habits. What are some of the things that I can do, subconsciously and involuntarily, that can help me pick the "correct" answer choice even when I'm nervous and pressed for time? Why did my intuition work for the easier questions but end up failing me when it came to harder questions? This was the most significant obstacle I faced, but at least I have located the key problem!

Reconstructing an LR stimulus

At this point, I began to drill LR questions by type. I worked through the easier questions and spent most of my time focusing on the more difficult ones. By comparing easier questions and the most difficult questions of the same type, I came to the most critical realization thus far:

> While the fundamentals of approaching a specific question type remain the same between easier and more difficult questions, the test makers will throw in a lot more variation in both the stimulus and the answer choices as the questions grow harder.

I actively sought out these variations, taking the hardest LR questions and simplifying them, stripping away the traps and difficult traits until just the barebones were left. Eventually, after looking at thousands of questions, many of them a dozen times or more, I boiled it down to five different areas where the test makers can tinker to increase the difficulty of a question.

***

Let's look at an example now and you'll immediately see what I'm talking about.

The majority of LR stimuli will contain an argument. Let's start with something super simple.

Original Argument: *All JD students need to have completed an undergraduate degree. Joshua is going to law school; therefore, he must have graduated college.*

This is simple enough, right? You probably had no trouble figuring out what's the premise and what's the conclusion in this argument.

The first area where test makers can mess with us is by adding uncertainty to the **structure** of the argument. Simply put, analyzing an argument's structure is to differentiate the supporting premises from the main conclusion. Let's throw some confusion into the mix:

Variation 1: *Joshua is going to law school and has graduated college; thus all JD students need to have completed an undergraduate degree.*

Or:

Variation 2*: Joshua is going to law school and must have graduated college; we know all JD students need to have completed an undergraduate degree.*

By simply switching up the sequence of statements and adding certain keywords into the mix, detecting the main conclusion of the argument suddenly became a lot more treacherous. Variation 1 is using Joshua as an example and making a generalization about "all JD students." The conclusion is that "all JD students need to have completed an undergraduate degree." In Variation 2; however, the conclusion is that "Joshua must have graduated college."

***

Let's keep on building up Variation #2. This time let's crank up the difficulty of the **logic** behind the argument:

Variation 2.1: *Joshua is going to law school and must have graduated college; we know all JD students need to have completed an undergraduate degree. As a result, Joshua's studiousness will cause him to become a successful attorney.*

The argument is now getting more convoluted, gaps are starting to appear in its reasoning. The main conclusion of the argument has changed yet again. The previous main conclusion is now the intermediate conclusion. Now the main conclusion is about Joshua's studiousness causing him to become a successful attorney. The conclusion contains causal logic (studiousness *cause him to become* a successful attorney). The premises, on the other hand, contain conditional logic (*all* JD students *need* to have completed an undergraduate degree).

***

How did we go from premises about Law Students → Completed Undergraduate to a conclusion about studiousness *causing* Joshua to become a successful attorney? I've deliberately made this unwarranted jump in the argument. Test makers do this all the time. In both assumption family questions and harder non-assumption family questions, the test makers will leave out critical parts of the argument on purpose. It's our job to fill in the blanks or to come up with the author's **assumptions** as we dissect an argument.

Here, I'm assuming that JD students go on to become attorneys, and that completing college is a sign of a student's studiousness. These were left unsaid in the argument, but they are just as crucial to understanding the argument.

> Variations in structure, logic, and unstated assumptions are the three key areas that distinguish harder question stimuli from easier question stimuli. We will look at all of these in turn.

***

Even when we get good at simplifying/clarifying a complex stimulus, the test makers will throw in additional traps in the answer choices. This can happen in three ways:

Deliberately vague answers

In questions such as Role, Method, and Flaw types, the answer choices can be so *abstract* that we won't, at first glance, have any idea of what it's trying to say. In the chapters on these question types, we will practice drills in translating vague and abstract answer choices and try to match them up with the stimulus.

Answer choices that are *open to interpretation* are also especially tricky, especially in Strengthen/Weaken Question types. These answer choices can either help or hurt an argument, depending on how you view it. Because they are so pressed for time, many students end up only seeing one side of the picture.

Seemingly legitimate answers with one or two bad keywords

You have seen these trap answers before. Everything looks fine except for one or two words. **Keyword Extraction** is a habit that we will practice again and again throughout this book. We will examine how certain keywords can make or break an answer choice.

Multiple attractive answer choices

In Strengthen, Weaken, and MSS Questions (and a few other question types to a lesser extent), we often find multiple answer choices that all seem to fit the bill. Many intermediate/advanced students will have no problem narrowing the answer choices down to two attractive answers but still end up picking the wrong one. We will look at different types of correct answer choices, why certain types of answer choices are preferable, and practice the habit of **ranking answers**.

Answer choice ranking is also a core skill in RC, but that's another topic reserved for another book.

***

Structure, Logic, Assumptions, Keywords, and Ranking answers form the five core sectors we must strive to improve during our practice (SLAKR). The goal is to practice these incessantly until they become natural habits to us. These core skills are the tools we need to navigate the hardest LR questions successfully, and when these habits become second nature to us, so will the results speak for themselves. By analyzing these five elements of all the questions that I had gotten wrong or flagged, I was finally able to consistently score in the -1, -0 range on the LR section. On the eve of my test, I made an average one mistake per four sections of LR. I got extremely lucky and eventually scored a 180.

The Final Element: Intra-Question Pattern Perception

After taking the LSAT, I began to tutor the test. It was recreationally at first, but as more students approached me, it soon became a full-time job. Due to COVID restrictions, I quit my job at a fintech start-up to teach the LSAT. I will be applying to law school this year or the next.

I've worked with over 200 students preparing the LSAT during the last two years. More than half scored over 170, and just under a third scored in the 175-180 range. While score inflation since COVID is a real phenomenon, I'm nonetheless convinced that my methods are truly effective in helping students attain the score they desire.

Working with students had an added benefit that learning the test on my own didn't provide. It forced me to explain a question so that others may understand it as clearly as I did. Knowing how to do a question is one thing, but being able to explain it is different.

We also must know *why* students got this question wrong, and most importantly, devise drills and recommend similar questions for them to practice, so they can upgrade their knowledge and habits to never make the same mistake again.

The last two years also forced me to look at the test more in-depth than I had ever anticipated. Other than the knowledge and habits I discovered were crucial to LR success, I saw additional patterns emerging within each question type. I returned to the drawing board, redid all the questions of harder and hardest difficulty from PT1 to PT90, and categorized them according to the patterns that I perceived.

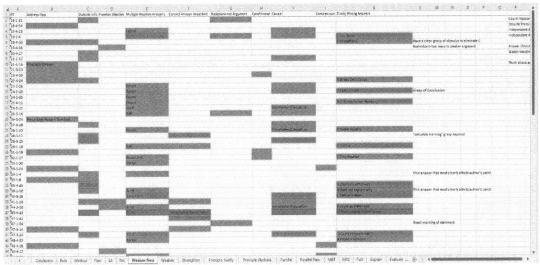

Categorization of harder LR questions by intra-question type features

Recognizing patterns within a specific question type had an unforeseeable hidden benefit: it made my tutoring much more efficient. Whenever a student came to me with a specific question, we would not only dissect it via the SLAKR method, but I could pinpoint the error they committed and point to another dozen additional questions with similar traps as additional practice. This was truly helpful in preventing one from making the same mistake again.

Finally, recognizing certain archetypes within a specific question type will help you save precious time on the exam. While others are busily trying to understand a stimulus, you already see the potential traps and pitfalls and can spend most of your time analyzing each question on a deeper level.

In this book, I've listed the most representative patterns pertaining to the hardest questions of each question type. You don't need to memorize these, only to recognize them if they appear in practice or on the actual exam.

In order to attain perfection, focus on the hardest questions of each type

I strongly recommend the intermediate/advanced student to focus on the hardest questions of each type in practice. As we saw in the example from the beginning of this book, if you can learn to dissect a question with a complicated structure, confusing logic, and gaps in its reasoning, easier questions will almost seem like a joke. By focusing on the hardest questions, we are also saving our energy to reflect on our mistakes, upgrading our knowledge and habits as needed, and avoiding burnout. Lastly, because the hardest questions have so many issues that needs to be considered, they force us to be more observant in the test-taking process, thus simultaneously helping us avoid careless mistakes.

The LR questions contained in this book are among the hardest to ever appear on the LSAT. Don't be afraid to get them wrong. Each failure is an opportunity to upgrade our test-taking strategies.

The book's last chapter (22) gives you a detailed outline on how to practice LR questions in conjunction with this book. **Go ahead and take a look now**. We want to read each chapter, familiarize ourselves with the difficult traits associated with that question type, and practice as many questions of that type as we can.

> After each chapter, practice that question type to consolidate the knowledge that you've just learned! Think about the difficult traits that fooled you in each of the chapters and take those insights with you into practice. Are you still making the same mistakes? Can your mistakes be tied into the traps described in this book?

I would say at least **50** practice questions per question type would be the minimum, and upwards of a **hundred** questions was not uncommon for my students. For rarer types, practice at least 10-20 of the hardest questions, make sure you've mastered all the content from the associated chapter, before moving on.

For example, after reading Chapter 3, Find the Conclusion. You should use a program like adeptLR, lsatlab, or 7sage and start practicing Find the Conclusion Questions. I would keep in mind all the things I learned in Chapter 3 and see if I can spot these patterns as I practice.

Start at a difficulty level that you are comfortable with. LR questions are commonly divided into five difficulty levels. For example, if Level 3 Find the Conclusion questions are where I am beginning to make mistakes, I would continue to drill them until my accuracy and timing are consistent. Then I would move to Level 4 questions and, finally, level 5. If your goal is to perfect the LR section, only move to the next question type **after** you feel comfortable with the Level 5 questions of the previous type.

After finishing the entire book, I would keep it on the side as a reference book as you move into drilling entire sections or full PTs. Whenever you encounter difficult questions, refer back to the relevant chapters and see if what you are struggling with is one of the difficult traits we've discussed.

Throughout this book, over 200 of the hardest LR questions are discussed, 125 of them in painstaking detail. Try to figure out these questions before looking at the answer choices. Also be sure to read my explanations not just for the questions you got wrong, but all of them. Be sure to know why all the wrong answers were incorrect, rather than jumping straight to the correct answer.

Do you really need a tutor?

Before we finish this chapter, I just wanted to say a few words about the proper role of a tutor in your LSAT prep journey. Are tutors helpful, and who would benefit from hiring one? What should we look for in one?

First, a tutor is only helpful when you are stuck. If you are a beginner, then the materials available on the market are more than enough to get you started. If you are an intermediate/advanced student and are showing steady improvement from self-studying, then keep doing what you are doing! No need for a tutor either.

A tutor can be helpful if your progress is stagnating, or when you have a list of specific questions you can't find answers to anywhere else. But even then, there are certain qualities that we should look for in a tutor.

Most tutors will simply explain your question and leave it at that. But as we have seen, the LSAT will be a test of habits and understanding. So understanding one question doesn't help us unless we can repeat the process on a similar question down the road.

As a result, you want someone who can look at the mistake you made and tell right away *WHY* you made such a mistake. Is it due to bad habits? Is it due to insufficient knowledge? Can they give you drills to overcome such deficiencies and point to similar questions for you to practice?

Lastly, do not become too dependent on your tutor. The LSAT heavily relies on your ability to recognize patterns and traps. This ability is something you need to actively train for to succeed on the actual exam. A tutor may point you in the right direction and give you hints, but come exam day, you alone are reading over each argument, simplifying them, and evaluating them.

In terms of tutor recommendations I would go with someone who has an established track record and verifiable publications. You want someone who is not just a high scorer doing this just for the summer before law school, but someone who has experience teaching and can adapt their methods to your learning style. You also want someone who has published books or articles on the topic, so that you can look at what they have written and decide whether that fits your particular learning style as well. Don't be afraid to challenge your tutor, get on their nerves and see if they become defensive. You want someone who provides a safe learning environment. Only when you are completely comfortable can you start to learn. You want someone who is not trying to convince you that they are right but show you how you can tweak your methods so that you can be right too. This narrows down the field exponentially. I no longer tutor students, although there are tutors that I've vetted active in the LSAT Dragon discord.

My goal in writing this book

Some of my students went on to become tutors for test prep companies, and I was approached in early 2022 with a book deal by an internationally based education company. I ultimately went my own way, self-publishing since I wanted to retain the book's IP. Materials currently on the market are either rudimentary or rely on intuition that only caters to the most perceptive of students.

I wanted to write an all-encompassing book for the student aiming for 170+, for the student set on becoming a master of Logic Reasoning. I wanted to reveal the secrets of the LR section, along with its hidden traits and traps, information that can help all intermediate/advanced students attain a perfect score. I hope this book does the job and is worth your time.

The intended audience of this book is someone who already has a grasp of the fundamentals of LR, someone who has plateaued at maybe 3-5 errors per section and just wants to do better. (Although I've had readers who were making 5+ mistakes per LR section tell me they found the book helpful as well!)

If you are an absolute beginner though, it may be better to check out some resources intended for a more novice audience. I have written a **Beginner Guide** and a **175 Mastery Guide** on my website where I list my recommendations on resources and tips on studying for someone just starting out.

If you are struggling with RC, be sure to check out my other book, **RC Perfection**, also available on Amazon. Four chapters of that book are also available as a free preview on my website, so go take a look if you haven't already.

My apologies for any mistakes or typos you may encounter. This was a one-person effort until Sabrina, my editor, bravely came to my rescue. If you spot any issues, have any advice for improvement, or any LSAT-related questions or comments, do email me at joshua@dragontest.org. If you would like additional information or guidance, you can also check my website www.dragontest.org or join my discord group where I try to provide help and advice regularly.

Chinese speaking students may opt to add me on WeChat (作者微信号)：Lsatdragon（可获取一节免费一对一答疑课）

Lastly, I'd like to thank Yibo Zhang for giving me the courage to embark upon this endeavor, and Sabrina Musgrave, my editor, who tireless sought out the shortcomings I could not see.

Good luck and I'll see you on the other side!

2. Core Habit:
STRUCTURE

Always correctly identify the conclusions and supporting premises whenever there is an argument in the stimulus

Why is it important to understand the structure of an argument?

In the previous chapter, we discussed the five most important questions to ask ourselves when facing a challenging Logical Reasoning question. By asking ourselves these questions, we are developing the habits crucial to LR success:

- How is the stimulus **structured**, or what are the author's premises and conclusion?

- What kind of argumentative technique or type of **logic** is used?

- Are there any gaps or logical leaps in the author's reasoning? Does the author make any **assumptions** in the argument?

- Are there **keywords** (nouns, verbs, adjectives/adverbs) in answer choices that seem unclear or suspicious?

- If there are no seemingly perfect answer choices, how would you **rank** them?

For most LR questions, we need to follow these five steps in linear fashion. We cannot try to identify gaps in the author's reasoning if we don't know what is the reasoning employed; similarly, we cannot be sure of the type of logical reasoning/argumentative technique the author used to go from premise to conclusion if we don't know which sentence is the premise or which sentence is the conclusion. So, to answer question 3, we must have already answered question 2, and to answer question 2, we must have already answered question 1.

To solve Find the Conclusion/Main Point Questions, all we do is determine the argument's **structure**.

That's why we start our journey by looking at Find the Conclusion/Main Point questions.

For the student who already has an intermediate grasp of Logical Reasoning questions, we know that LR questions can be divided roughly into the following types:

- Find the Conclusion/Main Point
- Role
- Method of Reasoning
- Sufficient Assumption
- Necessary Assumption
- Flaw
- Strengthen
- Weaken
- Parallel (Parallel Argument + Parallel Flaw)
- Principle (Principle Justify + Principle Example)
- Must be True/Must be False
- Most Strongly Supported
- Explain a Result/Explain a Difference
- Point of Agreement/Disagreement

Out of these questions, only Must be True, Most Strongly Supported, Explain a Result, and Point of Agreement/Disagreement questions are **not** dependent on structurally analyzing the stimulus.

> In other words, in most LR question types, your first and foremost job is to determine the author's conclusion, and the support provided for it. Understanding an argument's structure basically means knowing which statement is the conclusion, and which statements are the premises.

Success in Find the Conclusion/Main Point Questions, and to a lesser extent, Role and Method of Reasoning Questions, are so heavily dependent on having a solid grasp of the structure of the stimulus that in all my tutoring sessions, I've always started with these. Not only do they force us to get into the habit of systematically looking at each question's structural makeup, but they also lay the foundation for having a coherent method for tackling the most challenging LR questions down the road.

Arguments and Conclusions

Before we dive into Find the Conclusion/Main Point Questions, it is important to remember that behind every conclusion, there is an argument. The word "argument" often appears on the LSAT; too often, we don't think too much about it, but it's a word not to be taken lightly.

So what is an argument?

An argument is an author's viewpoint, opinion, or decision supported by additional premises and evidence.

An argument is not simply a statement of fact or opinion without any support.

> An argument will always contain a premise, main conclusion, and maybe an intermediate conclusion.

Take a look at the following:

- *George Washington was the first president of the United States.*
- *Russia is the largest country in the world; its official language is Russian.*
- *Justice Scalia was a member of the Supreme Court of the United States.*
- *Water consists of hydrogen and oxygen.*

All of the above are FACTS. They are not independent arguments. Facts can be used in a logical reasoning stimulus as support and evidence. They can be used as premises to support a conclusion and as background information to better explain or situate the argument, but they are not arguments by themselves.

Now take a look at these:

- *We should attend the highest-ranked law school that we got into.*
- *I will take the train from New York to Boston instead of flying.*
- *Punishment should be proportional to the crime committed.*
- *All swans are white.*

Are these facts also? The first and second statements most definitely are not. The first, "*we should attend the highest ranked law school that we got into*" is an OPINION, and a common one at that, but it is not set in stone and thus debatable. I can argue that we should go to the school that gave us the most scholarship, or the one closest to my home. An OPINION, by itself, is not an argument.

The second statement is a DECISION. Independently, it does not suffice as a standalone argument either. But decisions, like opinions, can play the part of either the premise or the conclusion in an ARGUMENT. (Remember FACTS can only ever be used as premises in an Argument.) If we only slightly modify the statement above, we can come up with a pretty good argument:

> *Because I enjoy train travel and hate airport security, I will take the train from New York to Boston instead of flying.*

Here, simply by adding a premise ("*because I enjoy train travel and hate airport security*"), we have a coherent argument. By providing the rationale behind my decision to take the train, I have support for a decision/opinion, and together, they constitute an argument.

But the same statement can be equally effective as a premise as well:

> *Because I will be taking the train from New York to Boston instead of flying, I can bring full-sized toiletries in my carry-on luggage.*

Here, the same statement just used as a conclusion is now a premise. It's being used to support the statement on what I can bring with me on my trip to Boston.

The third and fourth statements are a little bit trickier. The third statement can potentially be construed as a fact, but I prefer to consider it a PRINCIPLE. Principles will come up later on in related chapters, but for now, all we have to keep in mind is that principles have two important characteristics:

> A principle can be used to guide our actions or decisions; it is normative/directive in nature.

Principles can be debated: we can argue that proportionality shouldn't apply in all situations (perhaps heavier punishment is called for when the crime is especially heinous), or that they shouldn't apply to all people (perhaps exceptions should be made for underaged offenders). As a result, PRINCIPLES can appear as premises OR conclusions in an LR stimulus. For example:

> *Because punishment should be proportional to the crime committed, John should not receive the death penalty for stealing a loaf of bread.* (Principle as a premise)

> *Because justice is the heart and soul of any form of legal sanction, punishment should be proportional to the crime committed.* (Principle as a conclusion)

Now the last statement, "*all swans are white*":

What we have here is a GENERALIZATION. A generalization can often look and feel like a fact or a principle, but there are subtle differences involved:

> Generalizations take individual findings and come up with an overarching summary or rule; it is descriptive in nature.

Principles are concerned with what should be done or ought to be done; generalizations are concerned with what things actually are.

Sometimes, the distinction between the two is blurred. What appears to be a generalization may also work as a guiding principle in the author's argument, and vice versa. But for now, just be aware of the existence of these two discrete concepts.

Generalizations, like principles, appear in LR stimuli and answer choices frequently. Like principles, opinions, and decisions, generalizations can work as both premises or conclusions:

> *All swans are white; the birds I saw in the lake are swans, so they must be white.*

> *All the swans I have ever seen were white; therefore, all swans are white.*

So that's a short introduction on the nature of statements appearing in LR stimuli: Facts, opinions, decisions, principles, and generalizations make up the majority. Facts cannot appear as conclusions in an argument, but the others can. Keep in mind that arguments will always have support, and individual statements without support are NOT considered arguments.

Elements of a Logical Reasoning Stimulus

So now that we have taken a closer look at how facts, opinions, decisions, principles and generalizations can all make up an LR argument, let's look at how arguments are structured in the LR stimulus.

At the core of most LR stimuli will be an argument (I would say > 80% of all LR stimuli contain an argument). An argument will consist of premises and a conclusion, and if that's the only information presented in a stimulus, our job would be so much easier.

But instead, most LR stimuli will also contain many peripheral elements.

When reading an LR stimulus, our job is to *separate* the **core information** (premise, intermediate conclusion, and main conclusion) from the **peripheral information** (background information, opposing viewpoints, and concessions).

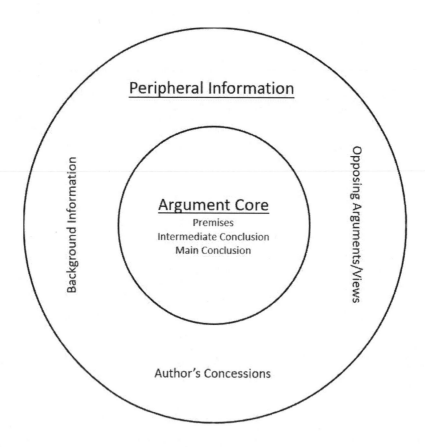

Let's look at each of these elements in detail:

The Argument Core:

<u>Main Conclusion</u>:

Hands down the most important part of any LR stimulus. *It is the point the author is trying to get across.* The conclusion is supported by premises and sometimes the intermediate conclusion. Every time I approach a question that is NOT a Must be True, Most Strongly Supported, Explain a Result, and Agree/Disagree question, I'm always sifting through the stimulus and asking myself, what is the author's conclusion?

<u>Premise</u>:

The premise *directly* supports the conclusion, the information presented in the premise/premises should *make the conclusion more believable.* An LR stimulus can contain a single premise or multiple premises.

Premises also independently support the conclusion; they are different from the intermediate conclusion. *Many students confuse a multi-premise argument with one that has both premises and an intermediate conclusion.* We will now look at this.

<u>Intermediate Conclusion</u>:

The intermediate conclusion is a statement that is supported by the premise/premises, which in turn, supports the conclusion. It is a part of a chain of reasoning which starts with the premise and ends with the main conclusion.

Let's look at a few different examples and clear up any confusion:

Electric vehicles are so much more enjoyable to drive than traditional cars, more and more people will buy electric cars in the future.

Here we have a simple premise-conclusion format argument. *EVs being more enjoyable to drive* is a premise being used to support the conclusion that *EV sales will grow in the future.*

Now let's mix it up a little:

Electric vehicles are so much more enjoyable to drive than traditional cars. The price of gas is going through the roof. More and more people will buy electric cars in the future.

Here the argument consists of three statements, with two *independent* premises and a main conclusion. Note that each of the two premises independently supports the conclusion. There isn't really any logical connection between statements 1 and 2.

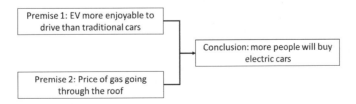

While in the above example, Premise 1 and Premise 2 are independent supporting statements for the conclusion, the LR stimulus has another trick up its sleeve, the intermediate conclusion:

Look at the following example:

The price of gas is going through the roof, more and more people will buy electric cars, the internal combustion engine car is doomed.

We have borrowed Premise 2 and the Conclusion from the previous example and added a new piece of information to the argument.

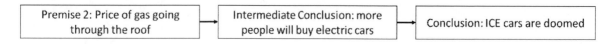

Here, we have taken the logic chain a step further and come up with the main conclusion of *internal combustion engine cars being doomed.* How is this conclusion supported? By the statement *more people will buy electric cars.*

But wait, wasn't this statement the conclusion itself in the previous example? If it is now used to support another conclusion, doesn't this make it a premise as well?

Absolutely.

The intermediate conclusion serves a *dual function* in an argument: it is a premise used to support the main conclusion, while simultaneously being a conclusion that is supported by another premise.

And that is how we distinguish an intermediate conclusion from a regular premise or main conclusion. We ask ourselves, *does it sit in the middle of an argument's logic chain in such a way that it is both a premise AND a conclusion?* Does a piece of information support it, and is in turn used to support another piece of information?

Let's try a final variation of the previous example and see if you can identify the function of each statement:

Electric vehicles are so much more enjoyable to drive than traditional cars. The price of gas is going through the roof. More and more people will buy electric cars in the future. Governments across the world are increasingly restricting the sale of internal combustion engine cars, the ICE car is doomed.

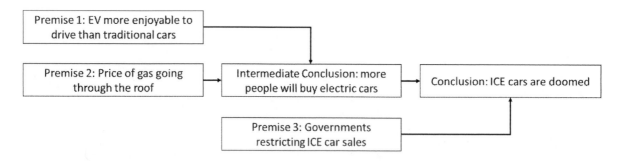

Here, we have a third premise, *governments restricting ICE car sales,* being used to support the main conclusion. It is an independent piece of information that supports only the main conclusion, and as a result, it is simply another premise.

So in summary, *the core of any LR stimulus is its argument.* Three components of any argument are its premises, intermediate conclusion, and main conclusion. When we are reading through any Find the Conclusion Questions, we are essentially identifying the author's argument, figuring out which statement is the premise, which is the intermediate conclusion, and which is the main conclusion.

Peripheral Information Found in a Stimulus (Not Part of the Argument!):

Outside of the argument core, we must be aware of another three types of statements. They are opposing viewpoints, concessions, and background information.

<u>Opposing Viewpoints:</u>

Often, the LR stimulus is structured so that the author is responding to another person's claim, which may or may not be explicitly stated. Sometimes the author will agree with the other person's view or claim, but more frequently, they will disagree. Let's look at two quick examples:

William: The law school admissions process should take a more holistic approach and place less weight on standardized tests.

Harry: I disagree. Standardized testing is the only way to ensure that candidates meet a high standard for facing the rigorous challenges of law school.

Here, Harry disagrees with William's viewpoint, and provides evidence to support his own perspective. Harry would conclude that *Law schools should NOT place less weight on standardized tests;* his premise is that standardized tests are the only way to ensure students are ready for law school. William's view, in this example, would be the OPPOSING VIEWPOINT, and does not constitute a core part of the argument. (Note also that William only provides an opinion, and does not provide support for it, therefore William's statement is not an argument in itself.)

Sometimes the opposing viewpoint is not explicitly stated, as seen in the example below:

Harry: Contrary to what many people believe, standardized testing should form an integral part of the law school admissions process. Standardized testing is an important indicator of whether a student is ready to face the rigorous challenges of law school.

Here, the opposing viewpoint can be inferred from Harry's argument, but it is not a core part of it.

<u>Concession:</u>

In an LR stimulus, the author will sometimes concede a point before defending their conclusion/main point. In a concession, the author's voice is discernible, so sometimes students will mistake a concession for the argument's conclusion. So remember that the author will often make a concession before bringing out their main point.

Here is an example of what concessions look like:

While it may be true that pulling an all-nighter writing a paper will get you a pass with the least amount of time spent, the best way to write a paper for a class would be to start early, conduct meticulous research, and revise iterative drafts until the final version is completed.

In short, a concession is where the author seemingly takes a step back and acknowledges that the opposing view has some valid points.

But granting the opponent a valid point is not the same as admitting defeat. Quite the opposite: a concession is ALWAYS followed by the author's actual viewpoint. So every time we sense that the author is conceding a point, be prepared for the author's actual main point.

Background Information:

Lastly, background information is any piece of information that appears in the stimulus to explain the importance, relevancy, or setting of the issue discussed in the argument. It could be used to define key terms that appear in the argument, or provide us with a better understanding of what is being argued. Background information usually appears as statements of fact and are always peripheral to the author's argument.

When we read through the stimulus of an LR question, a habit we must foster and turn into second nature is the ability to **categorize**. We must constantly be asking ourselves, what is the nature of the sentence I just read, and what's its job in the author's argument? There are six types of statements; three are crucial to the argument, and three are not. Which of them am I looking at now?

***

Finally, let's wrap up the theoretical section with the step-by-step construction of a detailed example.

Step 1: Let's start with the conclusion, the very heart and soul of any argument, and by extension, any LR question:

The Industrial Revolution led to the turmoil of World War II.

Step 2: Hmmm…that seems like a somewhat far-fetched idea, can we add in a premise to support our claim?

The Industrial Revolution led to the turmoil of World War II. As gaps in income and living standards widened due to industrialization, many people flocked to demagogues who promised a better life through extreme means.

Step 3: There seems to be a gap between our premise and conclusion, how does popular support for demagogues lead to war? I think an intermediate conclusion is needed:

The Industrial Revolution led to the turmoil of World War II. As gaps in income and living standards widened due to industrialization, many people flocked to demagogues who promised a better life through extreme means. As a result, wealth disparity caused people to embrace ideologies that espoused war and persecution of minorities as a means of solving their problems.

Note here that the intermediate conclusion is the last sentence of the paragraph. It's also preceded by the words "as a result." **The LSAT uses this common tactic to throw test-takers off balance.** Too often, undiscerning test takers would assume this to be the main conclusion, when it is in fact only the intermediate conclusion. More on this later.

Steps 1-3 conclude the argument phase of the stimulus. This is the core of any LR stimulus and what we should focus on when tackling the majority of LR questions.

Step 4: Let's add in some background information to explain the topic at hand better:

The Industrial Revolution, which spread from Britain across Europe during the nineteenth century, was a period of rapid change. The Industrial Revolution led to the turmoil of World War II. As gaps in income and living standards widened due to industrialization, many people flocked to demagogues who promised a better life through extreme means. As a result, wealth disparity caused people to embrace ideologies that espoused war and persecution of minorities as a means of solving their problems.

Step 5: Let's add in an opposing viewpoint to the mix:

The Industrial Revolution, which spread from Britain across Europe during the nineteenth century, was a period of rapid change. <u>Some historians have argued that the Industrial Revolution provided only benefits to humanity, bringing the world into modernity.</u> The Industrial Revolution led to the turmoil of World War II. As gaps in income and living standards widened due to industrialization, many people flocked to demagogues who promised a better life through extreme means. As a result, wealth disparity caused people to embrace ideologies that espoused war and persecution of minorities as a means of solving their problems.

Step 6: Finally, let's include a concession from the author:

The Industrial Revolution, which spread from Britain across Europe during the nineteenth century, was a period of rapid change. Some historians have argued that the Industrial Revolution provided only benefits to humanity, bringing the world into modernity. <u>Although it's true that the rapid industrialization of Europe in the nineteenth century saw the introduction of many new technologies and improvements to life</u>, it also indirectly led to the turmoil of World War II in the twentieth century. As gaps in income and living standards widened due to industrialization, many people flocked to demagogues who promised a better life through extreme means. As a result, wealth disparity caused people to embrace ideologies that espoused war and persecution of minorities as a means of solving their problems.

There you have it! The entire stimulus is complete with the argument (premise, intermediate conclusion, conclusion); and the peripheral information (background information, opposing viewpoint, concession). Read it over one more time and try to categorize every statement as it comes up:

The Industrial Revolution, which spread from Britain across Europe during the nineteenth century, was a period of rapid change. Some historians have argued that the Industrial Revolution provided only benefits to humanity, bringing the world into modernity. Although it's true that the rapid industrialization of Europe in the nineteenth century saw the introduction of many new technologies and improvements to life, it also indirectly led to the turmoil of World War II in the twentieth century. As gaps in income and living standards widened due to industrialization, many people flocked to demagogues who promised a better life through extreme means. As a result, wealth disparity caused people to embrace ideologies that espoused war and persecution of minorities as a means of solving their problems.

2. Core Habit: STRUCTURE

3: Find the Conclusion

A Selection of the Hardest Find the Conclusion/Main Point Questions:

Here is a selection of the hardest/most representative Find the Conclusion Questions. For the student just exposed to LR, the best thing we can do is to practice different questions by type and difficulty. We use the easier questions to build up and solidify our knowledge and familiarity with the question type, and gradually progress towards harder questions.

For the student stuck in the 150s or 160s, the most effective strategy would be to study the harder/hardest questions in excruciating detail. The intermediate student already has a fairly comprehensive understanding of the quirks of different question types and the different approach/knowledge required to solve them.

LR questions are categorized by type. It is important to note that the only difference between the easier and harder questions is that in the harder questions, the test makers have thrown in more things for us to consider, made the language more abstract, blurred the logical relationship within the stimulus, or laid out more trap answers. In other words, between the easiest and hardest LR questions of the same type, the fundamentals are still the same, albeit now you have to consider not just the fundamentals, but also to identify and avoid all the extra tricks and traps.

So by looking at the harder questions, we are essentially forcing ourselves to operate at higher capacity and analyze the questions on a deeper level. This will not only make us more confident with these harder questions, but also make tackling the easier questions a much more manageable process.

When we look at the questions presented in this book, and harder questions in general, it is crucial to think about the features that made the question difficult to answer. This is especially true for questions that we get wrong or the ones that we had a hard time with. (The final chapter of this book lays out a detailed plan on how to attain LR perfection with the relevant milestones.)

Take just as much time to look over the answer choices as the stimulus, if not more. Half the battle to success in Logic Reasoning is to differentiate between the answer choices, choose the best one, and have a clear rationale for your choice.

In this book, I lay out in detail my analysis of the stimulus and the answer choices, as well as the reason why these questions are tricky and the knowledge and habits we can derive from them. Use my analysis as a guide for doing LR questions on your own. The **most important thing about LR practice** is not getting the question right or understanding why you got this specific question wrong, but to use the takeaway from this one specific question to upgrade our skills and habits for subsequent questions. This can only be achieved through in-depth analysis.

So take a look at the questions, and more importantly, my explanations. Don't worry too much about timing the first time around, and when you are finished with the whole book, come back and redo the questions. If you can get questions of this difficulty done within 2-3 minutes and still see all the patterns that I saw, I'd say you are in a pretty good place.

Difficult Trait #1: The stimulus contains a trap statement which really sounds like the author's main point, but there's no premise to support it

PT58 S1 Q13

It is a given that to be an intriguing person, one must be able to inspire the perpetual curiosity of others. Constantly broadening one's abilities and extending one's intellectual reach will enable one to inspire that curiosity. For such a perpetual expansion of one's mind makes it impossible to be fully comprehended, making one a constant mystery to others.

Which one of the following most accurately expresses the conclusion drawn in the argument above?

A. To be an intriguing person, one must be able to inspire the perpetual curiosity of others.
B. If one constantly broadens one's abilities and extends one's intellectual reach, one will be able to inspire the perpetual curiosity of others.
C. If one's mind becomes impossible to fully comprehend, one will always be a mystery to others.
D. To inspire the perpetual curiosity of others, one must constantly broaden one's abilities and extend one's intellectual reach.
E. If one constantly broadens one's abilities and extends one's intellectual reach, one will always have curiosity.

This question is quite a handful, complete with abstract terms. Let's break it down:

Remember how we mentioned that Find the Conclusion/Main Point Questions are first and foremost a *categorizing exercise*? To be sure that we have found the correct conclusion, we also have to know what the other sentences are; are they premises, intermediate conclusions, background information, concessions, or opposing viewpoints?

Let's start with the first sentence:

- *It is a given that to be an intriguing person, one must be able to inspire the perpetual curiosity of others.*

Ok, this looks like an opinion of the author's, and a pretty strong one at that. It has the potential to be our argument's conclusion.

It's also a conditional statement, so let's diagram it out:

Intriguing Person → Inspire Perpetual Curiosity

So the first sentence is a conditional statement and also looks like an opinion, let's move on:

- *Constantly broadening one's abilities and extending one's intellectual reach will enable one to inspire that curiosity.*

Tricky! Conceptually, this statement is linked to the previous one: the first statement talks about the requirement for being an intriguing person is to inspire perpetual curiosity; this sentence talks about how to satisfy that requirement.

Constantly broadening one's abilities + extending one's intellectual reach → Inspire that (perpetual) curiosity

This is getting complicated: now we have two statements, both opinions, both conditional statements. Each statement presents a sufficient condition for *inspiring perpetual curiosity*, but neither statement seems to be supporting the other. Let's move on to the last sentence:

- *For such a perpetual expansion of one's mind makes it impossible to fully comprehend, making one a constant mystery to others.*

This last statement supports the second statement. It explains how extending one's intellectual reach (expansion of one's mind) will inspire the curiosity of others (by making one a constant mystery to others).

Here, the author is using slightly different terms to express the same idea. **This is something we should always be on the lookout for.**

So, in terms of this stimulus's structure, we are fairly clear now: sentence 3 is supporting sentence 2, which does not support any other point; while sentence 1 seems to be on its own, but it's actually a premise. If you combine S1 and S3, you get:

Perpetual Expansion of One's Mind → Impossible to Fully Comprehend → Constant Mystery to Others/Intriguing Person → Inspire Perpetual Curiosity

(the author is making a pretty reasonable assumption here that if you are a constant mystery to others, you are an intriguing person, we will look at assumptions in greater detail in Chapter 9)

S2, on the other hand, states that:

Constantly broadening one's abilities + extending one's intellectual reach → Inspire that (perpetual) curiosity

Remember how we said that the correct conclusion will ALWAYS have support?

You can have a statement in the stimulus that is clearly the author's opinion, at the end of the stimulus, or even have the words "as a result" predicating it. But the correct conclusion will have two important features:

> 1.   It is supported by at least another statement in the passage (both intermediate and main conclusion)
> 2.   It does not go on to support another statement (main conclusion)

So the conclusion of this stimulus is the second sentence: *Constantly broadening one's abilities and extending one's intellectual reach will enable one to inspire that curiosity.*

Let's move on to the answer choices:

> A.   *To be an intriguing person, one must be able to inspire the perpetual curiosity of others.*

This is the first sentence and not what we are looking for.

> B.   *If one constantly broadens one's abilities and extends one's intellectual reach, one will be able to inspire the perpetual curiosity of others.*

This looks like a word-for-word repetition of the second sentence, but always check all the answers just to be sure.

> C.   *If one's mind becomes impossible to fully comprehend, one will always be a mystery to others.*

This answer choice has two issues: one, it's a variation of the third sentence, which is a premise; and two, the third sentence as presented in the stimulus is NOT a conditional relationship, so there is a subtle shift in logic here. (We will cover logic later in the book)

> D.   *To inspire the perpetual curiosity of others, one must constantly broaden one's abilities and extend one's intellectual reach.*

Close but no. This answer choice reverses the conditional relationship as stated in the second sentence of the stimulus.

> E.   *If one constantly broadens one's abilities and extends one's intellectual reach, one will always have curiosity.*

This answer takes the first half of the correct answer but messes up the second half. Remember the stimulus is saying one will "*inspire the curiosity of others.*

***

Most students who got this question wrong ended up choosing answer choices A or D. But it does teach some valuable lessons:

> 1.   The main conclusion of the argument will be the last link in the author's chain of reasoning; meaning that it is supported by others but supports no one.
> 2.   Beware of tricky answer choices which differ from the correct conclusion as stated in the stimulus.

The correct answer is B.

PT85 S2 Q8

Normally, political candidates send out campaign material in order to influence popular opinion. But recent ads for Ebsen's campaign were sent to too few households to serve this purpose effectively. The ads were evidently sent out to test their potential to influence popular opinion. They covered a wide variety of topics, and Ebsen's campaign has been spending heavily on follow-up to gauge their effect on recipients.

Which one of the following most accurately expresses the conclusion drawn in the argument above?

   A.   Normally, political candidates send out campaign material to influence popular opinion.
   B.   The recent ads for Ebsen's campaign were sent to too few households to influence popular opinion effectively.
   C.   The recent ads for Ebsen's campaign were sent out to test their potential to influence popular opinion.
   D.   The recent ads for Ebsen's campaign covered a wide variety of topics.
   E.   Ebsen's campaign has been spending heavily on follow-up surveys to gauge the ads' effect on recipients.

Let's look at this question in detail:

- *Normally, political candidates send out campaign material in order to influence popular opinion.*

As soon as we start reading a stimulus, we should be ready to think on the implications of each sentence/statement. When I read this sentence, the first thought that went through my mind was "so, does the normal situation apply here? Why or why not?" Let's keep on going.

- *But recent ads for Ebsen's campaign were sent to too few households to serve this purpose effectively.*

So the normal situation doesn't apply here, why? Because too few were sent out. If we arrange the first two statements in logical order, it would look like this:

- *Normally, we send out campaign materials to influence public opinion, but Ebsen sent too few, so that could not have been his purpose.*

Let's look at the third statement:

- *The ads were evidently sent out to test their potential to influence popular opinion.*

So this is Ebsen's real purpose. It's not to influence popular opinion, but to test their potential in influencing popular opinion. Ebsen is testing the waters, so to speak.

An invaluable yet overlooked skill to have when reading for the LSAT is the ability to differentiate between related, but distinct concepts. "Influencing popular opinion" and "testing the potential to influence popular opinion" are two different things. Just because they look very similar, it's easy to assume they mean the same thing.

Now let's turn to the final statement, just like the previous example, the last sentence is crucial in getting this question right:

- *They covered a wide variety of topics, and Ebsen's campaign has been spending heavily on follow-up to gauge their effect on recipients.*

This statement details the scope of the study and Ebsen's follow-up. These are facts. Which one of the author's opinions is this statement supporting? Is it A. their purpose is not to influence popular opinion, or B. their purpose is to test their potential to influence opinion? I'm sure you would have chosen B: the last statement directly supports the third statement.

If we make the stimulus a bit more abstract, then the conclusion is not hard to find, if we use A to represent "influence popular opinion" and B to represent "testing the potential to influence popular opinion," this is what we get:

Normally political candidates do A, but Ebsen is not doing A. Ebsen is doing B, and this is why he is doing B

Remember, **the correct conclusion of any argument will always have support**. It's true that the second sentence expresses a strong opinion on the author's part, and may look and feel like a conclusion, but it does not have explicit support. The third sentence has the support we need, and as such, is the argument's conclusion.

The trait we saw in the last two questions is a **common trick** LSAT test makers apply in the harder Find the Conclusion Questions. The test makers will throw in something that looks like and feels like a conclusion but follow it up with the actual conclusion. It's our job to analyze and categorize the function of each statement and separate the wheat from the chaff.

Don't be afraid to rearrange the ordering of how information is presented in a stimulus when we are reading, if we simply switch up the positions of statement 3 and statement 4, doesn't it make more sense now?

Normally, political candidates send out campaign material in order to influence popular opinion. But recent ads for Ebsen's campaign were sent to too few households to serve this purpose effectively. They covered a wide variety of topics, and Ebsen's campaign has been spending heavily on follow-up to gauge their effect on recipients. The ads were evidently sent out to test their potential to influence popular opinion.

Watch out for the real/fake conclusion trap and remember that the correct conclusion will always have supporting evidence within the argument.

If you had chosen B, then you have committed the error we were warning against in the last question! Remember that the correct conclusion will ALWAYS be supported by other information.

<u>The correct answer is C.</u>

***

Let's look at one more question that has a similar trap:

<u>PT12 S1 Q1</u>

It is probably within the reach of human technology to make the climate of Mars inhabitable. It might be several centuries before people could live there, even with breathing apparatuses, but some of the world's great temples and cathedrals took centuries to build. Research efforts now are justified if there is even a chance of making another planet inhabitable. Besides, the intellectual exercise of understanding how the Martian atmosphere might be changed could help in understanding atmospheric changes inadvertently triggered by human activity on Earth.

The main point of the argument is that

    A. It is probably technologically possible for humankind to alter the climate of Mars.
    B. It would take several centuries to make Mars even marginally inhabitable.
    C. Making Mars inhabitable is an effort comparable to building a great temple or cathedral.
    D. Research efforts aimed at discovering how to change the climate of Mars are justified.
    E. Efforts to change the climate of Mars could facilitate understanding of the Earth's climate.

Notice a pattern here? The test makers are using the same trick again. The stimulus begins with a strongly opinionated statement, but is it the author's main point? By now we know the correct conclusion will have direct support, so we must tread carefully and think about the relationship between each statement before making a decision.

It is probably within the reach of human technology to make the climate of Mars inhabitable.

Ok, so human technology has the potential to allow us to colonize Mars. Is this the conclusion? Will the argument talk about how close we are in terms of technological advances, the feasibility of space travel? Let's read on.

It might be several centuries before people could live here, even with breathing apparatuses, but some of the world's great temples and cathedrals took centuries to build.

The second statement introduces a separate point from the first statement. In the first statement, the author talks about the technological feasibility of colonizing Mars; here, they talk about how long it might take.

What the author does in the second statement is called arguing by comparison. Essentially, they suggest that taking a long time to colonize Mars is okay, because historically, many of our most celebrated architectural projects also took a long time. Combined, the first and second statements are basically saying *"we have the technology to adapt Mars' climate for human habitation, it may take a long time, but that's not a problem."*

The third statement ties in subtly with the first and second:

Research efforts now are justified if there is even a chance of making another planet inhabitable.

If there is a chance of making another planet (Mars) inhabitable, research efforts are justified.

So does such a chance exist? Sure it does! The author just stated that the technology is close and time is not an issue. So essentially, what is the author saying in this statement? That research efforts now are indeed justified.

Besides, the intellectual exercise of understanding how the Martian atmosphere might be changed could help in understanding the atmospheric changes inadvertently triggered by human activity on Earth.

In the final statement, the author again lists a benefit of this research, namely that it will benefit our endeavors on earth as well.

Let's restate the argument in simple English:

- The technology to transform Mars' climate is close.
- It may take a long time but it's still worth it.
- This research is justified.
- This research will help us better understand the earth as well.

Does it make more sense now? Statements 1, 2, and 4 are all talking about the benefits of Martian research/why it's something we should pursue. All three are supporting premises for the conclusion, which is statement 3.

The correct answer is D.

Sometimes, the correct answer choice is not a verbatim quote of the conclusion from the passage; but rather, a summary of the idea the author is trying to convey. This is also quite common among the harder questions, and this is something that we will now turn to.

Difficult Trait #2: The main conclusion isn't explicitly stated in the stimulus, we need to derive it ourselves

PT19 S2 Q17

People cannot devote themselves to the study of natural processes unless they have leisure, and people have leisure when resources are plentiful, not when resources are scarce. Although some anthropologists claim that agriculture, the cultivation of crops, actually began under conditions of drought and hunger, the early societies that domesticated plants must first have discovered how the plants they cultivated reproduced themselves and grew to maturity. These complex discoveries were the result of the active study of natural processes.

The argument is structured to lead to the conclusion that

A. Whenever a society has plentiful resources, some members of that society devote themselves to the study of natural processes.
B. Plants cannot be cultivated by someone lacking theoretical knowledge of the principles of plant generation and growth.
C. Agriculture first began in societies that at some time in their history had plentiful resources.
D. Early agricultural societies knew more about the natural sciences than did early non-agricultural societies.
E. Early societies could have discovered by accident how the plants they cultivated reproduced and grew.

A notoriously difficult LR stimulus, complete with conditional reasoning chains to diagram and inferences that we must make by ourselves, let's break it down:

- *People cannot devote themselves to the study of natural processes unless they have leisure, and people have leisure when resources are plentiful, not when resources are scarce.*

Conditional 1: People cannot devote themselves to the study of natural processes unless they have leisure

Study natural process → Leisure

Conditional 2: People have leisure when resources are plentiful

Plentiful resources → Leisure

If resources are plentiful, they are definitely not scarce, right? So you can also go a step further and diagram Conditional 2 as Resources not scarce → Leisure.

Conditional 3: (People have leisure) not when resources are scarce

What does this even mean? Let's illustrate it with an analogy:

People go to T14 law schools when they get 170+ on the LSAT, not when they get a 140.

It's essentially saying that if you get a 140, you are not going to a T14 law school. Simple enough, right?

So the third conditional is basically saying that if resources are scarce, you don't have leisure.

Resources scarce → NO leisure

The contrapositive of this would be:

Leisure → Resources not scarce

So now we combine Conditional 2 and Conditional 3 and get a dual relationship (double arrow) :

Leisure ↔ Resources not scarce

Let's diagram the entirety of the first statement:

Study natural process → Leisure ↔ Resources not scarce

- *Although some anthropologists claim that agriculture, the cultivation of crops, actually began under conditions of drought and hunger, the early societies that domesticated plants must first have discovered how the plants they cultivated reproduced themselves and grew to maturity.*

Here we see an opposing viewpoint (something we talked about earlier in this chapter) that the author presents and argues against. I get the impression that the author disagrees with the anthropologists.

- *These complex discoveries were the result of the active study of natural processes.*

This final statement can be linked to the first statement, let's simplify it a little bit:

Agricultural discovery is the result of the study of the natural processes, which requires leisure, which in turn occurs if and only if resources are not scarce.

Let's simplify that even further:

Agricultural discovery occurred when resources were not scarce.

This is a direct refutation of the anthropologists' view. It is backed by supporting premises and the author's main point.

Let's look at the answer choices in detail:

A. *Whenever a society has plentiful resources, some members of that society devote themselves to the study of natural processes.*

This is the most commonly selected wrong answer, besides being based on information from our first sentence (premise), it has another problem with it: this statement, if diagrammed in the conditional form, is thus:

- Plentiful resources → Members devote to study of natural processes

Remember the conditional statement that can be inferred from the stimulus? It's

- People devote themselves to the study of natural process → Resources not scarce

Answer A mistakenly converses the sufficient and the necessary.

B. *Plants cannot be cultivated by someone lacking theoretical knowledge of the principles of plant generation and growth.*

Here is another conditional relationship, it can be diagrammed as

- Cultivation → Theoretical principles of plant generation and growth

Is this a conditional relationship that can be deduced from our stimulus? No. The passage does talk about the cultivation of crops, as a part of the agricultural process; but nowhere does the author mention the theoretical principles of plant generation and growth. We must watch carefully for answers that partially echo the passage's concepts. **Newly introduced and out-of-scope ideas are always wrong in Find the Conclusion answers.**

The distinction here is subtle. The people who discovered agriculture may have been scientists or temple priests. But those who cultivate may be farmers who were taught by others. The farmers don't really need theoretical knowledge.

C. *Agriculture first began in societies that at some time in their history had plentiful resources.*

This is an almost word for word restatement of our summarized conclusion above,

There is one caveat with this answer though. Can we equate "not scarce" with "plentiful?" In the most strict sense, no.

But although the LSAT is a test of logic, sometimes the correct answer choices will contain imperfections. We will look at this in greater detail in the Strengthen/Weaken Chapters. But for now, let's look at the rest of the answer choices.

D. *Early agricultural societies knew more about the natural sciences than did early non-agricultural societies.*

This answer is essentially a comparison of agricultural and non-agricultural societies. Do we know anything about non-agricultural societies from the information presented in the stimulus? No, we do not. The stimulus provides a tiny bit of tangential information in that we know early agricultural societies did actively study natural processes. But that's it.

E. *Early societies could have discovered by accident how the plants they cultivated reproduced and grew.*

This answer choice contradicts the stimulus's final sentence: "*These complex discoveries were the result of the active study of the natural process.*" So the discoveries were not an accident at all.

The correct answer is C.

While it's not perfect, it's the closest answer we have to the actual main conclusion of the stimulus. **We pick the best answer available, even if it contains imperfections**. This is a point that we will visit again and again.

So in the hardest questions, it's not as straightforward as finding the statement that is the main conclusion in the stimulus and matching it up with an answer choice. As we saw in this question, we had to link up the information given to us and derive the main conclusion ourselves. But sometimes even when we do actually find the main conclusion in the stimulus, the correct answer won't be a verbatim restatement either. We still have to **synthesize** or **rephrase** the information given to us in the stimulus to find the right answer. We will look at such an example now.

Difficult Trait #3: The correct answer choice is worded differently from the main conclusion in the stimulus, although the meaning is unchanged.

PT34 S2 Q18

Editorialist: The positions advanced by radical environmentalists often contain hypotheses that are false and proposals that are economically infeasible. But there is a positive role to be played even by extremists, for the social and political inertia that attends environmental issues is so stubborn that even small areas of progress can be made only if the populace fears environmental disaster, however untenable the reasons for those fears may be.

Which one of the following most accurately expresses the main conclusion of the editorialist's argument?

A. The little progress that has been made in improving the environment is mainly due to the fear created by radical environmentalists.
B. Radical environmentalists, by promoting their views, stimulate progress on environmental issues.
C. Social and political inertia is most effectively overcome by an extremely fearful populace, regardless of whether its fears are well founded.
D. Radical environmentalists often put forth untenable positions in order to produce the fear that is required to bring about moderate reforms.
E. Radical environmentalists advocate positions without regard for factual support or economic feasibility.

Let's look at the stimulus in detail, remember to separate opinions from facts and constantly think about which statement is supporting which other statement.

- *The positions advanced by radical environmentalists often contain hypotheses that are false and proposals that are economically infeasible.*

The stimulus begins by pointing out the shortcomings/faults espoused by radical environmentalists, but is this the author's main point? Let's read on:

- *But there is a positive role to be played even by extremists.*

The author is suggesting that even radical environmentalists have positive contributions to make. So the first statement is not the author's main opinion after all, but rather, a concession.

- *For the social and political inertia that attends environmental issues is so stubborn that even small areas of progress can be made only if the populace fears environmental disaster, however untenable the reasons for those fears may be.*

Quite a bit of information here, what the author is trying to say is this: in order to make any progress, we need the population to be afraid of environmental disaster, even though disaster may or may not happen.

How does this tie in with the positive contributions of the radical environmentalists? The assumption here is that the positions pushed by radical environmentalists are able to distill that sense of fear into the populace at large, which in turn makes progress easier. Even though the radical environmentalists' positions may be flawed, they nonetheless help make it easier to bring about positive change.

So what's the main conclusion of this stimulus? It is the first half of the second sentence, namely that even extremists play a positive role.

So if we were to simplify the stimulus, it would look something like this:

Radical environmentalists have many flaws. But they also make a positive contribution. Their warnings make the populace fearful of ecological disaster, and fear is necessary if progress is to be made.

In other words, the main conclusion should look something like "*radical environmentalists make some positive contributions to environmental protection.*"

Answer choice B most closely echoes this:

B.   *Radical environmentalists, by promoting their views, stimulate progress on environmental issues.*

Can we equate "*positive contributions to the environmental cause*" with "*stimulate progress on environmental issues?*" I think so. They essentially mean the same thing: radicals benefit the environment.

So although it's not an exact restatement of the words used in the stimulus argument, we'll let it slide. Because as we saw in the previous question, our job is to select the answer choice that **most closely** expresses the argument's main conclusion, even if it's not exact.

Answer choice D is a tricky one here. It's the most commonly selected wrong answer in this question. We must be extra careful when making answer selections and choose the answer that most closely matches the conclusion we found in the stimulus.

Answer choice D states that "*radical environmentalists put forth untenable positions IN ORDER TO produce fear,*" whereas the stimulus suggests that the fear produced by radical environmentalists can lead to progress. There is a significant difference here. If studying the LSAT has made me a more thorough reader, does it mean

I'm studying the LSAT in order to be more thorough in my reading? No. I'm studying the LSAT to go to law school and be a lawyer.

The correct answer is B.

Difficult Trait #4: Subtle scope shifts in wrong answer choices

PT23 S2 Q2

Veterinarian: a disease of purebred racehorses that is caused by a genetic defect prevents afflicted horses from racing and can cause paralysis and death. Some horse breeders conclude that because the disease can have such serious consequences, horses with this defect should not be bred. But they are wrong because, in most cases, the severity of the disease can be controlled by diet and medication, and the defect also produces horses of extreme beauty that are in great demand in the horse show industry.

The point of the veterinarian's response to the horse breeders is most accurately expressed by which one of the following?

A. Racehorses that have the genetic defect need not be prevented from racing.
B. There should not be an absolute ban on breeding racehorses that have the genetic defect.
C. Racehorses that are severely afflicted with the disease have not been provided with the proper diet.
D. The best way to produce racehorses of extreme beauty is to breed horses that have the genetic defect.
E. There should be no prohibition against breeding racehorses that have any disease that can be controlled by diet and exercise.

If we had been looking at this stimulus and categorizing each piece of information as they came up, while thinking about the structural relationship between each statement (which statement is supporting which other statement), then finding the author's main point shouldn't be too hard. Let's get right to it:

- *A disease of purebred racehorses that is caused by a genetic defect prevents afflicted horses from racing and can cause paralysis and death.*

This is a statement of fact, but what is it supporting? Let's look at statement 2.

- *Some horse breeders conclude that the disease can have such serious consequences, horses with this defect should not be bred.*

So statements 1 and 2 collectively form the argument of some horse breeders (opposing argument): because the disease is so dangerous, we should not breed these horses. Let's keep on going.

- *But they are wrong.*

This is definitely the vet's opinion, so what are they saying? Essentially, we should still breed these horses. Let's see why they thinks so:

- *Because, in most cases, the severity of the disease can be controlled by diet and medication, and the defect also produces horses of extreme beauty that are in great demand in the horse show industry.*

So why should we breed these horses? Because the disease can be controlled, and the horses are so pretty. This statement directly supports the vet's opinion, which in turn is the argument's conclusion.

I wanted to take a more detailed look at this question primarily for the answer choices. We talked about the common trap answer choices the test makers like to throw in to confuse us, and this question is full of them.

A. *Racehorses that have the genetic defect need not be prevented from <u>racing.</u>*

The vet's argument is about allowing the breeding of these horses, not about allowing them to race. Beware out of scope answers and subtle term shifts.

B. *There should not be an absolute ban on breeding racehorses that have the genetic defect.*

In other words, the breeding of these horses should be permitted. That is precisely the veterinarian's main point and therefore the correct answer. Notice how even though the words are different, it expresses the same idea as the main conclusion in the stimulus?

Answer choices C and D are so far removed from our prediction that they are fairly easy to eliminate. Let's look at answer choice E, which is also the most commonly selected wrong answer.

E. *There should be no prohibition against breeding racehorses that have <u>any</u> disease that can be controlled by diet and exercise.*

This answer starts off okay, but again, its scope subtly shifts. The veterinarian's argument is about this particular disease that afflicts purebred racehorses. Answer choice E is about ANY disease that can be controlled by diet and exercise. Furthermore, this answer choice talks about "exercise," whereas the original stimulus discussed "medication."

<u>The correct answer is B.</u>

Think back on the term-shift in answer choice C of PT19 S2 Q17. "*Plentiful*" and "*not scarce*" were used interchangeably in that question. Similarly, in PT58 S1 Q13, "*inspiring curiosity*" was used interchangeably with "*being a constant mystery*." While those terms weren't exactly identical, the differences are much smaller than what we have witnessed in the wrong answers here. Knowing when the author is legitimately using two terms interchangeably and when something is out of scope is an art that few master. I still struggle with it occasionally.

Difficult Trait #5: Wrong answer choices that are ideas the author would probably agree with, but are not the actual main conclusion of the argument

This is another common trap found in the hardest Find the Conclusion Questions. The test makers will throw in some valid MBT/MSS answers into the mix. The undiscerning student sees these, forgets that they are actually doing a Find the Conclusion/Main Point Question, and is led astray.

Take a look at the following example:

John: My flight was delayed and my friend, who came to pick me up from the airport, simply went home without waiting for me. Since my tardiness was due to a reason beyond my control. Her actions are extremely selfish and speaks volumes about her character.

What is John's conclusion here? His friend did something selfish and is (probably) a selfish person. This is fairly straightforward.

But you may also encounter an answer that read "*John doesn't think his friend leaving early is justified.*" This is ok for a MBT/MSS Question, because that's most likely what John thinks. But it's NOT the conclusion of the argument! Always know your task at hand when doing LR questions.

***

PT24 S2 Q12

For years scientists have been scanning the skies in the hope of finding life on other planets. But in spite of the ever-increasing sophistication of the equipment they employ, some of it costing hundreds of millions of dollars, not the first shred of evidence of such life has been forthcoming. And there is no reason to think that these scientists will be anymore successful in the future, no matter how much money is invested in the search. The dream of finding extraterrestrial life is destined to remain a dream, as science's experience up to this point should indicate.

Which one of the following most accurately states the main point of the argument?

A. There is no reason to believe that life exists on other planets.
B. The equipment that scientists employ is not as sophisticated as it should be.
C. Scientists searching for extraterrestrial life will not find it.
D. Only if scientists had already found evidence of life on other planets would continued search be justified.
E. We should not spend money on sophisticated equipment to aid in the search for extraterrestrial life.

The stimulus is actually fairly straightforward, summarize as you read through it and think about whether the statement you are reading is supporting or being supported. It's basically saying that *scientists have been looking for aliens (statement 1), but they haven't found any (statement 2). They won't find any in the future (statement 3), they will never find aliens (statement 4).*

Sometimes when the stimulus is relatively easier to understand, the traps will lay in the answer choices. The authors will include answer choices that closely mirror what was said in the stimulus but not quite true, or answer choices that can probably be inferred from the stimulus but are not the conclusion of the argument.

Let's take a quick look at the answer choices:

> A. There is no reason to believe that <u>life exists</u> on other planets.

Tricky! Remember the stimulus is about scientists not being able to FIND aliens, and NOT that aliens don't exist? This is the most commonly selected wrong answer. Be careful of closely related ideas that don't actually appear in the stimulus.

> B. The equipment that scientists employ is not as sophisticated as it should be.

Is this a possibility? Sure, if the goal is to find more aliens. But is this the conclusion of the argument? Remember that we cannot stray from the scope of what is discussed in the stimulus. So any could be true or most likely true answers will be wrong. We are doing a Find the Conclusion Question, not a MBT/MSS Question!

> C. Scientists searching for extraterrestrial life will not find it.

Here we go. <u>This is the correct answer</u> and matches our summary/understanding. Because the dream of finding aliens will just be a dream.

> D. Only if scientists had already found evidence of life on other planets would continued search be justified.

Whenever a conditional statement appears in Find the Conclusion answer choices, I immediately go back to the stimulus to check if this conditional relationship can be located/derived.

This answer choice is basically saying

- Continued search for aliens justified → Already found evidence of life

Does the author imply/assume that the search for aliens is unjustified? Yes, because the scientists will never find them. But again, this answer choice is another MSS answer. This is not a MSS Question.

> E. We should not spend money on sophisticated equipment to aid in the search for extraterrestrial life.

This answer choice makes the same mistake as the previous one: it's a could be true/most likely true statement that needs to be inferred from the stimulus. It's probably what the author believes, but if we analyze the structure of the stimulus, we realize that the argument is that *scientists have not found any aliens, therefore they will never find aliens.* The conclusion is that *scientists will never find aliens.*

Difficult Trait #6: Placing an attractive wrong answer next to the correct answer, which is worded in hard-to-understand language

<u>PT44 S2 Q16</u>

Sociologist: some economists hold that unregulated markets should accompany democratic sovereignty because they let people vote with their money. But this view ignores the crucial distinction between the private consumer and the public citizen. In the marketplace the question is, "What do I want?" At the voting booth the question is always, "What do we want?" Hence, supporters of political democracy can also support marketplace regulation.

Which one of the following most accurately expresses the conclusion drawn by the sociologists?

  A. Voters think of themselves as members of a community, rather than as isolated individuals.
  B. Unregulated markets are incompatible with democratic sovereignty.
  C. Where there is democratic sovereignty there should be unregulated markets.
  D. Private consumers are primarily concerned with their own self-interest.
  E. Opposition to unregulated markets is consistent with support for democracy.

As we have probably seen by now, sometimes even the correct answer choice will be dressed up in such a vague and abstract way that we end up missing it despite having located the main conclusion in the stimulus.

This is a common two-step trick the test makers employ in the hardest questions:

Step one, making an attractive wrong answer super close to the correct answer, but with just a tiny albeit material difference in detail.

Step two, rephrase the correct answer in hard-to-understand language so that you have no idea what you are looking at or just skip it altogether.

What is the conclusion of this argument? The sociologist believes democracy is compatible with regulation, so in other words, you can both support democracy and regulation.

Let's take a closer look at answer choices B and E. By looking at these two answer choices in conjunction, we can highlight one of the most lethal traps the test makers will lay out for you.

    B.   Unregulated markets are incompatible with democratic sovereignty.

This answer choice is tricky because at a first glance, it looks pretty close to what the sociologist is saying, namely that political democracy/democratic sovereignty is COMPATIBLE with REGULATED markets. Isn't saying unregulated markets are incompatible with democracy essentially the same thing?

No. If A is compatible with B, does it mean A is incompatible with B̶? Not necessarily: if exercising daily is compatible with a full work schedule, does that mean exercising daily is incompatible with a free schedule? Of course not. The sociologist's idea is not conditional in nature, so don't fall into the trap of thinking that democracy is only compatible with regulated markets.

    E.   Opposition to unregulated markets is consistent with support for democracy.

<u>This is the correct answer</u>. It's essentially saying that support of regulation is consistent with support for democracy, namely the conclusion of our argument. Instead of directly saying that, the authors have used the words "*opposition to unregulated markets,*" and if we are reading too fast or pressed for time, we may easily have eliminated this answer, thinking it out of scope.

But does opposition to unregulated markets really mean the same thing as support for regulation? Isn't this the same kind of reasoning gap which made answer choice B wrong? In some cases it may be, but here it's actually fine. If I oppose the Republican candidate, it doesn't mean I automatically support the Democratic candidate, because you have other alternatives. You can support the libertarian candidate, or simply abstain from voting, because there's a multitude of choices. But market regulation here is a binary choice, there is either regulation or no regulation. So by opposing the latter you are necessarily endorsing the former. Take the example of gun control, if you oppose unregulated sale of guns, does that necessarily mean you support some form of gun control? Yes.

The takeaway from this question is to keep in mind one of the most common traps on answer choice selections. We will have an attractive wrong answer which will be just slightly off, and the correct answer dressed up in a vague/abstract/confusing manner. Read the answer choices carefully, compare them, and refer back to the stimulus when in doubt. This habit is also essential in Must be True, Most Strongly Supported, Strengthen, and Weaken Questions, we will get to those in due time.

Let's look at another question where the correct answer is dressed up in super abstract wording:

<u>PT23 S3 Q25</u>

The end of an action is the intended outcome of the action and not a mere by-product of the action, and the end's value is thus the only reason for the action. So while it is true that not every end's value will justify any means, and even, perhaps, that there is no end whose value will justify every means, it is clear that nothing will justify a means except an end's value.

Which one of the following most accurately expresses the main conclusion of the argument?

    A. The value of some ends may justify any means.
    B. One can always justify a given action by appeal to the value of its intended outcome.
    C. One can justify an action only by appeal to the value of its intended outcome.
    D. Only the value of the by-products of an action can justify that action.
    E. Nothing can justify the intended outcome of an action except the value of that action's actual outcomes.

This is one of the most abstract and hard to understand stimuli I've come across. Let's break it down.

- Statement 1: *The end of an action is the intended outcome of the action and not a mere by-product of the action, and the end's value is thus the only reason for the action.*

So three pieces of information we can gather here:

The end of an action is the intended outcome of that action (end = intended outcome), the end is more than the by-product, and the reason for an action is the end's value (Reason for an action → End/intended outcome's value)

Notice how I'm already using the words "end" and "intended outcome" interchangeably, given the information in the stimulus.

- Statement 2: *So while it is true that not every end's value will justify any means, and even, perhaps, that there is no end whose value will justify every means.*

This statement is a concession (not part of the argument), and it's basically saying that to justify different means we need different end values.

- Statement 3: *It is clear that nothing will justify a means except an end's value.*

Justify means → End's value/intended outcome's value

Statement 2 and statement 3 are super confusing, but if we parallel it with an analogy, it will be much easier to understand:

> So while it is true that not every study method will make any student succeed, and even, perhaps, that there is no study method that will make every student succeed, it is clear that nothing will make a student successful except his or her study method.

What the stimulus's second half is saying is that while there is no single, universal end value which will justify all means, the end's value is a necessary condition to justify the means.

In this stimulus, the argument structure is not too difficult to categorize: we can probably figure out that the last statement is the author's conclusion without fully understanding the argument's content. What made this question difficult are its abstract answer choices.

A. The value of some ends may justify any means.

This is a corruption of the first part of the second sentence of the argument, which says "*not every end's value will justify any means.*" In diagrammed form, the stimulus is saying "not all A is B", but this answer choice is saying "some A is B".

In real life, we sometimes use "not all" to imply "some do", for example, when I say "not all Americans speak English," some may take it to also mean "some Americans do speak English". But on the LSAT, no such inferences can be made. **All = 100%, so "not all" simply means "not 100%". It could be anywhere from 0% to 99%.**

"Some", on the other hand, could be anywhere from 1% to 100%. So while there is indeed significant overlap between the two, they are not equal. If I make the statement that "not all people weigh 2000 lbs", does that mean some people do weigh 2000 lbs? No.

We will look at "some, most, all" relationships in greater detail in the Must be True Chapter.

Furthermore, from a structural standpoint, this statement is a concession and not the conclusion of the argument.

  B. *One can always justify a given action by appeal to the value of its intended outcome.*

"Always" is indicating the necessary condition here. Let's look at a few examples:

You can always get into a good law school with a 4.0 GPA and a 180 LSAT

- 4.0 GPA + 180 LSAT → Good law school (You don't need a 4.0/180, but it guarantees that you will be accepted at a good law school.)

You can always find taxis at the airport

- Airport → Taxi (If you are at the airport, you will find a taxi.)

So answer choice B is essentially saying that

- Appealing to the value of its intended outcome (end's value) → Justify a given action

This is an erroneous conversing of the sufficient and necessary as presented in the author's argument, which states that *nothing will justify a means except an end's value* (Justify a given action → End's value/intended outcome's value)

  C. *One can justify an action only by appeal to the value of its intended outcome.*

This is basically a rephrasing of the last statement. Remember, the end of an action IS its intended outcome, so if nothing will justify a means except an end's value, nothing will justify a means except its intended outcome's value.

  D. *Only the value of the by-products of an action can justify that action.*

This is in direct conflict with what the author is saying. The author is saying that it's the intended outcome and not the by-product's value that justifies the action.

  E. *Nothing can justify the intended outcome of an action except the value of that action's actual outcomes.*

This answer choice mirrors closely the language in the argument's conclusion but mixes up the terms. Remember the real conclusion says:

- Justify Action → Value of Intended Outcome

Answer choice E says:
- Justify Intended Outcome → Value of Actual Outcome

So again, when faced with harder Find the Conclusion questions, be extra careful when examining the answer choices. The correct answer is often presented in a confusing/abstract manner, while an attractive wrong answer is tempting you nearby.

The correct answer is C.

Difficult Trait #7: Placing the intermediate conclusion at the end of the stimulus, and prefacing it with words like "thus," "therefore," or "as a result."

Be extra careful here. If you see a statement at the very end of a stimulus/argument, beginning with words like "thus" or "therefore," it doesn't automatically mean that it's a trap intermediate conclusion posing as the main conclusion!

In easier questions, it may very well be the argument's main conclusion. But because the test makers know that we are so used to having the main conclusion as the very last sentence, they will sometimes put the intermediate conclusion last on purpose. Let's go back to our EV example from earlier:

The price of gasoline is going through the roof, more and more people are buying electric vehicles in order to save money. Thus, the internal combustion engine is doomed.

Nothing out of the ordinary here. The first statement is the premise, the second is the intermediate conclusion, and the last sentence is the main conclusion.

But what if we switched it up a little bit?

The internal combustion engine is doomed. The price of gasoline is going through the roof. As a result, in order to save money, more and more people are buying electric vehicles.

We have the exact same argument, but the intermediate conclusion is placed last this time. If we weren't careful, we might have easily mixed up the intermediate and main conclusions.

So the story's moral is to think about the support relationship between each statement within the argument.

Based on indicator words and location in the stimulus alone, there's just no way to determine which statement is the intermediate conclusion and which statement is the main conclusion.

Always look at the structure of the argument as a whole to determine the intermediate and main conclusions.

***

PT43 S3 Q23

Each of many different human hormones can by itself raise the concentration of glucose in the blood. The reason for this is probably a metabolic quirk of the brain. To see this, consider that although most human cells can produce energy from fats and proteins, brain cells can use only glucose. Thus, if blood glucose levels fall too low, brain cells will rapidly starve, leading to unconsciousness and death.

Which one of the following most accurately expresses the main conclusion of the argument above?

    A.   Each of many different human hormones can by itself raise blood glucose levels.

    B.   The reason that many different hormones can each independently raise blood glucose levels is probably a metabolic quirk of the brain.

    C.   Although most human cells can produce energy from fats and proteins, brain cells can produce energy only from glucose.

    D.   If blood glucose levels fall too low, then brain cells starve, resulting in loss of consciousness and death.

    E.   The reason brain cells starve if deprived of glucose is that they can produce energy only from glucose.

The reason we have included this question is to do a deeper dive into the importance of having a clear understanding of a stimulus's structure, to differentiate between what portion of the stimulus forms the argument and what forms the peripheral information. We also do this to further differentiate between premises, the intermediate conclusion, and the main conclusion.

Before we move to the actual question, I just wanted to clarify a persistent point of confusion many students face when discussing a stimulus's structure. Remember that most LR stimuli will contain an argument (premise, conclusion, and maybe an intermediate conclusion), and the LSAT will often use logic (most frequently conditional logic and causation logic, we will look at this soon) to advance the argument, to get from premise to conclusion.

But in an argument that uses causal logic, cause - effect does not mean premise and conclusion. Let's look at two different examples:

Smoking is a leading cause of lung cancer, John smokes two packs a day, therefore he will surely get lung cancer.

What is the causal relationship here? Smoking $\Rightarrow$ Cancer. John smokes: therefore, he will get cancer. The conclusion is that John will get cancer. Simple enough, right?

Now take a look at the next example:

Smoking is a leading cause of lung cancer, John has lung cancer, therefore he must surely have been a heavy smoker.

The causal relationship here is still the same, Smoking $\Rightarrow$ Cancer. But the premise is that John has lung cancer (effect), while the conclusion points to the cause for this effect (John is a smoker). So here, the logical relationship between cause and effect is essentially reversed in the argument's structural pattern. The effect is identified, and the cause is actually the conclusion.

Whenever we see a causal relationship in the stimulus, many students will erroneously assume that the cause is the premise, and the effect is the conclusion.

Don't make this mistake!

In a causation-based argument, the cause - effect relationship and the premise - conclusion relationship are two discrete elements that we must analyze independently.

In LR questions, the test makers will often present a result/situation, then provide an explanation or cause for it. In such instances, the conclusion is the explanation for the phenomenon described and thus the causation part of the cause - effect relationship. This brings us to the final trick employed in Find the Conclusion Questions:

> When there is a cause/effect relationship in the argument, sometimes the effect is the premise and the cause is the conclusion. Don't always assume that because cause $\Rightarrow$ effect, cause = premise, and effect = conclusion.

The stimulus describes a phenomenon (different hormones can raise glucose concentration), and then proceeds to offer up an explanation for it. In other words, metabolic quirk of the brain is the cause, and hormones raising glucose concentrations is the effect in this causal relationship. But that doesn't mean the effect is the conclusion of the argument!

The author then goes on to talk about why glucose is so important to the brain (brain cells can use only glucose…if glucose levels fall too low, brain cells will starve).

So the argument presents three different elements:

1. Different hormones can raise glucose levels.
2. This is due to the brain.
3. Glucose is really important to the brain.

When simplified, it is not hard to see that the first statement is a fact/background information, the second statement is the author's opinion, and the last statement is the support that the author provides for the second statement.

So from a causal **logic** perspective, metabolic quirk of the brain ⇒ different human hormones being able to raise glucose levels by themselves.

But from a **structural** perspective, glucose being important to the brain (third and fourth sentence of the stimulus) are the premise and intermediate conclusion, respectively; the second sentence, *"the reason for this is probably a metabolic quirk of the brain,"* is the conclusion.

    A. *Each of the many different human hormones can by itself raise blood glucose levels.*

This is the most commonly selected wrong answer: it's the phenomenon that the author is seeking an explanation for. Yes, it's the effect in the cause - effect relationship, but it is not the conclusion. If you had selected this as the answer, you would have fallen into the trap of not distinguishing between an argument's logical and structural pattern.

    B. *The reason that many different hormones can each independently raise blood glucose levels is probably a metabolic quirk of the brain.*

This is the correct answer.

    C. *Although most human cells can produce energy from fats and proteins, brain cells can produce energy only from glucose.*

This is the support/premise provided by the author for why it's the brain that is responsible for allowing different hormones to independently raise glucose levels.

    D. *If blood glucose levels fall too low, then brain cells starve, resulting in loss of consciousness and death.*

This is the intermediate conclusion of the argument. Structurally, as we mentioned previously, the argument goes like this:

Brain cells can only use glucose (premise) → Low glucose is fatal (intermediate conclusion) → Brain makes sure hormones can produce glucose (conclusion)

Frequently, as per **Trait #7**, the test makers will put the intermediate conclusion at the end of the stimulus and preface it with words like "thus," "as a result," or "therefore." They are trying to trick us into thinking it's the main conclusion when it's not. Remember, other elements of the argument will always support the actual main conclusion, whereas the intermediate conclusion, while supported, will go on to support another idea.

    E. *The reason brain cells starve if deprived of glucose is that they can produce energy only from glucose.*

This is a summary of the premise and intermediate conclusion of the argument.

4. Role Questions

Role Questions are one step removed from Find the Conclusion Questions, which we have covered in depth in the previous chapter. We say it's "one step removed" because the skills needed to succeed in Role questions are very much the same as those needed in Find the Conclusion Questions. We approach Role questions in almost the same way.

Well, "almost" the same way because there are a few additional steps involved, but the core skill set of tackling Role Questions is the ability to identify the structure of the argument (locating the premises, intermediate conclusion, and main conclusion), and the ability to categorize different statements as we read them (separating the argument from the peripheral information). In other words, how we approach a Role Question stimulus is no different from Find the Conclusion Questions. If you ever struggle with identifying the structural elements of the argument or cannot consistently identify the correct conclusion, go back and re-read Chapters 2 and 3.

But there are differences between how we approach Role Questions and Find the Conclusion Questions.

Role Questions will quote a sentence or a statement that appears in the stimulus and ask us what the role/function of this statement is. For instance, Role Questions will ask us, *"what is the role of statement X in the speaker's argument/stimulus?"*

So in Role Questions, we are not only reading the stimulus, looking for the main conclusion. We also need to keep an eye out for the quoted statement (statement X), and THINK about the relationship between the quoted statement and the main conclusion.

Tackling the Role Question Stimulus

Enough of the explaining, let's go through a few examples:

We will see a drastic increase in the cost of food in the near future. War in Ukraine has caused a significant disturbance in the global supply of grain and livestock feed. Inflationary pressure on the economy means that prices only have one place to go, which is up.

What is the role played by the statement about inflationary pressure?

***

The diligent LSAT student should devote as much time to their emotional and physical well-being as to the studying of the LSAT itself. Studying for the LSAT is akin to training for a marathon and requires long-term commitment and planning. As a result, ensuring one is in top shape mentally and physically will help the student in their performance.

What is the role played by the statement that ensuring one is in top shape mentally and physically will help the student?

***

The court system must remain vigilant of the attempts made by politicians to damage its effectiveness. It has been argued that the separation of powers already keeps a country's judicial system independent and free from political interference. But all political and legal institutions are made by humans, and as such, they are fragile and prone to error.

What is the role played by the statement that the separation of powers keeps a country's judicial system independent and free from political interference?

***

Let's look at these examples in more detail, starting with the first one:

The **first** thing I do when approaching Role Questions is to isolate the statement/sentence that the question is asking us about. You can do this either by highlighting or underlining it in the stimulus.

I do this to keep myself focused on the task at hand. If we make careless mistakes and choose the wrong statement to analyze, then whatever skills we have learned regarding this question type will be for naught.

We will see a drastic increase in the cost of food in the near future. War in Ukraine has caused a significant disturbance in the global supply of grain and livestock feed. Inflationary pressure on the economy means that prices only have one place to go, which is up.

What is the role played by the statement about inflationary pressure?

Now with the statement isolated, it's time to turn to the **second** step: reading the stimulus.

When reading the stimulus of Role Questions, the reading habits are no different from reading the stimulus of a Find the Conclusion Question. We are reading primarily for structure: we read the statements one by one, trying to decipher the author's argument. We are essentially doing two things: one, categorizing each statement according to its function, and two, finding the argument's main conclusion.

This example is essentially saying that food will get more expensive in the future. This is an opinion and not a fact, so it has the potential to be the example's main conclusion. With that in mind we look at the second and third statements to see what their relationship is to the first statement and to each other. The second statement says war has disrupted food supplies, and the third statement says prices are going up due to inflation.

So we have three statements in this example:

1. Food is going to be more expensive.
2. Food supply is disrupted.
3. Inflation is making things cost more.

Statement 1 is an opinion while Statements 2 and 3 are facts. As such, it appears that both 2 and 3 support 1. So statement 1 is the conclusion of this example.

Is there a supporting relationship between statements 2 and 3? Are they both independent premises, or is one of them a premise and the other an intermediate conclusion?

Disrupted supplies will lead to higher costs; inflation also means higher costs. Both are factors contributing to the predicted rise in food prices. Statements 2 and 3 are separate premises, each supporting the conclusion. There are no intermediate conclusions in this example!

Finally, it's time to turn to the **third** step of reading a Role question stimulus: we ask ourselves what is the relationship between the quoted statement to the conclusion of the stimulus?

It's a premise, independently providing support for the argument's conclusion.

***

Let's take a look at example 2:

Step 1: isolate the quoted statement within the stimulus.

The diligent LSAT student should devote as much time to their emotional and physical well-being as to the studying of the LSAT itself. Studying for the LSAT is akin to training for a marathon and requires long-term

commitment and planning. <u>*As a result, ensuring one is in top shape mentally and physically will help the*</u>
<u>*student on their performance.*</u>

What is the role played by the statement that <u>ensuring one is in top shape mentally and physically will help the</u>
<u>student?</u>

Step 2: examine the stimulus as you would a Find the Conclusion Question, keeping an eye out for the
highlighted/underlined statement.

It is clear from the example that the second statement supports the underlined statement. But is the underlined
statement the intermediate conclusion or the main conclusion? Consider the relationship between the first
statement (*The diligent LSAT student should devote as much time to their emotional and physical well-being*)
and the underlined statement (*ensuring one is in top shape mentally and physically will help the student in their*
performance).

Being in good shape mentally and physically will help with our performance on the LSAT, therefore we should
take care of ourselves mentally and physically. The underlined statement is the intermediate conclusion which
supports Statement 1, the conclusion.

Step 3: Double-check to ensure we haven't fallen into one of the structural traps test makers love to use to throw
us off balance. In other words, make sure we are not confusing an intermediate conclusion for a main
conclusion, an independent premise for an intermediate conclusion, and that we have correctly differentiated the
peripheral information in the stimulus (background information/concession/opposing views) from the core
elements of the argument.

***

Great work. Let's look at example 3 before moving on to the more advanced stuff.

Step 1: isolate the quoted statement.

The court system must remain vigilant of the attempts made by politicians to damage its effectiveness. It has
been argued that <u>the separation of powers already keeps a country's judicial system independent and free from</u>
<u>political interference</u>. But all political and legal institutions are made by humans, and as such, they are fragile
and prone to error.

What is the role played by the statement that <u>the separation of powers keeps a country's judicial system</u>
<u>independent and free from political interference</u>?

Step 2: read the stimulus as you would a Find the Conclusion Question but pay special attention to the
underlined statement.

The example is arguing for vigilance on the part of judges and the court system and resisting undue influence
from politicians. That's the main conclusion of this argument and is the essence of statement 1. Statement 3, by
supporting statement 1, is acting as the premise. That leaves the second statement, the one we are interested in.
What is statement 2 saying? Essentially, the separation of powers (institutional judicial independence) is a
defense against political interference. Does this support our conclusion that we need to remain vigilant? No, it
runs contrary to the spirit of our conclusion and is therefore either a concession or an opposing viewpoint.

Some students confuse a "concession" and an "opposing viewpoint." They are similar yet different in one key
aspect. An **opposing viewpoint** is simply what the other party thinks or believes. The author disagrees with it.
A **concession**, on the other hand, is a point made by the opponent explicitly acknowledged and granted by the
author.

As a result, the statement *"the separation of powers already keeps a country's judicial system independent and free from political interference"* is an opposing viewpoint with which our author disagrees. On the other hand, had the statement read, *"Granted, the separation of powers keeps a country's judicial system independent and free from political interference somewhat,"* then the statement would be a concession because the author has expressed a partial agreement with the statement.

Step 3: reconsider the relationship between the quoted statement and the argument's conclusion and confirm that our reasoning indeed makes sense.

As we have already explained, this statement functions as an opposing viewpoint in the argument.

***

In summary, how we approach Role Questions initially is no different from how we approach Find the Conclusion Questions. We must analyze the stimulus statement by statement, look for the main conclusion and the premises/intermediate conclusion. We then take the statement in question and ask ourselves, how does it fit into the argument?

Here is a quick list of the habits that will make the process go a lot smoother:

1. Locate the statement that the question is asking us about. I usually highlight/underline the statement in the question and in the stimulus to provide a constant visual reminder of what I am supposed to focus on.

2. Read the stimulus as you would a Find the Conclusion Question. Categorize each sentence/statement and find what the argument core is. In other words, identify the main conclusion, premise, and intermediate conclusion (if there is one).

3. Think about the relationship between the quoted statement and the argument's conclusion; what is their relationship?

***

Deconstructing the Role Question Answer Choice

While how we read the stimulus of any Role Question is similar to how we approach Find the Conclusion Questions, the answer choices we face in Role Questions will be much more difficult. Life would be so simple if all the answer choices just asked us whether the statement in question is a premise or a conclusion, but the test makers love to describe a relatively straightforward concept in abstract and vague language in Role Question answer choices.

As a result, the successful student should devote most of their time and energy to answer choices when approaching Role Questions. As you get comfortable with analyzing the structure of the stimulus, it should become second nature to you. I use about 60% of all the time to examine answer choices in Role Questions, with the other 40% set aside for reading the question and the stimulus.

The ability to deconstruct answer choices (translating vague and abstract terms that appear in answer choices into their stimulus equivalents) and know exactly what they are referring to is one of the most important skills that the advanced student needs to master. If you do not have this ability, often you will end up choosing a wrong answer choice even if you knew what you were looking for. You simply did not understand what the answer choice was trying to say. In other words, advanced students can read through a list of abstract answer choices and know exactly what they refer to.

Take a look at the following answer choice examples, and see if you can decipher what it is that they are referring to, or even better, try to make up an argument with the components that would function as these answer choices describe:

1. *It is used to illustrate the general principle that the argument presupposes.*

2. *It is an illustration of a premise that is used to support the argument's conclusion.*

3. *It is used to counter a consideration that might be taken to undermine the argument's conclusion.*

4. *It makes an observation that, according to the argument, is insufficient to justify the claim that the argument concludes is false.*

5. *It describes a phenomenon for which the argument's conclusion is offered as an explanation.*

6. *It is a general principle whose validity the argument questions.*

7. *It denies a claim that the argument takes to be assumed in the reasoning it rejects.*

8. *It is a claim for which no justification is provided but that is required to establish the argument's main conclusion.*

9. *It is a claim for which justification is provided and that, if true, establishes the truth of the argument's main conclusion.*

10. *It is what the author's argument purports to explain.*

11. *It is a hypothesis that the argument attempts to undermine by calling into question the sufficiency of the evidence.*

12. *It is the conclusion of the argument as a whole but is not the only explicitly stated conclusion in the argument.*

13. *It is a statement that the argument is intended to support but is not the conclusion of the argument as a whole.*

14. *It is a statement for which some evidence is provided and that itself is offered as support for the conclusion of the argument as a whole.*

15. *It is the conclusion of the argument as a whole and is supported by another statement for which support is offered.*

Yep, that was brutal. You probably had no idea what many of these even meant. Not to worry, let's break them down one by one:

1. <u>It is used to illustrate the general principle that the argument presupposes.</u>

Whenever we are faced with an answer choice that looks super abstract, the first thing to do is to always **extract** what **keywords** we can to try to make sense of the whole thing. Three words stand out in this answer choice: "illustrate", "general principle", and "presuppose".

Now certain words have specific meanings within the LSAT. All three of these words repeatedly appear in LR questions and we need to memorize them:

> **Presuppose**: in daily usage, a presupposition can mean either an assumption or something that is necessary. On the LSAT presuppose simply means "assume." (It's talking about a necessary assumption here, something that we will soon cover.)

> **Illustrate**: an illustration, as it appears in an LR question, is simply referring to an example/examples

> **General Principle**: we briefly touched upon the nature of principles on the LSAT in the last chapter and will do so again further down the road. But for now, just know that a principle is a rule on what we should/shouldn't do and that it applies to multiple conditions and scenarios.

For example, "*John is always tired in the morning, he should go to bed earlier*" is not a principle, we are just talking about one person here. "*Those who are tired in the morning should strive to get to bed earlier*" is a principle. It's no longer just about John anymore, it is a recommendation for a certain category of people.

So now there are three requirements that must be met if we were to select this hypothetical answer choice as the correct answer: first, the statement in question must be an example; second, behind this example is a principle on what we should or shouldn't do; and lastly, this principle is required in order for the author to advance their argument.

Take a look at this example:

<u>Despite a high paying job, John was extremely stressed out and depressed</u>, so there are intangible things in life that we must pursue to find true happiness.

John's situation is the illustration of a general principle; namely that having a lot of money isn't enough to make you happy. Is this principle required in order for the conclusion to stand? Yes, the conclusion says factors other than money must be considered in order to be happy. The underlined statement satisfies all three requirements and if this was a Role question, this would be the correct answer.

2. <u>It is an illustration of a premise that is used to support the argument's conclusion.</u>

Again, "**illustration**" means example. So we know this answer choice is referring to an example in the stimulus. Furthermore, it is an illustration of a premise. So when examining this answer choice, we must isolate the premise/premises that appear in the argument and ask ourselves, is the quoted statement an example of what the premise is trying to say?

Here is an example to illustrate what this answer choice is trying to say:

<u>John has been smoking two packs a day since he was sixteen, last week he was diagnosed with lung cancer.</u> Smoking is a direct cause of lung cancer. We must avoid cigarettes at all costs if we want to stay healthy.

What is the premise here? Smoking causes lung cancer. What is the conclusion? Don't smoke. John's case is an illustration of the causal relationship between smoking and lung cancer. Requirement satisfied.

3.   It is used to counter a consideration that might be taken to undermine the argument's conclusion.

So right away, we should realize that *"a consideration that might be taken to undermine the argument's conclusion"* refers to a real or potential counterargument. A counterargument runs contrary to the author's conclusion. If I say, "Going to college is a great way to enjoy a higher standard of living down the road," but you respond with "But many college graduates have to take years to pay back debt," you are making a counterargument opposing me.

Continuing with our example, if I had anticipated your potential objection/counterargument, I could say that "college graduates enjoy higher income than their non-college counterparts even with the cost of debt factored in." What I'm doing, essentially, is anticipating your potential objection and shutting you down in advance. That's what is meant by countering a consideration that might be taken to undermine the argument's conclusion.

College graduates make more money than they would if they didn't go to college, even if they are paying off student loans plus interest. So going to college is a great way to make more money and enjoy a better life.

Here, the underlined statement is both a premise and a pre-emptive strike against a potential objection, namely that graduates end up with so much debt that going to college doesn't make sense.

4.   It makes an observation that, according to the argument, is insufficient to justify the claim that the argument concludes is false.

A key piece of information we can extract from this answer choice is that there is a *claim that the argument concludes is false.* In other words, the author of this argument is arguing AGAINST a claim. Someone has made a claim, and the author is saying that the claim is false.

So we have two viewpoints in this potential stimulus. The author's argument is directed against an adversary.

Further, we know that the opponent *"made an observation"* in support of their view, but the author is saying that the observation is not enough to prove anything, and subsequently goes on to argue that the opponent's claim is false.

So in order for this answer choice to be correct, the stimulus must satisfy the following requirements: there must be an opposing view and the author must be arguing against this opposing view and declaring it false. The opponent must have provided an observation as a basis of support for their view, and the author must have claimed that this observation is not enough to demonstrate the truth of the opponent's view.

Let's go a step further with a concrete example:

John: Celebrities have the biggest smiles in front of the camera, so they must be the happiest people alive.

David: That is not true. Many celebrities suffer from depression and substance abuse. Smiling in front of the camera doesn't mean a thing. They could simply be putting on a show for the audience.

Does the underlined statement fit the requirement for this answer choice? Yes, David is arguing that John's claim is false. David also suggests that John's observation in support of his claim is insufficient to justify his claim.

5.   It describes a phenomenon for which the argument's conclusion is offered as an explanation.

Here is another key term that we must familiarize ourselves with: explanation.

> **Explanation**: on the LSAT, the word "explanation" has a very strict and precise meaning, it simply means "cause."

So whenever you see the word "explanation" in an answer choice, check the stimulus for cause-effect reasoning. If it's not there, then this answer would be wrong.

What this answer choice is referring to is something we have seen before. We talked about questions where there is a cause-and-effect relationship in the argument, but instead of the cause being the premise and the effect being the conclusion, the order is reversed. The author describes a phenomenon and concludes what caused it. See PT43-S3-Q23 in the Find the Conclusion Chapter if you had forgotten.

We will reuse our example from the previous chapter:

Smoking is a leading cause of lung cancer, <u>John has lung cancer</u>, therefore he must surely have been a heavy smoker.

John having lung cancer is the phenomenon; the author subsequently concludes that it must be smoking that caused his lung cancer. The cause-effect relationship goes like this: Smoking ⇒ Lung cancer, and the cause/explanation is in fact the conclusion in this example.

6. <u>It is a general principle whose validity the argument questions.</u>

Again, this answer choice refers to a general principle, but it's a general principle that the argument is questioning/attacking. So if we are confronted with this answer choice, we must go back to the stimulus to ensure it satisfies two requirements: one, the quoted statement is indeed a general principle; and two, the author is arguing against the truth of this principle. Here is an example that would match what this answer choice is saying:

It has been said that <u>the best way to approach any situation is to be yourself</u>. But this cannot be true. What if you are a selfish, egotistical or horrible person? Surely we must strive to better ourselves and be the best we can?

7. <u>It denies a claim that the argument takes to be assumed in the reasoning it rejects.</u>

This one is very similar to example 4. The argument rejects another person's reasoning. So the author is arguing against someone else here. But are they rejecting that view outright? No, the author does something much more nuanced than that. The author thinks the reasoning used by their opponent contains an assumption. Instead of going after the opponent's explicit argument, our author is going after their assumption.

So this answer choice describes a stimulus in which there are two arguments, the author's argument and the opponent's argument. This particular statement is the author rejecting an assumption made in the opponent's argument.

(We will look at the nature of assumptions in a subsequent chapter and in Sufficient and Necessary Assumption question types.)

John: I've studied so hard for finals, I'm definitely going to ace the exam!

David: <u>Studying hard doesn't guarantee you will do well.</u> The exams are graded on a curve, and everyone else has studied just as hard.

8. <u>It is a claim for which no justification is provided but that is required to establish the argument's main conclusion.</u>

This answer choice has two important pieces of information that can help us determine whether it's the correct answer. First, it is "*required*" to establish the argument's main conclusion. That means it's necessary for the main conclusion to be valid. So there's no way this answer choice is describing the main conclusion itself, it's therefore either a premise or an intermediate conclusion.

Second, the answer choice says it's a claim for which no justification is provided. Remember what we said about differentiating between premises and intermediate conclusions in the previous chapter? Premises support the conclusion but do not have any other statements supporting them, whereas intermediate conclusions both support the conclusion and are supported by premises. So when we have a statement which supports the conclusion but is not supported by others, it can only mean one thing: we are talking about a premise here.

So we are essentially talking about a premise that is required to establish the truth of the conclusion. In other words, if the premise was untrue, the conclusion would not stand. Take a look at the following example for more clarity:

I found an Olympic gold medal in the swim team locker room. It must have originally belonged to John. John is always losing things and <u>he participated in the Olympics</u>.

John's participation in the Olympics is a requirement for the example's conclusion to stand. In order for John to be the original owner of the medal, he MUST have been a participant at least.

John's participation in the Olympics is also a premise that supports the example argument's conclusion.

9. <u>It is a claim for which justification is provided and that, if true, establishes the truth of the argument's main conclusion.</u>

Very similar to the example listed above, but with two important caveats. This answer choice HAS justification provided, while supporting the main conclusion, so it's an intermediate conclusion. It also **guarantees/establishes** the truth of the conclusion.

All practicing lawyers must have passed the bar. John is a partner at a prestigious law firm and therefore <u>he is a practicing lawyer</u>, so he must have passed the bar.

John being a practicing lawyer is supported by the fact that he is a partner at a law firm. This satisfies the intermediate conclusion requirement. Does John being a practicing lawyer establish the fact that he has passed the bar? Yes, it is mentioned in the first statement/premise that all practicing lawyers must have passed the bar.

10. <u>It is what the author's argument purports to explain.</u>

This is identical to example 5: the author describes an effect/result/phenomenon and argues for a specific cause.

11. <u>It is a hypothesis that the argument attempts to undermine by calling into question the sufficiency of the evidence.</u>

What is a hypothesis? In science, a hypothesis is offered by scientists to try to explain a phenomenon in the physical world or universe. Why did different types of birds have physical features that are adapted to their physical environments? Darwin hypothesized that it is because species can change over time, adapting to their environments via physical modifications generation after generation. Darwin came up with a hypothesis, which today we know as The Theory of Evolution, that has been supported by evidence gathered both by him and subsequent scientists. In other words, a hypothesis is simply a posited causal explanation of a phenomenon, explaining WHY something is the way it is.

 On the LSAT, the word "**hypothesis**" can be understood as a "potential explanation/theory not yet proven"; it usually appears in science/medicine themed LR stimuli.

So what is this answer choice saying? The argument attempts to undermine this hypothesis. It does so by saying that the evidence out there is not enough to support such a hypothesis. So when we are going through answer choices and come to this, we must make sure that there is a hypothesis present in the stimulus (the quoted statement being that hypothesis), the author is challenging this hypothesis, and the author does so by suggesting that the available evidence is not enough to support this hypothesis.

12. It is the conclusion of the argument as a whole but is not the only explicitly stated conclusion in the argument.

Two pieces of key information here. The first is straightforward: we are talking about the main conclusion here. But note that it "*is not the only explicitly stated conclusion in the argument.*" That can only mean one thing: we also have an intermediate conclusion in the argument. So if confronted with this answer choice, make sure that one, the statement we are talking about is in fact the main conclusion of the argument; and two, the argument contains a separate intermediate conclusion.

13. It is a statement that the argument is intended to support but is not the conclusion of the argument as a whole.

Something that is supported by the argument but is not the main conclusion; that's an intermediate conclusion we are talking about here.

14. It is a statement for which some evidence is provided and that itself is offered as support for the conclusion of the argument as a whole.

Same as above. The statement in question is supported by something, and supports the main conclusion. This is also the intermediate conclusion.

15. It is the conclusion of the argument as a whole and is supported by another statement for which support is offered.

Same as example 12: the statement referred to by the answer choice is the main conclusion and is supported by *another statement for which support is offered.* So the main conclusion is supported by an intermediate conclusion. When faced with an answer choice like this, make sure it is indeed the main conclusion that the question is asking us to analyze, and make sure the argument contains an intermediate conclusion.

A Selection of the Hardest Role Questions

Take a look at the following questions. Try to go through the questions practicing the skills developed earlier in the chapter. Try to follow the steps outlined above, paying particular attention to the answer choices! Do the questions first before looking at my explanations!

Again, if you struggle with some questions, don't worry too much about timing. Use the opportunity to develop a systematic approach to these questions, fill in knowledge gaps, and familiarize yourself with how to deconstruct an abstract answer choice. For the advanced test taker, try to aim for under 3 minutes per question. 2 minutes per question is good, granted that you are getting them correct and following the steps.

Structurally analyzing the stimulus is the first step to successfully tackling Role Questions. In fact, complicated arguments with multiple premises, intermediate conclusions, and background information are harder Role Questions' most common characteristics.

Difficult Trait #1: Make sure you are clearly categorizing each statement in the stimulus and argument as you read it. Don't confuse the intermediate conclusion for the main conclusion.

PT34 S3 Q14

People's political behavior frequently does not match their rhetoric. Although many complain about government intervention in their lives, they tend not to re-elect inactive politicians. But a politician's activity consists largely in the passage of laws whose enforcement affects voters' lives. Thus, voters often re-elect politicians whose behavior they resent.

Which one of the following most accurately describes the role played in the argument by the claim that people tend not to re-elect inactive politicians?

A. It describes a phenomenon for which the argument's conclusion is offered as an explanation.
B. It is a premise offered in support of the conclusion that voters often re-elect politicians whose behavior they resent.
C. It is offered as an example of how a politician's activity consists largely in the passage of laws whose enforcement interferes with voters' lives.
D. It is a generalization based on the claim that people complain about government intervention in their lives.
E. It is cited as evidence that people's behavior never matches their political beliefs.

Let's break this question down step by step:

First things first, let's make a note of what it is exactly that we are going to analyze in this question:

People's political behavior frequently does not match their rhetoric. Although many complain about government intervention in their lives, they tend not to re-elect inactive politicians. But a politician's activity consists largely in the passage of laws whose enforcement affects voters' lives. Thus, voters often re-elect politicians whose behavior they resent.

Which one of the following most accurately describes the role played in the argument by the claim that people tend not to re-elect inactive politicians?

So it's the second half of the second statement that we are concerned with. Let's now break down the stimulus structurally.

Look at this stimulus. What is the argument that the author is trying to make? What is their conclusion, and what premises do they use to support that conclusion?

- Statement 1: *People's political behavior frequently does not match their rhetoric.*

This can be an author's opinion or observation. At this point it can either be used to support or be supported by another statement. Let's keep on reading and try to situate this statement when we have more information.

- Statement 2: *Although many complain about government intervention in their lives, they tend not to re-elect inactive politicians.*

This statement seems like a further development of the first statement. It offers more details. So people say they want governments to leave them alone, but they don't like politicians who don't do anything. (In other words, politicians who actually do leave them alone don't get any support.)

It seems to me that statement 1 is a summary of what statement 2 is actually describing. Statement 2 seems like a premise at the moment; maybe statement 1 is the conclusion or intermediate conclusion. Let's keep on going.

- Statement 3: *But a politician's activity consists largely in the passage of laws whose enforcement affects voters' lives.*

Stop and think. How does this piece of information tie in with what we have read and learned previously? In statement 2 voters say they don't like interference, but don't vote for inactive politicians. This statement is saying what political activities are; in other words, what active politicians do. Active politicians interfere in voters' lives. Inactive politicians don't get the votes; active ones do. So voters say they don't want interference but will go on to vote for interfering politicians.

Statements 2 and 3 are premises. Statement 1 seems like the conclusion so far. Let's look at the last sentence.

- Statement 4: *Thus, voters often re-elect politicians whose behavior they resent.*

How the last statement is presented should already be familiar to the discerning student. It's the last statement and begins with "thus". It could signify the actual main conclusion of the argument, but we must remember that often the test makers will present an intermediate conclusion this way. So always make sure. Here it is the intermediate conclusion, while the first statement is the main conclusion. Here is the argument in simplified form:

- Premise 1: *People want governments to leave them alone, but they don't vote for politicians who are inactive. (Assumption: It's the active politicians who get the votes)*
- Premise 2: *Active politicians don't leave people alone.*
- Intermediate Conclusion: *People end up voting for politicians that do things they don't like (interference).*
- Conclusion: *What people say (leave me alone!) doesn't match what they do (vote for interfering politicians).*

Now let's think about the relationship between the underlined statement and the main conclusion, and how the underlined statement functions in the author's argument.

Before approaching the answer choices, we have come to an understanding that the statement in question is a premise, the argument contains two premises, an intermediate conclusion, and a main conclusion.

Now for the hard part, deconstructing and differentiating between answer choices:

> *A. It describes a phenomenon for which the argument's conclusion is offered as an explanation.*

We have seen this kind of structure before, once in the previous chapter on Find the Conclusion Questions, and again in the exercise earlier in the chapter. A phenomenon is presented, and a cause is provided. Why is John grumpy? It's because he didn't have his morning coffee. Why is David late? Because his car broke down. The statement in question is not a phenomenon that the conclusion provides the cause for. If the argument in the stimulus read like this, then A would be the correct answer:

> *Voters tend not to re-elect inactive politicians. This is because people forget about politicians who haven't done anything and people vote for those that have made a strong impression.*

Let's keep on going.

> *B. It is a premise offered in support of the conclusion that voters often re-elect politicians whose behavior they resent.*

Looks good on a first pass: it is indeed a premise, and it supports the (intermediate) conclusion that voters often re-elect politicians whose behavior they resent. But the premise is calling the intermediate conclusion a conclusion, is that grounds for elimination?

Remember this answer choice from our exercise earlier?

It is the conclusion of the argument as a whole but is not the only explicitly stated conclusion in the argument.

On the LSAT, the word "**conclusion**" can refer to both the main conclusion and the intermediate conclusion. More specifically, "Conclusion of the argument as a whole" means main conclusion. So while the wording of this question should raise some eyebrows, it's not wrong per se.

> *C. It is offered as an example of how a politician's activity consists largely in the passage of laws whose enforcement interferes with voters' lives.*

Active politicians interfere with voters' lives is the message of the next statement, this statement is about voters not re-electing inactive politicians.

> *D. It is a generalization based on the claim that people complain about government intervention in their lives.*

> **Generalizations** and **Examples** are related concepts.
>
> In an LSAT stimulus, a generalization is when you infer a rule based on specific facts/findings. If I saw 500 swans and they were all white, I can **generalize** by saying that all swans are white. Conversely, I can have a rule that I back up with a specific example. I can say that, as a general rule, people who work hard on the LSAT will succeed. For **example**, John studied 10 hours a day for a year, and he got a 180.

So a "*generalization based on the claim that people complain about government intervention in their lives*" should look something like this:

All my neighbors complain about government interference, all my coworkers too: so people tend to complain when they perceive government intervention in their lives.

E. *It is cited as evidence that people's behavior never matches their political beliefs.*

Two things I dislike about this answer: one, the conclusion is about people's behavior not matching rhetoric. So what they do doesn't match up with what they say. It's not about what they believe. Two, "never" is too strong a word here; remember to be careful with answer choices that are too strong. Degree-based errors are frequent in wrong answer choices.

The correct answer is B.

***

PT70 S4 Q24

Biologist: Scientists have discovered fossilized bacteria in rocks 3.5 billion years old. The fossils indicate that these bacteria were quite complex and so must have already had a long evolutionary history when fossilized 3.5 billion years ago. However, Earth is only 4.6 billion years old, so the first life on Earth must have appeared soon after the planet's formation, when conditions were extremely harsh. This suggests that life may be able to arise under many difficult conditions throughout the universe.

Which one of the following most accurately describes the role played in the biologist's argument by the claim that fossilized bacteria discovered in rocks 3.5 billion years old must have had a long evolutionary history?

A. It is a claim for which no support is provided in the argument, and that is used to illustrate the conclusion of the argument as a whole.
B. It is a claim for which no support is provided in the argument, and that is used to support a claim that in turn lends support to the conclusion of the argument as a whole.
C. It is a claim for which some support is provided in the argument, and that itself is used to support another claim that in turn lends support to the conclusion of the argument as a whole.
D. It is a claim for which some support is provided in the argument, and that itself is not used to support any other claim in the argument.
E. It is a claim for which some support is provided in the argument, and that itself is used to support two distinct conclusions, neither of which is intended to provide support for the other.

Biologist: Scientists have discovered fossilized bacteria in rocks 3.5 billion years old. The fossils indicate that these bacteria were quite complex and <u>so must have already had a long evolutionary history when fossilized 3.5 billion years ago</u>. However, Earth is only 4.6 billion years old, so the first life on Earth must have appeared soon after the planet's formation, when conditions were extremely harsh. This suggests that life may be able to arise under many difficult conditions throughout the universe.

Which one of the following most accurately describes the role played in the biologist's argument by the claim that <u>fossilized bacteria discovered in rocks 3.5 billion years ago must have had a long evolutionary history</u>?

Notice how I only underlined the second half of the second statement. This is because the second statement actually contains two pieces of information: "*bacteria were complex*" AND that "*they must have had a long evolutionary history*". The question is asking about the part regarding "*long evolutionary history*", it never mentioned the "*complex*" part. So the lesson is to always focus on exactly what the question is asking about, never just automatically assume we are looking at the entire sentence in which our underlined statement is situated.

What is the structure of the author's argument?

The main conclusion is the last sentence of the stimulus*: life may arise under difficult conditions in the universe.*

How is this conclusion supported? Let's take a look at the rest of the stimulus.

- Statement 1: *Scientists have discovered fossilized bacteria in rocks 3.5 billion years old.*

This is a fact and most likely background information; let's continue.

- Statement 2: *The fossils indicate that these bacteria were quite complex and <u>so must have already had a long evolutionary history when fossilized 3.5 billion years ago</u>.*

Be careful with this one; it may only be one sentence, but a lot of information is involved. The bacteria were complex, so they must have had a long evolutionary history. There is a mini-argument here! The author is probably assuming that a bacteria's complexity means it has had a long time to develop. So even within this sentence, there is both a premise and an intermediate conclusion.

Premise (bacteria were complex) + Assumption (more complex the bacteria, more time they had to evolve) → Intermediate Conclusion (these bacteria had already been around for a long time when they fossilized 3.5 billion years ago)

- Statement 3: *However, Earth is only 4.6 billion years old, so the first life on Earth must have appeared soon after the planet's formation, when conditions were extremely harsh.*

At a first glance, we may not clearly see how this relates to the information we have read previously. Remember statement 2 said that the bacteria had been around for a long time. They fossilized 3.5 billion years ago, so they must have been much older than that. If the earth is only 4.6 billion years old, and the bacteria have been around a lot longer than 3.5 billion years, then we can infer that the bacteria have been around soon after the earth was formed.

Statement 3 also contains a piece of new information, namely that conditions were harsh when earth was just formed.

As we said before, the last statement, *"life may be able to arise under many difficult conditions throughout the universe"*, is the conclusion. Because bacteria appeared under harsh conditions on earth, the author concludes that life can arise under harsh conditions in the universe.

This argument is structurally quite complex, if we diagram it we get this:

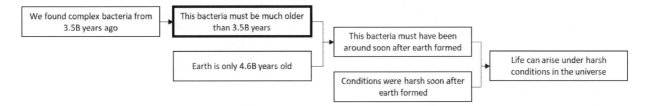

I've paraphrased the underlined statement (bacteria must have had a long evolutionary history when they fossilized 3.5 billion years ago) for ease of understanding. As the diagram makes clear, this statement is right in the middle of the argument chain. It has support, making it an intermediate conclusion; but it also supports another intermediate conclusion. Let's take a look at the answer choices:

A. It is a claim for which no support is provided in the argument, and that is used to illustrate the conclusion of the argument as a whole.

Does our statement have support in the argument? It's easily missed but still there: because the bacteria were complex, they must have a long evolutionary history. The complexity of the bacteria is the support. Is it an illustration (example) of the main conclusion? No.

B. It is a claim for which no support is provided in the argument, and that is used to support a claim that in turn lends support to the conclusion of the argument as a whole.

The same problem as the previous answer choice, there is support for the claim. The rest of the answer has no problems, but that only makes it a partially correct answer.

C. It is a claim for which some support is provided in the argument, and that itself is used to support another claim that in turn lends support to the conclusion of the argument as a whole.

Support is indeed provided, and the statement is being used to support Intermediate Conclusion #2, which further supports the main conclusion.

D. It is a claim for which some support is provided in the argument, and that itself is not used to support any other claim in the argument.

The main conclusion is the only statement not used to support anything else in an argument. What D is referring to here is the main conclusion.

E. It is a claim for which some support is provided in the argument, and that itself is used to support two distinct conclusions, neither of which is intended to provide support for the other.

This describes an intermediate conclusion, and the stimulus described in this answer choice has two separate main conclusions. It is similar to answer choice E of the previous question and does not fit with our understanding of this question's stimulus.

The correct answer is C.

Let's look at another question where we may get confused between the premise and the intermediate conclusion.

PT70 S1 Q17

Meteorologist: Heavy downpours are likely to become more frequent if Earth's atmosphere becomes significantly warmer. A warm atmosphere heats the oceans, leading to faster evaporation, and the resulting water vapor forms rain clouds more quickly. A warmer atmosphere also holds more moisture, resulting in larger clouds. In general, as water vapor in larger clouds condenses, heavier downpours are more likely to result.

Which one of the following most accurately describes the role played in the meteorologist's argument by the claim that, in general, as water vapor in larger clouds condenses, heavier downpours are more likely to result?

A. It is the only conclusion in the argument.
B. It is the conclusion of the argument as a whole but is not the only explicitly stated conclusion in the argument.
C. It is a statement that the argument is intended to support but is not the conclusion of the argument as a whole.
D. It is used to support the only conclusion in the argument.
E. It provides a causal explanation of the phenomenon described by the conclusion of the argument as a whole, but it is not intended to provide support for that conclusion.

Before we dive into this question, I just wanted to return to the topic of **causality vs. argument structure** and examine it further. It's a subject that confuses even the most advanced students.

Remember how we mentioned that if there is a cause-and-effect relationship in an LR argument, don't automatically assume that the cause is the premise and effect is the conclusion? Take a quick look at the following example:

John couldn't wake up on time for his morning class. John usually has trouble waking up in the morning when he stays up late watching Netflix. Therefore John probably was binge watching Netflix again last night.

What is the cause-and-effect relationship here? Watching Netflix (Cause) ⇒ Cannot wake up early (Effect)

What are the premises and conclusion of this argument?

- Premise 1: *John couldn't wake up early.*
- Premise 2: *John has trouble waking up early when he watches Netflix late into the night.*
- Conclusion: *John was probably watching Netflix last night.*

So we know to analyze the logical aspect of an LR argument (in this case, causality) separate from its structure (premise/conclusion). But when we have a causational chain in the argument, that's when things get even more confusing. Take a look at the following example:

Because Megan missed her morning coffee she was not paying attention to her surroundings. As a result, she fell down the stairs on her way to school. So not getting your daily dose of caffeine can cause dangerous accidents.

The cause/effect chain is pretty apparent here:

No Coffee (A) ⇒ Not Paying Attention to Surroundings (B) ⇒ Accident (C)

But structurally, how should we diagram this argument?

We know that the main conclusion is A ⇒ C, and we have two pieces of information supporting that conclusion: A ⇒ B and B ⇒ C. Is there an intermediate conclusion here?

Remember that the intermediate conclusion is ALWAYS supported by a premise? Does A ⇒ B support in any way B ⇒ C? No. They are two independent causal relationships. Yes it's true that they form a single causal chain in our argument. But there is no supporting relationship between the two.

So structurally, what we have essentially is this:

- Premise: A ⇒ B
- Premise: B ⇒ C
- Conclusion: A ⇒ C

 Just because there is a causal logic chain, A ⇒ B ⇒ C, don't assume that A is the premise, B is the intermediate conclusion, and C is the conclusion!

If the argument is in conditional form, the essential difference between an argument's structure and its logic is still there:

If you went to Yale Law School, then you must have gotten a great LSAT score. Every high LSAT scorer is a proficient computer user. So all YLS students are proficient computer users.

Conditionally: YLS → Great LSAT → Computer Skills

Structurally:

- Premise: YLS → Great LSAT
- Premise: Great LSAT → Computer Skills
- Conclusion: YLS → Computer Skills

Is "Great LSAT → Computer Skills" an intermediate conclusion? No. Because the conditional premise "YLS → Great LSAT" is not supporting "Great LSAT → Computer Skills". They are each independent premises, when combined, lead to the conclusion.

> In other words, just because a statement/idea/condition forms the middle part of a causal or conditional chain, that doesn't make it the intermediate conclusion. Always treat the structure of an argument (premise, intermediate conclusion, main conclusion) and the logical aspects of the argument (cause/effect, sufficient/necessary) as **two distinct and separate issues**!

So Cause ⇒ Effect is not the same thing as Premise – Conclusion!

Similarly, Sufficient → Necessary is also not the same thing as Premise – Conclusion.

With that in mind, let's break up the stimulus structure.

Statement 1: *Heavy downpours are likely to become more frequent if Earth's atmosphere becomes significantly warmer.*

- Warmer atmosphere ⇒ More frequent heavy downpours

Statement 2: *A warm atmosphere heats the oceans, leading to faster evaporation, and the resulting water vapor forms rain clouds more quickly.*

- Warm atmosphere ⇒ Hotter ocean ⇒ Faster evaporation ⇒ Faster rain cloud formation

Statement 3: *A warmer atmosphere also holds more moisture, resulting in larger clouds.*

- Warm atmosphere ⇒ More moisture ⇒ Larger clouds

Statement 4: *In general, as water vapor in larger clouds condenses, heavier downpours are more likely to result.*

- Larger clouds ⇒ More frequent heavy downpours

Let's reorganize the information in structural form:

- Premise 1: Warm atmosphere ⇒ Faster rain cloud formation
- Premise 2: Warm atmosphere ⇒ Larger clouds
- Premise 3: Larger clouds ⇒ More frequent heavy downpours
- Conclusion: Warm atmosphere ⇒ More frequent heavy downpours

The statement we are analyzing is the last statement of the stimulus, and as we have seen, is a premise (Premise 3).

The correct answer is D.

***

In the next question, practice not only reading the argument for its structure, but also pay specific attention to the keywords in each answer choice.

Difficult Trait #2: Be extra careful of vague/abstract terms in answer choices; try to match them up with what actually happened in the stimulus.

PT87 S3 Q8

Astronomer: Conditions in our solar system have probably favored the emergence of life more than conditions in most other solar systems of similar age. Any conceivable form of life depends on the presence of adequate amounts of chemical elements heavier than hydrogen and helium, and our sun has an unusually high abundance of these heavier elements for its age.

Which one of the following most accurately describes the role played in the astronomer's argument by the claim that any conceivable form of life depends on chemical elements heavier than hydrogen and helium?

A. It is a statement for which no evidence is provided and that is part of the evidence offered for the argument's only conclusion.
B. It is a statement for which no evidence is provided and that is offered as support for another statement that in turn is offered as support for the conclusion of the argument as a whole.
C. It is a statement for which some evidence is provided and that itself is offered as support for the conclusion of the argument as a whole.
D. It is the conclusion of the argument as a whole and is supported by another statement for which support is offered.
E. It is one of two conclusions in the argument, neither of which is offered as support for the other.

First things first, let's isolate the statement in question:

Astronomer: Conditions in our solar system have probably favored the emergence of life more than conditions in most other solar systems of similar age. <u>Any conceivable form of life depends on the presence of adequate amounts of chemical elements heavier than hydrogen and helium</u>, and our sun has an unusually high abundance of these heavier elements of its age.

Which one of the following most accurately describes the role played in the astronomer's argument by the claim that <u>any conceivable form of life depends on chemical elements heavier than hydrogen and helium</u>?

Now, let's go through the stimulus, reading for structure:

The first statement has the word "*probably*," indicating that it's an opinion of the author. The author believes that our solar system is better suited to life than other solar systems. Let's see why.

Statement 2 says that life needs a lot of chemicals heavier than hydrogen and helium, while statement 3 says that our solar system has plenty of both. Statements 2 and 3 are INDEPENDENT statements supporting statement 1, the main conclusion. There is no intermediate conclusion here.

    A.   *It is a statement for which no evidence is provided and that is part of the evidence offered for the argument's only conclusion.*

Answer choice A says the underlined statement is a premise (no evidence provided), and the argument contains no intermediate conclusion (argument's only conclusion). Take a look at our stimulus, is it the premise that we are examining? Yes. Does the argument contain an intermediate conclusion? No.

    B.   *It is a statement for which no evidence is provided and that is offered as support for another statement that in turn is offered as support for the conclusion of the argument as a whole.*

Answer choice B also calls the underlined statement a premise, but according to this answer choice, there is an intermediate conclusion in the stimulus. Do we have an intermediate conclusion present? No. Earth having a lot of heavy elements does not support the fact that we need these elements to support life, nor does life needing heavy elements support the fact that the Earth contains a lot of these elements.

    C.   *It is a statement for which some evidence is provided and that itself is offered as support for the conclusion of the argument as a whole.*

C is essentially talking about an intermediate conclusion. Again, there is no intermediate conclusion in this stimulus.

    D.   *It is the conclusion of the argument as a while and is supported by another statement for which support is offered.*

Answer choice D is saying that the underlined statement is the main conclusion (it isn't), and that there is an intermediate conclusion in this stimulus/argument (there isn't).

    E.   *It is one of two conclusions in the argument, neither of which is offered as support for the other.*

Hmmm, interesting. Answer choice E describes an interesting scenario. So there are two conclusions in the argument, but no intermediate conclusion. Take a look at the following example; that's what answer choice E is talking about:

To go to Yale Law School you need a high GPA and a high LSAT. John has been admitted to YLS. John therefore has a high GPA and a high LSAT score.

Two conclusions here: John has a high GPA; John has a high LSAT score. Neither of them are intermediate conclusions. Having one doesn't mean you will more likely have the other.

The correct answer is A.

As we can see, clearly understanding the stimulus structure is crucial to tackling Role Questions. Furthermore, we also need to constantly practice deconstructing what each answer choice is saying and matching that up with the stimulus. In the hardest questions, sometimes it's not enough to simply identify the premise, intermediate conclusion and main conclusion. We must also read the answer choice word for word and refer back to the stimulus to prove or reject the answer based on the evidence available.

***

PT79 S1 Q22

Consumer advocate: Economists reason that price gouging – increasing the price of goods when no alternative seller is available – is efficient because it allocates goods to people whose willingness to pay more shows that they really need those goods. But willingness to pay is not proportional to need. In the real world, some people simply cannot pay as much as others. As a result, a price increase will allocate goods to people with the most money, not to those with the most need.

Which one of the following most accurately describes the role played in the consumer advocate's argument by the claim that willingness to pay is not proportional to need?

A. It disputes one explanation in order to make way for an alternative explanation.

B. It is the overall conclusion of the argument.

C. It is a component of reasoning disputed in the argument.

D. It is a general principle whose validity the argument questions.

E. It denies a claim that the argument takes to be assumed in the reasoning that it rejects.

The structure of this stimulus has tripped up countless students, let's break it down step by step:

- Statement 1: *Economists reason that price gouging – increasing the price of goods when no alternative seller is available – is efficient because it allocates goods to people whose willingness to pay more shows that they really need these goods.*

This is an opposing argument, or what the consumer advocate is arguing against. What is the economists' argument?

If you are willing to pay more for a good, you must need it more. So price gouging is efficient. (The economists believe that allocating goods to those who need it the most is an efficient strategy)

- Statement 2: <u>But willingness to pay is not proportional to need.</u>

This is the consumer advocate's opinion. they are attacking the reasoning behind the economists' premise.

- Statement 3: *In the real world, some people simply cannot pay as much as others.*

At a first glance, how this statement ties in with the rest of the stimulus is a little bit unclear. Whenever I read a statement that seems to be disconnected from the rest of the information available, my first reaction is "**so what**?" If some people cannot pay as much as others, then the person needing something the most (for example, an urgent medical treatment) may not necessarily be able to offer the highest price for it. So in other words, statement 3 supports statement 2.

Statement 4: *As a result, a price increase will allocate goods to people with the most money, not to those with the most need.*

This directly opposes the economists' reasoning and therefore the consumer advocate's conclusion. Let's diagram this:

Economists:

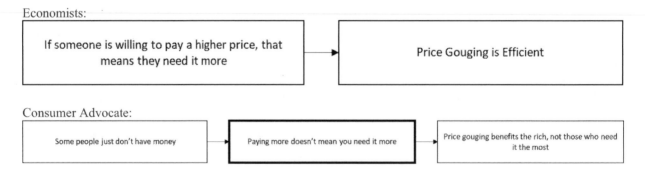

So, structurally, statement 2 (*willingness to pay is not proportional to need*) is the consumer advocate's intermediate conclusion in their response to the economists. It's an attack on the economists' premise.

Let's look at the answer choices:

A. *It disputes one explanation in order to make way for an alternative explanation.*

Tricky! Remember what the word "explanation" means on the LSAT? It has an exact definition and means "causation." So what this answer choice is saying is that the author is disputing one cause in order to make way for another cause. If this is the correct answer, the stimulus would look something like this:

John: A is caused by B.

David: No, A is not caused by B, it's caused by C.

Does this happen in our stimulus? No. If the consumer advocate had said that *price gouging is efficient NOT because it allocates goods to people whose willingness to pay more shows that they really need those goods; BUT that it is efficient because allows companies that make products people want to earn more profits and make better products,* then this could potentially be the correct answer.

This is the most selected wrong answer. **The takeaway here is that we must get into the habit of reading answer choices word for word.** Right off the bat, the word "explanation" should be a red flag, and if we dive deeper into this answer with a healthy dose of skepticism, we soon find more issues with it.

  B.   It is the overall conclusion of the argument.

The overall conclusion is the last statement of the stimulus.

  C.   It is a component of the reasoning disputed in the argument.

What the consumer advocate disputes is the second half of the first statement, namely the reasoning offered by the economists in support of their opposing view. The statement we are concerned with forms a part of the consumer advocate's reasoning.

  D.   It is a general principle whose validity the argument questions.

Again, this statement is a part of the consumer advocate's argument; its validity is not questioned.

  E.   It denies a claim that the argument takes to be assumed in the reasoning that it rejects.

As we have seen in the previous chapter, the correct answer will often be packaged in an abstract/vague way to throw the test taker off track. Many students will eliminate this answer simply because they had no idea what it's saying or failed to think on a deeper level about what it's describing. Answer E is basically suggesting that there is an assumption in the economists' reasoning (the reasoning that it rejects), and that statement 2 ("*willingness to pay is not proportional to need*") is denying that assumption.

Does the economists' reasoning contain an assumption? Remember what the economists' argument was: *if you are willing to pay more, it means you need it more, so price gouging is efficient.* So the economists do believe that the willingness to pay IS proportional to need, a direct contradiction of statement 2.

<u>E is the correct answer.</u>

***

Let's look at another question where we must carefully consider each answer choice word for word. Take a look at the following question: after finding the structure of the argument, put your primary focus on the answer choices. For each answer choice, ask yourself, "Does this happen in the stimulus? If so, where?"

PT59 S2 Q7

Columnist: It has been noted that attending a live musical performance is a richer experience than listening to recorded music. Some say that this is merely because we do not see the performers when we listen to recorded music. However, there must be some other reason, for there is relatively little difference between listening to someone read a story over the radio and listening to someone in the same room read a story.

Which one of the following most accurately expresses the role played in the argument by the observation that attending a live musical performance is a richer experience than is listening to recorded music?

A. It is what the columnist's argument purports to show.
B. It is the reason given for the claim that the columnist's argument is attempting to undermine.
C. It is what the columnist's argument purports to explain.
D. It is what the columnist's argument purports to refute.
E. It is what the position that the columnist tries to undermine is purported to explain.

Let's break down the stimulus:

Columnist: It has been noted that <u>attending a live musical performance is a richer experience than listening to recorded music</u>. Some say that this is merely because we do not see the performers when we listen to recorded music. However, there must be some other reason, for there is relatively little difference between listening to someone read a story over the radio and listening to someone in the same room read a story.

Which one of the following most accurately expresses the role played in the argument by the observation that <u>attending a live musical performance is a richer experience than is listening to recorded music</u>?

- Statement 1 is the columnist's observation ("it has been noted"). Let's keep on going.
- Statement 2 presents one explanation (cause) for the observation made above.
- Statement 3 is the columnist's conclusion and the support they offer for it.

If we simplify the structure, we get something like this:

- Statement 1: There is a phenomenon that has been noted (X)
- Statement 2: Some believe X is caused by Y (Y⇒X)
- Statement 3: X cannot be caused by Y (conclusion), because…(premise)

So the first statement is a scenario/phenomenon that the author is concerned with. It's not a part of the author's argument, it is background information. The second statement is a classic opposing viewpoint. The author's argument comes in the last statement, in which they reject the cause offered by the people in the second statement and provide reasons for it.

Remember this example?

John has lung cancer. Smoking causes lung cancer. Therefore John must be a smoker.

Compare and contrast this example with the stimulus; what are the similarities and differences between the two?

Similarities: in both arguments, we start off with a phenomenon, and in both arguments, we attempt to find a cause to explain that phenomenon.

Differences: in John's case, the author provides a cause for his lung cancer (smoking). In the stimulus, does the author provide a cause/explanation? No. The author's conclusion only rejects the cause offered by others, without going all the way to provide a cause/explanation of his own.

   A. *It is what the columnist's argument purports to show.*

Answer choice A refers to the main conclusion of the argument. We know that in our stimulus, statement 1 is a phenomenon for which we are looking for the cause. It's not the main conclusion.

   B. *It is the reason given for the claim that the columnist's argument is attempting to undermine.*

This answer choice reverses the cause-effect relationship in our stimulus. In the stimulus, some people think that because we do see the performers when we listen to live music (cause) ⇒ live music is a richer experience (effect). According to B, statement 1 is the reason for the view attacked by the columnist. So in other words, if we fully expand answer choice B, it should look like this:

Because attending a live musical performance is a richer experience, we do not see the performers when we listen to recorded music.

C. *It is what the columnist's argument purports to explain.*

This is the most commonly selected wrong answer: read the keywords in the answer choice and ask yourself, does this happen in the stimulus? All correct answers will NEED to be matched with information in the stimulus.

Does the author explain (offer a cause) in their argument? Why is attending a live performance a richer experience? No, the author rejects another cause, but doesn't offer any new alternatives.

D. *It is what the columnist's argument purports to refute.*

Does the author reject the observation that *"attending a live musical performance is a richer experience than listening to recorded music?"* No, the author doesn't. The author refutes an explanation for why this is the case but doesn't reject the phenomenon itself.

E. *It is what the position that the columnist tries to undermine is purported to explain.*

Two words: **keyword extraction**. When an answer choice is suspiciously vague and makes us run in circles in an attempt to understand its meaning, break it up into pieces (deconstruction) and see if we can match it up with information from the stimulus.

"Position that the columnist tries to undermine" = because we do not see the performers when we listen to recorded music

What is this position purporting to explain? In other words, this position is a cause for what effect?

The effect is none other than the observation that "attending a live musical performance is a richer experience." Bingo.

The correct answer is E.

Sometimes it's not just the answer choices that are vague/abstract, stimuli and arguments can be too, and that brings us to:

Difficult Trait #3: Role Questions are famous for brutally abstract stimuli/arguments. When faced with an abstract argument in the stimulus, don't be afraid to slow down, summarize each statement, and rearrange the information structurally (deconstructing the stimulus).

PT 51 S3 Q23

Ethicist: it would be a mistake to say that just because someone is not inclined to do otherwise, she or he does not deserve to be praised for doing what is right, for although we do consider people especially virtuous if they successfully resist a desire to do what is wrong, they are certainly no less virtuous if they have succeeded in extinguishing all such desires.

The assertion that people are considered especially virtuous if they successfully resist a desire to do what is wrong plays which one of the following roles in the ethicist's argument?

A. It is a claim for which the argument attempts to provide justification.
B. It makes an observation that, according to the argument, is insufficient to justify the claim that the argument concludes is false.
C. It is a claim, acceptance of which, the argument contends, is a primary obstacle to some people having an adequate conception of virtue.
D. It is, according to the argument, a commonly held opinion that is nevertheless false.
E. It reports an observation that, according to the argument, serves as evidence for the truth of its conclusion.

Ethicist: it would be a mistake to say that just because someone is not inclined to do otherwise, she or he does not deserve to be praised for doing what is right, for although we do consider <u>people especially virtuous if they successfully resist a desire to do what is wrong</u>, they are certainly no less virtuous if they have succeeded in extinguishing all such desires.

The assertion that <u>people are considered especially virtuous if they successfully resist a desire to do what is wrong</u> plays which one of the following roles in the ethicist's argument?

Let's rearrange the stimulus and see if this will make more sense:

<u>Although we do consider people especially virtuous if they successfully resist a desire to do what is wrong</u>, they are certainly no less virtuous if they have succeeded in extinguishing all such desires. It would be a mistake to say that just because someone is not inclined to do otherwise, she or he does not deserve to be praised for doing what is right.

According to the author's reasoning, if John was a recovering alcoholic and David doesn't like alcohol, and both of them abstained from binge drinking, who is the more virtuous and more deserving of praise?

Neither: both are equally virtuous and deserving of praise. According to the author, it doesn't matter if you resist an especially strong temptation or urge to do what is wrong. As long as you refrain from doing the wrong thing, you are virtuous and deserving of praise.

Here, the underlined statement is a concession that the author makes.

>   A.   *It is a claim for which the argument attempts to provide justification.*

Answer choice A describes an intermediate conclusion or main conclusion. What we are looking for is a concession here.

>   B.   *It makes an observation that, according to the argument, is insufficient to justify the claim that the argument concludes is false.*

What does the argument conclude is false? The argument concludes that people who have no inclination to do wrong still deserve praise for doing right. (It would be a mistake to say that just because someone is not inclined to do otherwise, they do not deserve to be praised for doing what is right)

The claim that the argument concludes is false would basically be the opposite of the view that the author holds, or the view that the author thinks is mistaken. (If you are not inclined to do otherwise, you do not deserve praise for doing what is right)

Is the underlined statement insufficient to justify the claim that the author rejects? Yes, this is precisely how the author advances their argument. Even though we think alcoholics especially virtuous if they resist binge drinking, it doesn't mean those who don't like alcohol in the first place don't deserve praise for not binge drinking.

>   C.   *It is a claim, the acceptance of which the argument contends is a primary obstacle to some people's having an adequate conception of virtue.*

Is the fact that we consider recovering alcoholics especially virtuous if they resist the urge to drink a primary obstacle to people having an adequate conception of virtue? It's certainly a possibility. But there is simply too much inferred information in this answer choice that we cannot match it up with the stimulus or derive support from it. How do you define primary obstacle? What about an adequate conception of virtue?

Like Find the Conclusion answer choices, correct Role answer choices **must be provable** via the information available in the stimulus. Be careful of answer choices that sound reasonable but do not have explicit support, could be true, and most likely true answer choices!

> D.   *It is, according to the argument, a commonly held opinion that is nevertheless false.*

Is this claim a commonly held opinion? Probably. Is it false? No, the author argues that despite the truth of this claim, we should have a certain conception of virtue. The author is not arguing that this opinion is false.

> E.   *It reports an observation that, according to the argument, serves as evidence for the truth of its conclusion.*

What answer E describes is a premise. A premise supports the conclusion. What we have here is a concession: something that runs counter to the argument. *Despite the traffic jam, John arrived at work on time.* In this example, the traffic jam is the concession, John did not arrive at work on time because of the traffic jam; quite the contrary, it's something he had to overcome.

The correct answer is B.

Difficult Trait #4: Some correct answer choices won't actually describe the role played by the statement in question, but rather, a trait or characteristic of it.

In most Role Questions, as long as we have figured out whether the statement in question is a premise, intermediate conclusion, or main conclusion, we can get the question right without further complication.

But sometimes, the correct answer won't actually describe the statement's role in the argument. Instead, it will describe a quality or trait of that statement. When we can't simply match up our anticipated answer with one in the answer choices, it's okay to choose an answer choice that describes a quality or trait of the statement in question.

These answer choices are like Must be True Question answers, a topic we will cover in a subsequent chapter. Whenever I can't find an answer choice to match what I already have in mind, I go down the list and ask myself, "Which of the following is true of the statement in question?"

PT3 S4 Q20

Politician: Homelessness is a serious social problem, but further government spending to provide low income housing is not the cure for homelessness. The most cursory glance at the real-estate section of any major newspaper is enough to show that there is no lack of housing units available to rent. So the frequent claim that people are homeless because of a lack of available housing is wrong.

That homelessness is a serious social problem figures in the argument in which one of the following ways?

> A.   It suggests an alternative perspective to the one adopted in the argument.
> B.   It sets out a problem the argument is designed to resolve.
> C.   It is compatible either with accepting the conclusion or with denying it.
> D.   It summarizes a position the argument as a whole is directed toward discrediting.
> E.   It is required in order to establish the conclusion.

The conclusion of this argument is in the second half of the first sentence:

"But further government spending to provide low-income housing is not the cure for homelessness."

This is supported by statement 2 and statement 3 of the stimulus:

"The most cursory glance at the real-state section of any major newspaper is enough to show that there is no lack of housing units available to rent."

And,

"So the frequent claim that people are homeless because of a lack of available housing is wrong."

The relationship between statement 2 and 3 is not hard to detect. The author is arguing that *because there is enough housing, homelessness is not due to a lack of housing.* In other words, statement 2 is supporting statement 3.

How do these relate to the argument's conclusion? Statement 3 is direct support for the conclusion. So what we have here is a classic premise – intermediate conclusion – main conclusion structural pattern:

- Premise: There is enough housing.
- Intermediate Conclusion: Homelessness is not due to a lack of housing.
- Main Conclusion: Providing low-income housing will not cure homelessness.

But wait, what is the statement with which we are concerned? The question is asking us about the first half of the first sentence of the stimulus, *"homelessness is a serious social problem."* This is not a part of the argument. It's actually background information! It's providing the context for our argument.

So with that in mind, let's look at the answer choices.

　　　A.　　It suggests an alternative perspective to the one adopted in the argument.

What is meant by "alternative perspective?" It means that it is different and perhaps contrary to the author's view/conclusion. I think that means an opposing viewpoint. What we are looking for is background information. This answer choice can be eliminated.

　　　B.　　It sets out a problem the argument is designed to resolve.

Does it set out a problem? Yes: the problem of homelessness.

But be careful! Do you find any issues with the second half of this answer choice? Is the argument *designed to resolve* the problem of homelessness? I'm not so sure. The argument doesn't actually talk about how to solve homelessness but rejects a potential solution. Let's keep this one for now.

　　　C.　　It is compatible either with accepting the conclusion or denying it.

This is one weird answer choice. It's certainly true. Whether or not you agree or disagree that low-income housing is a viable solution to homelessness, you can't deny that homelessness is a serious problem.

　　　D.　　It summarizes a position the argument as a whole is directed toward discrediting.

We are not trying to argue that homelessness *isn't a serious problem* here.

　　　E.　　It is required in order to establish the conclusion.

Is this piece of information *required?* If homelessness wasn't a serious problem, then does it mean that the conclusion "low-income housing is not the solution" is no longer valid? No: how serious the situation is with regards to homelessness has no bearing on whether or not government-provided housing is a viable solution. Maybe homelessness was just a minor problem; maybe we can solve it by providing low-income housing; maybe low-income housing will still be ineffective. We just don't know.

This answer is too strong. Furthermore, we know that the statement in question is a piece of background information, not part of the core argument. As such, it's not a required component of the argument.

So we are left with B and C. Answer choice B is somewhat problematic because of its second half. Answer choice C, on the other hand, has nothing wrong with it. Although it doesn't really describe what "role" the statement in question actually plays, it has no specific problem that we could point to.

C is the correct answer.

> When it comes down to it, it's better to choose an answer that is further from your anticipated answer choice but don't have any particular issues than something close to what you had in mind but with clear additional problems.

Lastly, this question really reminded me of Difficult Trait #6 in the Find the Conclusion Chapter. The correct answer, which appears out of place, is placed next to two attractive wrong answers, answer choices B and E.

> When we are practicing, don't eliminate an answer choice simply because we are unclear about what it means. Eliminate an answer only when we can pinpoint what's wrong with it.

***

PT59 S2 Q18

Contrary to Malthus's arguments, human food producing capacity has increased more rapidly than human population. Yet, agricultural advances often compromise biological diversity. Therefore, Malthus's prediction that insufficient food will doom humanity to war, pestilence, and famine will likely be proven correct in the future, because a lack of biodiversity will eventually erode our capacity to produce food.

The statement that human food producing capacity has increased more rapidly than human population plays which one of the following roles in the argument?

- A. It is a hypothesis the argument provides reasons for believing to be presently false.
- B. It is a part of the evidence used in the argument to support the conclusion that a well known view is misguided.
- C. It is an observation that the argument suggests actually supports Malthus's position.
- D. It is a general fact that the argument offers reason to believe will eventually change.
- E. It is a hypothesis that, according to the argument, is accepted on the basis of inadequate evidence.

Let's break down the stimulus structurally:

Contrary to Malthus' arguments, <u>human food producing capacity has increased more rapidly than human</u> <u>population</u>. Yet, agricultural advances often compromise biological diversity. Therefore, Malthus' prediction that insufficient food will doom humanity to war, pestilence, and famine will likely be proven correct in the future, because a lack of biodiversity will eventually erode our capacity to produce food.

The statement that <u>human food producing capacity has increased more rapidly than human population</u> plays which one of the following roles in the argument?

Here is another question on which we must differentiate the structure of the argument and its logic chain. Logically, the argument is causal in nature:

Increased food production/agricultural advances ⇒ Compromise biological diversity ⇒ Decreased food production capacity ⇒ Insufficient food ⇒ War/pestilence/famine

But remember, when approaching a Role Question, we are concerned with its structure, what its main conclusion is, what its premises are, and how we should categorize each piece of information. With that in mind, let's look again at the stimulus.

Statement 1: *Contrary to Malthus' arguments, human food producing capacity has increased more rapidly than human population.*

Malthus' argument is not explicitly stated but can be inferred: Malthus believes population growth will outpace food increase. But this is not the case at the moment: food production is growing faster than population. This statement is an observation/fact, it is not an opinion. It can either be a premise, background information, or a concession.

Statement 2: *Yet, agricultural advances often compromise biological diversity.*

So increased food production/agricultural advances can have negative effects as well. Let's keep on going.

Statement 3: *Therefore, Malthus' prediction that insufficient food will doom humanity to war, pestilence, and famine will likely be proven true in the future.*

This is the argument's main conclusion. The author argues that Malthus' prediction will come true in the future.

Statement 4: *Because a lack of biodiversity will eventually erode our capacity to produce food.*

This is the author's support for his conclusion that Malthus will be correct after all.

If we simplify the argument and rearrange it structurally, we will get this:

Malthus believes we won't have enough food. This is currently not the case: we now have more food than people. But food production can compromise biological diversity, leading to decreased food production. So eventually Malthus will be right, in the future we probably won't have enough food.

The statement "*human food production capacity has increased more rapidly than human population*" is a concession. The author argues that although what Malthus predicted hasn't come to pass, it will eventually happen.

    A. *It is a hypothesis the argument provides reasons for believing to be presently false.*

Remember what a hypothesis is? A hypothesis is a causal explanation for a scientific/medical phenomenon. The statement in question is a factual statement, and it's also not a causal explanation. Also, the author believes it to be presently true.

> B. *It is a part of the evidence used in the argument to support the conclusion that a well known view is misguided.*

The conclusion of the argument is that Malthus will be proven right eventually, not that Malthus is misguided.

> C. *It is an observation that the argument suggests actually supports Malthus' position.*

This is the most commonly selected wrong answer, and a very tricky one at that. Remember that only premises and intermediate conclusions will support a main conclusion. Does the fact that Malthus is currently wrong support Malthus' position? No, the argument is suggesting that despite the fact that Malthus is currently wrong, he will be right in the future. What we have here is a concession. A concession does not support the conclusion.

> D. *It is a general fact that the argument offers reason to believe will eventually change.*

Is the underlined statement a general fact? Yes, it's a fact. Does the argument offer reason to believe it will eventually change? Yes: currently we have more food than people; eventually we won't have enough food for everyone due to the loss of biodiversity.

> E. *It is a hypothesis that, according to the argument, is accepted on the basis of inadequate evidence.*

What we have here is not a hypothesis, but a fact. The author does not argue against the fact that currently, food-producing capacity has increased more rapidly than the human population.

The correct answer is D.

Ultimately, we must carefully look at each answer choice, **word for word**. In this question, the only thing wrong with answer choice C is one single word, "*supports*." Get into the habit of examining answer choices in excruciating detail, refer back to the stimulus at every opportunity. If you can't match up the keywords in the answer choices with the content and structure of the stimulus, it will be wrong.

In this question, what we were looking for in the answer choices is a "concession." But no such answer appeared. The only answer choice that correctly describes the statement in question was D. Does the author believe the population will grow faster than food production eventually? Yes.

5.Core Habit:
KEYWORDS

Read each answer choice word for word, pay special attention to terms that are unclear or suspicious looking

5.Core Habit: KEYWORDS

Focus on the Answer Choices

We have already seen in previous chapters that many wrong answers can be eliminated because they are out of scope. That is, what these answer choices describe is something different from what was discussed in the stimulus.

Indeed, out-of-scope answer choices can be eliminated in many types of LR questions. An answer choice about something different from what was described in the stimulus will can be a red flag.

It is important to note that for different categories of LR questions, there will be different types of wrong answers. For question types such as Find the Conclusion Questions or Must be True Questions, out of scope answer choices will be wrong, whereas for question types such as Strengthen, Weaken, and even Necessary Assumption Questions, where outside or unexpected information is acceptable in correct answer choices, an answer choice being out of scope is NOT automatic grounds for elimination.

Suspicious Answer Choices

Six types of suspicious answers frequently appear in LR questions. Some of them will be automatically wrong, some will be wrong depending on the question type, and still some need to be compared to the other answer choices available.

We are getting ahead of ourselves a bit here because there are still many question types that we haven't covered yet along with the traits we typically associate with their answer choice selection. Don't worry too much about this as we will revisit these concepts when we get to each specific chapter.

Come back after you have finished the entire book and take another look to get a more generalized overview of some of the most common characteristics of wrong LR answer choices.

Opposite Answers

Opposite answers will give us a result that is the exact opposite of what we want. For example, an answer choice attacking the conclusion will be wrong on a Strengthen Question, and an answer describing something that cannot be true will be wrong on a Must be True Question.

Opposite answers frequently appear in Strengthen, Weaken, MBT, MSS, and Point of Agreement/Disagreement questions.

Opposite answers will always be wrong. Make sure you know what the question is asking for.

Out-of-Scope Answers

An out-of-scope answer will usually discuss something unrelated to the specific subject in the stimulus. For example, in a question about dogs, an answer choice about cats can look very suspicious.

Simple enough, right? But in reality, the test makers have several techniques to mask out-of-scope answers, making them less obvious.

- Unwarranted connections: two discrete, independent concepts are discussed in the stimulus, and the answer choice draws an unsupported connection between the two. For instance, if the stimulus said that *both disease and war caused many deaths during WWI*, an answer choice that says *military injuries led to the spread of diseases* would be making an unwarranted connection.

- Scope too narrow: the answer is discussing a group that is a subset of the group mentioned in the stimulus. For instance, if the stimulus was discussing African primates, and the answer is about gorillas in Rwanda, then the scope is narrowing.

Narrow-scope answer choices can be correct for certain question types. In fact, for inference questions (MBT and MSS,) these often appear as the correct answer choice. For example, if New York is located in the US, then it must be true that Manhattan is also located in the US.

For other question types, we need to be more careful and review the answer choice on a case-by-case basis.

- Scope too wide: an answer choice that discusses a topic more general or broader than what was discussed in the stimulus.

These answers are more suspicious and often wrong. But in certain question types they can work as correct answers. In Strengthen, Weaken, and Explain Questions, where we can draw upon outside information, a seemingly out-of-scope answer choice is not automatic grounds for elimination.

Similarly, in SA and NA Questions, an answer choice that appears out of scope but either allows the conclusion to be established or is necessary to the author's reasoning, respectively, will be fine.

For MBT and MSS Questions, a widening of the scope of discussion is nearly always problematic.

Lastly, scope doesn't matter on Parallel and Parallel Flaw questions because the correct answer doesn't need to match the content of the stimulus argument.

Answers that are too strong/too weak

Answer choices worded too strongly or weakly are not automatic grounds for dismissal. We may have a penchant for either strongly worded or weakly worded answers for certain types of LR questions.

In general, for Sufficient Assumption Questions, we like strongly worded answers, whereas for Necessary Assumption Questions, we prefer more conservatively worded answers.

Strongly worded answer choices/answer choices that clearly impact the argument are also preferable in Strengthen/Weaken Questions, as opposed to answer choices whose impact is unclear.

We will look at these traits in detail when we get to these question types down the road.

Half right half wrong answers

An **essential habit** to have for the most challenging LR questions (and RC questions) is to carefully parse the answer choices, looking for suspicious keywords or concepts and connections that seem out of place.

The test makers love to offer us an answer choice that is only partially correct. The first half of the answer may be correct, but the second half will contain out-of-scope information, for instance. So it's crucial to review each answer word by word and look for red flags.

Answers describing something that did not happen

For questions whose correct answer describes a feature of the stimuli's argument (Role, Method, Flaw), we need to watch for answer choices describing something that does not happen in the argument.

In fact, identifying answer choices that deviate from the stimulus is a sure-fire way to eliminate erroneous contenders. For these types of questions, read the answer choice, think about what it means, isolate any suspicious words in them, and ask yourself, "Does the author do this in their argument?"

But of course, this depends on the question type we are working on. Similar to Out of Scope answer choices, answer choices describing something that does not occur in the stimulus can work as correct Strengthen/Weaken answers, among others.

<u>Answer choices that are too vague/abstract</u>

Finally, we have seen how the correct answer can be vaguely worded in the previous two chapters. We have even practiced the art of extrapolating what an answer is referring to by analyzing its keywords in Chapter 4. (Answer choice deconstruction)

Extracting certain keywords from vague or abstract answer choices in order to understand what that answer choice is actually talking about is also an invaluable skill. Unfortunately, it's one of the most underdeveloped skills and is often overlooked when students pursue speed at the expense of accuracy.

When faced with an abstract answer choice, this is what we do:

- Read the answer choice, and extract any keywords that stand out to you.
- Think about what these keywords mean in an LSAT-specific setting.
- If it's a **noun**, ask yourself, does this concept appear in the stimulus?
- If it's a **verb**, ask yourself, does the author do this in the argument?
- If it's an **adjective/adverb**, does it correctly describe the tone or strength of the author's argument?
- Reread the answer choice and see if you can match what the answer describes with the stimulus's structure.
- Don't be afraid to go back and forth between the answer choice and the stimulus, the more you practice this skill, the easier it will be.

<u>Answer choices that can go either way depending on your assumptions</u>

These trap answers pertain specifically to Strengthen/Weaken Questions, and are probably the hardest to eliminate. I've had many 175+ students who routinely fell for them.

To illustrate with an example, let's say that the end goal of the question is for us to strengthen the conclusion "smoking is a leading cause of lung cancer," and one of the answer choices read "some people who smoke regularly have lung cancer."

When faced with such an answer choice, we have to be especially careful. Because how this answer affects the conclusion really depends on our interpretation of the word "some." On the surface, the answer may be re-emphasizing the linkage between smoking and lung cancer; but on a deeper level, if by "some" the testmakers are only talking about 20 people out of 20 million, then this answer would seem to do more harm to the original argument. Conversely, if we interpret "some" to mean 19 out of 20 million smokers, then yes, that would be a reasonable answer for a Strengthen Question.

Now I wouldn't eliminate such an answer outright, but if another answer choice with a more definitive effect came along for a Strengthen/Weaken Question, that other anwer would be the one I want. Answers whose effects are dependent on how we chose to interpret them are yellow flags to me and only selected as a last resort. Don't worry too much about this just yet as we shall look at real examples pertaining to this in Chapters 13 and 14.

<u>Placement traps</u>

Lastly, a common trick the test authors employs is to have an almost perfect answer with a glaring error, usually due to one word. This attractive trap answer is placed right next to the correct answer, which is worded vaguely. This is a trap that we shall see repeatedly throughout the book.

6. Method Questions

Method vs. Conclusion vs. Role Questions

After Role questions, we move to Method of Reasoning Questions. Generally speaking, Method Questions are more complex than Conclusion and Role Questions. But how you tackle these questions, at least in terms of the skills involved, is very similar. In all three types of questions, we need to be able to analyze the structure of the stimulus, but for Role and Method Questions, there's the additional requirement to differentiate between abstract answer choices. Method Questions go a step further: now in addition to these two skills, you have to further summarize how the argument goes from premise to conclusion logically.

Here is a diagram of the core skills involved in these three types of questions. As we can see, each question type builds upon the previous one:

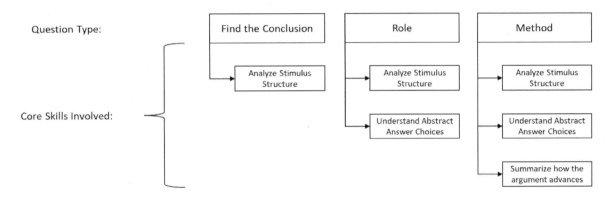

To analyze the stimulus structure, we have to distinguish between the argument components (premise/intermediate conclusion/main conclusion) and the peripheral information (background information/concession/opposing view) and categorize each statement. This is the most important skill in Find the Conclusion Questions, and half the battle for Role Questions.

In order to successfully differentiate between **abstract answer choices**, we have to read answer choices word for word, figure out the meaning behind certain LSAT-specific keywords, and make sure what the correct answer choice is describing can indeed be matched with the stimulus. Abstract answer choices are common in the hardest Role Questions, and we practiced deciphering these answer choices in the last chapter.

This is why we started with Find the Conclusion Questions, followed by Role Questions, and now turn to Method of Reasoning Questions. Each new question type requires us to master the previous one, and all three skills required for Method questions are invaluable for nearly every other type of LR question.

Method of Reasoning Questions, as we shall soon see, requires both of these skills and one more. When reading the stimulus, we must categorize the argument components (premise/intermediate conclusion/main conclusion); and when we approach the answer choices, we must deconstruct abstract and vague wording. (Just like we did for Role questions)

But there is an additional aspect to Method Questions not usually present in Conclusion or Role Questions: we now have to think about an additional element of the LR argument: How does the author advance their argument? How does the author go from the premise to the conclusion?

From Structure to Logic: How Arguments are Advanced in LR Questions

By now, we should have a strong understanding of how to analyze an LR stimulus structurally. We can identify the premises, intermediate conclusions, main conclusions that form the argument core, as well as the peripheral information within the stimulus. Once we can do this consistently, it's time to turn to another skill that we must possess, the ability to make sense of how the author advances their argument.

How the author advances their argument can be understood as the path they take from the premise to the conclusion. In each LR argument, the author starts at the premise (A) and ends at the conclusion (B). How the author goes from A to B is what we are interested in whenever we assess an argument's method of reasoning.

***

Let's look at an example and some of its variations, this will provide a better understanding of what we are dealing with:

We will start with a premise, *John consistently scores over 175 on his practice LSATs,* and end with the conclusion *John is a highly analytical person in his approach to life.* Let's look at all the different ways we can go from the premise to the conclusion. Some of these arguments may have gaps in their reasoning, but don't worry about this for now. Simply think about all the different ways in which we can move from premise to conclusion.

Conditional:

John consistently scores over 175 on his practice LSATs, only people who are highly analytical in real life situations score that high, so John is a highly analytical person in his approach to life.

Causation:

John consistently scores over 175 on his practice LSATs, constant practice and improvements on the LSAT causes a person to take a highly analytical approach to life as well, so John is a highly analytical person in his approach to life.

Another Causation variation (think about how this example differs from the previous one):

John consistently scores over 175 on his practice LSATs. Being a highly analytical person in real life is the most important reason that makes people succeed on the LSAT, so John is a highly analytical person in his approach to life.

Conditional and causal logic appears in a lot of LR questions. We often have to analyze the logic used in advancing the argument, especially in harder LR questions. Both conditional and causal logic are methods used by the author to advance the argument, to get from the premise to the conclusion; to go from A to B.

Other than conditional and causal logic, the author has a variety of other methods at their disposal to advance the argument:

Analogy/Comparable:

John consistently scores over 175 on his practice LSATs, David, who also scores in the same percentile, is a highly analytical person in his approach to life. So John must be as well.

Here, we are comparing John to David: John is a high scorer, David is too. David is highly analytical, so John must be too.

Generalization:

John consistently scores over 175 on his practice LSATs. John is a highly analytical person. In fact, every high scorer I know is a highly analytical person. So high scorers must all be highly analytical.

Correlation:

John consistently scores over 175 on his practice LSATs. There is a certain positive correlation between your performance on LSATs and the degree to which you approach life analytically. So John must be a highly analytical person in his approach to life.

Appeal to Authority:

John consistently scores over 175 on his practice LSATs. According to Professor Lin, the world's foremost expert on LSAT performance and real life performance, a high PT score is an indicator of a test taker's highly analytical approach to life. So John must be a highly analytical person in his approach to life.

Elimination of Alternatives:

John consistently scores over 175 on his practice LSATs. Nobody who approaches life in a non-analytical manner can ever attain such a high score. Even people who are only sometimes analytical in their approach to real life scenarios won't be able to score that high. Therefore John must be a highly analytical person in his approach to life.

Appealing to a Definition:

John consistently scores over 175 on his practice LSATs. The LSAT is defined as an exam that tests to what extent is someone analytical in their approach to life. Therefore John must be a highly analytical person in his approach to life.

***

Of course, all of the above examples are hypothetical scenarios. There is probably no well-defined correlation between your LSAT performance and your approach to life. These are just examples designed to show that there are different ways to advance one's argument. We know that we have premises and conclusions for each argument that appears on the LSAT. We must get into the habit of thinking about how we go from point A to point B, or from premise to conclusion.

Knowing how the author advances their argument is a crucial element that will help us succeed on the hardest questions.

The examples listed above are by no means exhaustive. Test makers love to come up with weird ways to advance the arguments in each stimulus. Make a note of these methods, you don't need to memorize them, but be familiar with the ways in which an LR argument is advanced.

Some Common Patterns of Reasoning that Appear in Method Questions

Look at the following descriptions of methods of reasoning and see if you can figure out for yourself what they mean. It's time to **deconstruct** the answer choices again.

1. *Providing an alternative explanation*

2. *Establishing the validity of one explanation by excluding alternative explanations*

3. *Reinterpreting an opponent's evidence so that they are also compatible with an alternative explanation*

4. *Infer a causal relationship from a correlation*

5. *Appeal to definition*

6. *Appeal to authority*

7. *Opponent's policy could have undesirable consequences*

8. *Pointing out that the opponent failed to take relevant information into account*

9. *Deriving a general principle from specific examples*

10. *Supporting a conclusion about a specific case by invoking a relevant generalization*

11. *Using a counterexample to attack a general claim*

12. *Attacking an opponent's premise*

13. *Conclude that members of two groups are likely to share a certain characteristic because of other characteristics they share*

14. *Pointing out that the opponent makes an inappropriate comparison/analogy*

15. *Using an analogy to advance one's argument*

16. *Pointing out an erroneous assumption in the opponent's argument*

17. *Showing that the opponent's conclusion, if true, leads to an impossible/unlikely result*

***

This is a list of all the most common patterns of reasoning that have appeared from PT 1 - 90. The list is by no means exhaustive. They are just patterns that have come up repeatedly in Method of Reasoning Questions. Again, you don't have to memorize the list; just read through them, make sure you understand the examples I provide and the reasoning pattern it is trying to describe. The goal here is that if you ever saw something similar on an actual test or a variation of it, you could quickly spot it.

- Providing an alternative explanation:

Remember, an **explanation** simply means cause on the LSAT.

A: I finally broke the 170 barrier on the LSAT. This was all because I had an awesome tutor.

B: Tutors can only point out the right way to study. Your success on the LSAT is rather due to your incessant hard work.

In the example above, A provides a cause/reason for getting over 170 on the LSAT. On the other hand, B disputes that cause and provides an alternative cause/explanation.

- Establishing the validity of one explanation by excluding alternative explanations:

We have briefly looked at this example earlier: the author will narrow in on one specific cause via the process of elimination. Take a look at the following example:

Gas prices have been increasing recently. Price increases can be caused by increased demand, limited supplies, or unforeseen geopolitical events. Demand and supply have remained constant, so the cause must be due to the war currently going on.

- Reinterpreting an opponent's evidence so that they are also compatible with an alternative explanation:

This is a tricky reasoning pattern that the test makers love to throw around. Notice how we are NOT rejecting the opponent's explanation, simply arguing that the reason they provide is compatible with ANOTHER explanation:

John: I saw Peter the other day, that guy lost over 40 lbs! He must have exercised like crazy.

David: It's also possible that he just watched his diet really carefully.

Notice how David isn't arguing that Peter didn't exercise. David is simply saying that it is also possible that Peter lost all this weight due to his diet.

Being aware of what the author is saying and what he isn't is really important on the LSAT. Know the limits of the author's conclusion.

- Infer a causal relationship from a correlation:

Correlation - Causation is one of the most common reasoning patterns to appear on the LSAT. Basically, the author will tell us that there is a positive correlation between A and B. They argue that there is causation behind this correlation, or that A ⇒ B.

A positive correlation is a statistical relationship where as one value increases, the other increases as well. As one value decreases, the other value also decreases. For example, as the temperature increases, the amount of sunscreen sold also increases. So we say that there is a correlation between the temperature and sunscreen sales.

Having a correlation between A and B doesn't automatically mean that there is causation involved between A and B. For instance, there is a positive correlation between how green the vegetation is and the number of people going swimming. Are people going swimming because trees are turning green or vice versa? No. There is a common cause for both phenomena, namely that the temperature is rising.

So whenever the stimulus presents us with a correlation, use your best judgment to determine whether there is a causal relationship behind it.

We will also look at correlations and causations in a later chapter in greater detail.

- Appeal to definition:

The author will give a dictionary/textbook definition of a certain term, and go on to argue that the action or event we are discussing fits or doesn't fit this definition.

- Appeal to authority:

We have also touched upon this earlier in the chapter: the author will invoke/appeal to an expert in the field to justify their point.

- Opponent's policy could have undesirable consequences:

In this type of reasoning, our author isn't attacking the opponent's reasoning per se, but instead they are suggesting that if we go through with what the opponent is recommending, it can lead to disastrous consequences.

John: Gasoline cars cause a lot of environmental damage, we should ban them outright.

David: But if you ban gasoline cars, how will millions of people survive? Most people need a car to go to work, and if you take away their cars, what will they do?

- Pointing out that the opponent failed to take relevant information into account:

This pattern of reasoning is very similar to the previous one. The author offers additional information or new evidence to attack/weaken the opponent's argument. It could be that what the opponent is arguing for has undesirable consequences, is impossible or difficult to enforce:

John: We should expose the government's corruption. Let's send the evidence to all the major media outlets in the country.

David: You forget that the government owns all the media outlets in our country. Doing so would only endanger yourself.

- Deriving a general principle from specific examples:

Remember that we briefly discussed generalizations and principles in the Find the Conclusion Chapter. A **principle** is essentially concerned with what you should do, or what should be done. Principles also have applicability to cases not explicitly discussed in the stimulus.

"People who break the law should be punished" is a principle. It is applicable regardless of who the person is, or what law was broken.

"All cars must pass the safety standard test before they can be marketed to the public" is also a principle.

"Taylor broke the law, so he should be punished" is NOT a principle. The statement is only talking about one person.

A **generalization** is very similar. It has applicability to cases not explicitly discussed in the stimulus. But a generalization doesn't have to be about what you should do or what should be done. If all the swans I saw were white, and I say *"All swans are white"*, I am generalizing.

A common pattern of reasoning in Method questions is to give a list of examples and derive a generalization/principle from them. This pattern of reasoning also appears in other types of questions. Here is an example:

Elon Musk failed many times before he succeeded, so did Steve Jobs, Thomas Edison, and all the great inventors and entrepreneurs that I know about. So in order to be successful, we must learn from our mistakes and never give up.

- <u>Supporting a conclusion about a specific case by invoking a relevant generalization:</u>

This is very similar to the preceding example, just done in reverse. Here, the author offers up a generalization, and uses it to justify their conclusion about a specific case/individual:

Every successful person has overcome many failures in order to be where they are today. So behind Elon Musk's great success story, there must have been countless painful failures.

- <u>Using a counterexample to attack a general claim:</u>

The opponent's argument will contain a generalization. Our author, in response, provides an example that doesn't fit into the opponent's generalization.

- <u>Attacking an opponent's premise:</u>

This demonstrates again why when faced with a rebuttal-type stimulus, we need to read the opponent's argument carefully, focusing on its structure. Is our author attacking the opponent's premise? If so, then this is the correct answer/method of reasoning.

- <u>Conclude that members of two groups are likely to share a certain characteristic because of other characteristics they share:</u>

This is essentially the most basic form of comparable reasoning. **Other than conditional logic and causal logic, comparable/making a comparison is the most common way to advance one's argument.** We will talk about this in the next chapter.

The author is basically saying that A and B have one similarity, so they are similar in another aspect. For example: *David and John are both from Chicago. David loves deep dish pizza, so John must love it as well.*

- <u>Pointing out that the opponent makes an inappropriate comparison/analogy:</u>

Comparable reasoning is again at play here, except this time our author is attacking the comparison made by the opponent. The author argues that just because two entities are similar in one aspect, it doesn't mean they are similar in another.

Continuing with the example above, we can argue that *just because two people are from the same city doesn't mean they will like the same food.*

- Using an analogy to advance one's argument:

An **analogy** is, according to the dictionary definition, *"a comparison between two things, typically for the purpose of clarification."* In other words, it is an advanced form of a comparison. For instance, physicists have used the analogy of a gun shooting bullets to better describe the process of radiation, where energy is "shot" out in the form of particles. The two processes are similar enough so that we can visualize one to better understand the other.

- Pointing out an erroneous assumption in the opponent's argument:

We will cover assumptions in more detail down the road, but the intermediate/advanced student should already know that an **assumption** is essentially an implicit/unstated premise. It would fill in the reasoning gap between the premise and conclusion, but for some reason, it has been left out by the author.

Take a look at the following argument:

All JDs must have taken the LSAT, so John must have taken the LSAT.

We have a premise (JD → LSAT) and a conclusion (John must have taken the LSAT), but clearly something is missing. We need an additional piece of information to make the argument complete:

John is a JD candidate/degree holder

This piece of missing information is the assumption. The whole argument, in its complete form, is like this:

All JDs must have taken the LSAT (premise), John is a JD candidate (assumption), so John must have taken the LSAT. (conclusion)

In Method Questions, arguments will sometimes contain assumptions. Both the opponent's argument and/or the author's argument can contain these assumptions. They are hard to spot because they don't appear in the stimulus. We have to understand the argument and find the gap between premise and conclusion, finally inferring the assumptions ourselves.

An especially tricky format that we will see in Method Questions is when the opponent's argument contains an assumption, and our author is attacking that assumption, rather than the opponent's premise or conclusion. When faced with such a reasoning pattern, many students will be at a loss of what to do, as what the author is saying seems to have no connection to what the opponent was saying. Continuing with the same example, the stimulus would look something like this:

Peter: All JDs must have taken the LSAT, so John must have taken the LSAT.

David: But John isn't a JD, he's an LLM.

Here, David is directly contradicting Peter's assumption that John has a JD. When looking at harder Method Questions, ask yourself if any of the arguments contain assumptions.

- Showing that the opponent's conclusion, if true, leads to an impossible/unlikely result:

This type of reasoning looks very similar to the conditional reasoning contrapositive. Remember that in a conditional relationship, A → B, its contrapositive is B̶ → A̶.

In this type of argument, the opponent will come to the conclusion A. Our author, on the other hand, will state that if conclusion A is true, it will lead to/likely lead to B. However, since B is not true, A cannot be true either. Here is an example:

John: The taller you are, the better you are as a basketball player. (A)

David: If that were true, the world's tallest person would be the best basketball player in the world. (If A were true, it leads to B)

Here, David assumes that the tallest person in the world is NOT also the best basketball player; hence John is mistaken in his belief about the correlation between height and basketball skills. (B is not the case; hence A is wrong as well. B̶ → A̶)

***

So far, we have covered some of the most common patterns of reasoning to appear in Method Questions. Make sure you are familiar with these examples and can readily spot them again when they appear in the LR stimulus. Whenever we approach a Method Question, always consider how the author advances their argument, how they get from the premise to the conclusion, and what reasoning technique or type of logic is used.

*Be sure to differentiate between an analogy and an example. These are two different things. Take a look at PT81 S3 Q21. What's the correct answer?

So we have looked at Find the Conclusion, Role, and Method of Reasoning questions.

In Find the Conclusion Questions, we learned to dissect an LR stimuli's **structure**: identifying its premises, conclusions, and peripheral information. In Role Questions, we learned to translate abstract **answer** choices into pieces of information that can be compared to the stimulus. In Method of Reasoning Questions, we have looked at many of the different ways in which the author can advance their argument, and the type of **logic** they have employed.

These three skills will form an important part of our approach to nearly all subsequent LR Questions, as well as a part of the SLAKR Approach to the most difficult questions.

A Selection of the Hardest Method of Reasoning Questions

Take a look at the following questions. I've included several questions where either the argument structure or the answer choices are especially tricky. Don't worry too much about timing in your first pass, just focus on the step-by-step process we discussed. Develop a systematic approach to these questions and apply that approach to your by-type practicing and your practice tests.

Try not to only select the correct answer, but to extract all the information you can from the stimulus, and have a reason for eliminating the answer choices you did. Then compare your reasoning to mine to see if we see eye to eye. On an actual test, since these are the hardest questions in this category, a time of under 3 minutes is acceptable, and around 2 minutes would be spectacular.

Difficult Trait #1: Beware of abstract/vague terms in the answer choices, practice the core habit of keyword extraction, and make sure you know what certain words mean specifically to the LSAT.

PT18 S4 Q21

Jane: Professor Harper's ideas for modifying the design of guitars are of no value because there is no general agreement among musicians as to what a guitar should sound like and, consequently, no widely accepted basis for evaluating the merits of a guitar's sound.

Mark: What's more, Harper's ideas have had enough time to be adopted if they really resulted in superior sound. It took only ten years for the Torres design for guitars to be almost universally adopted because of the improvement it makes in tonal quality.

Which one of the following most accurately describes the relationship between Jane's argument and Mark's argument?

- A. Mark's argument shows how a weakness in Jane's argument can be overcome
- B. Mark's argument has a premise in common with Jane's argument
- C. Mark and Jane use similar techniques to argue for different conclusions
- D. Mark's argument restates Jane's argument in other terms
- E. Mark's argument and Jane's argument are based on conflicting suppositions

We start by thinking about the structure of the stimulus. As we can see, the stimulus has two people engaged in a conversation, Jane and Mark. We must look at both when two people are talking in the stimulus.

Jane's argument is pretty straightforward. She concludes that *Harper's ideas are of no value.* It's at the very beginning of her argument. Her entire argument, if diagrammed, looks like this:

- Premise: *There is no general consensus on what guitars should sound like*
- Intermediate Conclusion: *There is no basis for evaluating the merits of a guitar's sound*
- Main Conclusion: *Professor Harper's ideas for modifying guitar design have no value*

Now let's look at Mark's argument:

Mark's argument is interesting because he appears to agree with Jane's conclusion. We have discussed instances where the second person is rebutting the first person in the stimulus, but this is different. We must always beware of these little variations that can throw us off track.

So if Mark agrees that Harper's ideas are of no value, how does he support his argument? Mark's argument is slightly more hidden than Jane's, but if we dig deeper, we can find it.

It took only ten years for the Torres design for guitars to be almost universally adopted because of the improvement it makes in tonal quality

So designs that do improve sound quality are quickly adopted, as the Torres guitar demonstrates.

But has Harper's ideas been adopted? No. This can be gleaned from Mark's first statement: *Harper's ideas have had enough time to be adopted if they really resulted in superior sound.*

So Mark's argument is this:

- Premise: *Like the Torres guitar, if the design improves sound quality, they are quickly adopted*
- Assumption: *Harper's designs haven't been adopted*
- Conclusion: *Harper's designs do not improve sound quality (Harper's designs have no value)*

So Mark and Jane agree in their conclusions but arrive at that conclusion via different means. Let's take a look at the answer choices:

   A.   *Mark's argument shows how a weakness in Jane's argument can be overcome*

Remember the skills we learned in the chapter on Role Questions? (**keyword extraction**) What is the so-called weakness contained in Jane's argument? Jane and Mark are indeed arguing for the same conclusion, but they come from different places. Mark is not using his argument to plug a gap/weak point in Jane's argument.

Let's go a bit deeper with a hypothetical. Let's have two people, A and B, arguing for the same conclusion but using different support.

A: *All men are mortal, Socrates is a man, therefore Socrates is mortal.*
B: *I was there when the Athenians killed him, Socrates died in front of my eyes, he's definitely mortal.*

Even though A and B are arguing for the same conclusion, it doesn't mean one is helping the other overcome a weakness in their argument.

   B.   *Mark's argument has a premise in common with Jane's argument*

We know they have different premises but the same conclusion.

> *C.   Mark and Jane use similar techniques to argue for different conclusions*

First of all, they argue for the same conclusion. Even the techniques they use are different. For Jane, I'd say that she uses a fact or maybe a generalization (*no standard to evaluate how a guitar ought to sound like*) to support her conclusion. Mark, on the other hand, shows that if Harper's ideas had merit, it would lead to an impossible/unlikely result. (*If Harper's ideas had merit, they'd have been adopted already, since they haven't been adopted, Harper's ideas don't have merit.*)

> *D.   Mark's argument restates Jane's argument in other terms*

Careful here, the word of concern is "argument." As we know, an argument will contain not just the conclusion but also the premise and intermediate conclusion. Mark restates Jane's conclusion, not her entire argument.

> *E.   Mark's argument and Jane's argument are based on conflicting suppositions*

On the LSAT, a **supposition** means premise. (Remember that a **presupposition** means assumption).

So this answer choice is basically saying that their arguments have conflicting premises. Jane's intermediate conclusion (remember that an intermediate conclusion is also a premise to the main conclusion, it has a dual role) states that *there is no basis for evaluating the merits of a guitar's sound*. Mark, in his Torres example, believes the Torres guitar was adopted so quickly *because of the improvement it makes in tonal quality*.

E is the correct answer.

As you can see, getting this question right requires knowing what "*supposition*" means. Words like "explanation," "generalization," and "assumption" all refer to specific things on the LSAT.

Once you have isolated the keywords in a Method Question, ask yourself what they mean. Then go back to the stimulus and see if it fits.

Difficult Trait #2: Watch out for assumptions in the author's argument, not just the premises and conclusions.

I know that we haven't properly covered assumptions yet and are getting ahead of ourselves a little bit. But the intermediate/advanced student should already have a general idea of what an assumption is on the LSAT, In fact, you have most likely come across Sufficient and Necessary Assumption questions previously.

As we will soon see in later chapters, an assumption is a piece of missing information. It can either be a premise or intermediate conclusion of the argument that the author has deliberately left out. Basically, to detect an assumption, we must look for gaps in the author's reasoning and try to come up with a statement that would fill the gap to the best of our ability.

Identifying a missing assumption is one of the core skills that we will soon look at. As a result, we won't go into further detail here. Don't worry if you are having trouble following the questions below or my explanations. Make a note to yourself and return after finishing the chapters on Assumptions.

PT58 S1 Q26

Philosopher: Wolves do not tolerate an attack by one wolf on another if the latter wolf demonstrates submission by baring its throat. The same is true of foxes and domesticated dogs. So it would be erroneous to deny that animals have rights on the grounds that only human beings are capable of obeying moral rules.

The philosopher's argument proceeds by attempting to

    A.   Provide counterexamples to refute a premise on which a particular conclusion is based
    B.   Establish inductively that all animals possess some form of morality
    C.   Cast doubt on the principle that being capable of obeying moral rules is a necessary condition for having rights
    D.   Establish a claim by showing that the denial of that claim entails a logical contradiction
    E.   Provide evidence suggesting that the concept of morality is often applied too broadly

Look carefully at the philosopher's argument. Are they making a point, or rebutting an opponent?

The philosopher is responding to someone who wishes to deny animal rights. So this stimulus is actually a "rebutting an opponent" type question, even though it's not explicitly laid out in a two-person conversational type format. Again, beware the tricky variations that appear in these questions!

So what is the opponent arguing? The opponent believes *only humans are capable of obeying moral rules,* so *animals DON'T have rights.*

However, if *only humans are capable of obeying moral rules,* the opponent is essentially saying that animals can't obey moral rules, right?

So if we expand the opponent's argument, what they are essentially saying is this:

- Premise: *animals don't obey moral rules*
- Assumption: *rights → obeying moral rules*
- Conclusion (via the assumption's contrapositive): *animals don't have rights*

So how does the philosopher argue AGAINST this?

The philosopher lists examples of animals that don't attack those who submit. How do these examples relate to our argument?

There is an assumption that the philosopher makes here. Not attacking those who have submitted IS a moral rule in the animal kingdom. In other words, such behavior demonstrates that wolves, foxes, and dogs are capable of obeying moral rules. So the philosopher's argument, complete with assumption, is this:

- Premise: *animals don't attack those who submit*
- Assumption: *not attacking those who submit is a moral rule*
- Conclusion: *animals obey moral rules*

The philosopher is essentially attacking the opponent's premise with their examples.

Before we turn to the answer choices, it is also important to note that the philosopher is simply arguing that the opponent can't use this type of reasoning to conclude that animals don't have rights. The philosopher's argument doesn't demonstrate that animals actually do have rights. So as we mentioned previously, just be aware of the degree/scope of the author's conclusion.

Let's take a look at the answer choices:

A. *Provide counterexamples to refute a premise on which a particular conclusion is based*

This is precisely what our explanations are getting at, let's keep on going.

B. *Establish inductively that all animals possess some form of morality*

Inductive reasoning is where you are moving from a list of examples to a generalization. So what this answer is saying is that "wolves have morality, foxes have morality, dogs have morality, so all animals have morality."

C. *Cast doubt on the principle that being capable of obeying moral rules is a necessary condition for having rights*

Does the philosopher attack the conditional relationship Rights → Obey Moral Rules? No, they do not dispute this. The philosopher is simply arguing that animals ARE capable of obeying moral rules.

D.   Establish a claim by showing that the denial of that claim entails a logical contradiction

A **logical contradiction** is where a state and its denial exist simultaneously. This cannot happen. If A → B and A → B̶ are placed together, that entails a logical contradiction. "New York is in the US" and "New York is NOT in the US", together, forms a logical contradiction. This doesn't happen in our stimulus.

E.   Provide evidence suggesting that the concept of morality is often applied too broadly

The philosopher isn't suggesting that the concept of morality is applied too broadly and should be narrowed down. Quite the opposite, the opponent restricts morality to humans, but the philosopher also believes it applies to animals.

The takeaway from this question is that we must look at the **structure** of the stimulus carefully; having a clear grasp of the premises, conclusions, and assumptions within an argument is crucial to success on Method Questions.

We also need to have a clear and discrete understanding of the answer choices. Know what each **keyword** is referring to, and don't choose an answer choice if you can't match it up with the stimulus!

The correct answer is A.

***

Let's look at another question where assumptions play an important role in the stimulus:

PT56 S2 Q9

Rifka: We do not need to stop and ask for directions. We would not need to do that unless, of course, we were lost.

Craig: The fact that we are lost is precisely why we need to stop.

In the exchange above, the function of Craig's comment is to

A.   Contradict the conclusion of Rifka's argument without offering any reason to reject any of Rifka's implicit premises
B.   Deny one of Rifka's implicit premises and thereby arrive at a different conclusion
C.   Imply that Rifka's argument is invalid by accepting the truth of its premises while rejecting its conclusion
D.   Provide a counterexample to Rifka's generalization
E.   Affirm the truth of the stated premise of Rifka's argument while remaining noncommittal about its conclusion

This question, again, is a "rebutting an opponent" type question. Craig disagrees with Rifka. Let's break down each person's argument.

Rifka concludes that *we do not need to stop and ask for directions.* Her premise is a conditional statement: *We would not need to do that unless we were lost.*

So how does Rifka go from "Stop and ask for directions → Lost" to "We do not need to stop and ask for directions?"

Rifka's argument, just like in the previous question, contains an assumption. Rifka is assuming that we are NOT lost.

- Rifka's Premise: *Stop and ask for directions → Lost*
- Rifka's Assumption: *We are NOT lost.*
- Rifka's Conclusion: *We do NOT need to stop and ask for directions.*

Now look at Craig's argument, Craig says that *the fact that we are lost is precisely why we need to stop.*

What does Craig want to do? He wants to stop. Why does he want to stop? Because he thinks we are lost.

So Craig is essentially denying Rifka's assumption and coming to the opposite conclusion.

- Craig's Premise: *We ARE lost*
- Craig's Conclusion: *We DO need to stop and ask for directions*

Let's take a look at the answer choices:

A. *Contradict the conclusion of Rifka's argument without offering any reason to reject any of Rifka's implicit premises.*

An **implicit premise** is the same thing as an assumption.

This answer is only half correct. Craig rejects both the implicit premise and the conclusion.

B. *Deny one of Rifka's implicit premises and thereby arrive at a different conclusion*

This is good, Craig denies Rifka's implicit premise and arrives at the opposite conclusion.

C. *Imply that Rifka's argument is invalid by accepting the truth of its premises while rejecting its conclusion.*

Extract the keywords from this answer choice: does Craig accept the truth of Rifka's premises? Rifka has one explicit premise, Stop → Lost. Craig does not acknowledge this conditional in his argument. Rifka has one implicit premise (assumption), which Craig denies.

D. *Provide a counterexample to Rifka's generalization.*

No generalizations or counterexamples here.

E. *Affirm the truth of the stated premise of Rifka's argument while remaining noncommittal about its conclusion*

Again, Craig doesn't affirm Rifka's conditional statement and he explicitly denies Rifka's conclusion. The correct answer is B.

Difficult Trait #3: Watch out for the common wrong answer traps we discussed in "Core Habit: Keywords." Be careful of out-of-scope, half right/half wrong, and too strong/too weak answer choices!

PT69 S1 Q23

Anthropologist: every human culture has taboos against eating certain animals. Some researchers have argued that such taboos originated solely for practical reasons, pointing out, for example, that in many cultures it is taboo to eat domestic animals that provide labor and that are therefore worth more alive than dead. But that conclusion is unwarranted; taboos against eating certain animals might have arisen for symbolic, ritualistic reasons, and the presence of the taboos might then have led people to find other uses for those animals.

In the argument, the anthropologist

A. Calls an explanation of a phenomenon into question by pointing out that observations cited as evidence supporting it are also compatible with an alternative explanation of the phenomenon
B. Establishes that an explanation of a phenomenon is false by demonstrating that the evidence that had been cited in support of that explanation was inadequate
C. Rejects the reasoning used to justify a hypothesis about the origins of a phenomenon, on the grounds that there exists another, more plausible hypothesis about the origins of that phenomenon
D. Argues in support of one explanation of a phenomenon by citing evidence incompatible with a rival explanation
E. Describes a hypothesis about the sequence of events involved in the origins of a phenomenon, and then argues that those events occurred in a different sequence

I specifically included this question because there are two essential lessons here. **First**, as we mentioned earlier in the chapter, we really must watch *the scope of the conclusion*. We have to be aware of what the author is arguing for and, more importantly, what they are not. In this stimulus, the author's conclusion is simply that *the opponent's conclusion is unwarranted.* Our author isn't pushing for an alternative conclusion, our author isn't flat out rejecting the opponent's conclusion; they are simply suggesting that the opponent's conclusion does not follow from their premise.

Secondly, there's a treasure trove of LSAT-specific key terms in the answer choices; words like "explanation," "hypothesis," and "phenomenon." It's a great opportunity to refresh our understanding of these key terms, so let's look at the question now:

The first statement is background information telling us that there are animals that we just don't eat. The second statement presents the researchers (opponents) and their view. They believe we don't eat certain animals because they can provide labor.

Does the format of this stimulus look familiar? A phenomenon is described at the beginning of the stimulus, and the researchers have offered an explanation/causation. Why are there animals that people refuse to eat? It's because of practical reasons.

So if we reorganize the researchers' argument, which attempts to find the cause for why is it that we have taboos against eating certain animals, it should look like this:

In many cultures people don't eat labor animals, so it is because of practical reasons that we have taboos against eating certain animals.

What is the anthropologist's view towards the researchers' viewpoint? Like we said before, the anthropologist only offers a very limited rebuttal. They simply say the researchers' conclusion is unwarranted. What does this mean? Let's take a look at the following example:

John: I scored a 170 on the LSAT, my IQ must be really high as well.
David: The LSAT is a learnable test, IQ tests are not. Your conclusion is unwarranted.

Is David saying that John doesn't have a high IQ? No, that's not what he is saying. He simply says that you cannot conclude that you have a high IQ based on LSAT performance.

The test makers love to place a **limited conclusion** in the stimulus, and **subtly shift** its strength/scope in attractive wrong answer choices.

So if the author's conclusion is so limited, are his premises also limited? Yes, note the support given: *"taboos against eating certain animals MIGHT instead have arisen for symbolic, ritualistic reasons, and the presence of the taboos MIGHT then have led people to find other uses for those animals."* So the author is simply suggesting that there is another possibility. He is not arguing that people first decided to stop eating certain animals, and then put them to work. He is only demonstrating that there's another potential possibility, but he is not actually committing to this second possibility.

Let's take a look at the answer choices:

> A. *Calls an explanation of a phenomenon into question by pointing out that observations cited as evidence supporting it are also compatible with an alternative explanation of the phenomenon*

Let's break this answer choice down into actionable parts:

- *"Calls an explanation of a phenomenon into question"* – what's the phenomenon that we are concerned with? Every culture has taboos against eating certain animals. What's the explanation the author questions? The author thinks the researchers' explanation/causation is unwarranted.

- *"By pointing out that observations cited as evidence supporting it are also compatible with an alternative explanation of the phenomenon"* – This is how the author questions the opposing view. What's the evidence supporting the opposing view? Namely that many cultures don't eat labor animals. Does our author think this evidence is also compatible with another explanation for the phenomenon? Yes, the author says that it's also possible that we first refused to eat these animals, and then put them to work.

Everything in this answer choice matches the stimulus's structure and reasoning.

> B.   *Establishes that an explanation of a phenomenon is false by demonstrating that the evidence that had been cited in support of that explanation was inadequate*

Does the author think the researcher's evidence is inadequate? I think so. Because we don't eat labor animals doesn't necessarily mean we don't eat them *because* they are labor animals. It could be that we refuse to eat them first, then found work for them. The problem with this answer choice is in the first part. Our author didn't *establish* that the researcher's explanation is false. They simply think its unwarranted.

> C.   *Rejects the reasoning used to justify a hypothesis about the origins of a phenomenon, on the grounds that there exists another, more plausible hypothesis about the origins of that phenomenon*

The second half of this answer choice is problematic. Our author does raise another possibility, an alternative explanation of the phenomenon. But they do not think the alternative *more plausible.*

Take a look at the following example:

John: I saw Peter today, he must have flown in early this morning.
David: You don't know that, he could have also taken the train.

Does David think it more likely that Peter took the train? Does David argue that Peter took the train and not the plane? Not necessarily, he is simply pointing out that John is too quick in his conclusion and there's an alternative that he has failed to consider.

So always be on the lookout for answer choices that are stronger/weaker than what was argued in the stimulus. These are usually **trap answers** in Method of Reasoning Questions.

> D.   *Argues in support of one explanation of a phenomenon by citing evidence incompatible with a rival explanation*

Our author isn't arguing *in support* of their alternative explanation. They are only raising the possibility to show that the opponent's premise doesn't automatically lead to their conclusion.

> E.   *Describes a hypothesis about the sequence of events involved in the origins of a phenomenon, and then argues that those events occurred in a different sequence*

Same issue here, this answer is way too strong. If the answer choice had read "*described a hypothesis about the sequence of events involved in the origins of a phenomenon, and then raises the possibility that those events occurred in a different sequence,*" then it would probably be okay.

The correct answer is A.

***

We actually saw this in the previous question. In the previous question, the author concludes that the opponent's conclusion is "unwarranted." Answer choice B, on the other hand, describes an argument in which the author flat-out rejects the opponent's conclusion. Think about the subtle differences:

John: A caused B.

David: But it's also possible that C caused B.

Here, David is merely raising the possibility that something else caused B. David isn't committed to the position that A did not cause B. Perhaps he is hinting at it, but it's not a position that he is explicitly committed to. In the language of the LSAT, David is *suggesting another potential explanation,* but he has not demonstrated the *falsity of John's explanation.*

Similarly, David is not arguing that C had indeed caused B.

This second point encapsulates the differences between what was described in answer choice C and the actual argument itself. The author is simply questioning one explanation by providing a potential alternative. The alternative explanation is not the author's conclusion.

The test makers love to place a limited conclusion in Method Questions and provide us with tempting wrong answers that describe a scenario either too strong or too broad.

So **focus on the wording of the conclusion** and think about the exact position to which the author is committed.

Let's look at another question where we have to put all the skills we have learned so far to use: think about assumptions hidden in the stimulus structure, decipher abstract reasoning patterns, use keyword extraction techniques to deconstruct and differentiate between answer choices, and finally match them up with the stimulus.

Difficult Trait #4: Pay attention to the scope/strength of the author's conclusion!

<u>PT70 S4 Q26</u>

People may praise the talent of a painter capable of realistically portraying a scene and dismiss as artistically worthless the efforts of abstract expressionists, but obviously an exact replica of the scene depicted is not the only thing people appreciate in a painting, for otherwise photography would have entirely displaced painting as an art form.

The argument proceeds by

    A.   Using a claim about what most people appreciate to support an aesthetic principle
    B.   Appealing to an aesthetic principle to defend the tastes that people have
    C.   Explaining a historical fact in terms of the artistic preferences of people
    D.   Appealing to a historical fact to support a claim about people's artistic preferences
    E.   Considering historical context to defend the artistic preferences of people

This is one of those questions that at a first glance looks fairly straightforward. But when you analyze it, you find it hard to fully explain what is going on, because there's so much more going on beneath the surface.

The entire stimulus is one long sentence, divided into three parts:

People may praise the talent of a painter capable of realistically portraying a scene and dismiss as artistically worthless the efforts of abstract expressionists

This is a phenomenon; perhaps the author will strive to find an explanation for why it is so? People praise realism in art but think abstract expressionism (non-realistic art) worthless. Is it because people judge an artwork by how realistic it is? Let's read on.

But obviously an exact replica of the scene depicted is not the only thing people appreciate in a painting

This is the author's main point. The author believes that an exact replica (the most realistic painting) is not the only thing people care about. So the author thinks realism is not the only factor in people's judgment of art. Does the author deny that realism is important? No. Does the author say what these other factors are? No. The author simply says it's not the only factor.

For otherwise photography would have entirely displaced painting as an art form

This supports the author's conclusion that there are factors other than realism to consider. We have seen this type of reasoning pattern in our examples earlier in the chapter. Just to refresh your memory, here is an analogy:

John: it obviously didn't rain last night, for otherwise the ground would still be wet.

So what is John's argument here?

- Premise: *if it rained last night the ground would still be wet.*
- Assumption: *the ground isn't wet*
- Conclusion: *it didn't rain last night*

So here, the author is arguing that because an implication if the conclusion is true did not occur, the conclusion is false. If you think about it as conditional reasoning, then the author is basically saying A → B, ~~B~~, therefore ~~A~~.

So in the author's reasoning:

- Premise: *If the only thing people appreciated in art was realism, photography would have entirely displaced paintings*
- Assumption: *Photography didn't entirely displace paintings*
- Conclusions: *People appreciate factors other than realism in art*

Clear now? Two things that stood out to me in this stimulus are the **assumption** we just talked about and the fact that the author's conclusion is restricted. (They are not saying realism is not a factor, just saying that there are other factors to consider.)

A.   *Using a claim about what most people appreciate to support an aesthetic principle*

What do people appreciate? We know from the stimulus that people appreciate realism. Is there an aesthetic principle in the argument? Hidden in the author's conclusion there seems to be the view that *realism is not the only factor to consider.*

Does the fact that most people appreciate realism *support* the conclusion that there are factors beside realism to be considered? No, the author is arguing that there are other factors to consider *despite the fact that* most people appreciate realism. Also, how do we know whether it's *most people* who appreciate realism? The stimulus only mentioned *people,* we simply don't know if it's most people, some people, or a few people.

B.   *Appealing to an aesthetic principle to defend the tastes that people have*

Using a principle to support a conclusion is a pattern we have looked at before. The principle in this question, if there is one, is that *people appreciate qualities in art other than realism.* This is the conclusion and not the premise. Furthermore, the author isn't really defending people's tastes here. They are not really taking a side in this fight; there is no defense, judgment, or evaluation of whether people are right to appreciate realistic art.

C.   *Explaining a historical fact in terms of the artistic preferences of people*

So basically using the artistic preferences of people to explain a historical fact. In other words, because people have a certain preference for art, a certain historical fact happened. What is the historical fact in this stimulus? The only possible historical fact that we can discern is that *photography hasn't entirely displaced painting as an art form.*

So this answer choice is saying either one of two things: *because people prefer realistic paintings, photography didn't displace art;* or *because people appreciate more than realism, photography hasn't displaced art.* The actual argument is sort of the reversal of the second possibility: *Since photography hasn't displaced art, people must care about factors other than realism in art.* But the fact that photography hasn't displaced art is not a *cause/explanation* for why people have certain tastes in art. It's a premise, sure, but causal logic isn't in play here. So there's several issueswith this answer.

D.   *Appealing to a historical fact to support a claim about people's artistic preferences*

So using a historical fact (photography didn't replace art) to support a claim about people's artistic preferences (people care about factors other than realism). This seems to match up well with what actually happens in the stimulus. The author is making a claim, they are not defending people's tastes.

E.   *Considering historical context to defend the artistic preferences of people*

Again, the word "defend" is too strong. Had the answer read *considering historical context to make a claim about the artistic preferences of people,* then it would have been okay.

The correct answer is D.

Difficult Trait #5: During answer choice elimination, when all else fails, pick the answer you didn't understand over answer choices in which you detected errors.

We have already seen variations of this several times in the previous chapters. There will be time and time again when the correct answer will not match up with what we had anticipated from reading the stimulus. As a result, we had to turn to the process of elimination to choose the best available answer.

More so than Find the Conclusion and Role Questions, where you can mostly anticipate the correct answer, Method Questions are largely answer choice driven: this means that there be a lot of times when you will have no idea what the correct answer should look like upon reading the stimulus.

When faced with such a scenario, all we can do is carefully go over the answer choices and pick the one that most closely matches the stimulus. We don't really know what we are looking for, so we have to look at each answer choice one by one and think about whether it deviates from the stimulus's argument.

But what happens when we have gone through all the answers, but still can't find an answer we like?

As we have seen in Difficult Trait #6 in the Find the Conclusion Chapter, test makers love to make the correct answer super abstract while throwing attractive wrong answers into the lot. This happens on the hardest LR questions of nearly every type, and Method Questions are no exception.

Knowing this, when I'm going through a Method Question, I always have my highlighter in hand, highlighting suspicious keywords, words that are out of scope, too strong, too weak, or simply describing something that does not appear in the author's argument. In other words, I'm looking for grounds to eliminate each and every answer choice.

But occasionally, we get to an answer choice that is phrased in such a way that we have no idea what it's trying to say. There's nothing wrong with it, at least in the sense that it does not appear to be out of scope, worded too strongly/too weakly, or describes something that does not happen in the stimulus.

When all else fails and with time running out, and knowing that test makers love to make the correct answer extra complicated, it's time to take a leap of faith. Wrong answers are always wrong for a reason, so I trust my instincts and go with the unclear answer choice rather the answer choice that I understand but I know contains problems.

***

PT86 S1 Q24

Andy Warhol's Brillo Boxes is a stack of boxes that are visually indistinguishable from the product packaging of an actual brand of scouring pads. Warhol's Brillo Boxes is considered a work of art, while an identical stack of ordinary boxes would not be considered a work of art. Therefore, it's not true that appearance alone entirely determines whether or not something is considered a work of art.

The argument proceeds by

    A.   Highlighting the differences between things that are believed to have a certain property and things that actually have that property
    B.   Demonstrating that an opposing argument relies on an ambiguity
    C.   Suggesting that two things that are indistinguishable from each other must be the same type of thing
    D.   Questioning the assumptions underlying a particular theory
    E.   Showing that something that would be impossible if a particular thesis were correct is actually true

The author concludes that it's not true that appearances alone determine if something is art. In other words, we have to look at something more. Maybe it's the artist, the history behind the piece, or the value placed upon it by collectors…the author doesn't say, so we don't really know for sure.

- • Premise: *Two boxes look identical, but one is art and the other isn't.*
- • Conclusion: *It's not appearance alone that determines what is art.*

How does the author go from the premise to the conclusion? The reasoning pattern at play here is one we have seen before. What would happen if appearance alone determined what is art? Then both would be art, or both would not be art. That clearly isn't the case. So there's more to this than appearances alone. In other words, the opponent's conclusion has an implication that cannot be true, so that conclusion is false as well.

A. Highlighting the differences between things that are believed to have a certain property and things that actually have that property

This answer choice is saying that there are two things (Warhol's boxes and commercial boxes), both of which are believed to be art, and the author is trying to say that they are actually different. On the other hand, our author is using the differences between the two boxes (one is art and one isn't) to support a view about what determines art.

B. Demonstrating that an opposing argument relies on an ambiguity

Is the author demonstrating that the opponent's argument is ambiguous? Is the opponent using one word in two different meanings? No. We are not disputing whether one box is art and the other isn't. We are pretty clear on that. What we are disputing is what determines art, is it appearances alone or is there something more?

C. Suggesting that two things that are indistinguishable from each other must be the same type of thing

The author does not argue that because Warhol's box and commercial boxes look the same, they are in fact the same.

D. Questioning the assumptions underlying a particular theory

Can the view that the author argues against, "appearances alone determine what is art," be considered a theory? Possibly, we do not have enough support to negate this part of the answer choice. But even if it is a theory, does it have assumptions? No. The author attacks the theory by showing that this theory's implications are false.

There is a difference between **assumptions** and **implications**. As we mentioned earlier, an assumption is an unstated premise or intermediate conclusion linking the supporting information and the main conclusion of an argument. An implication, on the other hand, is something that will follow if you accept the truth of the conclusion.

Assumption: an unstated premise

Implication: an unstated inference if you accept the truth of the argument

Inferences and implications play a big role in MBT and MSS Questions, we will look at them in a later chapter.

E. Showing that something that would be impossible if a particular thesis were correct is actually true

We've mentioned before that the test makers love to dress up the correct answer in vague and convoluted language. This is a clear example of that. What is this answer saying?

Let's try to rearrange the wording sequence of this answer choice to see if you can figure it out for yourself:

"If a particular thesis were correct, something would be impossible...showing that something is actually true."

What is the thesis that we are concerned with? It's the belief that *appearances alone determine what is art.*

So what would be impossible if a particular thesis were correct? We can extrapolate this from the author's argument. Remember the author argues that "*since the two boxes are identical in appearance but only one is art, so it's not true that appearances alone determine what is art.*"

If appearances alone DID determine what is art, then both boxes would be art, or none of them would be art (since they are identical in appearance). If that is the case, then it is impossible to have one box be art, and the other not.

But wait, the so-called impossible situation is actually true! The box by Warhol is art, the other regular box isn't. So the aforementioned thesis can't be right.

Remember the reasoning pattern in the previous question?

- *Premise: If the only thing people appreciated in art was realism, photography would have entirely displaced paintings* (A → B)
- *Assumption: Photography didn't entirely displace paintings* (B̶)
- *Conclusion: People appreciate factors other than realism in art* (A̶)

The reasoning in this question is a variation along the same theme:

- *Assumption: If appearances alone determined what is art, two things that look the same would both be art, or neither would be.* (A → B)
- *Premise: One is art, and the other isn't.* (B̶)
- *Conclusion: So appearances alone do not determine what is art.* (A̶)

The correct answer is E.

7.Core Habit: LOGIC

Conditional, Causal, and Analogical reasoning play oversized roles in LR arguments, look for these in every argument and know their implications for the specific question type you are tackling.

A Refresher on LSAT Logic

So we have covered Conclusion, Role and Method Questions. During this process we have emphasized the importance of reading the stimulus for structure, deciphering hard-to-understand answer choices, and being mindful of the reasoning the author uses to advance their argument. Next, we will move to Assumption Family Questions (Flaw, Sufficient Assumption, Necessary Assumption, Strengthen, Weaken). But before we do so, I think it is important to look at the different types of logic used in Logic Reasoning Questions in greater detail. Conditional and Causal logic repeatedly appear on the LSAT, and the intermediate student should already have an awareness. But here, we will focus more on the advanced logic patterns that appear in LR questions.

Conditional Reasoning: The Basics

Most of us should be able to spot a conditional relationship embedded in the LSAT without much difficulty. Simply put, a conditional relationship involves two parts, the sufficient and the necessary. If we have S, we definitely have N. The correct contrapositive is that without N, we do not have S.

$S \rightarrow N$
$\cancel{N} \rightarrow \cancel{S}$ (contrapositive)

The **contrapositive** is the ONLY inference we can make from any conditional relationship. Get into the habit of diagramming out any conditional relationships AND their contrapositives whenever they appear on the LSAT.

As you get more familiar with conditional logic, you can try to mentally diagram conditional relationships. I personally use the highlight function in the online test interface to denote conditional relationships. Whenever a conditional relationship pops up in a stimulus, I automatically use yellow to mark sufficient conditions and red to mark necessary conditions. This habit gives me clarity of thought during the test process and saves me valuable time.

The following terms are the most common indicators of sufficient conditions:

- **If**
- **When**
- **Whenever**
- **Every**
- **All**
- **In order to**
- **The only***

The following terms are the most common indicators of necessary conditions:

- **Then**
- **Only**
- **Only if**
- **Must**
- **Required**
- **Need**
- **Depend on**

*Make sure we are not confusing "the only" with "only". "The only" introduces a sufficient condition, while "only if" introduces a necessary condition:

The only people who are accepted by law schools are college graduates.

- Accepted student → College graduate

Law schools accept students only if they have graduated from college.

- Accepted student → College graduate

With terms like "only if" and "only when," even though they contain both sufficient and necessary indicators, since "only" comes before "if" and "when", they are still necessary condition indicators.

***

The following terms are also necessary conditional indicators, but with a caveat:

- **Unless**
- **Until**
- **Without**

Take a look at the following examples, what is the sufficient and what is the necessary?

You can't legally drive unless you have a driver's license.
You can't drive legally until you have a driver's license.
You can't drive legally without a driver's license.

In all three the examples, the conditional is Drive legally → Driver's license. Whenever we approach a conditional relationship with these keywords, we take the term that comes after the keyword, make it the necessary, and the negated version of the other condition automatically becomes the sufficient.

You can't legally drive unless you have a driver's license.

So the condition "having a driver's license" comes after "unless," that becomes the necessary condition.

The remaining condition "can't legally drive" is negated, becoming "can legally drive," and is now the sufficient condition.

***

The following are also indicators of conditional logic, but appear less commonly in LR stimuli:

- **No***
- **Not until/no one but/no one except**
- **Cannot coexist**
- **If and only if**
- **All but/All except**

"No" is a tricky one. Sometimes it is simply negating a piece of information, but other times it can indicate a conditional:

No sane person takes John seriously.

- Sane Person → Do not take John seriously

- Takes John seriously → Not a sane person (contrapositive)

No Lakers fan dislikes Kobe

- All Lakers fans → Like Kobe
- Dislike Kobe → Not a Lakers fan (contrapositive)

"None except" / "Not until" indicates a necessary condition.

None except those with driver's licenses can legally drive.

- Legally drive → Driver's License

Not until you have finished residency can you practice as a doctor.

- Practice as a doctor → Finished residency

Keep in mind that with "until", you have to negate the sufficient; but with "not until", there is no need to do so.

"No one but" and "no one except" are similar to "not until", they indicate necessary conditions also:

No one except Vladimir believes the war can be won.

- Believe the war can be won → Vladimir
- Everyone else (not Vladimir) → Don't believe the war can be won (contrapositive)

Cannot coexist: either condition can be the sufficient condition, the remaining one is negated and becomes the necessary condition. A mutually exclusive relationship is created.

A and B cannot coexist

- A → B̶
- B → A̶

(A third possibility exists, both A and B are absent)

***

The following two indicate two-way relationships, diagrammed as ←→

"If and only if"

This creates a two-way relationship. *A comes to the meeting if and only if B comes also.*

- A ←→ B

This means that either both A and B are present, or none of them are.

"All but" and "All except":

This creates a two way, mutually exclusive relationship.

All except John graduated.

From the example above, we can actually derive two separate conditional relationships. We know that John didn't graduate, so John → ~~Graduate~~.

But we also know John is the only person not to graduate. So everyone else (not John) graduated. So ~~John~~ → Graduate is also a valid conditional here. Its contrapositive is ~~Graduate~~ → John.

Now let's combine both conditional statements, John → ~~Graduate,~~ and ~~Graduate~~ → John, what we get is a two-way relationship: John ←→ ~~Graduate~~. So in other words, if you are John, you didn't graduate. If you didn't graduate, you must be John.

We can also infer that ~~John~~ ←→ Graduate from this two-way relationship. If you are not John (everyone else), then you definitely graduated; and if you graduated, you are definitely not John.

So All except/but A are B can be diagrammed as:

A ←→ ~~B~~ or ~~A~~ ←→ B

***

Advanced Conditional Reasoning

<u>False and Hidden Conditionals</u>

Once we can consistently distinguish and diagram the conditional relationships present in LR questions, we should pause and think on the nature of conditional relationships. What is the one absolute essential quality that defines all conditional relationships? It's the fact that when the sufficient condition is true, the necessary condition **will definitely be true**. No exceptions, period. Sometimes the stimulus will dress up a non-conditional relationship in conditional-like language in order to throw you off, take a look at the following example:

If you are going to law school, then you most likely enjoy writing.

Is this a conditional relationship? If the sufficient is true, is the necessary definitely true? No. If someone is not likely to enjoy writing, or doesn't enjoy writing at all, will that person go to law school? Maybe, maybe not. We just don't know for sure. With logical relationships where we do not know for sure that when the sufficient occurs, the necessary will definitely occur, we are **not** dealing with a conditional relationship.

So whenever we are faced with a conditional-like relationship, and we are not sure whether it's truly a conditional, use the **contrapositive test** to find out for sure:

> Every proper conditional relationship S → N can be placed in the contrapositive: N̶ → S̶. If we negate the potential necessary condition and it does not lead to the negation of the potential sufficient condition 100% of the time, we are not dealing with a conditional relationship.

So always be careful when you face an advanced conditional reasoning question. Make sure it's actually a conditional relationship in play before proceeding.

Similarly, when we apply the contrapositive test, many statements that at first glance don't appear to be conditional statements can be construed as conditionals. Take a look at the following example:

A triangle has three sides.

Is this a conditional statement? There are no conditional indicators, but if we ask ourselves, "if a shape doesn't have three sides, is it still a triangle?" The answer, of course, is no. So if we wanted to, we can diagram this statement as Triangle → 3 sides.

Look at PT10 S4 Q5 for a flawed argument that appears to be conditional at first glance.

<u>Multiple Sufficient and Necessary Conditions</u>

Most students, especially those well versed in the Logic Games section, will know that when we take the contrapositive of multiple sufficient or necessary conditions, "and" becomes "or".

A and B → C
C̶ → A̶ or B̶ (contrapositive)

A or B → C
C̶ → A̶ and B̶ (contrapositive)

A → B and C
B̶ or C̶ → A̶ (contrapositive)

A → B or C

~~B~~ and ~~C~~ → ~~A~~ (contrapositive)

Hidden Sufficient Conditions

Students should have no problems with the information above, but one thing we should beware of is a technique that I call a **"hidden sufficient."** It's a trick test makers will often use in more difficult conditional logic questions. Essentially, the test makers will set a location, time, or similar limitation in addition to a conditional relationship. Take a look at the examples below:

Whenever Peter is at home, he plays video games only when there are no good shows on Netflix.

In authoritarian countries, if you criticize the government you will face repercussions.

If you do drugs in China, you will be arrested.

What do all three examples have in common? In all three examples, the author has set limitations to the applicability of the conditionals, or in other words, prequalified them. In the first example, the conditional (Video games → No good shows on Netflix) only applies when Peter is at home. When he is not at home, say he is at a friend's house, the rule no longer applies. So what we have here are essentially two sufficient conditions: (At home AND Play video games → No good shows on Netflix).

If we take the contrapositive of this conditional, what we get is (Good shows on Netflix → Not at home OR not playing video games). If there are good shows on Netflix, and Peter is at home, he is definitely not playing games; similarly, if there are good shows on Netflix, and he is playing video games, he is not home.

In example 2, the conditional is

- Authoritarian Country AND Criticize Government → Face Repercussions
- ~~Face Repercussions~~ → ~~Authoritarian Country~~ OR ~~Criticize Government~~ (contrapositive)

If you haven't faced repercussions, you are either not in an authoritarian country, or you are not criticizing the government. There is of course a third possibility, namely that you are neither in an authoritarian country nor criticizing the government.

Similarly, in example 3, if you are not arrested, you could have done drugs but just not in China, or in China but have abstained from drugs, or not in China and are drug free.

- China + Do Drugs → Arrested
- Not Arrested → Not in China OR Not Doing Drugs (contrapositive)

So beware of hidden sufficient conditions!

We will look at these in real questions in later chapters.

Causal Reasoning

Causal reasoning frequently appears on the LSAT as well. It is different from Conditional Reasoning. As we mentioned before. A conditional relationship indicates that if A happens, B will always happen. But A does not make B happen or vice versa. If every time John puts on his hat, David takes a sip of water in a galaxy far, far, away, then this is a conditional relationship. Perhaps John and David aren't even aware of each other's existence. Maybe it's just a coincidence. But if it's a coincidence that happens every single time, it is conditional. Conditional Reasoning is also a part of formal logic, meaning that if the rules are accepted, the contrapositive is also 100% true.

On the other hand, causal reasoning is where the cause contributes to the effect, meaning that there is a more direct relationship between the two. There is also a temporal requirement present in causal reasoning that isn't present in conditional reasoning. The cause must happen earlier than the effect, as *David Hume*, the English philosopher, tells us. Conditional Logic, on the other hand, does not.

Take a look at the following example:

If you are a five year old human child, then you are a carbon based life form.

This is a conditional relationship:

- 5 years old human child → Carbon based life form

What came first? Carbon based life, or the child's fifth birthday? It's pretty obvious that the child was carbon based even before he turned five. In this case, the necessary condition came before the sufficient.

Take a look at the following:

If you scored a 180 on the LSAT and have a 4.0 GPA, then you are guaranteed admissions to a T14 law school.

In this conditional example, the sufficient comes before the necessary in terms of timing.

But for causal reasoning, the cause **must** come before the effect.

> Causal reasoning or causality is defined as when one event, action, or state (cause) contributes to the creation of another event, action, or state (effect). In other words, we have a cause that leads to an effect.

Identifying causal reasoning in LR questions is a bit harder than identifying conditional reasoning. We do not have a distinct list of keywords that can remind us that sufficient or necessary conditions are present. What we look for instead are **action verbs** that indicate A has caused B.

Some examples that indicate causal reasoning A ⇒ B:

- **A caused B**
- **A contributes to B**
- **A is a contributing factor to B**
- **A led to B**
- **A produces B**
- **Because of A, B happened**
- **A is an explanation for B (remember explanation means causation on the LSAT)**
- **B is a result of A**
- **B is a consequence of A**

- **B is a product of A**

This list is only the tip of the iceberg. The important habit to develop is to constantly double check the information in the stimulus and ask yourself if one event, action, or state is contributing to the likelihood or production of another event, action, or state?

For the academically curious student, I would recommend looking into John Stuart Mill's five methods for discovering causes in his work, "*System of Logic*." Mill lists five methods (agreement, difference, agreement and difference, residues, and concomitant variation) to detect causation. This may be indirectly helpful to your understanding of causation, but for the student who is still struggling with the basics, it may further confuse you. So be careful!

Causal vs. Conditional

We should think critically about the differences between causal reasoning and conditional reasoning. This is where many students get confused. The best way to put it is this:

LSAT reasoning can be **both** causal and conditional at the same time, but they are not the same thing. There are reasoning patterns that are strictly conditional, and there are reasoning patterns that are strictly causal. So we check arguments for conditional reasoning and causal reasoning separately.

Take a look at the following example, is it conditional or causal in nature?

When the temperature falls below zero degrees Celsius, water freezes.

It is certainly a conditional, Below zero → Water freezes.

But hidden within the conditional relationship is also the element of causality: we know that the cold temperature is causing the water to freeze.

Let's look at a more obvious one:

If smoking causes lung damage, then hanging around smokers must lead to lung damage as well.

This example also contains conditional and causal reasoning. Two causal relationships are present, Smoking ⇒ Lung damage, and Hanging around smokers ⇒ Lung damage. The first causal relationship happens to be the sufficient condition, the second is the necessary condition.

However, the majority of reasoning on the LSAT are either exclusively conditional or causal. Take a look at the following examples:

If you have fingernails, then you must have fingers.

If you have a Social Security number, then you are a human being.

Is having fingernails contributing to you growing fingers or vice versa? No, the necessary condition is simply bound to the sufficient condition in the sense that if S is true, N must be true as well. Similarly, does having an SSN make you a person or vice versa? No, this conditional is simply saying that only humans can possess an SSN.

Similarly, we can have causal reasoning without conditional reasoning appear in the stimulus:

Because Megan didn't have her morning coffee, she fell asleep at the wheel and caused an accident.

Causality is involved here: Not having coffee (cause) led to the car accident (effect). But is there a conditional element to this example? No: we don't know if Megan will cause an accident *every time* she misses her morning coffee, what if she didn't drive that day?

Thinking outside the box: the non-exclusive nature of causal reasoning

One important aspect we must consider when confronting causal reasoning in Logic Reasoning questions is that we have to critically evaluate the soundness of the reasoning.

With conditional logic, we usually accept the conditional relationships presented to us as is. If there are no flaws in the stimulus's conditional reasoning, we do not have to consider whether the conditional makes sense. But with causal reasoning, we have to consider whether the cause and effect determined by the author is actually reasonable.

So one thing to realize about causal reasoning is that it's non-exclusive. If A causes B, A being the cause and B being the effect, B can also potentially have many other causes. Even if A causes B, a variety of other factors (C, D, E…) can also cause B.

When we trace the cause-and-effect relationships presented in LR questions, we have to think about potential **alternative causes** and **contributing causes**. This will help us critically evaluate the soundness of the causal reasoning in the questions and be of tremendous help when we look at Assumption family questions.

Alternative Causes: So the author says A is the cause of B, which we agree is a possibility. But could it be possible that in this specific case, it's C or D or an alternative that actually caused B? Take a look at the following example:

Smoking is a leading cause of lung disease. Kai, the foreman at the local chemical factory, has just been diagnosed with lung cancer. It's very likely that he had been a smoker.

So we look at the causation provided by the author, Smoking ⇒ Lung disease: it's not this cause and effect relationship we are directly challenging. Rather, we ask ourselves, is it possible that there is an alternative cause in this scenario? If Kai works at the local chemical factory, is it possible that noxious fumes damaged his lungs?

Contributing Causes: As we have mentioned previously, an effect can have multiple causes. Sometimes we can have these multiple causes contributing *simultaneously* to the same effect. So the key to approaching causal reasoning is to keep an open mind and think about other potential causes for the effect described.

Correlations vs. Causation

Correlation - Causation is a common reasoning pattern on the LSAT. Again, whenever we see correlation-causation, we must evaluate its validity and likelihood critically.

A **correlation**, simply put, is when two things occur in conjunction with one another. A **positive correlation**, as we have touched upon previously, is a statistical relationship between two variables where an increase in value X is mirrored by an increase in value Y. Similarly, a decrease in X will see a decrease in Y. If we say that the number of people going to the beach is correlated with increase in temperature, that means *as temperature increases, more and more people will go to the beach; and as the temperature decreases, less and less people will go to the beach.*

When diagramming, I use A ~ B to signify a correlation.

In statistics, the correlation coefficient is used to denote how strong the correlative relationship is between values X and Y. A correlation coefficient value of 1 means that there is a perfect positive correlation (more X - more Y), a correlation coefficient value of -1 means a perfect negative correlation (more X - less Y), and a correlation coefficient of 0 means that there is no correlation.

In all the LR questions so far, all the correlations that have appeared have been perfect correlations. So unless otherwise stated, we can safely assume that when the test makers say there is a correlation between X and Y (X ~ Y), they mean a perfect positive or negative correlation (more X - more Y) or (more X - less Y).

With perfect positive correlation, we can infer that since X increases in correlation with Y, the highest X value also corresponds with the highest Y value. Conversely, the lowest X value also corresponds with the lowest Y value.

For example, if we assume that aircraft speed has a perfect positive correlation with G-force, we know that the fastest plane will experience the highest G-force, and the slowest plane will experience the lowest G-force.

For the mathematically inclined students, taking a look at concepts such as direct variation and inverse variation can be helpful. These are the proper names for what we have labelled positive and negative correlations above. There are more complicated correlative relationships known as combined variations and joint variations. But you don't need to know these to spot correlations on the LSAT (for now.)

Now that we understand what a correlation is, let's think about the relationship between a correlation and causation.

The most important thing to remember is that there is no automatic relationship between a correlation and causality. You can have a correlation between X and Y, but no cause-and-effect relationship between the two. Similarly, you can have a causal relationship between A and B, but no correlation between A and B. For further understanding, take a look at the following two examples, one of which we have seen before:

The more leaves deciduous trees in our city have, the less layers of clothing people wear.

Here we have a negative correlation between tree leaves and layers of clothing. But is there causality between the two? Do more leaves cause people to wear less clothing or vice versa? No.

The nation's authoritarian model of government has contributed to the success of its economy.

Here we have a causal relationship, Authoritarian government ⇒ Economic success. But is there a correlation? Does the country's economic growth increase more as the government becomes more dictatorial? We don't know.

So whenever the author presents a correlation and assumes or concludes that the relationship is causal, question the causality to see if it makes sense and seek out alternative explanations.

Two common ways to question the validity of correlation-causation reasoning patterns is to ask ourselves whether the causal relationship could be reversed, and whether there could be a common cause for both correlating variables.

If the author concludes that A ⇒ B because A ~ B, ask yourself, is it possible that

B ⇒ A? (Could the author have reversed the causal relationship?)

Or

C $\Rightarrow$ A and B? (Could another factor have caused both A and B?)

<u>A good habit to have: verifying causality</u>

So whenever faced with causal reasoning, our first and foremost job is to verify its validity. Whenever the author presents a causal relationship, or derives one from a correlation, think about potential alternatives.

Given A $\Rightarrow$ B

Is it possible that

B $\Rightarrow$ A ?

C $\Rightarrow$ A + B ?

D, E, F... $\Rightarrow$ B ?

Reasoning by Analogy (Comparable Reasoning)

Before we conclude the chapter, I think a special mention of the use of comparisons in LR questions is warranted. We have looked at conditional and causal reasoning, two of the more popular types of logic involved in arguments. Comparable reasoning, although not a branch of logic like the other two, is also seen frequently on the LSAT. Together, conditional, causal, and comparable reasoning can be found in a large majority of LR questions. As such, we will quickly look at the nature of comparable reasoning and its relationship to conditional and causal reasoning.

As we have mentioned previously, making a comparison is a technique where the author sees A and B being similar in one aspect, and assumes that they must be **similar** in another aspect. Conversely, the author sees A and B different in one aspect and assumes that they must also be **different** in another aspect.

Take a look at the following two examples:

James and Shawn are both Brazilian, James is good at soccer, Shawn must be too.

I am a conscientious person, while my brother is not. So while my room is tidy, his room must be really messy.

In the first example, the author sees one similarity/commonality between James and Shawn (both Brazilian) and concludes that they share another similarity/commonality (both being good at soccer).

In the second example, the author distinguishes himself from his brother based on a personality trait (conscientiousness) and derives an additional difference from that (one's room being tidy, the other's room being messy).

***

 An **analogy**, as we mentioned before, is *a comparison between two things, for the purpose of explanation or clarification.* In making an analogy, the author is already assuming that the action, situation or event in the analogy shares a similarity with the original action, situation, or event.

Take a look at the following example:

Just as in war, it is a sign of tactical genius to surprise your enemy when he is unaware in order to gain a great victory; so the best boxers in a boxing competition should hit their opponents when they are talking to their coaches or have their backs turned.

This, of course, is a horrible analogy. But we can see that the author is comparing war and boxing matches. The author assumes that these two activities are similar enough so that what is applicable in war is also applicable in boxing.

But of course, the analogy is not apt. The rules are different in war and in sports competitions.

This is how we critically analyze comparable reasoning and analogies: **we ask ourselves if the two things compared are really similar, and if there are any differences that the author has ignored.**

So when faced with comparable reasoning, we have to evaluate it to see if it's strong or weak. In general, there are four questions that I ask myself when evaluating a comparable argument/analogy:

1. Are the two things **really comparable**? Is there a similarity or multiple similarities between the two?

2. If there are similarities, is it **relevant** to the author's conclusion or is it just a superficial similarity?

- For example, if the argument is *"A and B are both redheads, A is a musician, so B is too"*, how is your hair color relevant to whether you are a musician or not?

- But if the first comparison is actually relevant to the comparison made in the conclusion, then the argument is stronger, as in this example: *"A and B are both heavy smokers, A's lungs are in terrible shape, so B's must be too."*

3. Are there **material differences** between the two things that the author ignored?

4. Even if the similarity exists, is the author's conclusion **too strong**? Is the conclusion warranted?

- A more conservative conclusion is always more welcome than a conclusion that is too strong.

  - For example, suppose the argument was *"Kepler 22b is a planet situated in a similar environment as Earth, so it must be habitable"*. In that case, the argument is somewhat problematic, because we do not know if there are differences between Kepler 22b and Earth that we have overlooked.

  - However, if the argument was *"Kepler 22b is a planet situated in a similar environment as Earth, so it's possible that it is also habitable,"* it is a perfectly valid argument because the conclusion is much more limited.

Hybrids

We have seen previously that an argument can be both causal and conditional in nature; in fact,

> advanced arguments can contain multiple types of reasoning, sometimes even elements of comparable, causal, and conditional reasoning all at once.

Take a look at the following example:

Throughout Asia, land reform has contributed to the success of the country's subsequent industrialization. So if countries in Africa want to industrialize, land reform is necessary.

This argument has a comparable element: the author is comparing Asia to Africa, assuming what worked in Asia will also work in Africa.

According to the first part of the argument, there is cause and effect reasoning in the argument: land reform caused the success of industrial policies in Asia.

The argument also has conditional reasoning: the author's conclusion is conditional, arguing that land reform is necessary to industrialization.

Having a clear understanding of the type of reasoning used in an argument, whether it be conditional, causal, or comparable, is crucial to success in Assumption Family Questions and many other types of questions, as we shall see down the road. For now, practice getting into the habit of trying to identify the types of reasoning each time we approach a stimulus. Be vigilant, there can be more than one!

Look at PT17 S3 Q11 for a stimulus containing both conditional and causal logic. Can you identify and differentiate the two? How do they relate to each other in advancing the argument?

Three Final Points

Conditional Reasoning, Causal Reasoning, and Analogies are all just ways to advance one's argument.

To end this chapter, I just wanted to use three famous philosophical examples to illustrate the nature of the three types of reasoning which we have covered. Condition, Causal, and Comparable reasoning are tools the author uses to reach their conclusion. To use an analogy, you can fly, drive, or take the train from New York to Boston. Similarly, one can use conditional, causal, and comparable reasoning to go from premise to conclusion. The logic used by the author in the argument is not the destination, it is simply a means of transportation.

Saint Thomas Aquinas, the great scholastic theologian, attempts to prove the existence of God via causal reasoning. Aquinas argues that there is a cause for everything and that nothing can be the cause for itself. It's not possible to have an infinite number of causes. So there must be a first cause, the cause that started everything. That cause has to be God.

Leibniz, the German philosopher and co-inventor of calculus, echoes this argument but adds an element of conditionality to it. Leibniz's Principle of Sufficient Reason states that there must be a reason for everything that exists. That reason must then have its own reason, and so on. At the end of this conditional chain is the Necessary Being, or God.

Finally, there is the watchmaker argument for the existence of God. According to this argument, just as a watch, with all its mechanical intricacies and complications, points toward the existence of a watchmaker, so the universe, with all its complications, point towards the existence of a God.

I have grossly oversimplified both Aquinas and Leibniz's ideas, but I wanted to illustrate how three separate arguments were made, one using causation, the second using conditionals, and the third using an analogy, to come to the same conclusion. The goals in all three arguments were the same, to prove the existence of God. They just used different means of transportation to get there.

Differentiating between structure and logic

We have seen this in arguments that contained causal reasoning in several earlier examples. The argument will contain both a premise and a conclusion, but either of these can be the cause or effect.

Similarly, the argument can contain two causal chains, $A \Rightarrow B$, and $B \Rightarrow C$, with the conclusion $A \Rightarrow C$. But this doesn't mean the first causal relationship is the premise, the second the intermediate conclusion. In fact, both are premises supporting the main conclusion.

This is also true of conditional reasoning. The author can use the contrapositive ($\cancel{N} \rightarrow \cancel{S}$) as the premise, and the main conditional relationship ($S \rightarrow N$) as the main conclusion; or vice versa.

It is absolutely crucial to analyze an argument's structure and logic separately. Do not confuse the two elements!

Conditional, Causal, and Comparable Reasoning exist in over half of all LR arguments, but they are not present in all cases

Together, conditional, causal, and comparable reasoning are present in over half of all LR arguments. So it's important to look for potential elements of each whenever we come across an argument. But in the remaining

30-40% of LR arguments, the author will use other means to advance their argument. They can cite a study, appeal to an expert, a survey, or come to a decision via the process of elimination…

We have seen many of the ways in which the author advances their argument in the previous chapter on Method questions. So definitely look for conditional, causal, and comparable reasoning in an argument, but don't worry even if it's not there.

8. Flaw Questions

Analyzing Flaw Stimuli from a Structural Perspective

Flaw Questions are the most common questions to appear on the Logic Reasoning section, making up over 20% of all questions in total. It is also the only question type that can only be solved via outside knowledge. For nearly every other type of question, we can learn them by practicing and examining the questions, but for Flaw Questions, there are material that we must learn and memorize.

Flaw Questions are also noted for their hard to decipher answer choices, so we will continue to practice the art of matching keywords from answer choices with information in the stimulus. (Just as we did with Role and Method Questions.)

Flaw Questions will contain a problematic argument in the stimulus (remember we mentioned before that for the majority of LR questions, the stimulus will contain an argument). Flaw Question stimuli will ALWAYS contain an argument, which means that it will have a main conclusion, premises, and maybe an intermediate conclusion. As usual, the **first step** when approaching Flaw Questions is to **dissect the stimulus and identify components of the argument**, just as we did in Find the Conclusion, Role, and Method Questions.

Once we have identified the support and the conclusion in the author's argument, we need to find what's wrong with the argument. Take a look at the following argument:

All men are mortal.
Socrates is a man.
Therefore, Socrates is mortal.

This is Aristotle's most famous syllogism. You have probably seen it before. It is a valid argument, we can find no fault with it, and as a result, it is without flaw.

An argument may be logically valid but still false, as seen in the example below:

All men are unicorns.
Socrates is a man.
Therefore, Socrates is a unicorn.

This is still a valid argument, despite all its ridiculousness. In real life, you could refute this argument by pointing out the falsehood of its premise: the statement all men are unicorns is false. So even though the argument is still **valid**, it's not a **sound** argument.

But on the LSAT, we are not here to dispute the truthfulness/falsity of the argument's premises. In other words, we do not care whether the statements in the argument are true in real life. All we care about is the validity of the argument.

But how do we determine whether an argument is valid or not? Take a look at the following example:

All men are mortal.
Socrates is probably a man.
Therefore, Socrates is mortal.

This argument is imperfect. In fact, it is invalid. We accept each premise as true, but the author's premises do not warrant the conclusion. If Socrates is probably a man, then the only conclusion you can derive is that Socrates is *probably* mortal. There is a shift in the language of the argument going from premise to conclusion. The author makes a certain conclusion based on what is probable.

In fact, in every flaw argument, there will be an unsupported leap made going from the premises to the main conclusion. Sometimes it's between one of the premises and the main conclusion, sometimes it's between the intermediate conclusion and the main conclusion. But it will always involve the main conclusion and another supporting statement.

Because the author has made a "leap of reasoning," there will be gaps in the author's reasoning, as a result. Our **second step** is therefore to **think about the gap in the author's reasoning and ask ourselves whether this leap is reasonable.**

Take a look at the following example:

David is going to law school, therefore he must have taken the LSAT.

What is the premise in this argument?

David is going to law school,

What is the conclusion in this argument?

David has taken the LSAT.

Are there any gaps in the author's reasoning? Well, we know that not everyone who is going to law school will have taken the LSAT. Maybe they took the GRE instead. Perhaps the law school David is attending doesn't require the LSAT. Perhaps David is attending an LLM or JSD program.

In other words, the premise in the example above does not automatically lead to the conclusion. When analyzing the Flaw Question stimulus, our job is to find that gap in the author's reasoning. Sometimes the gap is pretty obvious, as we saw in the first example. But other times, we must think about whether the premise/intermediate conclusion will automatically lead to the main conclusion, or has something less obvious been overlooked.

Shifts from Premises/Intermediate Conclusions to the Main Conclusion

A technique that really helped me find the gap in the author's reasoning is to compare the wording of the supporting premises and the conclusion, looking for shifts in scope, quantity, intensity, logic, and concepts. Let's look at a question stimulus.

The probability of avoiding heart disease is increased if one avoids fat in one's diet. Furthermore, one is less likely to eat fat if one avoids eating dairy foods. Thus the probability of maintaining good health is increased by avoiding dairy foods.

The stimulus of this question is not hard to understand. There is no peripheral information in this stimulus; it contains two premises and a conclusion. Let's rearrange it in logical order:

- Premise: *One is less likely to eat fat if one avoids eating dairy foods*

- Premise: *The probability of avoiding heart disease is increased if one avoids fat in one's diet*

The premises, when linked, give us this: *Avoid dairy ⇒ Less likely to eat fat ⇒ More chance of a healthy heart/higher chance of avoiding heart disease*

Now let's look at the conclusion of the argument:

- Conclusion: *Thus the probability of maintaining good health is increased by avoiding dairy foods*

In other words, *Avoid dairy* ⇒ *More chance of maintaining good health*

Notice the term shift? The scope of the conclusion widened considerably compared to that of the premises. The premises tell us that avoiding dairy can help us avoid heart disease, but the conclusion is now about health in general.

***

So remember to look at the supporting premises and the conclusion of Flaw Questions **separately**. Compare and contrast the differences between the two, and ask yourself if the author has made any leaps of reasoning or left gaps in the argument when deriving the conclusion from the premises.

Let's look at another question where we have to consider the differences between what the author is talking about in the premises and what they are talking about in the conclusion.

<u>PT40 S3 Q19</u>

Fishing columnist: When an independent research firm compared the five best-selling baits, it found that Benton baits work best for catching trout. It asked a dozen top anglers to try out the five bestselling baits as they fished for speckled trout in a pristine northern stream, and every angler had the most success with a Benton bait. These results show that Benton is the best bait for anyone who is fishing for trout.

Each of the following describes a flaw in the reasoning in the fishing columnist's argument EXCEPT

A. The argument overlooks the possibility that some other bait is more successful than any of the five best selling baits.
B. The argument overlooks the possibility that what works best for expert anglers will not work best for ordinary anglers.
C. The argument overlooks the possibility that the relative effectiveness of different baits changes when used in different locations.
D. The argument overlooks the possibility that two best selling brands of bait may be equally effective.
E. The argument overlooks the possibility that baits that work well with a particular variety of fish may not work well with other varieties of that fish.

What is the author's conclusion in this question?

- *Benton is the best bait for anyone who is fishing for trout.*

So the author concludes that Benton is the best, not one of the best, not the second best, but number one, and for everyone who is fishing for trout. That's a pretty big claim. How does the author support their conclusion? Let's go through the author's supporting premises one by one, looking for gaps between the premise and the conclusion.

- *When an independent research firm compared the five best selling baits, it found that Benton baits work best for catching trout.*

Ok, so the study was done by an independent research firm, that's good, perhaps there is no conflict of interest here. But why did they only compare the five best selling baits? We know already that the conclusion is that Benton is the best for anyone looking to catch trout, not just the best among best selling baits. There is a significant gap here. Is it possible that the best bait is not the best-selling bait? Yes. The best-selling cars are probably Corollas, Camrys, Civics, etc. But are these the best cars? It's possible that some products sell well due to their price point or availability in stores.

- *It asked a dozen top anglers to try out the five bestselling baits as they fished for speckled trout in a pristine northern stream*

There are three potential issues here: the people testing the bait were all top fishermen. If Tiger Woods thinks a golf club is the best, does it mean it's the best for anyone looking to golf? Not necessarily: something that works for the pros might not work for beginners. Secondly, they were fishing for a very specific type of trout. If something works for speckled trout, would it work equally well for other types of trout, like rainbow trout? Thirdly, the fishermen were fishing in a pristine northern stream. Would it work equally well in a lake or elsewhere?

When we line up the premises and compare it to the conclusion, we find significant gaps in the reasoning. The differences in scope between the two are glaring. This is what we know:

Premises:
- Pros liked Benton bait
  - Gap: just because pros think its good doesn't mean it's suitable for everyone
- Only five top selling brands were tested
  - Gap: could there be really good brands that don't sell well that the study missed out on?
- The testing was done in a pristine northern stream
  - Gap: what about trout living in lakes? Or in the south?
- They were fishing for a very specific species of trout
  - Gap: would the bait work for other species of trout

Conclusion
- Benton is the best for anyone looking to fish for trout

So once we have isolated and compared the premises and the conclusions, we try to think of potential objections to the author's reasoning. Is the author's reasoning valid? Can we brainstorm potential ways to rebut the author's argument? **The third step** of analyzing a Flaw question stimulus is therefore to **think of potential objections we can make to the author's reasoning once we have identified the gap between the premise and conclusion.**

Let's take a look at the answer choices:

One thing to note here is that this is an EXCEPT question. This means that the way we approach the answer choices is essentially reversed: instead of looking for the flaw in the question, we are eliminating the four answer choices that correctly state flaws that appeared in the argument. The correct answer is in fact irrelevant to the argument.

A. *The argument overlooks the possibility that some other bait is more successful than any of the five bestselling baits.*

If something is overlooked, then that information can potentially hurt the argument. We will look at "overlook" answer choices in further detail later in the chapter.

Is this piece of information something that can potentially hurt the argument? Yes: the best bait is not necessarily the best selling. This is one of the gaps in reasoning we have discovered previously.

B. *The argument overlooks the possibility that what works best for expert anglers will not work best for ordinary anglers*

This answer choice also matches up with one of the gaps in reasoning we have identified.

C. *The argument overlooks the possibility that the relative effectiveness of different baits changes when used in different locations.*

We have also identified this as a gap in the author's reasoning. The testing was done in a pristine northern stream. Would it also work as well in a lake in the south?

D. *The argument overlooks the possibility that two best selling brands of bait may be equally effective*

This is NOT one of the gaps we have identified. Is it possible that there is another brand of best-selling bait that is just as good as Benton's? No: the stimulus clearly states that Bentons is the best among the five best selling baits.

E. *The argument overlooks the possibility that baits that work well with a particular variety of fish may not work well with other varieties of that fish*

Something that works with speckled trout may not work with rainbow trout. This is also a gap that we have identified.

The correct answer is D.

Most Commonly Seen Flaw Patterns (Fallacies)

However, simply noticing the gap between the premise and the main conclusion is not enough to guarantee success on Flaw Questions. Many of the invalid arguments in Flaw Questions correspond with famous reasoning fallacies such as the slippery slope, the strawman, or ad hominem. (By my count, about 40-50% of all Flaw arguments correspond with one of the following fallacies.) Here is a list of 21 fallacies that have commonly appeared in Flaw Questions.

Commit each of these to memory, google them for examples if need be, and try to match up the gap in the stimulus argument with these if you can.

1. Sampling bias

Sampling errors occur when the author extrapolates the qualities of a sample unto the whole population. Whenever we see the argument stimulus talking about a survey, sample, or study, we ask ourselves whether sampling bias is involved.

Having a survey/sample present in an argument **doesn't automatically mean** bias is present (as we can see from the question earlier in the chapter). In fact, sampling bias is one of the most frequent red herrings to appear in Flaw questions. More specifically, the author will talk about a survey in the argument, thereby tricking the test taker into thinking it's a sampling flaw we are dealing with. But in reality, the survey itself has no problems, and the flaw is hidden deeper in the argument.

So whenever we see that a sample/survey is present, ask ourselves the following questions: is the sample size representative of the population? Are there flaws or biases in the survey methodology? If not, then the flaw will lay elsewhere.

Questions to consider: 59-2-20, 74-4-18

2. Ad hominem

Ad hominem, or personal attacks are less frequent in harder Flaw Questions. But look out for arguments where the author is refuting another point of view by criticizing the source rather than the opponent's argument. Perhaps the opponent doesn't practice what he preaches, or they can have questionable motives. Be careful when the opponent's argument is not directly addressed.

Questions to consider: 77-2-18

3. Appeal to authority

Appealing to authority is problematic in two scenarios:

First, when the only support provided for a point of view is that the person voicing the claim or supporting the claim is an expert. For example, if we argue that *"we should believe John simply because he is an expert,"* the author commits the appeal to authority fallacy. Experts, just like everyone else, need to back up their claims with credible evidence.

Second, whenever an expert's voice is thrown into the mix, we have to ask ourselves whether the expert is the appropriate authority in this case. Are they qualified to speak on the matter? Does what we are discussing fall into the scope of their expertise?

Questions to consider: 21-2-25

4. Appeal to ignorance

Appeal to ignorance, or "*unproven vs. untrue*," as many like to call it, is where we accept a view due to the lack of evidence to the contrary. The argument "*aliens exist because there is no evidence to prove that they don't*", or "*there is no God because you can't prove his existence*" are both appeals to ignorance.

In other words, you can't prove/disprove a thesis or conclusion simply because there is no way to prove the contrary.

Appeal to ignorance fallacies are quite common in Flaw Questions. But in the majority of cases, the test makers will present a variation of this fallacy. Instead of suggesting that the opponent's view is false because there is no evidence to prove it true, the author will argue that the opponent's view is false because the opponent's argument is weak. The author may point out the opponent's reasoning has gaps in it, and then hastily rejects the opponent's conclusion.

I call this the "Weakness - Reject" variation. The author in the stimulus finds certain weaknesses in the opponent's reasoning, and jumps to the conclusion that the opponent's view is thereby wrong and rejects it. It's a more commonly seen variation of the Appeal to Ignorance/Unproven vs. Untrue fallacy.

Let's take a look at the following example:

John: Socrates died in his old age, therefore all men are mortal.

David: You cannot extrapolate from one person to all men, therefore there must be some men who are immortal.

Here, David points out a legitimate issue with John's argument (weakness), and goes on to deny wholesale John's conclusion (reject). Pointing out a weakness in the opponent's reasoning doesn't automatically negate their conclusion, it only weakens it.

Questions to consider: 20-4-18, 20-4-22, 26-2-21, 29-1-17, 45-4-24, 64-3-14, 72-3-11

5. False dichotomy

False dichotomy or false choice fallacies do not appear frequently. It occurs when two options are presented, the author rejects one, and concludes that the alternative option is the only possibility left. If the stimulus clearly states that only two choices are available, then rejecting one and being left with only one choice is *not* flawed reasoning. However, sometimes we do not know if the two choices presented are the only options available. In this case just because one option is unavailable, it doesn't mean we have to choose the alternative. Take a look at the following example:

The only ways to go to Hawaii are by plane or boat, no boats will sail due to the hurricane, so we have to fly. (This reasoning is valid because we know that only two choices are available.)

*You can go to Canada by flying or driving. Flights have all been grounded due to Covid, so we have to drive up there. (*This argument suffers from the false dichotomy fallacy. Flying and driving are possibilities, but we don't know if they are the only possibilities. So potentially, you can go by train as well.)

Be sure to distinguish the false dichotomy fallacy from the selective attention fallacy, which we will look at down the road.

Questions to consider: 44-4-22

6. Fallacy of Composition/Division

The fallacy of composition/division is an informal logical fallacy commonly called "part vs. whole" on the LSAT. This fallacy occurs when there is an entity that can be divided into multiple parts in the stimulus. The author erroneously extrapolates the entity's properties unto its composites (believing what is true of the whole must be true of its parts). Alternatively, the author takes a property of the composite and believes it is also applicable to the entire entity (believing what is true of the parts must be true of the whole).

For instance, the erroneous argument *"The US military is the most lethal fighting machine in the world, so each of its individual soldiers must also be the best fighters in the world as well"* makes the mistake of extrapolating a property of the whole to an individual part of that entity.

It is important to note that extrapolating a property of the whole to the part or vice versa is NOT automatically fallacious. We have to examine the reasoning on a case-by-case basis. For instance, if I said, *"Every part of this ship is made out of steel, therefore this ship is made of steel,"* then there is nothing wrong with the statement. However, if we try to extend a property that should not be extended from parts to the whole or vice versa, then it becomes problematic. If my argument was instead, *"Steel components sink in water, so this ship, made entirely of steel, will no doubt sink as well,* " I would have committed the part vs. whole fallacy.

It is important to note that the fallacy of composition is not the same as sampling bias. These two fallacies are similar in the sense that you are extrapolating a property from a part to a whole. But with the sampling bias, you are estimating some characteristic of a population based on a subset or sample. In contrast, with the fallacy of composition, there is no requirement for the whole entity to consist of a population.

Questions to consider: 23-3-16, 44-4-11, 77-2-22,

7. Equivocation

Equivocation occurs when a specific word with multiple meanings is used in the author's argument, but the word's meaning subtly shifts as the argument moves from premise to conclusion. Look at the following example: *"Bringing a gun into the classroom is a criminal offense, so we should arrest all the gunners in my law school class."*

Equivocation flaws frequently appear in harder Flaw Questions, and it's important to read the stimulus carefully and closely examine recurring words.

In the hardest equivocation flaw questions, the second equivocate usage of the word will not appear explicitly in the stimulus. Instead, **they form a part of the author's assumptions**. Because assumptions are unstated, we will not find the word by simply parsing the stimulus's text.

John: my opponent argues that political candidates must do whatever they can to enhance their credit. But unsustainable spending surely carries over from one's personal life into one's political agenda. I rather prefer the fiscally responsible candidate.

In the example above, the word "credit" means "trust" in the first sentence, but in John's subsequent argument, he interprets "credit" to mean financial obligations. Even though the word "credit" only appears once in the example, the argument's flaw is based on a misinterpretation of the word "credit."

Questions to consider: 1-3-22, 22-2-12, 22-2-24, 22-4-18, 26-2-15, 59-2-15

8. Percentage vs. Amount

Confusing a percentage change with a change in net amount is also a common flaw. For example, the author mistakenly assumes that a greater percentage increase means a greater net increase.

When the concept of percentages appears on any Flaw Question, I will immediately check for such an error. Three figures are at play in percentage vs. amount questions: **total sum**, **percentage change**, and **change in amount**. We need two to derive a conclusion about the third figure. Take a look at the following example:

Rwanda's GDP increased at 15% last year, while the US only increased 5%. So Rwanda's economic expansion was bigger than the US's last year.

Percentage is based on the pre-existing size of the pie: the American economy is much larger than the Rwandan economy.

Any question that only gives us one out of the three figures (**total sum, percentage change, change in amount**) and makes a conclusion about another figure will have committed the percentage vs. amount flaw. **We need to provide the other two to come to a proper conclusion about any of these figures.**

Questions to consider: 6-3-24, 48-4-25, and an especially tricky/well-disguised one: 71-3-22

9. Circular Reasoning

Circular reasoning is essentially the conclusion repeating the information stated/assumed in the premise. In its most basic form, it looks like this:

Premise: A
Conclusion: A

Because of A, therefore A.

Of course, circular reasoning flaw conclusions on the LSAT will not simply repeat what was stated in the premise verbatim. The language will be slightly different but still express essentially the same idea. Take a look at the following two examples:

New York is the best city in the world because no city is better.

Premise: no city is better than New York (New York is the best)
Conclusion: New York is the best city in the world

Surely the egg came before the chicken, otherwise where would the first chicken have come from?

Premise: if the egg didn't come before the chicken, then we can't adequately explain chickens' origins. (Assumption: the egg came before the chicken)
Conclusion: the egg came before the chicken.

In the second example, the author's conclusion is not a simple restatement of the supporting premise, but rather, the point made in the conclusion is assumed in the premise's reasoning. **This is more common in the harder circular reasoning type questions.** So always beware of arguments that contain no new information going from the premise to the conclusion, and keep an eye out for unstated assumptions.

Questions to consider: 49-2-23, 82-1-22

10. Self Contradiction

Self-contradiction flaws occur when the conclusion contradicts some of the information already presented in the rest of the stimulus/argument. This is quite easy to spot in easier questions. However, the contradiction will be harder to spot in the hardest questions. The author will often mask the contradiction behind complicated language and assumptions or require the test taker to make the inference themselves. Take a look at the following examples:

Although high cholesterol levels have been associated with the development of heart disease, many people with high cholesterol never develop heart disease, while many without high cholesterol do. Recently, above average concentrations of lipoprotein were found in the blood of many people whose heart disease was not attributable to other causes. Dietary changes that affect cholesterol levels have no effect on lipoprotein levels. Hence, there is no reason for anyone to make dietary changes for the sake of preventing heart disease.

In the example above, the author concludes that because lipoprotein is unaffected by dietary changes, there is no reason to make dietary changes if your goal is to prevent heart disease. (The author is assuming that lipoprotein levels are the only factor in play here). However, the author also states that high cholesterol levels can cause heart disease (*above-average concentrations of lipoprotein were found in the blood of many people whose heart disease was not attributable to other causes).* Herein lies the contradiction: the author states that high cholesterol levels sometimes cause heart disease, then goes on to a conclusion that assumes only lipoprotein causes heart disease.

To hold criminals responsible for their crimes involves a failure to recognize that criminal actions, like all actions, are ultimately products of the environment that forged the agent's character. It is not criminals but people in the law abiding majority who by their actions do most to create and maintain this environment. Therefore, it is law abiding people whose actions, and nothing else, make them alone truly responsible for the crime.

Can you find the self-contradiction in this example? The author concludes that it is law abiding people who are responsible for the crime. Why aren't criminals responsible? Because their actions are products of the environment? But what about the actions of law-abiding citizens? The author states that *all actions are ultimately products of the environment.* According to the author's reasoning, no one would be responsible, right? How can you argue that because criminals' actions are products of the environment, so they are not responsible; but normal people are responsible even though their actions are also products of the environment?

These two examples represent the **most challenging** Self Contradiction flaws in general. The argument's author can either present but then **ignore** a piece of contrary evidence or present a piece of information that can lead us to an **inference** that contradicts the author's conclusion.

Questions to consider: 9-2-22, 12-1-24, 20-1-22, 33-3-17, 43-3-20, 47-3-19, 67-2-13, 83-1-22, 84-3-22

11. Inducing future from past events

This fallacy is quite easy to understand: the author assumes what was true in the past will continue to hold true in the future. **Sometimes the author will dress this flaw up in conditional-like language to confuse you.** Take a look at the following example:

All presidents in the past have only been white males. So Barack Obama, who is black, cannot become president.

Some students, seeing the words "all" and "only," mistakenly believe the argument to be conditional. But remember, as we have discussed in Chapter 7, true conditionals should have universal applicability. Limited statements like these aren't true conditionals, so you can't contrapositive them and come to a valid conclusion.

Questions to consider: 54-2-19, 74-4-20

12. Gambler's Fallacy

The gambler's fallacy occurs when we mistakenly believe occurrences in the past will influence the likelihood of random events occurring in the future. When you have a series of random events occurring in sequence, such as flipping a fair coin, or betting on black or red on the roulette table, each flip or roll is an independent event in itself. Just because you flipped five tails in a row, the probability of getting heads on the next coin toss is still 50/50.

Gambler's Fallacy vs. Law of Large Numbers:

Here is where some students get confused. The law of large numbers states that over an extended period of time or a large number of trials/coin tosses, we can expect a gradual regression to the mean. In other words, continuing with our coin toss example, assuming the coin is fair and we get 10 heads in a roll,

Law of Large Numbers:

First 10 tosses: 10 Heads (Heads 10 : Tails 0)
Next 100 tosses: 50 Heads/50 Tails (So 60 Heads/50 Tails after 110 tosses) (Heads 6: Tails 5)
Next 1000 tosses: 500 Heads/500 Tails (560 Heads/550 Tails after 1110 tosses) (Heads 56: Tails 55)
So on and so forth…

So the probability of each individual coin toss is not affected by previous results, but rather, the effect is lessened when you toss more and more, with the overall result getting closer to 1:1 (*regression toward the mean*).

A Special Note: There are instances when past occurrences WILL affect the probability of events occurring in the future. In such cases, the Gambler's Fallacy is not applicable. For instance, if we are attempting to draw the Queen of Spades from a deck of 52 cards. Initially, the probability is 1/52. But after drawing 10 cards and still not getting the Queen of Spades, the likelihood that we get this card on the next draw has increased. It is now 1/42. For the curious student intent on doing additional research into the topic of conditional probability, start by looking into the *general multiplication rule formula*, or $P(A \cap B) = P(A) P(B|A)$.

13. Non sequitur fallacy (Unnecessary Extrapolation of Belief)

A non sequitur fallacy is where the conclusion does not follow the premise. On the LSAT, this flaw is manifested by extending an implication or result of a view unto the view holder:

I love junk food, junk food destroys the body, therefore I love to destroy my body.

I believe studying hard will get me into law school, but going to law school will put me into a lot of debt, so I believe studying hard will put me into a lot of debt.

Priests from the Middle Ages believed the plague to be a punishment from God. We now know that the plague was caused by bacterial infection. So medieval priests saw bacteria as a tool of God.

In reality, the argument's conclusion in both examples above do not follow from the premise. I can either be unaware of the additional result of my view, disagree with it, or hold my view despite that result. The scope shifts/widens going from the premise to the conclusion, and that's why we must keep in mind to compare the exact wording of the supporting premises and the main conclusion on Flaw Questions.

14. Confusing conditional with causation

Essentially, the author argues that because B is necessary to A, B is the cause for A. So in other words, confusing $A \rightarrow B$ with $B \Rightarrow A$ or $A \Rightarrow B$.

As we have mentioned previously, harder LR questions can contain conditional and causal reasoning elements. But they must be considered independently, so don't mix up the two.

Alternatively, the author can present us with a causal relationship A ⇒ B, and derive a conditional relationship from it. This would be wrong as well.

15. Appeal to probability/possibility

This fallacy assumes that just because something could be true or is probably true, then it must be true.

Questions to consider: 29-4-18, 32-1-6, 35-1-17, 88-4-21

16. Selective Attention fallacy

The selective attention fallacy, or cherry-picking, occurs when we are presented with two or more alternatives, and the author arbitrarily chooses one of them. The author selects one or the other without additional elaboration. So we are left wondering why the author chose A over B. In other words, the author overlooks the other possibility and selects one over the other in a seemingly random manner.

Questions to consider: 83-3-15, 87-3-26

17. Relative/Absolute confusion

The relative/absolute confusion is specific to the LSAT, and not considered an official informal fallacy in the philosophical sense. In the relative/absolute flaw, the author confuses a relative value with an absolute value. For example, the author will claim that because *being slightly overweight is healthier than being severely underweight, being slightly overweight is a healthy condition.*

Another way the relative/absolute flaw appears is with the words "more" and "most." This ties in directly with the equivocation and percentage vs. amount flaws. This kind of reasoning has appeared several times in Flaw and other types of questions: the author can argue that *because Candidate X has the most votes out of all the candidates, more people voted for him than those who didn't.* The validity of this argument depends on the total number of candidates. If there are more than two candidates in the running, being the first past the polls doesn't necessarily mean that you received more than 50% of the votes.

Questions to consider: 53-1-22, 54-4-16, 65-4-26, 51-1-18

18. False Conversion

(We will look at this in greater detail in the chapter on Must be True Questions)

False conversion fallacies have to do with reversing the order of relationships in "all" and "most" relationships. We will look at some/most/all relationships in greater detail in the Must be True chapter, but for now, remember that "all" and "most" relationships cannot be reversed without committing a logical fallacy.

All law students are college grads
All college grads are law students (false conversion)

Most Americans are English speakers
Most English speakers are Americans (false conversion)

"Some" relationships can be reversed,

Some Japanese people are English speakers
Some English speakers are Japanese (valid)

The only correct way in which we can reverse "most" and "all" relationships is by turning them into "some":

All law students are college grads
Some college grads are law students (valid)

Most Americans are English speakers
Some English speakers are Americans (valid)

In some of the harder false conversion questions, the stimulus will not use terms such as "most" or "some", these would be too obvious. Instead, percentages or likelihood will be substituted. Take the following example:

70% of all smokers have lung disease, John has lung disease, so he is most likely a smoker.

The argument in the example above is essentially a variation of the false conversion of "most". In other words, *most smokers have lung disease,* so most people with lung disease are smokers (this is the flawed assumption of the argument and where the false conversion happens), *John has lung disease and therefore his probability of being a smoker is high.*

Questions to consider: 4-1-23, 13-2-24, 27-1-23, 41-3-20

19. Appeal to extremes/slippery slope

This fallacy has rarely appeared in more recent tests, I would keep an eye out for it. The author appeals to extreme cases or improbable cases to justify their conclusion.

Question to consider: 86-1-21, 57-3-8

20. Appeal to belief

In the appeal to belief fallacy, the author argues that because people believe X, X is true. This is similar to the informal fallacy of *argumentum ad populum*, or appeal to popularity, which states that because most people/segments of the population believe X, X is true. In other words, the author confuses the opinion/beliefs of certain people with factual information.

Questions to consider: 15-2-17, 32-4-13

21. Comparable Flaw (False Analogy)

We have examined comparable reasoning/analogies in greater detail at the end of the previous chapter. The author will compare two concepts and argue that since A and B are similar in one aspect, they will be similar in another. Conversely, the author will argue that since A and B are dissimilar in one aspect, they must be dissimilar in another.

The hardest comparable flaw questions will often contain traces of other types of reasoning in them as well, the most frequent being causal reasoning. Suppose the argument read, *"Air pollution is the leading cause of lung disease in China, so to decrease incidents of lung disease here in the US, we must make every effort to clean up the air."* This is a hybrid argument (we discussed hybrid arguments in the previous chapter). It contains causal reasoning (air pollution as a cause of lung disease), but don't forget that the argument, at its core, assumes a similarity between China and the US.

Look at 23-2-21, 33-3-15, 46-2-11, 49-2-18, 52-3-16, 81-2-20, and 86-4-24 for a deeper understanding of how comparable reasoning/analogies are used in Flaw questions.

Here is a quick summary of what we have covered so far:

Find the Conclusion.

How is the Conclusion supported? (Isolate the premises provided for the conclusion)

Think about how the author goes from the premises to the conclusion: are there any gaps in the author's reasoning, does the author make any unwarranted leaps going from premise to conclusion?

If we accept the author's premises, can we make potential objections to the author's conclusion?
Are there any term shifts between the wording in the premises and the conclusion? Have the scope, intensity, logic, and concepts discussed subtly changed?

Does the reasoning pattern match up with one of our classical fallacies?

Analyzing Flaw Stimuli from a Logical Perspective

At the same time as we analyze the argument's structural shifts, we must also keep a close eye out for the presence of **conditional** and **causal** logic in the author's argument.

We have covered conditional and causal logic in depth in "Core Habits: Logic," so here, we will focus on these relationships' flawed/invalid variations.

A Flaw argument may contain conditional or causal reasoning, but that doesn't necessarily mean that they will be erroneous. Roughly 30-40% of all Flaw Questions will contain either conditional or causal reasoning, but only 3/4 of these questions have a conditional or causal flaw.

Just as I try to analyze the argument's structure as soon as I start to read the stimulus, I am also looking for signs of conditional and causal logic. I do this by specifically looking for indicator words (see the previous chapter). If I do find either conditional or causal logic, the first thing I do is check to see if it is valid.

Conditional Flaws

Given the conditional relationship A → B, the only valid extrapolation is that B̶ → A̶. Other than the contrapositive, there is absolutely nothing that we can derive from a conditional relationship. Conditional flaws come in two forms: the author can erroneously reverse the relationship without negating the conditions, or the author can negate both sides of the conditional without reversing the relationship.

A → B (original conditional relationship)
B̶ → A̶ (proper contrapositive, this is correct)
B → A (reversed original relationship without negation, this is wrong)
A̶ → B̶ (negated conditions without reversing relationship, this is also wrong)

The same rule applies when the conditional relationship involves and/or relationships. Only now the "and" is turned into "or," and vice versa.

A → B and C (original conditional relationship)
B̶ or C̶ → A̶ (proper contrapositive)

A and B → C (original conditional relationship)
C̶ → A̶ or B̶ (proper contrapositive)

A → B or C (original conditional relationship)
B̶ and C̶ → A̶ (proper contrapositive)

A or B → C (original conditional relationship)
C̶ → A̶ and B̶ (proper contrapositive)

Whenever you recognize conditional logic in the author's argument, make sure to check to see if they commit a conditional logic flaw. If a conditional relationship is present, does the author reverse the relationship without negating it in his subsequent reasoning? Does the author negate the terms without reversing the relationship? Both would be wrong.

Conditional flaws are fairly easy to detect, because once you are comfortable identifying conditional relationships, you can mechanically check for errors without having to think too much about it.

Another benefit of recognizing conditional flaws is that when you are trying to match up a conditional error with the correct answer choice, the process is also straightforward. Here are some examples of answer choices describing conditional flaws:

Takes a condition necessary to be a condition sufficient

Takes for granted that an assumption required to establish the argument's conclusion is sufficient to establish that conclusion

Treats a statement whose truth is required for the conclusion to be true as though it were a statement whose truth ensures that the conclusion is true

Confuses a stated requirement with a sufficient condition

***

In the hardest conditional flaw questions, the test makers will try to throw you off by dressing up the error committed in the argument as another flaw type. Misdirection, or "Red Herrings," are a recurrent technique used in the most challenging flaw questions. We will talk about this once we have covered all 23 flaws.

Take a look at the following question:

PT22 S2 Q25

A recent survey showed that 50% of people polled believe that elected officials should resign if indicted for a crime, whereas 35% believe that elected officials should resign only if they are convicted of a crime. Therefore, more people believe that elected officials should resign if indicted than believe that they should resign if convicted.

The reasoning above is flawed because it

    A.   Draws a conclusion about the population in general based only on a sample of that population
    B.   Confuses a sufficient condition with a required condition
    C.   Is based on an ambiguity of one of its terms
    D.   Draws a conclusion about a specific belief based on responses to queries about two different specific beliefs
    E.   Contains premises that cannot all be true

The stimulus starts off talking about a survey. As soon as I see this, I make a note to double-check if this is a *sampling bias* flaw question. The stimulus also contains conditional logic, so it could also be a conditional flaw hiding in the stimulus somewhere. Let's dissect the argument:

- Premise: *A recent survey showed that 50% of people polled believe that elected officials should resign if indicted for a crime*

Poll: 50% believe Indicted → Resign

- Premise: *whereas 35% believe that elected officials should resign only if they are convicted of a crime*

Poll: 35% believe Resign → Convicted

- Conclusion: *more people believe that elected officials should resign if indicted than believe that they should resign if convicted*

Number of people who believe Indicted → Resign > number of people who believe Convicted → Resign

Notice the subtle shift from the premises to the conclusion? The author has swapped the ordering between "resign" and "convicted" going from the premise to the conclusion. In the second premise, 35% of the people believe that elected officials should resign *only if* they are convicted of a crime. "Resign" is the sufficient, while "convicted" is the necessary.

In the conclusion, however, the author is talking about whether officials should *resign if convicted.* Here, "convicted" is the sufficient condition, and "resign" is the necessary condition.

This argument contains an obvious conditional flaw. But it also contains a survey, so does it have a sampling problem too? We don't know: we don't have enough information to decide whether the sample size is adequately representative, whether there is sampling bias, and whether the methodology has flaws. In other words, it could be a problematic sample, or it could be a perfectly fine sample.

As we mentioned previously, a flawed argument often contains multiple or **multiple potential flaws**. Don't rest on your laurels after you've found just one. In addition, if there is one certain flaw and one possible flaw in an argument, as seen here, we always go with the most certain one. (The conditional flaw in this case.)

Let's take a look at the answer choices:

A. Draws a conclusion about the population in general based only on a sample of that population

What the test makers are describing here is a *sampling bias fallacy.* The previous question where the author concludes anyone fishing for trout based on how the best fishermen felt about the best selling bait would be such a flaw. Here, even though a survey and sampling are involved, we simply do not have enough information to know whether such a flaw is committed. On the real test, I would keep this answer and move on.

B. Confuses a sufficient condition with a required condition

This is the flaw we are looking for, the conditional logic flaw. (required condition = necessary condition)

C. Is based on an ambiguity of one of its terms

The flaw this answer is talking about is called *Equivocation*, where one word has two meanings and the meaning of the word shifts through the argument.

D. *Draws a conclusion about a specific belief based on responses to queries about two different specific beliefs*

This answer is tricky because it's half wrong half right. The author drew a conclusion about *two* specific beliefs (more people believe Indicted → Resign than Convicted → Resign) based upon two specific beliefs, one of which is the same (Indicted → Resign), and *one of which is different.* (Resign → Convicted)

E. *Contains premises that cannot all be true*

This is the *Self Contradiction* flaw, it does not appear here.

Causal Flaws

We discussed different types of logic used in the LSAT in detail in the previous chapter and explored the nature of causal logic in depth. Here is a refresher:

Causal logic is not exclusive. Just because A can cause B doesn't mean C, D, or E cannot also cause B. Take the following example:

Cardio helps one lose weight. Peter lost so much weight, he must have done some insane cardio.

What's wrong with this argument? It's possible that Peter did other things which caused him to lose weight, for example, maybe he dieted, or lifted weights, or got surgery, or a combination of the above.

Whenever the argument presents us with some form of causal logic in a Flaw question stimulus, always ask yourself, could there be **alternative causes** or **contributing causes**?

See 6-3-16 for an example of this type of causal flaw.

Similarly, one cause can have multiple effects. **One trick the test makers use in flaw questions is to confuse side effects with the intended effect.** For instance, drinking wine can have the side effect of giving you a headache, but the reason you drank wine wasn't to get a headache. Just because A causes B, doesn't mean A is intended to cause B.

So whenever the author presents causal logic in the argument, ask ourselves the following questions:

* Is the cause provided reasonable? Could there be **alternative causes** that the author has ignored?
* Even if the cause provided is reasonable, could it be only one of many **contributing causes** all leading to the effect in question?
* Can the cause provided by the author lead to **multiple effects**?
* Even if the cause-effect relationship the author provides exists, is the effect in question an intended or **side effect**?

A common way causal flaws appear in Logic Reasoning questions is in the famous Correlation-Causation format. The author presents a correlation, A ~ B, and concludes that the relationship is causal, or A ⇒ B.

A correlation could be due to causation, other reasons, or even a statistical fluke. **Don't automatically assume cause and effect when presented with a correlation.** Whenever the argument presents a correlation and concludes that there is a causal relationship, we ask ourselves three questions:
If the author sees A ~ B, and concludes A ⇒ B, is it possible that

C/D/E $\Rightarrow$ B? (Could it be that alternative factors caused B?)
C $\Rightarrow$ A and B? (Could it be that there is a third common cause?)
B $\Rightarrow$ A? (Could the author have reversed the causal relationship?)

Sometimes the author will make the argument slightly more complicated by negating the correlation in the premise and thereby negating causation in the conclusion. For example, the author will argue that because *there is no correlation between coffee consumption and work performance, drinking coffee does not cause you to work more effectively.* This variation of the Correlation - Causation argument type is more common in Strengthen/Weaken Questions but will occasionally pop up in Flaw Questions. Just be aware that even without correlation, causation can exist as well.

Take a look at 58-1-11 and 62-4-19 for this type of flawed argumentation.

***

Let's look at a more complicated variation of the causation flaw:

<u>PT86 S1 Q19</u>

Researcher: In an experiment, 500 families were given a medical self-help book, and 500 similar families were not. Over the next year, the average number of visits to doctors dropped by 20 percent for the families who had been given the book but remained unchanged for the other families. Since improved family health leads to fewer visits to doctors, the experiment indicates that having a medical self-help book in the home improves family health.

The reasoning in the researcher's argument is questionable in that

A. It is possible that the families in the experiment who were not given a medical self-help book acquired medical self-help books on their own
B. The families in the experiment could have gained access to medical self-help information outside of books
C. A state of affairs could causally contribute to two or more different effects
D. Two different states of affairs could each causally contribute to the same effect even though neither causally contributes to the other
E. Certain states of affairs that lead families to visit the doctor less frequently could also make them more likely to have a medical self-help book in the home

This question is hard because it's not the usual Correlation - Causation variation we have encountered so many times before. The test makers came up with a slightly more complicated alternative.

As we read the first half of the stimulus, we discover a correlation between having the medical help book and fewer visits to the doctor's office. Those who have the book didn't go to the doctor's as much, while those who didn't have the book had the same number of visits as before. So there is a correlation, but is there causation? I suppose having the medical self-help book can *cause* you to go to the doctor's office less. You can probably find some treatments or diagnose your disease on your own with the help of the book. Let's see what the author's reasoning is.

Instead of arguing that because Medical Self-Help Book ~ Less Visits to the Doctor, Medical Self Help Book ⇒ Decreased Visits to the Doctor, the author comes up with a more complicated, alternative causal possibility. The author says that *since improved family health leads to fewer visits to the doctors, the experiment indicates that having a medical self-help book in the home improves family health.*

If we diagram out the author's reasoning? It will look like this:

- Medical Self-Help Book ~ Less Visits to the Doctor's Office (correlation found in the experiment)
- Improved Family Health ⇒ Less Visits to the Doctor's Office
- Medical Self-Help Book ⇒ Improved Family Health

In abstract notation form, it will look like this:

- A ~ B,
- Because C ⇒ B,
- A ⇒ C (in the author's view, A ⇒ C ⇒ B)

The author's causal chain is certainly a possibility, but could it also be possible A ~ B can simply be explained by A ⇒ B.

Take a look at the following analogy if you are still a little confused:

- *Law students have stronger reading skills than students who didn't go to law school*
- *Since reading Shakespeare improves one's reading ability,*
- *Going to law school causes students to read Shakespeare.*

This example is a direct parallel to the author's reasoning above. The author's explanation, while a possibility, ignores a glaring alternative: it's also very possible that having the medical book was the direct cause for fewer doctor visits, just as a legal education can be the direct cause for students having stronger reading ability.

So the flaw in this question, while a little non-conventional, is still causal in nature. The author has overlooked an alternative cause.

Let's now take a look at the answer choices:

A. *It is possible that the families in the experiment who were not given a medical self-help book acquired medical self-help books on their own*

Even if the families who were not given the book got the book on their own, where does that lead us? Their visits to the doctor's office were not affected. So that can only mean one thing: the correlation between having the medical self help book and less visits to the doctor's office isn't as clear as the stimulus makes it out to be.

This answer is sowing doubt in our minds about the *phenomenon*, rather than the author's *explanation*. It is not attacking the author's premise - conclusion core itself.

B. *The families in the experiment could have gained access to medical self help information outside of books*

If the families gained access to medical information outside the books, how do we explain the correlation between those given the books and decreased visits to the doctor? Did only those who were given the books do extra research? We can't be sure. If everybody did outside research, how is it that only those given the books visited doctors less?

C. *A state of affairs could causally contribute to two or more different effects*

This answer is saying that a cause can have many different effects. For instance, eating sugary food can make you happy but also make you gain weight. In the stimulus, the author's mistake was to assume that one effect can only have one cause. The author thinks less visits to the doctor is caused by improved health, which is in turn caused by having the medical book. The more likely alternative is that people with the books simply consulted the books when they got sick and saved a trip to the doctor's.

D. *Two different states of affairs could each causally contribute to the same effect even though neither causally contributes to the other*

This is the correct answer, but in super abstract format. So we have two causes that can contribute to the same effect. Cause 1 (medical book) and Cause 2 (improved family health) each *independently* contribute to the same effect (less visits to the doctor), and there is no causal relationship between cause 1 and cause 2.

The correct answer, as we will see over and over again, will often be worded more vaguely and in more abstract terms than the wrong answers. So don't eliminate an answer simply because we are unclear on what it means. Try to extract what keywords we can from it and match it to the stimulus to have a better idea of what it's trying to say.

E. *Certain states of affairs that lead families to visit the doctor less frequently could also make them more likely to have a medical self help book in the home.*

This answer choice is suggesting that instead of A ⇒ B, there is a common cause for both A and B. But in this question, we know that people who received the medical books did so because of their participation in the experiment, could participation in the experiment also have led to them going to the doctor less? This sounds rather far-fetched to me.

The correct answer is D.

Causation flaws are fairly common in Flaw Questions. Whenever we sense causal logic at play in an author's argument, ask ourselves whether there are alternative causes or contributing causes that the author has willfully ignored. Similarly, whenever there is a correlation involved in a stimulus, and the author provides a causal explanation for it, try to think of alternative ways to explain the correlation.

Now that we have a complete list of the structural and logical flaws to frequently appear in Flaw Questions, we must strive not only to memorize them, to commit them to heart, but also to be able to detect such flaws even when the stimulus arguments get vague, abstract, or are enshrouded in complicated language. Personally, I found the best way to quickly come to a strong grasp of these fallacies is to do some additional research (google these fallacies) and try to come up with your own examples.

Being able to quickly figure out what flaw each of the answer choices are describing is also a skill that will greatly aid in our Flaw Question successes. The advanced test takers will be able to take a look at the answer choices, quickly realize the flaws many of the answer choices are describing and be able to match up/eliminate these choices accordingly.

Lastly, before we turn to the next segment of the chapter, the academically oriented student can further explore the topic of formal and informal fallacies in Douglas Walton's Informal Logic: A Pragmatic Approach.

Focusing on Answer Choices

But questions that can be solved simply by looking at the gap between premise and conclusion, or those that can be matched up with the 23 flaws mentioned above only form a majority of the Flaw Questions on the LSAT (approximately around 70%). In the remaining Flaw Questions, the key to getting them right lies in careful analysis of the answer choices. In this sense Flaw Questions are similar to Role and Method Questions. A large portion of our attention should be focused on identifying and understanding the keywords presented in the answer choices and trying to match them up with the stimulus.

Similarly, you will often read the stimulus but cannot definitively answer what exact fallacy the argument's reasoning has committed. This is also when we turn to the answer choices and proceed via the process of elimination. Before we look at how to use the answer choices to guide us to success, let's look at two commonly seen types of answer choices:

Two types of Flaw Questions don't really fit into the categories we have discussed above, they are Overlook and False assumption flaws. These flaws can always be identified via the wording of the answer choices. These flaws are hard to identify when we have just read the stimulus, so instead, we let the answer choices guide us in coming to the correct answer. Let's call them "**Overlook Flaws**" and "**False Assumption Flaws**."

Overlook Flaws

Whenever the answer choice contains the following,

the author has overlooked,
the author has failed to consider,
the author disregarded the possibility,

we look at the rest of the answer choice and ask ourselves, "*Which one of the following, if true, would hurt the author's argument and conclusion?*" To see why, look at the example below:

Argument: *John is a JD student, therefore he must have taken the LSAT.*

Question: what is the flaw in this argument? What has the author overlooked?

The answer to this question is simply that not all JD students have taken the LSAT in order to gain admissions to law school. Some may have taken the GRE, some schools allow for transfers from their LLM or LLB programs. So being a JD doesn't automatically mean that you have taken the LSAT.

By rephrasing the answer choice as *the author has overlooked the fact that not all JD students take the LSAT,* or *the author failed to consider the possibility/disregarded the possibility that some JD students have not taken the LSAT,* we are simply introducing a potential objection to the argument itself. In other words, the author's flaw in such a question is that they have *ignored* a piece of evidence that may cast doubt on their argument.

So whenever we see the question or answer choices in a Flaw question beginning with "the author has overlooked/failed to consider/disregarded the possibility", we ask ourselves whether the rest of the information in the answer choice is an objection to the author's original argument. **Does the rest of the answer choice attack the author's argument, do they hurt the original conclusion?**

PT50 S4 Q19

Recent studies have demonstrated that smokers are more likely than non-smokers to develop heart disease. Other studies have established that smokers are more likely than others to drink caffeinated beverages. Therefore, even though drinking caffeinated beverages is not thought to be a cause of heart disease, there is a positive correlation between drinking caffeinated beverages and the development of heart disease.

The argument's reasoning is most vulnerable to criticism on the grounds that the argument fails to take into account the possibility that

- A. Smokers who drink caffeinated beverages are less likely to develop heart disease than are smokers who do not drink caffeinated beverages
- B. Something else, such as dietary fat intake, may be a more important factor in the development of heart disease than are the factors cited in the argument
- C. Drinking caffeinated beverages is more strongly correlated with the development of heart disease than is smoking
- D. It is only among people who have a hereditary predisposition to heart disease that caffeine consumption is positively correlated with the development of heart disease
- E. There is a common cause of both the development of heart disease and behaviors such as drinking caffeinated beverages and smoking

This question contains keywords with which we are no doubt familiar by now: words like "more likely", "not thought to be a cause", and "positive correlation" are seemingly pointing us towards a correlation - causation flaw. But be careful! Since we only look at the hardest LR questions in this book, you should know that often things are not what they appear to be. Let's look at the argument in detail:

- *Recent studies have demonstrated that smokers are more likely than non-smokers to develop heart disease.*

So there is a correlation between smokers and heart disease: smoking ~ heart disease.

- *Other studies have established that smokers are more likely than others to drink caffeinated beverages.*

Another correlation, smoking ~ drink caffeinated beverages.

We have two correlations so far, what will the author do next?

- *Therefore, even though drinking caffeinated beverages is not thought to be a cause of heart disease,*

The test makers put a "therefore" here to trap you, this is not the conclusion! The "even though" introduces a concession that is not essential to the argument, but let's diagram it out anyway:

Drinking caffeinated beverages does NOT cause heart disease

- *There is a positive correlation between drinking caffeinated beverages and the development of heart disease.*

This is the conclusion of the argument, the author concludes that drink caffeinated beverages ~ heart disease.

What we are looking at is the author deriving an additional correlation from two original correlations. This argument contains no causal reasoning. Some students, after seeing the correlation, assume it's a correlation - causation argument. Remember that in the hardest LR questions, always expect variations in the author's reasoning!

If we diagram the author's argument out in abstract form, it yields:

A ~ B
A ~ C
Therefore B ~ C

This reasoning is problematic, take a look at the following analogy:

Law students are more likely than non law students to have better reading skills. Law students are also more likely than non law students to be stressed out. So there is a positive correlation between better reading skills and stress.

For anyone who has tried to do LSAT RC under timed conditions, we know that this correlation is absurd. Being stressed out doesn't make you a better reader, quite the opposite. When given a correlation, we know that there is the potential for causation behind it. But to derive B ~ C from A ~ B and A ~ C is just another form of erroneous reasoning thrown at us by the test makers.

Now a new problem arises: this error doesn't quite fit in with any of the flaws we have discussed above. So all that's left to do is turn to the answer choices, hopefully they will give us a clue.

The question asks us what the argument *fails to take into account*, that makes it fall into the Overlook Flaw category. So we look at the answer choices and ask ourselves, which one of the following attacks the original argument and conclusion?

    A.   *Smokers who drink caffeinated beverages are less likely to develop heart disease than are smokers who do not drink caffeinated beverages*

This is stating the opposite of what the author's conclusion is suggesting. The author's conclusion states that *there is a positive correlation between drinking caffeinated beverages and the development of heart disease.* In other words, a coffee drinker is more likely to develop heart disease than a non coffee drinker.

This answer, on the other hand, suggests that drinking coffee actually lessens your chances of developing heart disease. In other words, it's attacking the author's original conclusion.

    B.   *Something else, such as dietary fat intake, may be a more important factor in the development of heart disease than are the factors cited in the argument*

This answer itself suffers from the relative vs. absolute fallacy which we have talked about earlier. Does it matter if there are more important factors? Just because John runs faster than David doesn't mean David isn't fast. Similarly, just because dietary fat intake is a more important factor in the development of heart disease doesn't mean drinking caffeinated beverages isn't a factor. This answer is irrelevant to the author's argument and conclusion.

However, if the author had concluded that drinking caffeinated beverages was the *most important factor* in the development of heart disease, then this answer could potentially be acceptable.

    C.   *Drinking caffeinated beverages is more strongly correlated with the development of heart disease than is smoking*

This answer basically repeats the author's conclusion, but in a stronger manner. It's the opposite of what we want.

    D.   *It is only among people who have a hereditary predisposition to heart disease that caffeine consumption is positively correlated with the development of heart disease*

This answer choice confirms the positive correlation between caffeine consumption and heart disease, albeit in a qualified way. Compared to answer choice A, it's a much weaker way to attack the conclusion, if it does so at all.

    E.   *There is a common cause of both the development of heart disease and behaviors such as drinking caffeinated beverages and smoking*

This answer claims there is a common cause behind A, B, and C. It is irrelevant, remember, we are trying to find an answer that is attacking the author's conclusion. So we are looking for an answer that suggests there is no correlation between drinking caffeinated beverages and the development of heart disease.

The correct answer is A.

False Assumption Flaws

Like Overlook Flaws, False Assumption Flaws are determined on a case by case basis when we look at answer choices. Unlike Overlook answer choices, where we look for the answer that is attacking the author's argument/conclusion, False Assumption answers state an assumption that the author makes in coming to their conclusion.

False Assumption Flaw answer choices will typically contain the phrases *the author takes for granted, assumes without evidence,* or *fails to establish.* What is the nature of the information introduced by these phrases? Let's go back to our previous example:

Argument: *John is a JD student, therefore he must have taken the LSAT.*

Question: What is the flaw in this argument? What has the author taken for granted?

The author takes for granted that if you are a JD student, then you must have taken the LSAT. In other words, JD → LSAT. What's the nature of this conditional statement to the author's argument? It helps the author's argument. So when we examine false assumption flaw answer choices, we are looking for something that is helping the author's argument/conclusion. This is the opposite to what we do in Overlook type answer choices.

Some students confuse "fail to consider" and "fail to establish" answer choices. The former is an Overlook type answer choice, and the latter is a False Assumption type answer choice.

There is an additional step to consider when looking at False Assumption Flaw answer choices. We must make sure what the answer choice says the author has assumed is *truly* what the author has assumed. In other words, we approach False Assumption answers like we would Necessary Assumption answer choices. We use the **Assumption Negation Technique** to make sure that by negating the answer choice, it is hurting the author's original conclusion. (The intermediate/advanced student should already have an understanding of the Assumption Negation Technique, we will take a deeper look at it in the chapter on Necessary Assumptions, including its rationale and usage.) Take a look at 59-2-20 Answer Choice B for an incorrect answer that satisfies step 1, but not step 2.

So there's two steps involved when evaluating a false assumption type answer choice, we ask ourselves:

1.	Does the answer choice help the author's argument?
2.	Even if it helps the author's argument, is it something really assumed by the author? (Does negating the answer choice hurt the validity of the author's conclusion?)

PT44 S4 Q20

Advertisement: Each of the Economic Merit Prize winners from the past 25 years is covered by the ACME retirement plan. Since the winners of the nation's most prestigious award for economists have thus clearly recognized that the ACME plan offers them a financially secure future, it is probably a good plan for anyone with retirement needs similar to theirs.

The advertisement's argumentation is most vulnerable to criticism on which one of the following grounds?

    A. It ignores the possibility that the majority of Economic Merit Prize winners from previous years used a retirement plan other than the ACME plan

    B. It fails to address adequately the possibility that any of several retirement plans would be good enough for, and offer a financially secure future to, Economic Prize winners

    C. It appeals to the fact that supposed experts have endorsed the argument's main conclusion, rather than appealing to direct evidence for that conclusion

    D. It takes for granted that some winners of the Economic Merit Prize have deliberately selected the ACME retirement plan, rather than having had it chosen for them by their employers

    E. It presumes, without providing justification, that each of the Economic Merit Prize winners has retirement plan needs that are identical to the advertisement's intended audience's retirement plan needs

The argument is not hard to understand, what is hard about this question is determining the fallacy that the author commits. Is it the comparable flaw, where the author makes an inappropriate comparison between the needs of Economic Prize winners and regular customers? Is it the appeal to authority fallacy, are these economists qualified to recommend retirement plans to regular people? Perhaps it is something else?

The comparable fallacy is tempting but it's not the case here. Does the author make an inappropriate comparison? Not really: the author qualifies his conclusion by making it applicable only to people with retirement needs similar to the economists. As a result, what the author is really comparing is the choice of economists and people with similar needs.

Could it be an inappropriate appeal to authority fallacy? Potentially. Just because you are an accomplished academic in economics doesn't mean you make sound financial planning decisions. Furthermore, the stimulus doesn't really tell us if the economists actively chose the retirement plans, only that they are covered by it.

To have a more detailed picture of where potential flaws can arise, let's break down the argument structurally:

- Premise: *Winners covered by ACME plan*
- Intermediate Conclusion: *Winners recognize benefits of ACME plan*
- Conclusion: *ACME plan good for those with similar needs*

What are the gaps in this argument, and what potential objections can we make to it?

Well, for starters, is it possible to be covered by a retirement plan without actively recognizing its benefits? Certainly: perhaps it was a sponsorship offered by the awards committee, perhaps they were covered by their academic institutions, or perhaps there was only a limited number of plans available and they chose the less bad from two terrible options. In other words, being covered by the ACME plan doesn't automatically mean the economists chose it due to its benefits.

Secondly, perhaps even though the needs of the winners and regular people are the same, the benefits are different? For example, if the winners receive royalties for subscribing to the ACME plan for being prize winners and celebrities, while regular people don't receive such benefits, then the conclusion would also not make sense.

In short, after a detailed analysis of the author's argument, we still only have a vague idea of the type of fallacy this question entails. As such, we now turn to the answer choices to see if it can be solved via the process of elimination.

A. *It ignores the possibility that the majority of Economic Merit Prize winners from previous years used a retirement plan other than the ACME plan*

This answer choice begins with "*ignores the possibility*," so let's see if it attacks the author's argument and conclusion. If it turned out that the winners had multiple retirement plans, does it weaken the author's argument? Not really, you can't really argue that because they had multiple plans, they don't recognize the benefits of the ACME plan. Also, the answer choice says a majority of winners used other plans, but we know every winner was covered by the ACME plan. So this answer is too vague for my liking. I will keep it for now and return for a closer look if I don't find a better answer.

B. *It fails to address adequately the possibility that any of several retirement plans would be good enough for, and offer a financially secure future to, Economic Merit Prize winners*

Again, "fails to address" means it's supposed to attack the argument/conclusion. This answer doesn't really do that. What if there are multiple good plans? Does that make the ACME plan less suitable to our needs? No.

C. *It appeals to the fact that supposed experts have endorsed the argument's main conclusion, rather than appealing to direct evidence for that conclusion*

What is the argument's main conclusion? Namely that the ACME plan is good for regular people too. Have the experts endorsed this conclusion? No. In order to tackle this answer choice, we use the technique of "keyword extraction" that we practiced in Role and Method Questions. Does what is described in the answer choice match up with the stimulus?

> D. *It takes for granted that some winners of the Economic Merit Prize have deliberately selected the ACME retirement plan, rather than having had it chosen for them by their employers*

A "*takes for granted*" answer choice, which means looking at it as a Necessary Assumption answer choice. First of all, does this help the author's argument? Yes, if the winners deliberately chose ACME, that overcomes the first gap we identified in our analysis of the argument. Secondly, does the author really assume this? Yes, the author must have assumed this, because if he didn't, and we negate the answer into "*none of the winners deliberately selected ACME, it was chosen for all of them*", then there is no way to extrapolate that they actually recognize some benefits to ACME. This answer passes the two-pronged test for false assumption answer choices.

> E. *It presumes, without providing justification, that each of the Economic Merit Prize winners has retirement plan needs that are identical to the advertisement's intended audience's retirement plan needs*

Another False Assumption answer choice here. Does it help the conclusion? Yes, it strengthens the idea that what is good for the winners is good for the audience. But is it something truly assumed by the author? No. The author states that the plan is good for people with retirement needs *similar* to the winners, not identical. So if we negate this answer choice, the conclusion still stands.

Answer choice E is a tricky one, so whenever faced with false assumption answer choices, always go the additional step to make sure it's **truly** something that the author had assumed in their reasoning.

All that's left are A and D. A leaves something to be desired. Just because the economists didn't use ACME's plan, it doesn't imply that they don't recognize its benefits, and we can't therefore say that it isn't good for those with similar needs. To use an example, you can very well recognize the benefits of one insurance plan but chose another due to more offices or friendlier customer service. Answer choice A leaves us with more uncertainties than I'd like.

Answer choice D has its own issue too though, it is actually addressing the gap between the premise and the intermediate conclusion, sidestepping the main conclusion. I know that we said in the beginning of the chapter that the correct answer will address the gap between the supporting information and the main conclusion, and I still believe that to be true. In all the Flaw Questions that I've encountered, this is one of the few that doesn't directly address the gap between the main conclusion and the rest of the information.

I do not think one exception warrants a modification of our rules for tackling Flaw Questions, but be aware that freak accidents do occur from time to time on the LSAT.

There is another core habit, one which we will cover later on in the book, that involves the criteria for **ranking answer choices**. There will be times when we have multiple attractive answer choices available, and it is our job to find the most appropriate answer depending on the question type. For Strengthen, Weaken, and Most Strongly Supported Questions, as well as RC Infer questions, it's an absolutely crucial skill. We will cover this core habit down the road.

In this question, D wins over A, albeit not by much.

The correct answer is D.

False Leads and Multiple Flaws in the Stimulus

As we have seen in the previous question, there will be times when we have trouble figuring out what fallacy the author has committed even when we have a strong grasp of the 23 fallacies listed above. This is because the test makers love to throw in tempting information to mislead us toward a **fake flaw** (remember how PT22 S2 Q25 was a conditional flaw question, even though the stimulus started off talking about a survey), or leave signs for **multiple potential flaws** in the stimulus.

I call these red herrings, and they are quite common in the hardest Flaw Questions. Unfortunately, the only thing we can do to successfully navigate these questions is to have a strong grasp of the fallacies we have listed and practice until you have an instinctive knowledge of what these fallacies are and the similarities and differences between each of them.

A good way to practice Flaw Questions is to try to find as many fallacies as you can in the stimulus before turning to the answer choices. Think about the potential flaws the argument contains, list them out, and gradually narrow it down by truly thinking about which fallacy fits and which one doesn't.

We also have to study the answer choices extra carefully. If we were able to identify a few potential flaws in the stimulus, we can simply turn to the answer choices to see which ones are represented. The questions will ALWAYS have only one correct answer, so if you find two fallacies which both appear in the stimulus and the answer choices, there's usually something wrong with the wording of one of the answers.

Lastly, there will be times when we are completely lost and will need to use the answer choices to guide us to the correct answer. This happens frequently in Overlook and False Assumption answer choices. So pay extra attention to the answers!

Take a look at 9-2-22, 15-2-17, 22-2-25, 24-2-1, 44-4-20, 45-4-24, 47-3-23, 48-4-25, 49-2-18, 54-2-19, 56-3-10, 65-4-26, 68-3-21, 72-3-11, 81-2-20, and 84-3-22. See how many potential fallacies, real or imagined, you can identify in the stimulus before moving on to the answer choices.

Answer Choice Elimination

Before we conclude this chapter, I just wanted to dive a little deeper into tricky answer choices. As we have seen in the previous questions, getting a Flaw Question right not only depends on having a strong grasp of the logic and standard fallacies that we have encountered, but also being able to tactically navigate through vague and abstract answer choices. This is also the reason why we have placed the Flaw Questions chapter before all the other Assumption family questions. The skills we need to approach Flaw answer choices are similar to the ones we used in Role and Method questions. Use the habit of "keyword extraction" and comparing what is described in the answer choices with the stimulus just as we have learned in the previous chapters.

We have already seen how important answer choices are to Flaw Questions. As we have seen in the Overlook and False Assumption type answer choices, sometimes getting the question right is not just about being able to decipher what fallacy lies behind the author's argument, but also to correctly eliminate all the wrong answers presented to us. With these types of questions, it's not as simple as finding the flaw in the stimulus and picking it out from the answer choices, we have to individually go through each answer choice, checking if "Overlook" answers attack the argument, and "False Assumption" answers are in fact assumed by the author in their reasoning.

I personally spend **just over half of my time per question on answer choices**, figuring out what they are trying to say, comparing and contrasting them. When I started doing Flaw Questions, the majority of my time was spent on reading the stimulus and trying to match it up with a potential fallacy, but as I got more familiar with the process, I can now devote more time to the answers. This should be your ultimate goal as an advanced test taker.

On the hardest Flaw Questions, expect the author to lay down all kinds of traps for you. Here are four questions that you should ask yourself whenever you are faced with difficult or hard-to-understand answer choices:

The information presented in this answer choice, does it **happen/appear** in the stimulus? (focus on nouns and verbs)

Is the order **correct structurally**? If the stimulus is using A to support B, does the answer say something like using B to support A? (this would be wrong)

Is this answer choice **out of scope**?

Is this answer choice **too strong or too weak**? (focus on adjectives and adverbs)

Let's turn to some questions with tricky answer choices: I've deliberately only included the correct answer and a notoriously tricky wrong answer.

PT18 S4 Q25 (Partial)

George: a well-known educator claims that children who are read to when they are very young are more likely to enjoy reading when they grow up than are children who are not read to. But this claim is clearly false. My cousin Emory was regularly read to as a child and as an adult he seldom reads for pleasure, whereas no one read to me and reading is now my favorite form of relaxation.

Which of the following describes a flaw in George's reasoning?

A. He treats his own experience and the experiences of other members of his own family as though they have more weight as evidence than do the experiences of other people.

B. He attempts to refute a general claim by reference to nonconforming cases, although the claim is consistent with the occurrence of such cases.

I've only included the correct answer and the most selected wrong answer to this question. Statistically speaking, about half of all test takers chose the wrong answer. Let's look at the stimulus first.

The first statement is a view held by the opponent (well known educator), who prescribes to the view that if you were read to as a child, you are more likely to enjoy reading as an adult.

The second statement is the conclusion of George's argument. George denies the educator's view, so George is saying that if you were read to as a child, you are NOT more likely to enjoy reading as an adult.

The last statement is the support provided by George, it's the premise. He uses his cousin and himself as examples to support his conclusion.

What is the flaw with this question? There appears to be two, one quite clear and the other not so obvious. Let's look at the obvious one first:

There appears to be a sampling flaw here. The flaw here is actually called an appeal to anecdotal evidence, where you support your conclusion with evidence that is atypical, personal, or cannot be verified. Both the appeal to anecdotal evidence and sampling bias fall into the same family of fallacies (hasty generalization), but it's not a fallacy tested on the LSAT, and it's closely related to the sample bias fallacy. So for the argument's sake, we can categorize it as a sampling flaw.

Of course, there is no survey involved here, but one of the key issues that can arise with a sampling flaw, the problem of the unrepresentative sample, is also reflected in George's argument. George attempts to refute the educator's view using only himself and his brother. While we don't know what evidence the educator bases his view on, deriving a conclusion from the experiences of two people is surely problematic.

The second flaw is somewhat harder to find. Remember at the beginning of the chapter we talked about getting into the habit of comparing the wording of the premises and the conclusion, looking for shifts? Let's do that here:

George's premise: Emory was read to as a child but he rarely reads, I was never read to as a child but reading is my favorite form of relaxation.

George's conclusion: being read to as a child does not increase your likelihood of enjoying reading as an adult.

Increasing one's likelihood of enjoying reading doesn't necessarily mean you have to actually enjoy reading, right? It's an issue of confusing the relative with the absolute here. Maybe if Emory wasn't read to as a child, he would never even go near a book as an adult. Although he seldomly reads now, perhaps he would have read even less if not for his parents reading to him as a child? Same with George: reading is his favorite form of relaxation. But if he was read to as a child, perhaps his passion for reading would have been even more intense?

In other words, even if we ignore the sampling issue, George's evidence doesn't really conflict with the educator's claims.

Let's take a look at the first answer choice. Remember what we talked about in the previous chapters, trying to match up what the answer describes with the structure of the stimulus:

Does George treat his own experience and the experiences of other members of his own family as though they have more weight? Yes, he believes his own experiences more than the view of the educator. The first half of the answer choice is ok.

But does he think his experiences have more weight than the experiences of other people?

Who are these other people, and what are their experiences? We don't really know. There's the educator, but we only know what his view is, not their experiences. Perhaps this answer is talking about people who conform to the educator's view, people who were read to as children and who actually do enjoy reading as adults. But this is only a guess, it's never mentioned in the stimulus. Furthermore, the educator never uses the experiences of other people to back up their claim.

If this answer had read "*he treats his own experience and the experiences of other members of his own family as though they have more weight than the view of another*", then it would have been an okay answer.

The second answer choice is the correct answer, simply because everything from it matches up with what happened in the stimulus. Does George attempt to refute a general claim? Yes, the educator's point of view is a general claim (people read to as children are more likely to enjoy reading). Does George reference non-conforming cases? Yes, he provides himself and Emory as examples. Are these examples consistent with the educator's claim? Yes, even though Emory dislikes reading now, he may have disliked it even more had he not been read to as a child. Even though George loves reading now, he may have loved it even more had he been read to as a child. As we mentioned earlier, George and Emory's cases are not in contradiction to the educator's view.

Had George's conclusion been "*so it's not guaranteed that adults read to as children will enjoy reading, nor adults not read to as children will dislike reading*", then his argument would have been flawless.

***

PT26 S2 Q21 (Partial)

Attorney for Ziegler: my client continued to do consulting work between the time of his arrest for attempted murder and the start of this trial. But I contend that Ziegler was insane at the time that he fired the shot. This is the only reasonable conclusion to draw from the fact that the accusers have submitted no evidence that he was sane at the time he pulled the trigger, only that he was sane some time after he did so.

Which one of the following most accurately describes a flaw in the reasoning of Ziegler's attorney?

A. It concludes on the basis of evidence against Ziegler's being sane that there is a lack of evidence for Ziegler being sane.
B. It fails to consider the possibility that Ziegler's being sane after the shooting is an indication that he was sane at the time of the shooting.

Again, we have included only the correct answer choice and the most commonly selected wrong choice here, having only two answer choices to select from will force the student to slow down and really think about the options available. Can you match up the keywords from this answer choice with what was described in the stimulus? Can you match up the structure of the argument described in the answer choice with the structure of the argument in the actual stimulus?

What is the attorney's conclusion? Ziegler was insane when he fired the shot.

What's the premise the attorney offers for this conclusion? Accusers offered no evidence that he was sane when he pulled the trigger.

This is a very typical appeal to ignorance flaw (unproven vs. untrue). The opponent did not offer evidence for A, so A is false.

Let's take a look at the answer choices:

A.   *It concludes on the basis of evidence against Ziegler's being sane that there is a lack of evidence for Ziegler being sane.*

What is this answer choice saying? What is the structure of the hypothetical argument this answer choice is describing? What is its premise and what is its conclusion?

Premise: *existence of evidence against Ziegler being sane* (in other words, we have evidence Ziegler is insane)

Conclusion: *there is a lack of evidence for Ziegler being sane* (so we have no evidence that Ziegler is sane)

Notice the subtle shift of this answer choice from the appeal to ignorance fallacy that we have identified in the stimulus argument?

The argument in the stimulus: *we have no evidence Z was sane, so he must be insane.*
The argument in this answer choice: *we have evidence Z was insane, so there is no evidence he was sane.*

Some students get confused by the differences between the two, so let's try an example:

Author's argument: *we have no evidence that OJ was innocent, so he must be guilty.*

Answer choice's argument: *we have evidence that OJ did it, so there can't be evidence demonstrating his innocence.*

This is a really tricky answer choice and trapped a lot of students. Because on the actual exam, we only have just over two minutes for even the hardest questions. We often end up reading the answer choices without truly delving into their structure, much less compare what they describe to what actually happens in the stimulus. This answer choice is even more tempting because we can figure out the flaw here is an appeal to ignorance, and this answer choice looks really close to being a description of that type of flaw.

So, like I mentioned before, your goal in Flaw Questions is to get as familiar as you can with the flaws, be able to quickly decipher the author's argument and try to match up the flaws. Only when you can do this with relative ease and faster, will you be able to have enough time to **actually examine the answer choices** in greater detail.

If we changed this answer choice into "*it concludes on the basis of a lack of evidence for Ziegler was sane that Ziegler was insane,*" then it will be a good answer choice.

B. *It fails to consider the possibility that Ziegler's being sane after the shooting is an indication that he was sane at the time of the shooting.*

This answer choice begins with "*fail to consider*", so we check to see if what it's describing damages the author's argument and conclusion. What is the author's conclusion? Ziegler was insane. But if we follow the reasoning in this answer choice we can argue that "*if Ziegler was sane right after the shooting, then there is a high possibility that Ziegler was sane during the shooting.*" This is in direct opposition to the author's conclusion, and forms a direct challenge to it.

This is the correct answer.

***

Let's look at another example, read the answer choices in detail and go back to the stimulus to try to match it up before you select it.

PT47 S3 Q23 (Partial)

Television network executive: Some scientists have expressed concern about the numerous highly popular television programs that emphasize paranormal incidents, warning that these programs will encourage superstition and thereby impede the public's scientific understanding. But these predictions are baseless. Throughout recorded history, dramatists have relied on ghosts and spirits to enliven their stories, and yet the scientific understanding of the populace has steadily advanced.

The television network executive's argument is most vulnerable to criticism on which one of the following grounds?

A. It fails to consider that one phenomenon can steadily advance even when it is being impeded by another phenomenon.
B. It takes for granted that the contention that one phenomenon causes another must be baseless if the latter phenomenon has persisted despite steady increases in the pervasiveness of the former.

***

There are two potential flaws in this argument. The first one is a comparable fallacy. The author doesn't think TV programs that portray paranormal incidents will impede the public's scientific understanding, because dramas have portrayed ghosts and spirits while science still advanced. In other words, the author's argument is basically this: "*if dramas and plays had ghosts in them and people's scientific understanding advanced, TV programs that have ghosts in them won't impede people's scientific understanding.*"

They are assuming that there is enough similarity between dramas and plays vs. TV programs so that what holds true with dramas will hold true with TV programs.

To argue against this point we must point out that dramas and TV programs are actually not comparable. Perhaps when people see dramas or plays they are perfectly aware that what we are seeing are fictional depictions. Whereas a lot of TV programs such as documentaries or realistically shot horror movies can pull the audience in and blur the lines between fiction and reality.

The second flaw, like we saw in one of the examples earlier, is again the fallacy of confusing the relative and the absolute. You see, in absolute terms, scientific understanding could have advanced, but relatively speaking, it could have been advancing at a slower pace, being impeded by the abundance of ghost stories and paranormal dramas. Just because scientific knowledge has been steadily advancing doesn't mean it wasn't impeded by some external force. Take the following absurd analogy for example: "*John scored a 175 on his LSAT, 15 points more than his previous score, so he is surely lying when he said slow internet was an impediment on his test.*"

The answer choices, however, don't give us the flaws in a straightforward manner. As soon as we realize that we can't simply match up the flaws that we have detected in the stimulus with an answer choice, we go into keyword analysis mode and start nitpicking at all the little details in each answer choice. Are the answer choices Overlook or False Assumption types? Can we match up the keywords and order of the answer choice with what occurred in the stimulus?

Answer choice A is an Overlook type answer, and as such we check to see if it can damage the author's argument and conclusion. If it contains vague and abstract terms we try to match that up with the stimulus as well.

Which phenomenon can steadily advance even when it is being impeded by another phenomenon?

If we said the first phenomenon referred to scientific understanding of the public, and the other phenomenon referred to TV programs featuring ghosts, does that make sense? If we replied "*scientific understanding can advance even when it's impeded by depictions of ghosts and spirits in the media*" to the author, does that weaken his argument? Yes, in fact, this is an indirect way of saying advancement and impediments can coexist.

Answer choice B is a False Assumption answer, let's break it down and try to understand what it is saying before deciding if it passes the Assumption Negation test.

It takes for granted that the contention that one phenomenon (X) causes another (Y) must be baseless…

What causal relationship does our author think is baseless? According to the author, the view that TV programs emphasizing paranormal activities impedes the public's scientific understanding is baseless. So this is the causal relationship that the author rejects.

X = TV programs with ghosts and spirits

Y = Impeded scientific understanding

…if the latter phenomenon has persisted despite steady increases in the pervasiveness of the former

The latter phenomenon refers to Y, while the former is referring to X, so in other words, "*if impeded scientific understanding has persisted despite steady increases in the pervasiveness of ghost stories.*"

Does the author assume this? No, the author believes that TV programs emphasizing ghosts impedes the public's scientific understanding is baseless if depictions of paranormal activities have continued through the ages despite a steady increase in scientific understanding.

<u>A is the correct answer.</u>

Summary and Habits

Here is a simplified chart of how to approach Flaw Questions. When we are reading the stimulus, make a note of its **structure**. What is the gap between the author's supporting premises and main conclusion? Is it a shift in details, concepts, or scope? Or does it fit in with one of the classical fallacies which we have looked at?

We also look for indications of conditional and/or causal **logic** in the argument. If such logic is present, is it flawed?

Lastly, we are to analyze **answer choices** in a critical way: are we looking at an Overlook or False Assumption answer choice? Can we match up the answer choice with the stimulus? Do the answer choice's scope and structure match the stimulus? Is the answer choice too weak or too strong?

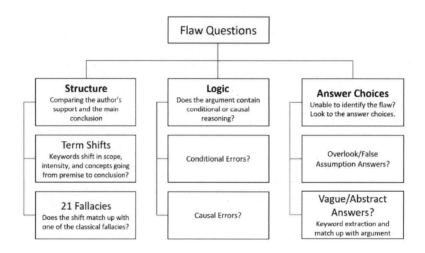

9.Core Habit:
ASSUMPTIONS

Think about gaps in the argument. What kind of statement can we come up with to connect these gaps, to make the author's reasoning more understandable, to make their arguments more coherent and valid?

A Mini Review on Core Habits Covered So Far

So far, we have looked at many of the essential skills needed to succeed in the Logic Reasoning section. In the chapter on Find the Conclusion Questions, we examined how to differentiate between the author's argument and peripheral information, and to distinguish premises from intermediate conclusions and main conclusions. In the chapters on Role and Flaw Questions, we emphasized the importance of investigating all the little details contained in answer choices and matching up what the answer choices said with what actually occurred in the stimulus. Finally, in Method and the Logic chapters, we studied how the author advances their argument, what techniques are used, and the type of logic (conditional/causal/analogy) employed to go from premise to conclusion.

Indeed, mastering these skills will prove to be invaluable help with the hardest LR questions. Whenever we approach a question that is giving us trouble, keep the following three things in mind:

1. Analyze the stimulus's **structure**: isolate the argument core from the peripheral information. What is the author's conclusion, and what information is used to support this conclusion?

2. Analyze the **logic** behind the author's reasoning. We have already isolated the premises and conclusions, now think about HOW the author advances their argument. (Are there Causal and Conditional reasoning present in the argument?)

3. Get into the habit of reading answer choices word for word, and compare what is described in the answer choices with information in the stimulus. Extract the relevant **keywords**.

On the actual test, we have on average 1 minute 45 seconds per question. We want to aim for one minute for the easiest questions and just over two minutes for the harder questions.

In this 1-2 minute window, you have to look at the question, realize the type of question it is and adjust your strategy accordingly, read the stimulus, figure out its structure, maybe look for assumptions hidden within the argument, think about the author's reasoning, come up with a viable answer, look over the answer choices, eliminate obviously wrong answers, compare attractive leftover answers, possibly refer back to the stimulus, and finally pick the correct answer choice. All this time you are dealing with the adrenaline rush of test day, possibly coping with fatigue and stress, while trying hard not to get distracted by the proctor, your environment, or think about what mistakes you might have made in earlier sections of the test.

With so much on your mind it's going to be extremely difficult to follow a step-by-step process that encompasses every aspect of every question. Instead, we will be falling back on our intuition and involuntary habits as the stress and pressure begins to mount. What really matters in LR, and on the rest of the LSAT, is the ability to improve our test taking habits. We do this through constant practice and drilling. We do this until we no longer have to remind ourselves to look for the premises/conclusion, until we can spot conditional or causal reasoning automatically, until we are intuitively underlining suspicious keywords in answer choices.

Arguments and Assumptions

The intermediate/advanced student will know that "assumption" questions nominally consists of Flaw, Sufficient Assumption, Necessary Assumption, Strengthen, and Weaken Questions. Principle Strengthen/Justify questions also belong to this category. Assumptions are really important in LR questions!

But what I want to tell you is that assumptions can and do appear in question types that are not a part of the "assumption family" as well. We already saw this in Method questions (Difficult Trait #2). In other question types such as Point of Agreement/Disagreement Questions, assumptions also abound.

We must always be on the lookout for gaps and assumptions in an argument. The test writers will deliberately leave gaps in an argument's reasoning to further confuse us.

So that's why now I'm asking you to think of assumptions in a different light. Most of us have only really thought about assumptions when looking at Sufficient Assumption or Necessary Assumption Questions, or questions from the Assumption Family. But what I'm suggesting is that we think of potential assumptions in any stimulus where we don't have a clear idea of what the author is trying to say.

Think back on the very first question we encountered, in Chapter 3, Find the Conclusion. (PT58 S1 Q13)

> *It is a given that to be an intriguing person, one must be able to inspire the perpetual curiosity of others. Constantly broadening one's abilities and extending one's intellectual reach will enable one to inspire that curiosity. For such a perpetual expansion of one's mind makes it impossible to fully comprehend, making one a constant mystery to others.*

Recall that the first and last sentences are the premises, with the main conclusion sandwiched in between.

- Intriguing Person → Inspire Perpetual Curiosity (S1, Premise)
- Expansion of One's Mind → Impossible to Comprehend → Constant Mystery (S3, Premise)
- Broadening One's Abilities and One's Intellectual Reach → Inspire Perpetual Curiosity (S2, Conclusion)

In this argument, the author essentially links S3 and S1 in a longer chain to derive the main conclusion. But notice that there's a slight gap between S3 and S1: what the author has left unsaid is the relationship between "*being a constant mystery to others*" and "*being an intriguing person.*" So if we were to help the argument a little bit by adding in an assumption, the argument becomes much more straightforward:

It is a given that to be an intriguing person, one must be able to inspire the perpetual curiosity of others. Constantly broadening one's abilities and extending one's intellectual reach will enable one to inspire that curiosity. For such a perpetual expansion of one's mind makes it impossible to fully comprehend, making one a constant mystery to others. (Being a constant mystery to others makes one an intriguing person.)

Now, we can see right away that S1 can be appendaged to the end of S3, creating the relationship Perpetual Expansion of One's Mind → Inspire Curiosity, which also happens to be what S2, the main conclusion, is expressing. **Term-shifts** like these abound in more complicated stimuli, sometimes we are able to spot these "mini-jumps" in the author's chain of reasoning, other times they perplex us and lead us astray.

***

Now take a look at the following argument, there will be gaps and uncertainties in it, try to plug in our own understanding to help make the argument flow and more understandable:

Scientist: Given the human tendency to explore and colonize new areas, some people believe that the galaxy will eventually be colonized by trillions of humans. If so, the vast majority of humans ever to live would be alive during this period of colonization. Since all of us are humans and we have no reason to think we are unrepresentative, the odds are overwhelming that we would be alive during this period, too. But, because we are not alive during this period, the odds are slim that such colonization will ever happen.

This comes from one of the hardest all time Method Question stimulus (PT 68 S3 Q20), read it over, think about its structure and reasoning, what is the author's conclusion, and how do they come to it?

Don't worry too much if you are having trouble connecting the dots. Think about the gaps between each statement and try to add in whatever information you can to make the author's argument more understandable. In other words, edit the stimulus by inserting additional statements to make it more straightforward.

***

This is what I had come up with:

The underlined statements are the extra information I added to make the argument more understandable. I am essentially filling in the gaps that the test makers have left for us.

Given the human tendency to explore and colonize new areas, some people believe that the galaxy will eventually be colonized by trillions of humans. (<u>But the total number of humans ever to live from when we began as a species until our extinction cannot be much more than this number.</u>) If so, the vast majority of humans ever to live would be alive during this period of colonization. Since all of us are humans and we have no reason to think we are unrepresentative, (<u>we are in fact representative of humanity and are probably just like everybody else. And if the majority of humanity ever to live are alive during this period,</u>) the odds are overwhelming that we would be alive during this period, too. But because we are not alive during this period, the odds are slim that such colonization will ever happen.

The underlined statements are my own additions. The author commits a series of flaws in their reasoning. Let's flesh it out with a hypothetical scenario:

Assume 2.5 trillion humans have existed from the Big Bang to the end of time, and 2 trillion of them are alive during the colonization of the galaxy. That means 80% of all humans ever to exist lived during this age of colonization. Since we are representative of humanity, and 80% of humanity is alive during this time, we should be alive during this time as well. (Imagine if we said John is representative of the law student population, and we know that most law students are easily stressed out, then we can probably infer that John is also easily stressed out.)

Does it make more sense now? The author deliberately left gaps in their reasoning to make the argument hard to understand and follow. Sometimes we will read an LR stimulus, understand all the words in it, but still have no idea what just happened. Sometimes we can isolate the premises and the conclusion, but if someone asked us to describe the argument to them, we would have no idea where to begin.

What I have done here is essentially fill in some of the pieces of information that the author believes and uses in their reasoning but never explicitly mentioned. In fact, that's what assumptions are on the LSAT.

> Whenever there are gaps in the author's reasoning, **assumptions** are additional pieces of information along the author's line of reasoning that we can place into the argument to help it make more sense.

Let's turn to another really confusing stimulus:

Think about the author's reasoning as you read through the stimulus, are there assumptions that we can place within the author's argument to make it clearer?

PT12 S1 Q24

Until recently it was thought that ink used before the sixteenth century did not contain titanium. However, a new type of analysis detected titanium in the ink of the famous Bible printed by Johannes Gutenberg and in that of another fifteenth century Bible known as B-36, though not in the ink of any of numerous other fifteenth century books analyzed. This finding is of great significance, since it not only strongly supports the hypothesis that B-36 was printed by Gutenberg but also shows that the presence of titanium in the ink of the purportedly fifteenth century Vinland Map can no longer be regarded as a reason for doubting the map's authenticity.

The reasoning in the passage is vulnerable to criticism on the ground that

    A. The results of the analysis are interpreted as indicating that the use of titanium as an ingredient in fifteenth century ink both was, and was not, extremely restricted.

    B. If the technology that makes it possible to detect titanium in printing ink has only recently become available, it is unlikely that printers or artists in the fifteenth century would know whether their ink contained titanium or not.

    C. It is unreasonable to suppose that determination of the date and location of a document's printing or drawing can be made solely on the basis of the presence or absence of a single element in the ink used in the document.

    D. Both the B-36 Bible and the Vinland Map are objects that can be appreciated on their own merits whether or not the precise date of their creation or the identity of the person who made them is known.

    E. The discovery of titanium in the ink of the Vinland Map must have occurred before titanium was discovered in the ink of the Gutenberg Bible and the B-36 Bible.

Here is my reworked version of the stimulus, with additional clarifying information added. Compare your understanding of the stimulus with what I have below, does it make more sense now on what flaw the author commits?

Until recently it was thought that ink used before the sixteenth century did not contain titanium. However, a new type of analysis detected titanium in the ink of the famous Bible printed by Johannes Gutenberg and in that of another fifteenth century Bible known as B-36, though not in the ink of any of numerous other fifteenth century books analyzed. (So in all the books from the fifteenth century, only two Bibles were printed with titanium ink: the Gutenberg Bible and the B-36 Bible, so Gutenberg was probably the only person to have used titanium ink.) This finding is of great significance, since it not only strongly supports the hypothesis that B-36 was printed by Gutenberg but also shows that the presence of titanium in the ink of the purportedly fifteenth century Vinland Map can no longer be regarded as a reason for doubting the map's authenticity. (So there must have been a map printer who also used titanium ink.)

The flaw committed here is the fallacy of self contradiction. But unlike most self contradiction flaw questions we will have seen, in this argument the self contradiction occurs in the author's assumptions.

The author has two distinct conclusions:

Conclusion 1: B-36 was printed by Gutenberg.

Assumption: the use of titanium ink is extremely rare and only used by Gutenberg. (The author must assume this because if multiple people printed with titanium ink, you can't attribute B-36 to Gutenberg solely based on the titanium.)

Conclusion 2: Vinland Map is authentic.

Assumption: there must have been a map printer in the fifteenth century who also used titanium ink.

The correct answer is A.

***

When reading a hard-to-understand stimulus, keep an open mind and search for information that the author may have deliberately omitted. Information that when included, will help the argument actually make sense. When analyzing a stimulus/argument, try to systematically ask yourself the following three questions:

1. Did I identify the conclusion correctly? What about the premises and intermediate conclusion?

2. Do I have a clear understanding of how the author advances the argument? What type of logic and techniques are employed? (conditional/causal/comparable/eliminate an alternative…)

3. Are there gaps in the author's reasoning? What additional statements can I insert into the argument to help it make more sense? (Does the author make any assumptions in this argument?)

You will notice that these also match up with the three Core Habits needed to successfully navigate a stimulus argument: **Structure**, **Logic**, and **Assumptions**.

The **SLAKR** Method to tackle the hardest LR Questions

By now we have looked at four of the five elements that we must consider when faced with a harder LR question. Structure, Logic, Assumptions, and Keywords in Answers. While every different type of LR question will have their own distinct approach, these five elements are usually where the test makers will throw in tricks to throw the student off track. So whenever you are unsure about a question, systematically think about these five elements and their implications.

The fifth core habit, ranking answer choices, will be covered once we have looked at Strengthen, Weaken, and Most Strongly Supported Questions.

Structure: Did I identify the premises and conclusions correctly, what about other parts of the argument?

Logic: Does the author use conditional and/or causal logic to advance the argument? What other reasoning techniques are employed?

Assumptions: Does the argument contain gaps between premises and the conclusion? Are there gaps elsewhere in the author's reasoning? Can we identify them?

Keywords in Answers: Am I aware of the meaning of all the keywords in the answer choices? Do they match up with what I observed in the stimulus?

Ranking Answers: Is there one answer choice head and shoulders above the rest? If not, then what are the top two answer choices? What are their respective issues? Which one is less problematic than the other? What is the specific goal of the question type that I am faced with? What's my exact criterion for determining which answer is better? (Chapter 19)

The Role of Assumptions in Assumption Family Questions

We have just seen that assumptions are a recurring theme in LR question stimuli, regardless of question type. But the need to clearly identify assumptions is the greatest in Assumption Family questions. In Flaw Questions, we start by isolating the shift between the premises and the conclusion, and the rest of our work stems from there. In other words, the authors of flawed arguments are committing fallacies in their assumptions.

In most Assumption Family Questions (Flaw, Sufficient Assumption, Necessary Assumption, Principle Strengthen), our primary focus when analyzing the stimulus should be to think about what assumptions the author made going from premises to the conclusion.

Strengthen and Weaken Questions, although still technically a part of Assumption Family questions, are somewhat different. A majority of Strengthen and Weaken Questions are solved by first isolating gaps between the premises and the conclusion, identifying the corresponding assumptions. However, a small proportion of Strengthen and Weaken Questions are solved by other means, something that we will talk about when we get to Chapters 13 and 14.

For now, all you need to remember is that Strengthen and Weaken Questions are part of the Assumption Family, but think of them as distant cousins rather than members of the immediate family.

Before we turn to Sufficient and Necessary Assumption Questions in Chapters 10 and 11, I just wanted to speak a little more on the concept of assumptions on a more macroscopic level. Attaining a conceptual grasp of what assumptions are and how to situate sufficient and necessary assumptions within the larger theoretical framework will make tackling the next two chapters a lot easier.

As we have seen, an **assumption** is the piece of information hurdling a reasoning gap within the author's argument. The author doesn't always list out all his premises in explicit detail, and it is our job to discover what was deliberately left unsaid.

In **Assumption Family** questions, all the questions will contain a reasoning gap, but unlike other question types, this reasoning gap occurs between the premises/intermediate conclusion and the main conclusion. We call this the **Main Assumption**. A Main Assumption perfectly connects the premises and the conclusion. It hurdles the biggest gap of the argument, the gap between the author's support and his main conclusion.

Take a look at the following example:

John scored 180 on the LSAT. Hard working students will succeed in law school. So John will have a successful life.

The conclusion of this mini argument is that *John will have a successful life.* There are two reasoning gaps at play in this argument.

The first gap is between "*John scored 180 on the LSAT*" and "*hard working students will succeed in law school.*" The author is assuming that those who scored 180 on the LSAT must be hard workers. We can use conditional logic to express the assumption that would bridge the gap: "*if you scored 180 on the LSAT, then you must be a hard-working student.*"

This assumption, however, is **not** the main assumption that we have to identify when tackling Assumption Family questions. Remember, the main assumption bridges the gap between the premises/intermediate conclusions and the MAIN CONCLUSION. Let's look at the second gap and assumption needed in this argument.

The second gap is between the intermediate conclusion and the main conclusion. The author goes from *"success in law school"* to *"success in life."* The assumption here is that *"those who succeed in law school will succeed in life."* This is the Main Assumption of the argument, as it directly links the main conclusion with the argument's supporting elements.

> In Assumption Family questions (Flaw, SA, NA, Principle Strengthen, and to a lesser extent Strengthen and Weaken), the question stimulus will contain a **Main Assumption**. It may contain other, less significant assumptions, but our primary job is to isolate and analyze the Main Assumption.

So always find the reasoning gap that is connected to the Main Conclusion and come up with a Main Assumption to address this specific gap.

Sufficient Assumptions

The next two chapters will look at Sufficient Assumption and Necessary Assumption Questions. We will examine the theory behind SA and NA Question types in more detail then. But in this chapter, we will explore a bit further the relationship between Sufficient Assumptions and Necessary Assumptions, as well as their relationship to the Main Assumption.

As we have seen just now, the Main Assumption is the assumption that bridges the gap between an argument's main conclusion and supporting premises. It links the two bodies of information in such a way that the argument is logically valid, and the reasoning gap is overcome.

> The Sufficient Assumption is an assumption that is greater or equal to the Main Assumption in strength, degree, scope, or quantity. If the Sufficient Assumption is true, the Main Assumption must be true.

The Sufficient Assumption can be the main assumption we have identified, or it can be bigger/stronger than it. Take a look at the following examples:

Law school costs 200,000 dollars, John has enough savings to pay for law school.

The Main Assumption here would be that *"John has 200,000 dollars in the bank."* If we plug in the Main Assumption, the argument flows and is valid. The Main Assumption here is also a Sufficient Assumption. However, the statement *"John has a million dollars in the bank"* is also a Sufficient Assumption. It is stronger than the Main Assumption, in terms of quantity, one million dollars is more than 200,000 dollars. If John has a million dollars, it must be true that he has at least 200,000 dollars.

Could statements like "John makes 300,000 dollars a year" or "John has billionaire parents" work as Sufficient Assumptions in this argument? Not really, because maybe John spends all his money on drugs and gambling, or maybe his parents refuse to pay for law school. Just because he makes a lot of money or comes from money doesn't necessarily mean that he will have the savings to pay for law school.

In other words, if you plug the correct Sufficient Assumption back into the author's argument, the argument's conclusion is **guaranteed**.

If we plug in our original SA into the argument, both times the argument is valid and the conclusion stands:

"Law school costs 200,000 dollars, John has 200,000 dollars in the bank, John has enough savings to pay for law school."

"Law school costs 200,000 dollars, John has one million dollars in the bank, John has enough savings to pay for law school."

If John had a million dollars in the bank, he has the 200,000 needed for law school. In fact, any amount equal to or more than 200,000 dollars would constitute a Sufficient Assumption.

***

Those who got above average grades are conscientious students, John is a conscientious student.

What is the main assumption here? "*John got above average grades.*" Can we think of an alternative SA? Remember, sufficient assumptions are equal to or stronger than the main assumption that we have envisaged.

"*John got straight As while the class average was a B+*" or "*John is the top student of his school*" will work as Sufficient Assumptions. They are more specific than our main assumption. If either of these statements are true, we know that the Main Assumption will also hold true.

Similarly, statements like "*John works really hard*" or "*John got an A on his final exam*" won't work as Sufficient Assumptions, because neither of these guarantees the truth of the main assumption, and by extension, the argument's conclusion.

People from New York live fast paced lives. John lives a fast-paced life.

What is the main assumption in this argument? "*John is from New York.*"

Can we think of an alternative Sufficient Assumption? What about "*John is born in Manhattan and has never left the island.*"

This statement is much stronger than what is required. It's more than enough to ensure the truth of our main assumption.

Would a statement like "*John works in New York*" be a valid Sufficient Assumption? No, because just because he works in NYC doesn't mean he is from there.

***

But when we are faced with an answer choice that doesn't seem obvious at first glance whether it's a valid Sufficient Assumption, what do we do then?

It's simple really, we have already identified the main assumption in our reading of the author's argument in the stimulus. We simply ask ourselves, **does this answer choice guarantee the truth of the main assumption?** Remember the examples we have just looked at, if John was born in and has never left Manhattan, he is definitely from New York; if John is the top student of his class, he is definitely an above average student, if John has a million dollars saved, he definitely has the 200,000 needed for law school.

***

So in summary, here are the two essential traits of valid Sufficient Assumptions:

Sufficient Assumption ≥ Main Assumption (the correct SA answer will guarantee the truth of the main assumption)

If we plug the correct Sufficient Assumption back into the author's argument, it will be just **enough** or **more than enough** to hurdle the author's reasoning gap, and in turn **guarantee** the truth of the author's main conclusion.

The next chapter will apply these two ideas to the hardest SA Questions.

Necessary Assumptions

Necessary Assumptions are another type of assumptions that we look at on the LSAT. We will look at NA Questions in Chapter 11, right after we look at SA Questions in Chapter 10.

Just like how we explained Sufficient Assumptions by thinking about their relationship to the Main Assumption, Necessary Assumptions are also looked at in relationship to the Main Assumption:

We already know that the Main Assumption is a statement we come up with to perfectly connect the author's premises and main conclusion, making the argument valid.

> The Necessary Assumption is a statement that must be true if the Main Assumption is true.

What does this mean? Let's revisit our examples from the previous section:

***

Law school costs 200,000 dollars, John has enough savings to pay for law school.

Main Assumption: John has 200,000 dollars in savings.

If the Main Assumption is true, what else must also be true? Take a look at the following extrapolations and ask yourself which one of the following must be true?

John is a frugal person.

Is this a valid extension of the main assumption? Can we extrapolate this from the main assumption alone? If John has 200,000 dollars in savings, does that mean he is definitely a frugal person? Not necessarily: maybe he won the lottery, blew most of it, and decided to go to law school. In other words, the statement that "*John is a frugal person*" is not necessarily true given the Main Assumption, so it's NOT a valid Necessary Assumption.

John has a habit of saving money.

This is NOT a valid Necessary Assumption either, because just like the example above, maybe John was given the money or he just won the lottery.

John has money.

This is a valid Necessary Assumption. If John has 200,000 dollars, he definitely has some money.

John has a bank account.

This is a tricky one, but it is also NOT a valid Necessary Assumption. All we know from the argument is that John has money saved. Maybe he hides it under his mattress?

John has a good credit score.

Again, not a valid extrapolation that we can make based on the Main Assumption alone, so not a valid Necessary Assumption either.

John has 200,000 dollars in savings.

This is the Main Assumption we had come up with, it is also a valid Necessary Assumption. This may seem a little redundant, but it will help you understand the nature of NAs better. If John has 200,000 dollars in savings, is it necessarily true that John has 200,000 dollars in savings? Yes, we are just repeating ourselves, but it's valid nonetheless.

John has 500,000 dollars in savings.

This is NOT a valid Necessary Assumption, it is a valid Sufficient Assumption. The test makers love to throw in SA answers in NA Questions or vice versa. Make sure you are constantly aware of the question type being dealt with.

***

In summary, we think about Necessary Assumptions as a **must be true extrapolation** that can be made based upon the Main Assumption. If the Main Assumption is true, then the correct Necessary Assumption answer will *necessarily* be true.

Also, the correct Necessary Assumption will be **weaker and more limited** in language than the Main Assumption. Its scope, certainty, degree, or strength, or quantity **cannot exceed** that of the Main Assumption.

In other words, NA ≤ Main Assumption.

***

Two final notes before we turn to Sufficient Assumption questions in the next chapter:

Do not confuse Sufficient/Necessary Assumptions with Sufficient/Necessary Conditions!

Even though they are similarly worded, they are two distinct concepts that must be understood separately and discretely.

The Sufficient Assumption is called "sufficient" because it ensures the truth of the argument's main assumption, and by extension, the validity of the argument's main conclusion.

The Necessary Assumption is called "necessary" because it is a required trait of the argument's main assumption, and by extension, required if we accept the validity of the argument's main conclusion.

In conditional logic, $A \rightarrow B$, A is the sufficient condition because it is *sufficient* to ensure B occurs. So if A, definitely B. B is the necessary condition because when the sufficient A occurs, B *necessarily* occurs.

Arguments containing a reasoning gap between the premises and the conclusion must be filled by a main assumption. The argument can have conditional logic, but it doesn't have to. The argument can be causal or analogical in nature, and still contain Sufficient and Necessary Assumptions. Take a look at the following example:

John smokes two packs a day, John will get lung cancer.

I've left the reasoning gap here deliberately vague so we can look at it in two different ways. To hurdle the gap, we can come up with a Main Assumption that is either conditional or causal in nature. Remember that in harder LR questions, we have to think about whether the author uses a multitude of logical techniques to advance the argument. Is it conditional? Is it causal? Comparable? A mix of both?

If we had come up with a conditional Main Assumption, "*if you smoke two packs a day, you will get lung cancer,*" then the conditional relationship is

- Smoking two packs a day → Lung Cancer

"*Smoking two packs a day*" is the *sufficient condition*, while "*lung cancer*" is the *necessary condition*.

But a **Sufficient Assumption** can be worded as "*if you have ever smoked in your life, you will get lung cancer.*" It is NOT a sufficient condition, but rather, simply sufficient to ensure the argument's conclusion when you plug it back into the argument.

A **Necessary Assumption** in this case could be "*inhaling some chemicals can make you sick.*" If we believe Smoking two packs a day → Lung Cancer, then this statement is *necessarily* true.

We HAVE to think about an argument's structure and logic separately. We find assumptions embedded in an argument by analyzing the argument's structure. That means finding its premises/intermediate conclusion and the main conclusion, and comparing the two to find the gaps in the author's reasoning.

***

Let's go back to the example one more time, but this time we'll look at it from a different perspective.

John smokes two packs a day, John will get lung cancer.

Maybe you came up with a causal statement as the Main Assumption, this is fine too. Let's use the statement "*smoking two packs a day <u>causes</u> lung cancer*" as our Main Assumption here.

"*Even light smoking leads to lung cancer*" would be a great SA answer choice in this case. If smoking just a few cigarettes lead to lung cancer, smoking two packs a day will give you lung cancer. It's *sufficient* to ensure the conclusion stands.

"*Smoking can affect our body in a negative way*" would be a great NA answer choice. If we take our Main Assumption to be true, then this statement must be true as well.

So be flexible when we are trying to come up with a Main Assumption, we will get more practice in the subsequent two chapters.

How we approach the stimulus is DIFFERENT from how we approach answer choices

Some of us may have recognized a potential contradiction by now. We have stressed as one of our Core Habits the need to read each answer choice carefully and word by word. Some of the hardest wrong answer choices will deviate from the right answer choice in the tiniest degree. Maybe one adjective was too strong, maybe the scope was just too broad, or maybe it described a method of reasoning that simply did not happen in the stimulus.

But when we look at the stimulus and the argument within, we can sometimes input our own understanding to fill in the gaps. In other words, we are plugging additional information into the stimulus, while accepting the answer choices at face value.

Bringing our own understanding into the stimulus can, in the hardest questions, help us understand what the author is trying to say, what their argument is, and the logic they employ. In other words, **we should try to help the stimulus/argument.**

Bringing our own understanding into analyzing the answer choices, on the other hand, is a big no. We must evaluate and eliminate answer choices based on each individual word, and only on these words. We may think about the implications of such an answer choice, but we must not make additions to help the answer choices. **We must take the answer choices at face value, without bringing in our own assumptions.**

9.Core Habit: ASSUMPTIONS

10.Sufficient Assumption

We have just looked at Sufficient Assumptions from a conceptual perspective in the previous chapter. Let's go over it again with a quick review.

Sufficient Assumption Questions' stimuli will contain a gap between the information presented in the supporting premises/intermediate conclusion and the main conclusion. Sometimes it's a shift in terms, quantity, or a missing conditional link. In order to identify this reasoning gap we need to make sure we have correctly identified the structural elements of the stimulus.

After we have isolated the supporting information and the main conclusion, we compare the two and try to find a "main assumption" that would link them together, hurdling the gap left deliberately by the author and in the process justifying the author's argument.

Once we have come up with this "main assumption", it's time to compare it with the selection of answer choices. Remember, the nature of Sufficient Assumptions is that they *guarantee* the truth of the conclusion of the argument. When you plug the correct answer choice back into the author's argument in the stimulus, it fixes up whatever gap that has been left and ensures the conclusion drawn by the author is valid. As a result, the correct SA answer choice should be stronger or equal to the main assumption.

Here is a step-by-step guide to tackling SA Questions:

Identify the argument's **main conclusion** and supporting evidence (**premises** and **intermediate conclusion**)
Compare the two, **looking for shifts** or differences in information.
Ask yourself **what did the author miss** in making this argument? What is the **main reasoning gap**?
Create a "**main assumption**" to overcome that gap.
Compare your "main assumption" to the answer choices.
Plug back into the argument the answer choice you have selected, **can the conclusion be proven**?

***

We will now look at some of the hardest SA Questions that have appeared from PT1 to PT 90. As we go through the questions we will also shed light on some of the typical tricks and traps the test makers throw at us so they can be avoided.

Difficult Trait #1: Using a conditional relationship to link the premise and the conclusion is the most straightforward way to come up with a main assumption. Most of the time, I use it to pre-phrase my answer before looking at the answer choices.

<u>PT45 S1 Q21</u>

Although the geological record contains some hints of major meteor impacts preceding mass extinctions, there were many extinctions that did not follow any known major meteor impacts. Likewise, there are many records of major meteor impacts that do not seem to have been followed by mass extinctions. Thus the geological record suggests that there is no consistent causal link between major meteor impacts and mass extinctions.

Which one of the following assumptions enables the argument's conclusion to be properly inferred?

A. If there were a consistent causal link between major meteor impacts and mass extinctions, then all major meteor impacts would be followed by mass extinctions.
B. Major meteor impacts and mass extinctions cannot be consistently causally linked unless many mass extinctions have followed major meteor impacts.
C. Of the mass extinctions that did not follow any known major meteor impacts, few if any followed major meteor impacts of which the geological record contains no hints.
D. If there is no consistent causal link between major meteor impacts and mass extinctions, then not all mass extinctions could have followed major meteor impacts.
E. There could be a consistent causal link between major meteor impacts and mass extinctions even if not every major meteor impact has been followed by a mass extinction.

We should be familiar with the basic reasoning pattern behind this question. It is causal in nature. The argument is a variation of the "no correlation hence no causation" argument we discussed in Chapter 7. Let's go through it as we would any other question.

The conclusion of the argument is fairly obvious, the author believes that "there is no *consistent* causal link between major meteor impacts and mass extinctions." Note the language of the conclusion, the author isn't arguing that there is no causal relationship at all. Instead, the author believes there is no consistent causality. So in other words, maybe sometimes meteor impacts cause mass extinctions, but not all the time.

What is the support provided for this conclusion? The author suggests that sometimes you have meteor impacts but extinctions didn't follow; and sometimes you have extinctions but no meteor impacts came before it. In abstract terms, the author's argument is basically that sometimes A is not followed by B, and sometimes B is not preceded by A, so A does not always cause B.

Let's try an analogy if you still have trouble:

Sometimes I drink alcohol but don't get a headache, sometimes I have a headache but didn't drink alcohol. So drinking alcohol doesn't always cause headaches for me.

Can we think of a "main assumption" to link the premises and the conclusion? We can throw in a conditional relationship that states "*if not every impact is followed by mass extinctions, then there is no consistent causal link between impacts and mass extinctions.*"

What we have done here is essentially recast the author's argument in a conditional relationship.

Look at the following example to understand why conditionals are so helpful in hurdling the author's reasoning gap.

- Premise: John is in law school.
- Conclusion: John has taken the LSAT.

- Main Assumption: Law School Students → Taken the LSAT

Regardless of whether this argument is sound or not, when we combine the premise and the main assumption, it makes the conclusion logically valid.

So in the event that you have trouble coming up with the specific information needed to hurdle the gap between the premise and the conclusion, **conditionally linking them** can be a helpful tool to consider.

Let's now look at the answer choices:

A. *If there were a consistent causal link between major meteor impacts and mass extinctions, then all major meteor impacts would be followed by mass extinctions.*

This is the contrapositive of our "main assumption", it is good enough as a Sufficient Assumption answer choice. If the answer choice had said "all meteor impacts" rather than "all major meteor impacts", it would be stronger, but since the stimulus is only talking about "major impacts", this answer is good enough. This is the correct answer.

B. *Major meteor impacts and mass extinctions cannot be consistently causally linked unless many mass extinctions have followed major meteor impacts.*

The issue with this answer choice is the word "many". For students already familiar with "some, most, all" relationships, we will know that "many" just means "more than one." (If not, don't worry, we will cover "some, most, all" relationships in the chapter on Must be True Questions down the road.)

"*Many mass extinctions have followed major meteor impacts*" can mean potentially one of two things. Either each impact is followed by several extinctions, or there were many major impacts followed by extinctions. Either way we cannot know for sure if either is the case according to the stimulus. All we can gather from the stimulus is that some impacts were not followed by extinctions, how many or what proportion, we do not know. Similarly, for the impacts that were followed by extinctions, we don't know if it was just one or multiple.

As a result, we cannot take this conditional relationship and use it to connect the premise and the conclusion given by the author. It does not match up with the wording of the premise.

C. *Of the mass extinctions that did not follow any known major meteor impacts, few if any followed major meteor impacts of which the geological record contains no hints.*

What this answer is essentially saying is that for the extinctions that were not preceded by meteor impacts, it's not because the impacts were not recorded in the geological record. This could potentially work as a Strengthen answer, but remember our job here, we *need* to use the answer choice to connect the information in the premise (some impacts were not followed by meteors) with the information in the conclusion (no consistent causal link).

D. *If there is no consistent causal link between major meteor impacts and mass extinctions, then not all mass extinctions could have followed major meteor impacts.*

This answer choice reverses the order of our main assumption. Remember, we want an answer that gets us from Premise to Conclusion (P→C), this answer choice is the reversal.

E. *There could be a consistent causal link between major meteor impacts and mass extinctions even if not every major meteor impact has been followed by a mass extinction.*

This would be a correct Weaken answer choice, it's suggesting that even if the premise is true, the conclusion doesn't have to be true. Remember, in SA Questions, we are looking for an answer that when combined with the premises, makes the conclusion true.

PT53 S1 Q20

Biologist: Lions and tigers are so similar to each other anatomically that their skeletons are virtually indistinguishable. But their behaviors are known to be quite different: tigers hunt only as solitary individuals, whereas lions hunt in packs. Thus, paleontologists cannot reasonably infer solely on the basis of skeletal anatomy that extinct predatory animals, such as certain dinosaurs, hunted in packs.

The conclusion is properly drawn if which one of the following is assumed?

A. The skeletons of lions and tigers are at least somewhat similar in structure in certain key respects to the skeletons of at least some extinct predatory animals.

B. There have existed at least two species of extinct predatory dinosaurs that were so similar to each other that their skeletal anatomy is virtually indistinguishable.

C. If skeletal anatomy alone is ever an inadequate basis for inferring a particular species' hunting behavior, then it is never reasonable to infer, based on skeletal anatomy alone, that a species of animals hunted in packs.

D. If any two animal species with virtually indistinguishable skeletal anatomy exhibit quite different hunting behaviors, then it is never reasonable to infer, based solely on the hunting behavior of those species, that the two species have the same skeletal anatomy.

E. If it is unreasonable to infer, solely on the basis of differences in skeletal anatomy, that extinct animals of two distinct species differed in their hunting behavior, then the skeletal remains of those two species are virtually indistinguishable.

While the previous question had elements of causal reasoning in it, this one is analogical in nature. Let's look at it in more detail:

- Premise: *Lions and tigers have similar skeletal anatomy but different hunting behavior.*
- Conclusion: *We cannot infer that extinct animals hunted in packs based on their skeletal anatomy.*

On the surface the author seems to be comparing lions and tigers but remember that comparable reasoning is used to get us from premise to the conclusion. So how does the author go from lions vs. tigers to extinct predatory animals like dinosaurs?

What is the author really trying to say in the premise? If lions and tigers have nearly identical skeletons but different hunting behavior, then you can't determine an animal's hunting behavior from its skeletal structure alone, right? This is an assumption of the authors, but not the argument's Sufficient Assumption nor its main assumption.

To find the Main Assumption we again turn to the author's conclusion. The conclusion is about prehistoric animals such as dinosaurs. How does the author go from lions and tigers to a conclusion about dinosaurs? That's the real gap in the author's reasoning. What kind of assumption can we come up with to link the two?

Again, we can turn to a conditional statement to link the premise and the conclusion, for example: "*if surviving animals can have similar skeletons but different hunting behavior, then extinct animals with similar skeletons will have different hunting behavior as well.*"

This would work as a Sufficient Assumption, but if we wanted something that more closely mirrored the argument's language, we can try something like this: "*if lions and tigers have similar skeletons but different hunting behaviors, then extinct animals' hunting behavior cannot be inferred solely based on their skeletal structure.*" Again, we are simply using a conditional relationship to firmly link the information presented in the premise and the information presented in the conclusion.

A. *The skeletons of lions and tigers are at least somewhat similar in structure in certain key respects to the skeletons of at least some extinct predatory animals.*

What this answer is saying is that the two items the author compares share some similarities. But remember, the correct SA answer choice will be equal to or stronger than our main assumption. We also want an answer that links the premise and conclusion in an explicit way. We want an answer that says "*if you can't predict hunting behavior based on bone structure for lions and tigers, then you can't make a similar prediction for extinct animals either.*"

B. *There have existed at least two species of extinct predatory dinosaurs that were so similar to each other that their skeletal anatomy is virtually indistinguishable.*

This is potentially an assumption of the author's. But it doesn't meet our criteria for establishing sufficiency. For example, if the conclusion in a hypothetical argument read "*we cannot reasonably infer solely on the basis of LSAT performance how students will perform in law school,*" then maybe the author is assuming that there are high performers who do well in law school. But the author doesn't really have to assume that. In SA Questions, it's important to have come up with a main assumption before even tackling the answer choices. This way, we are not led astray by vague or weaker answer choices that could potentially be true.

C. *If skeletal anatomy alone is ever an inadequate basis for inferring a particular species' hunting behavior, then it is never reasonable to infer, based on skeletal anatomy alone, that a species of animals hunted in packs.*

This answer choice matches up with not only the structure of the author's argument, but is basically a restatement of our main assumption:

If skeletal anatomy alone is ever an inadequate basis for inferring a particular species' hunting behavior (*lions and tigers have the same skeletal anatomy but different hunting behavior*), then it is never reasonable to infer, based on skeletal anatomy alone, that a species of animals hunted in packs (*for example, extinct animals like dinosaurs*). This is the correct answer.

    D.   *If any two animal species with virtually indistinguishable skeletal anatomy exhibit quite different hunting behaviors, then it is never reasonable to infer, based solely on the hunting behavior of those species, that the two species have the same skeletal anatomy.*

This answer suffers from two problems: first, it's going from "hunting behavior" to "skeletal anatomy", the reverse of how the author advances the argument. Second, it's only talking about lions and tigers. We need an answer that connects lions and tigers with extinct animals like dinosaurs.

Remember the last step of SLAKR is to look at keywords in answer choices. We try to match up the information in the answer choices with the stimulus argument. Let's do that here:

If any two animal species with virtually indistinguishable skeletal anatomy exhibit quite different hunting behaviors (*that's lions and tigers we are talking about*), then it is never reasonable to infer, based solely on the hunting behavior of those species (*which species? Lions and tigers*), that the two species (*again, lions and tigers*) have the same skeletal anatomy.

    E.   *If it is unreasonable to infer, solely on the basis of differences in skeletal anatomy, that extinct animals of two distinct species differed in their hunting behavior, then the skeletal remains of those two species are virtually indistinguishable.*

Answer choice E starts off with the conclusion, that's already a sign of a wrong answer. Remember, we want an answer that goes from Premise to Conclusion. This answer is saying "if the conclusion is true, then there are extinct species with the same skeletal structure."

***

So far, we have been able to hurdle the gap in the author's argument by simply linking the premise and the conclusion in a conditional relationship to create the main assumption, and then comparing that main assumption to the answer choices. This technique can be used on many of the harder SA Questions. However, sometimes we really do have to isolate the information presented in the premises and that presented in the conclusion, and think about what it is that we are missing.

Take a look at the following question, make sure not to rush, really think about the premises and the conclusion separately, and then ask yourself what do I need to ensure that the conclusion is true?

Difficult Trait #2: The correct answer may not be a direct linkage of the premises and the main conclusion, but as long as it will help prove the main conclusion, it's the correct answer.

<u>PT85 S2 Q21</u>

Economist: Currently the interest rates that banks pay to borrow are higher than the interest rates that they can receive for loans to large, financially strong companies. Banks will not currently lend to companies that are not financially strong, and total lending by banks to small and medium companies is less than it was five years ago. So total bank lending to companies is less than it was five years ago.

The economist's conclusion follows logically if which one of the following is assumed?

A. Banks will not lend money at interest rates that are lower than the interest rates they pay to borrow.
B. Most small and medium sized companies were financially stronger five years ago than they are now.
C. Five years ago, some banks would lend to companies that were not financially strong.
D. The interest rates that banks currently pay to borrow are higher than the rates they paid five years ago.
E. The interest rates that small and medium sized companies pay to borrow are higher than those paid by large, financially strong companies.

We start with the conclusion: *total bank lending to companies is less than what it was five years ago.*

What are our premises?

- *SME (small medium enterprise) bank lending is less than what it was five years ago.*
- *Banks will not lend to companies not financially strong.*
- *Current interbank lending rates are higher than loan rates to large, financially strong companies.*

If we organize the information into table format, it's much easier to comprehend.

	Now	Five Years Ago
Financially strong small and medium companies	less	more
Not financially strong companies	0	?
Financially strong large companies	?	?
Total	Less	More

Some students get confused by the number of factors at play here. We can think of it this way:

Companies are either financially strong or not financially strong. Banks will only lend to financially strong companies. So if a company is not financially strong, doesn't matter whether it's small, medium, or large, it's not getting a loan currently.

So only financially strong companies are getting loans currently. That means financially strong small, medium and large companies.

So the author divides companies into those that are financially strong and those that are not financially strong. Among financially weak companies, current total lending is 0. We don't know what it was five years ago, but whatever it is, it can't be less than 0. So we can disregard this category and focus on the other types of companies. Remember, our goal is to get total lending to less than that of five years ago.

Lending to SMEs is less now than five years ago, so we can disregard this category as well. All that's left to consider are financially strong large companies.

In order to establish the conclusion, we want bank lending to financially strong large companies to be less or equal to what it was five years ago. There is also the possibility that lending to large, financially strong companies increased a small amount that has been offset by the larger decrease in lending to SMEs. But that is way too complicated, even for the LSAT.

So what we can do is to connect what the argument said about large financially strong companies (banks will not lend at negative real interest rates) with what we need to establish the conclusion (lending to financially strong large companies is less now than five years ago).

This is what I came up with:

"If lending rates are lower than borrowing rates for banks, then bank lending to large, financially strong companies will not be more than what it was five years ago."

A. *Banks will not lend money at interest rates that are lower than the interest rates they pay to borrow.*

If this is true, then bank lending to large financial institutions at present will be zero. Which means:

	Now	Five Years Ago
SME	less	more
Not financially strong companies	0	≥ 0 (whatever banks loaned out to these companies 5 years ago, it cannot be less than 0)
Financially strong large companies	0	≥ 0 (loans cannot be less than 0)
Total	Less	More

So total lending will definitely be less now than what it was five years ago. SME lending went down, lending to other types of companies either went down or stayed the same. <u>This is the correct answer</u>.

> B. *Most small and medium sized companies were financially stronger five years ago than they are now*

This is the most commonly selected wrong answer. We know that banks don't lend to companies that are not financially strong. But if SMEs have gotten weaker, perhaps the lending has decreased also? Either way, it is simply echoing what was already stated in the argument.

> Remember, Sufficient Assumptions are first and foremost, assumptions. That means the correct answer will be something that was not mentioned in the stimulus. Any repetition or restatement of either premises or conclusions will be wrong. **Beware answers that simply restate the premise or conclusion without any additional input.**

> C. *Five years ago, some banks would lend to companies that were not financially strong.*

This answer is along the author's line of reasoning, but it doesn't guarantee that total lending has decreased. The decrease in lending to companies that are not financially strong could simply be offset by a potential increase in lending to strong, large companies.

> D. *The interest rates that banks currently pay to borrow are higher than the rates they paid five years ago.*

Similarly, this answer choice also doesn't fully get us where we want to go. So borrowing rates for banks have gone up. But since we don't know how this affects bank lending patterns, it doesn't really affect our conclusion.

> E. *The interest rates that small and medium sized companies pay to borrow are higher than those paid by large, financially strong companies.*

This answer, like the previous one, does not give us the information to establish the conclusion as true. We need an answer that can prove that total lending has gone down. In order to do that, we must show that lending to large, financially strong companies has also gone down.

A lot of students get confused by this question because the main assumption for us here is not simply a matter of directly linking information in the premise with the conclusion. However, the correct answer choice, A, still serves as a Sufficient Assumption, because it guarantees the truth of the argument's conclusion.

10.Sufficient Assumption

Difficult Trait #3: In some SA Questions containing a conditional relationship, the correct answer will simply confirm the existence of the sufficient condition.

A common pattern in harder SA Questions is what I call "**Confirming the Sufficient**." It's actually quite simple once you learn to spot it. Basically, the premise provided by the author will be a conditional statement, A → B. The conclusion, on the other hand, is simply a restatement of the necessary condition. The correct answer choice is simply confirming that the sufficient condition presented in the premise does in fact exist.

Premise: A → B
Conclusion: B
Sufficient Assumption: A

Take a look at the following stimulus:

Moderate exercise lowers the risk of blockage of the arteries due to blood clots, since anything that lowers blood cholesterol levels also lowers the risk of hardening of the arteries, which in turn lowers the risk of arterial blockage due to blood clots; and, if the data reported in a recent study are correct, moderate exercise lowers blood cholesterol levels.

What is the conclusion of this argument? Moderate exercise lowers the risk of blockage of the arteries due to blood clots.

What about the premises of the argument?

If data is correct → moderate exercise lowers blood cholesterol levels → lowers the risk of hardening of arteries → lowers the risk of arterial blockage due to blood clots

In order for the argument's conclusion to stand, we must establish that moderate exercise does, in fact, lower blood cholesterol levels. If it were so, then we can properly make the connection between moderate exercise and lowered risk of arterial blockage.

How do we make sure that exercise lowers blood cholesterol levels? By confirming that the original sufficient condition does hold true, namely that the data reported are correct.
Take a look at the following example:

Premises: *If John is in law school, he must have graduated from college, which means he must have finished high school, which means he must have finished elementary school.*

Conclusion: *John has finished elementary school.*

The Sufficient Assumption here linking the information from the premises and the conclusion is simply a confirmation of the very first sufficient condition in the premises: *John is in fact in law school.*

Take a look at 36-1-18, 44-2-13, 69-4-21 for additional practice.

Missing Links in Conditional Chains as Sufficient Assumptions

By far the most common feature seen on harder SA Questions is when the author will present an incomplete conditional argument. The premise or premises will contain a conditional relationship, while the conclusion will also be conditional in nature. What is missing is a portion of the conditional chain. What we have to do is come up with an additional conditional relationship that in conjunction with the conditional relationships in the premises, lead to the conclusion.

Completing the argument's conditional logic chain is something many students have trouble with. It helps to practice the skill abstractly first, before moving on to actual test questions.

Take a look at the following exercise, try it out before turning to answers:

Premise: A → B
Conclusion: A → C
Sufficient Assumption: ?

Premise: A → B
Conclusion: C → B
Sufficient Assumption: ?

Premise: A → B
Conclusion: C → A
Sufficient Assumption: ?

Premise: A → B
Conclusion: B → C
Sufficient Assumption: ?

<u>Answer Key:</u>

Premise: A → B
Conclusion: A → C

We first find the element in the conclusion that also appears in the premise (the recurring element). In this case, it's A.

We take the new element that appears in the conclusion as well as the conditional arrow that came with it (→ C), and combine that with the conditional relationship in the premise (A → B).

So we combine A → B and → C, getting A → B → C.

The new linkage that we have made, between B → C, will be the Sufficient Assumption.

Sufficient Assumption: B → C or C̶ → B̶

Premise: A → B
Conclusion: C → B

Here, B is the recurring element, and C is the new element. We combine the new element and the conditional arrow associated with it (C →) with the conditional relationship in which the recurring element occurs (A → B).

So we have to connect C → with A → B. Resulting in C → A → B.

The new linkage we made, C → A, will be the Sufficient Assumption.

Sufficient Assumption: C → A or A̶ → C̶

Premise: A → B
Conclusion: C → A̶

The recurring element here is A, but it is negated in the conclusion (A̶). So we have to contrapositive the conditional relationship in the premise to get it to show A̶. Which then becomes B̶ → A̶.

We take the new element and its associated arrow from the conclusion (C →), and combine that with the conditional we just made the contrapositive for (B̶ → A̶).

So we get C → B̶ → A̶.

The new linkage we made is C → B̶.

Sufficient Assumption: C → B̶ or B → C̶

Premise: A → B
Conclusion: B̶ → C

Find the recurring element: B. Because it's negated in the conclusion we contrapositive the conditional from the premise (A → B), so B̶ appears.

So A → B becomes B̶ → A̶.

Now we take the new element and the arrow from the conclusion (→ C), and combine that with B̶ → A̶. We get B̶ → A̶ → C.

The new linkage we made is A̶ → C.

Sufficient Assumption: A̶ → C or C̶ → A

Even after you have found the Sufficient Assumption, make sure to keep an eye out for its **contrapositive** form in the answer choices. On the LSAT, a conditional relationship and its contrapositive are used interchangeably.

Sometimes the argument will contain two independent conditional chains in its premises, take a look at the following questions and see if you can come up with the correct answer:

Premise: A → B
Premise: C → D
Conclusion: A → D
Sufficient Assumption: ?

Premise: A → B
Premise: C → D
Conclusion: C → B
Sufficient Assumption: ?

Premise: A → B
Premise: C → D
Conclusion: D̶ → A̶
Sufficient Assumption: ?

Premise: A → B
Premise: C → D
Conclusion: B̶ → C̶
Sufficient Assumption: ?

Premise: A → B
Premise: C → D
Conclusion: C → A̶
Sufficient Assumption: ?

Premise: A → B
Premise: C → D
Conclusion: A → C̶
Sufficient Assumption: ?

Premise: A → B
Premise: C → D
Conclusion: D̶ → B
Sufficient Assumption: ?

Premise: A → B
Premise: C → D
Conclusion: B̶ → D
Sufficient Assumption: ?

Answer Key

Premise: A → B
Premise: C → D
Conclusion: A → D

We take the sufficient condition of the conclusion (A), situated it in the conditional containing it from the premises: A → B.

We then take the necessary condition of the conclusion (D), situate it in the conditional relationship from the premises (C → D). We then simply add this behind the first conditional we found from the premises.

A → B + C → D

Now we connect the two, the new linkage we made (B → C) will be the Sufficient Assumption.

Sufficient Assumption: B → C or C̶ → B̶

Premise: A → B
Premise: C → D
Conclusion: C → B

Take the sufficient condition from the conclusion (C), find the conditional relationship from the premise that contains C, so C → D.

Do the same for the conclusion's necessary condition (B), getting A → B. Add that behind C → D.

C → D + A → B

Sufficient Assumption: D → A or A̶ → D̶

Premise: A → B
Premise: C → D
Conclusion: D̶ → A̶

Sufficient condition of conclusion is D̶, it doesn't directly appear in the premises, so we have to contrapositive the premise C → D. We get D̶ → C̶.

Similarly, the necessary condition of the conclusion is A̶. So we have to contrapositive A → B, we get B̶ → A̶. Add this behind D̶ → C̶:

D̶ → C̶ + B̶ → A̶

The new linkage is C̶ → B̶

Sufficient Assumption: C̶ → B̶ or B → C

Alternatively, you can just contrapositive the conclusion D̶ → A̶ into A → D, and solve it accordingly. Either way is fine, just do whatever that you are comfortable with mentally. Let's do the next question this way.

Premise: A → B
Premise: C → D
Conclusion: B̶ → C̶

We notice that the conclusion ~~B~~ → ~~C~~ can be converted into C → B. So let's use that as our conclusion instead.

C → D + A → B

Sufficient Assumption: D → A or ~~A~~ → ~~D~~

Premise: A → B
Premise: C → D
Conclusion: C → ~~A~~

Conclusion's sufficient condition is C, so we take the conditional from the premise that contains C, which is C → D.

Conclusion's necessary condition is ~~A~~, we contrapositive A → B into ~~B~~ → ~~A~~ and tag that behind C → D.

C → D + ~~B~~ → ~~A~~

Sufficient Assumption: D → ~~B~~ or B → ~~D~~

Premise: A → B
Premise: C → D
Conclusion: A → ~~C~~

A → B + ~~D~~ → ~~C~~

Sufficient Assumption: B → ~~D~~ or D → ~~B~~ (this question is the same as the last one, its conclusion A → ~~C~~ is just the contrapositive of C → ~~A~~)

Premise: A → B
Premise: C → D
Conclusion: ~~D~~ → B

~~D~~ → ~~C~~ + A → B

Sufficient Assumption: ~~C~~ → A or ~~A~~ → C

Premise: A → B
Premise: C → D
Conclusion: ~~B~~ → D

~~B~~ → ~~A~~ + C → D

Sufficient Assumption: ~~A~~ → C or ~~C~~ → A

As you probably have figured out by now, half of these questions have the same answers, albeit in contrapositive form. A habit of mine is that whenever I see a conditional relationship on the LSAT, I'm automatically transcribing it in its original form and contrapositive form. I do this without thinking, and it saves a lot of time and energy in both Logic Reasoning and Logic Games.

Let's now put what we have just learned into practice on real SA Questions.

Difficult Trait #4: Master the steps needed to spot and fill in missing conditional linkages.

<u>PT38 S4 Q16</u>

People who do not believe that others distrust them are confident in their own abilities, so people who tend to trust others think of a difficult task as a challenge rather than a threat, since this is precisely how people who are confident in their own abilities regard such tasks.

The conclusion above follows logically if which one of the following is assumed?

    A.   People who believe that others distrust them tend to trust others.
    B.   Confidence in one's own abilities gives one confidence in the trustworthiness of others.
    C.   People who tend to trust others do not believe that others distrust them.
    D.   People who are not threatened by difficult tasks tend to find such tasks challenging.
    E.   People tend to distrust those who they believe lack self-confidence.

Let's divide this stimulus into supporting information and conclusion first. The supporting information are the first and last statements, while the conclusion is the second statement right in the middle. Let's diagram them out:

- Premise: *People who do not believe that others distrust them are confident in their own abilities*
  - Conditional: People who do not believe that others distrust them → Confident in their own abilities

- Premise: *People who are confident in their own abilities regard such tasks* (think of a difficult task as a challenge rather than a threat)
  - Conditional: People who are confident in their own abilities → Think of difficult tasks as a challenge rather than a threat

- Conclusion: *so people who tend to trust others think of a difficult task as a challenge rather than a threat*
  - Conditional: People who tend to trust others → Think of difficult tasks as a challenge rather than a threat

Now as you practice more and more conditional linkages in SA Questions you will be able to directly link the conditionals either on paper or in your mind. But for now, let's convert all the conditions into notation form so we don't get lost along the way.

- People who do not believe that others distrust them: A
- Confident in their own abilities: B
- Think of difficult tasks as a challenge rather than a threat: C
- People who tend to trust others: D

So in notation form, this argument is as follows:

Premise: A → B
Premise: B → C
Conclusion: D → C

We can combine the two premises to yield A → B → C.

We take the new element from the argument's conclusion and the conditional arrow (D →), and graft that on to A → B → C.

So our Sufficient Assumption is D → A, because (D → A) + (A → B) + (B → C) = D → C

D → B can also work as a Sufficient Assumption. In doing so, we are skipping over the first premise, giving us D → B → C. The result is still D → C.

So the correct answer will be either

People who tend to trust others (D) *are people who do not believe that others distrust them* (A).

Or

People who tend to trust others (D) *are confident in their own abilities* (B).

Let's quickly go over the answer choices:

A. *People who believe that others distrust them tend to trust others.*

This answer choice, if notated, is A̶ → D. We are looking for D → A, or D → B.

B. *Confidence in one's own abilities gives one confidence in the trustworthiness of others.*

"Confidence in the trustworthiness of others" I think can be interpreted as "trusting others". So if we really stretched it, we can read this as B → D. **I'm always really weary of subtle shifts in wording on answer choices in SA Questions, so that's already a red flag.** But regardless, it's not the conditional that we are looking for.

C. *People who tend to trust others do not believe that others distrust them.*

This is the correct answer, D → A.

D. *People who are not threatened by difficult tasks tend to find such tasks challenging.*

"People who are not threatened by difficult tasks" is really close to C, but not exactly. C is about "people who think of difficult tasks as a challenge rather than a threat", so this answer is really going in circles around C. We are looking for D → A, or D → B.

E. *People tend to distrust those who they believe lacks self-confidence.*

This answer's wording is similar to D̶ → B̶, some keywords are shared, but they are still talking about completely different things.

D is about "People who tend to trust others", B is about people who are confident. So D̶ → B̶ should read "people who distrust others are not confident."

So when we are reading answer choices, be sure to **refer back** to the exact wording of the conditional terms that we have isolated from the argument. Don't get carried away by answer choice wording that may look similar but are in fact talking about different things!

Difficult Trait #5: Beware subtle shifts in answer choices, make sure the conditional terms in the answers match up with the conditional terms stated in the stimulus, don't forget the contrapositive.

PT46 S2 Q23

Whoever is kind is loved by somebody or other, and whoever loves anyone is happy. It follows that whoever is kind is happy.

The conclusion follows logically if which one of the following is assumed?

A. Whoever loves someone loves everyone.
B. Whoever loves everyone loves someone.
C. Whoever is happy loves everyone.
D. Whoever loves no one is loved by no one.
E. Whoever loves everyone is kind.

Let's break down the conditional relationships, make a distinction between the premises and the conclusion.

- Premise: *Whoever is kind is loved by somebody or other*
     Kind (A) → Loved by somebody or other (B)
- Premise: *Whoever loves anyone is happy*
     Loves anyone (C) → Happy (D)
- Conclusion: *Whoever is kind is happy*
     Kind (A) → Happy (D)

So what we have is essentially this:

- Premise: A → B
- Premise: C → D
- Conclusion: A → D

The Sufficient Assumption that we are looking for here is B → C, or *whoever is loved by somebody or other loves someone.*

Or in contrapositive form (because authors love to throw contrapositives into the mix), *if you don't love anyone, you are not loved by anyone.* (Remember the negated form of "some" is "none". We look at "some, most, all" relationships in the chapter on Must be True Questions.)

Let's look at the answer choices:

   A.   *Whoever loves someone loves everyone.*

This answer choice starts with C, but introduces a new condition (loves everyone). We are looking for B → C. This answer choice is C → Loves Everyone

   B.   *Whoever loves everyone loves someone.*

Same issue here as answer choice A: "loves everyone" is not a part of our argument. This answer choice is Loves Everyone → C.

   C.   *Whoever is happy loves everyone.*

D → Loves Everyone, still not what we are looking for.

   D.   *Whoever loves no one is loved by no one.*

This is the correct answer, C̶ → B̶. Even after you've identified a conditional as the main assumption needed, the correct answer may be its **contrapositive**. Always contrapositive conditional answer choices just in case.

   E.   *Whoever loves everyone is kind.*

Loves everyone → A

Irrelevant Conditional Premises

In some of the hardest conditional linkage SA Questions, the test makers will throw in extra conditionals in the premises as red herrings. Remember we looked at two types of conditional linkage arguments:

Type 1 (Premises contain one conditional relationship)

Premise: A → B
Conclusion: A → C
Sufficient Assumption: B → C

Type 2 (Premises contain multiple conditional relationships)

Premise 1: A → B
Premise 2: C → D
Conclusion: A → D
Sufficient Assumption: B → C

But there is also another correct answer, B → D. If this appears in the answer choices, it would be correct as well, we are essentially skipping over Premise 2 and still the truth of the conclusion is guaranteed. A → C will also work.

Sometimes the conditional relationship in one of the premises is completely irrelevant, as seen below:

Premise 1: A → B
Premise 2: C → D
Conclusion: A → E
Sufficient Assumption: B → E

Here, premise 2 has no purpose other than to throw you off track. That's why we always ask ourselves if the sufficient or necessary conditions in the argument's CONCLUSION recur in the argument's premises first.

Difficult Trait #6: In a stimulus containing multiple conditional premises, you don't need to use all of them to come up with the main assumption, there may be an irrelevant conditional premise.

PT49 S2 Q7

Any fruit that is infected is also rotten. No fruit that was inspected is infected. Therefore, any fruit that was inspected is safe to eat.

The conclusion of the argument follows logically if which one of the following is assumed?

    A. It is not safe to eat any fruit that is rotten.
    B. It is safe to eat any fruit that is not rotten.
    C. It would have been safe to eat infected fruit if it had been inspected.
    D. It is not safe to eat any fruit that is infected.
    E. It is safe to eat any fruit that is uninfected.

- Premise 1: Infected → Rotten
- Premise 2: Inspected → ~~Infected~~
- Conclusion: Inspected → Safe to Eat

In notational form:

- Premise 1: A → B
- Premise 2: C → ~~A~~
- Conclusion: C → D

What is the recurring element here from the conclusion? It's C.

However, C only appears in Premise 2, C → ~~A~~.

Let's take the new element from the conclusion (D) and the arrow together, combine that with C → ~~A~~.

(→ D) + (C → ~~A~~)

What we end up with is C → A → D, the Sufficient Assumption in this case is ~~A~~ → D, or ~~Đ~~ → A.

The answer choice that we are looking for will either be "*All uninfected fruits are safe to eat*" or "*If a fruit is not safe to eat, then it's infected.*"

    A. *It is not safe to eat any fruit that is rotten.*

Remember that "any" introduces the sufficient condition. So Rotten → Not Safe to Eat, or B → ~~Đ~~.

    B. *It is safe to eat any fruit that is not rotten.*

~~B~~ → D here, not what we are looking for.

    C. *It would have been safe to eat infected fruit if it had been inspected.*

This answer choice is a little hard to diagram, but what it's essentially saying is that if a fruit has been inspected, then it's safe to eat, regardless of whether it's infected or not. So what we have is Inspected → Safe to eat, which is a repetition of the conclusion. **Remember, we are looking for an assumption, which has not been explicitly mentioned in the argument, repetitions or restatements of the premise or conclusion will not be correct.**

    D. *It is not safe to eat any fruit that is infected.*

Infected → ~~Safe to Eat~~, so A → ~~Đ~~. This is the reversal of what we want.

    E. *It is safe to eat any fruit that is uninfected.*

Uninfected → Safe to Eat, so ~~A~~ → D. <u>This is the correct answer.</u>

As we can see from this stimulus, the first premise, *any fruit that is infected is also rotten*, or A → B, is completely irrelevant. This has occurred periodically in conditional linkage SA Questions. Take a look at 53-1-20 and 89-4-11 to get a better grasp of the concept.

Difficult Trait #7: In the hardest SA Questions, the correct answer may need to be recombined with easily overlooked information from the stimulus in order to make sense!

For our final tip on tackling more difficult SA Questions, we will look at a feature that has caused trouble for countless students. Throughout the history of the LSAT, there has been a few SA Questions where the correct answer choice doesn't seem to have anything to do with our stimulus at a first glance. However, if we combined that correct answer choice with a pre-existing statement from the stimulus, only then does it match up with what we are looking for.

Let's jump straight into one of the more difficult questions, and we will look at this feature in greater detail during the explanations.

PT21 S2 Q20

Ann will either take a leave of absence from Technocomp and return in a year or else she will quit her job there; but she would not do either one unless she were offered a one-year teaching fellowship at a prestigious university. Technocomp will allow her to take a leave of absence if it does not find out that she has been offered the fellowship, but not otherwise. Therefore, Ann will quit her job at Technocomp only if Technocomp finds out she has been offered the fellowship.

Which one of the following, if assumed, allows the conclusion above to be properly drawn?

    A. Technocomp will find out about Ann being offered the fellowship only if someone informs on her.
    B. The reason Ann wants the fellowship is so she can quit her job at Technocomp.
    C. Technocomp does not allow any of its employees to take a leave of absence in order to work for one of its competitors.
    D. Ann will take a leave of absence if Technocomp allows her to take a leave of absence.
    E. Ann would be offered the fellowship only if she quit her job at Technocomp.

Let's break down the stimulus:

- *Ann will either take a leave of absence from Technocomp and return in a year or else she will quit her job there.*

We have stressed in Chapter 7 to be actively look for statements that have a hidden conditional element to them. This is one of those. The "either…or" relationship here is also conditional in nature. We know that Ann cannot both take a leave of absence and quit, simultaneously. In other words, if she took a leave of absence, she isn't quitting. If she quit, she isn't taking a leave of absence. There is, of course, the possibility that she stays at her job and does neither.

- *But she would not do either one unless she was offered a one year teaching fellowship at a prestigious university.*

So in other words, Leave of Absence → Offered Fellowship, and Quit → Offered Fellowship.

- *Technocomp will allow her to take a leave of absence if it does not find out that she has been offered the fellowship, but not otherwise.*

This creates a two-way relationship: Technocomp Allow Ann to take Leave ←→Does Not Find Out About Fellowship

- *Therefore, Ann will quit her job at Technocomp only if Technocomp finds out she has been offered the fellowship.*

Quit → Technocomp Finds Out

Let's convert everything to notational form for ease of understanding:

- Leave of Absence: A
- Quit: B
- Offered Fellowship: C
- Technocomp Allow Leave of Absence: D
- Technocomp Find Out About Fellowship: E

Note how Ann taking a leave of absence is a different concept from Technocomp allowing her to take a leave of absence; similarly, being offered the fellowship is different from Technocomp finding out about the fellowship. So we use different letters to symbolize these different concepts.

Statement 1, which is a premise, gives us: A → B̶, or B → A̶

Statement 2, also a premise, tells us A → C, and B → C

Statement 3, yet another premise, tells us that D ←→ E̶

Finally, the last statement, our conclusion, tells us that B → E

We must further develop the conditional presented in statement 3, D ←→ E̶

We know that a dual relationship actually consists of two separate relationships, in this case, D → E̶ and E̶ → D.

D → E̶ can be turned into a contrapositive: E → D̶, similarly, E̶ → D can be turned into a contrapositive, D̶ → E.

Our main conclusion, similarly, can be turned into a contrapositive also: ~~E~~ → ~~B~~

We can look for something that would connect B → ~~A~~ and B → E, ~~A~~ → E would work in this case, giving us B → ~~A~~ → E, or B → E.

~~A~~ → E would read as "*if Ann did not take a leave of absence, that means Technocomp found out about the fellowship.*"

This would be our potential SA answer #1.

Similarly, we can come up with a conditional to connect the second statement B → C with B → E, the conclusion, so C → E.

That would read as "*if Ann was offered the fellowship, Technocomp will find out about it.*"

This would be our potential answer #2.

***

However, there is one more possibility, one that isn't easily discovered:

In the dual relationship of statement 3, we know that ~~E~~ → D, or "*if Technocomp does not find out, Technocomp will allow leave of absence.*"

Now let's look at the conclusion's contrapositive form, or ~~E~~ → ~~B~~

Can we throw in a conditional relationship to derive the conclusion? Yes: D → ~~B~~ works. Because if we combine ~~E~~ → D with D → ~~B~~, we get ~~E~~ → ~~B~~.

D → ~~B~~, or "*if Technocomp allows Ann to take a leave of absence, then Ann isn't quitting*" will also work as a SA answer.

***

For this question, we will focus on the <u>correct answer choice, D</u>, in order to drive home the point expressed in Difficult Trait #9.

Answer choice D reads: *Ann will take a leave of absence if Technocomp allows her to take a leave of absence.*

In notational form, that's D → A.

We were anticipating A → E, C → E, or D → ~~B~~ as the correct answer. At a first glance, this doesn't match any of them.

But remember that in our first statement, we know that Ann will either take a leave of absence or quit her job? So if she took a leave of absence, she isn't quitting. (A → ~~B~~)

What happens when we combine answer choice D (D → A) with A → ~~B~~?

We get D → ~~B~~, which was the third possible SA answer.

Here, the correct answer choice might not directly match up with our anticipated answer, but if we take an additional step, and combine the answer with a pre-existing conditional premise in our stimulus argument, we can come to a more straightforward conditional statement that perfectly links one of the premises with the main conclusion, allowing the conclusion to be properly drawn.

Let's take a look at another such question:

PT62 S4 Q18

If there are sentient beings on the planets outside our solar system, we will not be able to determine this anytime in the near future unless some of these beings are at least as intelligent as humans. We will not be able to send spacecrafts to planets outside our solar system anytime in the near future, and any sentient being on another planet capable of communicating with us anytime in the near future would have to be at least as intelligent as we are.

The argument's conclusion can be properly inferred if which one of the following is assumed?

A. There are no sentient beings on planets in our solar system other than those on Earth.
B. Any beings that are at least as intelligent as humans would want to communicate with sentient beings outside their own solar systems.
C. If there is a sentient being on another planet that is as intelligent as humans are, we will not be able to send spacecrafts to the being's planet anytime in the near future.
D. If a sentient being on another planet cannot communicate with us, then the only way to detect its existence is by sending a spacecrafts to its planet.
E. Any sentient beings on planets outside our solar system that are at least as intelligent as humans would be capable of communicating with us.

We start by structurally dissecting the argument, splitting it into supporting information and main conclusion.

The first sentence of the stimulus is the author's conclusion, while the second sentence contains two separate premises.

- Premise 1: *We will not be able to send spacecrafts to planets outside our solar system anytime in the near future.*
- Premise 2: *Any sentient being on another planet capable of communicating with us anytime in the near future would have to be at least as intelligent as we are.*
- Conclusion: *If there are sentient beings on planets outside our solar system, we will not be able to determine this anytime in the near future unless some of these beings are at least as intelligent as humans.*

Let's convert all this to conditional format:

- Premise 1: ~~Send Spacecraft in near future~~
- Premise 2: Alien capable of communicating with us → Alien at least as intelligent as humans
- Conclusion: Determine if there are aliens outside the solar system → Alien at least as intelligent as humans

And if we wanted to further clarify this and convert it to notational form?

- Premise 1: ~~A~~
- Premise 2: B → C
- Conclusion: D → C

What we want as a Sufficient Assumption or Main Assumption would be D → B. *"If we wanted to determine if there are aliens outside the solar system, we need these aliens to be capable of communicating with us."*

Is there another way to express this relationship? If you are not sure, take a look at the following analogy:

If John is planning to attend law school, he cannot go unless he learns conditional logic. He cannot take the GRE because he doesn't know any math, and anyone taking the LSAT would have to have a strong grasp of conditional logic.

What's the Sufficient Assumption here? It's that John needs to take the LSAT. The argument says that he can't take the GRE, so the GRE and the LSAT must be the only two options for someone wanting to attend law school.

So an alternative way to express the Sufficient Assumption is: *"In order to attend law school, one must take either the GRE or the LSAT."*

Or we can rephrase this statement as *"if a law school applicant can't take the GRE, they must take the LSAT."* (~~GRE~~ → LSAT)

We can also contrapositive this statement (~~LSAT~~ → GRE), or *"if a law school applicant can't take the LSAT, they must take the GRE."* These two statements are exactly the same thing.

Now back to the question at hand, along the same line of reasoning, what are the four possible variations of our Main Assumption?

- *In order to determine whether sentient beings exist outside our solar system, sentient beings must be capable of communicating with us.*

- *There are only two ways to determine whether sentient beings exist, either by sending space crafts, or have sentient beings capable of communicating with us.*

- *If sentient beings are not capable of communicating with us, we can only find them by sending space crafts to their planets.*

- *If we can't send space crafts to a sentient being's planet, we can't discover them unless they are capable of communicating with us.*

Now let's look at the answer choices:

A.   *There are no sentient beings on planets in our solar system other than those on Earth.*

Always keep in mind what we are looking for before approaching SA answer choices. We want an answer that says "if we cannot send space crafts, then the only way to discover aliens is for them to be capable of communicating with us."

B.   *Any beings that are at least as intelligent as humans would want to communicate with sentient beings outside their own solar systems.*

I suppose this could be a potential assumption of the author's. Perhaps the author is assuming that some aliens would want to communicate with us, and that's how we'll discover them. But not only is this answer too strong, it's also not the Sufficient Assumption we are looking for. Whether or not aliens want to communicate with us is not important. We just need aliens to be capable of communicating with us. Desire and capability are two separate concepts. (Keyword analysis)

This answer is tricky because on the surface, it seems to go along with the author's reasoning. But remember the requirements for SA answers.

C.   *If there is a sentient being on another planet that is as intelligent as humans are, we will not be able to send spacecraft to the being's planet anytime in the near future.*

This answer if diagrammed, is C → A̶. We are looking for something along the lines of D → A or B.

D.   *If a sentient being on another planet cannot communicate with us, then the only way to detect its existence is by sending a spacecraft to its planet.*

This is a variation of the answer we wanted, it's harder to detect at first because it's in contrapositive form: Cannot communicate → Send spacecraft. It's the same as Cannot send spacecraft → Capable of communicating. This is the correct answer.

Remember to always be aware of a conditional's contrapositive form on the LSAT. Otherwise, you might miss a question even though your train of thought was correct.

If you are having trouble understanding the conditionality of this answer choice, take a look at the following analogy:

If a law school applicant cannot take the LSAT, then the only way to go to law school is by taking the GRE.

What is the conditional logic behind this statement? We are essentially saying that in order to go to law school, you must take either the LSAT or the GRE.

Similarly, in order to detect alien existence, we must either send spacecrafts or have aliens capable of communicating with us.

We know that we cannot send spacecrafts from the stimulus, so the only way to detect alien existence is to have them capable of communicating with us.

> E. *Any sentient beings on planets outside our solar system that are at least as intelligent as humans would be capable of communicating with us.*

This answer is the reversal of the second premise, C → B.

In this question again, the correct answer choice needed to be combined with a piece of pre-existing information from the stimulus first, before it can be used to justify the author's main conclusion.

Tricky Answer Choices and the Plug Back Verification Test

So before we finish this chapter, let's take a look at some key characteristics of SA answer choices, as well as what to avoid. We have already covered some of this information previously in the chapter. We know that correct answer choices can be stronger than our main assumption. As long as the answer choice guarantees the truth of the conclusion, we are ok. Sometimes these correct answer choices are tricky because at a first glance, they appear to have nothing to do with the argument at hand. That's why we always plug the answer we have back into the stimulus.

We take the premises and the answer choice which we have chosen, and see if we can guarantee the outcome of the conclusion based on this information.

By far the most tricky wrong answer choices are answers which restate an existing premise/conclusion, or answer choices that are not strong enough to guarantee the conclusion. We will look at one more question, pay close attention to the answer choices, and try to give a specific reason for eliminating them.

So after you have selected an answer choice:

> 1. Go back to the argument and cover up the conclusion, read only the premises
>
> 2. Combine the premises and the answer choice you just picked, and ask yourself what conclusion would they lead to?
>
> 3. Is this conclusion stronger or equal to the original conclusion given by the author?

***

PT42 S2 Q23

Physics professor: Some scientists claim that superheated plasma in which electrical resistance fails is a factor in causing so-called "ball lightning." If this were so, then such lightning would emit intense light and, since plasma has gas like properties, would rise in the air. However, the instances of ball lightning that I observed were of low intensity and floated horizontally before vanishing. Thus, superheated plasma with failed resistance is never a factor in causing ball lightning.

The physics professor's conclusion follows logically if which one of the following is assumed?

    A. Superheated plasma in which electrical resistance fails does not cause types of lightning other than ball lightning.
    B. The phenomena observed by the physics professor were each observed by at least one other person.
    C. Ball lightning can occur as the result of several different factors.
    D. Superheating of gas like substances causes bright light to be emitted.
    E. All types of ball lightning have the same cause.

Let's break down the argument quickly, isolate the gap in the author's reasoning, and come up with our main assumption for it.

The author concludes, "*superheated plasma with failed electrical resistance is never a factor in causing ball lightning.*" Notice how strongly it is worded. In order to guarantee such a conclusion, as per our SA requirements, the answer choice would have to be strongly worded also. I would automatically be suspicious of answer choices with weaker wording.

How is the rest of the stimulus organized?

The first sentence is an opposing viewpoint that our author denies. Some scientists claim superheated plasma with failed electrical resistance is a cause for ball lightning.

The second and third sentences are the author's support. Notice how while the author's conclusion is about the causes of ball lightning (causal), they advance the argument via conditional means. So always be aware of the different elements of reasoning/logic in an argument.

This is the author's argument:

If superheated plasma causes ball lightning (A), lightning would be intense and rise in the air (B).

I've only seen low intensity and horizontal ball lightning (C), therefore superheated plasma is never a cause (A̶).

In notational form:

A → B
C → A̶

The main assumption would link together C and B̶. C → B̶ would give us "*if the physics professor has never seen ball lightning that is intense and rises in the air, then such ball lightning doesn't exist.*"

Indeed, this is the main gap in the author's reasoning. To challenge this argument, we can argue that just because the physics professor has never observed ball lightning, it doesn't mean such ball lightning doesn't exist. To guarantee the conclusion of the stimulus, we have to hurdle this gap.

   A.   *Superheated plasma in which electrical resistance fails does not cause types of lightning other than ball lightning.*

Whenever I get an answer choice that is nowhere close to our main assumption, I automatically try to connect it to the conclusion of the argument. I ask myself, if answer choice A is true, does it guarantee the conclusion's outcome? Am I missing something?

This answer doesn't do that. Remember we talked about the non-exclusive nature of causal reasoning. Remember how just because A can cause B, A can also cause C, D, E... Similarly, just because A doesn't cause B, it doesn't mean it's not a cause for C.

So if superheated plasma never causes other types of lightning, does it cause ball lightning? We can't be sure.

   B.   *The phenomena observed by the physics professor were each observed by at least one other person.*

If other people have also seen low intensity, horizontal ball lightning, I suppose it would make the professor's view more believable. It could work as a very weak Strengthen answer. But our goal is to ensure the conclusion's outcome. Maybe there are other people who have seen intense and rising ball lightning as well.

> C.   *Ball lightning can occur as the result of several different factors.*

This is attacking the author's reasoning. Maybe he is overlooking the possibility that plasma causes some, but not all ball lightnings?

In Sufficient and Necessary Assumption Questions, any answer choice that is **attacking** or **weakening** the author's conclusion **will be wrong**. Remember, we are looking for an assumption of the author's, the author will not assume something contradictory to their reasoning.

> D.   *Superheating of gas like substances causes bright light to be emitted.*

This is a repetition of the information in the author's premise. Repetitions or restatements of premises/conclusion are always wrong answers in SA Questions.

> E.   *All types of ball lightning have the same cause.*

This answer, at a first glance, looks a little off too. "But we still don't know if the cause is superheated plasma!" We might protest.

But if we plugged this answer choice back into the argument, it actually does work:

We know that if plasma caused ball lightning, such lightning would be bright and rise vertically. But the ball lightning the professor observed was dim and floated horizontally. So the ball lightning observed by the professor was not caused by superheated plasma. Now we also know all ball lightning has the same cause. (Note "cause" is singular, so there can be only one cause.) So if some ball lightning were not caused by plasma, none of them can be caused by plasma.

This answer choice is much stronger in its wording than the main assumption that we previously came up with. Answer choices that are much stronger than our main assumption are perfectly fine, as long as they guarantee the truth of our main assumption and conclusion. It is also more indirect in leading to the argument's conclusion.

<u>E is the correct answer.</u>

Luckily, we have the **Plug Back Verification Test** to help us. So with less obvious answer choices, always test the answer choice by taking it back, read it in conjunction with the premises, and ask yourself if the outcome in the conclusion is guaranteed.

For another question where the correct answer may not match up exactly with our main assumption, but does allow the conclusion to be properly drawn, check out 15-3-18.

11. Necessary Assumption

What is a Necessary Assumption?

We have looked at the nature of assumptions in Chapter 9 and Sufficient Assumptions in Chapter 10. We now turn to another frequently seen question type, the Necessary Assumption. We have talked at length about the differences between Sufficient Assumptions and Necessary Assumptions in Chapter 9, so return to that chapter and refresh your memory if needed. Here's a quick summary just to get us warmed up for a more in-depth look at Necessary Assumption Questions.

Remember, all Assumption Family questions (Flaw, Sufficient Assumption, Necessary Assumption, Principle Strengthen, and most of Strengthen/Weaken Questions) will contain an argument gap. In other words, there will be a jump in the author's reasoning between their premises and the main conclusion.

To discover the gap, we must first isolate the premises from the main conclusion. Doing this will also help us look at the argument's structure (S in the SLAKR method). Once we have the supporting information and the main conclusion figured out, we can compare the two, discover the jump in the author's reasoning, what unsupported leaps they made, and come up with our **Main Assumption** to help connect the two and make the author's argument watertight.

While the Sufficient Assumption is an assumption that would guarantee the author's conclusion, the Necessary Assumption is an entirely different beast. Up to this point, the strategies for both question types are identical, but they begin to differ here.

> The correct Necessary Assumption answer choice **must be true** if your Main Assumption is taken to be true.

This is different from Sufficient Assumptions: with SA Questions, the correct answer choice guarantees the truth of the argument's main assumption.

Let's revisit our example from Chapter 9:

Law school costs 200,000 dollars, John has enough money saved up to pay for his entire law school education.

The Main Assumption here, of course, is that "John has 200,000 dollars saved up." This perfectly hurdles the gap in the example's reasoning and validates the argument.

A correct Necessary Assumption will be true if our main assumption is true. The number of possibilities are endless. We can say that "John has money," or "John has saved money," or "John has more savings than the average American," or "John is not bankrupt", etc. All of these are legitimate Necessary Assumptions. Because they are all by extension true if we accept the truthfulness of our main assumption.

Answer Choice Negation Test

Let's imagine that we are playing a game of Yes or No. For those who don't know, it's where person A has a person/object in mind, person B tries to guess who or what it is by asking a series of questions. Person A can only answer "Yes" or "No." Person B tries to guess who or what it is based on Person A's responses.

If you have trouble understanding the conceptual basis of Necessary Assumptions, I strongly recommend giving this game a shot with a friend and coming back to read the rest of the information.

So let's say we have two people playing this game, John and Amber. John has someone/something in mind, and Amber is guessing.

John: I'm ready.

Amber: Ok, is it a person?

John: Yes.

Amber: Is this person male?

John: Yes.

Amber: Is he alive?

John: No.

Amber: Was he a professional musician?

John: No.

Amber: Was he an actor?

John: No.

Amber: Was he a professional athlete?

John: No.

Amber: Was he a politician?

John: Yes.

Amber: Was he American?

John: Yes.

Amber: Did he die of unnatural causes?

John: Yes.

Amber: Was he shot?

John: Yes.

Amber: Was it JFK?

John: No.

Amber: Was it Lincoln?

John: No.

Amber: Was he a President?

John: No.

Amber: Was it Alexander Hamilton?

John: Yes.

***

So in the scenario above, John had someone in mind, Alexander Hamilton. Every question he answered yes/no to, are linked traits or characteristics associated with Hamilton. These traits or characteristics *are definitely true/must be true* if the person we are talking about is in fact Hamilton. For instance, Hamilton *must* be a person, he *must* be male, he *must* not be alive, He *must* have been shot, he *must* not have been the President of the United States. In other words, they are *necessary* traits or characteristics associated with Alexander Hamilton.

How do we determine the *necessity* of a trait or characteristic? We simply negate the trait in question and ask ourselves if it affects the identity of the person or thing we are talking about? In other words, in the example of Alexander Hamilton, if this person *wasn't male,* or *wasn't shot,* or *was the President of the United States…,* then there is no way that it's Alexander Hamilton we are talking about.

Necessary Assumptions work in the same way. The correct NA answer choice *must be true* given our Main Assumption. Necessary Assumptions are mandatory extensions of the Main Assumption, just as being a politician is a mandatory/must be true characteristic of Alexander Hamilton.

Similarly, this is why with NA Question answer choices, we negate them to see if they hurt the argument's conclusion. Back to the Alexander Hamilton example, if we were not sure whether "not being a professional athlete" is a necessary trait to being Alexander Hamilton, we simply negate it. So let's say that the person we are talking about is in fact a professional athlete, that puts serious doubt on the likelihood that the person we are guessing is Alexander Hamilton.

And that's how we test out the *necessity* of NA answer choices. If it's truly an assumption that is necessary, then it would be integral to the argument. **If by negating the answer choice in question, we cast doubt on the conclusion's outcome, then it's the correct answer.**

So there's two things to think about when we are looking at NA answer choices:

> Given our Main Assumption, which of the following answers are definitely true?
>
> Which answer choice, if negated, would hurt the author's conclusion?

Difficult Trait #1: Many correct NA answers can be derived by coming up with the main assumption connecting the author's supporting premises and the main conclusion.

Let's start with a rather straightforward, albeit still difficult, question. Find the reasoning gap between premises and conclusion and come up with your own Main Assumption.

PT46 S3 Q15

Critic: Works of literature often present protagonists who scorn allegiance to their society and who advocate detachment rather than civic mindedness. However, modern literature is distinguished from the literature of earlier eras in part because it more frequently treats such protagonists sympathetically. Sympathetic treatment of such characters suggests to readers that one should be unconcerned about contributing to societal good. Thus, modern literature can damage individuals who appropriate this attitude, as well as damage society at large.

Which one of the following is an assumption on which the critic's argument relies?

A. Some individuals in earlier eras were more concerned about contributing to societal good than is any modern individual.
B. It is to the advantage of some individuals that they be concerned with contributing to societal good.
C. Some individuals must believe that their society is better than most before they can become concerned with benefitting it.
D. The aesthetic merit of some literary works cannot be judged in complete independence of their moral effects.
E. Modern literature is generally not as conducive to societal good as was the literature of earlier eras.

The first sentence of the stimulus is background information, notice its scope. It's talking about *works of literature*, whereas the author's argument is actually about *modern literature*.

The second and third sentences are the support of the argument:

Modern literature is distinguished from the literature of earlier eras in part because it more frequently treats such protagonists sympathetically.

Sympathetic treatment of such characters suggests to the readers that one should be unconcerned about contributing to societal good.

The conclusion is the final sentence.

Modern literature can damage individuals who appropriate this attitude, as well as damage society at large.

Look at the support and the main conclusion, do you see the gap in the author's reasoning?

The gap is between the second premise and the conclusion, between the ideas that "*one should be unconcerned about contributing to society good*" and "*damage individuals who appropriate this attitude.*"

I don't think there is a reasoning gap between "*unconcerned about contributing to society good*" and "*damage society at large,*" the second part of the author's conclusion. If people don't contribute to society, then society can be damaged. This seems reasonable.

So what kind of Main Assumption can we come up with to hurdle the gap? We can say "a person who is unconcerned about contributing to societal good *can* be damaged by this lack of concern." (Maybe it damages their soul, I don't know.) Note how I used the word "can" in my Main Assumption, mirroring the language of the conclusion. **We don't want something too strong and inadvertently turn it into a Sufficient Assumption.** We want something that perfectly mirrors the author's reasoning and language.

Now we turn to the answer choices, looking for something that must be true if *a person who is unconcerned about contributing to societal good can be damaged by this lack of concern.*

> A. Some individuals in earlier eras were more concerned about contributing to societal good than is *any* modern individual.

Remember what we mentioned previously, be suspicious of weak wording in SA answer choices, but **strong wording** in NA answer choices. Necessary Assumptions by nature cannot be stronger than our Main Assumption, so conservative and moderate language is usually preferred.

What this answer choice is saying is that there were some people in the past (exactly how many we don't know) who were more concerned about society than *any* modern individual. In other words, the person most concerned with society is from the past.

We can't really be sure of that. Our Main Assumption is that "if a person doesn't care about society, that attitude can damage him." We also know that modern literature can have a damaging effect on people. But is every modern individual worse off? Even those who haven't read modern literature?

Our main Assumption does not guarantee the truth of this answer choice. Even if we negate this answer choice and say "no individual in the past is more concerned about society than any modern individual. The most altruistic individual in the past is equally concerned with societal welfare as the most altruistic modern person", our conclusion still stands. Perhaps the most concerned individuals in both past and present only read historical works of literature.

> B. It is to the advantage of some individuals that they be concerned with contributing to societal good.

Given our main assumption, does this have to be true? Let's think of an analogy: if smoking *can* damage a person's health, is it to the advantage of some people that they don't smoke? Yes. The wording of this answer choice is also quite conservative in nature. The conclusion says "lack of concern *can* damage individuals," this answer choice says it's to the advantage of "some individuals". So that matches up quite nicely.

> C. *Some individuals must believe that their society is better than most before they can become concerned with benefitting it.*

This answer choice is talking about a prerequisite for some people before they can benefit their society, the answer we are looking for should be an extension of the view that being unconcerned with the betterment of society can actually damage yourself. This is off topic.

> D. *The <u>aesthetic merit</u> of some literary works cannot be judged in complete independence of their moral effects.*

Remember the K in our SLAKR method. Keywords will make or break an answer choice. We are not talking about the aesthetic merit of literary works here. We are talking about the attitude fostered by modern literature having a behavioral and social impact on readers which can ultimately damage them. Out of scope answer choices are frequently among the attractive wrong answer choices in NA Questions.

> E. *Modern literature is generally not as conducive to societal good as was the literature of earlier eras.*

This answer choice is very tricky. In terms of the general direction of where this answer choice is taking us, it's along the same lines of what the author had in mind. The author will potentially agree with this. But remember, what we are looking for is a *necessary assumption*, which means something that is necessary, mandatory, and HAS to be true.

If lack of concern with social welfare caused by modern literature can damage individuals, does it mean modern literature is generally not as conducive to societal good as historical literature? It's certainly very tempting to think so. But remember, we do not know if there are other factors at play here. We don't know if historical literature has negative effects that weren't mentioned here, or if modern literature has any benefits not mentioned here.

Let's think about an extreme case just to demonstrate my point:

> *Running is distinguished from playing video games because it more frequently leads to knee damage. Knee damage can be bad for your health. So running can damage an individual's health. Running is generally not as conducive to bodily health as playing video games.*

So just because A can have a negative effect that B doesn't have, doesn't mean that A is worse than B overall. We will look at specific types of wrong answers particular to NA Questions at the end of the chapter, overly strong and out of scope answers being two of them.

<u>The correct answer is B.</u>

Positive and Negative Wording in Answer Choices

Remember our hypothetical game of Yes/No about Alexander Hamilton. All the questions to which John answered "yes" or "no" were *necessary* traits associated with Alexander Hamilton. Hamilton was definitely male, he was definitely shot, he was definitely not a professional athlete…

If we separate all these answers by "yes" and "no", then we get a list like this:

Alexander Hamilton:

Positive	Negative
Is a person	Isn't a professional musician
Was shot	Isn't alive
Was killed by unnatural causes	Wasn't the President
Was a politician	Wasn't JFK
Was American	Wasn't Lincoln

So essentially, we can divide Alexander Hamilton's necessary traits and characteristics into what he *was*, and what he *wasn't.* I call these positively and negatively worded answers. They are basically two sides of the same coin, and the way we determine if these traits are actually necessary to Alexander Hamilton's identity is the same. We negate these traits and see if the person we are talking about can still possibly be Alexander Hamilton.

So "being shot" is definitely one of Hamilton's necessary traits, because if this person wasn't shot, then it can't possibly be Hamilton that we are talking about. Similarly, "not being a professional athlete or musician" is also another necessary trait, because if the person we are talking about is a professional athlete/musician, then the person in question cannot be Hamilton.

Notice how we have categorized Hamilton's traits into positive ones, which are what Hamilton *must be,* and negative ones, which are what Hamilton *must not be.*

Take a look at the following example:

John wants to go to law school, so he has to take the GRE or the LSAT.

Main Assumption: if you want to go to law school, you need to take the GRE or the LSAT.

Positively worded necessary assumption: you need to take a standardized test to go to law school. (What must be the case)

Negatively worded necessary assumption: you cannot take the GMAT or MCAT to gain admissions to law school. (What cannot be case)

A lot of test prep materials divide answer choices into "bridges" or "defenders", respectively. But I believe this is a more intuitive way of looking at the wording of answer choices. Our Main Assumption will have multiple necessary traits associated with it, some of them positive, some of them negative. The only material difference between them is how they are worded, and how we approach these answers is the same.

For every positively worded trait, there is a matching negatively worded trait. For instance, a positively worded trait of Hamilton would be "Hamilton is dead." You can express the exact same idea in a negatively worded way, simply by saying "Hamilton is not alive." **So just be aware that answer choices can come worded in two ways.**

***

We now turn to one of the hardest NA Questions ever to reinforce the understanding that we have acquired so far. Remember the SLAKR method, think about the structure, logic, assumptions, and keywords in answer choices as you tackle this question. If the argument is too hard to understand, try to make additions to the argument to help it make more sense.

Again, for this question, really focus on what the main conclusion is, and the gap between that and its support. Isolate that gap, come up with a main assumption, and derive your answer choice from it.

PT88 S2 Q21

A study of 30 years of weather pattern records of several industrialized urban areas found that weekend days tend to be cloudier than weekdays. Thus it can no longer be denied that human activity has appreciable, large-scale effects on weather, because the few seven day cycles that occur naturally are of too little significance to cause measurable weather patterns.

Which one of the following is an assumption on which the argument depends?

A. Industrial activity tends to decrease significantly on weekend days in the large urban areas studied.
B. There are no naturally occurring seven day cycles in the areas studied.
C. If living organisms have an appreciable large-scale effect on weather patterns, then this is due at least partly to the effects of human activity.
D. If something appreciably affects large-scale weather patterns, it is probably cyclical in nature.
E. If a weather pattern with a natural cause has a seven-day cycle, then that cause has a seven-day cycle.

Remember to use the SLAKR method whenever you are at a loss of what to do. Systematically going down the list checking the structure, logic, assumptions and keywords of an LR question will usually give us some insights into it.

Structure: The first sentence describes a phenomenon, weekends (Saturday to Sunday) tend to be cloudier than weekdays (Monday to Friday). As I was reading this, I knew this was background information for sure, I just wasn't sure whether this was going to be a "author provides a cause for a natural phenomenon" type of stimulus, or a correlation - causation type of stimulus. (I thought there could potentially be a correlation between working days and cloudy weather, maybe that's what the author's trying to get at.)

Either way, it just goes on to show that **advanced test takers** aren't simply reading the stimulus to understand it, they are simultaneously processing the information they read and thinking about its **implications** and **formulating potential strategies** to attack the question.

The second sentence is both the main conclusion and the premise rolled into one:

Main Conclusion: human activity has appreciable, large-scale effects on the weather.

Premise: Because the few seven-day cycles that occur naturally are of too little significance to cause measurable weather patterns.

The author's argument is fairly simple to understand once you have extracted the premise and the conclusion: because cloudier weekends can't have natural causes, they must have human causes.

Logic: Ok, so this isn't a correlation - causation type of argument. Rather, it's what we suspected in the beginning: the author presents a phenomenon, eliminates a potential cause, and decides on an alternative cause. The logic is definitely causal.

Assumptions: Are there any gaps in the author's reasoning? If a phenomenon doesn't have a natural cause, must it have a human cause? Furthermore, if the cause is not a seven-day natural cycle, can the cause still be natural? Why can't we have a natural eight-day cycle or a fourteen-day cycle as its cause?

The author is basically assuming that if the cause is not a naturally occurring seven-day cycle, then it must be man made. This is our Main Assumption.

Are there peripheral gaps in the author's reasoning elsewhere? Yes there are, but we will look at that when we get to the correct answer choice.

Again, remember our Main Assumption: if cloudier weekends aren't caused by a natural seven-day cycle, that cause is human.

A.   *Industrial activity tends to decrease <u>significantly</u> on weekend days in the large urban areas studied*

This can be tempting on a first pass, but we must not forget that it's the weekends that are cloudier, and not the weekdays. The author believes cloudier weekends are caused by human activity in industrialized urban areas. So maybe that's because of heavier industrialized activity during the week? This doesn't really make sense because why would the weather be more cloudy when the factories aren't running? Shouldn't it be the other way around?

The second issue with this answer choice can be derived when we think about certain keywords within it. The word "significantly" is one which I do not particularly like. Is it mandatory for the author to assume a *significant* decrease in industrial output on weekdays in order for their conclusion to stand? Not necessarily. **Remember the K in SLAKR, keywords will make or break an answer choice.**

B. There are no naturally occurring seven day cycles in the areas studied

The author doesn't assume it's because there are no naturally occurring cycles in the area, the cause must be man made. The author explicitly states that the few seven-day cycles in the area are of too little significance to be the cause, so the cause must be man made. This answer choice directly contradicts the stated information in the argument, and that makes it obviously wrong.

C. If living organisms have an appreciable large-scale effect on weather patterns, then this is due at least partly to the effects of human activity

This answer shows why keeping a clear grasp of our Main Assumption *before* we even look at the answer choices is so important. Our Main Assumption is that "*if it's not due to 7-day natural causes, it's due to humans.*" This answer choice is saying "*if living things can affect weather, humans must be part of the cause.*" The conclusion matches, but the premise doesn't.

D. If something appreciably affects large scale weather patterns, it is probably cyclical in nature

This is the opposite to what the author is arguing, the author argues that natural seven days cycles are not the reason (cyclical in nature). The author believes the cause is ultimately human activity, and we do not know if that's cyclical in nature.

E. If a weather pattern with a natural cause has a seven-day cycle, then that cause has a seven day cycle

This is the correct answer, to truly understand what it's saying, we turn to the A and K of the SLAKR method. Remember in Chapter 9 we looked at a few extra hard questions and practiced the art of filling the stimulus with our own understanding to make the argument clearer? We can also do that here.

How many days are in a week? Seven. So in seven days, days 1 - 5 are sunny, while days 6 - 7 are cloudy. The whole thing repeats again on day 8. So in other words, the phenomenon of cloudier weather on weekends is also cyclical in nature, every seven days it repeats itself.

Let's add that extra bit of information into our reworked stimulus.

A study of 30 years of weather pattern records of several industrialized urban areas found that weekend days tend to be cloudier than weekdays. So in every seven-day cycle, the first five days are less cloudier than the last two days. Thus it can no longer be denied that human activity has appreciable, large-scale effects on weather, because the few seven day cycles that occur naturally are of too little significance to cause measurable weather patterns.

Now we can look at the answer choice.

If weekends being cloudier (weather pattern that has a seven-day cycle) has a natural cause, then that cause (naturally occurring causes) has a seven-day cycle. (Matching up the keywords from answer choices with information from the stimulus)

In conditional form:

Weekends being cloudier has natural cause → Natural cause has seven-day cycle

What is our author's argument? they basically argue that because the phenomenon of cloudy weekends cannot be caused by seven-day natural cycles, it must have a man made cause.

In other words, the author's reasoning is based on the contrapositive of this answer choice. Cause does not have a seven-day cycle → Cause is not natural → Cause must be man made.

Remember our Main Assumption: *if cloudier weekends aren't caused by a natural seven-day cycle, that cause is human.*

Must this answer be true given our Main Assumption? Yes, this answer choice essentially eliminates all the other non seven-day cycles as potential causes. Ten-day cycles, eight-day cycles are all eliminated even if they are naturally occurring. If you are still confused, take a look at the following analogy:

Our Main Assumption: *if it isn't caused by a natural seven day cycle, then the cause is human.*

Analogy: *if John cannot fly business, he must travel by car*

Answer Choice E: *if it has a natural cause, that cause must be seven days (can't be eight days or ten days...)*

Analogy for Answer Choice E: *if John is flying, he must fly business (can't fly economy)*

As we can see, having a strong grasp of the structure and logic of the argument as we read it can help immensely with coming up with a Main Assumption. Using assumptions to fill in gaps, major and minor, in the author's argument will make the process a lot less painful. Finally, focus on the keywords in answer choices and try to match them up with the information contained in the stimulus to eliminate wrong answer choices.

The correct answer, E, is also a positive trait of our Main Assumption. Natural causes must only be seven days in nature. Because the author thinks that if it isn't, then it's due to human activity.

If we tried negating answer choice E, we would see why it is the correct choice. If a naturally occurring weather cycle doesn't need to have a seven-day cause, then the cause can be, let's say, ten days. So you can potentially argue that even though the cause is not a seven-day cycle, it's not man made either. It can just be due to a ten-day cyclical cause.

> The hardest arguments will require us to think about the **structure**, **logic**, **assumptions** as well as **keywords**, four of the core habits that we have already emphasized.

***

PT28 S3 Q16

Historian: we can learn about the medical history of individuals through chemical analysis of their hair. It is likely, for example, that Isaac Newton's psychological problems were due to mercury poisoning. Traces of mercury were found in his hair. Analysis is now being done on a lock of Beethoven's hair. Although no convincing argument has shown that Beethoven ever had a venereal disease, some people hypothesize that venereal disease caused his deafness. Since mercury was commonly ingested in Beethoven's time to treat venereal disease, if researchers find a trace of mercury in his hair, we can conclude that this hypothesis is correct.

Which one of the following is an assumption on which the historian's argument depends?

A. None of the mercury introduced into the body can be eliminated.
B. Some people in Beethoven's time did not ingest mercury.
C. Mercury is an effective treatment for venereal disease.
D. Mercury poisoning can cause deafness in people with venereal disease.
E. Beethoven suffered from psychological problems of the same severity as Newton's.

Quite often the author will load up a stimulus with extra information that we don't really need in order to come to the right answer. But as we are reading the stimulus, there's no way to know what's relevant and what isn't until you have finished reading it all. That's why it's so important to have a strong grasp of the argument's **structure**.

> Whenever I'm reading a longer or more convoluted stimulus, or if I'm pressed for time, I will make sure I've found the main conclusion after reading the argument, and then retrace the argument to confirm which statements are premises.

The conclusion of the argument is at the very end of the stimulus: "*if researchers find a trace of mercury in his hair, we can conclude that this hypothesis is correct.*"

What is the hypothesis? Namely that venereal disease caused Beethoven's deafness. We currently don't have evidence that Beethoven ever had VD, so the hypothesis is just something researchers put out there as an idea. Remember a hypothesis doesn't require supporting evidence (Chapter 2). Some people are saying, "well, maybe Beethoven had a VD/STD." (For the rest of the explanations, we will use the terms "venereal disease" and "sexually transmitted disease" interchangeably.)

So in other words, the conclusion says, if we find mercury in Beethoven's hair, Beethoven had venereal disease and it caused his deafness.

Once I have the conclusion down, I ask myself "**why**?" I do this in order to find the most direct support the author provides for the conclusion. This helps me isolate the supporting premises and the main conclusion quickly, **so I can focus on the main gap in the author's reasoning.**

So why does the author think if we find mercury in Beethoven's hair, he had an STD?

Is it because we found mercury in Isaac Newton's hair? No. The author isn't arguing from an analogy here. It's not as if the author is saying "Isaac Newton had an STD and mercury in his hair, so if Beethoven had mercury in his hair he also had an STD."

So why would the presence of mercury indicate Beethoven had an STD?

It's because mercury was commonly taken to treat STDs during his time.

So if we simplify the whole argument, it really boils down to this:

- Premise: *mercury was taken to treat venereal disease*
- Conclusion: *if we find mercury in Beethoven's hair, Beethoven had venereal disease*

Now we try to find the gap between the premise and the conclusion and come up with our Main Assumption. Here is where thinking about the **logic** behind the author's reasoning can help. Does the author employ conditional logic or causal logic in this argument?

There is an element of causality involved. The author believes that STDs caused one to ingest mercury.

The conclusion is in conditional format: Mercury → STD, or in other words, if Beethoven took mercury, it's because he had an STD.

If we contrapositive that, we get ~~STD~~ → ~~mercury~~. In other words, if Beethoven didn't have a STD, we wouldn't find mercury in his hair. So people who didn't have STDs did not ingest mercury.

Now the gap between the premise and the conclusion is somewhat more obvious:

The premise says that mercury was commonly ingested to treat STDs, the conclusion is basically saying if you ingested mercury, it's definitely for the treatment of STDs.

Let's throw in an analogy to help us understand this better:

> *Tylenol is commonly taken to treat headaches. So if we find acetaminophen (the medical ingredient of Tylenol) in your blood, you must have had a headache.*

What is the gap in this analogy? We are assuming that the only use for Tylenol is for the treatment of headaches. Maybe you took Tylenol for muscle cramps or the flu?

Similarly, here the author is assuming that the only reason people ingested mercury was to treat STDs. We can use this as our Main Assumption.

We can also look at this argument using causal logic to guide our framework. Let's go back to our analogy: having a headache (cause) leads you to take Tylenol (effect), but how can you be sure that if someone has taken Tylenol, it's because they had a headache? That can only work when you are assuming there are no other reasons to take Tylenol. Similarly, in the author's argument, the author is assuming that there are no other reasons to ingest mercury besides the treatment of STDs. The author is assuming that there is only one reason to ingest mercury.

| If you are stuck thinking about the author's argument, try to analyze it from both a conditional and causal perspective. |

So our Main Assumption can be presented in a multitude of ways. We can present it as a positive trait:

People ingested mercury only to treat venereal disease; or as a negative trait: *People did not ingest mercury to treat other diseases.*

>   A. <u>*None*</u> *of the mercury introduced into the body can be eliminated.*

Absolute words like "all", "every" and "none" are really strong, and I will be extremely suspicious of them in NA answer choices. I suppose the author does assume that "some mercury will still be detectable after hundreds of years", but the language of this answer choice is just way too strong. Suppose we negate this answer choice into "some mercury can be eliminated after one thousand years". In that case, it is still feasible to discover mercury in Beethoven's hair, because he has only been dead for a few centuries. But even so, with our improved and more moderate alternative, it would only be a potential assumption and not a necessary assumption. Here is why:

The author's conclusion is conditional in nature: "if researchers find a trace of mercury…" Which means the author is not committed to the outcome that we will definitely find mercury. The author is only saying that in the event we do find mercury, then he had a STD. It's also possible that we don't find mercury, then it's a whole different story.

Take a look at the following analogy if you are somewhat confused:

John: if you get into law school, you will have to work super hard.

Is John assuming that you will definitely get into law school? No. Similar to the author's conclusion in this question, John's statement is conditional. You may or may not get in, but if you do get in, you will need to work hard.

B.   *Some people in Beethoven's time did not ingest mercury.*

Remember our Main Assumption, *if you ingested mercury, it was to treat STDs.* So if you didn't have a STD, then you did not ingest mercury. We know that there are some people who didn't have STDs, so by extension, some people didn't ingest mercury. This answer must be true given our Main Assumption, as a result, it is the correct answer.

In harder questions, the test makers will frequently dress up the correct answer in vague, unclear, or complicated language. This is a prime example. So always try to think of the implications of each answer choice, and if you must guess between an answer that seems to have something wrong with it and an unclear answer, go with the unclear answer. (Like we talked about before)

Alternatively, if we negate this answer, it becomes "everyone in Beethoven's time ingested mercury." (When we negate "some", it becomes "none", we will cover "some, most, all" relationships in greater detail in the Must be True Chapter.)

If everybody ingested mercury, then you can't conclude that because Beethoven ingested mercury, he had a STD. Because that would imply everybody had STDs.

C.   *Mercury is an <u>effective</u> treatment for venereal disease.*

Whether or not mercury is effective or not is irrelevant. It is out of scope.

D.   *Mercury poisoning can cause deafness in people with venereal disease.*

This answer choice is very tricky. It takes the concepts discussed in the stimulus and mixes them up. If you were pressed for time or didn't have a clear grasp of the main gap/Main assumption we have to be focused on, then you could easily be led astray by this answer.

Back in the stimulus, we know that:

<u>Mercury poisoning</u> likely caused Isaac Newton's psychological problems.

It's possible that venereal disease caused Beethoven's <u>deafness</u>.

Venereal disease caused some people to take mercury.

Mercury poisoning doesn't cause deafness! The author believes venereal disease causes deafness, and mercury poisoning doesn't cause venereal diseases.

E.   *Beethoven suffered from psychological problems of the same <u>severity</u> as Newton's.*

We don't know if Beethoven had psychological problems. The author thinks if we find mercury in Beethoven's hair, then he had a STD. Isaac Newton had psychological problems, and the author thinks it's due to mercury poisoning.

All in all, that was a brutal question, and the takeaway is to explore the argument's structure and logical reasoning fully before turning to the answer choices. If you have a clear idea of the reasoning gap and Main Assumption required to hurdle that gap, then we can be much more discerning when tackling the answer choices, which can be narrowed down via keyword elimination. <u>B is the correct answer.</u>

Conditional Answer Choices (What happens when you negate a conditional?)

We have seen examples of the correct NA answer worded as both positively worded and negatively worded, now we turn to another common type of correct answer choices, conditional connectors.

Conditional answer choices that contain a conditional relationship frequently appear in correct answer choices. By my count, on the 100 most difficult NA Questions, just under twenty had conditional relationships as the correct answer choice.

Conditional answers are tricky for two reasons. First, we can't effectively use the answer choice negation test on a lot of them. Remember we said earlier in the chapter that a way to test whether an answer choice is truly necessary is by negating it. If the negated answer choice hurts the author's conclusion, then it's the correct answer choice.

Negating a conditional statement brings up additional complications, take a look at the following example and try to negate it.

All lawyers are rich. (Lawyer → Rich)

What is the negated form of this conditional? Is it "all lawyers are not rich?" No, we know that there are some extremely wealthy lawyers out there. The correct negation is "not all lawyers are rich." Some are rich, and some are not rich. **So negating a conditional DOES NOT yield a new conditional relationship.**

Let's try another example, one that hits a little closer to home:

John: all law students must take the LSAT. (Law Student → LSAT)
David: that is not true, some of them also take the GRE.

If we negate Law Student → LSAT, can we come up with a new conditional relationship? Can we say "law students never take the LSAT?" No. In negating a conditional relationship, all we are doing is voiding the pre-existing relationship, but no new relationship is created. Maybe some law students will still take the LSAT, or maybe not. Some will take the GRE, some will not. Even after we negate Law Student → LSAT, you can still have law students who have taken the LSAT.

All we have done is break the linkage between the two, that's it.

A lot of students mistakenly believe that if we negate A → B, we get A → B̶. That is not true. Even after negating a conditional, the sufficient condition and the necessary condition can still coexist. You can have both A and B, A without B, B without A, or neither A nor B. Essentially what we have done by negating A → B is saying that "A does not guarantee B, anything can happen now."

So if an answer choice is in conditional form, and we tried to negate it, it would often just leave us even more confused about the author's argument.

Let's run one more example just to reinforce our understanding of what happens when you negate a conditional:

John: All swans are white, if you are a swan, you must be white.
David: No, that's completely false. There are black swans.

If David were to negate John's conditional, what do we come up with?

Let's say there is a swan named Larry, is Larry white or black?

The answer is simply "we don't know." Larry can be white or black or any other color. He can be white, but he doesn't have to be. **A negated conditional doesn't yield any useful inferences.**

So the Answer Choice Negation Test doesn't really work well with a lot of conditional answer choices.

***

The second issue with conditional answers is that often even the correct answer will look too strong. When I was practicing NA Questions, I knew strongly worded answer choices were suspect, and as a result I often eliminated correct conditional answers for being too strong.

When I began to review the questions I had gotten wrong, I manually typed them all up and began to review them side by side to see if there is a pattern to my shortcomings. (Great habit by the way, it uncovers a lot of hidden weaknesses that you simply can't isolate by normal PTing.) I realized that a lot of NA Questions where the correct answer choices were conditional in nature are in fact worded very strongly. Upon further examination, I realized that these answer choices all shared a common characteristic. They are simply our Main Assumption worded as a conditional relationship.

Remember in Chapter 9 we talked about Main Assumptions as a piece of information that we can add to the argument to link the information presented in the premise with the information presented in the conclusion. It's something we can come up with before we even look at the answer choices to perfectly hurdle the author's reasoning gap. The Main Assumption is also where Sufficient Assumptions and Necessary Assumptions overlap. So in terms of language, Main Assumption ≥ Necessary Assumption.

In other words, the Main Assumption is the weakest SA answer choice we can have, but the STRONGEST NA answer choice we can have. That's the reason why they often appear to be too strong but are still correct NA answers!

Conditional answer choices that are simply linking the author's premises and conclusion are identical to our Main Assumptions, so they are correct in both SA and NA Questions.

Difficult Trait #2: Keep an eye out for conditional relationships in answer choices, does the conditional chain connect our premise and conclusion?

<u>PT38 S4 Q20</u>

Shy adolescents often devote themselves totally to a hobby to help distract them from the loneliness brought on by their shyness. Sometimes they are able to become friends with others who share their hobby. But if they lose interest in that hobby, their loneliness may be exacerbated. So developing an all-consuming hobby is not a successful strategy for overcoming adolescent loneliness.

Which one of the following assumptions does the argument depend on?

- A. Eventually, shy adolescents are going to want a wider circle of friends than is provided by their hobby.
- B. No successful strategy for overcoming adolescent loneliness ever intensifies that loneliness.
- C. Shy adolescents will lose interest in their hobbies if they do not make friends through their engagement in those hobbies.
- D. Some other strategy for overcoming adolescent loneliness is generally more successful than is developing an all consuming hobby.
- E. Shy adolescents devote themselves to hobbies mainly because they want to make friends.

We start, as always, by trying to come up with a Main Assumption to hurdle the gap between the argument's supporting information and main conclusion. In order to do that, we need to identify both of these elements via structural analysis.

The conclusion of this argument is not hard to find, it's the final sentence of the stimulus: *"So developing an all-consuming hobby is not a successful strategy for overcoming adolescent loneliness."*

To find the most relevant premises for this conclusion, we ask ourselves why. So why isn't developing an all-consuming hobby not a successful strategy for overcoming adolescent loneliness?

The only premise and the reason to the question "Why" is the second to last sentence of the stimulus: *"But if they lose interest in that hobby, their loneliness may be exacerbated."*

The gap that we need to address ALWAYS lies in between the premises and the conclusion. As a result, our Main Assumption will need to link the two pieces of information and create a watertight argument.

What we have to do, essentially, is create a relationship that connects "loneliness may be exacerbated" and "not a successful strategy." We can do that by creating a sentence that contains a conditional relationship: Loneliness may be exacerbated → Not a successful strategy. For example:

A strategy that attempts to address shy adolescent loneliness but has the potential to worsen that loneliness is not a successful strategy.

If losing interest in a hobby will exacerbate an adolescent's loneliness, then devoting oneself totally to a hobby is not a successful strategy for overcoming loneliness.

These are just two possible ways to present the Main Assumption that I have come up with, the correct answer choice must be true according to our Main Assumption.

> A. *Eventually, shy adolescents are going to want a wider circle of friends than is provided by their hobby.*

Answers like these are what trips up a lot of students. This answer choice is along the line of reasoning of the argument in the stimulus, and after reading the argument, this will seem to make sense. It offers a possible explanation of why getting a hobby may eventually exacerbate loneliness. But this is not an Explain a Result/Paradox Question, it's a Necessary Assumption Question. The answer choice must be an extension of our Main Assumption.

> B. *No successful strategy for overcoming adolescent loneliness ever intensifies that loneliness.*

This answer choice is conditional: Intensify Loneliness → Not a Successful Strategy. This is identical to the Main Assumption we envisioned prior. As it is our Main Assumption, it would be a correct answer for both Sufficient Assumption and Necessary Assumption Questions. <u>This is the correct answer.</u>

Recognizing conditionality in answer choices is crucial here. Because conditional relationships will contain strong words such as "must", "required", "only" ... they will appear too strong and susceptible at a first glance. **But that's not grounds for eliminating them**. If an answer choice is conditional but also identical to our Main Assumption, it would be correct.

> C. *Shy adolescents will lose interest in their hobbies if they do not make friends through their engagement in those hobbies.*

This is also a conditional relationship, but it doesn't address the gap between the premise and the conclusion.

- Premise: *if adolescents lose interest in their hobbies (A), it may exacerbate their loneliness (B)*

- Conclusion: *hobbies are not a successful strategy for overcoming loneliness (C)*

What we need is B → C, or something connecting A → B and C. (This is our Main Assumption)

What this answer gives us is D → A, *if they do not make friends (D), shy adolescents will lose interest in their hobbies (A).*

It has nothing to do with our conclusion.

> D. *Some other strategy for overcoming adolescent loneliness is generally more successful than is developing an all consuming hobby.*

This answer is also like answer choice A, it's certainly a possibility. It presents an idea that is closely related to what was said in the author's argument. If hobbies are not a successful strategy, maybe there is a better one? But the author doesn't have to assume this. Perhaps there are no successful strategies for overcoming loneliness, period. Beware could be true or even most likely true answers that are **not necessary** to the author's reasoning.

> E. *Shy adolescents devote themselves to hobbies <u>mainly</u> because they want to make friends.*

We know from the stimulus that shy adolescents <u>often</u> devote themselves to hobbies to distract themselves from loneliness, and <u>sometimes</u> they make friends from that hobby. Making friends is more like a side effect here, it's not the main reason why shy adolescents devote themselves to hobbies. This contradicts the information presented in the stimulus.

***

There are a few takeaways that I want to re-emphasize:

> 1. Don't get too fixated on trying to negate potential answer choices as a test in conditional answer choices on NA Questions.
>
> 2. Strongly worded answer choices are usually wrong, but less so if the answer choice is conditional. Out of scope answers are most likely wrong.
>
> 3. Conditionals are by nature strong (they contain words such as "only," "must," "required"). Focus instead on whether the conditional answer can link the premise with the main conclusion instead. (AKA the Main Assumption)

Take a look at 9-2-25, 28-3-22, 34-3-17, 51-3-18, 52-3-7, 57-2-24, 63-3-11, 67-4-18, 67-2-14, 72-2-12, 76-2-24, and 85-3-19 to familiarize yourself with conditional answer choices in NA Questions.

Good Habits to Have and Things to Pay Special Attention to in Harder NA Questions

So far we have looked at the steps to tackle NA Questions and different answer choices, now we will use some tricky questions to reinforce the good habits we have emphasized. On the actual exam, because we will be so pressed for time, there won't be enough time to actively think about each of the steps needed to solve a question individually, which step you are on right now, and what is the next step every time you see a new LR question.

That is why it's so important to internalize the proper sequence of steps when we are practicing. When we are faced with a harder question in practice, it's okay to slow down, mentally remind yourself of the steps we need to take, and to conduct SLAKR analysis.

With repeated practice, the step-by-step process of attacking a certain question type will feel like second nature to you. It will become habitual. That way, we can divert more and more of our attention to dealing with the hidden nuances and traps present in the hardest questions.

Difficult Trait #3: Pay special attention to the wording and scope of the conclusion.

Having a clear understanding of the main conclusion and its scope, as well as not forgetting it as we read through the answer choices is the first habit we need to emphasize. It's so easy to read through the stimulus, not having a clear idea of what we are looking for, and then getting misled by a tempting wrong answer choice. If you are constantly selecting out of scope answer choices, it might help to read the conclusion twice before looking at the answer choices.

This was also a trait that we have covered in Method Questions previously.

Take a look at the following question:

PT46 S3 Q17

Traditionally, students at Kelly University have evaluated professors on the last day of class. But some professors at Kelly either do not distribute the paper evaluation forms or do so selectively, and many students cannot attend the last day of class. Soon, students will be able to use school computers to evaluate their professors at any time during the semester. Therefore, evaluations under the new system will accurately reflect the distribution of student opinion about teaching performance.

Which one of the following is an assumption required by the argument?

- A. Professors who distribute the paper evaluation forms selectively distribute them only to students they personally like.
- B. Students can wisely and insightfully assess a professor's performance before the end of the semester.
- C. The traditional system for evaluating teaching performance should not be used at any university.
- D. Nearly all professors who fail to distribute the paper evaluation forms do so because they believe the students will evaluate them unfavorably.
- E. Dissatisfied students are in general not more likely than satisfied students to submit a computerized evaluation.

Let's quickly go over the information presented in the stimulus:

The author advances the argument here via comparable reasoning. Paper evaluation forms are problematic because they are not representative. (Some students don't get an opportunity to fill them out.) The school is switching to a computer-based evaluation system. As a result, the new system will accurately reflect the distribution of student opinion.

The author is assuming that the computer-based evaluation system will not run into/can overcome the issues faced by the paper evaluation system. Some students didn't fill out the evaluation forms on paper because they didn't come to the last day of class. What if you need a specific login to do the computer evaluations and the professor only gives it out on the last day of class? Such possibilities must be eliminated in order for the argument to stand. What if the computer lab is located in an off-campus location and some busy but well performing students can't be bothered to submit an evaluation? Then the evaluation will not be representative either. I know these potential objections sound a little far fetched, but they are all legit possibilities that must be eliminated in order for the conclusion to stand.

So our Main Assumption, connecting our premises and conclusion, should look like this: *computer evaluations do not face the same issues as paper evaluations, so they will accurately reflect the distribution of student opinion.*

Before we look at the answer choices, **remember to really think about the conclusion here**. What is the author's conclusion about? To what position are they committed?

The author thinks that the new system will *accurately reflect the distribution of student opinion.* That means if there were a hundred students in the class, and 50 students liked the class but the others didn't, that will be reflected in the evaluations. Even if only ten evaluations were submitted, as long as there are five positive ones and five negative ones, it's still an accurate reflection of student opinion.

Secondly, all we need is that the surveys reflect *student opinion*, does it matter if student opinion is biased or opinionated? Not really. If the class was super early in the morning but the professor was awesome, but all the students gave negative evaluations, is that still an accurate reflection of student opinion? Yes.

I wanted to focus on answer choices B and E:

> B. *Students can wisely and insightfully assess a professor's performance before the end of the semester.*

Those who selected this answer forgot to really think about the **scope** of the author's conclusion. As we just mentioned, the author is committed to the position that the evaluations will accurately reflect student opinion. Whether or not they are an accurate reflection of the professor's performance is irrelevant.

> E. *Dissatisfied students are in general not more likely than satisfied students to submit a computerized evaluation.*

This is the correct answer choice, it's a negatively worded statement that must be true if the author's argument were to stand. If dissatisfied students were 10x more likely to submit an evaluation, would the results accurately reflect student opinion? No. If there were 100 students, 50 satisfied and 50 dissatisfied. All 50 dissatisfied students leave bad reviews and only 5 satisfied students left good reviews, the evaluation results would appear as 91% negative.

Let's look at one more question where we must pay special attention to the conclusion:

PT61 S2 Q16

Engineer: Thermophotovoltaic generators are devices that convert heat into electricity. The process of manufacturing steel produces huge amounts of heat that currently go to waste. So if steel manufacturing plants could feed the heat they produce into thermophotovoltaic generators, they would greatly reduce their electric bills, thereby saving money.

Which of the following is an assumption on which the engineer's argument depends?

A. There is no other means of utilizing the heat produced by the steel manufacturing process that would be more cost effective than installing thermophotovoltaic generators.
B. Using current technology, it would be possible for steel manufacturing plants to feed the heat they produce into thermophotovoltaic generators in such a way that those generators could convert at least some of that heat into electricity.
C. The amount steel manufacturing plants would save on their electric bills by feeding heat into thermophotovoltaic generators would be sufficient to cover the cost of purchasing and installing those generators.
D. At least some steel manufacturing plants rely on electricity as their primary source of energy in the steel manufacturing process.
E. There are at least some steel manufacturing plants that could greatly reduce their electricity bills only if they used some method of converting wasted heat or other energy from the steel manufacturing process into electricity.

The author's argument is straightforward. Manufacturing steel wastes heat, TP generators can convert heat to electricity. If we can input the heat from steel manufacturing into TP generators, we would be able to produce some of our own electricity and use less electricity from the grid. We will therefore save money.

The argument's conclusion has two interesting traits: it's conditional in nature (if plants...they would greatly reduce) and two-pronged (greatly reduce electric bills AND saving money). Let's start with the conditional nature of the conclusion.

Remember our explanation for answer choice A in PT28 S3 Q16 earlier in the chapter.

> Whenever we see a conditional relationship in the conclusion, the sufficient condition is not something assumed by the author.

Let's revisit our example from previously.

If you get into law school, you will have to work super hard.

Am I making that assumption that you will get into law school? Not necessarily. My point only stands if and when you get into law school. Whether you get in or not is a whole separate issue and not something I'm committed to.

So here, whether or not the plants can input heat into the generators is not an issue the author is concerned with. Whether or not this process is feasible is not an assumption of the authors. So answer choice B can be eliminated.

The conclusion also makes two separate points:

1. If we can recycle heat into electricity we would <u>greatly</u> reduce electric bills.
2. Doing so will save money.

Let's look at each of them:

The first assumption the author makes is that the electricity generated from TP generators can cover a significant proportion of the electricity currently used at the plant. What if the generators can generate 1 megawatt of electricity from recycling heat, but the plant uses 100 megawatts of electricity? That wouldn't be a great reduction in electric bills now would it?

Secondly, the author assumes that the whole process of purchasing, installing, running and maintaining the generators will be less than the cost of electricity it saves. Only then will you be able to save money in the process. That is exactly what answer choice C, the correct answer, is saying.

Mentally making a note of what the conclusion is saying and keeping this memory fresh as we examine the answer choices will prove to be an invaluable habit on NA Questions. You can even double check the **conclusion's scope** as you are comparing answer choices.

Let's look at one more question quickly.

<u>PT15 S3 Q3</u>

Organization president: The stationery and envelopes used in all of the mailings from our national headquarters are made from recycled paper, and we never put anything but letters in the envelopes. When the envelopes have windows, these windows are also made from recycled material. Therefore, the envelopes, and thus these mailings, are completely recyclable.

Which one of the following is an assumption on which the organization president's argument depends?

A. All the paper used by the organization for purposes other than mailings is recycled.
B. The mailings from the organization's national headquarters always use envelopes that have windows.
C. The envelope windows made from recycled material are recyclable.
D. The envelopes and stationery used in the organization are always recycled.
E. The organization sends mailings only from its national headquarters.

This is a relatively simple question compared to the rest of them, but it helps to drive our point home.

Let's focus on the wording of the conclusion:

Therefore, the envelopes, and thus these mailings, are completely recyclable.

Note how the conclusion is about whether the mailings are *recyclable.* That means the envelopes, the windows, and the letters within *can be recycled.*

We are not concerned with whether they are *actually* recycled. Even if in reality, these are thrown out with the rest of the garbage, it would have no bearing on our conclusion.

With this in mind, we can easily eliminate A and D right away.

Answer choice B can also be eliminated. Because even if some of the envelopes use other material of windows, that has no bearing on whether the envelopes being discussed in the stimulus are recyclable or not.

Similarly, with answer choice E, where the company sends mail from has no bearing on whether the envelopes with windows being sent from HQ are recyclable.

The correct answer is C.

Difficult Trait #4: Harder NA Questions may have multiple assumptions possible within the argument. Get into the habit of trying to think of potential assumptions as you read through the argument.

Take a look at the following:

Archaeologist: Our team discovered 5000 year old copper tools near a Canadian river, in a spot that offered easy access to the raw materials for birchbark canoes – birch, cedar, and spruce trees. The tools are of a sort used by the region's Aboriginal people in making birchbark canoes in more recent times. It is likely therefore that Aboriginal people in Canada built birchbark canoes 5000 years ago.

Think about the language of the conclusion, the support provided for it, what are some potential necessary assumptions that the author has? I came up with three.

***

The author's conclusion is the last sentence: *it is likely that Aboriginal people in Canada built birchbark canoes 5000 years ago.*

Why does the author think that? What is the supporting evidence provided?

First, they found a tool from 5000 years ago that is similar to the tools Native Americans today use to build birchbark canoes.

Second, the location where they found the tool was located near a river, where they had birch trees.

What are some assumptions of the author?

For one, the author is assuming that the usage of the tools hasn't changed significantly from 5000 years ago. Historically, people used swords to fight, but today they are largely ceremonial. So maybe the tool is used today to build canoes, but they had a different use historically?

Furthermore, there were birch, cedar, and spruce trees where the tool was found. Did Native Americans use the tool to make cedar and spruce canoes also? The author is assuming that the tool is likely used to build birch canoes in the past, but is it also possible that cedar and spruce canoes were built instead?

Lastly, the location where the tool was discovered, had it always been a river? What if it was a desert 5000 years ago? Were the birches here back in the day?

This is the stimulus from question 83-1-21, take a look at that question and try to figure out the answer for yourself.

***

In Chapter 9, we practiced brainstorming and identifying potential assumptions that would clarify the author's argument. We need to take it a step further in NA Questions. Thinking of potential necessary assumptions as we read the stimulus will help us immensely with NA Questions.

So try this strategy: look at the following questions untimed, try to come up with as many tentative necessary assumptions as possible, then check to see if they satisfy the requirements for correct NA answer choices as we have learned in this chapter.

65-1-18, 75-3-25, 76-2-24, 88-2-21, 51-3-18, 65-4-13

***

Take a look at the following question, focus on the conclusion, and also see if you can come up with more than one potential necessary assumption before tackling the answer choices.

PT17 S2 Q23 (Partial Stimulus)

Magazine editor: I know some of our regular advertisers have been pressuring us to give favorable mention to their products in our articles, but they should realize that for us to yield to their wishes would actually be against their interests. To remain an effective advertising vehicle we must have loyal readership, and we would soon lose that readership if our readers suspect that our editorial integrity has been compromised by pandering to advertisers.

The magazine editor's argument assumes which one of the following?

   A. A magazine editor should never be influenced in the performance of his or her professional duties by the wishes of the companies that regularly advertise in the magazine.
   B. The magazine cannot give away any favorable mention in its articles to its regular advertisers without compromising its reputation for editorial integrity.
   C. Favorable mention of their products in the magazine's articles is of less value to the advertisers than is the continued effectiveness of the magazine as an advertising vehicle.
   D. Giving favorable mention to a product in a magazine article is a more effective form of advertisement than is an explicit advertisement for the product in the same magazine.
   E. Carrying paid advertisements can never pose any threat to the magazine's reputation for editorial integrity nor to the loyalty of its readership.

Here, I've deliberately omitted the Magazine editor's opponent's argument from the stimulus, which is not relevant to solve this question.

This argument actually has multiple necessary assumptions within, but only one present in the answer choices. That's why the second last step of **SLAKR** (keyword analysis) is so important.

What is the conclusion of this argument?

- *But they (regular advertisers) should realize that for us to yield to their wishes would actually be against their interests.*

So what are the advertisers' wishes?

The advertisers wish for favorable reviews in the magazine. This is presented in the first sentence of the stimulus. So giving favorable reviews to advertiser products is actually going against their interests. The author presents a two-component conditional as supporting evidence.

- *To remain an effective advertising vehicle we must have loyal readership, and we would soon lose that readership if our readers suspect that our editorial integrity has been compromised by pandering to advertisers.*

    - Effective Advertising Vehicle → Loyal Readership

    - Readers Suspect Integrity Compromised → Lose Loyal Readership
        - Contrapositive: Keep Loyal Readership → Readers Do Not Suspect Integrity Compromised

If we link the two conditionals, then we get:

Readers Suspect Integrity Compromised → Lose Loyal Readership → Magazine No Longer an Effective Advertising Vehicle

So essentially the author's argument is this:

- Premise*: Readers Suspect Integrity Compromised (A) → Magazine No Longer an Effective Advertising Vehicle (B)*
- Conclusion*: Giving Favorable Reviews (C) → Not in Advertisers' Interests (D)*

Let's turn that into notational form and see if you can spot the missing Necessary Assumptions:

- Premise: A → B
- Conclusion: C → D

Necessary Assumptions: C → A, B → D
Necessary Assumptions + Premise = **C → A** + A → B + **B → D** = C → D = Conclusion

If you still have issues with conditional linkage, remember to revisit Chapter 10, where we devote a whole section to this skill.

So the argument contains two Necessary Assumptions,

Giving favorable reviews to advertisers will make readers suspect that the magazine's editorial integrity has been compromised.

It is in the interest of the advertisers that the magazine remains an effective advertising vehicle.

Both will work as answer choices, if you negate them, then the author's conclusion doesn't come to pass. For instance, if giving favorable reviews will not trigger readership suspicion, then there is no harm done to the magazine or the advertisers; similarly, if the advertisers are more interested in short term profits via product placements and don't care about the magazine's viability, then the editor's protestations are equally ineffective.

With that in mind, let's take a look at the answer choices B and C.

> B. *The magazine cannot give away <u>any</u> favorable mention in its articles to its regular advertisers without compromising its reputation for editorial integrity.*

This is very close to one of our answer choice ideas (C → A), but it's not perfect! Remember our proposal: *Giving favorable reviews to advertisers will make readers suspect that the magazine's editorial integrity has been compromised.* So in other words, Giving Favorable Reviews → Readers Will Get Suspicious.

What is this answer choice saying? Giving Favorable Reviews → Compromise Reputation

As you can see, this answer choice is way too strong ("any"), and arguably out of scope, two of the most common problems we see with wrong answer choices. The differences between the Main Assumption and this answer choice are very nuanced; take a look at the following analogy if you are still having trouble:

Proctors will suspect cheating if you repeatedly go to the bathroom during an exam.

You will have the reputation of a cheater if you repeatedly go to the bathroom during an exam.

So being suspected by readership that editorial integrity has been compromised AND actually having a bad reputation are two different things.

This is the most commonly selected wrong answer on an NA Question, ever. More than half of all test takers selected this answer choice. Now you probably won't be able to eliminate this answer right away during the test, but if you compare it closely with Answer Choice C and really think about the differences between the two, then your chances of getting this question right rises significantly.

> C. *Favorable mention of their products in the magazine's articles is of less value to the advertisers than is the continued effectiveness of the magazine as an advertising vehicle.*

This is an alternative way of presenting our second Necessary Assumption, which says that *it is in the interest of advertisers that the magazine remains effective.* The editor argues that advertisers shouldn't expect the magazines to give good reviews to their products, because it is not in their interest to do so. In other words, having the magazine be an effective advertising vehicle is of greater interest to advertisers than product placements.

When deliberating between answer choices B and C, two things ultimately persuaded me to go with C, the correct answer. One, answer choice B appeared a little too strong for my liking. I thought there was a difference between *being suspected of compromising integrity* and actually *compromising your reputation.* Answer C had another thing going for it: it ties in directly with the conclusion. As we have mentioned earlier, **focus on the wording of the conclusion** in NA Questions. The conclusion is about what is really in the interest of the advertisers (effective magazine vs. product reviews), and answer choice C directly addresses that.

This is an analogy that I've used to explain answer choice C to confused students:

Staying up all night to finish your paper on time is not in your best interest. Not getting enough sleep will lead to stress and deteriorating health.

Answer choice C, <u>the correct answer</u>, essentially says that to make this argument, we have to assume that *the benefits incurred from a good night's sleep are greater than the benefit you might incur from handing in your paper on time.*

***

Let's look at one more question that contains multiple NAs:

<u>PT37 S4 Q19</u>

Large scale government projects designed to benefit everyone – such as roads, schools, and bridges – usually benefit some small segment of society, initially at least, more than others. The more equally and widely political power is distributed among the citizenry, the less likely such projects are to receive funding. Hence, government by referendum rather than by means of elected representatives tends to diminish, not enhance, the welfare of a society.

Which one of the following is an assumption on which the argument depends?

  A. Large scale government projects sometimes enhance the welfare of society.
  B. Large scale projects are more likely to fulfill their intended purposes if they are not executed by the government.
  C. Government by referendum actually undermines the democratic process.
  D. The primary purpose of an equal distribution of political power is to enhance the welfare of society.
  E. Government by referendum is the only way to distribute political power equally and widely.

There is a disconnect in the information presented in the conclusion and that presented in the premises. Let's isolate each by looking at the argument structurally.

- **Premise:** *Large scale government projects designed to benefit everyone start off by benefitting a small segment of society more than others.*
- **Intermediate Conclusion:** *More equally and widely political power is distributed, large scale government projects less likely to receive funding.*
- **Main Conclusion:** *Government by referendum rather than elected representatives diminish the welfare of a society.*

There are gaps between the premise and the intermediate conclusion, and between the intermediate and main conclusions.

Let's start with the gap between the premise and the intermediate conclusion: the author is assuming that under more equal political systems, everyone will have an equal voice in deciding policy. So the majority who won't see immediate benefits from large scale government projects will not likely support these projects. A small segment benefits initially, so support for these projects are limited. As a result large projects are less likely to receive funding.

But this is NOT the Main Assumption that we are looking for.

This is a Necessary Assumption question, and we know that the correct answer will be a mandatory trait of our Main Assumption, which in turn addresses the gap between the supporting evidence and the main conclusion. The Main Assumption hurdles the main gap of the argument, which can be between the premise and the main conclusion, or between the intermediate and main conclusions. But it always involves the main conclusion. (That's why we have repeatedly emphasized paying special attention to the wording of the main conclusion.)

Refer back to Chapter 9 for a deeper understanding of the nature of the assumptions that we are looking for in both SA and NA Questions.

We need to establish two things to hurdle the gap between the intermediate and the main conclusion. One, compared to elective representational democracy, government by referendum is more equal and political power is more widely distributed. Two, if large scale government projects are less likely to receive funding, the welfare of society tends to be diminished.

These two, together, make up our Main Assumption for this question. The correct answer will be a trait of either of these.

So what we are looking for is this, or an extension of this:

Political power is more equally and widely distributed among the citizenry in a referendum system than elected representational democracy,

OR

If large scale government projects are less likely to receive funding, the welfare of a society tends to be diminished/not enhanced.

The correct answer will be either of these, or something that must be true given either of these.

   A.   *Large scale government projects sometimes enhance the welfare of society.*

This is a "Must be True" extension of our second NA proposal. *If large scale government projects are less likely to receive funding, the welfare of a society tends to be diminished/not enhanced.* So if we don't do large projects, welfare is diminished or not enhanced, then large projects *must at least* sometimes enhance social welfare. This is the correct answer.

> B. *Large scale projects are more likely to fulfill their intended purposes if they are not executed by the* *government.*

I guess the validity of this answer choice depends on the type of government we are talking about. If it's government by referendum, then it doesn't really matter. Also, if the government does not execute it, is it executed by large corporations? What is their success rate? This answer is out of scope compared to the potential necessary assumptions that we came up with.

> C. *Government by referendum actually undermines the <u>democratic process.</u>*

This answer choice is either out of scope or too strong. We know that government by referendum diminishes the welfare of a society. But does diminishing the welfare of society undermine the democratic process? Does the government turn to authoritarianism? We simply don't know.

> D. *The <u>primary purpose</u> of an equal distribution of political power is to enhance the welfare of society.*

We know that a government that has an equal distribution of political power (referendum) tends to diminish the welfare of society. But we don't know if the <u>primary purpose</u> of such a government is to achieve the opposite effect.

There are two issues with this answer choice. Firstly, just because A causes B doesn't mean the purpose of A is to cause B. Just because smoking leads to lung cancer doesn't mean I smoke in order to get lung cancer. Secondly, the author argues that an equal distribution of political power diminishes the welfare of society, this answer choice is the opposite of that.

> E. *Government by referendum is <u>the only way</u> to distribute political power equally and widely.*

This answer choice is very close to being correct. Remember our first NA proposal, "*Political power is more equally and widely distributed among the citizenry in a referendum system than elected representational democracy.*" This answer choice is too strong. What we want is that the government by referendum is MORE equal and power is MORE widely distributed THAN elected representatives. But we don't know if it's the only way.

So this argument had three assumptions needed to clarify its reasoning completely. An assumption was needed to address the gap between the premise and the intermediate conclusion, and two more to address the gap between the intermediate and main conclusion. The latter two, together, make up our Main Assumption, and the correct answer choice had to come out of our Main Assumption.

Tricky Answer Choices

In previous questions, if you looked carefully at the answer choices and the problems with wrong answer choices, we should already know that wrong answers frequently come in the following flavors:

Answer choices that **contradict** information presented in the argument, or even **weaken** the author's argument.

Answer choices that **repeat** the premise or the conclusion (These are not assumptions, assumptions must be *unstated*)

Out-of-scope answer choices (These can be detected by paying close attention to the wording of the conclusion)

Answer choices that are worded **too strongly** (These are not wrong, per se. I would just be extra careful with these answer choices. Remember, a correct NA answer would be an assumption that is *necessary* to the author's reasoning. Beware of answers that assume a little too much. Check out PT73-4-26, can you spot the answer choice that is too strong?) Correct conditional answers can be worded strongly, though.

Let's look at a final trick test makers love to use to mess with students:

Answer choices that would be ok for SA Questions but wrong on NA Questions

Remember the differences between a correct SA answer and a correct NA answer. SA answer choices are sufficient to guarantee the truth of our Main Assumption, they don't have to be true. NA answer choices are necessarily true given our Main Assumption. They must be true. If an answer choice is an exact restatement of our Main Assumption, then it is correct as both SA and NA answer choices. Otherwise, a correct SA answer will be wrong in NA Questions, and a correct NA answer will be wrong in SA Questions.

***

PT30 S2 Q22

The folktale that claims that a rattlesnake's age can be determined from the number of sections in its rattle is false, but only because the rattles are brittle and sometimes partially or completely break off. So if they were not so brittle, one could reliably determine a rattlesnake's age simply from the number of sections in its rattle, because one new section is formed each time a rattlesnake molts.

Which of the following is an assumption the argument requires in order for its conclusion to be properly drawn?

    A.   Rattlesnakes molt exactly once a year.
    B.   The rattles of rattlesnakes of different species are identical in appearance.
    C.   Rattlesnakes molt more frequently when young than when old.
    D.   The brittleness of a rattlesnake's rattle is not correlated with the length of the rattlesnake's life.
    E.   Rattlesnakes molt as often when food is scarce as they do when food is plentiful.

Let's focus specifically on the answer choices for this question as we have already covered how to analyze the stimulus in detail previously.

- Premise: *A new section is formed each time a rattle snake molts.*
- Conclusion: *if rattlesnake tails were not so brittle, one could reliably determine a rattlesnake's age from the number of sections in its tail.*
- Main Assumption: *Rattlesnakes molt at regular time intervals that we are aware of.*

Rattlesnakes *must* molt at regular time intervals, be it once every year, or once every month. If they molted once every year, and the tails weren't brittle, then a rattlesnake with 12 sections in its tail would be 12 years old. Similarly, if they molted once every month then a rattlesnake with 12 sections in its tail would be one year old.

We must also eliminate the possibility that rattlesnakes can molt at irregular times. If a rattlesnake molted once every year AND when it's in an especially good mood, then we won't be able to tell the age of a rattlesnake simply by looking at its tail section. Because we wouldn't be able to know how frequently it was in a good mood.

Lastly, we also have to be aware of the time interval each tail section represents. If we know the molting is regular, but we don't know if each section represents a month, six months, a year, or five years, then we wouldn't be able to determine a snake's age.

With that being said, let's look at the answer choices:

A.   *Rattlesnakes molt exactly once a year.*

This answer choice would work perfectly as an SA answer, but it's not a *necessary* assumption of the author's. If rattlesnakes molted exactly twice a year, then the argument will still work. All we need for the argument to work is that the snakes molted at *regular time intervals.*

B.   *The rattles of rattlesnakes of different species are identical in appearance.*

This answer choice is out of scope.

C.   *Rattlesnakes molt more frequently when young than when old.*

This answer choice is the opposite of what our Main Assumption is.

D.   *The brittleness of a rattlesnake's rattle is not correlated with the length of the rattlesnake's life.*

This answer choice is an extension of the sufficient condition in our conclusion. Remember earlier on in the chapter (61-2-16) we looked at conditional conclusions. The author is not assuming the truth of the sufficient condition in a conditional conclusion.

E.   *Rattlesnakes molt as often when food is scarce as they do when food is plentiful.*

This is the correct answer, it *must be true* if our Main Assumption is true. If rattlesnakes molted at regular time intervals, then their molting frequency must not change due to food scarcity.

Always remember whether you are working on an NA Question or an SA Question.

Take a look at 39-4-19 and 60-1-20 for further practice. Ask yourself which answer choice is a good SA answer, but would not be a suitable NA answer?

At the same time, just because an answer choice is a correct SA answer doesn't mean it's automatically *wrong* in a NA Question. Answer choices that match our Main Assumption will be ok for both SA and NA Questions. Take a look at 37-2-19, 62-2-25, and 71-1-22.

12. Weaken and Strengthen: A Short Intro

A Quick Review

So far, we have covered several of the question types belonging to the Assumption Family. We have looked at Flaw, Sufficient Assumption, and Necessary Assumption questions. In all three types, if you remember, one of the most important jobs when reading the stimulus is to find the gap between the premises and the conclusion. We need to isolate the premises, isolate the main conclusion, and think about how the author gets from one to the other. All Assumption Family questions are interconnected, because the gap in the argument that you need to focus on when analyzing the stimulus will be crucial to getting to the correct answer choice.

Take a look at our now overused hypothetical:

- Premise*: John is a JD candidate*
- Conclusion*: Therefore he has taken the LSAT*

The gap in this argument is quite obvious, the author goes from JD to LSAT in a jump in reasoning. It's what the author believes without explicitly stating, it's what they assume in the argument.

A correct flaw answer would state this and tell us what error the author committed, what the author had mistakenly assumed, or overlooked:

The author assumes without justification that all JD candidates need to take the LSAT.
The author overlooks the fact that not all JD candidates take the LSAT in order to gain admissions to law school.

In a correct sufficient assumption answer choice, we devise a Main Assumption to connect the two concepts presented in the premise and the conclusion; in other words, our thinking is still evolving around the concepts of "JD" and "LSAT." Our Main Assumption can be presented in conditional form, JD → LSAT, or "*if you are a JD candidate, then you must take the LSAT.*"

A correct SA answer choice would be either stronger or just as strong as our Main Assumption:

All JD candidates need to take the LSAT.
Anyone planning to pursue post college education must take the LSAT.

Notice how neither of these states are factually correct or sound, but they fulfill their purposes as sufficient assumptions, and as such, are valid SA answer choices.

In a correct necessary assumption answer choice, the correct answer can either be as strong as our Main Assumption or a weaker, must be true trait of that Main Assumption:

All JD candidates need to take the LSAT.
Some students who are JD candidates have taken the LSAT.

As you can see, with flaw, SA, and NA Questions, success is inseparable from having a clear and defined grasp of the argument's premises, conclusion, and gaps in between. We identify the ideas they present and compare and contrast the two according to the need of the question type.

Weaken and Strengthen Questions: The Black Sheep of the Assumption Family

Strengthen and Weaken Questions still form a part of the Assumption Family, and how we approach these questions is largely the same. But there are essential key differences between Strengthen/Weaken Questions and the rest of the Assumption Family. We will look at Weaken and Strengthen Questions in detail in Chapters 13 and 14, but for now, I just want you to have a macroscopic view of what's the same and what's different about these questions compared to the rest of them.

All the Assumption Family questions that we have looked at so far have premises and a main conclusion, which means they will contain an argument in the stimulus. (Reread the chapter on Find the Conclusion Questions if your skills in analyzing argument structures are rusty.)

Strengthen and Weaken Questions; however, might not even contain an argument.

Take a look at the stimulus of <u>PT42 S2 Q18</u>:

While it is true that bees' vision is well suited to the task of identifying flowers by their colors, it is probable that flowers developed in response to the type of vision that bees have, rather than bees' vision developing in response to flower color.

Which one of the following, if true, most strongly supports the statement above?

***

What we have here is a Strengthen Question, still technically a part of the Assumption Family of Questions. But look at this stimulus, does it have the elements we associate with an argument? Does it have premises, intermediate conclusions, or a main conclusion?

The answer is no. The author believes that *flowers developed in response to the type of vision that bees have.* (In other words, bees' eyes are better at seeing colors like red and yellow, rather than black or gray; so red and yellow flowers have a better chance of getting pollinated because they stand out more. So as time passed, we have more and more red and yellow flowers, and black or gray flowers just went extinct.)

This is the author's viewpoint, belief, opinion, or hypothesis. But it is NOT the main conclusion of an argument. Why? Because the author doesn't provide any supporting premises to back it up. An argument requires BOTH premises and a conclusion.

The majority of Strengthen and Weaken Questions will have an argument, **but some don't.** So what do we do? We begin our approach to a Strengthen/Weaken stimulus just as we would in any other Assumption Family question. We try to locate the gap. But just keep in mind that sometimes there won't even be an argument, much less a gap, in these types of questions.

***

This brings us to the second important thing to note when tackling Strengthen and Weaken Questions: answer choices which **independently** help make the author's viewpoint or conclusion more or less believable are acceptable answers.

If we are faced with a Strengthen Question, and we come across an answer choice that supports the author's view, but **has nothing to do with the information presented in the stimulus**, it's still an eligible answer choice. Similarly, if we are faced with a Weaken Question, and an answer choice is sowing the seeds of doubt in our mind about the validity/soundness of the author's view, then it's also a contender.

If the stimulus doesn't contain an argument, then our job is simple: we find the answer choice that confirms the author's point of view (strengthen) or disaffirms the author's point of view (weaken).

But even if the stimulus did contain an argument, these types of answer choices are still acceptable. Of course, if the argument contains a gap, we want an answer that addresses the gap. But if no such answer exists, then answers that aid or attack the conclusion or premises independently are still ok.

I know this probably sounds a little confusing right now. We will delve into this in more detail in the next two chapters, but for now, let's illustrate the point with our previous example.

- Premise*: John is a JD candidate,*
- Conclusion*: John has taken the LSAT*

Gap: JD…LSAT

If this was a Strengthen Question, then three types of answer choices are acceptable, in terms of preference:

- Answer choices that address the gap in the author's reasoning. (Best type of answer choice)

   o Example: *I am a law school professor, and every JD candidate I knew had taken the LSAT*

- Answer choices that are unrelated to the gap, but still make the conclusion more believable. (Not as common as an answer choice that connects the gap, but still an acceptable answer)

   o Example: *I was using John's computer the other day, I saw that he set his homepage to lsac.org*

- Answer choices that are unrelated to the gap, but make the premise more believable. (Even rarer than the previous two, but nonetheless still acceptable if the other two don't exist)

   o Example: *John is applying for summer internships at New York's top law firms.*

Note how in all three of the examples above, the truth of our original argument's conclusion is not guaranteed. Having your homepage set to lsac.org doesn't automatically mean that you have taken the LSAT, and being a summer associate at Cravath or Skadden doesn't mean that you are a JD candidate. They are weak examples and I have deliberately made it so. But more on this later.

If it's still not clear, let us use a slightly different approach to illustrate:

Let's take Aristotle's famous syllogism and slightly modify it, let's say that we see the following argument:

- Premise: *All men are mortal.*
- Conclusion: *Socrates is mortal.*

How would I strengthen this argument?

The best answer would be one to directly bridge this gap, and as we all know, the missing assumption is that *Socrates is a man.*

An equally valid answer for Strengthen and Weaken Questions would be one that skips the gap altogether and addresses the conclusion directly.

So an answer choice that read "*Socrates died thousands of years ago*" would be acceptable too. Because it strengthens the conclusion that *Socrates is mortal*.

Finally, an answer choice that boosts the validity of the premise have occasionally appeared as the correct choice. So an answer choice that said "*men are animals, and animals will eventually die*" can be the correct answer too. But I would choose such an answer only when the previous two types of answers cannot be found.

> Answer choices that strengthen/weaken the argument's premises are very rare, but they CAN be correct answer choices.

Unlike other question types in the Assumption Family, premise boosters/attackers are ONLY acceptable in Strengthen and Weaken Questions.

***

So we now know that there exists a wide variety of potentially correct answer choices for Strengthen/Weaken Questions. The observant student will naturally ask: "then how do we pick the correct answer if more than one correct answer exists?" This brings us to our third and final special observation about Strengthen and Weaken Questions: we need to compare and contrast answer choices to find the most suitable one.

There are three question types that can have MORE THAN ONE potentially acceptable answer, it is our job to compare each of the answer choices. They are:

- STRENGTHEN
- WEAKEN
- MOST STRONGLY SUPPORTED

Other question types can have multiple acceptable answers, but in much rarer quantities than these three. When there are multiple acceptable answers, we need to rank the answer choices and find the most suitable AC. In fact, **ranking** answers is a habit that we can apply to our overall approach, it's so important that we will devote a whole chapter to it later on in the book. This is the final element of our approach to the ultra difficult LR questions. (R in SLAKR)

We will look at MSS Questions down the road, so let's focus on Strengthen and Weaken Questions for now. Again, the correct answer to most other type of question can be derived via the **process of elimination**, but for these three question types, we also need to **compare and contrast** attractive answer choices in order to determine the best option available to us.

When tutoring students and trying to drive this nuanced nature of Strengthen/Weaken Questions home, I like to use the following hypothetical analogy:

John is broke, and he has been accepted to Columbia Law School. Unfortunately, because he is an international student, he is ineligible for financial aid. What's even worse is that because he barely met the median for both GPA and LSAT scores, he didn't receive any kind of scholarship. So he goes to his friends for help.

Which friend helped John the most?

A.   The first friend gave words of encouragement and wished him the best of luck.
B.   The second friend bought him a suit, because you need a suit for interviews.
C.   The third friend paid for his dinner and uber home.
D.   The fourth friend said he had no money, but gave him his old law school textbooks.
E.   The fifth friend agreed to lend John five thousand dollars.

You would probably agree that the fifth friend helped the most. To an extent, all five friends helped him in some ways, some more than others. But since our goal here is monetary support to attend law school, the fifth friend helped the most.

And this is how I would like you to think about Strengthen and Weaken Questions. In all the questions we have covered so far, our job was to find the one correct answer and eliminate the rest because there was something wrong with them.

But in Strengthen and Weaken Questions, our job is to find the BEST answer out of five possibilities: we need to find the answer that **most strengthens** or **most weakens** the author's viewpoint, argument, or conclusion. This is especially important on the hardest questions, where we can often eliminate two or three options, but end up stuck on the remaining answers. This is where we need to shift our mentality from wrong answer elimination mode to compare and contrast mode. This skill is essential in not just Strengthen, Weaken, and MSS Questions, but also in RC questions as well.

In the next two chapters, we will look at some of the hardest Weaken and Strengthen Questions, we will look at different types of stimuli, both those that contain an argument and those that don't; we will look at different types of answer choices, and most importantly, we will look at exactly how do we differentiate between two answer choices, both seemingly reasonable, and decide on which answer is the better option.

***

One final note on correct answer choices in Strengthen and Weaken Questions:

Quite often, even the correct answer choice will leave something to be desired. The correct answer is NOT correct per se, but correct simply by the virtue of being the best of the bunch.

Take our hypothetical above for example, we know that law school can cost upwards of 200,000 dollars. Is the five thousand dollar loan from friend #5 really going to make a material difference? Probably not. But given the answer choices we have, it's really the best of what we got. If there was another answer choice, answer choice F, where friend #6 offered to pay for John's tuition in its entirety, then that would be the right answer – answer choice E would then be an easy target for elimination. So when you are approaching Strengthen and Weaken Questions, try to think in **relative** rather than **absolute** terms. Remember, we are looking for the best answer *relative* to the other alternatives, not the perfect answer.

We will also look at questions with "imperfect correct answers" in the next two chapters in greater detail.

13. Weaken

In the last chapter we had a general overview of Weaken and Strengthen Questions, how they are a part of the Assumption Family of questions, and how they can still differ. In short, we have to remember the following three things when facing a Weaken/Strengthening Question:

A. Every Assumption Family question type will contain a gap between the premises and the main conclusion. Most Weaken and Strengthen Questions also contain this gap, but not all of them.

B. Weaken and Strengthen answer choices are more varied than other AF questions as well: correct answer choices can address the gap, or they can be outside information that independently affect the main conclusion or even the premise.

C. Harder Strengthen and Weaken Questions can have more than one acceptable answer. So we have to compare the answer choices to find the most suitable one.

The Differences between Weaken and Flaw Questions

Weaken Questions are similar to Flaw Questions, but with fundamental differences: with Flaw Questions, you are putting a label on what the author of the argument did wrong; whereas with Weaken Questions, you are essentially trying to come up with a piece of information as retort against the author's argument or conclusion.

Take a look at the following hypothetical:

David: Why are you going to law school? Teddy Roosevelt dropped out of law school and still became the President of the United States.

What reasoning flaw does David commit?

If this is a Flaw Question, then we have to refer to the list of standard logical fallacies that we talked about in Chapter 8. We have structure-based flaws, as well as flaws associated with conditional, causal, and comparable reasoning.

Here, David uses comparable reasoning/analogy to argue that going to law school is not a good idea, because Roosevelt didn't finish law school but still had an amazing life. But we know that Roosevelt is an extreme case and probably not a good example for regular people. The flaw David commits is a Flaw of Comparable Reasoning, where he compares two different things as if they are alike.

If we wanted to express David's flaw in different language, we can say that "David overlooks the possibility that there are significant differences between Roosevelt and I so that his analogy is not applicable." We can also say that "David assumes without providing justification that what worked for Roosevelt will also work for me."

In short, with Flaw Questions, we have a checklist of standard flaws that we try to match with the stimulus's argument.

Weaken Questions bring us many more possibilities in terms of potential answer choices. For instance, if I wanted to weaken David's argument, I can point out any one of the differences between me and Roosevelt. I can say "but Teddy Roosevelt came from a Boston Brahmin family, he is basically an American aristocrat." I can say "Roosevelt had a distinguished career as a military officer and was a national hero," or I can say that "Roosevelt became President a hundred years ago, the times have changed."

Or I can focus on my situation and use that as an objection. I can say "I have no desire to run for President, I just want to be a lawyer," this would also weaken the applicability of David's analogy. I can even offer up an objection that has nothing to do with Roosevelt. I can respond to David by saying "I enjoy reading legal analysis."

All of these are ways in which we can respond to David. Weaken answer choices are essentially objections to the statement/argument/conclusion presented in the stimulus. Think about it, in a real life situation, we don't need to point out what logical fallacy our opponent has committed in order to object to their reasoning. There are many different ways in which we can object to, protest, or challenge an opponent's argument.

And that is the essential difference between Flaw Questions and Weaken Questions. In Flaw Questions, we are identifying the reasoning error committed by the author and giving it an official label; whereas in Weaken Questions, we are trying to think of something that would challenge the believability of the author's argument.

One important thing to note, however; is that with "Overlook" type of Flaw Questions, we treat those exactly as we would Weaken Questions. Go back and take a look at those again after you have finished this chapter.

Tackling Weaken Questions from a Structural Perspective: Three Ways to Weaken

In the chapter on Flaw Questions, we saw that we can approach the question by analyzing it structurally, or by thinking about the conditional or causal logic behind the argument. There are two ways to approach those questions. Weaken Questions, similarly, can be approached from a structural as well as logical perspective. As we have seen in the previous chapter's overview of Strengthen and Weaken Questions, there are three ways to weaken an argument structurally in LR questions:

I. Acknowledge the information presented in the author's premises but show that it doesn't necessarily lead to the author's conclusion. (Addressing the gap)

Structurally, the vast majority of Weaken Questions will contain an argument (premises + conclusion). I did a manual count of the one hundred hardest Weaken Questions when preparing to write this chapter, and only four of them had stimuli that did not contain an argument. So for our purposes, we can make our initial approach to a Weaken stimulus as we would any other Assumption Family stimulus.

So we identify the supporting premises/intermediate conclusion, along with the argument's main conclusion. We then find the gap in the author's reasoning when they make the leap from the premises to the conclusion. But unlike Flaw Questions, where we give this fallacious leap an official name, or in SA and NA Questions, where we try to think of a Main Assumption to perfectly overcome this gap, in Weaken Questions, we try to brainstorm an answer that could demonstrate that the author's premises don't necessarily lead to their conclusion.

***

Let's look at a question:

PT22 S4 Q19

Speaker: Contemporary business firms need to recognize that avoiding social responsibility leads to the gradual erosion of power. This is Davis and Blomstrom's Iron Law of Responsibility. "In the long run, those who do not use power in a manner which society considers responsible will tend to lose it." The law's application to human institutions certainly stands confirmed by history. Though the "long run" may require decades or even centuries in some instances, society ultimately acts to reduce power when society thinks it is not being used responsibly. Therefore, a business that wishes to retain its power for as long as it can must act responsibly.

Which one of the following statements, if true, most weakens the speaker's argument?

  A. Government institutions are as subject to the Iron Law of Responsibility as business institutions.
  B. Public relations programs can cause society to consider an institution socially responsible even when its not.
  C. The power of some institutions erodes more slowly than the power of others, whether they are socially responsible or not.
  D. Since no institution is eternal, every business will eventually fail.
  E. Some businesses that have used power in socially responsible ways have lost it.

There is a lot of information in this stimulus, so let's cut to the essential parts by analyzing it structurally (S in SLAKR):

The main conclusion is the last sentence of the stimulus, "*a business that wishes to retain its power for as long as it can must act responsibly.*" The conclusion is in conditional form: Retain power for as long as it can → Act responsibly.

The first sentence of the stimulus confused me for a little. I initially thought it was a premise, but the information it's trying to convey is just another way of expressing what we have established in the conclusion. This statement reads "*Contemporary business firms need to recognize that avoiding social responsibility leads to the gradual erosion of power.*" So avoiding social responsibility leads to the gradual erosion of power; if you don't want your power eroded, you must not avoid social responsibility. That's the same as saying "if you want to retain power for as long as you can, you must act responsibly."

So this is a restatement of the conclusion, it's not new information designated to support our conclusion. To find the supporting premises, let's move on.

The author quotes Davis and Blomstrom's Iron Law of Responsibility as support: if you don't use power in a manner in which society considers responsible will tend to lose it. This is repeated in the second to last statement of the stimulus: "*society ultimately acts to reduce power when society thinks it is not being used responsibly.*" If we put it into conditional form, then it will look like this:

> Society thinks you are irresponsible → You will lose power
> To maintain power → Society thinks you are responsible (contrapositive)

Now go back and have a look at the conclusion again, do you notice the gap/shift between the premise and the conclusion?

- Premise: To maintain power → Society thinks you are responsible
- Conclusion: To maintain power → Act responsibly

Remember our goal here, to weaken the argument, we need to show that the premises don't necessarily lead to the conclusion. In other words, *having society think you are responsible doesn't necessarily mean that you actually have to act responsibly.*

Let's look at the answer choices:

> A.   Government institutions are as subject to the Iron Law of Responsibility as business institutions.

Because Strengthen and Weaken answer choices often bring in outside information, some of which can seem irrelevant at first, a good habit to have is to ask yourself "**so what**" after reading an answer choice.

So what if government institutions are subject to the ILR? Does that weaken our conclusion? Just because governments are subject, does it make businesses *less* subject to the law? No. This answer choice does nothing to the believability of our conclusion, nor does it relate to the gap in the author's reasoning.

> B.   Public relations programs can cause society to consider an institution socially responsible even when its not.

This matches up with what we had in mind when analyzing the stimulus. So what if PR programs can trick the public into thinking that some irresponsible companies are actually responsible? Well, then irresponsible companies can just hire PR companies to make them look good, right? So if the requirement for holding on to power is to have society think you are responsible, then we'll just do whatever we want and hire a PR company to take care of the rest. We don't actually have to act responsibly. Having society think that you are responsible doesn't necessarily mean that you are responsible, because you can hire a PR company to make you look good.

This is the correct answer.

> C. The power of some institutions erodes more slowly than the power of others, whether they are socially responsible or not.

This answer seems to weaken at a first glance, because what it is essentially saying is that the *relative* speed at which power erodes is different for different institutions, regardless of whether they are socially responsible or not.

For example, the public might have more prejudices against an investment bank than a private university. So a socially responsible investment bank might be influential for 50 years, and a socially irresponsible university might be influential for 100 years. But the author isn't arguing that being socially responsible will give you an *absolute* advantage over all the other institutions. The author is arguing that using power responsibly will help your institution last longer than it otherwise would. So a socially responsible investment bank might last 50 years, but if it acts irresponsibly, it might last only 20 years.

Always make sure you are aware of the specific point the author is making in the argument, and more specifically, what exactly is the main conclusion trying to convey. We will see countless irrelevant answer choices in Weaken Questions. So always ask yourself how does the answer choice presented affect the validity/believability of the author's conclusion.

> D. Since no institution is eternal, every business will eventually fail.

So what if every business will fail? If you want to stick around for longer, use power responsibly! This does not run contrary to the author's argument, so it doesn't weaken it.

> E. Some businesses that have used power in socially responsible ways have lost it.

This is the most commonly selected wrong answer. I try to think of **analogies** that hit closer to home whenever there is an attractive answer that I'm not sure about. So the argument's conclusion is Retain power → Act responsibly. This answer choice is Some who acted responsibly → Did not retain power.

Let's go back to the JD → LSAT example we are constantly using:

Let's assume that we have a statement, "*a person wishing to go to law school must take the LSAT.*"
Does the statement "*some people who have taken the LSAT didn't get into law school*" weaken our first statement?

No it doesn't. It is attacking the reversal of the conditional statement JD → LSAT: it's essentially saying, "no, not everyone who takes the LSAT gets into law school." So it's attacking this conditional instead: LSAT → JD

Same here with answer choice E, it's weakening/attacking/contradicting the reversal of the author's conclusion, and not actually the author's conclusion itself.

So if you selected answer choice E, here are two takeaways:

*   Always try to be extra careful when reading the main conclusion, don't forget what you are trying to weaken when you are looking over answer choices (we will look at this specifically near the end of the chapter).
*   Try using analogies involving concepts familiar to you to test the effectiveness of the answer choices.

***

So in the last question, we saw that the correct answer choice, B, gave us information that cast doubt on the author's reasoning. The author thinks that because companies need society to think they are responsible, they actually need to be responsible. Answer choice B introduces outside information that casts doubt on this train of thought. A new entity/concept is introduced in answer choice B, namely public relations programs. Now we know that if we take into account the role of public relations programs, the author's conclusion doesn't necessarily follow from his premise. If your goal is to have society think that you are responsible, you don't actually need to be responsible.

What answer choice B did, essentially, was to bring in **outside information that shows the author's premises don't necessarily lead to their conclusion.** We are weakening the argument in question by bringing in new information that objects to the author's line of reasoning.

***

Let's look at another example:

PT33 S3 Q24

Dietician: "The French Paradox" refers to the unusual concurrence in the population of France of a low incidence of heart disease and a diet high in fat. The most likely explanation is that the French consume a high quantity of red wine, which mitigates the ill effects of the fat they eat. So North Americans, with nearly the highest rate of heart disease in the world, should take a cue from the French: if you want to be healthier without cutting fat intake, drink more red wine.

Which one of the following statements, if true, most seriously undermines the conclusion of the dietician's argument?

    A. French men consume as much red wine as French women do, yet French men have a higher rate of heart disease than do French women.
    B. A greater intake of red wine among North Americans would likely lead to a higher incidence of liver problems and other illnesses.
    C. Not all French people have a diet that includes large amounts of fat and a high quantity of red wine.
    D. All evidence suggests that the healthiest way to decrease the chance of heart disease is to exercise and keep a diet low in fat.
    E. Many other regions have much lower rates of heart disease than France, though their populations consume even less red wine than do North Americans.

Let's break it down structurally, as we always do:

The conclusion states that drinking more wine will make you healthier if you don't want to reduce fat intake.

Why?

Because French people, who eat a lot of fat and drink a lot of wine, have low incidences of heart disease.

Notice the gap in the author's reasoning? The information in the premise supports the idea that drinking wine can improve heart health. But the conclusion is talking about health in general. Being healthier is not just about having a healthy heart, maybe you need to factor in other elements like bone health or mental health.

So we are looking for an answer, maybe introducing outside information, that tells us just because the heart is healthier doesn't mean you are healthier overall.

> A. *French men consume as much red wine as French women do, yet French men have a higher rate of heart disease than do French women.*

Is this because wine is less effective in mitigating the effects of fat intake on hearts in males? Or is it because of genetic, gender, or lifestyle related reasons? Is the rate of heart disease among French men still lower than that of Americans? This answer leaves a lot of questions unanswered. It seems to be casting doubt on the premise, but not really.

> B. *A greater intake of red wine among North Americans would likely lead to a higher incidence of liver problems and other illnesses.*

This answer hits the spot. It introduces outside information that objects to the author's reasoning. The author believes healthier heart = healthier, but what this answer choice tells us is that even though drinking more wine may give you a healthier heart, it doesn't necessarily mean you are healthier in general. Despite having a healthier heart due to increased red wine intake, you now have a bunch of other diseases, so maybe you are not healthier after all. This is the correct answer.

> C. *Not all French people have a diet that includes large amounts of fat and a high quantity of red wine.*

Ok, so some French people don't drink a lot of wine nor do they eat a lot of fat. Are they healthier than the rest of the population? What is their likelihood of suffering from heart disease? Like answer choice A, this answer choice C is introducing another layer of complexity to the premise, but it doesn't really attack the premise's validity, much less the conclusion.

> D. *All evidence suggests that the healthiest way to decrease the chance of heart disease is to exercise and keep a diet low in fat.*

Here is where we need to keep an eye on the conclusion of the argument. The author says that drinking wine will make you healthier, they never said that it's the healthiest way.

> E. *Many other regions have much lower rates of heart disease than France, though their populations consume even less red wine than do North Americans.*

Same problem here. So let's assume that this region that we are talking about is Scandinavia. Scandinavians drink less wine than Americans, but have healthier hearts than the French. Why? Maybe it's genetics, maybe it's exercise, maybe it's because they don't eat too much fat? So all this answer can tell us is that there is a better way than drinking red wine to avoid heart disease, but that doesn't mean drinking red wine isn't a viable way in itself.

13. Weaken

II. Outside information that independently attacks the author's main conclusion.

We just saw two questions with correct answer choices that threw a wrench into the author's reasoning, so that the premise, when considered in conjunction with the correct answer choice, no longer leads to the author's conclusion.

An equally valid form of correct answer choices will circumvent the author's premise - conclusion move completely, and offer up an objection that directly casts doubt on the likelihood of the author's conclusion.

Let's go back to our previous example:

John is a JD candidate, so he must have taken the LSAT.

We have already looked at **Type I** Weaken answers, those that fit into the gap between the premise and the conclusion, so that the conclusion doesn't necessarily follow from the premise. An example would be:

Some JD candidates take the GRE instead

What happens when we combine "John is a JD candidate" and "some JD candidates take the GRE instead," can we still guarantee that John "must have taken the LSAT?" No, the conclusion no longer follows.

Type II Weaken answers will skip the gap in the argument; instead, it will simply present us with a piece of information that only targets the conclusion itself instead. Some possible examples are:

But John doesn't even have an LSAC account

John doesn't have a computer

Neither of these answers challenges the author's JD → LSAT reasoning; instead, they are much more localized attacks against the conclusion "John must have taken the LSAT."

If John doesn't have an LSAC account, then he can't possibly have taken the LSAT. This is a pretty strong Weaken answer.

If John doesn't have a computer, could he still have taken the LSAT? Maybe he was able to write the paper exam, maybe he borrowed one. This is still a legitimate Weaken answer, albeit really feeble.

Both Type I and Type II answer choices are valid in Weaken Questions. However, Type I answer choices as correct answers are much more common. By my count probably around 70% of all correct Weaken answers are Type I, and 20% are Type II.

So another type of less common but still acceptable answer choice will introduce information **unrelated** to the premises to cast doubt on the author's conclusion.

Take a look at the following question:

PT88 S2 Q24

Until recently, experts have been unable to identify the artist who created a Renaissance painting depicting aristocrats in a historic battle. But the mystery has been solved by the discovery of a self-portrait of a well-known artist from very early in his career, dated to the same year that the painting of the battle scene was created. One of the figures in the battle scene closely resembles the young man in the self-portrait. It is likely, therefore, that the artist who painted the self-portrait also painted the battle scene.

Which one of the following, if true, most weakens the argument?

A. The painting of the battle scene depicts several other people who appear to be roughly the same age as the man depicted in the self-portrait.
B. Most of the figures depicted in the painting of the battle scene resemble real people from history.
C. It was not uncommon in the Renaissance for painters to use live models in depicting people in their paintings.
D. It would have been a violation of etiquette for so young an artist to include himself among aristocrats in a painting of a historic battle.
E. The historic battle that is the subject of the painting took place a number of years before the birth of the artist who painted the self-portrait.

The author believes that the painter of the self portrait is also the artist behind the painting of the battle. Why? Because there was this one person in the painting of the battle who closely resembles the subject of the self portrait. Let's try to make up a more concrete hypothetical based on the author's line of reasoning:

Let's say that we discovered a painting of the battle of Thermopylae (Leonidas and the three hundred Spartans). We don't know who the painter was, but we know from carbon dating that the painting was created in 1500.

Coincidentally, someone noticed that one of the soldiers in the painting had a face that closely resembled Michelangelo. Because we also have a self-portrait by Michelangelo from 1500, and the two faces look alike. So Michelangelo must have painted this battle scene.

How can we weaken this argument? **Type I** answer choices are the most frequent correct answers, so we can look for something that would make us say, "just because there was a subject in the historical painting that looked like Michelangelo's self portrait, it doesn't mean Michelangelo was the painter?"

We could say that perhaps Michelangelo's friends, Da Vinci and Raphael, had a habit of putting Michelangelo in their paintings as a prank; or perhaps we can say that Renaissance painters often painted faces in such a stylistic way so that they are not accurate representations, so even though the two subjects look alike, they were both idealized creations and didn't really resemble Michelangelo. Maybe we can also try to argue that there were other potential painters who looked like Michelangelo.

But **Type II** answer choices, though less common, also appear as correct answer choices. So if we can't find a Type I answer choice, we try to find something that is directly objecting to/contradicting the author's conclusion. So essentially, we are looking for an answer choice that would make us think that Michelangelo didn't paint the Battle of Thermopylae.

> A. *The painting of the battle scene depicts several other people who appear to be roughly the same age as the man depicted in the self-portrait.*

So there were other young men portrayed in the paintings. So it's a battle scene, a lot of soldiers will be young men. But does this tell us anything more about whether the artist of the portrait also painted the painting? Not really: these other young men in the painting of the battle, did they resemble the artist, or other artists? Did they resemble anyone? We simply don't have enough information to deduce what this answer is trying to say.

> B. *Most of the figures depicted in the painting of the battle scene resemble real people from history.*

This might actually help the author's reasoning, rather than weaken it, right? Because the artist obviously drew inspiration from reality. So maybe the painter put himself into the painting? Or the painter was someone else, but decided to put the painter of the self portrait into his war painting? It doesn't have a clearcut and direct weakening effect on our argument/conclusion.

> C. *It was not uncommon in the Renaissance for painters to use live models in depicting people in their paintings.*

So Renaissance painters used models. Did our painter use a model? Remember that the guy from the self portrait looked like the guy from the painting of the battle, right? Did the model paint the self-portrait? This answer doesn't really make any sense.

> D. *It would have been a violation of etiquette for so young an artist to include himself among aristocrats in a painting of a historic battle.*

I didn't like this answer at first, because it doesn't really guarantee that Michelangelo didn't paint the Battle of Thermopylae, to use our example. Maybe Michelangelo was a rebel and didn't care about etiquette?

But remember, while ideally, we would find an answer that would destroy the author's conclusion; there are countless questions where the correct answers will be imperfect. As we covered in the previous chapter, **we pick the best answer available to us in Weaken Questions, even if it's not perfect.**

Comparing answer choices is crucial in Weaken/Strengthen Questions, and we will cover it before this chapter finishes.

What does this answer tell us? I suppose we can say that it's rare for young artists to include themselves in their paintings, because it's frowned upon. So that at least opens up the possibility that the artist who painted the self portrait *didn't* also paint the battle scene. Does this answer mean that he definitely didn't paint the battle scene? No. But it's nudging us in the direction of believing that it's not very likely.

Furthermore, if we compare this answer choice to the rest of them, it becomes clear that this answer is the only one that offers up a direct objection to the author's conclusion. As such, it is a Type II answer choice.

This is the correct answer.

> E. *The historic battle that is the subject of the painting took place a number of years before the birth of the artist who painted the self-portrait.*

Yes, this doesn't contradict any of the information as presented in the stimulus. The painting dates from the Renaissance, but the actual battle itself could be from any time prior to that. Remember, the author's argument is that because there's a guy in the painting who looked like Michelangelo, Michelangelo painted it.

So in summary, make sure to keep an eye out for Type II answer choices. Since we are so used to dealing with Type I answer choices being the usual correct answer, I know it's easy to forget that Type II answer choices are also valid. In addition, remember that imperfect answer choices are ok, as long as they are the best of the bunch, but more on that later.

III. Information that suggests the premises provided in support of the author's conclusion may be inaccurate.

We now come to the third and final type of correct answer choice, let's call them **Type III** answers. These are the very rare **Premise Attacker** type answer choices. In every other type of LR question besides Strengthen and Weaken Questions, Premise Attackers will be wrong. But in Strengthen/Weaken Questions, answer choices that challenge the validity of the premises are actually ok.

That being said, they are the rarest type of correct answer choices. Less than 10% of correct answers are Type III answer choices (I counted 9 out of the hardest 100 Weaken Questions when preparing for this chapter).

Let's go back to our JD → LSAT hypothetical:

John is a JD candidate, so he must have taken the LSAT.

- Type I: *not all JD candidates take the LSAT.* (Challenges JD → LSAT relationship)
- Type II: *John doesn't have an LSAC account.* (Challenges the conclusion "John has taken the LSAT" directly)
- Type III: *But John is only 16 years old, are you sure he is in law school?* (Challenges the premise "John is a JD candidate.")

Type III answer choices, the Premise Attackers, will challenge the accuracy or believability of the author's premises. REMEMBER, these answer choices are only acceptable for Strengthen/Weaken Questions, and even then, they are acceptable if we don't have a better Type I or Type II answer choice.

***

PT53 S1 Q8

Doctor: In three separate studies, researchers compared children who had slept with night-lights in their rooms as infants to children who had not. In the first study, the children who had slept with night-lights proved more likely to be nearsighted, but the later studies found no correlation between night-lights and nearsightedness. However, the children in the first study were younger than those in the later studies. This suggests that if night-lights cause nearsightedness, the effect disappears with age.

Which one of the following, if true, would most weaken the doctor's argument?

    A.   A fourth study comparing infants who were currently sleeping with night-lights to infants who were not did not find any correlation between night-lights and nearsightedness.
    B.   On average, young children who are already very nearsighted are no more likely to sleep with night-lights than young children who are not already nearsighted.
    C.   In a study involving children who had not slept with nightlights as infants but had slept with nightlights when they were older, most of the children studied were not nearsighted.
    D.   The two studies in which no correlation was found did not examine enough children to provide significant support for any conclusion regarding a causal relationship between nightlights and nearsightedness.
    E.   In a fourth study involving 100 children who were older than those in any of the first three studies, several of the children who had slept with nightlights as infants were nearsighted.

13. Weaken

What is the author's conclusion? If nightlights cause nearsightedness, the effect disappears with age.

Why does the author think so? What are his supporting premises?

The author cites three studies. In the first study, a correlation was found between nightlights and nearsightedness, but no correlation was found between the two in the second and third studies. Also, the children were younger in the first study and older in the second and third studies.

	Age	Correlation
Study 1	Younger	Yes
Study 2	Older	No
Study 3	Older	No

Also, the author's conclusion is conditional. As we have seen in previous chapters, in a conditional conclusion, the author isn't committed to the occurrence of the sufficient condition. For instance, if my conclusion was "if you get into law school, you'll need to work hard." I'm not committed to the position that you will or will not actually get into law school. The conclusion is about when and if you actually did get into law school, whatever your chances may be.

Similarly, here the author isn't actually committed to the position that Nightlight ⇒ Nearsightedness. The author is saying that "if the cause exists, and it may very well not exist; but if it did, then the effect disappears with age." Before even looking at the answer choices, I can already sense that the test makers will throw in an attractive wrong answer that will try to convince us that nightlights do not cause nearsightedness.

What are the ways in which we can weaken this argument?

Let's start with a Type I answer choice. We want an answer choice that will make us think that *despite the three studies, the effects don't actually disappear with age.*

We can potentially say that "the studies were done in different countries, and the second and third studies were conducted in countries where the standard for nearsightedness is less strict."

For instance, if Study 1 was conducted in country A, where anyone with less than 0.0 vision is classified as being nearsighted; whereas Studies 2 and 3 were conducted in country B, where myopia is defined as worse than -0.50.

If this were the case, you can't conclude that myopia disappeared with age. Because the standards are different, and maybe there will be an equal number of nearsighted kids in Study 2 and 3 if the standards were uniform across the board.

Can we also think of a Type II answer choice? We want something that can independently object to the author's conclusion. The author is open to the possibility that myopia disappeared with age, so let's find something that argues the opposite. We can potentially say "nearly all optometrists agree that myopia is irreversible."

Now let's think about Type III answer choices. These Premise Attackers are extremely rare. We can argue that there is something wrong with the studies, or that they are flawed.

All three types of answer choices are acceptable, but in terms of order of preference, I > II > III.

    A. *A fourth study comparing infants who were currently sleeping with night-lights to infants who were not did not find any correlation between night-lights and nearsightedness.*

So the author is suggesting that the correlation is unclear. But remember that the author isn't committed to the position that nightlights cause myopia. This is the trick answer we talked about earlier.

>   B. *On average, young children who are already very nearsighted are no more likely to sleep with night-lights than young children who are not already nearsighted.*

This answer choice eliminates the possibility that the correlation in Study 1 is due to nearsighted children sleeping with nightlights on, rather than vice versa. This answer choice is actually strengthening the causal relationship between nightlights and myopia. We don't want that.

>   C. *In a study involving children who had not slept with nightlights as infants but had slept with nightlights when they were older, most of the children studied were not nearsighted.*

So older children are less likely to become nearsighted due to nightlights. If you didn't sleep with nightlights as a baby, but started doing so when you were five years old, your chances of myopia are small. If older children are less susceptible to the damaging effects of nightlights, maybe for those who did use nightlights as infants, the effects disappear with age? This answer could potentially be a strengthening answer.

>   D. *The two studies in which no correlation was found did not examine enough children to provide significant support for any conclusion regarding a causal relationship between nightlights and nearsightedness.*

This is a **premise attacker**, it's saying that the evidence used by the author is no good. The author based his conclusion on the results of three studies, this answer is saying that two of them are invalid. **Because we did not find any Type I or Type II answer choices, this is the correct answer.**

>   E. *In a fourth study involving 100 children who were older than those in any of the first three studies, several of the children who had slept with nightlights as infants were nearsighted.*

So in the fourth study, most of the children who had slept with nightlights were not nearsighted. These children were also older than the children in the first three studies. So there is still no correlation between nightlights and myopia. This answer is strengthening the validity of the results of Studies 2 and 3.

Type III Premise Attackers are extremely rare in Weaken Questions, I would only pick it as a last resort. Like we mentioned before, the ratio of Types I, II, and III answers in Weaken Questions is probably 70% - 20% -10%, respectively.

Take a look at 11-4-11, 19-4-26, 41-1-16, 44-2-20, 50-4-12, 75-3-13, 80-1-19, and 86-4-22 for additional practice.

Tackling Weaken Questions from a Logic Perspective

We have just looked at how to analyze a Weaken stimulus from a structure perspective, either by targeting the gap between the premise and the conclusion, the conclusion, or just the premise. (S in SLAKR)

Now we will look at Weaken Questions from a different perspective. This time, we will look at how to analyze a Weaken stimulus from a logical perspective. (L in SLAKR)

We should be familiar by now with the L in SLAKR. It stands for logic, more specifically, the logic used by the author to advance their argument. There are two types of logic commonly used in Logic Reasoning questions: **conditional logic** and **causal logic**.

We have devoted the entirety of Chapter 7 to the use of these two types of logic in LR questions, their similarities and differences, as well as the traps and complications associated with them.

In Weaken Questions, just like other LR questions, the author will sometimes use conditional or causal logic to advance their argument. Obviously, they don't appear in every question, by my count only half of all Weaken Questions contain them.

So whenever we are looking at a Weaken Question, our **first job** should be to try to come up with Type I, II, and III answers on our own by analyzing its structure. Think about the logic side of things **only** when you are sure the argument contains conditional or causal logic.

That being said, let's take a look at the common ways in which we can weaken an argument that contains conditional and causal reasoning.

Conditional

If the argument contains conditional logic A → B, how would we go about weakening it?

We do so by demonstrating that it's possible to simultaneously have A and B̶.

Why?

Because at the heart of it, a conditional relationship is about universality, it's absolute. A → B essentially means all As are Bs, or all As have Bs, or every time A happens, B happens. In a conditional relationship, there are no ifs or buts, no exceptions and special cases. If we have A, then we got to have B.

To attack a conditional relationship we just have to show that there are instances where we have A but not B. Let's reuse our JD → LSAT example to drive the point home:

How should we weaken the statement "all JDs have taken the LSAT?"

We need to find information that indicates "not all JDs have taken the LSAT," or there are some cases of JDs who haven't taken the LSAT.

Would the statement "I'm not a JD, but I haven't taken the LSAT" or "I'm not a JD, but I have taken the LSAT" weaken the conditional statement JD → LSAT?

No, because if you are not a JD, then the conditional no longer applies to you.

> So in order to weaken a conditional relationship, we are looking for a scenario where the sufficient condition exists, but the necessary condition doesn't exist.

Conditional reasoning is rare in Weaken Questions, but it's important to be aware of how to weaken a conditional relationship. It will come in handy in the chapter on Must be True/Must be False Questions.

Causal

Causal logic appears more frequently in Weaken Question arguments. By my count about 30% of all Weaken Questions contain some form of causal reasoning. A causal relationship will contain a cause and an effect, if we represent that in notational form, $A \Rightarrow B$.

How do we go about weakening a causal relationship, $A \Rightarrow B$?

First of all, because causation is non-exclusive (refer back to Chapter 4 if you are a little rusty), we can propose an **alternative cause**. We can say that C also causes B, or that it's more likely $C \Rightarrow B$ rather than $A \Rightarrow B$. By proposing an alternative cause/explanation, we are weakening the author's line of reasoning.

Secondly, we can demonstrate that there are instances where A is present, but B is not; or when B is present, but A is not. So in other words, **show a scenario where the cause is without the effect, or the effect occurs without the cause.**

Remember, in Weaken Questions our job is to make the author's reasoning *less believable.* We don't have to completely refute the argument. A relevant objection would suffice.

If my opponent says "exercising causes stress," and I respond by saying "I know many people who are stressed all day but have never worked out," or "I know fitness buffs who are never stressed out," do they make the opponent's view somewhat less believable? Yes, even though they don't fully refute the causal relationship between exercise and stress a hundred percent (for example, it may only be applicable to some but not all people,) they are still valid ways to weaken a causal argument, albeit somewhat feebly.

Remember, our job in Weaken Questions is not to find the perfect answer, but the best answer available.

The third way to weaken a causal relationship $A \Rightarrow B$ is to simply **introduce evidence that suggests A does not cause B**. That's right, a flat out denial of the causal relationship also constitutes an acceptable way to weaken it.

Take a look at PT18 S4 Q23 for additional practice.

Correlation - Causation

When the author derives a causal relationship from a correlation, we can weaken it in four possible ways:

One, we can propose that the causal relationship is actually **reversed**. Instead of $A \Rightarrow B$, maybe it's $B \Rightarrow A$.

Two, we can propose a **common third cause** for both A and B, so $C \Rightarrow A + B$.

Thirdly, a Type II answer choice can just challenge the causal relationship in the conclusion by itself, and suggest that **A does not cause B**.

Lastly, a Type III answer choice can even **challenge the correlation** stated in the premise, suggesting that the correlation itself is faulty, based on erroneous data, flawed methodology, etc.

With this in mind, let's look at a stimulus:

The interstitial nucleus, a subregion of the brain's hypothalamus, is typically smaller for male cats than for female cats. A neurobiologist performed autopsies on male cats who died from disease X, a disease affecting no more than 0.05% of male cats, and found that these male cats had interstitial nuclei that were as large as those generally found in female cats. Thus, the size of the interstitial nucleus determines whether or not male cats can contract disease X.

Which of the following statements, if true, most seriously weakens the argument?

***

Before we go any further, I'd like you to try to list all the ways you could potentially weaken this argument. Try to think about it from both structure and logic perspectives. Brainstorm before moving on.

The conclusion of the argument is the last sentence of the stimulus: *the size of the interstitial nucleus determines whether or not male cats can contract disease X.*

The supporting premises make up the rest of the argument: male cats normally have smaller nuclei than female cats, but those suffering from disease X had bigger nuclei (as big as those found in female cats).

This looks like a correlation to me, *enlarged nuclei ~ likelihood of disease X.*

Whenever I see a correlation in an argument, I immediately try to look for a causal relationship elsewhere in the argument. So I reread the conclusion, parsing it to see if there is a causal relationship in there somewhere.

The conclusion looks like a causal relationship to me, *the size of the interstitial nucleus determines whether or not male cats can contract disease X.* "Determine" is an action verb, something we look for in causal relationships. I think I can restate the conclusion as "enlarged nuclei cause male cats to contract disease X."

So what we have here is a correlation - causation reasoning pattern. The premises describe a correlation between an enlarged nuclei in male cats and incidences of disease X, while the conclusion says the enlarged nuclei causes disease X.

How do we weaken a correlation-causation argument again? There are four possible ways:

1. Argue that the causal relationship is reversed. So instead of an enlarged nuclei determining whether or not male cats can contract disease X, we can say that a symptom of disease X is the enlargement of the nuclei.

2. Argue that there is a common cause C for both A and B. We can say that a genetic mutation causes both an enlarged nucleus and raises the risk of contracting disease X.

3. We can object to the causal relationship itself, and suggest that A does not cause B. For example, we can say that disease X is an infectious disease, and that cannot be caused by physiological changes.

4. We can object to the correlation itself. Because so few cats are affected by disease X, we can say that the neurobiologist only had two cats to work with, so the correlation isn't as strong as we might think.

Let's now try to look at it from a structural perspective.

1. A Type I answer would tell us that just because there is a correlation A ~ B, there isn't necessarily causation A ⇒ B involved (conclusion doesn't follow from premise). How do we do that? We can propose that the causal relationship is reversed, or there is another cause for both A and B.

2. A Type II answer would directly attack the conclusion, and provide information that would suggest A doesn't cause B.

3. A Type III answer would attack the premise A ~ B.

***

Notice something really neat here? The answers we had come up with, regardless of whether we are using the argument's structure to guide us, or its causal logic to guide us, were the same. They are just different routes we can take to arrive at the same destination.

That's why I'd like to think about the logic behind an argument, whether it be causal or conditional, as a shortcut. First of all only half of all Weaken Questions will contain these three types of logic, so thinking from a logic standpoint doesn't work for a lot of questions. **But when they do contain causal or conditional reasoning, it's almost as if we have standard, prepared answer choice templates that we can use, saving us a lot of time and energy in the process.**

So this is how I approach Weaken Questions. If the structure of the argument is a little confusing, or I'm having trouble pre-phrasing potential answer choices, **I switch up my strategy and try to think about the logic behind the author's argument.** If I notice that the author is employing conditional or causal techniques to advance the argument, then I know exactly how to weaken the argument.

Of course, if in the process of reading an argument, you are certain it contains conditional or causal reasoning, then you can jump right into the fray by analyzing the logical aspect of the argument.

***

Let's now look at the entire question:

PT28 S3 Q25

The interstitial nucleus, a subregion of the brain's hypothalamus, is typically smaller for male cats than for female cats. A neurobiologist performed autopsies on male cats who died from disease X, a disease affecting no more than 0.05% of male cats, and found that these male cats had interstitial nuclei that were as large as those generally found in female cats. Thus, the size of the interstitial nucleus determines whether or not male cats can contract disease X.

Which of the following statements, if true, most seriously weakens the argument?

- A. No female cats have been known to contract disease X, which is a subtype of disease Y.
- B. Many male cats who contract disease X also contract disease Z, the cause of which is unknown.
- C. The interstitial nuclei of female cats who contract disease X are larger than those of female cats who do not contract disease X.
- D. Of 1000 autopsies on male cats who did not contract disease X, 5 revealed interstitial nuclei larger than those of the average male cat.
- E. The hypothalamus is known not to be causally linked to disease Y, and disease X is a subtype of disease Y.

***

A. No female cats have been known to contract disease X, which is a subtype of disease Y.

Remember, we want to attack the correlation - causation reasoning, more specifically, we want an answer that tells us that the correlation between nucleus size and disease X does not mean that the enlarged nucleus is a cause for disease X in male cats.

So what if female cats don't contract disease X? We want an answer that pertains to *male* cats, that tells us there is no causal relationship between the enlarged nuclei and disease X.

B. Many male cats who contract disease X also contract disease Z, the cause of which is unknown.

If disease Z caused the nuclei of male cats to enlarge, then this would be a good answer. Because then you can argue that the enlargement of the nuclei is caused by disease Z, and there is an overlap in the population of male cats suffering from disease X and Z. Unfortunately, the author does not mention this, so this answer has no effect on our causal relationship.

C. The interstitial nuclei of female cats who contract disease X are larger than those of female cats who do not contract disease X.

This answer takes the correlation pertaining to male cats, and applies it to female cats as well. So it's actually *strengthening* the correlation between enlarged nuclei and disease X.

D. Of 1000 autopsies on male cats who did not contract disease X, 5 revealed interstitial nuclei larger than those of the average <u>male cat.</u>

This answer is so close. What helped me eliminate this answer is that it's talking about "male cats." In a given sample, you are going to have some members who are going to be above average, and some below average, that's how calculating the mean works. In fact, only five had nuclei of above average size, which means 995 were of average or below average size. That is actually reinforcing the correlation between disease X and enlarged nuclei because 995/1000 cats without disease X had smaller nuclei.

If this answer had said there were 5 whose nuclei were larger than the average *female cat*, then it would work as a (really weak) correct answer. Because that shows 0.5% of male cats without disease X had naturally occurring enlarged nuclei, larger than the female cat's. So in that sense, 5/1000 male cats had large nuclei, and 5/10000 male cats had disease X, you could potentially argue that there is an overlap between the two.

Keyword extraction in answer choices (K in SLAKR) will probably be the only way that you can avoid this answer choice. Refer back to earlier chapters to practice this skill.

E. The hypothalamus is known not to be causally linked to disease Y, and disease X is a subtype of disease Y.

Remember how we have mentioned earlier in the book that the test makers will often present the correct answer choice in vague or confusing language? So not understanding an answer choice is NEVER a good reason to eliminate it.

Let's see what this answer choice is trying to say.

So we know the interstitial nucleus is a part of the hypothalamus, and disease X is a subset of disease Y.

The argument concludes that enlarged nuclei cause male cats to contract disease X.

If there is no causal relationship between the hypothalamus and disease Y, then there is no causal relationship between the nucleus and disease X, because the nucleus is a part of the hypothalamus, and disease X is a part of disease Y. This is the correct answer.

Use **Keyword Extraction** (K in SLAKR) or **analogies** to test vague or unclear answers, just as we have done in previous chapters.

The Art of Answer-Choice Comparison

As we have seen in the previous question, even when we have a pretty strong grasp of the stimulus, its structure, its logic, and have thoroughly thought out potential ways to weaken the argument, we can still get tripped up by answer choices! We have seen tricky answer choices in nearly every type of question so far, and Weaken Questions are no exception. In fact, we ought to spend *more* time on Weaken answer choices, since there are so many ways to weaken an argument.

The correct answer choice is often unexpected in Weaken Questions, because it can take on a variety of shapes and sizes. We can have Type I, II, or III answers, the answer choice could involve outside information, it could be really strong, or it could be somewhat feeble in trying to get its point across. Unlike Flaw or Sufficient Assumption questions, where we usually have a good inclination of what the correct answer should look like after reading the stimulus, Weaken and Strengthen Questions are only solved by reading and comparing each answer choice.

We will now look at some of the common characteristics of wrong answers and right answers that leave something to be desired, and then throw in some questions where you really need to compare the answer choices to come to the right decision.

Tricky Answers

We will first look at some traits we should be suspicious of when seen in answer choices. First of all, remember that out of the five choices in a Weaken Question, you could potentially have multiple answers that each work to weaken the argument.

This means that we have to look at Weaken answer choices **relatively**. As mentioned earlier in the chapter, our job is to select the answer choice that does the *most* to weaken the argument/conclusion. The answer is correct simply because it is the best out of the five. If there were a better answer, we would select that instead.

This means that during the answer choice selection process, we should be suspicious of answer choices worded **feebly**, or answer choices that can potentially weaken the argument, but whose **impact is far from certain**. These answer choices are not wrong per se, and they shouldn't be eliminated outright, but rather, we hold on to them to see if there is a better alternative.

Difficult Trait #1: For Strengthen and Weaken Questions, practice by ranking the answer choices from best to worst. Be careful of weak and unclear answers.

So let's say that in a hypothetical question, I see answer choice A, it looks pretty good, so I move to B. I still think A is better than B, so now my job is to compare A to C. If C is better, then I compare C to D, so on and so forth. Ranking answers and choosing the best available, rather than chasing the only correct answer is a crucial to success in these questions.

Take a look at the following:

PT19 S2 Q4

Scientists analyzing air bubbles that had been trapped in Antarctic ice during the Earth's last ice age found that the ice-age atmosphere had contained unusually large amounts of ferrous material and surprisingly small amounts of carbon dioxide. One scientist noted that algae absorb carbon dioxide from the atmosphere. The scientist hypothesized that the ferrous material, which was contained in atmospheric dust, had promoted a great increase in the population of Antarctic algae such as diatoms.

Which one of the following, if true, would most seriously undermine the scientist's hypothesis?

A. Diatoms are a microscopic form of algae that has remained largely unchanged since the last ice age.
B. Computer models suggest that a large increase in ferrous material today could greatly promote the growth of oceanic algae.
C. The dust found in the air bubbles trapped in Antarctic ice contained other minerals in addition to the ferrous material.
D. Sediment from the ocean floor near Antarctica reflects no increase, during the last ice age, in the rate at which the shells that diatoms leave when they die accumulated.
E. Algae that currently grow in the oceans near Antarctica do not appear to be harmed by even a large increase in exposure to ferrous material.

In this stimulus, the author presents a phenomenon (air bubbles containing lots of iron and little CO_2) and seeks to provide a cause/explanation for it (iron $\Rightarrow$ increase in algae $\Rightarrow$ algae absorb CO_2).

It's a reasoning pattern we have covered in the chapter on Find the Conclusion questions. The author proposes a potential cause, and our job is to weaken this causation.

We need to find an answer choice that indicates iron did not lead to an increase in the algae, or that algae do not absorb CO_2 from the atmosphere.

A. *Diatoms are a microscopic form of algae that has remained largely unchanged since the last ice age.*

First of all, the author didn't say that it was diatoms specifically that increased during the last ice age. It was algae that included diatoms. Secondly, this answer choice talks about whether the diatoms have changed; we are concerned with population changes.

B. *Computer models suggest that a large increase in ferrous material today could greatly promote the growth of oceanic algae.*

So iron leads to an increase in algae, this is in line with the author's belief, it strengthens the author's position.

C. *The dust found in the air bubbles trapped in Antarctic ice contained other minerals in addition to the ferrous material.*

So there were other materials in the atmosphere. Let's say it was titanium. Does titanium promote the growth of algae? Is the presence of titanium a potential alternative explanation for why there is so little CO_2?

This answer choice starts well, leading us to think there is another element we haven't considered. But remember, one of the ways to weaken causation is to find an alternate *cause*. It would have been perfect if the answer choice had gone further and said that the additional mineral can also lead to an increase in algae or decrease in CO_2. So this answer could potentially weaken, if we knew more about the nature of this other mineral.

Tricky answer choices are notorious for this. The test makers will throw in a half-baked idea as an answer choice that doesn't really have an effect and use it **to tempt us to come to our own unsupported conclusions.**

D. *Sediment from the ocean floor near Antarctica reflects no increase, during the last ice age, in the rate at which the shells that diatoms leave when they die accumulated.*

If diatoms didn't increase, then it raises the possibility that iron didn't lead to a great increase in the algae population. This goes against the author's view that iron caused an increase in the algae population.

Is this answer perfect? No: it is talking about diatoms, which is only one type of algae. We have no idea whether other types of algae increased or not. But it is a better choice than answer choice C, because it directly targets the causal link proposed by the author, whereas C only hints at that possibility. <u>This is the correct answer.</u>

E. *Algae that currently grow in the oceans near Antarctica do not appear to be harmed by even a large increase in exposure to ferrous material.*

So algae is not harmed by iron, I suppose that the author's idea that iron causes algae increase is a possibility. This answer strengthens the author's view.

This question, at the end of the day, boils down to picking D over C. Take some time to examine C and D together, and ask yourself which one is the stronger objection?

Difficult Trait #2: Beware Open to Interpretation Answer Choices

As we can see from answer choice C from the previous question, which stated that the air bubbles contained another mineral other than iron, answer choices that can go either way are usually tempting but wrong. Does this second mineral lead to an increase in algae? If so, it weakens. But if this second mineral actually limits algae growth or has no effect on algae growth, all of a sudden it becomes a Strengthen answer. **Answer choices that are unclear, or are open to interpretation depending on your assumptions are very dangerous.**

That's why I recommend deliberately slowing down when navigating Weaken answer choices during practice. The majority of your time on a Weaken Question should be devoted to discerning between answer choices, and ranking them in terms of which one is the most suitable. On the actual test itself we have maybe 1 minute for easier questions, and 2 minutes for the harder questions. That is probably not enough time to fully think about the implications of each answer choice.

But if we don't think about the implications of each answer choice on the hardest questions, we will suffer in terms of accuracy. So what I would like you to do, especially with Weaken Questions, is to slow down at first, think about the structure and logic behind the argument, think about ways in which we can weaken the argument, and think about each answer choice in detail. Make this habit of tackling Weaken Questions second nature, something you don't have to actively remind yourself to do. Only then should we start to gradually cut down on speed.

Take a look at the following question, try to figure it out fully before looking at the answer choices, and pick an answer only when you are absolutely certain:

PT35 S4 Q20

Archaeologist: A skeleton of a North American mastodon that became extinct at the peak of the Ice Age was recently discovered. It contains a human made projectile dissimilar to any found in that part of Eurasia closest to North America. Thus, since Eurasians did not settle in North America until shortly before the peak of the Ice Age, the first Eurasian settlers in North America probably came from a more distant part of Eurasia.

Which one of the following, if true, most seriously weakens the archaeologist's argument?

A. The projectile found in the mastodon does not resemble any that were used in Eurasia before or during the Ice Age.
B. The people who occupied the Eurasian area closest to North America remained nomadic throughout the Ice Age.
C. The skeleton of a bear from the same place and time as the mastodon skeleton contains a similar projectile.
D. Other North American artifacts from the peak of the Ice Age are similar to ones from the same time found in more distant parts of Eurasia.
E. Climatic conditions in North America just before the Ice Age were more conducive to human habitation than were those in the part of Eurasia closest to North America at that time.

This stimulus is hard to understand because it contains a lot of rather vague, scientific/anthropological information. Let's try to clarify what the stimulus is trying to say:

- *A skeleton of a North American mastodon that became extinct at the peak of the Ice Age was recently discovered.*

A mastodon is basically a smaller version of the mammoth. They went extinct 20,000 years ago. It was a North American mastodon, so let's assume that it was discovered in Alaska.

- *It contains a human made projectile dissimilar to any found in that part of Eurasia closest to North America.*

So they found an arrowhead in the mastodon, meaning that it was hunted. This must have happened before the mastodon went extinct, or earlier than 20,000 years ago. So now we know that there was human activity in Alaska prior to 20,000 years ago.

Humans crossed the Bering land bridge into North America, from modern day Russian Siberia. The arrowhead found in the mastodon in Alaska is different from any found in Siberia.

- *Thus, since Eurasians did not settle in North America until shortly before the peak of the Ice Age,*

So let's say the peak of the Ice Age was 20,000 years ago, that means humans did not settle in North America just before 20,000 years ago. That means just a short time after humans settled in North America, the mastodon went extinct.

What does this mean? Basically human hunters only had a very limited window of opportunity to hunt the mastodon: humans arrived 20,500 years ago, the mastodon went extinct 20,000 years ago or 500 years after human arrival. So there was only a 500 year window to hunt the mastodon.

Human migration across the Bering land bridge into North America also took thousands of years, so the people who hunted the mastodon must have been one of the first people to come to North America.

- *The first Eurasian settlers in North America probably came from a more distant part of Eurasia.*

This is the conclusion of the argument. The author concludes that the first settlers/hunters who shot the arrow came from further away. In other words, they did not come from Siberia. Maybe they came from Mongolia.

So in essence, the author's argument is this:

Because the arrows used by the first settlers were not found in Siberia, the first settlers came from a more distant location, such as Mongolia.

How would we go about weakening this argument? There aren't elements of causal or conditional reasoning in the wording of the stimulus, so let's think about it in terms of Type I, II, and III answers.

Type I: we want an answer that would tell us that "even though the arrowheads were not found in Siberia, that doesn't mean the settlers came from a more distant location." or "even though the arrowheads were not found in Siberia, it's still possible that these settlers came from Siberia."

Some potential Type I answer choices would be:

The first settlers to North America didn't specifically craft arrowheads, they just took whatever resources that were available (bone, flint, etc.) and sharpened them. So as they traveled, their arrowheads differed considerably.

Type II answer choices would directly attack the conclusion, making us think that the first settlers did come from the part of Eurasia closest to North America.

During the last ice age it was basically impossible to travel long distances.

If the first settlers in Alaska came from further away, that means they had to travel longer distances.

A Type III answer attacks the premise, which could look something like this:

An arrow which struck the bone of an animal will deform significantly so that it no longer bears any resemblance to other, similar arrow heads.

This explains the dissimilarity aspect between Eurasian arrowheads and the arrowhead in the mastodon. Maybe they were similar to begin with?

Let's look at the answer choices:

> A.   *The projectile found in the mastodon does not resemble any that were used in Eurasia before or during the Ice Age.*

This is a Type I answer choice. If we plug it into our argument, see what happens to the conclusion?

Despite the fact that the arrowhead found in the mastodon was dissimilar to any that were found in parts of Eurasia closest to North America, the projectile found in the mastodon does not resemble any that were used in Eurasia.

Now you can't conclude that the settlers came from another part of Eurasia. Either the settlers came from another part of the world, or you can't draw any inferences on the origins of the settlers based on the arrowhead at all. This is the correct answer, but let's look at the others.

> B.   *The people who occupied the Eurasian area closest to North America remained nomadic throughout the Ice Age.*

This is a half-baked answer, one that can easily lead us astray. Maybe the reason we couldn't find the arrows in Eurasia is because they wandered around all the time. But again, if they remained nomadic, then they definitely didn't settle in North America, right?

Depending on how you look at it, this answer is open to interpretation. That's why we need to slow down when examining the answer choices. With answers that provide us limited information, we have to be aware that just because they can be interpreted to weaken the argument, they can also be interpreted to have no effect or even strengthen the argument.

> C.   *The skeleton of a bear from the same place and time as the mastodon skeleton contains a similar projectile.*

So the people who hunted the mastodon also hunted a bear, but where did these people come from?

> D.   *Other North American artifacts from the peak of the Ice Age are similar to ones from the same time found in more distant parts of Eurasia.*

This actually strengthens the argument, it's more likely that the settlers came from a more distant part of Eurasia.

> E. *Climatic conditions in North America just before the Ice Age were more conducive to human habitation than were those in the part of Eurasia closest to North America at that time.*

This answer weakens but is really feeble. It's a Type II answer. Maybe weather is a reason for people closest to North America to move, we can't be sure. If the answer had said that weather is the primary reason why people migrated during the ice age, then it would have been a contender.

If we look at this answer choice in conjunction with answer choice A, its shortcomings are much more obvious. Here is a simplified version of the essence of this question:

Author's argument: we didn't find the arrowheads in Siberia, so the settlers must have come from Mongolia.

Answer choice A: but the arrowheads weren't found in Mongolia either. (This is the correct answer.)

Answer choice E: but the weather in Alaska is better than Siberia.

In short, be careful of answer choices that are intentionally vague. You can interpret these in multiple ways, but by themselves they do not weaken the argument.

Similarly, get into the habit of comparing answers, this habit is absolutely crucial to Strengthen/Weaken Questions.

Imperfect Right Answers

So we have looked at some of the things to watch out for during answer choice selection, let's now turn to some questions where even the right answers have their share of issues. This has become more prevalent in more recent PTs, so take note!

This for me personally, was the hardest thing about Weaken Questions. Because so much of what you do relies on picking out the problems with each answer choice and eliminating them, you develop an overly critical attitude towards answer choices. And once you are faced with a correct answer choice that has its own issues, you are paralyzed and unable to make an effective decision.

The solution to this is NOT to look at answer choices more forgivingly, we want to be overly critical of answer choices. But rather, when faced with a question where every answer choice seems to have its own issues, we compare them to find the most suitable one. In other words, **we find the answer choice with the least amount of problems.**

Difficult Trait #3: Sometimes it's our job to find the "least bad" answer, rather than being fixated on finding the perfect one.

<u>PT85 S3 Q22</u>

Insurers and doctors are well aware that the incidence of lower-back injuries among office workers who spend long hours sitting is higher than that among people who regularly do physical work of a type known to place heavy stress on the lower back. This shows that office equipment and furniture are not properly designed to promote workers' health.

Which one of the following, if true, most undermines the reasoning above?

- A. When they are at home, laborers and office workers tend to spend similar amounts of time sitting.
- B. Insurance companies tend to dislike selling policies to companies whose workers often claim to have back pain.
- C. People who regularly do physical work of a type known to place heavy stress on the lower back are encouraged to use techniques that reduce the degree of stress involved.
- D. Most of the lower back injuries that office workers suffer occur while they are on the job.
- E. Consistent physical exercise is one of the most effective ways to prevent or recover from lower back injuries.

This argument is causal in nature. The author observes a phenomenon (office workers who sit a lot have higher incidences of lower back injury than laborers) and decides that it must be because office furniture is at fault.

Can we suggest an alternative cause here? Perhaps it's not the office furniture's fault, perhaps it's the lack of exercise. Even if you had the best Herman Miller chairs, you would still have a stiff back after long hours of sitting and get injured more easily if you are not doing yoga or stretching.

Perhaps the reason these people became office workers is because they are not capable of hard physical work? Perhaps the people who chose to become office workers were more prone to injury in the first place?

Alternatively, perhaps the people who regularly do physical work are injured less because they are physically fitter to begin with, or they take care of their bodies more carefully simply because they know how important it is in their line of work?

Let's look at the answers. There are two answers that I want to focus on in greater detail than the others:

> A.   *When they are at home, laborers and office workers tend to spend similar amounts of time sitting.*

So it must be due to work then. If there isn't much difference outside of work, it must be office work that is the culprit. This strengthens the argument.

> B.   *Insurance companies tend to dislike selling policies to companies whose workers often claim to have back pain.*

So what? We still do not know what caused the back injuries.

> C.   *People who regularly do physical work of a type known to place heavy stress on the lower back are encouraged to use techniques that reduce the degree of stress involved.*

This looks pretty good, let's save it for later.

> D.   *Most of the lower back injuries that office workers suffer occur while they are on the job.*

This strengthens the argument, so they get injured in the office, maybe it has something to do with the office furniture and equipment.

> E.   *Consistent physical exercise is one of the most effective ways to prevent or recover from lower back injuries.*

What is this answer choice trying to say, who does consistent physical exercise?

***

So now we are left with C and E, let's look at them in greater detail:

Both of these answers can be construed to weaken the argument. With answer choice C, if laborers actually do use good techniques, that explains why they don't suffer from lower back injuries. Office workers don't get injured more than laborers because of bad chairs, but because laborers really do take care of themselves.

But there is one issue with this answer choice, the word "encouraged." Remember we said to ask ourselves "so what" after each answer choice? So what if laborers are encouraged to use good techniques? Do they follow this advice? If they did, then the answer weakens, but if they didn't, the answer would actually strengthen the argument a little bit.

Answer choice E also has something that I particularly disliked. What does the author mean by "physical exercise?" Does physical labor count as physical exercise? Do they share similarities? If by physical exercising the author just means moving around a lot, getting your heart rate up, or burning calories, then this answer would work.

Ultimately, this question boils down to choosing between E and C. Answer choice C is really open to interpretation, I suppose there is a 50/50 chance that the laborers follow good techniques, and we know that answers open to interpretation are common trap answers. With answer choice E; however, you really have to believe that physical work doesn't count as any form of physical exercise in order to eliminate it.

Answer choice E is the slightly better answer, and as such, <u>it's the correct answer</u>.

***

Let's look at one more question where our job is to find the least bad answer:

<u>PT81 S2 Q22</u>

In a recent study, one group of participants watched video recordings of themselves running on treadmills, and a second group watched recordings of other people running on treadmills. When contacted later, participants in the first group reported exercising, on average, 1 hour longer each day than the other participants. This shows that watching a recording of yourself exercising can motivate you to exercise more.

Which one of the following, if true, most weakens the argument?

A. In another study, people who watched recordings of themselves lifting weights exercised for more time each day than did people who watched recordings of themselves running.
B. Another study's members exhibited an increased willingness to give to charity after hearing stories in which people with whom they identified did so.
C. Participants who were already highly motivated to exercise did not report exercising for any longer each day than they had before the study.
D. In studies of identical twins, participants who observed their twin read overreported by a significant amount how much time they themselves spent reading in the days that followed.
E. A third group of participants who watched recordings of themselves sitting on couches afterwards reported being sedentary for more time each day than did the other participants.

Let's look at this argument from both a logic and structural perspective.

The conclusion seems to be causal in nature. The author believes that watching a recording of yourself can cause you to exercise more.

Can we think of an alternative cause? Perhaps the people who participated in the group that watched themselves were narcissists to begin with? Perhaps they were people who are obsessed with their self image, the kind of people who spend a lot of time looking in the mirror? And people who didn't care about their own self image chose to be in the second group. People who are obsessed with how they look will have higher motivation to workout. Of course, I'm assuming that group selection is voluntary, so I'll admit that it's a little bit far-fetched.

Perhaps examining the argument from a structural perspective will yield more results:

The author cites a study as his supporting premises: people who watched themselves reported exercising more. The conclusion is that watching a recording of yourself can motivate you to actually exercise more.

Notice the glaring gap between the premise and the conclusion. The author goes from "reported exercising more" to "actually exercising more."

There is a potential Type I answer here: people who reported exercising more didn't actually do the exercise: they either lied, or the experience of watching themselves exercise in videos made them over-estimate the amount of time they spent exercising.

> A. *In another study, people who watched recordings of themselves lifting weights exercised for more time each day than did people who watched recordings of themselves running.*

How much did the weightlifters exercise prior to watching recordings of themselves? More or less? We don't know. As a result, the effect of this answer choice is unclear.

> B. *Another study's members exhibited an increased willingness to give to charity after hearing stories in which people with whom they identified did so.*

This answer choice strengthens the argument. Watching similar people do something increased your willingness to do the same thing. So perhaps it's possible that watching yourself exercise will increase your willingness to exercise too.

> C. *Participants who were already highly motivated to exercise did not report exercising for any longer each day than they had before the study.*

In Chapter 5, we practiced matching keywords in answer choices with information from the stimulus. We called this skill "**keyword extraction**." (K in SLAKR)

So who are these "participants who were already highly motivated to exercise?" Are they in the first group or the second group?

Well they can't be in the first group, because the first group did report exercising more. So they must be in the second group, the group that watched other people. So the people watching others were already highly motivated. Whereas the people watching themselves were not motivated.

But we also know that the first group also reported exercising more after watching themselves. They were unmotivated to begin with, but after watching the videos of themselves, reported exercising more. This fits in with the author's reasoning: watching yourself exercise can motivate you to exercise more.

D. In studies of <u>identical twins</u>, participants who observed their twin read overreported by a significant amount how much time they themselves spent reading in the days that followed.

This answer has two things about it that I want to emphasize, one of them I really liked, the other, not so much. I really liked the part about "overreporting." It fits in nicely with our anticipated answer. It weakens the author's movement from "reported increase in exercise" to "exercise more."

The thing I didn't like about this answer is its scope. This answer is about people who watched their identical twins, rather than people who watched themselves. Can watching a person who looks exactly like you have a similar effect as watching yourself?

If you answered yes, then this answer will work. If you answered no, then this answer will be wrong. Let's keep it for now and look at answer choice E.

E. A third group of participants who watched recordings of themselves sitting on couches afterwards reported being sedentary for more time each day than did the other participants.

This answer choice strengthens the author's argument. Watching yourself perform an activity reinforces your behavior.

Ultimately, we have four answers that I'm pretty sure are wrong, and one answer that I'm not too sure about. Since we pick the best answer out of the bunch, it's got to be D. <u>D is the correct answer.</u>

I would have gone back and looked at C and D more carefully, just to make sure I didn't miss anything from C. But ultimately, I would have bit the bullet and selected D.

Two Rarely Seen Weaken Question Variations

EXCEPT Questions

EXCEPT questions are the opposite of regular Weaken Questions. Instead of asking for the answer that *most* weakens the argument, we are looking for the answer choice that *least* weakens the argument.

The good thing about these questions is that the stimulus/argument will usually be easier to comprehend, but the hard thing is that you now have to manually switch up your mode of thinking. It will feel a little weird at times, because you are so used to looking at the answer choices, sensing that a certain selection has no bearing on the argument, and eliminating it. But now, if something truly weakens, you have to eliminate it.

There will be four answer choices that definitely weaken the argument, and one answer choice whose impact is either unclear, irrelevant, or actually strengthening. The correct answer will have no bearing on the argument.

While normal Weaken Questions can have multiple answers that all achieve the "weakening" effect, and we pick the most effective/strongest answer, Weaken EXCEPT questions don't have multiple correct answers.

My habit of tackling Weaken EXCEPT questions is as follows:

- Even before reading the stimulus, remind myself that this is an EXCEPT question.

- When reading the stimulus for the author's argument, try to anticipate *as many* potential ways to weaken the argument as possible. I know that there will be four answers that I need to eliminate, so I try to anticipate as many as I can.

- With the answer choices, there will usually be two to three choices that can be eliminated outright. In other words, I find the strongest answers and cross them out.

- I spend the majority of my time and attention on the remaining two answer choices, try to think about what each of their implications are, and if these answers were true, is there any way in which they can affect the argument? I will also compare them to each other. Find the one that weakens less than the other.

Take a look at 10-1-19, 18-4-23, 23-2-26, 24-2-19, 24-2-20, 25-4-11, 28-1-23, **32-1-17**, **40-3-26**, **48-4-23**, 71-3-21, 89-2-24 for additional practice. The bolded questions deserve special attention, the differences in weakening effect between some of the right and wrong answers are very subtle.

No Argument Stimulus

We have called Strengthen and Weaken Questions the "black sheep" of the Assumption Family for several reasons, one of them being that Strengthen and Weaken Questions sometimes don't even contain an argument. Without an argument, there are no premises and conclusions, only statements of opinion, or just a particular point of view without any support.

As a result, we can no longer anticipate answers by thinking about Type I, Type II, and Type III possibilities. Instead, I will do the following:

- Make sure there is no supporting evidence to the author's statement, If there is, then it becomes a legitimate argument. If there isn't, then I isolate the point that the author is trying to convey.

- I negate the language of this particular statement.

- I go down the list of answer choices and find the answer choice that will do the most in convincing me of the credibility of the negated statement.

Weaken stimuli containing no argument have been rarely seen in recent years, take a look at 18-2-21, **19-2-4**, **26-3-14**, and 47-1-24 for additional practice. Take note of the bolded questions, and make sure you compare answer choices.

13. Weaken

14. Strengthen

LR Perfection   dragontest.org

We have just covered Weaken Questions in the previous chapter, looking at how to analyze a Weaken Question's argument structurally, how the author can use causal and conditional logic to advance their argument, the types of answer choices acceptable for these questions, and how to select the most suitable answer.

Strengthen Questions are the polar opposite of Weaken Questions. All the concepts and knowledge from the previous chapter are still applicable here, with one exception.

Instead of trying to think of ways to poke holes in the author's argument, or to make it less believable; we are now trying to fortify it and make it more believable. In other words, we now have the opposite goal, but the techniques are still the same.

The Strengthen Question Stimulus

Like Weaken Questions, most Strengthen Question stimuli will contain an argument. (Very few questions will contain stimuli that have no arguments, containing an unsupported viewpoint or hypothesis instead: see 44-4-17, 42-2-18, 72-2-23, and 73-2-22.) An argument will contain supporting information and a main conclusion. So dividing the argument into premises and the main conclusion is still our **first** order of action.

The **second** step is still to compare the supporting premises and the main conclusion, and try to anticipate an answer that hurdles the shift between the two.

Remember, in Weaken Questions, our foremost job was to emphasize the reasoning gap that existed between the premises and the conclusion, highlighting it and demonstrating how the existence of this gap prevents us from deriving the conclusion from simply the premises. In Strengthen Questions, our job is to find an answer choice that covers up the gap so it's no longer a liability or hurting the author's argument's validity. We are looking primarily for a piece of connecting information that helps the author's conclusion follow more smoothly from their supporting premises.

Take a look at the following stimulus. Can you locate the gap that exists between the premises and the conclusion? (There's more than one)

PT69 S4 Q23

Botanist: In an experiment, scientists raised domesticated radishes in a field with wild radishes, which are considered weeds. Within several generations, the wild radishes began to show the same flower color as the domesticated ones. This suggests that resistance to pesticides, which is often a genetically engineered trait, would also be passed from domesticated crop plants to their relatives that are considered weeds.

Which one of the following, if true, most strengthens the botanist's argument?

A. It is much easier in principle for genetic traits to be passed from wild plants to their domesticated. relatives than it is for such traits to be passed from the domesticated plant to the wild relative.
B. When the ratio of domesticated radishes to wild radishes in the field increased, the speed with which the flower color passed to the wild radishes also increased.
C. Radishes are not representative of crop plants in general with respect to the ease with which various traits are passed among members of closely related species.
D. The flower color of the domesticated radishes had not been introduced into them via genetic engineering.
E. It is more difficult for flower color to be transferred between domesticated and wild radishes than it is for almost any other trait to be passed between any two similarly related plant species.

Let's take this argument apart structurally:

The conclusion of the argument is the last sentence of the stimulus: *This suggests that resistance to pesticides, which is often a genetically engineered trait, would also be passed from domesticated crop plants to their relatives that are considered weeds.*

Why does the author think *resistance to pesticides* will also pass from *domesticated crops* to *wild crops?* What are the author's premises?

The author uses the results of an experiment to back up the main conclusion. In this study, scientists raised wild and domesticated radishes together, the flowers of newer generations of wild radishes took on the same color as those of domesticated radishes.

This is where we ask ourselves whether there are gaps in the author's reasoning. Are there weaknesses that we need to address to make the author's argument sounder?

There are a few that I can think of: for one, can the results of the experiment be replicated in real life? Second, are different genetically inherited traits easier or harder to pass on? For instance, in humans, we know things like hair color or eye color are easily passed down, but what about rarer traits? What if flower color is something that can be easily passed from domesticated to wild radishes, but resistance to pesticide aren't? Lastly, radish is only one type of crop, even if pesticide resistance can be passed between radishes, does it also apply to other types of crop plants like wheat or barley?

What are some ways in which we can address these gaps in the author's reasoning? We can say that pesticide resistance is a trait that can be just as easily passed on as flower color, or that the experiment's results, although they are conducted only with radishes, can be replicated with other crops. These would be Type I answers.

We can also use Type II or Type III answers to strengthen the author's view, we can say that the experiment is well conducted, for example. This would be a premise helper and a Type III answer choice.

Let's look at the answer choices:

> A. *It is much easier in principle for genetic traits to be passed from wild plants to their domesticated relatives than it is for such traits to be passed from the domesticated plant to the wild relative.*

This answer goes contrary to the author's reasoning. It's saying that "going from wild to domesticated is easier than going from domesticated to wild." So our job is actually harder than we supposed.

> B. *When the ratio of domesticated radishes to wild radishes in the field increased, the speed with which the flower color passed to the wild radishes also increased.*

This answer choice is basically saying that "more domesticated radishes, faster colors passed on." Does this strengthen our argument? Remember our argument, in its crudest form is that "if it works for radish flower color, it will work for crop pesticide resistance."

It addresses neither the gap nor the conclusion, so it's neither a Type I nor II answer choice. Is it a Premise Helper then? Not really: we already know that flower color is a trait that passes from domesticated to wild radishes. The speed of the process is irrelevant.

> C. *Radishes are <u>not</u> representative of crop plants in general with respect to the ease with which various traits are passed among members of closely related species.*

This answer choice is the opposite of what we want.

D. *The flower color of the domesticated radishes had not been introduced into them via genetic engineering.*

This answer choice highlights one of the potential gaps in the argument. Pesticide resistance is introduced via genetic engineering, but flower color isn't. So maybe only traits that aren't introduced via genetic engineering can be passed from domesticated species to wild species. It weakens the argument.

E. *It is more difficult for flower color to be transferred between domesticated and wild radishes than it is for almost any other trait to be passed between any two similarly related plant species.*

This answer, while not perfect, strengthens our argument. According to this answer choice, most traits can be passed from domesticated to wild crops. Because flower color passed between radishes, and this is one of the hardest processes.

The answer has a little bit of weakness to it: we know flower color passage is harder than most other traits, but do these traits include pesticide resistance? We don't know. It doesn't guarantee the outcome of our conclusion. But since we are faced with a Strengthen/Weaken Question, and not a SA Question, answers that leave something to be desired are ok, as long as there are no better alternatives. <u>E is the correct answer choice.</u>

Difficult Trait #1: Hard-to-Discover Reasoning Gap

As you have probably figured out by now, thinking about the gap between the premises and the conclusion is absolutely crucial to ALL Assumption Family questions. Even though sometimes the correct answer won't address this gap, and in some extreme cases the stimulus contains no gap, the majority of questions can be solved this way. The hardest questions, however, will often obscure the connection between the premise and the conclusion so that the gap we are looking for isn't visible at first glance:

PT64 S3 Q17

Science writer: The deterioration of cognitive faculties associated with Alzheimer's disease is evidently caused by the activities of microglia – the brain's own immune cells. For one thing, this deterioration can be slowed by some anti-inflammatory drugs, such as acetylsalicylic acid. Furthermore, patients with Alzheimer's are unable to eliminate the protein BA from the brain, where it accumulates and forms deposits. The microglia attack these protein deposits by releasing poisons that destroy surrounding healthy brain cells, thereby impairing the brain's cognitive functions.

Which one of the following, if true, most helps to support the science writer's argument?

A. The inability of Alzheimer's patients to eliminate the protein BA from the brain is due to a deficiency in the brain's immune system.
B. Acetylsalicylic acid reduces the production of immune cells in the brain.
C. The activity of microglia results in a decrease in the buildup of protein deposits in the brain.
D. The protein BA directly interferes with the cognitive functions of the brain.
E. Immune reactions by microglia occur in certain diseases of the brain other than Alzheimer's.

The conclusion of this argument is the first sentence of the stimulus: *The deterioration of cognitive faculties associated with Alzheimer's disease is evidently caused by the activities of microglia – the brain's own immune cells.*

The conclusion is about a causal relationship, microglia being the *cause,* and the deterioration of cognitive faculties being the *effect.* In notational form, microglia ⇒ cognitive deterioration. For now, let's focus on finding ways to strengthen the argument structurally. We'll look at the argument's logical aspects after.

There are two premises in this argument. They are two independent premises, and not a premise and an intermediate conclusion.

- Premise 1: *For one thing, this deterioration can be slowed by some anti-inflammatory drugs, such as acetylsalicylic acid.*
- Premise 2: *The microglia attack these protein deposits by releasing poisons that destroy surrounding healthy brain cells, thereby impairing the brain's cognitive functions.*

Now our job is to see if there is a gap between Premise 1 and the Conclusion, as well as between Premise 2 and the Conclusion.

Premise 2 is a causal relationship as well, the microglia attacking BA protein deposits causes surrounding healthy brain cells to be destroyed as well, which in turn causes the brain's cognitive functions to be impaired. In notational form: microglia attack BA protein ⇒ healthy cells destroyed ⇒ cognitive impairment.

Is there a gap between Premise 2 and the Conclusion? I'm not too sure. Premise 2 talks about "cognitive impairment," while the Conclusion is about "cognitive deterioration." Maybe the author is talking about the same thing, just worded differently. But if he isn't, then we can argue that "cognitive impairment caused by the microglia leads to cognitive deterioration." This would fully bridge the gap between Premise 2 and the Conclusion.

The relationship between Premise 1 and the Conclusion is not as straightforward. The Premise is causal in nature: anti-inflammatory drugs lead to decreased deterioration. So if anti-inflammatory drugs lead to decreased deterioration, why does the microglia cause deterioration? What isn't the author telling us here?

It must be that anti-inflammatory drugs suppress or target the microglia. If anti-inflammatory drugs target the microglia and slow down the decreased deterioration, then we can reasonably infer that the microglia is at least partially responsible for cognitive deterioration.

So there we have it: two potential Type I answer choices:

1. Anti-inflammatory drugs target the activities of the microglia.
2. Cognitive impairment leads to cognitive deterioration.

We can also have potential Type II and III answer choices as well. Since this argument is causal in nature, we can strengthen this argument by affirming the causal relationship between the microglia and cognitive deterioration. (We will look at how to strengthen a causal relationship in detail later in this chapter.)

In the author's second premise *"The microglia attack these protein deposits by releasing poisons that destroy surrounding healthy brain cells, thereby impairing the brain's cognitive functions,"* we can potentially reinforce the premise by suggesting that the healthy cells destroyed by the microglia are in fact responsible for the brain's cognitive functions. Because if these cells were responsible for one's motor functions, the microglia would be responsible for movement impairment, not cognitive impairment. This would constitute a Premise Helper, a Type III answer.

Let's now look at the answer choices:

A.   The inability of Alzheimer's patients to eliminate the protein BA from the brain is due to a deficiency in the brain's immune system.

This answer choice is causal also, but it's talking about a different cause/effect relationship than the one with which we are concerned. We know from Premise 2 that microglia attacks these BA protein deposits and also inadvertently attacks healthy cells, leading to cognitive impairment. This answer is explaining why we have BA deposits in the first place. It has no bearing on the argument.

B.   Acetylsalicylic acid reduces the production of immune cells in the brain.

This looks similar to what we devised to connect Premise 1 and the Conclusion. We wanted something that would say "anti-inflammatory drugs target the microglia" and this is what the answer is trying to convey. Acetylsalicylic acid is a type of anti-inflammatory drug, and the microglia is the brain's immune cell. This answer choice hurdles the gap between Premise 1 and the Conclusion. It is also one of the answers that we had in mind. This is the correct answer.

C.   The activity of microglia results in a decrease in the buildup of protein deposits in the brain.

This repeats what we already know from the argument. Remember, it's NOT the protein deposits that cause cognitive impairment. Microglia attacks the protein deposits and kills healthy cells in the process. That's what causes the impairment. This answer doesn't hurt the argument, but it doesn't help it either.

D.   The protein BA directly interferes with the cognitive functions of the brain.

This answer weakens our argument. We know that the microglia attacks BA protein. If BA protein interferes with the brain's cognitive functions, the microglia should be helping improve the brain's cognitive functions if this answer is true.

E.   Immune reactions by microglia occur in certain diseases of the brain other than Alzheimer's.

So the microglia has effects on the brain in other diseases, let's say Parkinson's. What is our argument? What is our conclusion? Microglia is responsible for cognitive deterioration in Alzheimer patients. This answer is out of scope.

As we can see from the previous question, it would be very difficult to anticipate the correct answer, or to recognize it when we saw it, unless we had a clear grasp of the argument's structure. So divide the stimulus's argument into supporting premises and the main conclusion and think about the relationship between the two.

Type II and III Answer Choices

The last two questions that we looked at both had the correct answer choice address a weakness/gap in the author's move from premise to conclusion. These answers are my favorites as they are the most frequently occurring correct answer choice types in Weaken/Strengthen Questions. However, as we have seen in the previous chapter, answer choices that independently make the author's conclusion more believable (Type II) and answer choices that strengthen the author's premises (Type III) are also acceptable. Both are less frequent occurrences, and Type III answer choices have only appeared a few times in all of LSAT history.

There were a few questions that I got wrong when I was preparing for the LSAT because I was so fixated on finding a Type I answer that I ignored the Type II and III alternatives. So in order to remedy this, I constantly reminded myself to be mentally flexible enough to be open to different types of answer choices, and don't eliminate an answer choice just because it didn't address the gap in the argument.

***

PT60 S3 Q21

Safety consultant: Judged by the number of injuries per licensed vehicle, minivans are the safest vehicles on the road. However, in carefully designed crash tests, minivans show no greater ability to protect their occupants than other vehicles of similar size do. Thus, the reason minivans have such a good safety record is probably not that they are inherently safer than other vehicles, but rather that they are driven primarily by low-risk drivers.

Which one of the following, if true, most strengthens the safety consultant's argument?

    A.   When choosing what kind of vehicle to drive, low risk drivers often select a kind that they know to perform particularly well in crash tests.
    B.   Judged by the number of accidents per licensed vehicle, minivans are no safer than most other kinds of vehicles are.
    C.   Minivans tend to carry more passengers at any time than do most other vehicles.
    D.   In general, the larger a vehicle is, the greater the ability to protect its occupants.
    E.   Minivans generally have worse braking and emergency handling capabilities than other vehicles of similar size.

In this stimulus, we find the often-seen Phenomenon (Effect) → Explanation (Cause) reasoning pattern. The phenomenon is that minivans are the safest vehicles on the road. Why? Because the drivers are low risk.

This argument contains an intermediate conclusion, the structure of the argument is Premise → Intermediate Conclusion → Main Conclusion.

The author cites crash test results that show minivans aren't more protective of occupants than other cars, which means minivans are not inherently safer than other vehicles.

If minivans aren't safer than other vehicles, it must be because drivers are risk averse that the number of injuries are lower for minivans than for other vehicles.

So this is what we have as an argument:

Why are minivans the safest vehicles on the road?

Premise: Minivans are not more protective of occupants
↓
Intermediate Conclusion: Minivans are not safer than other vehicles
↓
Main Conclusion: Minivans are driven by low-risk drivers

The main gap that we should examine first is between the Intermediate Conclusion and the Main Conclusion. While we have always emphasized that Type I answers address the gap between the supporting premises and the conclusion, an intermediate conclusion, while performing the role of conclusion in relation to the argument's premise, **is STILL considered a premise in relation to the main conclusion.**

So let's see if any gaps need to be addressed between the IC and the MC:

If minivans are not safer than other vehicles, is driver profile the only alternative explanation for their safety numbers?

Is it possible that minivans are used primarily for urban commutes, and hence primarily driven on well policed city roads? Or maybe because of urban traffic, you can't go very fast, hence the low incidence of injuries? If you have a 4x4, and go off-roading frequently, even if you are a careful driver, you can still have a higher chance of injury from accidents than a minivan that is used to pick up and drop off kids from school.

So to strengthen the argument, we can try something that eliminates this possibility, we can say that "the environment in which a vehicle is driving is NOT a significant factor in causing injury to occupants in the event of a crash."

Or even better, we can try something like "how safe a vehicle is can be determined by two factors: it's inherent safety and driver habit." This eliminates the gap all together, because it tells us that if it's not because the vehicle is safer inherently, the safety numbers can only be explained by risk averse drivers.

Both of these would be good Type I answers.

A Type II answer would directly strengthen the idea that minivans are safe because of safe drivers, our main conclusion. We could say that "parents with children, statistically the most risk averse of all drivers, overwhelmingly purchase minivans to ferry their families around."

A rarer Type III answer would strengthen the argument's premises or minimize any gaps that we find outside the main conclusion. That can mean either the Premise or the Intermediate Conclusion in this case. Is there a gap between our Premise and Intermediate Conclusion? The author argues that because minivans didn't perform better in crash testing, they aren't inherently more safe. Are there additional features like blind spot monitoring, early warning radar, or auto hi-beams that can make a vehicle safer? Maybe minivans don't perform better in actual crashes, but they are so loaded up with features that they just avoid getting into accidents. This is a potential objection that we can make.

So to strengthen our argument, we can also eliminate such a possibility.

A Good Habit to Have When Examining Answer Choices

Another problem I had specifically with Strengthen/Weaken Questions is this:

In a lot of question types like Flaw and SA, I will have a pretty good idea of what the correct answer will look like. So by the time I get to the answer choices, the job is simple. I'm here to read the answer choices carefully and eliminate answer choices with problematic keywords in them.

With Weaken/Strengthen answer choices, because there are so many ways to weaken/strengthen, I won't have as clear an idea of what exactly it is that I'm looking for. So I end up getting lost in the answer choices, get carried away by the possibilities, or end up forgetting key information from the stimulus.

Many students mistakenly believe that tackling LR questions should be a linear process: you read the stimulus, you try to think of an answer, you go down the list and pick the best one.

But what helped me immensely was to **refer back** to the stimulus whenever I'm unsure about an answer choice. We put this tactic to good use in SA Questions and NA Questions, where we plugged the answer choice back into the author's argument to see if it would constitute a valid SA answer, or negated it to see if it would hurt the conclusion in NA Questions.

I'm here to tell you that in Strengthen/Weaken Questions, think about the implications of answer choices **in conjunction** with the information already given us in the stimulus.

In the previous chapter we talked about asking ourselves "**so what**" when confronted with an answer choice. This is in the same vein and in many ways a step up from that. Combine the information from the stimulus with what is being said in the answer choices and see where it leads us.

Difficult Trait #2: For answers with unclear implications, combine it with the argument to see how the main conclusion is affected.

> A.   *When choosing what kind of vehicle to drive, low-risk drivers often select a kind that they know to perform particularly well in crash tests.*

Let's practice the habit we just talked about. Let's try to relate this answer choice to the information from the stimulus:

Which vehicles performed particularly well in crash tests? We know it's not the minivans. So it must be some other cars. That means low risk drivers don't have a preference for minivans but some other vehicle. Where does this answer lead us? It's actually weakening the author's conclusion: minivan drivers aren't more low-risk than other drivers.

B. Judged by the number of accidents per licensed vehicle, minivans are no safer than most other kinds of vehicles are.

This answer choice is very tricky. On the surface, it seems like it's echoing our Intermediate Conclusion, which states that "minivans are not <u>inherently</u> safer than other vehicles." But be careful! Being "no safer" is NOT the same thing as being "not inherently safer." Being "no safer" can be due to various reasons, it can be because minivans aren't inherently safer, or it can be because of drivers, the roads driven on, etc.

Let's develop this answer choice a bit further: minivans are no safer than most other vehicles judged by number of accidents. Let's say per 100,000 miles driven, a typical Corvette gets into 5 accidents. A Toyota Sienna Minivan also gets into 5 accidents. Now all of a sudden it seems much less likely that the minivan driver is safer than the Corvette driver, right?

We also know from the stimulus that minivan occupants suffer less injuries. If the number of accidents are the same between the Corvette and the Sienna, 5 each, but only one injury for the Sienna but three for the Corvette, isn't it possible that the Sienna is the safer vehicle? This actually runs contrary to our Intermediate Conclusion.

C. Minivans tend to carry more passengers at any time than do most other vehicles.

More passengers, but less injuries, could be because the vehicles are safer, or that the drivers are more risk averse. This is one of those answers that is **open to interpretation**, an especially tricky variant we talked about in the previous chapter.

D. In general, the larger a vehicle is, the greater the ability to protect its occupants.

Referring back to the stimulus pays off again here, remember our study is about vehicles of a similar size. So all this answer can really tell us is that maybe minivans are safer than sedans but less safe than RVs. Why do they have such a low number of injuries? If a minivan is of the same size as a cargo van, which one is safer? We don't know. Even if the minivan is safer, is it due to the driver's habits? We don't know either.

E. Minivans generally have worse braking and emergency handling capabilities than other vehicles of similar size.

This answer makes us more inclined to believe that minivans aren't inherently safer than other vehicles. So their safety numbers aren't due to the vehicle itself, making it more likely to be due to a driver's aversion to risky driving. This is a Type III answer and <u>the correct one</u>.

Approaching Strengthen Questions from a Logic Perspective:

Conditional arguments have been extremely rare in Strengthen Questions, so we will focus our attention on causal logic instead here.

Just like Weaken Questions, a lot of Strengthen Questions will contain elements of causal reasoning. So it is crucial that we keep also approach the question by analyzing its logic. In the last few examples, we analyzed the argument by breaking it down into its premise and conclusion components, approaching them from a structural perspective. Let's now try to strengthen an argument by strengthening the causal logic behind it.

Remember back in Weaken Questions, we can weaken a causal relationship by proposing alternative causes, or suggesting that the causal relationship is actually reversed.

To strengthen a causal argument, we can simply do the reverse: we suggest that the causal relationship ISN'T reversed, or that there is NO alternative cause.

So if we had a causal relationship, A ⇒ B

To WEAKEN it, we could suggest that:

- There is an alternative cause: C ⇒ B
- The causal relationship is actually reversed: B ⇒ A
- A third cause C is responsible for causing both A and B: C ⇒ A + B

To STRENGTHEN it, we could suggest that:

- There is NO alternative cause: C̶ ̶⇒̶ ̶B̶
- The causal relationship is NOT reversed: B̶ ̶⇒̶ ̶A̶
- A third cause C is NOT responsible for causing both A and B: C̶ ̶⇒̶ ̶A̶ ̶+̶ ̶B̶

***

Of course, in the hardest Strengthen Questions containing causal reasoning, the cause-and-effect relationship might not be so obvious, as we can see in the following question:

Difficult Trait #3: When we spot causal reasoning in an author's argument, always think of ways in which we can strengthen that causal relationship.

<u>PT17 S3 Q12</u>

One year ago a local government initiated an anti-smoking advertising campaign in local newspapers, which it financed by imposing a tax on cigarettes of 20 cents per pack. One year later, the number of people in the locality who smoke cigarettes had declined by 3 percent. Clearly, what was said in the advertisement had an effect, although a small one, on the number of people in the locality who smoke cigarettes.

Which one of the following, if true, most helps to strengthen the argument?

    A.   Residents of the locality have not increased their use of other tobacco products such as snuff and chewing tobacco since the campaign went into effect.
    B.   A substantial number of cigarette smokers in the locality who did not quit smoking during the campaign now smoke less than they did before it began.
    C.   Admissions to the local hospital for chronic respiratory ailments were down by 15 percent one year after the campaign began.
    D.   Merchants in the locality responded to the local tax by reducing the price at which they sold cigarettes by 20 cents per pack.
    E.   Smokers in the locality had incomes that on average were 25% lower than those of non-smokers.

Let's look at this question from a causal logic perspective first. I tried approaching this question from both a structural perspective and a causal logic perspective, and it was much easier to solve the question by thinking about the causal logic behind the argument. That's why we've emphasized the habit of thinking about the type of logic, if any, that's behind an argument in Strengthen and Weaken Questions. If the argument contains conditional (rare) or causal (common) reasoning/logic, then it can help immensely to think about the ways in which we can strengthen or weaken conditional and causal reasoning.

The conclusion of the argument is definitely causal in nature: the government's anti-smoking ads have *caused* a decrease in the number of smokers. Once we have realized this, the different ways in which we can potentially strengthen a causal argument should automatically come to mind, the most commonly seen is **the elimination of an alternative cause**.

Simply put, by rejecting other potential causes, we are narrowing down the likelihood that the cause advocated by our author stands. Is there an alternative cause that you can think of in this case?

An alternative cause is hiding in plain sight in this argument. How did the government finance its advertising campaign? It did so by raising the tax on cigarettes. Would it be possible that the decrease in the number of smokers is due to the increase in tobacco prices, rather than the government's ad campaign?

Thus, in order to strengthen the author's argument, an answer that tells us the decrease in number of smokers is NOT due to the increase in tobacco prices would suffice.

Thinking about this question from a structural perspective is somewhat more difficult. In the argument's premises, the author presents three separate events (government raised taxes on tobacco, government ran an advertisement campaign against smoking, number of smokers decreased by 3% one year later), and concludes that there is a causal connection between the second and third event in the conclusion.

If we had been too fixated on the connection between the advertising campaign and the decrease in the number of smokers we might have easily overlooked this alternative possibility staring at us right in the face. I certainly did the first time I attempted this question. So the lesson here is to be flexible in our approach to Strengthen/Weaken Questions.

 I typically start by analyzing the argument's structure, but if I spot causation in the argument's conclusion, I will think about the ways we can strengthen a causal argument as well.

> A. *Residents of the locality have not increased their use of other tobacco products such as snuff and chewing tobacco since the campaign went into effect.*

This answer choice can potentially help our argument if we look at it this way: the 3% who stopped smoking didn't turn to other means of satisfying their tobacco cravings, so the decrease is real. But our argument is about cigarettes and the number of people who stopped smoking cigarettes. If the argument/conclusion was about tobacco consumption, this would be a more suitable answer. I would keep this answer choice as a potential contender and keep on going.

> B. *A substantial number of cigarette smokers in the locality who did not quit smoking during the campaign now smoke less than they did before it began.*

This answer, on the surface, seems to be helping the author's reasoning. People in general are smoking less, the advertisement must be working, right? However, remember the exact wording of the conclusion: the advertisement having an effect on the *number of people who smoked cigarettes.* The author's argument is strictly about the number of smokers who no longer smoke. Even if you are smoking less, you are still counted as a smoker.

When there is an attractive answer that I'm not so sure about, I like to think about its **implications** and **compare that to the exact wording of the conclusion**. It's a skill that has helped me immensely in the most difficult Strengthen/Weaken Questions, we will practice it later on in the chapter.

    C. *Admissions to the local hospital for chronic respiratory ailments were down by 15 percent one year after the campaign began.*

This answer also seems to be helping our premise: less smokers = less respiratory diseases. However, it still doesn't address the most crucial aspect of our argument: the causal relationship between government advertisement and a net decrease in the number of smokers. I think this answer choice is better than A or B, but still not something I particularly like.

    D. *Merchants in the locality responded to the local tax by reducing the price at which they sold cigarettes by 20 cents per pack.*

This is where the habit we had stressed about earlier comes in handy. Remember we talked about asking "**so what**" when new information is presented in the answer choices? We also talked about **connecting this information to what we already know from the stimulus** in order to fully explore its implications.

If merchants reduced the price of cigarettes by the exact amount of increase in taxes, then there is no net increase in the cost of cigarettes, which means a price hike cannot be responsible for the decrease in the number of smokers.

Remember, our argument presents two separate events and concludes that the relationship between them is causal. This answer choice eliminates the most tempting alternative cause out there. It is the most direct way to strengthen a causal argument. <u>This is the correct answer.</u>

    E. *Smokers in the locality had incomes that on average were 25% lower than those of non-smokers.*

What happens if smokers had lower income? Would they be more susceptible to quit smoking if cigarettes were more expensive? This answer can potentially weaken our argument, if it did have an effect.

Ultimately, causal reasoning appears very frequently in both Strengthen and Weaken Questions, so always remember to approach such a question not just from a **structural** perspective (S in SLAKR), but also a **logical** perspective (L in SLAKR).

Comparing Answer Choices

In the last question, we saw first handedly how several answer choices were contenders until the last minute. In other words, there were answer choices that we couldn't eliminate outright, because they had the potential of having a strengthening effect on the argument. We saw this repeatedly in Weaken Questions, and it's only become more frequent in more recent PTs. Thus, our approach to Strengthen answer choices is the same as our approach to Weaken ones: we try to fully think about the implications of each answer choice, how they affect the argument, and choose the strongest, most direct answer choice vis-a-vis the others.

PT15 S3 Q23

Asbestos, an almost indestructible mineral once installed as building insulation, poses no health risk unless the asbestos is disturbed and asbestos fibers are released into the environment. Since removing asbestos from buildings disturbs it, thereby releasing asbestos fibers, the government should not require removal of all asbestos insulation.

Which of the following, if true, most strengthens the argument?

    A. Asbestos poses far less risk to health than does smoking, drug and alcohol abuse, improper diet, or lack of exercise.
    B. Asbestos can pose a health threat to workers who remove it without wearing required protective gear.
    C. Some kinds of asbestos, when disturbed, pose greater health risks than do other kinds.
    D. Asbestos is inevitably disturbed by building renovations or building demolition.
    E. Much of the time, removed asbestos is buried in landfills and forgotten, with no guarantee that it will not be disturbed again.

This argument is not complicated. Basically, the author is saying that the disturbance and release of asbestos leads to health risks. (This information is presented in **conditional** format and in the first sentence of the stimulus: Health Risk → Disturbed + Released.) The second sentence of the argument is **causal** in nature, the author says that *removing asbestos* causes the aforementioned disturbance and release.

So always be careful of elements of both causal and conditional reasoning that are sprinkled throughout arguments!

The author finally concludes that *the government should not require removal of all asbestos insulation.*

The gap between the premises and the conclusion is rather straightforward to decipher, the author argues that *because removing asbestos leads to something that could be a health risk, the government shouldn't do it.*

So a good Type I answer would tell us something along the lines of "the government shouldn't order anything that could lead to health risks."

Alternatively, we also have to keep our mind open for Type II or Type III answers that tell us why asbestos removal is a bad idea.

> A. *Asbestos poses far less risk to health than does smoking, drug and alcohol abuse, improper diet, or lack of exercise.*

This answer is kind of telling us that asbestos is not that dangerous after all, many things that people regularly do are much more dangerous. We want an answer that tells us the government shouldn't remove asbestos, or that the removal of asbestos is a bad idea. Furthermore, the answer doesn't really tell us how risky things like smoking, improper diet, or lack of exercise are, so this comparison is incomplete.

> B. *Asbestos can pose a health threat to workers who remove it without wearing required protective gear.*

I held on to this answer initially. It does suggest that asbestos can pose a risk. However, remember how we have repeatedly said to be careful of answer choices that can be interpreted in a multitude of ways? Answers that are open to interpretation are *usually* wrong answers. I can say that a significant number of workers don't wear protective gear, and this answer would *strengthen* the author's argument; whereas if I said that only a negligible number of workers don't wear required protective gear, then this might be interpreted as a *weaken* answer.

Beware of answer choices that are **open to interpretation** and can be construed in diametrically opposing ways! Don't bring in your own assumptions into your understanding of an answer choice.

> C. *Some kinds of asbestos, when disturbed, pose greater health risks than do other kinds.*

This answer, on the surface, helps to strengthen the argument. If we plug this back into the author's argument, and link this answer choice with the conclusion, we get this: "*some kinds of asbestos pose greater health risks than others, so the government shouldn't require the removal of all asbestos.*"

But there is something problematic about this answer choice: what this answer is really saying is basically "not all asbestos are equally risky." As such, it isn't telling us much. Remember we did mention to look suspiciously upon answer choices whose effects on the argument/conclusion aren't definitive.

> D. *Asbestos is <u>inevitably</u> disturbed by building <u>renovations</u> or building <u>demolition.</u>*

This is the most commonly selected wrong answer, and the students who have selected this answer probably haven't mastered one of the fundamental skills that we have taught in this book: **Keyword Extraction** from answer choices (K in SLAKR). If we paid attention to three keywords in this answer choice, we would come to realize that this is actually a Weaken answer.

Inevitably: This is telling us that no matter what we do, asbestos is disturbed.

Building Renovations and Building Demolition: Remember our stimulus is talking about *removing asbestos from buildings.* Here we are talking about two different things.

If asbestos is *inevitably* disturbed during *renovations* and *demolitions,* where does that lead us? Unless we never renovate or demolish buildings again, asbestos disturbance is unavoidable. So this answer is basically telling us that no matter what we do, asbestos will eventually be disturbed. So should the government remove it? The answer is unclear: some will say we should remove it, better now than later, when it's sure to cause harm; and perhaps some will say "what's the point?" The disturbance is inevitable anyways.

> E. *Much of the time, removed asbestos is buried in landfills and forgotten, with no guarantee that it will not be disturbed again.*

This answer is worded weakly, and that's grounds for suspicion. However, since every answer we've had so far except for Answer Choice A all left us more confused than ever, we should not be quick to eliminate this answer either.

What can we gather from this answer choice? This answer tells us that there is the risk of re-disturbance with removed asbestos. We also know from the stimulus that the disturbance of asbestos is a health risk, so combining that with this answer, we can say with relative certainty that *much of the time, asbestos removal can lead to increased health risks.*

The second thing I didn't particularly like was the phrase "much of the time." How much time is much? Unlike terms like "some" or "most", there aren't any quantitative guidelines for "much." I like to think of "much" to mean "many" or "a significant amount." In that sense, what this answer is essentially saying is that "removing asbestos can be a significant factor in causing health risks."

Now we come to the hardest part of the answer selection process, we have four options to contend with: B, C, D, and E. Let's look at them in conjunction:

Answer Choice:	B	C	D	E
Issues:	Answer choice open to interpretation	Doesn't have a definitive effect on our argument/conclusion	Effect on our argument/conclusion is unclear	Answer choice effect is weak/uncertain
	We don't know how many workers don't wear safety equipment	We know some are riskier than others, but is it risky enough to stop us from removing it?	Since disturbance is inevitable, should we remove it before it's too late?	Removing asbestos can lead to further disturbance, but how likely is it?
	Can potentially strengthen, but can also weaken		Or there's no point removing it in the first place?	How much is "much of the time?"

Answer choice E, at the end of the day, has a small, but perceptive and definitive effect on our conclusion. Removing asbestos can be forgotten, and it can be disturbed again. So the increase in risk is definitely there. It may be a miniscule effect on our conclusion, but it is telling us that the risk of asbestos disturbance is increased, and that's why we shouldn't remove it.

In terms of preference, I would say that E > D > B > C > A. So we go with E as our final answer.

E is the correct answer.

***

PT71 S1 Q12

Climatologist: Over the coming century, winter temperatures are likely to increase in the Rocky Mountains due to global warming. This will cause a greater proportion of precipitation to fall as rain instead of snow. Therefore, the mountain snowpack will probably melt more rapidly and earlier in the season, leading to greater spring flooding and less storable water to meet summer demands.

Which one of the following, if true, most strengthens the climatologist's argument?

A. Global warming will probably cause a substantial increase in the average amount of annual precipitation in the Rocky Mountains over the coming century.
B. In other mountainous regions after relatively mild winters, the melting of snowpacks has led to greater spring flooding and less storable water, on average, than in those mountainous regions after colder winters.
C. On average, in areas of the Rocky Mountains in which winters are relatively mild, there is less storable water to meet summer demands than there is in areas of the Rocky Mountains that experience colder winters.
D. On average, in the regions of the world with the mildest winters, there is more spring flooding and less storable water than in regions of the world with much colder winters.
E. The larger a mountain snowpack is, the greater the amount of spring flooding it is likely to be responsible for producing.

Let's take the argument apart: both the premises and the conclusion are causal in nature. Let's see what gap is there between the two and come up with an answer that can surmount this gap.

- Premises: *Over the coming century, winter temperatures are likely to increase in the Rocky Mountains due to global warming. This will cause a greater proportion of precipitation to fall as rain instead of snow.*

In causal form:

Global Warming ⇒ Winter Temperature Increase in the Rockies ⇒ Higher Proportion of Rain vs. Snow

- Conclusion: *Therefore, the mountain snowpack will probably melt more rapidly and earlier in the season, leading to greater spring flooding and less storable water to meet summer demands.*

Earlier and more Rapid Melting of Snowpack ⇒ Greater Spring Flooding + Less Storable Water

Basically we want an answer choice that would reinforce the linkage between the Premise and the Conclusion, and/or reaffirm the causal relationship stated in the conclusion.

A. *Global warming will probably cause a <u>substantial increase</u> in the average <u>amount of annual precipitation</u> in the Rocky Mountains over the coming century.*

We have to be aware of the precise concepts discussed in the stimulus, so that we are not tricked by subtle shifts in answer choices. The stimulus talked about a *greater proportion of precipitation to fall as rain instead of snow.* In other words, if previously, the ratio of snow to rain was 50/50, now it's 70/30. This answer is talking about the total amount, and since precipitation includes snow and rain, we still do not know if that increase is due to more rain or snow, or both are increasing at the same rate.

B. *In other mountainous regions after relatively mild winters, the melting of snowpacks has <u>led to</u> greater spring flooding and less storable water, on average, than in those mountainous regions after colder winters.*

What I liked most about this answer choice is that it reaffirms the *causal* relationship stated in the conclusion: snowpack melting ⇒ greater spring flooding + less storable water.

What I wished it had talked about also are two-fold: one, in the stimulus, the author thinks the *earlier* and *more rapid* melting of snow will lead to greater flooding and less storable water; in this answer choice it's only about the melting of snowpacks after mild winters. If it had talked about mild winters leading to earlier and more rapid melting of snow as well, it would have been even better.

Two, I wish it had addressed the gap between the premise and the conclusion. There is a gap between how a greater proportion of precipitation falling as rain will lead to earlier and more rapid snow melting. I suppose it could be common sense that if the winter was warmer, and it rained more than it snowed, existing snow would melt faster and earlier, but still it would have been nice to cover this in the answer.

In short, this answer connects the premise to the main conclusion *partially.* It links "mild winters," a concept that appears in the premises, with the conclusion. It also strengthens the causal relationship in the conclusion. There were shortcomings to this answer choice, but I would leave it as a contender and see if I can spot a better answer choice.

C. *On average, in areas of the Rocky Mountains in which winters are relatively mild, there is less storable water to meet summer demands than there is in areas of the Rocky Mountains that experience colder winters.*

This answer also strengthens, compared to the previous answer, it has one thing going for it and two things going against it. This answer is also talking about the Rocky Mountains, which is also what the stimulus is talking about, while answer choice B is a statement about other mountainous regions. So this is probably more relevant.

However, this answer is describing a *correlation*, while the previous answer choice is restating the *causation* that also appears in the argument's conclusion. A correlation could mean causation, but it doesn't have to be, so the previous answer choice is a more direct way to strengthen the causality that was stated in the conclusion.

Another issue I had with this answer choice was that it only covers the first part of the conclusion, it doesn't talk about greater spring flooding. Answer choice B, however, does talk about this.

So if I were to choose between B and C, I would go with B.

> D. *On average, in the regions of the world with the mildest winters, there is more spring flooding and less storable water than in regions of the world with much colder winters.*

This answer also strengthens, but even less so than C. It's also stating a *correlation*, when what we really want is *causation*. It is also less relevant than either B or C as it's just talking about regions with mild winters, not even mountainous regions.

This answer has both B and C's issues, but none of their strengths. My money is still on B.

> E. *The larger a mountain snowpack is, the greater the amount of spring flooding it is likely to be responsible for producing.*

This answer runs contrary to the reasoning in the stimulus. The argument's author thinks that more rain instead of snow and warm winters would lead to greater flooding. When there's warmer weather, more rain and less snow, the snowpack will be smaller.

B is the correct answer.

Ranking Answer Choices:

As we have seen in the last two questions, and also in the chapter on Weaken Questions, the hardest of these questions cannot be solved by our usual strategy. Some other types of questions and easier questions can be solved by anticipating the answer choice and eliminating answers that contain errors, ultimately allowing us to narrow it down to one. But with Strengthen/Weaken Questions, because there are so many possibilities, we really have to fully explore the possibilities behind each and every answer choice before picking the best one.

Many harder questions will have multiple answer choices that can all strengthen/weaken the argument. So trying to think about each answer **relative** to the other ones will really help us foster the habit of comparing answers. These are the things that I look for in Strengthen/Weaken answer choices:

- The answer choice has a **definitive effect** on the argument/conclusion. Even if the effect is tiny, it still makes the argument more believable for Strengthen Questions, and less believable for Weaken Questions. The correct answer WILL weaken/strengthen the argument, not maybe weaken/strengthen or possibly weaken/strengthen.

- In the same vein, answer choices that are **open to interpretation** are usually wrong. If an answer choice's effect on the argument is entirely dependent on our own assumptions, that's a huge red flag. In other words, a flexible answer choice that strengthens the argument if you believe A, weakens the argument if you believe B, and has no effect if you believe C will most likely be wrong.

- Answer choices that are **worded weakly** are not wrong per se, but I would only select them if there isn't a better alternative. Find the answer choice with the most clearcut, direct effect on the author's argument/conclusion. This involves analyzing the reasoning gap in the argument, as well as the type of logic the author used to advance the argument. Try to think about what an ideal strong answer would look like, and go for the choice that *least* falls short of it.

- Remember what we have said about different types of answer choices. Answer choices which directly links the argument's premise and conclusion are generally speaking, better than answer choices which use independent information to support the argument's conclusion. Both of these will be preferable to answer choices which only strengthen the argument's premises.

Focus on Wording of Conclusion

Another tip I would like to share with you for the times when you are stuck between different answer choices is to refer back to the main conclusion of the argument. There will be times when you are overwhelmed with information on a Strengthen/Weaken Question and are at a loss of what to do. With only 1 - 2 minutes per question you will not be able to think about all the things we have covered in this chapter and the previous one until you have trained your mind to do so with massive amounts of practice. Whenever I feel I'm running around in circles, or just getting confused, **I refocus my attention on the Main Conclusion of the author's argument.** I read it slowly and deliberately, and really *think about* the point the author is trying to make.

Difficult Trait #4: When ranking answer choices in terms of desirability, revisit the main conclusion and think about its scope.

<u>PT85 S2 Q18</u>

In grasslands near the Namib Desert there are "fairy circles" –large, circular patches that are entirely devoid of vegetation. Since sand termite colonies were found in every fairy circle they investigated, scientists hypothesize that it is the burrowing activities of these termites that cause the circles to form.

Which one of the following, if true, most supports the scientists' hypothesis?

A. Dying grass plants within newly forming fairy circles are damaged only at the roots.
B. The grasses that grow around fairy circles are able to survive even the harshest and most prolonged droughts in the region.
C. The soil in fairy circles typically has higher water content than the soil in areas immediately outside the circles.
D. Fairy circles tend to form in areas that already have numerous other fairy circles.
E. Species of animals that feed on sand termites are often found living near fairy circles.

Technically, this stimulus contains no argument. There are facts and a hypothesis. Scientists discovered termite colonies near the "fairy circles," so they hypothesized that it must be the termites who are responsible for these circles' formation.

Note the causal logic indicator in the conclusion, *it is the burrowing activities of these termites that caused the circles to form.* So we are looking for an answer choice that tells us it's the termites that caused these circles to form, or an answer choice that eliminates an alternative explanation, such as pesticides.

But this argument isn't just about the relationship between termites and the "fairy circles!" There is a very important keyword in the stimulus's main point:: "burrowing." Yes, the scientists believe it's the termites who are responsible, but not just that, they believe it's the termites' *burrowing activity* that is responsible.

So there's actually two concepts at play here: ideally, we want an answer choice that tells us not only it's the termites who are responsible, but more specifically, it's due to the termites' burrowing.

> A. *Dying grass plants within newly forming fairy circles are damaged only at the roots.*

This answer strengthens the likelihood that it's burrowing that caused the "fairy circles" to form. However, it doesn't specifically mention termites as the ultimate culprit. As such it's not a perfect answer, but that's no grounds for eliminating it. Let's keep it and move on.

> B. *The grasses that grow around fairy circles are able to survive even the harshest and most prolonged droughts in the region.*

This answer also strengthens the causal reasoning in the author's hypothesis. It's ruling out the possibility that the circles formed due to drought. It's eliminating an alternative explanation.

> C. *The soil in fairy circles typically has higher water content than the soil in areas immediately outside the circles.*

This answer is a potential Weaken answer. Perhaps the circles formed due to high water content, and not due to termites?

> D. *Fairy circles tend to form in areas that already have numerous other fairy circles.*

This answer has no effect on the hypothesis. So the "fairy circles" always come in groups, but what created them? The answer doesn't say.

> E. *Species of animals that feed on sand termites are often found living near fairy circles.*

This answer strengthens, somewhat. It's leading us to think that if the predators are around, termites must also be around, so it's more possible that the termites caused the circles.

But remember what we said about answer choices earlier on in the chapter?

Always take the information given in the answer choice and tie that back to the information in the stimulus if you can.

So this answer choice tells us that there are probably termites around these fairy circles. But what does the stimulus tell us? Termite colonies were found in every fairy circle investigated. This answer isn't telling us anything new. It is in fact not as strong as the information already given to us in the stimulus.

A, B, and E were answers that I kept around and therefore required a more careful second look. This is where the habit of focusing on the conclusion/main point of the stimulus comes in. I know that the hypothesis is about "burrowing." The scientists didn't just hypothesize that termites had something to do with the fairy circles, but more specifically, it's the termites' burrowing activities. By focusing on this keyword from the hypothesis, I chose A, which turned out to be the most direct strengthener and the <u>correct answer choice</u>.

This is an example of where zoning in on the exact wording of the conclusion will help us in choosing the more suitable answer choice.

Right Answers can be Imperfect

Just like Weaken Questions, Strengthen Question answer choices can be imperfect, leaving something to be desired. We have repeatedly emphasized the importance of **comparing** answer choices, rather than going down the list and eliminating problematic ones.

Ideally, going through Strengthen/Weaken answer choices, I would make an initial pass, eliminating answer choices which are obviously wrong to me. In the hardest questions, I would be left with maybe two or three attractive selections, and I try to narrow it down to two. Finally, I will think about their relationship to the information already presented in the stimulus, their effects on the argument/conclusion, which one is more direct and which one's effect is more definite. I will also think about what's wrong with these two answer choices, and which answer choice's problems are less glaring.

The correct answer choice having issues of its own has only become more frequent in more recent PTs (PT 70+). So it's crucial to keep this in mind and not be paralyzed by indecision when confronted by such a situation.

***

PT79 S1 Q10

The more sunlight our planet reflects back into space, the cooler the global atmosphere tends to become. Snow and ice reflect much more sunlight back into space than do ocean water or land without snow cover. Therefore, the greater the area of Earth's surface that is covered with snow and ice, the cooler, on average, the global atmosphere is likely to become.

Which one of the following, if true, would most strengthen the argument?

A. Low atmospheric temperatures are required for the formation of clouds that result in snow.
B. Other factors besides the reflectivity of ice and snow affect the cooling of Earth's atmosphere.
C. Ocean water and land heated by sunlight in turn warm Earth's atmosphere.
D. The atmosphere derives most of its heat from the passage of sunlight through it.
E. Lighter colored soil reflects more sunlight back into space than does darker colored soil.

This argument is interesting because it contains correlations, but no obvious causation. The first correlation is in the premise, *more sunlight reflected back into space, cooler the global atmosphere.* The second correlation is embedded in the argument's conclusion, and a little harder to detect: *greater the area of Earth's surface that is covered with snow and ice, the cooler, on average, the global atmosphere is likely to become.*

So if we break down the argument:

- Premise 1: More sunlight reflected back into space ~ Cooler the global atmosphere
- Premise 2: Snow and ice reflect more sunlight than water and land without snow and ice
- Conclusion: More area covered by snow and ice ~ Cooler the global atmosphere

The author's reasoning seems fairly ok to me, there doesn't seem to be a gap between the premises and the conclusion, so let's try to look for a Type II answer first, and if no Type II answers are available, a Type III answer.

   A.   *Low atmospheric temperatures are required for the formation of clouds that result in snow.*

So this answer tells us the atmosphere must already be cold in order for it to snow. What we are looking for is more snow on the ground, colder the atmosphere is likely to become. Although this answer does reaffirm the relationship between cold temperatures and snow, it doesn't directly strengthen the argument's reasoning nor its conclusion.

   B.   *Other factors besides the reflectivity of ice and snow affect the cooling of Earth's atmosphere.*

This answer choice actually weakens our argument. The existence of other factors that are influences on atmospheric temperature complicates things for us. Now we can't say with absolute certainty that the more snow there is on the ground, the cooler the atmosphere will be. Now we have to take additional factors into consideration.

   C.   *Ocean water and land heated by sunlight in turn warm Earth's atmosphere.*

I didn't really like this answer choice at first, and still don't like it now, because it's way too vague and open to interpretation. The water and land mentioned in the answer choice, are they covered by snow, or not? If it's uncovered water and land, then it's a good strengthen answer, because land without snow or ice cover are an additional source of heat for the atmosphere, so the more land and water covered by snow, the less heat there is for the atmosphere. But water and land covered by snow can still be heated by sunlight right? Is the warming effect significantly lessened for land and water with snow and ice cover?

   D.   *The atmosphere derives most of its heat from the passage of sunlight through it.*

This answer actually weakens the argument. We know regular land and water absorbs light, while snow-covered land and water reflect light. So light actually makes a return trip back through the atmosphere. So the atmosphere is warmed twice, once by light hitting the earth, and a second time by light reflected from the snow. Wouldn't it be warmer this way?

   E.   *Lighter colored soil reflects more sunlight back into space than does darker colored soil.*

This answer has two issues. First of all, the argument is talking about snow covered land/water, so even if light colored soil reflects more sunlight, it is irrelevant to our argument. Because for our purposes, the soil, dark or light, would be covered by snow.

Secondly, even if we take this to imply that lighter colored substances reflect more light, hence snow, which is white, will reflect more light than regular earth, it's not really a Type III premise helper either.

Remember in the previous question, PT85 S2 Q18, we eliminated answer choice E because the information we can derive from it is already given to us in the stimulus? **Strengthen answers should go above and beyond what we have already obtained from the stimulus.** This answer choice would only tell us that snow and ice reflect more sunlight than darker materials, and we already know that from the stimulus.

Answer choices that repeat what has already been said in the argument and don't add anything new to the argument are usually wrong in Strengthen/Weaken Questions.

Here comes the most difficult part. We are faced with five answer choices each with their own share of problems. B and D are most likely wrong, A is probably wrong, so that leaves us C and E.

C is open to interpretation, while E mirrors the author's reasoning but doesn't give us anything new. Answer choice C is the only answer that can be *construed* to help the author's argument. Answer choice C is talking about water and land *heated* by sunlight. Perhaps if sunlight is reflected, it no longer heats the earth? If we interpreted this answer choice in this manner, it could pass for a Strengthen answer, but just barely.

Remember we said that answer choices open to interpretation are *usually* wrong? This is a case where we must embrace uncertainty, just like we did in the chapter on Weaken Questions. **In nearly all Strengthen Questions, answer choice C would not be a top contender and likely a wrong answer, but here, it's the best we've got.**

C is the correct answer.

***

PT74 S1 Q17

How the pigment known as Han purple was synthesized by the ancient Chinese of Qin and Han dynasties has puzzled scientists. The Chinese chemists employed the same chemical ingredients used for Han purple in the production of a common type of white glass during that period. Both were produced in the processes that involved subjecting the mixtures to high heat and mixing in lead to decrease the melting temperature. Thus, Han purple was probably discovered by a fortuitous accident during glass production.

Which one of the following, if true, would most strengthen the argument?

A. Chemical analysis shows that most of the known fragments of both Han purple and the white glass were produced within a small geographical radius.
B. Han purple was used for luxury and ceremonial items, whereas the white glass was used to make certain household items.
C. The technique used for producing Han purple was known to very few people during the Qin and Han dynasties.
D. The ingredients used in producing both Han purple and the white glass were easily obtainable during the Qin and Han dynasties.
E. The white glass is found in more surviving artifacts from the Qin and Han dynasties than Han purple is.

In this argument, the author concludes that Han purple was discovered during glass production because the two shared the same chemical ingredients and chemical process.

There is an obvious gap here. Just because two things share the same ingredients and the same manufacturing process, it doesn't necessarily mean one is derived from the other. I mean, vodka, gin, and whiskey are all made from the same ingredient, wheat; and all made from the same process, distillation. But that doesn't mean vodka was discovered while making gin, or gin discovered while making whiskey, right?

We can try to anticipate an answer that closes this gap here. Something that tells us these ingredients or the manufacturing process wasn't used on anything else, or that in the making of porcelain, another pigment was discovered inadvertently, and these two also shared the same ingredients/process.

We must also watch for Type II and Type III answers that make the conclusion and premises more believable.

> A. *Chemical analysis shows that most of the known fragments of both Han purple and the white glass were produced within a small geographical radius.*

This answer strengthens the connection between Han purple and white glass, but it's far from definite or direct. Just because it's made in close proximity, doesn't mean the discovery of one derived from the other. It's a feeble strengthener at best, but let's hold unto it for now.

> B. *Han purple was used for luxury and ceremonial items, whereas the white glass was used to make certain household items.*

This answer weakens the likelihood that Han purple was discovered during the creation of white glass. The consumers, and perhaps the artisans too, of these two items belonged to different social groups.

> C. *The technique used for producing Han purple was known to very few people during the Qin and Han dynasties.*

This answer also weakens the conclusion. If only a few people knew how to produce Han purple, and the production of white glass was common knowledge, then it's doubtful that the producers of white glass discovered Han purple. If they did, wouldn't the knowledge of how to produce Han purple be less esoteric?

> D. *The ingredients used in producing both Han purple and the white glass were easily obtainable during the Qin and Han dynasties.*

If both ingredients were available to the general public, wouldn't it also be possible that they were discovered independent of each other? I mean, nearly anyone would have the resources to discover Han purple, right? This answer weakens.

> E. *The white glass is found in more surviving artifacts from the Qin and Han dynasties than Han purple is.*

This answer becomes problematic when we focus on the conclusion's wording and scope. We are concerned with how Han purple was discovered. Perhaps glass is more likely to survive, while pigment fades, but we still don't know if Han purple was discovered during glass production.

Answer choice A is the only answer that is helping to make the author's conclusion somewhat more plausible. It is essentially saying that "not only did Han purple and white glass share the same ingredients, the same manufacturing process, but were even made in the same location." It doesn't really help us decide that Han purple derived from glass manufacturing, but it does strengthen the relationship between the two.

A, despite its imperfections, is the best answer available. A is the correct answer.

15. Principles

15. Principles

Two Types of Principle Questions (What is a Principle?)

In the chapter on Find the Conclusion Questions earlier in the book we talked about the nature of **Principles** on the LSAT. Principles appear commonly on Logical Reasoning questions, but nowhere are they more prominent in two specific question types.

These two question types are **Principle Justify** and **Principle Illustrate** Questions. Although both question types contain principles, they are very different from each other. In this chapter, we will first review the nature of principles, then look at these two question types in succession.

So what is a principle?

The Merriam Webster dictionary defines a "principle" as a "fundamental law governing the rule of conduct," or a "general theorem that has numerous applications across a wide field."

For the purposes of the LSAT, there are three characteristics of "principles" that we need to be aware of. If you see a statement in the stimulus or answer choices possessing these three characteristics, chances are that you are dealing with a principle.

<u>A principle should have multiple and general applicability.</u>

In the first place, a principle has widespread applicability. It holds true not just for one specific instance, but across a wide range of situations and scenarios.

The statement "*John is a corrupt government official and he should be prosecuted*" is NOT a principle. It pertains to John, who is one single person. But the statement "*corrupt government officials should be prosecuted*" IS a principle because it applies to corrupt government officials in general, regardless of who you are. If this principle holds true, then it doesn't matter how many years of experience you have, which department you work for, or your position, if you are a corrupt government official, you should be prosecuted.

<u>A principle should apply equally across the board and at all times.</u>

When we say "as a matter of principle," we mean something that is non-negotiable. If honesty is one of my principles, then that means I strive to be honest all the time, not only when it provides me with advantages or only when I feel like it. I should be honest even if it could get me in trouble. Similarly, even if there are extenuating circumstances and exceptions, by being dishonest, I have still breached my principle.

<u>A principle should be the expression of a rule or standard, it can be both descriptive and prescriptive.</u>

Behind every principle there is a standard. A principle should tell us what is or ought to be. For example, scientific laws such as the Theory of Relativity or the Law of Thermodynamics should be considered principles. A principle can also govern our actions, it can have a moral component to it, as we can be held accountable to moral standards/principles.

Type 1: Principle Justify Questions

Principle Justify Questions are the last type of **Assumption Family** Questions. Like all Assumption Family Questions, the stimulus of a Principle Justify Question will contain an argument, with its premises and main conclusion. Between the premises and the main conclusion, there will be a main reasoning gap. Structure-wise, they are no different from Flaw, Sufficient Assumption, Necessary Assumption, Strengthen, and Weaken Questions.

In over 90% of the time, **Principle Justify Questions can be treated exactly like Sufficient Assumption Questions.** I highly recommend returning to the chapter on SA Questions for a refresher if you don't remember the steps to solving this type of question. Basically, we analyze the argument within the stimulus structurally, isolate the gap in the author's reasoning, come up with a Main Assumption to close that gap, and find an answer choice that is equal to or stronger than our Main Assumption.

In fact, the biggest difference between Principle Justify Questions and Sufficient Assumption Questions is that the answer choices in Principle Justify Questions will be worded as principles. So instead of finding a regular answer choice that, in conjunction with the premises, would guarantee the argument's conclusion; we are looking for a PRINCIPLE that would do the same thing.

So whenever we approach a Principle Justify Question, treat it as you would a Sufficient Assumption Question. (There will be certain exceptions, but we will cover them as we move forward.)

Principle Justify Questions will usually be worded thus:

Which of the following principles justifies/most justifies the author's reasoning/argument?

Occasionally, the question will also read like this:

Which of the following principles most supports/strengthens the author's reasoning/argument?

Regardless of whether the word "justify" or "support/strengthen" is used in the question, it does not make a difference to how we approach the question.

Let's try a question, tackle it as you would an SA Question:

PT24 S2 Q25

The publisher of a best-selling self-help book had, in some promotional material, claimed that it showed readers how to become exceptionally successful. Of course, everyone knows that no book can deliver to the many what, by definition, must remain limited to the few: exceptional success. Thus, although it is clear that the publisher knowingly made a false claim, doing so should not be considered unethical in this case.

Which one of the following principles, if valid, most strongly supports the reasoning above?

A. Knowingly making a false claim is unethical only if it is reasonable for people to accept the claim as true.
B. Knowingly making a false claim is unethical if those making it derive a gain at the expense of those acting as if the claim were true.
C. Knowingly making a false claim is unethical in only those cases in which those who accept the claim as true suffer a hardship greater than the gain they were anticipating.
D. Knowingly making a false claim is unethical only if there is a possibility that someone will act as if the claim might be true.
E. Knowingly making a false claim is unethical in at least those cases in which for someone else to discover that the claim is false, that person must have acted as if the claim were true.

Let's break down the author's argument structurally:

The conclusion is the last sentence of the stimulus, "*although it is clear that the publisher knowingly made a false claim, doing so should not be considered unethical in this case.*"

Why does the author think it's okay for the publisher to make a false claim here? In other words, what information is used to support this claim? What are the conclusion's supporting premises?

The answer lies in the second sentence of the stimulus: even though the publishers made a false claim, it's a claim that everyone knows to be false/unrealistic: "*Of course, everyone knows that no book can deliver to the many what, by definition, must remain limited to the few: exceptional success.*"

So the gap between the premise and the conclusion is pretty obvious now: if you lie, but everyone knows you told a lie, is it then okay? If you make a false claim, but everyone knows the claim to be false, then is it not unethical to do so?

In Principle Justify questions, just like SA Questions, we are looking for a Main Assumption that links the information between the premise and the conclusion, so that the gap in reasoning may be filled. In this question, we can do so via a conditional relationship:

Making a false claim is not unethical if everyone knows it to be false.
- *Everyone Knows Claim is False → Making this False Claim not Unethical*

Let's look at the answer choices, we are looking for something similar to this but expressed as a principle.

    A. *Knowingly making a false claim is unethical only if it is reasonable for people to accept the claim as true.*

This is a conditional statement. Let's diagram it:

- Knowingly making a false claim unethical → Reasonable for people to accept the claim as true

Let's restate this in contrapositive form:

- Unreasonable for people to accept truth of claim → Knowingly making a false claim not unethical

How does this compare to our anticipated answer? There are slight differences, but are they dealbreakers?

The sufficient condition we came up with was "*everyone knows the claim is false,*" does the sufficient condition in our contrapositive answer choice match up with that? If everyone knows the claim to be false, does it mean it's unreasonable for people to accept the truth of the claim? Seems okay to me, let's look at the second half: in the anticipated answer our necessary condition was "*making the false claim not unethical,*" whereas in the answer choice, it's "*knowingly making a false claim is not unethical.*" An additional word, "*knowingly,*" has been added to the mix. Is this problematic? No, because the stimulus already states that "*everyone*" knows the claim to be false, and that ought to include the publishers too. So they are knowingly making a false claim.

Looking carefully at keywords in answer choices (K in SLAKR) is an essential habit to success, but an answer choice with different wording doesn't automatically mean an answer choice is wrong. We need to actually think it over.

Throughout the book, we have seen **term shifts** occur in the stimulus. The author may be talking about the same thing but using different words, or they may have inadvertently made a problematic leap of reasoning, creating a gap in their argument. We must consider each of these shifts on a case-by-case basis.

So this answer seems fine, with tiny discrepancies when compared with our Main Assumption/Anticipated Answer, I would hold my horses and go through the other answer choices to see if there is a better alternative.

> B. *Knowingly making a false claim is unethical if those making it derive a gain at the expense of those acting as if the claim were true.*

Again, a conditional relationship masked in abstract language:

- Those making a false claim derive a gain at the expense of those acting as if the claim were true → Knowingly making a false claim is unethical

What does the sufficient condition mean? Basically, it's describing people who made a false claim, and people got tricked, and the tricksters derived a gain from tricking people.

Actively train yourself to **decipher abstract language** not only in the stimulus, but also in the answer choices, this will save you a lot of time on the actual exam.

So this conditional can be simplified as:

- If you made a false claim and gained something from people who actually believed it → Making the false claim is unethical

Two things from this answer choice don't match up with our Main Assumption conditional. First, according to the stimulus, people don't actually believe the false claim, and second, we want the necessary condition to be about "not unethical."

> C. *Knowingly making a false claim is unethical in only those cases in which those who accept the claim as true suffer a hardship greater than the gain they were anticipating.*

- Making false claim unethical → Those who accept the claim suffer more than they hoped to gain

This doesn't match our stimulus either: nobody accepted the claim, and we don't know what people hoped to gain and how much they actually suffered.

> D. *Knowingly making a false claim is unethical only if there is a possibility that someone will <u>act</u> as if the claim might be true.*

- False claim unethical → there is a possibility that someone will act as if the claim might be true
- In contrapositive form: No possibility someone will act as if the claim might be true → False claim not unethical

This answer is very, very close. We know from the stimulus that everyone knows the claim to be false. What this answer gives us is that no one will act as if the claim might be true. There is a subtle difference here: you may act like you'll live forever, but you know you won't. So these two aren't interchangeable ideas, and the habit of paying attention to the excruciating details of the answer choice will help us eliminate this answer.

> E. *Knowingly making a false claim is unethical in at least those cases in which for someone else to discover that the claim is false, that person <u>must have acted</u> as if the claim were true.*

This answer choice doesn't match up with our argument, we don't know if the publisher has acted like the book will bring success or not.

Ultimately, it boils down to choosing between A and D,

A is a closer version of our anticipated answer, while D contains a shift in scope, going from what people "know" to how people will "act."

<u>A is the correct answer.</u>

***

Difficult Trait #1: Harder Principle Justify Questions will contain complex conditionals, review Chapter 7 if need be.

Like SA Questions, complex conditionals abound in Principle Justify Questions.

<u>PT70 S1 Q23</u>

Columnist: Although most people favor the bill and the bill does not violate anyone's basic human rights, it will not be passed for many years, if at all; nor will any similar bill. Those people who would be adversely affected were it to become law are very influential. This shows that, if this country is a democracy at all, it is not a well functioning one.

Which one of the following principles, if valid, most helps to justify the columnist's reasoning?

A. In a well functioning democracy, any bill that would benefit most people will be passed into law within a few years if it does not violate anyone's basic human rights.
B. If a democracy is well functioning, then any bill that is opposed by influential people but favored by most other people will eventually pass into law.
C. In a well functioning democracy, a bill that is favored by most people will become law within a few years only if those who oppose it are not very influential.
D. Any bill passed into law in a well-functioning democracy will be favored by most people and be consistent with individuals' basic human rights.
E. A bill that most people favor will be passed promptly into law in a well-functioning democracy if the bill does not violate anyone's basic human rights.

The argument is conditional in nature and contains multiple sufficient conditions. (Refer to the "Hidden Sufficient Conditions" section in Chapter 7 if you had trouble diagramming the author's argument in this question.)

The author concludes that the country in question is not a well functioning democracy.

Why?

Because a bill that is favored by most people and does not violate anyone's basic human rights will not be passed for many years.

Why won't it pass for many years? Because the people who would be negatively affected by the law are very influential.

To recast this argument in conditional terms can be a little overwhelming, so let's mirror the author's argument with an analogy:

Although John has amazing extracurriculars and stellar references, he will not get into a good law school. His GPA and LSAT are very low. This shows that applying to law school is largely a numbers game.

Can we reword the author's argument as a conditional relationship? How about this:

If you have amazing extracurriculars and stellar references but still can't get into a good law school due to low GPA and LSAT, then applying to law school is largely a numbers game.

Can we take the contrapositive of this also?

If applying to law school isn't largely a numbers game, you'd be able to get into a good school with amazing extracurriculars and stellar references, even if your GPA and LSAT were low.

Similarly, back to our stimulus argument, if we were to restate the entire argument as a conditional statement, it would look like this:

In a well functioning democracy, a bill favored by most people and not violating anyone's basic human rights will be passed into law, even if those who would be adversely affected are very influential.

Well functioning democracy + Bill favored by most people + Bill does not violate basic human rights → Passed into law.

Whether or not the bill is opposed by influential people is irrelevant. According to our conditional, if it's a well functioning democracy, a bill favored by most people, and doesn't violate basic human rights, it will pass. If influential people opposed it, it will pass, if influential people didn't oppose it, it will pass too. The statement *"those people who would be adversely affected were it to become law are very influential"* is the author's reason why the bill will not pass, it is not a sufficient condition.

Let's take a look at the answer choices:

A.   *In a well functioning democracy, any bill that would <u>benefit</u> most people will be passed into law within a few years if it does not violate anyone's basic human rights.*

This answer is very close, however, one of the sufficient conditions that we are looking for is "favored by most people," not "benefit most people."

B.   If a democracy is well functioning, then any bill that is opposed by influential people but favored by most other people will eventually pass into law.

This answer is on the right track, it only has two of the three sufficient conditions we identified in the stimulus, I would keep this for now and see if there is another answer choice that is a perfect match.

C.   In a well functioning democracy, a bill that is favored by most people will become law within a few years only if those who oppose it are not very influential.

This directly contradicts the argument. We know from our argument that in a well functioning democracy, a bill favored by most people and not violating anyone's basic human rights (this part is missing) will pass into law *even if* the opposition is very influential.

D.   Any bill passed into law in a well-functioning democracy will be favored by most people and be consistent with individuals' basic human rights.

This misplaces the sufficient and necessary conditions as stated in the argument. This answer choice, when diagrammed, will look like this:

Well functioning democracy + bill passed into law → favored by most people + consistent with individuals' basic human rights

E.   A bill that most people favor will be passed promptly into law in a well-functioning democracy if the bill does not violate anyone's basic human rights.

Definitely go back and read the section on "hidden sufficient conditions" in Chapter 7 if you are having trouble diagramming this answer choice. Here, instead of going over all the theoretical stuff, we'll make up an analogy that mirrors the sentence structure of this answer choice:

A road that is rarely traveled will be closed to the public in Alaska if it is snowing.

There are three sufficient conditions here,

- Snowing + In Alaska + Road rarely traveled → Road closed

Similarly, this answer choice matches up with the argument:

- Favored by most people + Does not violate basic human rights + well functioning democracy → promptly passed into law

In contrapositive form:

- Not promptly passed into law → Not favored by most people OR violate basic human rights OR not a well functioning democracy

We already know that the bill is favored by most, and it does not violate basic human rights, so all that's left to negate is "well functioning democracy." If we apply the process of elimination to the contrapositive of this answer choice, we will get the conclusion we want: this country is not a well functioning democracy.

This answer covers all the sufficient conditions as listed in the stimulus, whereas B only covers two. I would take this over B.

<u>E is the correct answer.</u>

This question, I think, is one of the hardest Principle Justify Questions simply because the conditional relationships in the stimulus and the correct answer choice are so hard to decipher.

> As we mentioned before, complex conditionals are present in a majority of the hardest Principle Justify Questions, so it's of paramount importance that we get comfortable with conditional logic and correctly identify and diagram conditional relationships.

A conditional relationship in which there are multiple, hidden sufficient conditions have appeared several times in the harder Principle Justify Questions. We saw this at work here, take a look at 71-1-25 and 80-4-24 for additional practice.

***

Difficult Trait #2: Sometimes the question does not ask us to justify the conclusion of the argument; but rather, a specific outcome.

We mentioned earlier that Principle Justify Questions will usually look like this:

Which one of the following principles would most justify/strengthen the author's argument/conclusion?

However, instead of asking you for an answer choice that would justify/strengthen the argument's conclusion, some Principle Justify Questions will ask you to find the answer choice that leads to a specific outcome.

These types of questions were more common in earlier PTs but have become less and less frequent. Unfortunately, there are no tried-and-true rules here as each of these questions will be slightly different. The important thing is to read the question carefully, and ask yourself what is the outcome you are trying to justify?

PT17 S3 Q23

Arnold: I was recently denied a seat on an airline flight for which I had a confirmed reservation, because the airline had overbooked the flight. Since I was forced to fly on the next available flight, which did not depart until two hours later, I missed an important business meeting. Even though the flight on which I had a reservation was canceled at the last minute due to bad weather, the airline should still pay me compensation for denying me a seat on the flight.

Jamie: The airline is not morally obligated to pay you any compensation. Even if you had not been denied a seat on the earlier flight, you would have missed your business meeting anyway.

A principle that, if established, justifies Jamie's response to Arnold is that an airline is morally obligated to compensate a passenger who has been denied a seat on a flight for which the passenger has confirmed reservations

- A. If the only reason the passenger is forced to take a later flight is that the airline overbooked the original flight
- B. Only if there is a reason the passenger is forced to take a later flight other than the original flight's being canceled due to bad weather
- C. Only if the passenger would not have been forced to take a later flight had the airline not overbooked the original flight
- D. Even if the only reason the passenger is forced to take a later flight were that the original flight is canceled due to bad weather
- E. Even if the passenger would still have been forced to take a later flight had the airline not overbooked the original flight

Let's take a careful look at the question:

A principle that, if established, justifies Jamie's response to Arnold is that an airline is morally obligated to compensate a passenger who has been denied a seat on a flight for which the passenger has confirmed reservations

We are no longer looking for a principle to support the argument's main conclusion. Instead, we are focusing specifically on Jamie's response. So what is Jamie's response to Arnold?

Jamie thinks that the airline is NOT morally obligated to pay Arnold any compensation. So we are looking for an answer which would tell us that given Arnold's situation, the airline *doesn't* have to pay him.

So what exactly happened to Arnold?

Arnold booked a flight that departs at, say, 10:00 AM. He got to the airport on time, but could not get on the flight because it was overbooked. So he had to wait for the next flight, which departed at 12:00 PM. As a result, he missed his business meeting.

However, the earlier flight was canceled due to bad weather. Which means that had Arnold got on the earlier flight, he would have had to disembark anyway. Regardless of whether or not Arnold was able to get on the first plane, he would ultimately end up on the second flight.

That's exactly Jamie's argument. According to Jamie, regardless of whether or not Arnold was denied a seat, the outcome would have been the same. So essentially, we are looking for an answer choice that says "*if Arnold would have had to take the second flight/miss his business meeting even if he wasn't denied a seat on the first flight, the airline is not obligated to compensate him.*" Stated in a different way, we can also anticipate something that says "*if the overbooking was not the only reason why Arnold missed his meeting, then the airline doesn't have to compensate him.*"

If we take the contrapositive of these two statements, then we get:

Airline obligated to compensate Arnold → Arnold would have gotten to his meeting on time had he been able to get on the first flight

Or

Airline obligated to compensate Arnold → overbooking was the only reason why Arnold missed the meeting

Let's take a look at the answer choices:

A.   *If the only reason the passenger is forced to take a later flight is that the airline overbooked the original flight*

If combined with the information in the question itself, this answer choice would read like this:

An airline is morally obligated to compensate a passenger who has been denied a seat on a flight for which the passenger has confirmed reservations if the only reason the passenger is forced to take a later flight is that the airline overbooked the original flight
Let's simplify that a little bit:

The airline is morally obligated to compensate Arnold if the only reason Arnold had to take a later flight was because of the overbooking.

- The only reason Arnold had to take a later flight was because of the overbooking → Airline morally obligated to compensate Arnold

What we are looking for, however, is an answer choice that tells us the airline is NOT obligated to compensate Arnold. What we are looking for is this:

- Overbooking was not the only reason why Arnold took a later flight (the first flight was canceled anyway) → Airline not obligated to compensate Arnold

This answer negates both the sufficient and necessary without reversing the order. We are looking for A → B, this answer instead gives us ~~A~~ → ~~B~~.

B. *Only if there is a reason the passenger is forced to take a later flight other than the original flight's being canceled due to bad weather*

This answer says that the airline is morally obligated to compensate Arnold only if there is an additional reason Arnold had to take the second flight.

Was there a second reason? Yes, the flight was overbooked.

If we contrapositive this answer choice, we would get this:

- Flight being canceled due to bad weather was the only reason Arnold was forced to take the second flight → Airline not obligated to compensate Arnold.

If what we want is A → B, this answer gives us ~~A~~ → ~~B~~.

C. *Only if the passenger would not have been forced to take a later flight had the airline not overbooked the original flight*

This answer says: Airline morally obligated to compensate Arnold only if Arnold didn't have to take the later flight had the first flight not been overbooked

- Morally obligated to compensate Arnold → Had first flight not been overbooked, Arnold wouldn't have to take the second flight

The answer we are looking for is the contrapositive of this. We know that due to bad weather, even if the first flight wasn't overbooked, it was canceled, leaving Arnold with no choice but to take the second flight. Thus, the airline wasn't morally obligated to compensate Arnold.

This answer matches what we had in mind. <u>It's the correct answer</u>.

D. *Even if the only reason the passenger is forced to take a later flight were that the original flight is canceled due to bad weather*

This answer tells us that the airline is obligated to compensate Arnold even if the only reason he had to take a later flight was due to bad weather canceling the first flight.

But we know that it isn't the only reason why Arnold had to take a later flight. His first flight was also overbooked. This answer choice is a reversal of what we want.

This answer, if diagrammed, looks like this:

The only reason Arnold took later flight was due to cancellation of first flight → Morally obligated to compensate

> E. *Even if the passenger would still have been forced to take a later flight had the airline not overbooked the original flight*

This answer matches Arnold's situation, but the outcome, when combined with the information in the question, leads to the result of the airline being *morally obligated to compensate* him.

What we want instead is a principle supporting Jamie's view, which is that the airline is *not morally obligated to compensate* Arnold.

Difficult Trait #3: Don't loose track of what you are trying to justify/prove when reviewing the answer choices.

Since PJ Questions are so similar to SA Questions, many of the skills that we have learned in Chapter 10 will apply to PJ Questions as well. Remember in SA Questions, our goal is to ensure that the conclusion of the argument is established. So paying extra careful attention to the wording of the main conclusion will help us zone in on the correct answer.

Take a look at the following question:

PT77 S2 Q16

Some people see no harm in promoting a folk remedy that in fact has no effect. But there is indeed harm: many people who are convinced to use an ineffective remedy continue with it for years rather than pursuing conventional treatments that would almost certainly help them.

Which one of the following principles, if valid, most helps to justify the reasoning in the argument?

> A. One should not promote a remedy if one believes that using that remedy will cause harm.
> B. It is harmful to interfere with someone doing something that is likely to benefit that person.
> C. To convince people of something for which one knows there is no evidence is to be dishonest.
> D. A person is responsible for harm he or she does to someone even if the harm was done unintentionally.
> E. A person who convinces someone to take a course of action is in part responsible for the consequences of that action.

The conclusion of this argument is a combination of the first statement and the first half of the second statement, the author believes that there is *indeed harm in promoting folk remedies.*

What is the support given for this particular conclusion? Why does the author think there is indeed harm?

Because using an ineffective remedy can preclude you from seeking effective treatment alternatives.

So what we want as a correct answer choice would be something that says *doing something that precludes/prevents someone from actually getting the real help they need is the same as doing harm.*

> A.   One *should not promote* a remedy if one *believes* that using that remedy will cause harm.

This answer says nothing about the harmful qualities of promoting folk remedies, which is the essence of our main conclusion. Furthermore, we don't know what the promoter believes. Perhaps they are just ignorant. This does not connect the gap between our premise and conclusion.

> B.   It is harmful to interfere with someone doing something that is likely to benefit that person.

Does promoting folk remedies interfere with something that is likely to benefit that person?

Yes, it precludes them from getting effective treatment.

So, when we combine this answer choice with the premise, we can derive the conclusion that promoting folk remedies is harmful. This matches our conclusion. It's the correct answer.

> C.   To convince people of something for which one *knows* there is no evidence is to be *dishonest*.

Again, we don't know what the promoters know or don't know. Furthermore, being dishonest does not necessarily mean that the act is harmful. Let's move on.

> D.   A person is responsible for harm he or she does to someone even if the harm was done *unintentionally*.

This answer assumes that harm was done. We want an answer that tells us the act itself is in fact harmful.

> E.   A person who convinces someone to take a course of action is in part responsible for the consequences of that action.

The first part of the answer choice can be matched up with our premise, if you convince someone to use folk remedies, you are convincing them to take a course of action.

But the second part of this answer is problematic. From this answer, all we know is that the promoter would be responsible for the consequences of their actions. We can potentially stretch this argument by adding in our own assumptions: we can say that the promoter is responsible for the patient foregoing effective treatment. The consequences of which is that the patient is harmed. Therefore the promoter is responsible for the harm. Thus the promoter's actions are harmful.

But there are several leaps in reasoning that we must make in order to derive the conclusion. Moreover, there's an argument to be made that being responsible for an act is not the same as that act being harmful.

Ultimately, we want an answer that can prove the conclusion present in the stimulus, and answer choice B is more directly in line with our goal. So always keep in mind the exact wording of the main conclusion of the argument, even when looking at the answer choices.

Hard Answer Choices: Unclear Correct Answers (Plug-Back Test)

Back in the chapter on SA Questions we were introduced to the **Plug Back Test**. To determine whether an answer is correct or not, we take it and add it to the supporting premises of the argument. What kind of conclusion would these two pieces of information lead to? Is it stronger or equal to the actual main conclusion presented in the argument? If so, then it is the correct answer.

Premises + Correct Answer Choice ≥ Argument's Main Conclusion

In harder Principle Justify questions, the answer choices will often be more general and vague than we are used to, since we are dealing with principles. Because principles by nature are often expressed in vague or generalized language.

This raises a unique problem: sometimes the correct answer choice will be worded in such a way that it **may appear to be completely out of scope** at first glance.

The information presented in the answer choice may seem to have nothing to do with the information presented in the stimulus argument. But don't eliminate these "out of scope" answer choices just yet, **plug it back into the argument and see if it can guarantee the outcome described in the main conclusion.**

Let's take a look at a question:

PT37 S2 Q22

Political Theorist: Many people believe that the punishment of those who commit even the most heinous crimes should be mitigated to some extent if the crime was motivated by a sincere desire to achieve some larger good. Granted, some criminals with admirable motives deserve mitigated punishments. Nonetheless, judges should never mitigate punishment on the basis of motives, since motives are essentially a matter of conjecture and even vicious motives can easily be presented as altruistic.

Which one of the following principles, if valid, most helps to justify the political theorist's reasoning?

    A. Laws that prohibit or permit actions solely on the basis of psychological states should not be part of a legal system.
    B. It is better to err on the side of overly severe punishment than to err on the side of overly lenient punishment.
    C. The legal permissibility of actions should depend on the perceivable consequences of those actions.
    D. No law that cannot be enforced should be enacted.
    E. A legal system that, if adopted, would have disastrous consequences ought not be adopted.

Let's look at the argument in this stimulus.

Besides the argument, there's a lot of peripheral information in this stimulus. The first sentence is an opposing viewpoint, while the second sentence is a concession the author makes. The real argument is only in the last sentence of the stimulus: *judges should never mitigate punishment on the basis of motives, since motives are essentially a matter of conjecture and even vicious motives can easily be presented as altruistic.*

So the conclusion of the political theorist is that *judges should never mitigate punishment on the basis of motives.*

The premise that directly supports this is that *motives are essentially a matter of conjecture and even vicious motives can easily be presented as altruistic.*

These two pieces of information make up the author's argument. We talked at length about the different structural components of an LR stimulus and how to separate the argument from the peripheral information in Chapter 1.

So the author's argument is essentially this: because motives are a matter of conjecture and can be covered up in a favorable light, motives should not form a basis of legal judgments.

But doesn't that mean some people who were motivated by good motives are burdened with punishment harsher than they deserve? Isn't that unfair in itself?

So we are looking for a principle to hurdle this gap, something that tells us as long as there is the possibility that something can be abused, it should not be allowed to factor into judicial decision making, even if that means some people may be unfairly punished.

Let's look at the answer choices:

> A. Laws that prohibit or permit actions solely on the basis of psychological states should not be part of a legal system.

Due to the abstract nature of Principle Justify answer choices, we must take a minute to think about the full implications of each of these answer choices.

So let's assume that there is a law that prohibits an action if your motivation is not altruistic: a statute states that if you are motivated by reward, you are prohibited from helping strangers. Such a law should not form a part of the legal system.

Is this what our argument is talking about? Not really. What we are looking for is something like this:

Defense arguments based on psychological states should not be part of a judge's decision-making rationale.

If we take our premise (motives are essentially a matter of conjecture and even vicious motives can easily be presented as altruistic), and this answer choice, where does that lead us?

You can't really link these two together. The argument is talking about bringing up motivation as a defense, here we are talking about laws as a part of the legal system. That's the first issue.

Secondly, this answer is talking about laws *solely* based on psychological states. What if our defense is based only partially on motivation? Then this principle would no longer apply.

At the end of the day, there are enough issues with this answer choice that when you plug it back into the argument, we cannot guarantee the conclusion.

B.   *It is better to err on the side of overly severe punishment than to err on the side of overly lenient punishment.*

On the surface, this answer has nothing to do with what we were talking about in the stimulus. Our argument in the stimulus, essentially, is that the motivation defense can be abused, so it should not factor into the judge's reasoning. But there was also the element of people with good motivations being unfairly punished as a result of the author's conclusion, and the author is okay with that.

Assume in 100 trials, 50 people had good motivations and 50 people had bad motivations for the same crime. Ideally, we would lessen the sentencing of the people with good motivations from 10 years down to 8 years, while giving the people with bad motivations 10 years. But this is unrealistic. Everyone will claim that their motivations were good to begin with, so then everybody will get 8 years. This is the overly lenient punishment scenario.

So the judge says no, we will not factor in motivation in this trial. Everybody gets 10 years. Now the people with good motivations are faced with overly severe punishment, but the people with bad motivations are not let off easy. This is the scenario the author is indirectly arguing for.

If we take the premise and this answer choice, we will reach a conclusion that tells us it's better to not allow motivation to be factored into a court's decision-making process. Because even if this would mean that some are faced with overly severe punishment, no one got off on overly lenient punishment.

This answer indirectly leads to the result presented in the author's conclusion. It just takes a different route. This is the correct answer choice.

C.   *The legal permissibility of actions should depend on the perceivable consequences of those actions.*

So if we translate this answer choice and diagram it, it should look like this:

Action allowed by law → What consequences of those actions we can actually see

There's several things about this answer that stray from what's being discussed in the argument, just like answer choice A.

First of all, we are talking about people who have already committed crimes using motivation as a defense, this is not an action allowed by the law.

Secondly, the argument is about motivation, while this answer choice is about perceivable consequences.

D.   *No law that cannot be enforced should be enacted.*

Diagrammed as a conditional relationship, this answer is Enacted law → Enforced

What is the enacted law here? Can it be enforced? What our conclusion is about is whether judges should factor in the defendant's motivation when passing judgment. We are not interested in enacting any laws here.

E.   *A legal system that, if adopted, would have disastrous consequences ought not be adopted.*

This answer choice strays even further from the topic being discussed. We do not know whether permitting the motivation defense would have disastrous consequences, and we are not planning to adopt a new legal system. If this answer had read "a judicial practice that, if adopted, would have negative consequences ought not be adopted," then it's probably ok.

***

The last question is an extreme case of where a seemingly irrelevant answer choice actually turned out to be the correct answer. **So if an answer appears to be out of scope, that's not automatic grounds for dismissal.** None of the answer choices matched exactly what was discussed in the argument, and that's what made this question especially difficult. The correct answer is completely different from what we anticipated by analyzing the argument's structure.

This is where the **Plug Back Test** comes in handy. I will usually use it to confirm my answer choice selection, or to help myself decide on an answer choice when I have nowhere to turn to. So take the prospective answer choice and combine it with the premise, and see if you can independently arrive at the conclusion from them.

Secondly, the above question is also valuable because it demonstrates one of the differences between SA and Principle Justify questions.

Remember in SA Questions, we want an answer that connects the gap between the premise and the main conclusion. The correct answer can be as strong or stronger than our main assumption, but it always links the information presented in our premises and the information in our main conclusion.

For Principle Justify Questions, however, we can get a correct answer that has nothing to do with the premises. In the question we just saw, answer choice B *independently* guaranteed the author's main conclusion. These types of correct answers are few and far in between, but they are still acceptable.

Difficult Trait #4: Use the Plug-Back Test to verify answer choices that sidestep the author's argument and see if they can independently prove the main conclusion.

PT82 S4 Q21

Restaurant critic: Most people agree that food at Marva's Diner is exceptional, while the food at the more popular Traintrack Inn is fairly ordinary. This discrepancy should come as no surprise, since the Traintrack Inn's more convenient location is by itself almost enough to guarantee a steady flow of customers.

Which one of the following is a principle that, if valid, most helps to justify the restaurant critic's reasoning?

    A. The best way for a business to attract a steady flow of customers is to improve its products.
    B. Any restaurant can become more popular by moving to a more convenient location.
    C. The quality of the food at a restaurant is the most important factor in its popularity.
    D. A business will improve its products only when it is necessary to do so in order to attract customers.
    E. There is no relationship between the quality of a restaurant's food and the popularity of that restaurant.

Premise: Traintrack Inn's more convenient location is by itself almost enough to guarantee a steady flow of customers

Conclusion: It should not come as a surprise that Traintrack Inn's food is ordinary but it's more popular.

  A. *The best way for a business to attract a steady flow of customers is to improve its products.*

Premise + Answer Choice A = ?

Traintrack Inn's more convenient location is by itself almost enough to guarantee a steady flow of customers + the best way for a business to attract a steady flow of customers is to improve its products = ?

If we combine the premise and answer choice A, we would come to the conclusion that Traintrack Inn can do more to attract customers. Although they already have many customers, if they improve their food they can get even more customers.

Is this the conclusion from the argument? No, the conclusion is saying how it's not surprising that the popular restaurant Traintrack's food is mediocre.

  B. *Any restaurant can become more popular by moving to a more convenient location.*

Premise + Answer Choice B = ?

Traintrack's convenient location guarantees it more customers + any restaurant can become more popular by moving to a more convenient location = ?

What kind of conclusion does this lead to? Perhaps Marva can also become more popular by moving? We are not too sure, but it's definitely not the conclusion from the argument.

  C. *The quality of the food at a restaurant is the most important factor in its popularity.*

This answer leads to a self contradiction with the argument. Traintrack is popular but its food is mediocre. So it should come as a surprise that Traintrack is a popular restaurant.

  D. *A business will improve its products only when it is necessary to do so in order to attract customers.*

Traintrack's location guarantees it more customers + A business will improve its products only when it's necessary to do so in order to attract customers = ?

So we know it's not necessary for Traintrack to attract customers, they have no motivation to improve the quality of their food.

This explains why Traintrack's food is mediocre, it's due to their lack of motivation to improve. This is the correct answer.

  E. *There is no relationship between the quality of a restaurant's food and the popularity of that restaurant.*

If there is no relationship between the food and popularity, what kind of conclusion can we draw from the fact that Traintrack is more popular? None. We still don't know why its food is of lesser quality.

Difficult Trait #5: Watch out for the occasional Principle Necessary Assumption question.

Now this is an extremely rare type of question, only appearing a few times in all of LSAT history. I've included it here as many of my students have made the mistake of treating it as a regular Principle Justify Question. Take a careful look at the question itself, what do you see?

Really think about SA vs. NA differences before attempting this question.

PT56 S2 Q20

Psychologist: Psychotherapists who attempt to provide psychotherapy on radio or television talk shows are expected to do so in ways that entertain a broad audience. However, satisfying this demand is nearly always incompatible with providing high-quality psychological help. For this reason, psychotherapists should never provide psychotherapy on talk shows.

Which one of the following principles <u>must be assumed</u> in order for the psychologist's conclusion to be properly drawn?

A. It is never appropriate for psychotherapists to attempt to entertain a broad audience.
B. The context in which psychological help is presented has a greater impact on its quality than the nature of the advice that is given.
C. Psychotherapy should never be provided in a context in which there is any chance that the therapy might be of less than high quality.
D. Most members of radio and television talk show audiences are seeking entertainment rather than high quality psychological help.
E. Psychotherapists should never attempt to provide psychological help in a manner that makes it unlikely to be of high quality.

Unlike your typical Principle Justify Question, this is actually a Necessary Assumption Question disguised as a Principle Question, as evident from the words "must be assumed" in the question stem.

Let's look at answer choices C and E in particular:

> C.   *Psychotherapy should never be provided in a context in which there is any chance that the therapy might be of less than high quality.*

> E.   *Psychotherapists should never attempt to provide psychological help in a manner that makes it unlikely to be of high quality.*

Our Main Assumption should connect the premise and the conclusion, so what we want would look something like this:

If providing psychotherapy in a setting is nearly always incompatible with providing high quality help, then psychotherapists should never provide help in that setting.

Answer C would work perfectly as a Sufficient Assumption answer. If this was a regular Principle Justify Question, it would be fine too.

However, it is not a necessary assumption of the author's. It is stronger than our Main Assumption.

Answer choice E matches our Main Assumption in language and strength much better.

Answer E is the correct answer.

***

Before we turn to Principle Illustrate Questions, let's look at another rare variation of the Principle Justify Question.

While the vast majority of Principle Justify Questions can be treated as Sufficient Assumption Questions, sometimes the correct answer in a Principle Justify Question will not 100% establish the truth of the author's conclusion. This is the third difference/variation between Principle Justify and Sufficient Assumption Questions.

We know that in SA Questions, the correct answer will 100% guarantee the outcome of the conclusion.

But in a few Principle Justify Questions, even with the correct answer choice, **there is still a gap left** in the argument's reasoning.

Difficult Trait #6: In less than 10% of all Principle Justify Questions, even the correct answer won't 100% guarantee the conclusion. If you feel that the answer choices all leave something to be desired, pick the answer that *most* justifies the conclusion.

Take a look at the question below:

PT26 S2 Q23

In a certain municipality, a judge overturned a suspect's conviction for possession of an illegal weapon. The suspect had fled upon seeing the police and subsequently discarded the illegal weapon after the police gave chase. The judge reasoned as follows: the only cause for the police giving chase was the suspect's flight; by itself, flight from the police does not create a reasonable suspicion of a criminal act; evidence collected during an illegal chase is inadmissible; therefore, the evidence in this case was inadmissible.

Which one of the following principles, if valid, most helps to justify the judge's decision that the evidence was inadmissible?

    A. Flight from the police could create a reasonable suspicion of a criminal act as long as other significant factors are involved.
    B. People can legally flee from the police only when those people are not involved in a criminal act at the time.
    C. Police can legally give chase to a person only when the person's actions have created a reasonable suspicion of a criminal act.
    D. Flight from the police should not itself be considered a criminal act.
    E. In all cases in which a person's actions have created a reasonable suspicion of a criminal act, police can legally give chase to that person.

So the point that we are trying to prove here is that the *evidence in this case was inadmissible.*

We know, according to the argument, that *evidence collected during an illegal chase is inadmissible.*

So we are actually in need of two pieces of information in order to perfectly link the premise and the conclusion:

1. This particular chase was an illegal chase
2. The gun was collected during the chase

If we can answer "yes" to both of these, then we can be certain that the evidence in this case was inadmissible.

What does the argument tell us? What is the judge's reasoning?

The only cause for the police giving chase was the suspect's flight, by itself, flight from the police does not create a reasonable suspicion of a criminal act.

It is basically saying that running from the police, by itself, does not justify the police giving chase.

Or in the judge's words, there was no "*reasonable suspicion of a criminal act.*" Simply running away from the cops doesn't count.

We can now connect this premise with the main conclusion with a conditional relationship, we can say:

If there was no reasonable suspicion of a criminal act, then the chase was illegal.

If we take its contrapositive, we can say that:

In order for a police chase to be legal, there must be reasonable suspicion of a criminal act (on the part of the police.)

Let's move to the second point:

In order to guarantee the validity of the main conclusion, we must also establish that the gun was collected during the chase itself. If the gun was picked up again and surrendered by the suspect voluntarily a few weeks later, after the police promised leniency for cooperation; or it was found by a neighbor and brought to the police station, then it wouldn't count as "*evidence collected during an illegal chase.*"

So in order to ensure the truth of the conclusion, we need to establish both of these points.

Let's look at the answer choices.

A. *Flight from the police could create a reasonable suspicion of a criminal act as long as other significant factors are involved.*

This is contrary to the reasoning of the judge. This can be construed as a conditional relationship:

Other significant factors involved → Could create reasonable suspicion

We know there aren't other significant factors involved, but we can't negate the sufficient and then negate the necessary. That would be a logical flaw.

Furthermore, even if there was no reasonable suspicion, we already know that from the stimulus.

B. *People can legally flee from the police only when those people are not involved in a criminal act at the time.*

Legally flee → Not involved in criminal act

We know that the suspect ran away, but what was he doing at the time? We don't know.

> C. *Police can legally give chase to a person only when the person's actions have created a reasonable suspicion of a criminal act.*

This matches up with our anticipated answer.

Legal Chase → Reasonable Suspicion of Criminal Act

But this only touches on one of the points! We still don't know whether the gun was collected during the chase!

> D. *Flight from the police should not itself be considered a criminal act.*

Even if running away is not illegal, was the chase illegal? We need an answer choice that tells us that the chase was illegal.

If this answer had said "*Flight from the police should not be considered a criminal act, and the police can give chase legally only when someone is committing a criminal act,*" then it would work.

But as such, it's incomplete and does not lead us to the desired conclusion.

> E. *In all cases in which a person's actions have created a reasonable suspicion of a criminal act, police can legally give chase to that person.*

But we know that the suspect's actions *didn't* create a reasonable suspicion of a criminal act. So this conditional is out of scope.

There were two gaps that needed to be filled in this argument in order to guarantee the conclusion. Answer choice C only fills in one of them. Nonetheless, it's the only viable answer available, so that's what we'll take. C is the correct answer.

In a majority of Principle Justify Questions, the correct answer, just like Sufficient Assumption answers, will guarantee the outcome of the main conclusion. But occasionally, we will get an answer that still leaves minor gaps in the author's reasoning.

When this happens, we go with **the strongest answer available**. Take a look at PT86 S1 Q20 and PT16 S3 Q23 (this one will also test your mastery of complex conditionals) for such an example.

Difficult Trait #7: When the principle appears in the stimulus rather than the answer choices

One final note on Principle Justify Questions: in all the questions we have considered so far in this chapter, the principles have been in the answer choices. We found the reasoning gap in the stimulus and chose a principle from the answer choices to justify the author's argument/conclusion.

Occasionally, the test makers will present the principle in the stimulus, and each of the answer choices will contain a scenario/argument instead. The only difference is that the order is reversed. Instead of finding the best principle from the answer choices to justify the argument in the stimulus, we take the principle and see which argument in the different answer choices it will justify the most.

Principle Justify questions with the principle in the stimulus and arguments in the answer choices have become more common recently.

Take a look at 89-4-24, 18-4-19, 22-2-18, 82-1-21, 80-4-24 for additional practice.

Type 2: Principle Illustrate Questions

There's another type of LR question that involves a principle. These are Principle Illustrate Questions.

Unlike Principle Justify Questions, Principle Illustrate Questions are **not** a part of the Assumption Family.

Remember that in Assumption Family questions, our primary focus had been to find the gap in the author's reasoning in the stimulus argument. The correct answer would most likely be addressing an aspect of that gap or logical leap made by the author. This was the case with Flaw, Sufficient Assumption, Necessary Assumption, Strengthen, Weaken, and Principle Justify questions.

Principle Illustrate Questions are beasts of a different nature. Here, we are no longer concerned with finding the main conclusion and its supporting premises, nor the leap in reasoning between the two. With Principle Illustrate Questions, instead, we are either trying to decipher the principle behind a scenario described in the stimulus; or given a principle and trying to find a scenario that most exemplifies an application of that principle.

If this sounds a little too abstract, don't worry. We will now look at these subtypes in greater detail.

Type 2.1: When Principle is Explicitly Stated in the Stimulus (Principle Matching)

The first subtype of Principle Illustrate Questions is when the author gives us a principle in the stimulus, and then gives us five different scenarios or situations, and asks us which answer choice best exemplifies or illustrates the principle already given.

The questions will look something like this:

Which one of the following judgments most conforms to the principle stated above?

So right away, just by looking at the question, we know that **the stimulus will contain a principle**.

So our job, first and foremost, **is to isolate that principle from the stimulus.** The principle may be the only piece of information contained in the stimulus, it may be encased in an argument, or there may be multiple principles contained in the stimulus. It is important that we know exactly what the principle/principles we are supposed to use to derive the correct answer.

Take a look at the following stimulus:

If an act of civil disobedience – willfully breaking a specific law in order to bring about legal reform – is done out of self interest alone and not out of a concern for others, it cannot be justified. But one is justified in performing an act of civil disobedience if one's conscience requires one to do so.

Which one of the following judgments most closely conforms to the principles stated above?

***

So in this question stimulus, we have not just one, but two principles, both of which are conditional:

- Principle 1: *If an act of civil disobedience is done out of self interest alone and not out of a concern for others, it cannot be justified*

Conditional Relationship: ~~Concern for Others~~ → ~~Justified~~

Contrapositive: Justified → Out of Concern for Others

- Principle 2: *But one is justified in performing an act of civil disobedience if one's conscience requires one to do so*

Conditional Relationship: One's Conscience Requires one to do so → Justified

Notice something a little tricky here: in the first principle, "justified" is the sufficient condition, while in the second principle, it is the necessary condition. I'm sure the answer choices will throw in a whole bunch of flawed conditional reversals and negations to confuse us.

Now when there's multiple principles in the stimulus, we would ideally find an answer choice that matches up with both of these principles. But oftentimes the correct answer will only match one of the two principles stated.

But what happens if there are two answer choices, one of them matches up with the first principle, and another matches up with the second?

Luckily, this has never happened before:

if you feel like there are two equally valid answer choices, examine their respective wording carefully. One of the seemingly correct answers will have something wrong with it. (More on this later)

Let's take a look at the question again, this time with answer choices:

PT38 S4 Q23:

If an act of civil disobedience – willfully breaking a specific law in order to bring about legal reform – is done out of self interest alone and not out of a concern for others, it cannot be justified. But one is justified in performing an act of civil disobedience if one's conscience requires one to do so.

Which one of the following judgments most closely conforms to the principles stated above?

A. Keisha's protest against what she perceived to be a brutal and repressive dictatorship in another country was an act of justified civil disobedience, because in organizing an illegal but peaceful demonstration calling for a return to democratic leadership in that country, she acted purely out of concern for the people of that country.
B. Janice's protest against a law that forbade labor strikes was motivated solely by a desire to help local mine workers obtain fair wages. But her conscience did not require her to protest this law, so Janice did not perform an act of justified civil disobedience.
C. In organizing an illegal protest against the practice in her country of having prison inmates work eighteen hours per day, Georgette performed an act of justified civil disobedience: she acted out of concern for her fellow inmates rather than out of concern for herself.
D. Maria's deliberate violation of a law requiring pre-publication government approval of all printed materials was an act of justified civil disobedience: though her interest as an owner of a publishing company would be served by repeal of the law, she violated the law because her conscience required doing so on behalf of all publishers.
E. In organizing a parade of motorcyclists riding without helmets through the capital city, Louise's act was not one of justified civil disobedience: she was willfully challenging a specific law requiring motorcyclists to wear helmets, but her conscience did not require her to organize the parade.

The first thing that we should have done is to isolate the principles present in the stimulus, if you recall, they are:

1. Justified → Out of Concern for Others
2. Required to do so by one's conscience → Justified

So our job should be fairly straightforward, we have to parse each answer choice to find one that matches up with either or both of these conditional principles.

A. *Keisha's protest against what she perceived to be a brutal and repressive dictatorship in another country was an act of **justified** civil disobedience, because in organizing an illegal but peaceful demonstration calling for a return to democratic leadership in that country, she acted purely **out of concern** for the people of that country.*

This answer reads Out of Concern for Others → Justified, it's a flawed reversal of our first principle.

B. *Janice's protest against a law that forbade labor strikes was motivated solely by a desire to help local mine workers obtain fair wages. But her **conscience did not require** her to protest this law, so Janice **did not perform an act of justified** civil disobedience.*

This answer is a flawed negation of our second principle.

C. *In organizing an illegal protest against the practice in her country of having prison inmates work eighteen hours per day, Georgette performed an act of **justified** civil disobedience: she acted **out of concern** for her fellow inmates rather than out of concern for herself.*

This answer, like answer choice A, is a flawed reversal of our first principle.

D. *Maria's deliberate violation of a law requiring pre-publication government approval of all printed materials was an act of **justified** civil disobedience: though her interest as an owner of a publishing company would be served by repeal of the law, she violated the law because her **conscience required doing so** on behalf of all publishers.*

This answer choice matches up with our second principle.

E. *In organizing a parade of motorcyclists riding without helmets through the capital city, Louise's act was **not one of justified** civil disobedience: she was willfully challenging a specific law requiring motorcyclists to wear helmets, but her **conscience did not require her** to organize the parade.*

This answer choice is a flawed negation of our second principle.

The correct answer choice is D.

In the majority of cases, the process of answer choice elimination is fairly straightforward. We already know exactly what we want, so it's just a matter of not getting mixed up by all the extra information present in the answer choices.

However, the most challenging questions will have answer choices that are harder to differentiate. Take a look at the following question:

Difficult Trait #1: The scenarios presented in the answer choices may not cleanly match up with the principle given.

PT46 S2 Q21

Ethicist: As a function of one's job and societal role, one has various duties. There are situations where acting in accord with one of these duties has disastrous consequences, and thus the duties are not absolute. However, it is a principle of morality that if one does not have overwhelming evidence that fulfilling such a duty will have disastrous consequences, one ought to fulfill it.

Which one of the following most closely conforms to the principle of morality cited by the ethicist?

- A. A teacher thinks that a certain student has received the course grade merited by the quality of his work. The teacher should fulfill her duty not to raise the student's grade, even though the lower grade might harm the student's chance of obtaining an internship.
- B. A person should not fulfill his duty to tell his friend the truth about the friend's new haircut, because lying will make the friend happier than the truth would.
- C. A police investigator discovers that a contractor has slightly overcharged wealthy customers in order to lower rates for a charity. The investigator should not fulfill his duty to report the contractor provided that the contractor stops the practice.
- D. A psychiatrist's patient tells her about his recurring nightmares of having committed a terrible crime. The psychiatrist should fulfill her duty to report this to the authorities because the patient may have broken the law, even though the psychiatrist also has a duty of confidentiality to her patients.
- E. A journalist thinks there is a slight chance that a story about a developing crisis will endanger innocent lives. Therefore, the journalist should await further developments before fulfilling his duty to file the story.

The principle in this question is conditional in nature: *if one does not have overwhelming evidence that fulfilling such a duty will have disastrous consequences, one ought to fulfill it.*

- In conditional form: ~~Overwhelming Evidence that Fulfilling Duty will have Disastrous Consequences~~ → Fulfill this Duty
- Contrapositive: Don't fulfill duty → Have overwhelming evidence of fulfillment's disastrous consequences

The correct answer will express either one of these. The correct answer can argue that *because there is no overwhelming evidence of disastrous consequences, we should fulfill this duty,* or that *since this duty should not be fulfilled, there must be overwhelming evidence of disastrous consequences.*

Let's look at each of the answer choices:

A. *A teacher thinks that a certain student has received the course grade merited by the quality of his work. The teacher should fulfill her duty not to raise the student's grade, even though the lower grade might harm the student's chance of obtaining an internship.*

This hypothetical is essentially saying that even though fulfilling the duty of not inflating grades may harm the student's career opportunities, it's a duty that the teacher should fulfill.

Is there overwhelming evidence that not giving the student a higher grade will have disastrous consequences? I'm not too sure. It's not ideal for the student, but is it "disastrous?" Is there "overwhelming evidence?" The answer doesn't make it clear. Let's keep this answer choice for now.

B. *A person should not fulfill his duty to tell his friend the truth about the friend's new haircut, because lying will make the friend happier than the truth would.*

This answer choice says because lying makes the friend happier, you should lie. If the duty is to tell the truth, then it can be interpreted as "not fulfilling duty will make friend happier, so don't fulfill the duty."

There are two issues with this answer choice. In the first place, I'm not sure if the friend being unhappy would be a disastrous consequence, so in that respect this answer is unclear like answer choice A.

Furthermore, even if a friend's anger does count as a disastrous consequence, this argument is a flawed reversal of the principle's contrapositive. So there's no way this answer can be right.

C. *A police investigator discovers that a contractor has slightly overcharged wealthy customers in order to lower rates for a charity. The investigator should not fulfill his duty to report the contractor provided that the contractor stops the practice.*

So the investigator has a duty to report dishonest contractors. Does fulfilling this duty have disastrous consequences? Probably not. So if there isn't such evidence, the investigator should fulfill this duty. This answer is the opposite of what we want.

D. *A psychiatrist's patient tells her about his recurring nightmares of having committed a terrible crime. The psychiatrist should fulfill her duty to report this to the authorities because the patient may have broken the law, even though the psychiatrist also has a duty of confidentiality to her patients.*

What is the duty in question here? The answer choice talks about two duties here, let's look at each of them:

Duty to report: is there overwhelming evidence that reporting the patient will have disastrous consequences? We are not sure. Just like answer A, answer D doesn't explicitly talk about how disastrous the consequences are.

Duty to patient: is there overwhelming evidence that keeping the patient's nightmares confidential will have disastrous consequences? We don't know either.

These are conflicting duties at play in answer choice D. It's rather confusing on a first read. Let's keep it and compare it to A later.

> E. *A journalist thinks there is a slight chance that a story about a developing crisis will endanger innocent lives. Therefore, the journalist should await further developments before fulfilling his duty to file the story.*

Is there overwhelming evidence that filing the story will have disastrous consequences? No, the answer choice tells us explicitly that "there is a slight chance" it will endanger innocent lives. So the conclusion should be that the duty should be fulfilled, the journalist shouldn't wait.

Let's go back to A and D.

Remember, since both of these answer choices are concluding that the duty should be fulfilled, we just have to look at the original principle, and not the contrapositive.

The original principle:

~~Overwhelming Evidence that Fulfilling Duty will have Disastrous Consequences~~ → Fulfill this Duty

The evidence in answer choice A is far from overwhelming. There is just the possibility that the lower grade might hurt the student's internship opportunities. It's far from overwhelming evidence, and I'm not sure if not having an internship constitutes disastrous consequences. This closely mirrors the conditional principle as stated in the stimulus.

What about reporting a patient's dreams to the police? Do we have any indication from the answer choice that there is NO overwhelming evidence this act will have disastrous consequences? The answer choice doesn't say.

However, just to play the devil's advocate, we can argue that it doesn't either. Because what's the worst that could happen? The police will investigate and if the patient was culpable, justice will be served; and if he was innocent, nothing will come of it. If we think of it this way, answer choice D also fits the bill, right?

But remember, for these Principle Illustrate Questions, we are trying to find the answer choice that **most closely** mirrors the principle given. Answer choice A already tells us what the consequences are, and we know with a high degree of certainty that it doesn't count as overwhelming evidence of disastrous consequences. Answer choice D, on the other hand, needs quite a bit of additional input from us, information that is not already available within the answer choices. So in that sense, answer choice A already fits the bill, while answer choice D can be interpreted to fit the bill.

The correct answer choice is A.

A Quick Way to Deal with Conditional Principle Illustrate Questions Containing Too Much Information

Let's revisit <u>PT38 S4 Q23</u>, this time paying special attention to the conclusions of each answer choice:

If an act of civil disobedience – willfully breaking a specific law in order to bring about legal reform – is done out of self interest alone and not out of a concern for others, it cannot be justified. But one is justified in performing an act of civil disobedience if one's conscience requires one to do so.

Which one of the following judgments most closely conforms to the principles stated above?

A. Keisha's protest against what she perceived to be a brutal and repressive dictatorship in another country **was an act of justified civil disobedience**, because in organizing an illegal but peaceful demonstration calling for a return to democratic leadership in that country, she acted purely out of concern for the people of that country.

B. Janice's protest against a law that forbade labor strikes was motivated solely by a desire to help local mine workers obtain fair wages. But her conscience did not require her to protest this law, so Janice **did not perform an act of justified civil disobedience**.

C. In organizing an illegal protest against the practice in her country of having prison inmates work eighteen hours per day, **Georgette performed an act of justified civil disobedience**: she acted out of concern for her fellow inmates rather than out of concern for herself.

D. Maria's deliberate violation of a law requiring pre-publication government approval of all printed materials **was an act of justified civil disobedience**: though her interest as an owner of a publishing company would be served by repeal of the law, she violated the law because her conscience required doing so on behalf of all publishers.

E. In organizing a parade of motorcyclists riding without helmets through the capital city, Louise's act **was not one of justified civil disobedience**: she was willfully challenging a specific law requiring motorcyclists to wear helmets, but her conscience did not require her to organize the parade.

If you recall, the two conditional principles presented in the stimulus are:

Justified → Out of Concern for Others
Contrapositive: Not out of concern for others → **Not Justified**

Required to do so by one's conscience → **Justified**
Contrapositive: Not Justified → Not Required by one's conscience

Look at answer choices A, C, and D. In each answer choice, the author concludes that the act was justified. In order to properly conclude that an act is justified, we NEED to apply the second principle. (Required by conscience → Justified)

Can we use the first principle to come to the conclusion that an act is justified? No. Because "justified" is the sufficient condition here.

So for answer choices A, C, and D, we simply have to check to see if any of them matches up with principle #2.

Similarly, for answer choices B and E, because the conclusion states that this action involved was NOT justified, we can only match them up with the contrapositive of principle #1.

***

To put it simply, if the principle presented in the stimulus is conditional, A → B, then by looking at the conclusions of each of the answer choices we will be able to eliminate some obviously wrong answer choices. The contrapositive of A → B is B̶ → A̶, so if we see an answer choice with the conclusion B, we just have to check if its premise is A, if an answer choice has the conclusion A̶, we just have to check if its premise is B̶. Any answer choice with A or B̶ as its conclusion will be wrong.

***

Type 2.2: When the Principle is Among the Answer Choices (Principle Extraction)

The second subtype of Principle Illustrate Questions will NOT have an explicitly stated principle in the stimulus. In this type of question, our job is to discover and state what the principle actually is.

The wording of the question will look like this:

Which one of the following most accurately expresses a principle employed in the argument?

The argument most closely conforms to which one of the following principles?

In these questions, we are given an example, argument, or scenario in the stimulus.

Remember the characteristics of a principle, discussed earlier in this chapter:

A principle should have multiple and general applicability.

A principle should apply equally across the board and at all times.

A principle should be the expression of a rule or standard (normative), it can be both descriptive and prescriptive.

So we know what a principle ought to look like, but how do we come up with our own hypothetical principle when given a stimulus?

It's actually quite straightforward: **we carefully read the information presented in the stimulus, summarize it, and restate it in generalized language as a principle.**

Let's go over two examples so you'll know exactly what I'm talking about:

Copernicus' astronomical system is superior to Ptolemy's and was so at the time it was proposed, even though at that time all observational evidence was equally consistent with both theories. Ptolemy believed that the stars revolved around the earth at great speeds. This struck Copernicus as unlikely; he correctly thought that a simpler theory is that the earth rotates on its axis.

There are two pieces of information presented in this argument:

Even though Ptolemy's and Copernicus' theories are both consistent with observational evidence, Copernicus' theory is superior.

Copernicus' theory is the simpler of the two.

If we were to summarize this argument, we can say something like this:

Because Copernicus' theory is the simpler of the two, even though both theories are equally consistent with observable evidence, it is the superior theory.

Finally, let's restate this in more general terms:

When two theories are equally consistent with observable evidence, the simpler theory is the superior theory.

***

See what we did there? We summarized the author's argument, with its premise and conclusion, and then reworded it into a principle that had more generalized application.

Let's try another example:

The use of space-based satellites to study environmental conditions on Earth is an important development in the conservation movement's history. Environmental problems may now be observed long before they otherwise would be noticed, allowing intervention before they reach the crisis stage. It is no wonder that environmentalists fail to consider both that spacecraft may damage the ozone layer and that this damage could be serious enough to warrant discontinuing space flight.

Step 1: Identify the premises and the conclusion in the argument

- Premise: *Space satellites have helped the environmental conservation movement and helped detect problems early on.*
- Conclusion: *It's not surprising that environmentalists overlook the negative effects of space flight.*

Can we shorten this to one sentence?

Because space satellites have helped environmentalists in their quest, it's not surprising that they overlooked space satellites' negative impact on their cause.

Let's now restate this as a principle:

If something has a positive impact for people, they tend to overlook its negative impacts.

***

The two examples we just went over are actually real Principle Illustrate Questions. Let's look at the actual questions themselves:

PT24 S2 Q22

Copernicus' astronomical system is superior to Ptolemy's and was so at the time it was proposed, even though at that time all observational evidence was equally consistent with both theories. Ptolemy believed that the stars revolved around the earth at great speeds. This struck Copernicus as unlikely; he correctly thought that a simpler theory is that the earth rotates on its axis.

This argument most closely conforms to which one of the following principles?

   A. Simplicity should be the sole deciding factor in choosing among competing scientific theories.
   B. If one theory is likely to be true, and another competing theory is likely to be false, then the one likely to be true is the superior of the two.
   C. If all observational evidence is consistent with two competing theories, the one that is more intuitively true is the more practical theory to adopt.
   D. Other things being equal, the more complex of two competing theories is the inferior theory.
   E. Other things being equal, the simpler of the two competing theories is the more scientifically important theory.

***

PT33 S1 Q18

The use of space-based satellites to study environmental conditions on Earth is an important development in the conservation movement's history. Environmental problems may now be observed long before they otherwise would be noticed, allowing for intervention before they reach the crisis stage. It is no wonder that environmentalists fail to consider both that spacecraft may damage the ozone layer and that this damage could be serious enough to warrant discontinuing space flight.

The reasoning above most closely conforms to which one of the following principles?

   A. People tend to ignore possible objectionable consequences of actions that support their activities.
   B. A negative consequence of an activity may be outweighed by its great positive consequences.
   C. Technology usually has at least some negative impact on the environment, even if it is largely beneficial.
   D. Even well-intentioned attempts to solve problems sometimes make them worse.
   E. Attempts to employ technology often have unforeseen consequences that may be negative.

PT24 S2 Q22:

We know from our previous exercise that the principle behind this argument is going to look something like this:

When two theories are equally consistent with observable evidence, the simpler theory is the superior theory.

We want an answer choice that comes the closest in expressing this. Be extremely careful of answer choices that contain information alien to what was discussed in the stimulus.

A **difficulty I faced** when tackling Principle Extraction questions was mistakenly selecting answer choices which are super close to the principle but aren't the principle.

The test makers will often throw in answer choices that can possibly work as Most Strongly Supported answer types into the mix. Answer choices that will seem very reasonable if you accept the author's argument in the stimulus.

But this is not what we are looking for!

Difficult Trait #1: We want a principle that mirrors the reasoning of the argument and our anticipated principle as closely as possible. We don't want something that is most likely true or could be true but contains extra information.

The habit of Keyword Extraction (K in SLAKR) is also very helpful in Principle Extraction subtypes. Look for out of place keywords that pop up in answer choices when trying to eliminate wrong answers.

Let's look at the answer choices:

A. *Simplicity should be the <u>sole</u> deciding factor in choosing among competing scientific theories.*

This answer is very similar to what we have espoused. One red flag that popped up was the word "sole." Our principle should be "simplicity should be the overriding factor when two theories are both equally consistent with evidence."

The argument never talks about simplicity being the "sole" deciding factor. There could be a multitude of deciding factors, and simplicity is just the tie breaker.

B. *If one theory is likely to be true, and another competing theory is likely to be false, then the one likely to be true is the superior of the two.*

This strays from the argument. In our argument, both Copernicus' and Ptolemy's theory are equally consistent with evidence, so they are equally likely to be true. This answer also doesn't talk about the simpler theory being the superior one.

C. *If all observational evidence is consistent with two competing theories, the one that is more intuitively true is the <u>more practical theory to adopt.</u>*

This is a MSS answer, the simpler theory is probably more practical to adopt I suppose. But as we mentioned before, we don't want to stray from the meaning of what was given to us.

Be careful of answer choices that include any additional speculation/inferences.

     D.   Other things being equal, the more complex of two competing theories is the inferior theory.

Remember in the very early part of the book, we talked about tricky answer choices, and we said that **the correct answer choice will often be presented in a more abstract/confusing way**? Here the test makers are being indirect. The answer we are anticipating is that the simpler theory is the superior theory, and that's what this answer choice is saying, only in a different way.

     E.   Other things being equal, the simpler of the two competing theories is the <u>more scientifically important theory.</u>

This is probably either a MBT or MSS answer choice. The simpler/superior theory is probably more scientifically important. But again, the answer we want is that the simpler of two competing theories is the superior theory. This answer strays a bit and is inferior to answer choice D, which is the correct answer.

<u>D is the correct answer.</u>

***

<u>PT33 S1 Q18</u>:

Remember that the principle we have anticipated is this:

If something has a positive impact for people, they tend to overlook their negative impacts.

Let's look at the answer choices, keeping an eye out of out of place keywords and answer choices that don't directly mirror this.

     A.   People tend to ignore possible objectionable consequences of actions that support their activities.

This looks good, actions that support their activities = have a positive impact for them, ignore possible. objectionable consequences = overlook their negative impacts. It matches our anticipated answer.

     B.   A negative consequence of an activity may be outweighed by its great positive consequences.

This could be true, it certainly doesn't conflict with the reasoning in the stimulus. But remember, we are looking for something different. The author argued in the stimulus that because space travel is helpful, it's *not surprising* that environmentalists overlook its negative effects. That's what we want. Whether space travel has an overall net positive impact on environmental protection is an entirely different story. Don't get carried away by answer choices, always keep your eye on what we really want!

     C.   Technology usually has at least some negative impact on the environment, even if it is largely beneficial.

This could work as a Strengthen answer, it would explain why it's not surprising that environmentalists overlook space travel's negative impact. But we want an answer that closely mirrors our principle, and this answer doesn't match.

     D.   Even well intentioned attempts to solve problems <u>sometimes make them worse.</u>

This answer contains an unsupported inference. We know that space travel has both positive and negative effects on environmental protection. But is it making things worse?

     E.   Attempts to employ technology often have <u>unforeseen</u> consequences that may be negative.

We know environmentalists overlook these problems, and that should not come as a surprise. But are these "unforeseen" consequences? Maybe they saw them and overlooked them?

Again, don't get carried away by the answer choices, **know exactly what we are looking for before reviewing the answer choice selection.**

A is the correct answer.

16. Parallel and Parallel Flaw Questions

Part I: Parallel Arguments

In the latter half of the last chapter we looked at Principle Extraction Questions, a subtype of Principle Illustrate Questions. In these questions, we matched up the principle we found in the stimulus with the correct answer choice, looking for the answer choice that most closely conveyed the meaning of the principle we found.

How we tackle Parallel Questions is very similar. We are trying to match up the argument contained in the stimulus with an answer choice that most closely resembles it.

However, instead of extracting a principle by summarizing the premises and conclusion of the argument, here we are trying to find an answer choice that mirrors the argument in the stimulus as a whole. That means matching the following:

1. **Logic**: Does the argument contain conditional/causal logic? If so, the correct answer choice will also be conditional/causal in nature. (<u>Mandatory</u>)

2. **Validity**: Is the argument in the stimulus a valid argument, or does it contain flaws? A valid argument in the stimulus means that the argument in the correct answer choice will also be valid. (<u>Mandatory</u>)

3. **Structure**: Does the argument contain an intermediate conclusion? If so, then the correct answer will probably have one. Does the argument contain two premises? If so, chances are the correct answer will have two as well. The order in which these are presented don't really matter, as long as they are all there. (<u>Good to have, but not mandatory</u>)

4. **Premises and Conclusion**: I will usually compare the wording of the conclusion and the premises as a last resort especially when I have two answer choices that both have acceptable logic, validity, and structure. Is the conclusion/premise of one answer choice closer to that of the stimulus argument? If so, I will select this answer choice. (<u>Good to have, but not mandatory</u>)

***

We will now look at each of these in turn and illustrate each point with a representative question.

The trickiest thing about Parallel Questions is simply **the amount of information** you have to keep in mind:

When faced with a complicated stimulus/argument, you have to not only analyze its logic and structure, but also pay attention to the details in the way it's worded. Then you have to look through each answer choice and try to match up these things one by one. That's a lot of steps and you can easily get lost in the process, but it does get better with practice.

The best approach I found for Parallel Questions was to **adopt a checklist mentality** when looking at the answer choices.

If the logic matches, then check whether it's valid, if it's valid, make sure the structure also matches... Being systematic and exhaustive in our approach is the only sure way to perfection.

Matching the Logic (Conditional/Causal/Comparison)

A large portion of Parallel questions will contain conditional or causal reasoning. Make sure that if the argument contains either, you are not only able to spot it but also remember to look for something similar when you approach the answer choices.

PT83 S3 Q23

Each new car in the lot at Rollway Motors costs more than $18,000. Any car in their lot that is ten or more years old costs less than $5,000. Thus, if a car in Rollway's lot costs between $5,000 and $18,000, it is a used car that is less than ten years old.

The pattern of reasoning in which one of the following arguments is most similar to that in the argument above?

A. Each apartment above the fourth floor of the building has more than two bedrooms. But all apartments below the fourth floor have fewer than two bedrooms. Thus, any apartment on the fourth floor of the building has exactly two bedrooms.

B. Each apartment above the fourth floor of the building has two or three bedrooms. But no apartment below the fourth floor has more than two bedrooms. Thus, all of the building's three bedroom apartments are on the fourth floor or higher.

C. No apartment above the fourth floor of the building has fewer than three bedrooms. But all apartments below the fourth floor have fewer than two bedrooms. Thus, if there are apartments in the building with exactly two bedrooms, they are on the fourth floor.

D. No apartment above the fourth floor of the building has more than two bedrooms. But only three bedroom apartments have balconies. Thus, if any apartment in the building has a balcony, it is on the fourth floor or lower.

E. Each apartment above the fourth floor of the building has more than two bedrooms. The building has no vacant apartments on or below the fourth floor. Thus, if there is any vacant apartment in the building, it will have more than two bedrooms.

This question really tests our proficiency in conditional logic. Not only is the argument entirely conditional, all the answer choices are too. With a question like this, it is easy to get confused as you are progressing through the answer choices, so it's crucial that you have a clear grasp of the conditional relationships in the stimulus to start with.

- Premise 1: New Car → > 18K
- Premise 2: 10 Years or more → < 5K
- Conclusion: Between 5K and 18K → Used Car + Less than 10 Years old

Let's take the contrapositive of the premises:

- Premise 1: Equal to or less than 18K → Used Car
- Premise 2: Equal to or more than 5K → Less than 10 years old

The conclusion derives much more naturally from the contrapositives of premises 1 and 2.

If we were to put this into notational form, it would look like this:

- Premise 1: A → B
- Premise 2: C → D
- Conclusion: B̶ + D̶ → C̶ + A̶

This is a valid argument, let's look at the answer choices:

A. *Each apartment above the fourth floor of the building has more than two bedrooms. But all apartments below the fourth floor have fewer than two bedrooms. Thus, any apartment on the fourth floor of the building has exactly two bedrooms.*

Premise 1: Above 4th floor → More than two bedrooms
Premise 2: Below 4th floor → Less than two bedrooms

Ok, stop right here. Just by looking at the two premises, we already have an idea of what the conclusion will look like if this is the correct answer. If this answer choice is correct, the conclusion would say: *if an apartment has exactly two bedrooms, it will be on the fourth floor.*

Is this the actual conclusion of answer choice A? No, the conclusion here is reversed. We can eliminate it.

B. *Each apartment above the fourth floor of the building has two or three bedrooms. But no apartment below the fourth floor has more than two bedrooms. Thus, all of the building's three bedroom apartments are on the fourth floor or higher.*

Premise 1: Above 4th floor → 2 or 3 bedrooms
Premise 2: Below 4th floor → 2 or less bedrooms

What is the conclusion we want? *If an apartment has more than 3 bedrooms* (not 2 bedrooms, not less than 2 bedrooms, not 3 bedrooms), *it will be on the fourth floor.*

This answer choice doesn't match up with our argument either.

C. *No apartment above the fourth floor of the building has fewer than three bedrooms. But all apartments below the fourth floor have fewer than two bedrooms. Thus, if there are apartments in the building with exactly two bedrooms, they are on the fourth floor.*

Premise 1: Above 4th floor → 3 or more bedrooms
Premise 2: Below 4th floor → less than two bedrooms

The conclusion we want is that *if an apartment doesn't have 3 or more bedrooms AND is not less than two bedrooms (in other words, exactly 2 bedrooms), it will be on the fourth floor.*

This matches. <u>C is the correct answer.</u>

D. *No apartment above the fourth floor of the building has more than two bedrooms. But only three bedroom apartments have balconies. Thus, if any apartment in the building has a balcony, it is on the fourth floor or lower.*

Premise 1: Above 4th floor → No more than 2 bedrooms
Premise 2: Balconies → 3 bedrooms

What is the conclusion we want here? *If an apartment has more than 2 bedrooms and not 3 bedrooms (so 4 bedrooms or more), it's not above the 4th floor and doesn't have a balcony.*

This doesn't match either.

E. *Each apartment above the fourth floor of the building has more than two bedrooms. The building has no vacant apartments on or below the fourth floor. Thus, if there is any vacant apartment in the building, it will have more than two bedrooms.*

Premise 1: Above 4th floor → more than 2 bedrooms
Premise 2: 4th floor or below → Not vacant

We want a conclusion that says *if an apartment is 2 bedrooms or less and vacant, it's neither above, on or below the fourth floor.* Such an answer wouldn't make sense, and in addition, that's not what the conclusion of this answer choice says, we can eliminate it with certainty.

As you can see, conditional parallel questions are difficult because there is just **so much information**. By having a clear grasp of the **conditional relationship** in the stimulus argument, and by **anticipating** how the conclusion of the correct answer choice will turn out, we can save valuable time.

When the stimulus premises and conclusion all contain conditional relationships, you can go through the answer choices to check if their premises/conclusion mirror those in the stimulus. Once you have done that, ask yourself: if this is the correct answer choice, how should it turn out?

Let's look at a question that uses causal logic to advance the argument:

PT75 S1 Q25

The availability of television reduces the amount of reading children do. When television is made unavailable, a nearly universal increase in reading, both by parents and by children, is reported. When television is available again, the level of reading by both parents and children relapses to its previous level.

The reasoning in which one of the following is most similar to the reasoning above?

A. Whenever the money supply in an economy fluctuates, interest rates tend to fluctuate. When the money supply remains constant, interest rates tend to remain stable. Thus, the money supply's remaining constant stabilizes interest rates.

B. The consumption of candy between meals disrupts a child's appetite at mealtimes. When candy is not consumed, blood sugar declines until mealtime, so the child feels hungry. A child who eats healthy meals feels less desire for candy.

C. Global warming is caused by increased carbon dioxide in the atmosphere. Furthermore, industrial pollution causes increased carbon dioxide in the atmosphere. So industrial pollution causes global warming.

D. Voting behavior is affected by factors other than political candidates' records of political achievement. For example, a candidate who projects confidence will gain votes as a result, whereas a candidate with a supercilious facial expression will lose votes.

E. Adults read less than they once did because there are so many other activities to divert them. This can be seen from the fact that the more time they spend on such other activities, the less they read. Conversely, the less they read, the more time they spend on such other activities.

The reasoning behind this argument is causal in nature. If we had realized this from the very start, it would have made our job much easier. The author's main conclusion is that Television reduces the amount of reading children do. The cause is television, and the effect is a reduction in reading. If we break down the premises and the main conclusion, here is what it looks like:

Cause: TV (A)
Effect: Reduction in Reading (B)

- Premise 1 (Second Statement): *When television is made unavailable, a nearly universal increase in reading, both by parents and by children, is reported.*
  - Without TV, reading is increased. (Without A, no B)

- Premise 2 (Third Statement): *When television is available again, the level of reading by both parents and children relapses to its previous level.*
  - With TV, reading is reduced. (With A, B is here too)

- Conclusion: *The availability of Television <u>reduces</u> the amount of reading children do.*
  - A Causes B (A ⇒ B)

The argument is fairly straightforward, the author says "no A, no B; yes A, yes B; therefore A causes B."

That's what we will be looking for in the answer choices.

Causal reasoning is **harder to detect** than conditional reasoning, simply because there isn't a uniform list of keywords to indicate its presence. But **action verbs** like "reduce" can be good signs that causal reasoning is present. In Chapter 7 we devoted a significant portion to the detection and qualities of causal reasoning. Refer back if needed.

Let's look at the answer choices:

A. *Whenever the money supply in an economy fluctuates, interest rates tend to fluctuate. When the money supply remains constant, interest rates tend to remain stable. Thus, the money supply's remaining constant stabilizes interest rates.*

- Premise 1: money supply fluctuates, interest rate fluctuates (no A, no B)
- Premise 2: money supply constant (not fluctuating), interest rates stable (not fluctuating) (A, B)
- Conclusion: money supply remaining constant ⇒ interest rate stable (A ⇒ B)

This matches with our argument, <u>it's the correct answer</u>.

B. *The consumption of candy between meals disrupts a child's appetite at mealtimes. When candy is not consumed, blood sugar declines until mealtime, so the child feels hungry. A child who eats healthy meals feels less desire for candy.*

The first statement introduces us to a causal relationship: consumption of candy ⇒ disruption of appetite. Just by reading this, we already know what the rest of the answer should look like if it's indeed the correct answer: we want the rest of the answer choice to say "with cause present, effect is present; without cause present, effect is not present either."

Does this happen? The second statement is good, it is saying that when there's no candy, appetite comes back/is not disrupted. But the third statement is not what we want. Here an additional causal relationship is given, healthy meals ⇒ less desire for candy. What we want instead is when candy is consumed, appetite is gone.

C.   Global warming is caused by increased carbon dioxide in the atmosphere. Furthermore, industrial pollution causes increased carbon dioxide in the atmosphere. So industrial pollution causes global warming.

Ok, so a causal relationship at the very start: increased CO2 ⇒ Global Warming. But the rest of the answer choice doesn't add up. This answer gives us a causal chain, Pollution ⇒ Increased CO2 ⇒ Global Warming.

D.   Voting behavior is affected by factors other than political candidates' records of political achievement. For example, a candidate who projects confidence will gain votes as a result, whereas a candidate with a supercilious facial expression will lose votes.

Factors other than candidates' records of political achievement ⇒ Voting behavior change

So in order to match the argument in the stimulus, we want an answer that says with these factors, change is detected in voting behavior; when these factors are unavailable, behavior doesn't change. Does the author do this? No. The author gives two examples of additional factors (confidence/facial expression) that affect voting behavior. Premise 1 from the stimulus argument is missing.

E.   Adults read less than they once did because there are so many other activities to divert them. This can be seen from the fact that the more time they spend on such other activities, the less they read. Conversely, the less they read, the more time they spend on such other activities.

In Parallel questions, answer choices that discuss the same topic as the stimulus argument will **usually** be wrong. Here answer choice E is also talking about reading, so that should be a big red flag.

The causal relationship here is Many Activities to Divert Adults ⇒ Adults Read Less.

Can we anticipate the rest of the answer choice? Ideally, it should contain two premises:

- Premise 1: When activities are around ⇒ Adults read less
- Premise 2: When no more activities ⇒ Adults read more

Does this happen? No, instead the answer gives us an inverse correlation between activities and reading: more you act, less you read, less you read, more you act.

Again, **anticipating** what each answer choice should look like if it's correct can save us a lot of time during the elimination process. When we know the format of the stimulus's argument, we should have no trouble anticipating what each answer choice *should* look like even before we have finished reading them. If they look different, they are probably wrong.

Anticipate what the correct answer should look like as we read through the answer choices. This will save us valuable time.

Matching the Validity

The validity of the reasoning in the stimulus argument needs to be matched as well. Contrary to what many believe, parallel questions will contain flawed arguments as well!

Parallel Flaw Questions will have stimuli that are certain to be flawed, but regular Parallel Questions can have flawed arguments as well.

PT31 S3 Q18

It is impossible to do science without measuring. It is impossible to measure without having first selected units of measurement. Hence, science is arbitrary, since the selection of a unit of measurement – kilometer, mile, fathom, etc. – is always arbitrary.

The pattern of reasoning in which one of the following is most similar to that in the argument above?

A. Long hours of practice are necessary for developing musical skill. One must develop one's musical skill in order to perform difficult music. But long hours of practice are tedious. So performing difficult music is tedious.

B. You have to advertise to run an expanding business, but advertising is expensive. Hence, it is expensive to run a business.

C. It is permissible to sit on the park benches. To sit on the park benches one must walk to them. One way to walk to them is by walking on the grass. So it is permissible to walk on the grass.

D. It is impossible to be a manager without evaluating people. The process of evaluation is necessarily subjective. Thus, people resent managers because they resent being evaluated subjectively.

E. Some farming on the plains requires irrigation. This irrigation now uses water pumped from aquifers. But aquifers have limited capacity and continued pumping will eventually exhaust them. Thus, a new source of water will have to be found in order for such farming to continue indefinitely.

The argument in the stimulus, again, is conditional:

- Premise 1: Science → Measuring
- Premise 2: Measure → Units of Measurement
- Premise 3: Units of Measurements Arbitrary
- Conclusion: Science is arbitrary

This is a flawed argument, it commits the Part vs. Whole flaw. So when we look at the answer choices, **I'll be sure to look for an answer choice that commits the same flaw.**

A. *Long hours of practice are necessary for developing musical skill. One must develop one's musical skill in order to perform difficult music. But long hours of practice are tedious. So performing difficult music is tedious.*

- Premise 1: Develop musical skill → Long hours of practice
- Premise 2: Perform difficult music → Develop Music Skills
- Premise 3: Long hours of practice tedious
- Conclusion: Performing difficult music is tedious

This matches up with our stimulus argument perfectly. It also commits the part vs. whole flaw. While the order in which the first two premises appear is different, this doesn't really matter.

B. *You have to advertise to run an expanding business, but advertising is expensive. Hence, it is expensive to run a business.*

Run Expanding Business → Advertise → Expensive

The conclusion we want would be something like *"doing something expensive will make you feel pampered, so running an expanding business will make you feel pampered."* Basically, we want to take a trait associated with the final necessary condition and attach that to the initial sufficient condition. This doesn't happen here.

C. *It is permissible to sit on the park benches. To sit on the park benches one must walk to them. One way to walk to them is by walking on the grass. So it is permissible to walk on the grass.*

The statement *"one way to walk to them is by walking on the grass"* is NOT a conditional. If it had instead read "The only way to walk to them is by walking on the grass," then it would have been an ok answer.

D. *It is impossible to be a manager without evaluating people. The process of evaluation is necessarily subjective. Thus, people resent managers because they resent being evaluated subjectively.*

Manager → Evaluate People → Subjective

Again, the conclusion here is not what we are looking for. Instead, we want something that takes a trait of subjective actions and associate it with being a manager.

E. *Some farming on the plains requires irrigation. This irrigation now uses water pumped from aquifers. But aquifers have limited capacity and continued pumping will eventually exhaust them. Thus, a new source of water will have to be found in order for such farming to continue indefinitely.*

This answer choice isn't even conditional in nature, it can be eliminated outright.

The correct answer is A.

16. Parallel and Parallel Flaw Questions

Let's look at one more question where thinking about the argument/answer choice's validity can help us figure out the correct answer.

PT35 S4 Q23

The higher the altitude, the thinner the air. Since Mexico City's altitude is higher than that of Panama City, the air must be thinner in Mexico City than in Panama City.

Which one of the following arguments is most similar in its reasoning to the argument above?

A. As one gets older one gets wiser. Since Henrietta is older than her daughter, Henrietta must be wiser than her daughter.
B. The more egg whites used and the longer they are beaten, the fluffier the meringue. Since Lydia used more egg whites in her meringue than Joseph used in his, Lydia's meringue must be fluffier than Joseph's.
C. The people who run the fastest marathons these days are faster than the people who ran the fastest marathons ten years ago. Charles is a marathon runner. So Charles must run faster marathons these days than he did ten years ago.
D. The older a tree, the more rings it has. The tree in Lou's yard is older than the tree in Teresa's yard. Therefore, the tree in Lou's yard must have more rings than does the tree in Teresa's yard.
E. The bigger the vocabulary a language has, the harder it is to learn. English is harder to learn than Italian. Therefore, English must have a bigger vocabulary than Italian.

- The first premise contains a correlation. Higher altitude ~ Thinner Air. (A ~ B)
- The second premise states that Mexico City's altitude is higher than Panama City's, so MA > PA.
- The conclusion states that Mexico's air is thinner than Panama City's, so MB > PB.

This is a valid argument, let's take a look at the answer choices.

A. *As one gets older one gets wiser. Since Henrietta is older than her daughter, Henrietta must be wiser than her daughter.*

At a first glance, the statement "as one gets older one gets wiser" seems like a correlation, just like "the higher the altitude, the thinner the air." But what we really want is "older the person, wiser the person."

In our stimulus, the difference will be *absolute* according to its correlation. If Mt. Everest is higher than the Dead Sea, the air will be thinner on Mt. Everest than at the Dead Sea. Here, how wise you get will be *relative* to how wise you were before. The older Peter will be wiser than the younger Peter, but we don't know how he is compared to someone else. So this answer choice is actually a flawed argument, it commits the *relative vs. absolute* flaw.

This is a perfect example of where the premise from the answer choice doesn't quite match up with the premise from the argument.

B. *The more egg whites used and the longer they are beaten, the fluffier the meringue. Since Lydia used more egg whites in her meringue than Joseph used in his, Lydia's meringue must be fluffier than Joseph's.*

There is a correlation in the first statement, more egg whites AND longer they are beaten, the fluffier the meringue.

However, in the second premise, only the amount of egg whites is discussed. We don't know if Lydia beat her eggs longer than Joseph also. The premises don't match up perfectly in this answer choice either.

C. *The people who run the fastest marathons these days are faster than the people who ran the fastest marathons ten years ago. Charles is a marathon runner. So Charles must run faster marathons these days than he did ten years ago.*

This answer doesn't have the correlation we are looking for, and there is no comparison between two entities (e.g. Mexico City vs. Panama City).

D. *The older a tree, the more rings it has. The tree in Lou's yard is older than the tree in Teresa's yard. Therefore, the tree in Lou's yard must have more rings than does the tree in Teresa's yard.*

- Older ~ More Rings
- LO > TO (Lou's tree older than Teresa's tree)
- LR > TR (Lou's tree has more rings than Teresa's tree)

This matches up better than answers choices A and B, so all that's left is to compare D with E, and pick the better one.

E. *The bigger the vocabulary a language has, the harder it is to learn. English is harder to learn than Italian. Therefore, English must have a bigger vocabulary than Italian.*

- Bigger Vocabulary ~ Harder to Learn
- English Hardness Level > Italian Hardness Level
- English Vocabulary > Italian Vocabulary

Technically, there is nothing wrong with this answer choice. The reasoning, validity, and structure all match up with the argument in the stimulus. The only difference is that while the argument in the stimulus takes the first part of the correlation as its premise, and the second part of the correlation to be the conclusion, the ordering is reversed here.

While this is not wrong *per se,* I will eliminate this answer only because answer choice D *doesn't have this* issue. We always strive to pick the answer choice that mirrors the original argument the *closest,* and answer choice D is just a safer pick.

<u>The correct answer is D.</u>

Matching the Conclusion:

Oftentimes the amount of information in a Parallel Question can be overwhelming. So it's only natural that we miss some of the details and nuances when tackling these questions, especially under realistic testing conditions.

In harder questions the differences between the correct answer and some tempting wrong answers will be barely noticeable. A common trick test makers like to use in formulating trap answers is to come up with an argument that largely matches the argument in the stimulus but with subtle differences in the conclusion. Perhaps a causal relationship is reversed, perhaps a conditional relationship is reversed.

Whenever I am faced with several potential contender answer choices, I would quickly go back to the main conclusion of the stimulus argument, memorize it, and compare it to the conclusions of the answer choices I'm looking at. Which one is closer to the conclusion in the stimulus?

Difficult Trait #1: Beware subtle shifts in the answer choice's conclusion

PT68 S3 Q22

Radio producer: Our failure to attract new listeners over the past several years has forced us to choose between devoting some airtime to other, more popular genres of music, and sticking with classical music that appeals only to our small but loyal audience. This audience, however loyal, did not generate enough advertising revenue for us to pay our bills, so if we appeal to them alone, our station risks going out of business. We should not take that risk. We should, therefore, devote some airtime to other, more popular genres of music.

Which one of the following arguments is most similar in its pattern of reasoning to that used by the radio producer?

A. We should either buy blinds for the windows or make full length curtains. Blinds would be very expensive to purchase. Thus, if cost is our greatest concern, we should make curtains.
B. We should either make curtains for the windows or buy blinds. Since the windows are not standard sizes, if we buy blinds we will have to special order them. Since we do not have time to wait for special orders, we should make the curtains.
C. For the living room windows, we can make curtains or valances or both. We want to have privacy; and while curtains provide privacy, valences do not. So we should make curtains but not valances.
D. Since we have very little fabric, we will have to either buy more, or make valances instead of curtains. However, if we use this fabric to make valances, then we will have to buy blinds. Since it would be hard to buy fabric that matches what we already have, we should buy blinds.
E. We should either buy blinds or make curtains for the windows. If we buy blinds but do not make valances, the windows will look bare. We should not have bare windows. So if we do not make the curtains, we should make the valances.

This stimulus is a bit long winded, but this is what the argument is, essentially:

- Premise 1: We must choose between devoting some airtime to other genres VS. sticking with classical music.
- Premise 2: Classical music audience does not generate enough revenue, so sticking with classical music can lead to bankruptcy
- Premise 3: We do not want to risk bankruptcy
- Conclusion: So we should choose to devote airtime to other genres.

So the author presents two options, one option would lead to an undesired result, so the author concludes we should choose the other option.

Let's see if we can eliminate some answer choices based on our summary understanding of the stimulus.

A.   *We should either buy blinds for the windows or make full length curtains. Blinds would be very expensive to purchase. Thus, if cost is our greatest concern, we should make curtains.*

So its blinds vs. full length curtains. Blinds are expensive, so we should make curtains. The reasoning seems to match up with what we anticipated. Let's keep it for now.

B.   *We should either make curtains for the windows or buy blinds. Since the windows are not standard sizes, if we buy blinds we will have to special order them. Since we do not have time to wait for special orders, we should make the curtains.*

Again, the options are curtains vs. blinds. Getting blinds means special ordering them, which we cannot do. So curtains it is. This answer seems to work also, let's keep it as well.

C.   *For the living room windows, we can make curtains or valances <u>or both</u>. We want to have privacy; and while curtains provide privacy, valences do not. So we should make curtains but not valances.*

Here, we are no longer choosing between two options, we can have both. This answer choice has already strayed further from the original stimulus than A or B, so I think it's safe to eliminate it.

D.   *Since we have very little fabric, we will have to either buy more, or make valances instead of curtains. However, if we use this fabric to make valances, then we will have to buy blinds. Since it would be hard to buy fabric that matches what we already have, we should buy blinds.*

The choice is between valances and curtains. Curtains need additional fabric, which we cannot find. So we should buy valances. However, the conclusion of this argument is about blinds, not valances. This argument goes a step further than the original stimulus, I would eliminate it also.

E.   *We should either buy blinds or make curtains for the windows. If we buy blinds but do not make valances, the windows will look bare. We should not have bare windows. So if we do not make the curtains, we should make the valances.*

The choice here is between blinds and curtains. But does the author choose one over the other because the other option leads to an undesirable result? If we buy blinds but do not make valances, the windows will look bare, but the author never says not to buy blinds. He or she only says blinds should come with valances. Neither does the author object to buying curtains. The author never commits to one over the other in this answer choice.

By anticipating how each answer choice should turn out, we can eliminate C, D, and E. So let's go back and take a second look at A and B.

Here is where taking a close look at the argument's conclusion can be helpful. In the author's conclusion, they commit explicitly to option A, devoting airtime to popular music. Answer choice A's conclusion is conditional in nature: "if cost is our greatest concern, we should make curtains." Answer choice B, however, has an unequivocal conclusion: he or she thinks we should make curtains.

<u>The correct answer is B.</u>

Taking a closer look at the conclusion of the argument can help us further differentiate between the correct answer choice and tempting wrong answers.

This is essentially my second round of elimination. In the first round I was able to eliminate answer choices C, D, E based on my rather general understanding of the stimulus argument. Once I've narrowed the correct answer down to two options, A, and B, I would then read these two extra carefully, looking for areas where they differ from the stimulus argument.

Matching Premises:

After taking a more detailed look at the conclusion, I will also double check to make sure that the premises match up as well. As we have already seen in PT35 S4 Q23, and PT75 S1 Q25, some answer choices can be eliminated because their premises don't match up with the stimulus's argument.

Again, in my initial round of reading answer choices, I try not to get too bogged down in the details of comparing the premises of each answer choice. That would be too time consuming.

Instead, I save premise comparison and conclusion comparison for last, almost as a tie-breaker to help me choose the best answer choice possible.

PT20 S1 Q19

No one in the French department to which Professor Alban belongs is allowed to teach more than one introductory level class in any one term. Moreover, the only language classes being taught next term are advanced ones. So it is untrue that both of the French classes Professor Alban will be teaching next term will be introductory level classes.

The pattern of reasoning displayed in the argument above is most closely paralleled by that in which one of the following arguments?

A. The Morrison Building will be fully occupied by May and since if a building is occupied by May the new tax rates apply to it, the Morrison Building will be taxed according to the new rates.

B. The revised tax code does not apply at all to buildings built before 1900, and only the first section of the revised code applies to buildings built between 1900 and 1920, so the revised code does not apply to the Norton Building, since it was built in 1873.

C. All property on Overton Road will be reassessed for tax purposes by the end of the year and the Elnor Company headquarters is on Overton Road, so Elnor's property taxes will be higher next year.

D. New buildings that include public space are exempt from city taxes for two years and all new buildings in the city's Alton district are exempt for five years, so the building with the large public space that was recently completed in Alton will not be subject to city taxes next year.

E. Since according to recent statute, a building that is exempt from property taxes is charged for city water at a special rate, and hospitals are exempt from property taxes, Founder's Hospital will be charged for city water at the special rate.

So there are three statements in the stimulus, consisting of two premises and a conclusion:

- Premise 1: Professor Alban's French department → Teach one intro level class at most
- Premise 2: Taught next term → Advanced Classes
- Conclusion: Professor Alban's French classes cannot both be intro classes

Take a look at the relationship of each premise to the main conclusion. Each premise is *independently sufficient* to establish the conclusion.

In other words, if we just had premise 1, it's enough to establish the conclusion. Premise 1 tells us Professor Alban can teach one intro level class at most. Similarly, if we only had Premise 2, then neither of Professor Alban's classes next term can be intro level classes. So the conclusion stands as well.

But then again, it might be difficult to catch all this on a first read. That's why it can be helpful to come back and re-read the premises when we are stuck on the answer choices.

A. *The Morrison Building will be fully occupied by May and since if a building is occupied by May the new tax rates apply to it, the Morrison Building will be taxed according to the new rates.*

B. *The revised tax code does not apply at all to buildings built before 1900, and only the first section of the revised code applies to buildings built between 1900 and 1920, so the revised code does not apply to the Norton Building, since it was built in 1873.*

C. *All property on Overton Road will be reassessed for tax purposes by the end of the year and the Elnor Company headquarters is on Overton Road, so Elnor's property taxes will be <u>higher</u> next year.*

D. *New buildings that include public space are exempt from city taxes for two years and all new buildings in the city's Alton district are exempt for five years, so the building with the large public space that was recently completed in Alton will not be subject to city taxes next year.*

E. *Since according to recent statute, a building that is exempt from property taxes is charged for city water at a special rate, and hospitals are exempt from property taxes, Founder's Hospital will be charged for city water at the special rate.*

Answer choices A, C, and E can be eliminated without much difficulty, they have the same reasoning structure which is quite different from the argument in our stimulus.

Let's look at answer choices B and D in greater detail:

At a first glance both answer choices seem pretty good. Both conclusions say that the rules don't apply to the building. (Revised code does not apply to Norton Building in B, large building in Alton not subject to taxes in D.) Both seem to match the conclusion from the stimulus, which says Alban's classes won't be intro level classes.

So now we have to really look at the premises in both of these answer choices. The logic, structure, and the conclusion all matches up, so all that's left to do is look at the premises.

Answer choice B:

- Premise 1: Build before 1900 → Doesn't Apply
- Premise 2: 1900 - 1920 → Only first section applies
- Conclusion: Code doesn't apply to Norton Building, built in 1873

Answer choice D:

- Premise 1: Public space → Exempt for two years
- Premise 2: New buildings → Exempt for five years
- Conclusion: new building w/ public space exempt next year

Take a careful look at these answer choices, premise 2 from answer choice B is problematic. It doesn't have any effect on our conclusion. The Norton building was built in 1873, so premise 2 is irrelevant.

By now, you should have gone back to the stimulus to check both premises of the argument, realizing that both premises *independently* justify the outcome in the conclusion. As a result, <u>answer choice D is the correct answer.</u>

If there are multiple tempting answers, see if one answer's premises/conclusion are a closer fit with the original argument.

***

Things that don't need to match in the correct answer

So far, we have looked at matching an argument's logic, validity, and structure in a Parallel question. We also saw that focusing on the conclusion and premises can help us determine which answer choice is a better match ultimately.

There are a few things that we don't need to worry about in a Parallel question too. The first of these is the **peripheral information** in a stimulus. If you remember from the chapter on Find the Conclusion Questions, in the section on stimulus structure, we divided the information present in a stimulus into the argument and peripheral information. Peripheral information includes concessions, counterpoints, and background information.

Our job is to match the argument, the peripheral information is less relevant. For example in PT68 S3 Q22, the statement "*our failure to attract new listeners over the past several years*" is less relevant. It is background information for why we are faced with a dilemma of courting new listeners with pop music or sticking with classical music. It is not a part of the argument.

The second thing that is less relevant in a Parallel question is the **sequence in which argument components appear**. More specifically, if the argument in the stimulus has a Premise - Intermediate Conclusion - Conclusion format, then the correct answer can reorder these components in any way it pleases, as long as all three are still present. We can have the conclusion come first, followed by the premise, and finally the conclusion, for example.

We saw this in the correct answer choice of PT31 S3 Q18, take a look at PT76 S4 Q22, PT27 S1 Q26, and PT23 S3 Q18 if you want to get a closer feel for correct answer choices that have reordered argument components.

As a result, in the hardest questions, it's crucial to read for structure when looking at the answer choices as well. Ask yourself, which one is the conclusion, the premise, the intermediate conclusion? Do all these match up with the structure of the stimulus argument?

Part II: Parallel Flaw

Nearly all study material currently on the market categorize "Parallel Flaw" questions as a variant of Parallel Questions. This is actually quite misleading. Some of the rules that apply to Parallel questions may not necessarily apply to "Parallel Flaw" questions. Instead, we should think of these questions, first and foremost, as Flaw Questions. **The most important element to match up between the stimulus argument and the correct answer choice is the flaw.** They must be suffering from the same flaw. You can have an answer choice that matches the original argument's logic, its structure, even its premises and conclusion, but if it has not committed the same flawed reasoning as the original argument, that answer choice will be wrong.

For this exact reason I prefer to call these questions "Flaw Matching" questions. Our job is to find the flaw in the stimulus argument, and identify the answer choice that is suffering from the same flaw. Only when we have multiple answers that all share the same flaw as the original argument do we ask ourselves the question of which answer choice is a closer match. (Take a look at PT 65-1-11 for a question where the correct answer matches the flaw but not necessarily the logic of the stimulus.)

So essentially, the steps to tackling a "Parallel Flaw/Flaw Matching" question are three-fold.

Identify the flaw committed by the argument in the stimulus.

Identify the answer choice whose argument commits the same flaw.

If multiple answer choices commit this flaw, choose the answer choice that is closest to the original argument.

I have included Flaw Matching Questions in the same chapter as Parallel Argument Questions, as you, the intermediate - advanced student, has probably already gotten into the habit of associating these questions with Parallel Argument questions. But just remember that finding the flaw and matching the flaw is our most important job, and if we can't do that, nothing else matters.

I would strongly recommend revisiting the chapter on Flaw Questions. Having a mastery of Flaw Questions is a prerequisite for tackling Flaw Matching Questions. A Flaw Matching Question, answers included, is basically six Flaw Question stimuli rolled into one. There is an argument in the stimulus, you need to find its flaw, then there's five answer choices, and you have to study each of these to see what their flaws are as well.

The following is a list of the flaws that have appeared frequently in harder Parallel Flaw/Flaw Matching questions; pay special attention to these as you revisit the Flaw Question chapter.

- Conditional Flaws
- Causal Flaws
- Sampling Bias
- Appeal to Ignorance (Unproven vs. Untrue)
- Fallacy of Composition/Division (Part vs. Whole)
- Inducing Future from Past Events (Past vs. Future)
- Non Sequitur Fallacy (Extrapolation of Unnecessary Belief)
- False Conversion (Some/Most/All)
- Overlook Flaws

Now that you have revisited the Flaw Questions chapter, let's return our focus to Flaw Matching Questions.

The skills required to navigate Flaw Matching Questions can be divided into two categories: **Flaw Detection** and **Answer Choice Differentiation**. We will look at each in turn.

Flaw Detection

Multiple Flaws/Gaps in the Stimulus Argument:

Building upon our knowledge of Flaw Questions, a common yet often exasperating feature of Flaw Matching Questions is that the stimulus argument will often contain more than one flaw or potential flaw. Sometimes the question will tell us explicitly that there are two flaws in the argument, and that we will have to find the answer choice that contains both of these flaws. But sometimes the question will not give us such a hint, and it is up to us to detect for ourselves if there are multiple flaws in the argument.

The good thing about these, however, is that even if we detected multiple flaws in the argument, we don't need to match them all up in the answer choices unless the question explicitly asks us to.

Let's look at some examples, all drawn, as usual, from the hardest questions of this type.

PT2 S4 Q22

All intelligent people are nearsighted. I am very nearsighted. So I must be a genius.

Which one of the following exhibits both of the logical flaws exhibited in the argument above?

    A. I must be stupid because all intelligent people are nearsighted and I have perfect eyesight.
    B. All chickens have beaks. This bird has a beak. So this bird must be a chicken.
    C. All pigs have four legs, but this spider has eight legs. So this spider must be twice as big as any pig.
    D. John is extremely happy, so he must be extremely tall because all tall people are happy.
    E. All geniuses are very nearsighted. I must be very nearsighted since I am a genius.

The question makes it easy for us. We are told there are two flaws in this argument.

The first flaw is pretty easy to spot, the author erroneously reverses the sufficient and necessary.

- Premise: Intelligent → Nearsighted
- Premise: Very Nearsighted
- Conclusion: Genius

The second flaw is a little harder to detect, the author thinks that because they are *very* nearsighted, they must be *very* intelligent (genius). The author takes a conditional relationship and infers a correlation from it.

There's no specific name for this type of flaw, but take a look at the following analogy, and you'll see why it's problematic.

All good basketball players are tall, so Yao Ming, who is the tallest basketball player, must be the best.

A.   *I must be stupid because all intelligent people are nearsighted and I have perfect eyesight.*

This answer contains neither of the flaws present in the stimulus. The author here argues by contrapositive, which is valid. It's debatable whether being "not intelligent" equals "stupid," but that's something that needn't concern us.

B.   *All chickens have beaks. This bird has a beak. So this bird must be a chicken.*

This answer contains the first flaw we mentioned, but we need both flaws!

C.   *All pigs have four legs, but this spider has eight legs. So this spider must be twice as big as any pig.*

This answer choice doesn't contain the first flaw, the author does seem to assume there to be a correlation between the number of legs and size, but the correlation in our original argument derives from a conditional premise, not from an assumption.

D.   *John is extremely happy, so he must be extremely tall because all tall people are happy.*

The premise tells us Tall → Happy, the author commits the first flaw by thinking that happy people must be tall. The second flaw is also committed when the author thinks that those who are extremely happy are also extremely tall. <u>This is the correct answer</u>.

E.   *All geniuses are very nearsighted. I must be very nearsighted since I am a genius.*

This answer choice is logically valid.

The previous question told us at the onset that the argument contained two flaws, so in some ways, that makes our job easier. We know not to stop looking until we have found both flaws. But more often, we can be faced with a stimulus argument that contains multiple flaws/gaps, and we would not know which flaw is the one the test makers want until we have read all the answer choices.

Difficult Trait #1: Sometimes a stimulus's argument can contain more than one flaw.

<u>PT14 S4 Q14</u>

The commissioner has announced that Judge Khalid, who was on the seven-member panel appointed to resolve the Amlec labor dispute, will have sole responsibility for resolving the Simdon labor dispute. Since in its decision the Amlec panel showed itself both reasonable and fair, the two sides in the Simdon dispute are undoubtedly justified in the confidence they have expressed in the reasonableness and fairness of the arbitrator assigned to their case.

Which one of the following contains flawed reasoning most parallel to that contained in the passage?

A. Representing the school board, Marcia Barthes presented to the school's principal a list of recently elected school board members. Since only an elected member of the school board can act as its representative, Ms. Barthes' name undoubtedly appears on that list.

B. Alan Caldalf, who likes being around young children, has decided to become a pediatrician. Since the one characteristic common to all good pediatricians is that they like young children, Mr. Caldalf will undoubtedly be a very good pediatrician.

C. Jorge Diaz is a teacher at a musical school nationally known for the excellence of its conducting faculty. Since Mr. Diaz has recently been commended for the excellence of his teaching, he is undoubtedly a member of the school's conducting faculty.

D. Ula Borg, who has sold real estate for Arcande Realty for many years, undoubtedly sold fewer houses last year than she had the year before since the number of houses sold last year by Arcande Realty is far lower than the number sold the previous year.

E. The members of the local historical society unanimously support designating the First National Bank building a historical landmark. Since Evelyn George is a member of that society, she undoubtedly favors according landmark status to the city hall as well.

There are two flaws I found with this argument. In the argument, the author is essentially arguing that because the panel had been just and fair in its handling of the Amlec case, Judge Khalid, who was a member of that panel, will be just and fair in his handling of the Simdon case.

In the first place, just because the panel was just and fair, it doesn't mean that Judge Khalid will be just and fair as well. Perhaps the decision rendered was a majority decision and Judge Khalid wrote the dissenting opinion. This is the Part vs. Whole flaw.

Secondly, being just and fair in a past decision is no guarantee that you will be just and fair in a future decision. A court may have rendered a fair decision before, but it is still susceptible to mistakes down the road. This is the Past vs. Future flaw.

The question didn't explicitly state that we need to match both flaws in the answer choices. So when we are going through them, **I would try to find one that contains both of these flaws, and if none of them do, I will select the answer choice that matches one of the two.**

> A. *Representing the school board, Marcia Barthes presented to the school's principal a list of recently elected school board members. Since only an elected member of the school board can act as its representative, Ms. Barthes' name undoubtedly appears on that list*

The issue with this answer choice is that Barthes being an elected member of the school board doesn't necessarily mean she is recently elected, or that the list is exhaustive. This is an Overlook Flaw and not one of the flaws that we are looking for.

> B. *Alan Caldalf, who likes being around young children, has decided to become a pediatrician. Since the one characteristic common to all good pediatricians is that they like young children, Mr. Caldalf will undoubtedly be a very good pediatrician*

In this answer choice, the author commits a conditional flaw, reversing the sufficient and the necessary.

> C. *Jorge Diaz is a teacher at a musical school nationally known for the excellence of its conducting faculty. Since Mr. Diaz has recently been commended for the excellence of his teaching, he is undoubtedly a member of the school's conducting faculty*

This answer choice gets a little more tricky. It has some of the elements of a Part vs. Whole flaw: the author talks about a school's conducting faculty, and Mr. Diaz, who is a music teacher. But the author isn't arguing that because the faculty is excellent, Diaz is excellent, or vice versa.

This is actually either the False Conversion Flaw, Conditional Flaw, or Overlook Flaw. The argument is essentially this: Conducting Faculty is excellent, Mr. Diaz is excellent, so Mr. Diaz is a member of the conducting faculty.

This is akin to saying that MMA fighters are good fighters, Navy Seals are good fighters, so Navy Seals are MMA fighters.

> D. *Ula Borg, who has sold real estate for Arcande Realty for many years, undoubtedly sold fewer houses last year than she had the year before since the number of houses sold last year by Arcande Realty is far lower than the number sold the previous year*

This answer choice commits the Part vs. Whole flaw. Because Arcande Realty's numbers are down doesn't mean Ula Borg's numbers are necessarily down.

E.   *The members of the local historical society unanimously support designating the First National Bank building a historical landmark. Since Evelyn George is a member of that society, she undoubtedly favors according landmark status to the city hall as well*

This answer choice uses premises about the bank building to justify a conclusion about the city hall.

Luckily, we weren't faced with another answer choice which commits the Past vs. Future flaw, because that's also a valid option. **So what happens when more than one answer choice matches up with the flaws detected in the stimulus?** That's when we compare the answer choices to see which one is a closer match to the original argument. But more on this later.

The correct answer is D. Even though it didn't match both of the flaws we detected in the stimulus, it got one of them, and that's already better than the rest of the answer choices.

Difficult Trait #2: Beware mis-directions and false leads that appear in the Parallel Flaw argument.

We have seen the presence of False Leads in the Flaw Questions chapter. The test makers will word the stimulus argument in such a way that can mislead you into thinking it's one flaw when in fact it is another. That's why we must remain mentally flexible when reading the stimulus. Keep on asking yourself "is there another potential flaw in there" even after having detected one flaw is a great way to train ourselves to remain mentally flexible.

Similarly, sometimes after reading the stimulus, you may think that the flaw we are looking for is of one type, when it is in fact another. So as soon as you realize that the actual flaw isn't what you thought it was, start looking elsewhere.

Answer Choice Differentiation

Oftentimes in the harder Flaw Matching Questions, we are faced with multiple answer choices that all contain the same flaw as the original argument. This leaves many students paralyzed and unable to proceed.

So what happens when we have identified the correct flaw in the stimulus, but **there is more than one answer choice that also shares the same flaw?**

Difficult Trait #3: When more than one answer shares the same flaw as the original argument, pick the one that is a closer match in language and level of certainty.

<u>PT52 S1 Q16</u>

Anyone who believes in extraterrestrials believes in UFOs. But the existence of UFOs has been conclusively refuted. Therefore a belief in extraterrestrials is false as well.

Which one of the following arguments contains flawed reasoning most similar to that in the argument above?

- A. Anyone who believes in unicorns believes in centaurs. But it has been demonstrated that there are no centaurs, so there are no unicorns either.
- B. Anyone who believes in unicorns believes in centaurs. But you do not believe in centaurs, so you do not believe in unicorns either.
- C. Anyone who believes in unicorns believes in centaurs. But you do not believe in unicorns, so you do not believe in centaurs either.
- D. Anyone who believes in unicorns believes in centaurs. But there is no good reason to believe in centaurs, so a belief in unicorns is unjustified as well.
- E. Anyone who believes in unicorns believes in centaurs. But it has been conclusively proven that there is no such thing as a unicorn, so a belief in centaurs is mistaken as well.

The flaw in this argument feels like a non sequitur/unnecessary belief flaw but not quite. It also has conditional reasoning sprinkled into the argument. Whenever we can't quite pinpoint what the exact flaw is, it helps to diagram out the original argument in notational form:

- Premise: Believe ET → Believe UFO
- Premise: UFOs don't exist (Belief in UFOs false)
- Conclusion: Belief in ET is also false

Making the argument more abstract will help us when eliminating answer choices:

- Premise: Believe A → Believe B
- Premise: B is false
- Conclusion: A is false

In this argument, the author improperly contrapositives the conditional in the initial premise. The contrapositive of (Believe A → Believe B) should be *"People who don't believe in UFOs won't believe in ET"* (Don't Believe B → Don't Believe A). Instead of properly negating a condition about what people believe in, the conclusion is about whether something exists.

Let's take a look at the answer choices, notice how every answer choice begins with "anyone who believes in unicorns believes in centaurs," so let's make "unicorns" A, and "centaurs" B.

A. *Anyone who believes in unicorns believes in centaurs. But it has been demonstrated that there are no centaurs, so there are no unicorns either.*

- Believe A → Believe B
- B is false
- A is false

B. *Anyone who believes in unicorns believes in centaurs. But you do not believe in centaurs, so you do not believe in unicorns either.*

- Believe A → Believe B
- You don't believe in B
- You don't believe in A

This is a proper contrapositive of the initial premise, it's a valid argument.

C. *Anyone who believes in unicorns believes in centaurs. But you do not believe in unicorns, so you do not believe in centaurs either.*

- Believe A → Believe B
- You don't believe in A
- You don't believe in B

Compared to the original argument, the author mixes up the conclusion and the second premise.

D. *Anyone who believes in unicorns believes in centaurs. But there is no good reason to believe in centaurs, so a belief in unicorns is unjustified as well.*

- Believe A → Believe B
- B is false

- A is false

E. *Anyone who believes in unicorns believes in centaurs. But it has been conclusively proven that there is no such thing as a unicorn, so a belief in centaurs is mistaken as well.*

- Believe A → Believe B
- A is false
- B is false

This answer choice commits the same error as answer choice C.

Both answer choices A and D seem to match the original argument pretty well, let's take a look at them again:

Original Argument: *Existence of B conclusively refuted, belief in A false as well.*

Answer choice A: *It has been demonstrated there are no B, so there are no As either.*

Answer choice D: *There is no good reason to believe in B, so belief in A is unjustified.*

Which answer choice more closely mirrors the language of the original argument? The level of certainty expressed by the original argument can be seen in answer choice A. Answer choice D, on the other hand, is slightly weaker. Just because there's no good reason to believe in B *doesn't necessarily mean* the same thing as B is false. Ancient peoples had no good reason to believe that the earth is round, but that doesn't mean it isn't. Similarly, an unjustified belief could still hold true, however small the possibilities.

Answer choice A wins over answer choice D in this question, but just slightly. A is the correct answer.

So here, we had to take a second look specifically at A and D, and ended up picking the answer that **more closely mirrored the strength and language of the original argument.**

***

PT89 S4 Q22

The universe as a whole necessarily tends toward greater disorder, or entropy. From this alone, it follows that the earth's biosphere has always been moving toward increased disorder as well, in spite of appearances to the contrary.

Which one of the following is most similar in its flawed reasoning to the argument above?

A. Wooded Lake is one of the most beautiful lakes in the world. This follows from the fact that the extensive system of interconnected lakes of which Wooded Lake is a part is one of the most beautiful systems of its type worldwide.
B. This has been the coldest April in this region in the last half-century. So, on any given day this April, it is likely that the weather was unseasonably cold.
C. The manifest indicates that every deck on that cruise ship houses some commercial cargo, even though on some decks the cargo storage areas are difficult to find. Hence every deck on the ship is devoted to commercial cargo storage, even though this is not immediately obvious.
D. Although Hopper claims to have been working in another part of the plant when the accident occurred, company records show that every person on the cleanup crew of which Hopper is a member was in the grain area at the time. Hence Hopper either has misremembered events, or is not telling the truth.
E. Two of the seven critical parts in that gear assembly are unsafe to use, even though this is not obvious upon a casual inspection. The assembly therefore is unsafe to rely on and ought to be repaired.

The flaw here is a Part vs. Whole flaw (Fallacy of Composition/Division). In the premise, the author states that the *universe* tends toward greater disorder. The author then concludes that the earth's biosphere (a part of the universe) also tends toward greater disorder.

This is relatively easy to detect, so let's look at the answer choices:

A. *Wooded Lake is one of the most beautiful lakes in the world. This follows from the fact that the extensive system of interconnected lakes of which Wooded Lake is a part is one of the most beautiful systems of its type worldwide.*

The lake district (whole) is one of the most beautiful systems in the world, so Wooded Lake, a part of the lake system, is also one of the most beautiful lakes in the world. This commits the same flaw as the original argument.

B. *This has been the coldest April in this region in the last half-century. So, on any given day this April, it is likely that the weather was unseasonably cold.*

The month is really cold, so any day in the month is likely to be really cold. This also seems to commit the Part vs. Whole fallacy.

C. *The manifest indicates that every deck on that cruise ship houses some commercial cargo, even though on some decks the cargo storage areas are difficult to find. Hence every deck on the ship is devoted to commercial cargo storage, even though this is not immediately obvious.*

This argument goes "every deck *houses* some cargo, so every deck is *devoted* to cargo." The author takes for granted that if a deck houses some cargo, it's entirely devoted to cargo.

Some students may mistake this for a Part vs. Whole argument, they think that "the deck houses some cargo" is the "part", and "every deck is devoted to cargo" is the "whole." However, if you recall from the Flaw chapter, a proper Part vs. Whole argument should look like this:

Subcomponent is X, so entirety is X.

Entirety is X, so subcomponent is X.

If the argument had read "lower deck is devoted to cargo, so whole ship is devoted to cargo," or vice versa, then it would have been ok.

D. *Although Hopper claims to have been working in another part of the plant when the accident occurred, company records show that every person on the cleanup crew of which Hopper is a member was in the grain area at the time. Hence Hopper either has misremembered events, or is not telling the truth.*

Everyone in area X, so Hopper was also in area X.

Remember in the section on the Fallacy of Composition/Division we stated that not every Part vs. Whole argument is automatically fallacious. The valid example we used was "every component of this chair is made out of wood, so this chair is made out of wood."

The argument here is actually a valid one. Perhaps you can argue that the company records are mistaken, but for our purposes, this Part vs. Whole argument is not fallacious.

E. *Two of the seven critical parts in that gear assembly are unsafe to use, even though this is not obvious upon a casual inspection. The assembly therefore is unsafe to rely on and ought to be repaired.*

Parts unsafe to use, so assembly unsafe to use.

This seems to commit the Part vs. Whole fallacy as well. Although it may be a valid argument too (the parts that are unsafe to use are *critical* parts).

Let's compare the original argument with answer choices A, B, and E:

Original Argument: *universe moves toward greater disorder (whole), so earth's biosphere moves toward greater disorder as well (part).*

A: *Lake system one of the most beautiful (whole), so Wooded lake one of the most beautiful (part).*

B: *Coldest April (whole), any given day likely to be cold (part).*

E: *Two parts unsafe to use (part), assembly unsafe to use (whole).*

I will first eliminate answer choice E, because it goes from part to whole, rather than whole to part. The original argument as well as A and B all go from whole to part. So answer choice E is pretty low on my list.

The conclusion of answer choice B is also modified with the adverb "likely." The level of certainty in the original argument is fairly high, and so is the language of answer choice A. So I would choose A over B.

In many ways, answer choice B presents us with a *valid* argument. If the month is the coldest ever, we know that there will be many cold days during this month, and we can speculate that any given day is *more likely* to be cold than not.

A is the correct answer.

Again, we chose the answer choice that most closely mirrored the original argument in both its structure and strength of language.

Take a look at 76-2-21 for another question where just matching the flaw is not enough, we also have to pay attention to the structural elements of the argument (premise and conclusion.)

Difficult Trait #4: Match the flaw first, then worry about matching the other aspects of the argument.

PT32 S4 Q21

Experimental psychology requires the application of statistics to interpret empirical data and assess their significance. A person will not be able to understand such applications without training in statistics. Therefore, the more training one has in statistics, the better one will be at research in experimental psychology.

Which one of the following arguments exhibits a flawed pattern of reasoning most similar to that exhibited by the argument above?

A. Most people need the love and support of others; without it, they become depressed and unhappy. Therefore, in most instances, the more love and support a person receives, the happier that person will be.

B. Since in most jobs there are annual wage or salary increases, the longer one has worked, the more raises one will have received. Therefore, in a typical job, the longer one has worked, the greater one's income will be.

C. The main cause of heart attacks is arteriosclerosis, the buildup of plaque on the interior wall of the coronary arteries. It develops over an extended period of time. Therefore, if one is at risk for arteriosclerosis, one becomes more likely to suffer a heart attack as one gets older.

D. Since many disease processes are biochemical in nature, unless one understands chemistry one will not be able to understand the explanations for many diseases. Therefore, if one has no training in chemistry, one will not be able to master medicine.

E. Since most disease processes are biochemical in nature, an understanding of chemistry will enable one to understand most diseases. Therefore, one needs little more than training in chemistry to be able to master medicine.

In this argument, the author infers a correlation from a conditional relationship:

- Premise: Experimental Psychology → Application of Statistics → Training in Statistics
- Conclusion: More Training in Statistics ~ Better at Experimental Psychology Research

This can probably be categorized as a flaw that confuses different types of logic, something we mentioned in the Flaw chapter. Take a look at the following analogy to see why it's wrong.

Being a lawyer requires going to law school, going to law school requires taking the LSAT. So the higher you score on the LSAT, the better you will be as a lawyer.

This question is not difficult, I trust you were able to deduce the correct answer, which is A.

However, I just wanted us to take a closer look at answer choice A. We know that the original argument's premises contain a conditional chain. But the relationship presented in the premises of answer choice A aren't, strictly speaking, conditional. It's only applicable to "most people." We will look at Some/Most/All relationships in greater detail in the chapter on Must be True Questions, but just bear with me for now.

All As are Bs is a conditional, you can diagram it as A → B, and its contrapositive is B̸ → A̸

Most As are Bs is NOT a conditional, because it's only applicable to a part of the population.

Strictly speaking, answer choice A is problematic. But compared to it, the other answer choices fall short of the original argument even more. That's why we have no choice but to select A, and A is the correct answer in this case.

And that's the point I'm trying to convey here.

Just like Strengthen/Weaken Questions, and Most Strongly Supported Questions which we have yet to look at, we want to choose the best answer available. Sometimes we get a perfect answer, and that's great. But sometimes the perfect answer doesn't exist, so we pick the best answer available.

Take a look at 80-4-23, see if you can pick out the correct answer, do you notice its slight deviation from the original argument in the stimulus?

A Technique of Last Resort: When you can't find the flaw or the flaw you anticipated is not in the answer choices

Before we end the chapter, I just wanted to show you a technique that can help us when we have exhausted all other options. There will be times when you have read the stimulus but still have no idea what the flaw is. Other times, you will have found a flaw in the stimulus, only to realize that none of the answer choices exemplified the flaw you found. When this happens, the first thing I do is usually to reread the stimulus, trying to find additional information or see if I've missed anything. But sometimes, even a second or third read of the original argument doesn't really help. When this happens, there's something we can try:

This is going to be much more time consuming than usual, but if you are an advanced test taker, have enough time remaining (let's say three minutes or more), and this is the only question left in the section that you are unsure about, then it could very well be worth a try.

I will look at the answer choices, figure out what flaws they committed, and then go back to the stimulus to look for that specific flaw.

The arguments of answer choices are usually worded more simply than the original argument, so it shouldn't be too hard to discover the flaw that lies within. For example, if answer choice A describes a Part vs. Whole flaw, we go back and reread the stimulus, looking to see if the original argument can be understood as such.

17. Must Be True

Read, Stop, Summarize, Extract, Combine

Let's talk about Must be True (MBT) Questions. Unlike all the previous questions that we have looked at, MBT Questions and MSS (Most Strongly Supported) questions require a different way of thinking.

Assumption Family questions tested our ability to identify the structural components of an argument, isolate the gap between the premises and the conclusion, and find a suitable answer choice tailored specifically to the question type we are dealing with.

Parallel Questions tested our ability to match the logic, conclusion, and premises of the stimulus's argument with the correct answer choice.

***

On the other hand, MBT and MSS Questions test our ability to extract, organize, and link information present in the stimulus. **In a way, tackling an MBT Question is almost like tackling the rules of a Logic Games question.** Here is why:

In a logic game, we are given a series of conditional rules. We diagram each of the rules, and then look to see if we can combine/synthesize them to create additional rules.

Let's use an example to better explain how MBT Questions work. Assume in a hypothetical logic game, we are given three rules, "*if I eat steak, I will drink red wine*," "*whenever I drink red wine, my face turns red*," and "*if my face turns red, I will not take selfies*."

We can diagram these three rules in notational form:

Steak → Red Wine
Red Wine → Red Face
Red Face → ~~Selfies~~

These are all "must be true" statements according to the stimulus, but there are additional pieces of information that also must be true. By combining these rules, we can derive additional inferences:

Steak → Red Face
Steak → ~~Selfies~~
Red Wine → ~~Selfies~~

These synthesized rules are derived by combining pre-existing rules. These are also "must be true" statements. So we have six statements in total that all "must be true."

But wait, since we are dealing with conditional statements here, we know that each conditional relationship's contrapositive must also be true. So in total, we have derived twelve MBT possibilities from the original three conditionals.

***

How we tackle the stimulus of a MBT Question is very similar to the process we use in **Logic Games**. There will be pieces of "must be true" information sprinkled throughout the stimulus. Our job is to extract this information from the stimulus. Once we have multiple pieces of "must be true" information, we can try to combine them to see if we can come up with additional "must be true" inferences. The correct answer choice will usually come from one of these.

I've simplified the procedure of reading a MBT stimulus into a five-step process: Read, Stop, Summarize, Extract, Combine.

Read: Whenever I'm reading the stimulus of a MBT Question, I'm more interested in what it's telling me, and less focused on trying to figure out the structural elements. I'm not too worried about identifying the premises, conclusion, background information, etc. because the correct answer's only requirement is that it MUST BE TRUE. It can come from anywhere in the stimulus.

Stop: Some students try to read the entire stimulus in one go, but while that might work with easier questions, you can easily miss key information crucial to selecting the correct answer. I will take two or three pauses throughout the stimulus, and really try to think about the stuff I just read before moving on.

Summarize: But just reading and stopping to think about what you've just read isn't enough. You have to truly understand it. Every time I stop and think about what I've just read, I ask myself two questions: "what is this sentence telling me?" and "what can I take away from this that is definitely true?"

Reading MBT stimuli is also a little like going through a passage in RC. The biggest danger is to blindly go through the information but end up retaining none of it at the end. We have to *actively* read the information given to us, and in order to do that, we need to engage with the stimulus and mentally repeat to ourselves, in our own words, what we have read. This is the only way that we know for sure we have understood.

Extract: When practicing MBT Questions, I would highly recommend that students jot down on paper whatever information/rules that they have discovered while reading the stimulus. While on the actual test you may not have enough time to do this for all but the hardest MBT Questions, it provides invaluable aid in practice. As you get more comfortable with MBT Questions, you will need to jot down things less and less, as your mental capacity for retaining and combining information grows.

Combine: Like we did in the logic games example above, just extracting whatever information we can from the stimulus is not enough. We need to ask ourselves if we can derive additional must be true inferences from the information we already have. Every time we've extracted a new piece of information, ask "how does this fit in with the existing information? Can it lead to new inferences?

***

Let's look at a rather difficult stimulus and practice the five steps:

Whenever she considers voting in an election to select one candidate for a position and there is at least one issue important to her, Kay uses the following principle in choosing which course of action to take: it is acceptable for me to vote for a candidate whose opinions differ from mine on at least one issue important to me whenever I disagree with each of the other candidates on even more such issues; it is otherwise unacceptable to vote for that candidate. In the upcoming mayoral election, the three candidates are Legrand, Medina, and Norton. There is only one issue important to Kay, and only Medina shares her opinion on that issue.

Remember this is a MBT Question, so we don't need to worry about reading for structure. Let's go through the stimulus sentence by sentence, using our five step process.

- *Whenever she considers voting in an election to select one candidate for a position and there is at least one issue important to her, Kay uses the following principle in choosing which course of action to take*

What does this statement tell us? So Kay has a principle that she uses to select who to vote for. When can she use this rule? When there is "*at least one issue important to her.*" So that means if there is one issue important to her, or multiple issues at stake, Kay will apply this principle to determine who to vote for. If there are no issues that mattered to Kay, can she use this principle? We don't really know, as that's outside of the scope of this conditional.

So when there's one or more issue important to Kay, she uses a principle to see who gets her vote.

- *it is acceptable for me to vote for a candidate whose opinions differ from mine on at least one issue important to me whenever I disagree with each of the other candidates on even more such issues*

When she has disagreements with the candidates on certain issues (e.g. abortion, gun control), she can vote for them as long as she disagrees with the other candidates on a greater number of issues.

So let's say there's three candidates, A, B, and C. Kay disagrees with A on one issue, B with two issues, and C with three issues. It would be ok for Kay to vote for A, because she disagrees with B on two issues and C on three issues (more disagreements with B and C than A).

If we put this into our own language, it means that Kay can vote for someone with whom she disagrees with, as long as her disagreements with this candidate are less than the number of disagreements she has with other candidates.

- *it is otherwise unacceptable to vote for that candidate.*

This creates a ⟵⟶ relationship between the sufficient and necessary conditions in the previous statement. So what we have is this:

Vote for Candidate A with whom Kay has disagreements ⟵⟶ Have More Disagreements with Candidates B, C, D…

Let's say Kay is voting. The election is between Lincoln and Douglas. She disagrees with Lincoln on five issues important to her. Can she vote for Lincoln? Only if she disagrees with Douglas on six or more issues important to her.

- *In the upcoming mayoral election, the three candidates are Legrand, Medina, and Norton.*

So there are three candidates, I wonder how many disagreements she has with each candidate, that will be key to solving who she can actually vote for.

- *There is only one issue important to Kay*

We can combine this with the information gathered from the first statement, so now we know that the rule applies in this situation. There is one issue important to Kay, so Kay will use the principle to figure out who to vote for.

- *and only Medina shares her opinion on that issue.*

So we know exactly how many disagreements she has with each candidate now. She has one disagreement with Legrand, one with Norton, and zero with Medina.

Combine this with the information we have already extracted. Can she vote for Legrand? Remember, she has one disagreement with Legrand, so in order to vote for Legrand, she must disagree with Norton and Medina on two or more issues. This is not the case, so she can't vote for Legrand.

Similarly, she can't vote for Norton either.

Can she vote for Medina? Well, we don't know for sure. The rules in this stimulus only applies to voting for a candidate with whom Kay has a *disagreement*. She has no disagreements with Medina. It's probable that she can vote for Medina, but it's not certain based on the information we have available in the stimulus.

As you can see, we have painstakingly and exhaustively analyzed the stimulus. It may seem like a tedious process, but if you are really struggling with MBT Questions, this is the way to go. As you get more comfortable reading, summarizing, extracting, and combining information from a stimulus, the process will get easier and faster.

This example is the stimulus from one of the hardest MBT Questions ever. Now that we have fully explored and understood the stimulus, let's look at the question itself:

***

PT26 S3 Q22

Whenever she considers voting in an election to select one candidate for a position and there is at least one issue important to her, Kay uses the following principle in choosing which course of action to take: it is acceptable for me to vote for a candidate whose opinions differ from mine on at least one issue important to me whenever I disagree with each of the other candidates on even more such issues; it is otherwise unacceptable to vote for that candidate. In the upcoming mayoral election, the three candidates are Legrand, Medina, and Norton. There is only one issue important to Kay, and only Medina shares her opinion on that issue.

If the statements in the passage are true, which one of the following must also be true about Kay's course of action in any election to select one candidate for a position?

   A.   If there are no issues important to her, it is unacceptable for her to vote for any candidate in the election.
   B.   If she agrees with each of the candidates on most of the issues important to her, it is unacceptable for her to vote for any candidate in the election.
   C.   If she agrees with a particular candidate on only one issue important to her, it is unacceptable for her to vote for that candidate.
   D.   If she disagrees with each of the candidates on exactly three issues important to her, it is unacceptable for her to vote for any candidate in the election.
   E.   If there are more issues important to her on which she disagrees with a particular candidate than there are such issues on which she agrees with that candidate, it is unacceptable for her to vote for that candidate.

As we have already looked at the stimulus, let's jump straight to the answer choices:

A.   *If there are no issues important to her, it is unacceptable for her to vote for any candidate in the election.*

Correct MBT answer choices must be backed up by certain information from the stimulus.

We know that the principle only applies whenever there is at least one issue important to her. When there are no issues important to her, will or will she not use the principle? We simply don't know.

Stimulus: One or more issue important to Kay → Kay uses Principle

Answer Choice A: No issue important to Kay → ???

Answer choice A negates the sufficient condition from the stimulus and derives an inference from that. But as we know, negating the sufficient doesn't yield any inferences.

Take a look at the following example:

If John is in law school, then he must have graduated college.
If John isn't in law school, is he a college graduate or not?

We have no idea.

B.   *If she agrees with each of the candidates on most of the issues important to her, it is unacceptable for her to vote for any candidate in the election.*

Most means greater than 50%. Let's say that there are 10 issues, and she agrees with candidate A on 6 issues, B on 7 issues, and C on 8 issues.

But since our rule is about when she disagrees with the candidates, we have to think about that instead.

So assuming, for the argument's sake, that if she agrees with candidate A on 6 issues, they would disagree on 4 issues. With candidate B it's 3, and with candidate C it's 2.

She can vote for C, because they have two disagreements, which is less than what she has with A and B.

C.   *If she agrees with a particular candidate on only one issue important to her, it is unacceptable for her to vote for that candidate.*

So Kay agrees with a particular candidate on exactly one issue. But what we are really interested in is how many disagreements she has with this candidate and the others. If she has one disagreement with this candidate, she can vote for him or her as long as she has more disagreements with the others.

D.   *If she disagrees with each of the candidates on exactly three issues important to her, it is unacceptable for her to vote for any candidate in the election.*

So our rule would actually be applicable here. She has three disagreements with each candidate. Can she vote for A? No, because in order to vote for A, she must disagree with B or C on four or more issues. The same is true for B and C, so the rule creates an impasse for her, essentially preventing her from voting for anyone.

E. *If there are more issues important to her on which she disagrees with a particular candidate than there are such issues on which she agrees with that candidate, it is unacceptable for her to vote for that candidate.*

So let's say that she disagrees with A on three issues, and only agrees with A on two issues, can she vote for A? Yes, if she disagrees with B and C on four or more issues.

The correct answer is D.

Scales of Certainty

As we saw in the previous question, correct MBT answer choices are exactly what they claim to be. They *must be true*. Answers which are probably true, or possibly true will be incorrect.

John Locke, in his *Essay Concerning Human Understanding*, makes the distinction between what is *certain* and what is *probable*. That is a distinction which we must keep in mind when tackling a MBT Question also.

The correct answer will always be supported by concrete and certain evidence from the stimulus. In fact, the test we use to confirm that we have the correct answer choice will take us back to the stimulus to make sure the evidence we need is in place. I call this the **Evidence Check Test**, and we will look at it later in this chapter.

We can envision the degree of truth on the LSAT as a sliding scale. On a scale of 0 - 10, 0 being that it's definitely not true, definitely false; and 10 being most definitely and without a doubt true. The answers that we are looking for in MBT Questions will all be 10s on this 0 - 10 scale. The level of certainty must be absolute in the correct answer choice.

If we were to further break down the Scale of Certainty, answer choice on MBT Questions can be further divided into the following five categories:

100% True/Must be True (Cannot be False): These are the answer choices we want, and the only ones we want. These answers will always be true according to the stimulus, no exceptions.

Most Likely True: These are answer choices that are probably true. In fact, the reasonable person will probably agree with this given the information presented in the stimulus. These answers will be wrong in MBT Questions. Most Likely True answer choices are acceptable for MSS Questions, and you will have a better idea on how to distinguish these from MBT answers after reading the next chapter.

Could Be True (Could be False): These answer choices could go both ways, they can be true, but they don't have to be true.

Not Likely True (Most Likely False): these will be wrong as well, however, they can be attractive trap answers on Must be False questions.

100% Not True/Cannot be True (Must be False): These answer choices will definitely be false. They will be the opposite of MBT answer choices. So beware of opposite answer choices during the answer choice selection, unless the question is a Cannot be True/MBF question.

Difficult Trait #1: Beware probably true or could be true answer choices

With MBT Questions, we can be easily tricked by Most Likely True or Could be True answer choices.

One method I consistently use to test the truthfulness of an answer choice is to think of an exception to challenge the answer choice.

I will negate the answer choice and ask myself whether under any circumstances can that scenario occur without running afoul of the information given in the stimulus.

For example, if the answer choice states that "all birds have feathers," I will ask myself whether I can think of a bird that doesn't have feathers. If the answer choice states that "John must see the Dr. on Tuesday," I will ask myself whether it's possible for John to see the doctor on Monday, Thursday, etc. instead. If this answer really must be true, then the opposite cannot happen under any circumstances. If exceptions to the contrary can occur that do not contradict the stimulus, then it's not the correct answer.

Some/Most/All Relationships

Quantitative relationships are quite common in MBT Questions. By my count, in the hardest 100 MBT Questions, about 20-30% contained some/most/all relationships. We have seen these previously, especially in Flaw Questions, but here we will look at them in greater detail. These relationships are actually derived from Aristotle's figures of categorical syllogisms as presented in his work, *Prior Analytics*. If you are interested in formal logic, that's something to look into.

All As are Bs:

"All" relationships are rather straightforward. You can also think of an "all" relationship as a conditional relationship, A → B. That means "all" relationships can lead to a contrapositive, B̶ → A̶.

Technically, it's not a conditional relationship, but for the purpose of the LSAT, "all" relationships can be treated just like conditionals. See Ebrey, David., Why are there no conditionals in Aristotle's Logic? Journal of the History of Philosophy, vol. 53, no. 2 (2015) 185-205

Two "all" relationships can also be linked, if we know that all As are Bs, and all Bs are Cs, then we know that all As are Cs.

"All" relationships, however, cannot be reversed. All Americans speak English doesn't mean all English speakers are American.

"All" relationships can also be downgraded to a "most" and "some" relationship: if all fish can swim, then most fish can swim, and some fish can swim.

Most As are Bs:

"Most" relationships can neither be linked nor reversed. Most As are Bs and Most Bs are Cs together don't yield any inferences. For instance, if I told you that "most Japanese people use chopsticks," and "most chopstick users are Chinese," there are no inferences we can make between Japanese and Chinese people.

Similarly, you cannot reverse "most" relationships either, if most NBA players are over six feet tall, that doesn't mean most people over six feet tall are NBA players.

A "most" relationship, however, can be linked to an "all" relationship. As long as the "all" relationship comes second, then a valid linkage can be made:

Most As are Bs + All Bs are Cs = Most As are Cs

(here, the "most" relationship comes before the "all" relationship)

All As are Bs + Most Bs are Cs = No inferences

(here, the "all" relationship comes before the "most" relationship)

"Most" means "more than 50%" on the LSAT, sometimes it will be expressed in a veiled way. For instance, if the statement said "*of all the people in my class, more people preferred vanilla ice-cream to people who didn't,*" that just means most people preferred vanilla.

However, if the choice isn't binary (when we don't know how many flavors there are to choose from, or if there's more than two options), then we are NOT dealing with a "most" relationship. (We talked about this in the chapter on Flaws also.)

Similarly, if a statement said "few" As are Bs, then we can assume that "most" As are not Bs.

So be on the lookout for hidden "most" relationships!

"Most" relationships can also be automatically downgraded to a "some" relationship, most English people speak English means that some English people speak English.

Some As are Bs

The word "some," on the LSAT, has a very peculiar meaning. If there were one hundred dogs, "some dogs" can refer to anything as low as one dog, or as high as all one hundred dogs.

The word "many," on the other hand, ranges from "more than one" to "all." There is a distinction between "some" and "many," take a look at PT1-S4-Q21.

"Some" relationships are the only quantitative relationship that can be reversed. "Some As are Bs" can be reversed into "Some Bs are As."

Two "some" relationships cannot be linked together to form additional inferences, neither can a "some" and "most" relationship be linked.

However, if we link a "some" relationship with an "all" relationship, an inference can be made:

Some As are Bs + All Bs are Cs = Some As are Cs

Again, just like in "most" relationships, when connecting a "some" relationship with an "all" relationship, the "all" relationship has to come second in order for it to work.

***

Below is a summary of all the valid inferences we can make from "some," "most," and "all" relationships:

All As are Bs:

Valid: A → B
Valid: ~~B → A~~
Valid: Most As are Bs
Valid: Some As are Bs
Valid: Some Bs are As (some relationships can be reversed)

Linkages:

All As are Bs + All Bs are Cs = All As are Cs

Most As are Bs:

Valid: Some As are Bs
Valid: Some Bs are As

Linkages:

Most As are Bs + All Bs are Cs = Most As are Cs

Some As are Bs:

Valid: Some Bs are As

Linkages:

Some As are Bs + All Bs are Cs = Some As are Cs

***

Two additional linkage inferences appear on the LSAT, you must remember these:

Most As are Bs + Most As are Cs = Some Bs are Cs (and vice versa)
Most As are Bs + Most Bs are not As = More Bs than As

Take a shot at the following question and try your hand at "some/most/all" inferences:

PT88 S2 Q22

Art critic: All of Dolores Albarran's oil paintings are highly original, though few of them are critically acclaimed or popular with collectors. Remarkably, Albarran produced no highly original works until late in her career, and few of her abstract works demonstrate much originality.

If all of the art critic's statements are true, which one of the following must also be true?

    A.   Most of Albarran's works that are not popular with collectors are highly original.
    B.   Few of the works produced late in Albarran's career are abstract works.
    C.   Most, if not all, of the works produced late in Albarran's career are oil paintings.
    D.   Most, if not all, of Albarran's abstract works are not oil paintings.
    E.   Few or none of Albarran's critically acclaimed works are highly original.

Let's look at each statement, extracting whatever information we can:

> 1. *All of Dolores Albarran's oil paintings are highly original*

DA's Oil Paintings → Highly Original

> 2. *Though few of them are critically acclaimed or popular with collectors*

Most of DA's Oil Paintings are NOT popular or critically acclaimed

> 3. *Albarran produced no highly original works until late in her career*

Highly Original → Late in Career

> 4. *Few of her abstract works demonstrate much originality*

Most abstract works are NOT original

Now for the fun part, we have four quantitative relationships, which ones can be combined to create additional inferences?

#1 and #3 can be linked: DA's Oil Paintings → Highly Original → Late in Career, we can infer with certainty that <u>Albarran's oil paintings are produced late in her career.</u>

#1 and #2 can also be linked: we can first reverse #2 into a "some" relationship: "some works not popular or critically acclaimed by DA are oil paintings".

We can then combine this with #1, leading to the inference that "<u>some of Albarran's works not popular or critically acclaimed are highly original.</u>"

We can also appendage #3 to this new inference: "<u>some of Albarran's works not popular or critically acclaimed are produced late in her career.</u>"

Finally, we can combine #4 with the contrapositive of #1: <u>most of Albarran's abstract works are not oil paintings.</u>

> A. *Most of Albarran's works that are not popular with collectors are highly original*

This is an incomplete and erroneous inference from #2 and #1.

#2 tells us that "most of DA's oil paintings are not critically acclaimed or popular." We can downgrade this into a "some" relationship and then reverse it, getting us "some of DA's unpopular or unacclaimed works are oil paintings."

We can then combine it with #1 to get "SOME of Albarran's works that are not popular with collectors OR UNACCLAIMED are highly original."

It should have been "some" instead of "most," and it's missing the part about works not critically unacclaimed.

> B. *Few of the works produced late in Albarran's career are abstract works*

This is an improper linkage of #3 and #4.

#3 tells us Original → Late Career (Contrapositive: ~~Late Career~~ → ~~Original~~)

#4 tells us Most Abstract Works → ~~Original~~, we can downgrade this to a "some" relationship and then reverse it: Some ~~Original~~ Works → Abstract.

We cannot link these two together, because in order to make a proper linkage between an "all" relationship and a "some" relationship, the "some" relationship has to be in front.

> C.   *Most, if not all, of the works produced late in Albarran's career are oil paintings*

This is an improper reversal of #1 and #3, which when linked, tells us that "Albarran's oil paintings are produced late in her career." If we were to downgrade this to a "some" relationship and reverse it, we would get "SOME of the works produced late in Albarran's career are oil paintings."

> D.   *Most, if not all, of Albarran's abstract works are not oil paintings*

This is a combination of #4 and #1, one of our anticipated answers. <u>This is the correct answer</u>.

> E.   *Few or none of Albarran's critically acclaimed works are highly original*

This creates an unwarranted connection between rule #1 and #2.

#1 tells us that Oil Paintings → Highly Original

#2 tells us that MOST oil paintings are unpopular or unacclaimed

But there is no relationship we can derive from "highly original" and "unacclaimed."

Take a look at the following analogy:

All law students are hardworking.

Most law students are not good at math or engineering

Answer choice E is basically saying that few or none of the people good at math are hardworking.

PT80 S1 Q22

Most of the new cars that Regis Motors sold last year were purchased by residents of Blomenville. Regis Motors sold more new cars last year than it did in any previous year. Still, most new cars purchased by Blomenville residents last year were not purchased from Regis Motors.

If the statements above are true, which one of the following must also be true?

    A.   Regis Motors sold more new cars to residents of Blomenville last year than they had in any previous year.
    B.   The total number of new cars purchased by residents of Blomenville was greater last year than it was in any previous year.
    C.   A car retailer other than Regis Motors sold the most new cars to residents of Blomenville last year.
    D.   The number of new cars purchased last year by residents of Blomenville is greater than the number of new cars sold by Regis Motors
    E.   Regis Motors' share of the new car market in Blomenville last year increased over its share the year before.

So all the statements are about new cars sold in the last year, the correct answer will be about new cars sold in the last year as well.

- *Most of the new cars that Regis Motors sold last year were purchased by residents of Blomenville.*

Most new cars sold last year by RM were bought by residents of Blomenville.

- *Regis Motors sold more new cars last year than it did in any previous year.*

There is no some/most/all relationship in this statement, let's keep it in mind and move on.

- *Still, most new cars purchased by Blomenville residents last year were not purchased from Regis Motors.*

Most B are not RM.

This is the second additional "most" linkage we talked about:

Most As are Bs + Most Bs are not As = More Bs than As

The correct answer should be that more Blomenville residents purchased new cars than Regis Motor had sold in the past year.

To see why, look at the following hypothetical:

If RM sold 100 cars last year, let's assume that 51 were sold to residents of Blomenville.

But we also know that most Blomenville residents' new car purchases were not from RM. That means > 50% of new car purchases were not from RM. In other words, < 50% of new car purchases were from RM.

If 51 < 50 %, 100% will be > 51*2. The total number of vehicle purchases by residents of Blomenville will at least be 2x of what Regis had sold in the past year. So we know that the number of cars B purchased will be > 102.

We also know RM sold 100 cars in the past year.

If we assume RM sold 100 out of 100 cars to residents of B last year ("most" is defined as 51 - 100), then we know that these 100 cars will be < 50% of all cars purchased by B. So 100% of B's car purchases will be > 200. That's still more than what RM had sold in the past year.

The correct answer is D.

With a question like this, since we have already committed all the valid inferences regarding Some/Most/All relationships to heart, we can just pick the correct answer and move on. Memorizing and familiarizing yourself with these rules will save a lot of time. A question that would normally take two minutes to do will end up only costing us 30 seconds or so.

Correct Answer Choices: Repetition/Synthesis/Inference

We saw in previous questions how certain **inferences** can be made by combining conditional and some/most/all relationships. Valid inferences can be made in causal relationships as well. If A causes B, and B causes C, then A is also a cause for C. So be on the lookout for additional inferences that can be made if the stimulus contains conditional, causal, or some/most/all relationships.

The second type of correct answer choices on a MBT Question will be a simple restatement of a singular piece of information found in the stimulus. Answer choices that are just a **repetition** of a single statement/sentence from the stimulus are less common. I counted approximately 10% of the correct answer choices in the hardest 100 MBT Questions to contain this feature. So just be aware that the correct answer doesn't have to be something we come up with our own via inference or synthesis, it can simply be a sentence from the stimulus, just worded differently.

The last type of correct answer choices **synthesizes** the information we have extracted from the stimulus. We have developed the habit of extracting key pieces of information from the stimulus as we read through it, and a synthesized answer choice is simply a combination of two or more pieces of information we found in the stimulus. (Synthesize answers are also especially tricky in RC According to the Passage/Detail Questions, a topic we cover in RC Perfection.)

Let's look at a few questions now and see if you can figure out whether the correct answer is of the inference, repetition, or synthesis type.

Difficult Trait #2: Oftentimes we are so fixated on looking for inferences from the stimulus that we forget the correct answer can also be repeating a single statement from the stimulus.

PT32 S4 Q24

The increasing complexity of scientific inquiry has led to a proliferation of multi-authored technical articles. Reports of clinical trials involving patients from several hospitals are usually coauthored by physicians from each participating hospital. Likewise, physics papers reporting results from experiments using subsystems developed at various laboratories generally have authors from each laboratory.

If all the statements above are true, which one of the following must be true?

   A. Clinical trials involving patients from several hospitals are never conducted solely by physicians from just one hospital.
   B. Most reports of clinical trials involving patients from several hospitals have multiple authors.
   C. When a technical article has multiple authors, they are usually from several different institutions.
   D. Physics papers authored by researchers from multiple laboratories usually report results from experiments using subsystems developed at each laboratory.
   E. Most technical articles are authored solely by the researchers who conducted the experiments these articles report.

What are the pieces of information that we can extract from this stimulus?

- *The increasing complexity of scientific inquiry has led to a proliferation of multi authored technical articles.*

Causal relationship in this statement here, Complexity of Scientific Inquiry ⇒ Growth of Multi-Authored Articles

- *Reports of clinical trials involving patients from several hospitals are <u>usually</u> coauthored by physicians from each participating hospital.*

I think there is a hidden "most" relationship here. "Usually" can mean "more often than not." So let's rephrase this as a "most" relationship:

Reports involving patients from multiple hospitals →most→ authored by multiple physicians

- *Likewise, physics papers reporting results from experiments using subsystems developed at various laboratories <u>generally</u> have authors from each laboratory.*

Same as above,

Physics papers reporting results from multiple labs →most→ multiple authors

So we have two "most" relationships in this stimulus, they can't be combined but can be downgraded to a "some" relationship and reversed.

- A. *Clinical trials involving patients from several hospitals are never conducted solely by physicians from just one hospital.*

This runs contrary to our "most" relationship. If most of these trials involve multiple physicians from multiple hospitals, then it's very possible that a minority of them involve physicians from just one hospital.

- B. *Most reports of clinical trials involving patients from several hospitals have multiple authors.*

This is a repetition of our second statement. This is a **repetition** answer <u>and the correct choice</u>.

- C. *When a technical article has multiple authors, they are usually from several different institutions.*

What do we know from the stimulus? When a clinical report involves patients from different hospitals, authors are usually from different institutions. When a physics paper involved different labs, the authors are usually from different institutions.

But what about technical articles in general? This is out of the scope of our stimulus and cannot be proven using the available information.

- D. *Physics papers authored by researchers from multiple laboratories <u>usually</u> report results from experiments using subsystems developed at each laboratory.*

This is an improper reversal of the "most" relationship in our third statement. If the author had said "sometimes" instead of "usually," then it would have been fine.

E.   *Most technical articles are authored solely by the researchers who conducted the experiments these articles report.*

We know that *if* the article had patients/subsystems from multiple institutions, then usually there are multiple authors.

Whether or not these multiple authors conducted the experiments is not something that we know. Similarly, this answer choice is talking about technical articles in general, and that's out of scope, just like answer choice C.

Difficult Trait #3: The correct answer can combine two pieces of seemingly unrelated information from the stimulus. Correct answers can be synthesized.

<u>PT87 S2 Q21</u>

City Official: Landowners must clear the snow from the sidewalks along the edge of their property by 24 hours after the end of a snowstorm. The city has the right to clear any sidewalk that is still covered more than 24 hours after a snowstorm's end, and whenever it does so, it will bill the landowner for the service. All landowners whose sidewalks have not been cleared within 48 hours of the end of a snowstorm will receive citations, which always result in fines unless the landowners can demonstrate extenuating circumstances.

If all of the official's statements are true, which one of the following must be true?

A.   If the city clears a sidewalk of snow 50 hours after the end of a snowstorm, the owner will be billed for the service and will receive a citation.
B.   All landowners who fail to clear their sidewalks by 24 hours after the end of a snowstorm will be billed by the city for snow removal.
C.   All sidewalks in the city will be cleared of snow within 50 hours of the end of a snowstorm.
D.   Nearly all landowners who do not clear their sidewalks within 48 hours after the end of a snowstorm will be fined.
E.   Landowners who can demonstrate extenuating circumstances will not be billed by the city for snow removal service.

There's a lot of information in this stimulus. Let's try to break it down.

- *Landowners must clear the snow from the sidewalks along the edge of their property by 24 hours after the end of a snowstorm.*

After Snowstorm → Clear Within 24 Hours

- *The city <u>has the right to</u> clear any sidewalk that is still covered more than 24 hours after a snowstorm's end, and whenever it does so, it will bill the landowner for the service.*

Not Cleared Within 24 Hours → City Has Right to Clear
City Clear Snow → Charge Landowner

This is quite subtle: if a homeowner didn't clear the snow within 24 hours, does the city automatically step in? Not really: the city has the right to do so, but how often the city actually does is beyond the scope of this question.

- *All landowners whose sidewalks have not been cleared within 48 hours of the end of a snowstorm will receive citations*

Not Cleared Within 48 Hours → Receive Citations

Citations are guaranteed, so if the homeowner didn't clear the snow within 24 hours, the city can come and do it for them, charging them in the process. But if the city didn't clear the snow, and 48 hours have passed, and the homeowner still didn't do anything about it, they will definitely receive citations.

- *which always result in fines unless the landowners can demonstrate extenuating circumstances.*

This can be restated as "without extenuating circumstances, citations always result in fines."
~~Extenuating Circumstances~~ → Fines

   A. *If the city clears a sidewalk of snow 50 hours after the end of a snowstorm, the owner will be billed for the service and will receive a citation.*

So we know that after 24 hours, the city has the right to clear the snow and bill the owner. 50 hours after the snowstorm fits that requirement.

We also know that if the snow hasn't been cleared after 48 hours, landowners will also receive a citation.

This answer is within the purview of both of these conditional rules. <u>This is the correct answer</u>.

   B. *All landowners who fail to clear their sidewalks by 24 hours after the end of a snowstorm will be billed by the city for snow removal.*

Tricky! We know that the city has the right to clear the snow and bill the owner for removal. But how often the city actually goes through with it is unknown. Are all landowners billed? Does the city only catch some of them?

   C. *All sidewalks in the city will be cleared of snow within 50 hours of the end of a snowstorm.*

It's still possible that the owner didn't clear the snow, the city never got to it, and they received a citation/fine. But the snow is still there after 50 hours.

D. *Nearly all landowners who do not clear their sidewalks within 48 hours after the end of a snowstorm will be fined.*

We know all landowners who do not clear their sidewalks within 48 hours will receive a citation. The citation will always result in fines *unless* extenuating circumstances can be demonstrated.

It's possible that a majority of landowners can in fact demonstrate extenuating circumstances, and so escape the fine. This might work as a most likely true answer, but it's not good enough for a Must be True Question.

E. *Landowners who can demonstrate extenuating circumstances will not be billed by the city for snow removal service.*

This is a flawed negation of our last conditional relationship in the stimulus.

This statement can be diagrammed as:

Demonstrate Extenuating Circumstances → Will Not be Billed

Our stimulus's conditional is:

Cannot Demonstrate Extenuating Circumstances → Will Be Fined

As you can see, the correct answer choice is a **synthesis** of two different points in the stimulus.

Take a look at PT81 S3 Q19 for another difficult MBT Question with a synthesis type answer.

Difficult Trait #4: When testing answer choices, always try to think of an exception. If an exception can stand and not contradict the stimulus, then this answer choice is not 100% must be true.

<u>PT20 S1 Q24</u>

Each December 31 in Country Q, a tally is made of the country's total available coal supplies – that is, the total amount of coal that has been mined throughout the country but not consumed. In 1991 that amount was considerably lower than it had been in 1990. Furthermore, Country Q has not imported or exported coal since 1970.

If the statements above are true, which one of the following must also be true on the basis of them?

A. In country Q, more coal was mined in 1990 than was mined in 1991.
B. In country Q, the amount of coal consumed in 1991 was greater than the amount of coal mined in 1991.
C. In country Q, the amount of coal consumed in 1990 was greater than the amount of coal consumed in 1991.
D. In country Q, the amount of coal consumed in 1991 was greater than the amount of coal consumed in 1990.
E. In country Q, more coal was consumed during the first half of 1991 than was consumed during the first half of 1990.

Let's take a look at the stimulus:

Each December 31 in Country Q, a tally is made of the country's total available coal supplies – that is, the total amount of coal that has been mined throughout the country but not consumed.

This first sentence gives us the definition of total available coal supplies.

Be careful here, this is where a lot of students get confused. The total available coal supply is the *cumulative* amount of coal, not just the coal mined from a specific year. For instance, if on Dec 31, 1990, the total amount of coal is 500 tonnes, and 200 tonnes were consumed in 1990, that doesn't mean 700 tonnes of coal were mined in 1990 alone.

We also have to think about how much coal is left over from the year before. If there was 300 tonnes of coal left over from 1989, that means only 400 tonnes were mined in 1990.

Total amount of coal left over from previous year + coal mined this year - coal consumed this year = total coal for this year

In 1991 that amount was considerably lower than it had been in 1990.

In 1991 the total went down, so the net amount of coal dropped from Dec 31, 1990 to Dec 31, 1991.

What does this mean?

Let's think of an analogy: if you had 100K in your bank account on Dec 31, 2020; but only 50K in your bank account on Dec 31, 2021, what does that mean?

Does that mean you spent 50K in 2021? Not necessarily, because we don't know whether you made any money in 2021. If your income was 0, then you spent 50K in 2021. But if your income was 200K in 2021, and at the end of the year you are still down by 50K? That means you have spent 250K in 2021.

So in other words, if your account balance was significantly down, that means you spent more than you made in that year.

Furthermore, Country Q has not imported or exported coal since 1970.

This rules out another explanation, so it's a closed system we are talking about, the reason we have inferred above is the only explanation.

If total coal reserves are down from a year ago, that must mean the amount of coal consumed is greater than the amount of coal mined in that given year. **This is an inference we can make from the information in the stimulus.**

    A.   *In country Q, more coal was mined in 1990 than was mined in 1991.*

As we mentioned previously, in order to test the truth of an answer choice, we try to come up with an exception that would also work. Such an exception would mean the answer is not 100% true, thus helping us eliminate the answer.

So is it possible to have more coal mined in 1991 than 1990? Yes: let's say 500 tonnes were mined in 1990, 100 tonnes were consumed, and coal was only discovered in 1990. So 400 tonnes of coal carried over to 1991. But 700 tonnes of coal were mined in 1991. Unfortunately, due to an energy crunch, 1000 tonnes of coal were consumed in 1991. At the end of 1991, we have 400 + 700 - 1000 = 100 tonnes of coal remaining. That is considerably lower than the 400 we had at the end of the previous year.

Answer choice A doesn't have to be true in order for the stimulus to stand, thus, A is not the correct answer.

   B.   *In country Q, the amount of coal consumed in 1991 was greater than the amount of coal mined in 1991.*

This is the correct answer, the amount of coal consumed has to be greater than the amount of coal mined in order for there to be a *net decrease* in the total amount of coal.

   C.   *In country Q, the amount of coal consumed in 1990 was greater than the amount of coal consumed in 1991.*

Does this have to be true? No, the hypothetical we gave in answer choice A would also work here. 100 tonnes were consumed in 1990, and 1000 tonnes in 1991, and it still works.

   D.   *In country Q, the amount of coal consumed in 1991 was greater than the amount of coal consumed in 1990.*

This is a little more tricky, but it's not necessarily true either. If little or no coal was mined in 1991, then an overall decrease is still possible. Let's say 1000 tonnes were consumed in 1990, and 1500 tonnes were mined, so 500 tonnes were carried over into 1991. No coal was mined in 1991, and 400 tonnes were consumed in 1991, the net decrease from 1990 to 1991 would be 500 - 400 = 100 tonnes

   E.   *In country Q, more coal was consumed during the first half of 1991 than was consumed during the first half of 1990.*

We wouldn't know whether the coal was consumed in the first and second quarters of the year or later, this answer is out of scope.

The correct answer will always be provable via information from the stimulus. Out of scope answer choices are always wrong.

Incorrect Answer Choices/Textual Proof Test

Previously, we have looked at how to use an exception/counter-example to test the truth of an answer choice. If the information presented in an answer choice really must be true, then it would be impossible to find an exception that doesn't contradict the stimulus.

In earlier chapters (Role, Method) we placed a heavy emphasis on careful readings of answer choices, and how to select or eliminate answer choices based on certain keywords that appear in them (Keyword Extraction or the K in SLAKR).

In harder MBT Questions, we are often faced with attractive wrong answers that have made a subtle shift in either scope or intensity. Or perhaps the answer choice's terms shifted or deviated from the information discussed in the stimulus. **Remember, correct MBT answer choices MUST be certain, or 100% provable via the stimulus.** Answer choices that are probably true or could be true will be wrong.

Throughout this book we have used different tests to confirm the validity of our answer choice selection (Plug Back Test for SA Questions, Negation Test for NA Questions). For MBT Questions, we use the **Textual Proof Test** to really make sure that the answer choice we have selected is in fact correct. We take the answer choice in question, extract the relevant keywords from it (nouns, verbs, adjectives/adverbs), and find the corresponding textual support from the stimulus.

In essence, we need to find proof from the stimulus for a specific answer choice in order to select it.

If there is no direct textual evidence in the stimulus for the answer choice in question, then it's probably wrong.

When facing a particularly difficult answer choice, I would do the following three things:

Look carefully at the **keywords** in the answer choice, its nouns, verbs, and adjectives/adverbs; do any of these seem out of scope, too strong, or out of place?

Ask myself: "What kind of **evidence** would I need from the stimulus in order to **prove** this answer choice?"

Refer back to the stimulus, is such evidence/proof **present** in the stimulus?

Let's look at a question that contains several attractive wrong answer choices, read each answer choice carefully, paying special attention to its nouns, verbs, and adjectives/adverbs, and ask yourself whether the claim is supported by text from the stimulus.

Readers of RC Perfection will no doubt notice the similarity between this strategy and the "Reverse Confirmation" drill. These are very similar tactics to help us decipher difficult answer choices.

Difficult Trait #5: Beware subtle shifts in terms, strength of language, scope, and level of certainty in the answer choices. The correct answer will always have textual proof from the stimulus

PT33 S1 Q11

Researchers have discovered that caffeine can be as physically addictive as other psychoactive substances. Some people find that they become unusually depressed, drowsy, or even irritable if they do not have their customary dose of caffeine. This is significant because as many people consume caffeine as consume any one of the other addictive psychoactive substances.

Which one of the following can be logically concluded from the information above?

    A. There is no psychoactive substance to which more people are physically addicted than are addicted to caffeine.
    B. A physical addiction to a particular psychoactive substance will typically give rise to diverse psychological symptoms.
    C. Not all substances to which people can become physically addicted are psychoactive.
    D. If one is physically addicted to a psychoactive substance, one will become unusually depressed when one is no longer ingesting that substance.
    E. If alcohol is a physically addictive psychoactive substance, there are not more people who consume alcohol than consume caffeine.

There are three pieces of information contained in this stimulus, presented to us in three sentences:

1. Caffeine can be as physically addictive as other psychoactive substances.

2. For some people, without caffeine they become depressed, drowsy, or irritable.

3. As many people consume caffeine as any one of the other addictive psychoactive substances.

Let's look at each of these in turn:

1. Caffeine <u>can be</u> as physically addictive <u>as other psychoactive substances</u>

    1. Notice how it says "can be," not "is," that's pretty uncertain language. I'd watch out for an answer that says caffeine IS the most addictive substance.

    2. The second interesting thing here is the phrase "as other psychoactive substances. Does that mean caffeine is a psychoactive substance? I think so, if I said "John is as smart as the other law students," then it's very likely that John is a law student too.

2. For <u>some</u> people, a lack of caffeine leads to depression, drowsiness, or irritability.

    a. This statement is presented almost like a conditional ("if they do not have caffeine, they will be drowsy, etc.") but I think it's more causal in nature. It only applies to some people, so a true conditional answer that says something like "without caffeine, people will become depressed, drowsy, or irritable" will probably be too strong. Similarly, an answer that said *most* coffee drinkers will become depressed without coffee will probably be wrong as well.

3. As many people <u>consume</u> caffeine as any one of the other addictive psychoactive substances

    a. Here, the stimulus is talking about the number of people who *consume* caffeine, not the number of people who are *addicted to* caffeine. It's telling us the number of caffeine consumers is equal to or greater than the users of any other addictive psychoactive substances.

4. Finally, the stimulus is about "caffeine," so an answer choice about "coffee" will probably be wrong too. Be careful of these subtle term shifts.

Even as we are reading the stimulus, we are making careful notes about the scope and strength of the language, as well as the specific terms that are being used. This way, when we get to the answers, we can better spot the subtle shifts in terms, scope, and intensity that are prevalent in trap answer choices.

   A. *There is no psychoactive substance to which more people are physically addicted than are addicted to caffeine*

This answer is telling us that caffeine is the *most addictive* of all psychoactive substances (in terms of numbers). Does our stimulus tell us this? We are told that caffeine has the *most consumers,* and that it *can be* as addicting as other psychoactive substances.

This answer choice is certainly attractive, but the stimulus doesn't provide direct textual support for the claim made here, let's keep it for now, but I don't like it too much to be honest.

   B. *A physical addiction to a particular psychoactive substance will <u>typically</u> give rise to diverse <u>psychological</u> symptoms.*

The information present in the stimulus tells us that a physical addiction to a particular psychoactive substance (caffeine) will *sometimes* (some people) give rise to diverse symptoms. But are these symptoms psychological or physiological? Drowsiness is certainly a physiological symptom, maybe depression and irritability are psychological symptoms. But I think we need *most people* to suffer from these symptoms in order to support the word "typically," not just *some people*, as stated in the stimulus.

> C.   *Not all substances to which people can become physically addicted are psychoactive.*

This statement is telling us that some substances to which people are addicted are NOT psychoactive.

In order to select this answer choice, I would need information from the stimulus that tells me either caffeine is NOT a psychoactive substance, or that there are other, non-psychoactive substances to which people can be addicted to.

The stimulus doesn't mention any non-psychoactive substances. Neither is it claimed that caffeine is NOT a psychoactive substance. In fact, all evidence points to the contrary. The author says caffeine can be as addictive as other psychoactive substances. That seems to suggest caffeine is a psychoactive substance.

> D.   *If one is physically addicted to a psychoactive substance, one will become unusually depressed when one is no longer ingesting that substance.*

What does the stimulus tell us?

For some people, a withdrawal from a physical addiction to caffeine leads to depression. This answer choice is too strong for my liking. It doesn't have to be true for everybody.

> E.   *If alcohol is a physically addictive psychoactive substance, there are not more people who consume alcohol than consume caffeine.*

We know caffeine is a physically addictive psychoactive substance. We also know that it's the most consumed of all such substances. It holds the rank of number one consumed addictive psychoactive substance, any other substance's consumer number is equal to or less than the number of consumers who consume caffeine.

So alcohol consumers either jointly hold number one rank with caffeine consumers, or are less than caffeine consumers. There can't be more alcohol consumers than caffeine consumers according to the stimulus.

E is the correct answer.

Must be False

We talked about the Scales of Certainty earlier on in this chapter. On the one end, we have what must be true, no exceptions, ifs, or buts, things that are 100% certain, backed by evidence, whose truth is guaranteed.

On the opposite end, there are answer choices that cannot be true, or must be false. MBF questions are rare but do pop up now and then.

Most MBF questions can be answered by finding what *must be true* according to the stimulus, and then negating that.

There are, however, some MBF questions which are worded in really weird ways. We will end the chapter by looking at one of those. This question also happens to be one of the hardest MBT/MBF questions in LSAT history.

PT28 S1 Q20

If the economy is weak, then prices remain constant although unemployment rises. But unemployment rises only if investment decreases. Fortunately, investment is not decreasing.

If the statements above are true, then which one of the following must be false?

    A. Either the economy is weak or investment is decreasing.
    B. If unemployment rises, the prices remain constant.
    C. The economy is weak only if investment decreases.
    D. Either the economy is weak or prices are remaining constant.
    E. Either unemployment is rising or the economy is not weak.

The stimulus is conditional, so let's diagram it.

- Economy Weak → Prices Remain Constant + Unemployment Rises
- Unemployment Rises → Investment Decreases
- Investment is not decreasing.

By contrapositive, we know that unemployment is NOT rising.

Similarly, if unemployment is NOT rising, then the economy is NOT weak.

(Remember that "and" becomes "or" when taking the contrapositive of a compound conditional)

So it must be true that unemployment is NOT rising and the economy is NOT weak.

So it must be false that unemployment is rising and the economy is weak.

　　A.　*Either the economy is weak or investment is decreasing.*

The correct "either/or" answer choice in a MBF question must present two possibilities, both of which are false. For instance, if it must be false that either John or David is coming to the party, that means neither of them are coming.

Can the economy be weak? No. Can investment be decreasing? No, this is in direct contradiction to the last sentence of our stimulus. Neither of these can be true. This is the correct answer.

　　B.　*If unemployment rises, the prices remain constant.*

We don't know enough about the relationship between unemployment and prices. Both are necessary conditions in the same conditional relationship. No inferences can be made here.

If our first conditional is A → B + C, answer choice B is saying B → C.

　　C.　*The economy is weak only if investment decreases.*

This is a MBT answer. Remember that this is a MBF question!

　　D.　*Either the economy is weak or prices are remaining constant.*

We know that the economy is NOT weak. So part 1 of this answer choice must be false. Must "prices remaining constant" also be false? We actually don't know. All we can derive from "investment is not decreasing" is that it must be false that unemployment is rising and the economy is weak. Whether prices remain constant or not cannot be determined by the contrapositive of the conditionals in the stimulus.

　　E.　*Either unemployment is rising or the economy is not weak.*

If it had said either unemployment is rising (false) or the economy is weak (false), then it would have been the correct answer. This answer is half right half wrong.

18. Most Strongly Supported

Truth vs. Speculation and the Distinction between Certainty and Probability

Bertrand Russell, one of my favorite authors, makes an interesting point in his book, *The History of Western Philosophy*. Russell makes a distinction between science and religion. On the one end of the spectrum of certainty lies immutable truth. This is the realm of science. On the other end lies religion, which is based on faith alone. Science requires hard facts as proof, while religion doesn't require any. Philosophy, according to Russell, lies somewhere in the middle.

Russell's distinction between science, which is provable and religion, which he considers to be speculation, is something to note. The Must be True Questions we have studied in the previous chapter are akin to the scientific truths as described by Russell. Just like how science is based on real world evidence, data, and experimentation results, the correct MBT answer choice must also be based on evidence from the stimulus. The correct answer choice is true because the stimulus said so, or it can be deduced from the information in the stimulus.

We now turn to Most Strongly Supported Questions. Unlike MBT Questions, which must be provable via the stimulus, MSS Questions can have correct answer choices that leave room for doubt. But this is where a lot of students stumble. They mistakenly assume that just because the correct answer isn't a "must be true" answer, all they need to do is select an answer choice that "could be true." Unfortunately, since the most difficult MSS Questions can contain several answer choices that "could be true," they end up selecting an answer on a whim, and end up making a mistake.

In reality, just about half of MSS Questions are no different from MBT Questions. The correct answer choice in these questions is something that can be proven via the stimulus. If you think about it, it actually makes sense, MSS Questions ask us to find the *most strongly supported* answer choice, and an answer choice that is 100% supported, or provable via the stimulus, will obviously be the best answer.

So the **first step** to tackling any MSS Question is to treat it as a MBT Question. See if we can find a MBT answer choice that can be proven by the stimulus.

If we can find a suitable MBT answer, then great, that will be the correct answer. Only when there are no answers that are 100% provable by the stimulus do we look at the answer choices that are partially supported by the stimulus. This is the **second step** to MSS Questions.

The alternate strategy, which we should avoid, is to consider the answer choices in bulk. This was the mistake I made when I first started studying for the LSAT, and a mistake a lot of students still continue to make. Because not all correct answer choices can be proven by the stimulus, our process of eliminating incorrect answers will be much less straightforward. Now, you can't eliminate an answer simply because there's no certain proof. As a result, we end up with a whole bunch of answer choices none of which we particularly liked.

The **third step** to MSS Questions is to find the *most probable answer* from a shortlist of *possible* answers.

Remember that in Strengthen/Weaken Questions we had the additional job of *comparing* answers in order to find the best choice available?

In MSS Questions, just like Strengthen/Weaken Questions, sometimes the best answer will not be perfect. It will have certain keywords or gaps that leave something to be desired. But just like how in Strengthen Questions, the correct answer need not wholly justify the argument, it just had to be the most capable strengthener out of the five possibilities; and in Weaken Questions, the correct answer need not fully destroy the argument, only be the one that hurts the argument the most; the correct MSS answer choice, sometimes, will not be 100% certain. But it WILL be the *most certain* or *most reasonable* inference among the five answer choices.

We will devote the latter half of this chapter to the art of finding the correct answer out of five imperfect answer choices.

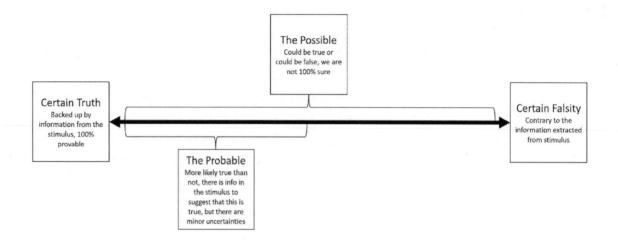

On our scales of certainty, on the very left are statements which **must be true**. These will be repetitions, synthesis, or inferences of the information presented in the stimulus.

On the opposite end will be statements which **cannot be true/must be false**, they will run contrary to the information we have extracted, synthesized, or inferred from the stimulus.

In the middle are statements which are **possible**, or in other words, **could be true**. Some are more likely to be true than others, but a common trait could be true statements all have is that we don't possess the absolute certainty as we do in MBT or MBF statements.

MBT Questions are relatively straightforward, we just have to find an answer choice that is a **Certain Truth**. No other answer choices are acceptable.

MSS Questions in contrast are more complicated. We start by looking for an answer that is also a **Certain Truth**, and only when we can't find that among the answer choices, do we find the **most probable** from all the **possible** answers.

***

So in summary, how we approach MSS Questions is a six step process:

When reading the stimulus, the process is exactly the same as in MBT Questions (refer back to the previous chapter for more practice on this):

> 1. Read each statement in the stimulus, extracting key information
> 2. Synthesis extracted information if possible
> 3. Come up with logical inferences via the extracted information if possible

When we look at the answer choices, however, there's a few extra steps involved:

> 1. See if there is a MBT answer choice, if so, select that
> 2. If not, determine which answer choices are possible outcomes according to the stimulus
> 3. Choose the answer choice with the most support/smallest uncertainty

Let's start with what I think is the hardest MSS Question, ever. Take it slow on this one and see if you can get it right!

PT18 S2 Q20

Oxygen-18 is a heavier than normal isotope of oxygen. In a rain cloud, water molecules containing oxygen-18 are rarer than water molecules containing normal oxygen. But in rainfall, a higher proportion of all water molecules containing oxygen-18 than of all water molecules containing ordinary oxygen descends to earth. Consequently, scientists were surprised when measurements along the entire route of rain clouds' passage from above the Atlantic Ocean, the site of their original formation, across the Amazon forests, where it rains almost daily, showed that the oxygen-18 content of each of the clouds remained fairly constant.

Which one of the following inferences about an individual rain cloud is supported by the passage?

A. Once it is formed over the Atlantic, the rain cloud contains more ordinary oxygen than oxygen-18.
B. Once it has passed over the Amazon, the rain cloud contains a greater than normal percentage of oxygen 18.
C. The cloud's rainfall contains more oxygen 18 than ordinary oxygen.
D. During a rainfall, the cloud must surrender the same percentage of its ordinary oxygen as of its oxygen 18.
E. During a rainfall, the cloud must surrender more of its oxygen 18 than it retains.

This stimulus is tricky for two reasons, one, it contains scientific information that may need a little background information. Two, this stimulus is also the stimulus for a Reconcile the Difference/Paradox question, so just by reading the stimulus, we may get carried away and end up thinking about a different question type altogether.

Let's start with the scientific information first: if you remember from high school chemistry, an isotope is an atom that has the same number of protons but a different number of neutrons. Most oxygen atoms contain 8 protons and 8 neutrons, O-18, on the other hand, contains 8 protons and 10 neutrons.

A water molecule comprises two hydrogen atoms and one oxygen atom. A regular water molecule will contain one oxygen atom, and a water molecule containing O-18 will also contain one oxygen atom.

The second tricky bit about this stimulus is the obvious paradox. If O-18 is rarer than O-16, but a higher proportion of O-18 is lost through rainfall, then why does the O-18 content remain constant? It must be because O-18 is replenished at a faster rate than O-16. But this inference might not be what we are looking for, as we are dealing with a MSS Question and not a Paradox question.

Now that we have this cleared up, let's look at the stimulus in detail. Remember, our job here is to extract, synthesize, and infer.

Oxygen-18 is a heavier than normal isotope of oxygen.

We've already talked about what is an isotope and its implications for the question.

In a rain cloud, water molecules containing oxygen-18 are rarer than water molecules containing normal oxygen.

Ok, so water molecules containing O-18 are rarer than those containing O-16. So that means most water molecules in rain clouds will contain O-16. Since each water molecule will contain one oxygen atom, it will either be O-18 or O-16, but not both. So we can extrapolate that in a given rain cloud, there are more O-16 atoms than O-18 atoms.

If a rain cloud contains 100 water molecules, there will be 51 or more water molecules containing O-16. In other words, there will be more O-16 atoms than O-18 atoms in that cloud.

But in rainfall, a higher proportion of <u>all water molecules containing oxygen-18</u> than of all water molecules containing ordinary oxygen descends to earth.

This statement is quite tricky and has tripped me up several times. Does this mean that in the rain fall, more O-18 falls to the ground than O-16? Not necessarily.

The statement says a higher proportion of ALL water molecules containing O-18 falls to the ground. That means a higher percentage of O-18 out of all the O-18 in the cloud falls as rain than O-16. The comparison here is between their relative proportions.

For example, we know O-18 is rarer than O-16 in a rain cloud.

So let's say that there is a rain cloud that contains 1000 water molecules/1000 oxygen atoms. Let's say 100 of these molecules fall to the ground as rain. How many O-16 and O-18 falls to the ground?

Well, we can't know for certain. All we know is that a higher proportion of all O-18 falls in the rain. Let's hypothetically assume that the ratio of O-16 to O-18 is 80:20 in the rain cloud. So we have 800 O-16 atoms in the rain cloud, and 200 O-18 atoms in the rain cloud.

Let's imagine that 25% of all O-18 falls to the ground, that's 50 O-18 atoms out of 100 molecules that fall as rain.

The remaining 50 molecules of water that fall as rain will contain O-16. We had 800 O-16 to start with. So 50/800 = 6.25%. So only 6.25% of O-16 fell in the rain.

But the rainfall contained exactly 50 O-16 atoms and 50 O-18 atoms. Just because the proportion relative to total is higher for O-18 in the rainfall, doesn't mean the net number of atoms that fell in the rain will be greater.

Be careful not to make a Percentage vs. Amount error here. Like we said in the Flaw Chapter, to derive net amount, we need not just the percentage, but also the total amount available.

Consequently, scientists were surprised when measurements along the entire route of rain clouds' passage from above the Atlantic Ocean, the site of their original formation, across the Amazon forests, where it rains almost daily, showed that the oxygen-18 content of each of the clouds remained fairly constant.

This statement tells us that the total amount of O-18 remained fairly constant. So in other words, if the rain cloud started with 800 O-16 and 200 O-18, and it was giving up 50 O-16 and 50 O-18 daily over the rain forest, after two days we should have 700 O-16 and 100 O-18, while after four days we should have 600 O-16 and no O-18.

But instead, the ratio remains constant at 8:2. That means although a higher proportion of all O-18 falls as rain, the same higher proportion of O-18 is replenished.

Let's look at the answer choices:

   A.   *Once it is formed over the Atlantic, the rain cloud contains more ordinary oxygen than oxygen-18.*

We know from our second statement that the rain cloud will contain more O-16 than O-18. This is a **repetition** statement and as a result, a good choice.

   B.   *Once it has passed over the Amazon, the rain cloud contains a greater than normal percentage of oxygen 18.*

This statement contradicts the final statement of the stimulus, which said that "the oxygen-18 content of each of the clouds remained fairly constant."

   C.   *The cloud's rainfall contains more oxygen 18 than ordinary oxygen.*

This answer is extremely tricky. As we explained earlier, the stimulus said that a *higher percentage of total O-18 falls in the rain,* not *a higher percentage of all the rainfall is O-18.*

To know whether more O-18 falls in the rain, we need to know not only that the percentage is higher, but also what the total amount of O-18 is in the cloud to start with.

   D.   *During a rainfall, the cloud <u>must</u> surrender the same percentage of its ordinary oxygen as of its oxygen 18.*

With **strongly worded** answer choices in MSS Questions, I treat them just as I would in MBT Questions. **I try to look for an exception that would negate this answer choice.** (Again, check out the last chapter for more practice)

So must the same percentage be surrendered? No, in our hypothetical, we saw that it's possible for the rain cloud to surrender 25% of its 200 O-18, and only 6.25% of its 800 O-16.

   E.   *During a rainfall, the cloud <u>must</u> surrender more of its oxygen 18 than it retains.*

Again, this is not necessary. The stimulus tells us that in the rain fall,

$$\frac{O-18 \; Atoms \; in \; the \; Rain}{Total \; O-18 \; Atoms \; in \; the \; Rain \; Cloud} > \frac{O-16 \; Atoms \; in \; the \; Rain}{Total \; O-16 \; Atoms \; in \; the \; Rain \; Cloud}$$

This answer choice is saying that the percentage of O-18 surrendered must be greater than 50%. It doesn't have to be. As long as this percentage is greater than the percentage of O-16, we'll be ok.

Think about it. If we had 1000 water molecules in the cloud, 900 containing O-16, and 100 containing O-18. Only 5% of O-16 were surrendered, or 45 O-16 atoms. 10% of O-18 atoms were surrendered, or 10 O-18 atoms.

This would still fit in with the stimulus, the cloud contains more O-16 than O-18 (900 > 100), and a higher proportion of O-18 fell in the rain than O-16 (10% > 5%).

But only 10% of O-18 has been surrendered, 90% have been retained.

<u>A is the correct answer.</u>

***

This question just goes to show how critical it is to have a careful understanding of the stimulus before moving to the answer choices in MSS Questions. Also, roughly about 50% of MSS Questions are no different from MBT Questions, so always start an MSS Question by treating it as a MBT Question.

That means painstakingly extracting information from the stimulus, creating our own synthesized and inferred statements. The whole six step process may seem too much to handle for now, but since we are still in our practice phase, we should strive to do everything we can to become familiar with the process, until we can internalize it to the point where the steps become second nature.

On the actual test we can afford a maximum of three minutes to complete a question like this. That means we won't have any time to think about the steps taught here. We need to forcefully change our habits so that we will unconsciously follow these steps even under stress and time constraints.

Difficult Trait #1: Just around half of correct MSS answers will also be MBT answers. So always try to look for an answer choice that can be 100% proven.

Let's look at another MSS Question. When you are looking at each answer choice, really think about which answer choice must be true, is probably true, or just possibly true.

PT32 S1 Q18

Until 1985 all commercial airlines completely replenished the cabin air in planes in flight once every 30 minutes. Since then the rate has been once every hour. The less frequently cabin air is replenished in a plane in flight, the higher the level of Carbon Dioxide in that plane and the easier it is for airborne illness to be spread.

Which one of the following is most strongly supported by the information above?

A. In 1985 there was a loosening of regulations concerning cabin air in commercial airline flights.
B. People who fly today are more likely to contract airborne illnesses than were people who flew prior to 1985.
C. Low levels of carbon dioxide in cabin air make it impossible for airborne illness to spread.
D. In 1980 the rate at which the cabin air was replenished in commercial airliners was sufficient to protect passengers from the effects of carbon dioxide buildup.
E. In 1980 the level of carbon dioxide in the cabin air on a two-hour commercial airline flight was lower than it is today on a similar flight.

The stimulus isn't hard to understand. There are three pieces of key information that can be extracted from it.

1.   Pre 1985 air was cycled once every thirty minutes, and only once every hour since.
2.   Less frequently air is cycled, the higher the CO2 (an inverse correlation).
3.   Higher the CO2, easier for airborne illnesses to spread (positive correlation).

Can we make the inference that it's easier for airborne illnesses to spread on modern flights than pre 1985 flights? That would depend on the length of the flight.

If a modern day flight from LAX to JFK takes 8 hrs, that's 8 replenishments of air. But if we compare that to a shorter flight pre 1985, let's say from LAX to SFO, which only takes an hour, that's 2 replenishments. The level of CO2 will be lower on the LAX to JFK flight, even though air was recycled more frequently pre 1985.

So whether or not a flight has a higher level of CO2 and whether it's easier for illnesses to spread on that flight depends not only on the time when it flew (pre vs. post 1985), but also on the length of the flight itself.

On the other hand, if the flying time is the same, then the CO2 levels will be lower on the pre 1985 flight, which will also have a lower chance for airborne illnesses to spread.

   A.   *In 1985 there was a loosening of regulations concerning cabin air in commercial airline flights.*

This would explain why air replenishment fell from every thirty minutes to once every hour. But it's only a potential reason and by no means supported by the stimulus.

   B.   *People who fly today are more likely to contract airborne illnesses than were people who flew prior to 1985.*

This is definitely a "could be true/probably true" answer choice. In fact, I had this selected until the very end.

There is just one thing though. We know that airborne illnesses spread more easily today. But just because an illness is spread more easily doesn't mean people are more likely to contract it. That would also depend on whether people's immune systems have gotten stronger, whether they have developed better hygiene habits, and whether they are vaccinated or wearing masks, etc. In other words, we can't know 100% that this is true.

So in other words, I would categorize this as a "probably true" answer choice. I would select this if nothing better came up.

   C.   *Low levels of carbon dioxide in cabin air make it <u>impossible</u> for airborne illness to spread.*

This can also be true. But maybe it just makes it harder to spread, not "impossible." **Again, watch out for strong wording in MSS answer choices.**

   D.   *In 1980 the rate at which the cabin air was replenished in commercial airliners was sufficient to protect passengers from the effects of carbon dioxide buildup.*

Were we ever told that the rate of replenishment was "sufficient?" No, just that it was higher than flights after 1985. Maybe neither were sufficient, and people still got sick on flights, both back then and now.

   E.   *In 1980 the level of carbon dioxide in the cabin air on a two-hour commercial airline flight was lower than it is today on a similar flight.*

I had my initial doubts when I saw this answer. I was thinking to myself, even if both flights were 2 hours long, what if the modern plane was bigger and seated more passengers? Wouldn't that mean more people breathing and hence more CO2 in the air at any given time?

But then I saw the phrase "on a similar flight," so I think in this case it would be safe to assume that factors such as the plane and number of passengers aren't external circumstances we need to take into consideration.

So both flights are two hours long. The 1980 flight would have replenished its air four times, and the flight today, only twice.

According to the last sentence of the stimulus, the less frequently air is replenished, higher the CO_2. 2 is less than 4, so CO_2 is higher on today's flight.

This is a MBT answer that **synthesizes** different information from the stimulus. Its level of certainty is higher than answer choice B, so E is the correct answer.

Answer choice B isn't wrong per se, but we chose E simply because even for MSS Questions, **certainly true answers are better than probably true answers.**

Finding the Most Probable Answer

When no MBT answer exists, which answer makes the most reasonable inference?

We saw in the previous question that **certainly true answers** > **probably true answers** > **possibly true answers**. But what happens when we don't have a MBT answer among the answer choices? How do we differentiate the likelihood or probability of the truth of answer choices?

Take a look at the following question:

PTC2 S3 Q21

Musicologist: Ludwig van Beethoven began losing his hearing when he was 30. This loss continued gradually, but was not complete until late in his life. While it may seem that complete hearing loss would be a severe liability for a composer, in Beethoven's case it gave his later music a wonderfully introspective quality that his earlier music lacked.

Which one of the following statements is most strongly supported by the musicologist's claims?

   A.   It was more difficult for Beethoven to compose his later works than his earlier ones.
   B.   Had he not lost his hearing, Beethoven's later music would have been of poorer quality than it is.
   C.   Had he not lost his hearing, Beethoven would have been less introspective than he was.
   D.   Beethoven's music became gradually more introspective as he grew older.
   E.   Had he not lost his hearing, Beethoven's later music would probably have been different than it is.

The author makes a causal claim in this stimulus: Complete Hearing Loss ⇒ Introspective Quality to Beethoven's Music.

We also know that Beethoven began losing his hearing when he was 30, the process was gradual, and according to some quick googling, Beethoven did not become completely deaf until he was 45.

We need to note that the author did not say that the *gradual* loss of hearing caused Beethoven's music to become more introspective. Rather, it's the *complete* loss of hearing which is the cause:

"*While it may seem that __complete hearing loss__ would be a severe liability for a composer, in Beethoven's case __it__ gave his later music a wonderfully introspective quality that his earlier music lacked.*"

The "it" here refers to "complete hearing loss."

> A. It was more <u>difficult</u> for Beethoven to compose his later works than his earlier ones.

Maybe, it would seem so if we appealed to common sense, but this is not supported by the stimulus.

Answer choices containing new and out of scope information are almost always wrong in MSS Questions.

> B. Had he not lost his hearing, Beethoven's later music would have been of poorer quality than it is.

It would probably lack the introspective quality, so it's possible that his music would be of poorer quality. But perhaps he would have found other inspiration, maybe the music would have been even better. This answer is just not something we can infer from the information in the stimulus.

> C. Had he not lost his hearing, Beethoven would have been less introspective <u>than he was.</u>

Throughout this book, we have emphasized keeping an eye out for particular keywords that can make or break an answer choice (K in the SLAKR method). We have underlined such keywords again and again.

The problem with this answer choice is at the very end: this answer suggests that Beethoven as a person had become more introspective. The stimulus, on the other hand, is talking about Beethoven's music. If your music is introspective, does that mean your personality is introspective as well? I don't think so: do you need to be a sad person to make sad music? Similarly, many artists or comedians who created joyful or hilarious, upbeat work were seriously depressed in real life. I just don't think the connection can be drawn.

> D. Beethoven's music became gradually more introspective as he grew older.

We know that Beethoven gradually became deafer as he grew older, and his *complete deafness* caused his music to become introspective.

Perhaps his music grew more introspective, or perhaps one day, when he was completely deaf, he had an epiphany and his music changed drastically. We just don't know.

Take the following analogy:

John saved more and more money as he grew older, until he became financially independent at the age of 40. His financial independence caused him to become a world traveler and adventurer.

This statement mirrors the stimulus. Did John travel more and more between the ages of 20 and 40? Maybe. But it's also possible that he carefully saved money, lived frugally, and only started traveling once he became financially independent.

E. *Had he not lost his hearing, Beethoven's later music would <u>probably</u> have been different than it is.*

We know that Complete Hearing Loss ⇒ Introspective Quality. What this answer choice is saying is that without the cause, we will <u>probably</u> not achieve the same effect.

But wait, haven't we learned that causation isn't exclusive in the chapter on Logic and Causal Reasoning? Just because A causes B, doesn't mean C or D cannot also cause B, right? If working out causes weight loss, does that mean if I don't work out, I won't lose weight? Of course not: I can also diet.

What saves this answer choice is the word "probably." If we didn't have the cause that made Beethoven's music introspective, how likely is it that his music turned out exactly the way it did? Would a Beethoven of good hearing have composed the same music as a deaf Beethoven? It's possible, maybe something else would have happened to him that had the same influence on him as deafness.

But if we had to guess what are the chances of finding an alternate cause that precisely mirrors the influence deafness had on Beethoven's music, I'd say that the chances are pretty slim.

So I'd say that had Beethoven not been deaf, his music would probably be different, maybe by a lot, and maybe by just a little.

Is answer choice E perfect? Far from it. But when we compare it to answer choices B, C, and D, all of which are merely "could be true," I would say answer choice E's likelihood is somewhat higher. In terms of ranking the answer choices, I think E > D > C > B > A. <u>E is the correct answer.</u>

Practice **ranking answer choices** in Strengthen, Weaken, and MSS Questions. It's the only way to really force ourselves to think in relative rather than absolute terms when targeting these question types.

***

Tricky Wrong Answer Choices

When we are ranking answer choices, we should obviously try to think about the probability that an answer is true according to the information presented in the stimulus. Which one is probably true, and which one is only possibly true?

But of course, to fully realize the implications of each answer choice is a skill only acquired after repeated and targeted practice. And that's something you should start doing as soon as possible. **Whenever we are looking at Strengthen/Weaken/MSS Questions, rank the answer choices in terms of preferability, and give your rationale for it.** (Why A is better than B, etc.)

In the meantime, we will look at some "red flags" that are often associated with wrong answer choices. By spotting these via the skill of Keyword Extraction, it will make our work of ranking answers and tackling MSS Questions a lot easier.

Strongly Worded Answers:

We have seen repeated in the previous questions that strongly worded answers ended up getting eliminated. Answer choices like

"During a rainfall, the cloud <u>must</u> surrender the same percentage of its ordinary oxygen as of its oxygen 18."

"Low levels of carbon dioxide in cabin air make it <u>impossible</u> for airborne illness to spread."

This is because a strongly worded answer choice would require a similarly strong level of proof from the stimulus. To show that the statement *"maybe John likes football"* is supported by the stimulus, we just have to find information that merely suggests it to be a possibility.

But in order to select an answer that says *"John loves football more than anything else,"* we need proof via the stimulus that football is indeed his number one passion. He loves it more than anything in the world.

Strongly worded answer choices are *usually* wrong in MSS Questions. I say "usually" because there will be times when a strongly worded answer is in fact supported by a strongly worded stimulus. **So treat strong, forceful words in answer choices as caution signs, but don't eliminate the answer only based on this.** (Readers of RC Perfection will no doubt recognize this concept as similar to the "Threshold of Proof" idea.)

Out-of-Scope Answers

Since all correct answers will be supported by information gleaned from the stimulus, answer choices containing information or keywords unrelated to the stimulus will be wrong.

We also have to get into the habit of reading the stimulus for its scope. Out of scope answer choices make up some of the most common traps in LR questions, something we discussed at the very beginning of the book. Be sure to have an exact idea of the precise nature of the topic and concepts being discussed in the stimulus. We have to be aware of not just what the author is talking about, but also what they are not talking about.

Unwarranted Connections and Term Shifts

A harder and more devious trap found often in MSS answer choices occurs when the author takes discrete, unrelated statements in the stimulus, and conjures up an answer choice that imagines a connection between the two. These are easy to miss, especially if you are reading quickly. All the information in this answer choice looks familiar, so you end up selecting it without much deliberation. These traps I call "**Unwarranted Connections**."

 Practice the art of Keyword extraction and underlining in the answer choices. Slow down your test taking speed until you can maintain a high rate of accuracy, only then should we attempt to speed up.

***

PT28 S1 Q22

Under the influence of today's computer-oriented culture, publishing for children has taken on a flashy new look that emphasizes illustrations and graphic design; the resulting lack of substance leads to books that are short-lived items covering mainly trendy subjects. The changes also include more humorous content, simplification of difficult material, and a narrower focus on specific topics.

Which one of the following is most strongly supported by the information above?

A. The inclusion of humorous material and a narrower focus detract from the substance of a children's book.
B. The substance of a children's book is important to its longevity.
C. Children of the computer generation cannot concentrate on long, unbroken sections of prose.
D. Children judge books primarily on the basis of graphic design.
E. The lack of substance of a children's book is unlikely to be important to its popularity.

There are two pieces of information in this stimulus that we should note:

1. Computer Oriented Culture ⇒ Flashy Children's Books that Lack Substance ⇒ Short Lived and Covering Trendy Subjects

2. Other changes associated with children's books (more humorous, simplification, and narrower focus)

What caused these "other changes?" Are they also due to the influences of computer oriented culture? Perhaps they are also an effect of "flashy children's books that lack substance?"

The author never says. It's certainly a possibility, but it's also possible that they were caused by something else. Perhaps the rise of the internet and people's need to be constantly stimulated by information caused these changes, perhaps education reform caused these changes.

As the author never links the second statement to the causal relationship in the first statement, we don't want to assume such a relationship. To do so would be stepping out of bounds on an MSS Question. We take what the stimulus gives us, and nothing more.

A. *The inclusion of humorous material and a narrower focus detract from the substance of a children's book.*

This statement connects the second statement with the first. This is an **unwarranted connection** never made by the author.

Let's put this answer choice into notation form, and you will see exactly what's wrong with it.

Statement 1: A ⇒ B ⇒ C

Statement 2: Other changes including D, E, and F

Answer choice A: D + F ⇒ B

Remember, just because something sounds or seems reasonable doesn't mean it is! Correct MSS answers need to be supported by the stimulus. **You need to find textual evidence to back up the answer choice that you have selected.** (More on this later)

B. *The substance of a children's book is important to its longevity.*

We know that a "*lack of substance*" leads to "*short-lived*" books. Can we deduce from this that "*the substance of a children's book is important to its longevity?*"

I believe that we can. Even when we take into account the non-exclusivity of causal logic, such an inference seems reasonable:

If we know that a "*lack of exercise leads to weight gain,*" can we say that "*exercising is important to weight loss?*"

Yes, even when we know that other things like dieting can lead to weight loss, we can't deny that exercising is an important factor as well. It may not be the only factor, but it's still an important factor.

C. *Children of the computer generation cannot concentrate on long, unbroken sections of prose.*

Maybe they can, they just prefer not to. They would much rather browse Reddit instead. This answer is both **out of scope** and **too strong**.

D. Children *judge* books *primarily* on the basis of graphic design.

Newer books have more graphic design elements to them. But we can't gather from the stimulus that children judge books primarily based on this. Maybe it's the parents who choose the books, or maybe the children judge the books based on illustrations and simplicity rather than graphic design.

Like the previous answer choice, D is both **out of scope** and **too strong**.

E. *The lack of substance of a children's book is unlikely to be important to its* *popularity*.

How popular are these newer books? We don't really know. If there are changes, then perhaps there is a market for it. So this answer can be construed as a "possibly true" choice.

But on the other hand, perhaps these books aren't popular at all, they will soon be pulled from the market because parents prefer books of substance for their children.

This answer choice can go both ways, remember to distinguish between the **probable** and the mere **possible**.

B is the correct answer.

***

PT79 S4 Q25

One way to compare chess playing programs is to compare how they perform with fixed time limits per move. Given any two computers with which a chess-playing program is compatible, and given fixed time limits per move, such a program will have a better chance of winning on the faster computer. This is simply because the program will be able to examine more possible moves in the time allotted per move.

Which one of the following is most strongly supported by the information above?

A. If one chess playing program can examine more possible moves than a different chess playing program run on the same computer under the same time constraints per move, the former program will have a better chance of winning than the latter.
B. How fast a given computer is has no effect on which chess-playing computer programs can run on that computer.
C. In general, the more moves a given chess playing program is able to examine under given time constraints per move, the better the chances that program will win.
D. If two different chess playing programs are running on two different computers under the same time constraints per move, the program running on the faster computer will be able to examine more possible moves in the time allotted.
E. If a chess playing program is run on two different computers and is allotted more time to examine possible moves when running on the slow computer than when running on the fast computer, it will have an equal chance of winning on either computer.

Let's take a look at this stimulus:

One way to compare chess playing programs is to compare how they perform with fixed time limits per move.

I'm not sure if there's anything useful in this statement. It seems like background information. Perhaps the words "one way" can be potentially of value? Perhaps there are other ways to compare chess programs too?

Given any two computers with which a chess-playing program is compatible, and given fixed time limits per move, such a program will have a better chance of winning on the faster computer.

So we have two computers, one faster and one slower. The faster computer will have a better chance of winning.

How many chess programs are we comparing? Are we comparing two different programs?

No, it's the same software. We are running the same software on two different computers. It's essentially playing against itself.

This is simply because the program will be able to examine more possible moves in the time allotted per move.

This explains why the same software would have a better chance of winning on a faster computer: the faster computer will process more moves in the same amount of time due to higher hardware specs.

    A. *If one chess playing program can examine more possible moves than <u>a different chess playing program</u> run on the same computer under the same time constraints per move, the former program will have a better chance of winning than the later.*

Notice the illicit **term shift** in this answer choice: in the stimulus, we were talking about the same program run on two computers, here we are talking about two different programs. What if one program has really buggy software and the other one doesn't? This is just not an inference we can make based on the stimulus alone.

    B. *How fast a given computer is has no effect on which chess-playing computer programs can run on that computer.*

We don't really know the answer to this. Perhaps some newer programs can't run on thirty-year-old machines? This is **out of scope**.

    C. <u>*In general*</u>, *the more moves a given chess playing program is able to examine under given time constraints per move, the better the chances that program will win.*

I didn't much like this answer choice to begin with. Do the chess programs which examine more moves usually have a better chance of winning? I guess it also depends on if the moves examined are relevant to the game being played? (For instance, would examining more opening moves help during the end game?)

Also, the stimulus did say that this method was only "one way" to compare chess programs. If there are other ways that we haven't considered, this answer choice seems to jump too hastily to conclusions.

But it did say "in general," so let's keep it for now.

    D. *If <u>two different chess playing programs</u> are running on two different computers under the same time constraints per move, the program running on the faster computer will be able to examine more possible moves in the time allotted.*

Again, we are talking about two different chess programs here, another **term shift.** So with the same time constraints, if we are talking about the same chess program, this answer choice would be true. But with two different programs, maybe the program running on the faster computer is a slower program to begin with?

> E. *If a chess playing program is run on two different computers and is allotted more time to examine possible moves when running on the slow computer than when running on the fast computer, it will have <u>an equal chance</u> of winning on either computer.*

In order to have an "equal chance," the slower speed of the computer will need to be offset by more allotted time. For instance, if the computer was twice as slow, in order to have an equal chance of winning, the program would need twice the time.

Let's go back to answer choice C:

> C. <u>*In general*</u>, *the more moves a given chess playing program is able to examine under given time constraints per move, the <u>better the chances</u> that program will win*

C appears to be the best option we have. Notice how it doesn't say that if you can examine more moves, you will win. It only says that you have better chances of winning. Furthermore, the stimulus does convey the message that if the same program can examine more moves under the same time constraints, it will have a better chance of winning. I guess you can't really find any support to argue the contrary.

The words "in general" is definitely a warning sign here, but I think it's something we can work with because the answer choice itself is worded in fairly mild language.

<u>C, although imperfect, is the correct answer.</u>

Textual Proof Test (Confirming your Answer Choice Selection)

In the last chapter, we talked about going back to re-check the stimulus to find the exact support for our answer choice once we've made a selection. The correct answer, we said, will always have direct, textual proof that can be underlined or highlighted within the stimulus.

This is mostly true for MSS Questions as well.

A habit I have found to be of great help is to read carefully the answer choice that I've selected, think about the type and kind of proof needed to make this answer choice stand, and **return to the stimulus** to make sure such proof is there.

Going back to the stimulus can help us root out not only careless misreads, but also force us to demonstrate that our answer choice doesn't suffer from scope, unwarranted connections, and term shift related issues.

Take a look at the following question, before finalizing on your answer choice selection, try to isolate the proof/evidence that you think is relevant to the answer choice chosen.

<u>PT49 S4 Q19</u>

Forester: The great majority of the forests remaining in the world are only sickly fragments of the fully functioning ecosystems they once were. These fragmented forest ecosystems have typically lost their ability to sustain themselves in the long term, yet they include the last refuges for some of the world's most endangered species. To maintain its full complement of plant and animal species, a fragmented forest requires regular interventions by resource managers.

The forester's statements, if true, most strongly support which one of the following?

    A.   Most of the world's forests will lose at least some of their plants or animal species if no one intervenes.

    B.   Unless resource managers regularly intervene in most of the world's remaining forests, many of the world's most endangered species will not survive.

    C.   A fragmented forest ecosystem cannot sustain itself in the long term if it loses any of its plants or animal species.

    D.   A complete, fully functioning forest ecosystem can always maintain its full complement of plant and animal species even without interventions by resource managers.

    E.   At present, resource managers intervene regularly in only some of the world's fragmented forest ecosystems.

For this question, let's try a different approach. Let's break down the answer choices first, then go back to the stimulus to look for the relevant evidence.

This will better simulate the textual proof test we have just talked about. Once we have selected an answer choice, the textual proof test tells us to double check our answer choice, think about the proof it would need if it was indeed the correct answer, and then return to the stimulus to find such corresponding proof.

> A. *Most of the world's forests will lose at least some of their plants or animal species if no one intervenes.*

Two things stood out to me about this answer choice: the word "most," and answer choice A's conditional nature.

We know this answer choice is conditional because of the phrase "if no one intervenes," which introduces a sufficient condition. So let's diagram it.

No One Intervenes → Most of the World's Forest will Lost some of their Plants or Animal Species

> B. *Unless resource managers regularly intervene in most of the world's remaining forests, many of the world's most endangered species will not survive.*

This is also conditional in nature, if we diagram it, it will look like this:

Some of the world's most endangered species' survival → Regular Intervention in Most Remaining Forests

Here, unlike answer choice A, which is talking about some plants and animal species, this answer is talking about "most endangered species."

Furthermore, the intervention has to be "regular," as well as conducted in "most" of the world's remaining forests.

> C. *A fragmented forest ecosystem cannot sustain itself in the long term if it loses any of its plants or animal species.*

Conditional again:

Lose any Plant/Animal Species → Fragmented Forest Ecosystem Cannot Sustain itself Long Term

> D. *A complete, fully functioning forest ecosystem can always maintain its full complement of plant and animal species even without interventions by resource managers.*

This is basically saying that intervention is not needed for a complete, fully functioning ecosystem.

> E. *At present, resource managers intervene regularly in only some of the world's fragmented forest ecosystems.*

This answer says current regular intervention is only partial.

Now let's look at the stimulus.

Forester: The great majority of the forests remaining in the world are only sickly fragments of the fully functioning ecosystems they once were.

So most of the forests are incomplete fragments, and not fully functioning ecosystems.

These fragmented forest ecosystems have typically lost their ability to sustain themselves in the long term, yet they include the last refuges for some of the world's most endangered species.

So most forests cannot sustain themselves in the long term, the world's most endangered species live in these incomplete, fragmented forests.

To maintain its full complement of plant and animal species, a <u>fragmented forest</u> requires regular interventions by resource managers.

We already know that most of the world's forests are fragmented, so this conditional applies to most of the world's forests.

For most forests to maintain all their plant and animal species → regular intervention by resource managers.

Let's go back again to the answer choices:

> A. *<u>Most</u> of the world's forests will lose at least some of their plants or animal species <u>if no one intervenes.</u>*

Two things stood out to me about this answer choice: the word "most," and answer choice A's conditional nature.

We know this answer choice is conditional because of the phrase "if no one intervenes," which introduces a sufficient condition. So let's diagram it.

No One Intervenes → Most of the World's Forest will Lost some of their Plants or Animal Species

This is a synthesis of statement 1 and statement 3 in the stimulus. <u>This is the correct answer.</u>

> B. *Unless resource managers <u>regularly</u> intervene in <u>most</u> of the world's remaining forests, many of the world's <u>most endangered species</u> will not survive.*

This is also conditional, if we diagram it, it will look like this:

Some of the world's most endangered species' survival → Regular Intervention in Most Remaining Forests

Here, unlike answer choice A, which is talking about some plants and animal species, this answer is talking about "most endangered species."

Furthermore, the intervention has to be "regular," as well as conducted in "most" of the world's remaining forests.

There is an **unwarranted connection** here. According to the stimulus, intervention is required to maintain all the plants and animal species. Endangered species also happen to live in these forests. It's two separate issues.

> C. *A fragmented forest ecosystem cannot sustain itself in the <u>long term</u> if it loses any of its plants or animal species.*

Conditional again:

Lose any Plant/Animal Species → Fragmented Forest Ecosystem Cannot Sustain itself Long Term

Another **unwarranted connection** is drawn here. We know from statement 2 that these forests cannot sustain themselves in the long term, period, whether or not they lose additional animals and plants.

> D. *A complete, fully functioning forest ecosystem can <u>always</u> maintain its <u>full</u> complement of plant and animal species even <u>without</u> interventions by resource managers.*

We know that fragmented forests need regular intervention, but does this mean non-fragmented forests don't need regular intervention? This would be a fallacious negation of the original conditional in the stimulus.

> E.   *At present, resource managers intervene regularly in only some of the world's fragmented forest ecosystems.*

This answer says current regular intervention is only partial.

This is **out of scope**. We know intervention is needed, but how often do they intervene at the present moment is something we cannot know from the stimulus alone.

Here, we looked at the answer choices first, and then went back to the stimulus to find corresponding support. It's a tactic that has helped me navigate some of the hardest MSS Questions. So give it a try when you are stuck!

Difficult Trait #2: If you are stuck, read the answer choice carefully, isolate its corresponding keywords, and go back to the stimulus to try to find the textual support needed.

Pick the Best Answer, Relatively Speaking

At the very end of the Chapter on Strengthen Questions, we reiterated the importance of adopting a different mindset for Strengthen/Weaken/MSS Questions. Instead of going through the answer choices, finding four problematic and one perfect answer, our job now is to find the best available answer choice. The correct answer choice may be imperfect, but still correct by virtue of being better than the rest of them. Keep this in mind and take a look at the next question.

PT14 S4 Q21

Monroe, despite his generally poor appetite, thoroughly enjoyed the three meals he ate at the Tip-Top Restaurant, but unfortunately, after each meal he became ill. The first time he ate an extra-large sausage pizza with a side order of hot peppers; the second time he took full advantage of the all-you-can-eat fried shrimp and hot peppers special; and the third time he had two of Tip-Top's giant meatball sandwiches with hot peppers. Since the only food all three meals had in common was the hot peppers, Monroe concludes that it is solely due to Tip-Top's hot peppers that he became ill.

If both Monroe's conclusion and the evidence on which he bases it are correct, they would provide the strongest support for which one of the following?

  A. Monroe can eat any of Tip-Top's daily all you can eat specials without becoming ill as long as the special does not include the hot peppers.
  B. If, at his third meal at Tip-Top, Monroe had chosen to eat baked chicken with hot peppers, he would have become ill after that meal.
  C. If the next time Monroe eats one of Tip-Top's extra-large sausage pizzas he does not have a side order of hot peppers, he will not become ill after his meal.
  D. Before eating Tip-Top's fried shrimp with hot peppers special, Monroe had eaten fried shrimp without suffering any ill effects.
  E. The only place Monroe has eaten hot peppers has been at Tip-Top.

This stimulus may seem familiar, it is also the stimulus for a Flaw Question, but that is outside of the scope of our discussions here.

We accept the information presented in the stimulus, both the premises and the conclusion. As a result, we know that:

1. Monroe had three meals at Tip-Top, each time he had hot peppers, and each time he got sick.
2. Hot peppers caused him to become sick. (Causal)

The stimulus is relatively simple to understand, so let's dive right into the answer choices:

A. *Monroe can eat any of Tip-Top's daily all you can eat specials without becoming ill as long as the special does not include hot peppers.*

The causal relationship given in the stimulus is between hot peppers and Monroe getting sick, or Hot Peppers (Cause) ⇒ Sick (Effect).

Answer choice A is saying that if the cause is not present, neither will the effect.

Let's keep this answer choice for now.

B. *If, at his third meal at Tip-Top, Monroe had chosen to eat baked chicken with hot peppers, he would have become ill after that meal.*

Answer choice B extrapolates the Hot Peppers ⇒ Sick causal relationship to an additional scenario. Let's keep it as well.

C. *If the next time Monroe eats one of Tip-Top's extra-large sausage pizzas he does not have a side order of hot peppers, he will not become ill after his meal.*

This answer choice is similar to A, no cause, no effect.

D. *Before eating Tip-Top's fried shrimp with hot peppers special, Monroe had eaten fried shrimp without suffering any ill effects.*

This answer is **out of scope**, we simply don't know, based on available information, whether he had gotten sick eating shrimp previously.

E. *The only place Monroe has eaten hot peppers has been at Tip-Top.*

This answer is also out of scope. We don't know if he had eaten hot peppers elsewhere.

So we have A, B, and C left to choose from:

The stimulus gives us a cause/effect relationship, Hot Peppers ⇒ Sick.

Both answer choices A and C suggest that without the cause, there will not be the effect either.

Answer choice B restates the causal relationship.

Which answer is more supported by our stimulus?

Let's go back to our Workout ⇒ Lose Weight hypothetical:

If given the causal relationship between working out and weight loss, which of the following statements is more likely to be true?

1. John doesn't work out, so he won't lose weight
2. David works out, so he will lose weight

Based on the causal relationship alone, the answer choice that is a **repetition** will be closer to the original meaning. While it's possible that without the cause, we won't have the corresponding effect, it's also possible that something else causes John to lose weight.

Similarly, answer choice B is better supported because it's a **repetition** of the original causal relationship in the stimulus. B is the correct answer.

18. Most Strongly Supported

19. Core Habit: RANKING

Let's start by revisiting two of the MSS Questions which we have covered in the previous chapter:

PTC2 S3 Q21

Musicologist: Ludwig van Beethoven began losing his hearing when he was 30. This loss continued gradually, but was not complete until late in his life. While it may seem that complete hearing loss would be a severe liability for a composer, in Beethoven's case it gave his later music a wonderfully introspective quality that his earlier music lacked.

Which one of the following statements is most strongly supported by the musicologist's claims?

    A. It was more difficult for Beethoven to compose his later works than his earlier ones.
    B. Had he not lost his hearing, Beethoven's later music would have been of poorer quality than it is.
    C. Had he not lost his hearing, Beethoven would have been less introspective than he was.
    D. Beethoven's music became gradually more introspective as he grew older.
    E. Had he not lost his hearing, Beethoven's later music would probably have been different than it is.

                                        ***

PT14 S4 Q21

Monroe, despite his generally poor appetite, thoroughly enjoyed the three meals he ate at the Tip-Top Restaurant, but unfortunately, after each meal he became ill. The first time he ate an extra-large sausage pizza with a side order of hot peppers; the second time he took full advantage of the all-you-can-eat fried shrimp and hot peppers special; and the third time he had two of Tip-Top's giant meatball sandwiches with hot peppers. Since the only food all three meals had in common was the hot peppers, Monroe concludes that it is solely due to Tip-Top's hot peppers that he became ill.

If both Monroe's conclusion and the evidence on which he bases it are correct, they would provide the strongest support for which one of the following?

    A. Monroe can eat any of Tip-Top's daily all you can eat specials without becoming ill as long as the special does not include hot peppers.
    B. If, at his third meal at Tip-Top, Monroe had chosen to eat baked chicken with hot peppers, he would have become ill after that meal.
    C. If the next time Monroe eats one of Tip-Top's extra-large sausage pizzas he does not have a side order of hot peppers, he will not become ill after his meal.
    D. Before eating Tip-Top's fried shrimp with hot peppers special, Monroe had eaten fried shrimp without suffering any ill effects.
    E. The only place Monroe has eaten hot peppers has been at Tip-Top.

If you still remember, the correct answer to PTC2 S3 Q21 is E.

The stimulus tells us that Loss of Hearing ⇒ Beethoven's music more introspective.

Answer choice E essentially says that without the cause, the effect would have been different too. (No cause, no effect)

For PT14 S4 Q21, the causal relationship in the stimulus is that Hot Peppers ⇒ Sick. The correct answer is B, which restates this causal relationship.

But take a look at answer choices A and C, both of which are saying that if no hot peppers are eaten, Monroe won't get sick. (No cause, no effect)

Now go back and look at the Beethoven question again.

Isn't the correct answer in PTC2 S3 Q21 sort of like answer choices A and C here, by saying that without the cause, the effect won't exist either?

This is exactly the point I wanted to convey: in the Beethoven question we chose this answer choice because it was the best available. All the other answer choices had bigger issues.

Here, in this question, answer choices A and C are not wrong, *per se.* They are wrong because answer choice B is a better alternative. If answer choice B wasn't around, I would probably go with answer choice C, and if C wasn't around, I would have no choice but to pick A.

> We pick the best answer choice available to us, rather than get frozen in fear because no answer choice is perfect.

***

Take a look at the following question, train your mind to find the better/best answer, rather than the correct answer:

PTJ2007 S3 Q16

Philosopher: Nations are not literally persons; they have no thoughts or feelings, and literally speaking, they perform no actions. Thus they have no moral rights or responsibilities. But no nation can survive unless many of its citizens attribute such rights and responsibilities to it, for nothing else could prompt people to make the sacrifices national citizenship demands. Obviously, then, a nation _____.

Which one of the following most logically completes the philosopher's argument?

    A. Cannot continue to exist unless something other than the false belief that the nation has moral rights. motivates its citizens to make sacrifices.
    B. Cannot survive unless many of its citizens have some beliefs that are literally false.
    C. Can never be a target of moral praise or blame.
    D. Is not worth the sacrifices that its citizens make on its behalf.
    E. Should always be thought of in metaphorical rather than literal terms.

| Fill in the Blank questions can be treated as MSS Questions unless otherwise stated. |

Let's break down this stimulus:

- *Philosopher: Nations are not literally persons; they have no thoughts or feelings, and literally speaking, they perform no actions.*

Why aren't nations persons? Because they have no thoughts or feelings and perform no actions.

There seems to be a conditional relationship in here, let's extract that:

Thoughts AND Feelings → Person
Contrapositive: Person → Thoughts OR Feelings

Perform No Actions → Not Person
Contrapositive: Person → Perform Actions

- *Thus they have no moral rights or responsibilities.*

Who has no moral rights or responsibilities? Nations. Why? Because they are not literally persons.

Person → Rights AND Responsibilities
Contrapositive: Rights OR Responsibilities → Person

(The phrase "No A or B," when diagrammed, becomes "A AND B." Think about the statement "John has no house or car," does that mean John has either a house and no car, a car but no house, or neither? John has no house and no car.)

The first two statements, combined, yields Nation → Literal Person → Rights AND Responsibilities

- *But no nation can survive unless many of its citizens attribute such rights and responsibilities to it,*

National Survival → Citizens Attribute Rights and Responsibilities

- *for nothing else could prompt people to make the sacrifices national citizenship demands.*

"Nothing else" is another way of saying "only." So only by attributing rights and responsibilities to the nation could people be prompted to make sacrifices for it.

Make Sacrifices → Attribute Rights and Responsibilities to the Nation

There is an assumption made when we look at the last two statements in conjunction: National survival requires citizens making sacrifices. (Refer back to the Chapter on Sufficient Assumptions on extracting conditional assumptions.)

So the second half of the stimulus can be expressed as:

National Survival → Citizens Make Sacrifices → Attributing Rights and Responsibilities to the Nation

When we combine the first and second halves of the stimulus, we end up with two discrete conditional chains:

- Nation → Literal Person → Rights AND Responsibilities
- National Survival → Citizens Make Sacrifices → Attributing Rights and Responsibilities to the Nation

So in other words, a nation has no rights or responsibilities. But in order for the nation to survive, rights and responsibilities have to be attributed to it.

This seems paradoxical, let's take a look at the answer choices and see which is supported by the stimulus.

> A. Cannot continue to exist unless something other than the false belief that the nation has moral rights motivates its citizens to make sacrifices.

National Survival → Attributing Rights and Responsibilities to the Nation + Another Belief

This is directly contradicting the third statement, *"But no nation can survive unless many of its citizens attribute such rights and responsibilities to it"*

This answer choice would be a **Must be False** answer, not what we are looking for.

This answer might sound reasonable at a first glance, because the stimulus already told us that "nations are not persons," so we would be tempted to think that since the belief in the personhood of nations is false, we would need a new belief.

But remember, we can only select an answer choice that is supported by evidence. This answer choice directly contradicts our stimulus.

> B. Cannot survive unless many of its citizens have some beliefs that are literally false.

If we combine the two conditional statements derived from the stimulus, we end with something like this:

"National survival requires attributing something that nations don't have to them anyways."

National survival requires attributing moral rights and responsibilities to nations, which they can't have, because only people have rights and responsibilities, and nations aren't people.

This answer choice matches up nicely with our stimulus, it's a **Must be True** inference, and <u>the correct answer.</u>

> C. Can <u>never</u> be a target of moral <u>praise</u> or <u>blame.</u>

Nations can't have rights or responsibilities, but can they be a target of moral praise or blame? I'm not so sure. I guess it all depends on how high your moral standards are. If I saw a stranger get mugged and did nothing, some will say that since I had no responsibility towards him, I should not be a target of censure. On the contrary, others may judge me cold-hearted and selfish. The implications of this answer choice are unclear. It's most likely both **too strong** and **out of scope**.

> D. Is <u>not worth</u> the sacrifices that its citizens make on its behalf.

Can we derive an evaluation of worth from the fact that citizens have false beliefs? If I make a sacrifice based on a false belief, does that mean the recipient is not worthy? The implication of this answer, like the previous one, is unclear. If I sacrificed myself to save a child that I mistakenly believed to be my brother, does that mean the child is not worthy to be saved? This answer is similarly **out of scope**, as it cannot be supported by the information provided.

> E. Should always be thought of in metaphorical rather than literal terms.

This answer is complicated. I think it's partially supported. If we only look at the first half of the stimulus, then we know nations are not literal persons. To think of nations as persons in literal terms would be erroneous.

But why "metaphorical?" Does the "metaphorical" person also have rights and responsibilities? We don't know. If the "metaphorical person" has no rights and responsibilities, then thinking of nations as metaphorical rather than literal persons doesn't change a thing.

In order to make this answer choice work, we'd have to add in a premise that states "metaphorical persons have rights and responsibilities." **But we can't bring our assumptions into MSS answer choices!**

Only then can we argue that since national survival requires attributing rights and responsibilities to nations, and because nations aren't literal persons, we have to think of nations as metaphorical persons. Because metaphorical persons can have rights and responsibilities.

But then again, this might contradict the first half of the stimulus: "Nations are not literally persons…thus they have no moral rights or responsibilities."

We can argue that "metaphorical persons are not literally persons either, so they can't have rights and responsibilities either."

To make E work, we would have to bring in an assumption that would potentially contradict the stimulus.

B, on the other hand, is an MBT answer, and the only one suitable.

We had mentioned in the last chapter that for MSS Questions, **strongly worded answer choices** should raise some red flags, unless they are directly supported by the stimulus.

The correct answer choice here is a conditional statement, and it doesn't get stronger than that. But here, it's the correct answer choice because it's **provable via the stimulus**.

Always Compare Answers

Let's revisit two more questions from the chapter on Strengthen Questions:

<u>PT79 S1 Q10</u>

The more sunlight our planet reflects back into space, the cooler the global atmosphere tends to become. Snow and ice reflect much more sunlight back into space than do ocean water or land without snow cover. Therefore, the greater the area of Earth's surface that is covered with snow and ice, the cooler, on average, the global atmosphere is likely to become.

Which one of the following, if true, would most strengthen the argument?

A. Low atmospheric temperatures are required for the formation of clouds that result in snow.
B. Other factors besides the reflectivity of ice and snow affect the cooling of Earth's atmosphere.
C. Ocean water and land heated by sunlight in turn warm Earth's atmosphere.
D. The atmosphere derives most of its heat from the passage of sunlight through it.
E. Lighter colored soil reflects more sunlight back into space than does darker colored soil.

***

<u>PT74 S1 Q17</u>

How the pigment known as Han purple was synthesized by the ancient Chinese of Qin and Han dynasties has puzzled scientists. The Chinese chemists employed the same chemical ingredients used for Han purple in the production of a common type of white glass during that period. Both were produced in the processes that involved subjecting the mixtures to high heat and mixing in lead to decrease the melting temperature. Thus, Han purple was probably discovered by a fortuitous accident during glass production.

Which one of the following, if true, would most strengthen the argument?

A. Chemical analysis shows that most of the known fragments of both Han purple and the white glass were produced within a small geographical radius.
B. Han purple was used for luxury and ceremonial items, whereas the white glass was used to make certain household items.
C. The technique used for producing Han purple was known to very few people during the Qin and Han dynasties.
D. The ingredients used in producing both Han purple and the white glass were easily obtainable during the Qin and Han dynasties.
E. The white glass is found in more surviving artifacts from the Qin and Han dynasties than Han purple is.

If we were to only remember one rule from the two chapters on Strengthen and Weaken Questions, then it is to remember that no answer is inherently correct. We said to avoid answer choices that are open to interpretation, but the correct answer to 79-1-10 is exactly that. We said to find an answer that has a direct effect on the conclusion, but the correct answer to 74-1-17 doesn't really do that.

In both cases, the correct answer is the ***best available answer***. Finding the best answer choice, relatively speaking, is something that has only gotten more crucial in recent years, as more and more correct answers that still leave something to be desired show up on the test.

For Strengthen, Weaken, and Most Strongly Supported Questions, our job is to find the *best available answer,* rather than the one correct answer.

Reading Comprehension Questions too, require this approach. But that's another topic reserved for another book.

***

The ability to take a "relative" perspective has only grown more important in recent times. Since PT70, we are witnessing more and more questions which contain multiple acceptable answer choices. Our job now is to find the best answer available, despite its imperfections; rather than simply eliminating four wrong answers and ending up with the right one.

Take a look at the following questions just to get an idea of how ranking your answer choices has become an absolute must in recent tests: 84-3-6, 84-3-19, 83-1-20, 79-4-22, 79-1-23, 75-3-21

Ranking answers will force us to face the subtle and nuanced differences between each answer choice, and more in depth thinking about answer choices and their implications is always a good idea.

Let's look at one more recent question where we need to rank and compare the answer choices:

PT90 S3 Q15

One should only buy a frying pan that has a manufacturer's warranty, even if it requires paying more, and even if one would never bother seeking reimbursement should the pan not work well or last long. Manufacturers will not offer a warranty on a product if doing so means that they will need to reimburse many customers because the product did not work well or last long.

The conclusion of the argument is strongly supported if which one of the following is assumed?

    A.   Most people who buy a frying pan with a manufacturer's warranty would seek reimbursement should the pan fail to work well or last long.
    B.   All of the frying pans currently on the market that are covered by a manufacturer's warranty work at least as well at the time of purchase as any of the frying pans not covered by a warranty.
    C.   The more a frying pan costs, the more likely it is to be covered by a manufacturer's warranty.
    D.   The most expensive frying pans are the ones most likely to work well for many years.
    E.   Most frying pan manufacturers' warranties provide for full customer satisfaction.

This is a Strengthen Question, so let's start off by dissecting the structure of the argument in the stimulus:

What is the conclusion of the argument? The author is trying to convince us to always buy a frying pan that has a warranty. This is straightforward enough.

The support they offer for this conclusion is somewhat more convoluted. We know that the author thinks frying pans covered by warranties are superior, but why?

Manufacturers will not offer a warranty on a product if doing so means that they will need to reimburse many customers because the product did not work well or last long."

Need to reimburse many customers due to shoddy product → Manufacturer will not offer warranty

So if we take the contrapositive of this, we would get something like this:

If the manufacturer offers a warranty, then there is no need to reimburse customers due to the shoddy quality of the product.

This may seem paradoxical at a first glance, but the author's reasoning is essentially this:

If the manufacturer knows that their product is subpar, customers will most likely return or refund it, so it's in the manufacturer's best interest not to offer a warranty. (If they offered a warranty on a terrible product, they would lose so much money due to returns and refunds.) Essentially, they are arguing that offering a warranty means the manufacturer is more likely to stand by their product, that incentivizes them to create a superior product.

If you are still a little confused about the argument:

Manufacturers do not like returns, so if you offer returns/warranty you are more inclined to offer a good product.

Conversely, if a product came with a warranty, it would be a better product in general.

In this line of reasoning, the author is making two assumptions:

1. Manufacturers are prepared to honor the warranty offered.

Think about it, if the manufacturers offered fake warranties that aren't honored, then the incentives of offering a better product due to warranties is no longer existent. Offering a warranty won't necessarily mean that the manufacturer will make an effort to produce a better product, because the warranty doesn't mean anything.

2. Customers will take the manufacturer up on their warranty offer.

If the frying pan cost 19.99, but in order to get a replacement, you had to pay to ship the pan to China, and pay for return shipping, which costs 100 dollars. Yes, the warranty is still honored, but will people realistically return the product?

A Type I answer would address one of these assumptions. A Type II answer, in contrast, would give us another reason to believe why products with warranties are better than those without.

Let's take a look at the answer choices:

> A. *Most people who buy a frying pan with a manufacturer's warranty would seek reimbursement should the pan fail to work well or last long.*

This addresses the second gap/assumption in the argument: if nobody bothered to use the warranty, and the manufacturer knows this, then there is no incentive to produce a better product when warranties are offered.

> B. *All of the frying pans currently on the market that are covered by a manufacturer's warranty work <u>at least as well</u> at the time of purchase as any of the frying pans not covered by a warranty.*

This answer is telling us that warrantied pans are *just as good* as those without warranties. Does this strengthen the argument? A little bit. If the answer choice had said that all warrantied frying pans *worked better* than non-warrantied pans, it would be a much better answer.

Think about it this way: you got accepted to both Yale and Harvard. Your friend is trying to convince you to go to Yale. He says: "Yale is at least as good as Harvard."

Is this a convincing argument? Not really, what he should really be telling you are the advantages Yale has over Harvard.

> C. *The more a frying pan costs, the more likely it is to be covered by a manufacturer's warranty.*

This answer choice has no effect on our argument or conclusion. We want something that tells us that pans with warranties are better.

> D. *The most expensive frying pans are the ones most likely to work well for many years.*

This answer is just like answer choice C. It's telling us that expensive pans are better. But that's not the author's point. they are arguing that pans with warranties are superior, so we should buy pans with warranties, regardless of cost.

If the author had stated that warrantied pans are more expensive, and more expensive pans work better, then this answer could work. But the author never commits to the position that warrantied pans are more expensive. He just says that they are better, even if they are more expensive. Very tricky!

> E. *Most frying pan manufacturers' warranties provide for full customer satisfaction.*

This answer also strengthens the author's position, to an extent. This answer is essentially telling us that warranties are great. It also seems to address our #1 potential gap. So manufacturers do honor their warranties. But remember the scope of our conclusion: our author is arguing that warrantied products are better, even if you don't use that warranty. So the reason why they are superior is not due simply to the warranty, but something more.

<u>Answer choice A more directly addresses that, which is the correct answer.</u>

A Final Word on Answer Choice Ranking

We have seen in this chapter (and on many Strengthen/Weaken/MSS Questions previously) how adopting a relative mentality during the answer choice selection process can benefit us. While it has been easier to differentiate between the one correct answer choice and four incorrect ones on earlier LSATs, more recent tests have been slowly taking away that logical certainty.

When stuck on two answers that both leave something to be desired, try to approach it from a holistic perspective. Ask yourself, "what kind of answer are you looking for in this particular question type?" For Strengthen and Weaken Questions, answer choices with a more direct effect will be more desirable; while for MSS Questions, more conservatively worded answers that are easier to meet the stimulus's threshold of proof are safer guesses. Think about the gaps contained in the argument, if any. Which answer choice best addresses those? Parse the answer choices for their keyword selection, any words stand out to you or make you more suspicious?

In short, know what your job is for the question type you have encountered, and go with the answer choice that gets the job done better.

But occasionally, even the habit of ranking is not enough to come to the correct answer. From my experiences tutoring the LSAT, this happens most frequently when you have skipped over the correct answer choice in your first passthrough. Perhaps you went with your gut feeling and quickly eliminated three ACs without truly thinking about their implications. Perhaps the correct answer is worded in such an abstract and vague way that you just didn't understand what it was trying to express. Either way, you are ranking the answers, except that you are looking in the wrong place.

So whenever I end up with **two imperfect/problematic answer choices**, I will quickly check the three ACs that I have already eliminated. I will make sure I didn't eliminate a contender without fully understanding it, before I zone in on the two ACs that truly need to be compared.

Similarly, if you are left with **two answer choices that both look good**, chances are that you have missed a keyword here and there. Think about the implications of every noun, verb, and adjective/adverb with a critical mindset if this is the case.

20. Point of Disagreement

We now turn to Point of Disagreement/Agreement Questions. In these questions, the stimulus will have two speakers engaged in a conversation. Each person will present their viewpoint, which could either be in argument form, with supporting evidence; or simply a statement stating their position. Our job is to find the specific issue on which these two speakers disagree or agree.

In my experience, Point of Disagreement Questions can be quite challenging, especially for the students who go through the Logical Reasoning section mainly driven by intuition. Many students prepare for the LSAT by going through PT after PT without critically reflecting on either the type of question they are dealing with, or the specific traits and characteristics unique to that question type. Their decision-making process relies largely on "gut feeling" or experience accumulated from practice. After reading the stimulus, they jump straight to the answer choices without anticipating what the correct answer ought to look like and pick the answer choice that seems "right." In the event that they did get the correct answer, if you ask them why they picked it and not the others, they will be hard pressed to find a reasonable answer.

While this process might work for easier questions, our accuracy takes a brutal hit once we are faced with more difficult questions. **As we have seen time and time again, different types of questions require different strategies.** What might be a correct answer choice for one question type will be wrong for another. Furthermore, the test makers love to lay out traps for the unwitting student throughout the question in the structure and logic of the stimulus, hide assumptions in the arguments, or sprinkle the answer choices with inappropriate keywords.

Point of Disagreement (POD) Questions are difficult to answer because there are simply too many things to watch out for. There are two speakers in the Stimulus, you have to keep track of each of their viewpoints, then you have to find the point of contention between the two, and that requires not only understanding each person's perspective, but also comparing and contrasting each statement with one another. In other words, you have to dig through two opposing statements/arguments, delineate all the separate points each person brings up, get to the crux of the argument, and find out exactly what is the point of disagreement/agreement between the two.

And that's only half the battle. Even when we have an anticipated answer, we now have to match it up with the answer choices. The answer choices are often worded vaguely, and sometimes the differences between the right and wrong answers are tiny. Finally, in the hardest questions, our anticipated answers will not necessarily match up with the correct answer, and we will need to take each answer choice back to the stimulus to see if we can find support for it.

For this chapter, let's try a different approach. Since we do not have to cover a lot of theoretical background for Point of Disagreement Questions, we shall take a pragmatic approach.

Difficult Trait #1: There are too many issues to keep track of in the stimulus

The first area of difficulty faced by students in POD Questions is the overwhelming amount of information we have to process in the stimulus. POD stimuli are structured differently in the sense that we normally have two speakers each presenting their point in the form of a conversation. Unlike the traditional LR stimulus, where we often find a coherent argument, POD stimuli will often throw even the most seasoned student off track because now we are dealing with two people with different views simultaneously.

Sometimes, even the points conveyed by each of the speakers don't form a real argument. For instance, Speaker A will make a claim, which consists of three statements; while Speaker B will refute that claim, with a reply consisting of two more statements. But if we look carefully at Speaker A's statements, they don't form a real argument, meaning that although we understand the point they are trying to make, we can't simply categorize each of the statements into premises, intermediate conclusions, or even main conclusions. So what happens in this case is that we are left with five discrete statements, with the logical and structural relationship between them unclear. With this much information on our hands, we literally don't know where to start. So quite often, even reading and processing the POD stimulus can be quite a daunting task, leaving us flustered and even more confused.

Solution: Summarize, Infer, and Extract

We tackle this problem by systematically reading and processing the information presented in the stimulus. **I treat a POD stimulus as two separate MBT/MSS stimuli.** I will start with Speaker A's statements, read each of them, and ask myself, **"what is this sentence saying, and what knowledge about Speaker A's point of view can I extract from this?"** I will repeat the process for the entirety of Speaker A's argument/viewpoint.

Now it's probably a good idea to take notes for POD Questions. Due to the varied and numerous nature of the ideas present in POD stimuli, it is a good idea to write down whatever information you can extract or summarize. This may seem tedious at first, but as you get better, you will be able to go through the process much faster, until eventually you may or may not need to write things down at all. (I still keep pen and paper beside me for POD Questions and will take notes for the hardest questions.)

***

Take a look at the following question stimulus, and try to exhaustively list all the views/points pertaining to each speaker:

Henry: Some scientists explain the dance of honeybees as the means by which honeybees communicate the location of whatever food source they have just visited to other members of the hive. But honeybees do not need so complicated a mechanism to communicate that information. Forager honeybees returning to their hive simply leave a scent trail from the food source they have just visited. There must therefore be some other explanation for the honeybees' dance.

Winifred: Not necessarily. Most animals have several ways of accomplishing critical tasks. Bees of some species can navigate using either the position of the Sun or the memory of landmarks. Similarly, for honeybees, scent trails are a supplementary not an exclusive means of communicating.

Let us treat this stimulus as two MBT/MSS stimuli. We will now go through each of them, extracting whatever information we can, with a special focus on the positions of each speaker:

Henry: <u>Some</u> scientists <u>explain</u> the dance of honeybees as the means by which honeybees communicate the location of whatever food source they have just visited to other members of the hive.

Henry is introducing the opinion of some scientists, we don't know just yet whether he agrees with them or not.

The word "explain" should stand out to us. We know that on the LSAT, "explain" means "cause." So essentially, some scientists believe that the cause for honeybees dancing is to communicate food location.

But honeybees do not need so complicated a mechanism to communicate that information.

This is Henry's opinion now. Does Henry agree with the scientists? No. Why?

Because he thinks using dance to communicate food location is overly complicated, which might mean that there's a simpler way to communicate food location for honeybees.

Forager honeybees returning to their hive simply leave a scent trail from the food source they have just visited. There must therefore be some other explanation for the honeybees' dance.

There are two separate issues here, hidden nicely in this statement.

One, how do bees communicate food location? Henry believes it's done by leaving a scent trail.

Two, if honeybees don't dance to communicate food location, then why do they dance? Henry doesn't say explicitly, but it's probably something else.

We can extract/summarize Henry's viewpoints as the following:

1. Honeybees don't dance in order to communicate food location
2. They can do that by leaving a scent
3. They must dance for some other reason

Let's now look at Winifred's rebuttal.

Winifred: Not necessarily. Most animals have several ways of accomplishing critical tasks.

Not necessarily what? We know Winifred is arguing against Henry, but exactly which point?

Remember that Henry thinks that if honeybees can communicate food location via scent, then dancing is not used for food communication?

> As we read/summarize/extract information from the stimulus, we are always trying to relate new ideas to the earlier statements.

So Winifred is basically saying that honeybees can use BOTH scent trails and dancing to communicate food. They don't have to be mutually exclusive.

Bees of some species can navigate using either the position of the Sun or the memory of landmarks.

Winifred is giving an example/analogy to back up her claim: two ways to accomplish the same task is a possibility for bees.

Similarly, for honeybees, scent trails are a supplementary not an exclusive means of communicating.

Remember what Henry had said about scent trails? Henry said that because bees use scent trails to communicate food location, they won't use dances for communicating food location. Winifred is saying that bees use both.

This is the information that I extracted from Winifred's argument.

1. There are multiple ways to accomplish the same task.
2. Bees can navigate by sun and landmarks.
3. Bees can communicate food location by scent and dance.

***

Extracting and listing the points/views made by each speaker is the **first step** we should take to get better at POD Questions. If you have trouble retaining the information presented in the stimulus, you need to slow down and really THINK about the different issues being discussed by both people.

Taking notes in bullet form for both Speaker A and Speaker B, as I did above, is an effective way to train ourselves to read systematically and exhaustively. As we get more comfortable with the process, we will notice a subconscious change in our reading habits. As we go through a POD stimulus (or MBT/MSS stimuli for that matter), we are automatically making mental notes and compartmentalizing the information that we've just read.

Difficult Trait #2: I understand both views, but don't know how they relate to each other

Once the student has learned to process the information presented in the stimulus, however numerous they may be, another challenge arises. Sometimes even after listing all the relevant issues, we still have trouble figuring out exactly which point it is that both parties disagree/agree on.

There will be times when the relationship between A and B's statements are far from clear. A and B may disagree with each other, but we can't be sure of the exact point on which their views diverge.

It would be simple if Speaker A had said a, b, and c; and Speaker B had said a, d, and e. We would know right away that the point of disagreement between the two is on issue a. But more often, we won't find a direct negation/denial of one person's claims in the other person's statements. Even after listing all the issues espoused by both speakers, we may end up with something like this:

Speaker A: a, b, and c

Speaker B: d, e, and f

On the surface, none of the issues relate to each other, and we can't figure out on which point do the two disagree/agree. The student, confused, resorts to reading over the answer choices, trying to stretch or help the answer choice to make them fit the stimulus, leaving greater room for error.

On a side note, this is also a frequent problem for many students doing comparable reading passages in the RC section. After having read both passages and seemingly having understood both, we still have no idea how they relate to each other.

Solution: Look for overlaps in scope between the issues discussed by the two speakers

This problem was something that plagued me as well, both in POD Questions and in comparative reading passages on the RC section. What really helped me overcome this difficulty was a readjustment of my reading strategy: I would still read the Speaker A's statements normally, as we have done above, understanding and extracting concrete pieces of information from it. But once I get to Speaker B's statements, I do one more thing: **In addition to making a note of what each sentence/statement is saying, I ask myself if this statement can be related to Speaker A's points.**

Let me demonstrate, using the previous stimulus as an example again:

Henry: Some scientists explain the dance of honeybees as the means by which honeybees communicate the location of whatever food source they have just visited to other members of the hive. But honeybees do not need so complicated a mechanism to communicate that information. Forager honeybees returning to their hive simply leave a scent trail from the food source they have just visited. There must therefore be some other explanation for the honeybees' dance.

We read Henry's statements as we had done before, and we end up extracting the following points from his argument:

1. Honeybees don't dance in order to communicate food location.

2. They can do that by leaving a scent.
3. They must dance for some other reason.

Now, we turn to Winifred's argument:

Winifred: Not necessarily. Most animals have several ways of accomplishing critical tasks. Bees of some species can navigate using either the position of the Sun or the memory of landmarks. Similarly, for honeybees, scent trails are a supplementary not an exclusive means of communicating.

Now, instead of simply reading each statement and writing down whatever information we can extract, we have to go a step further. We need to ask ourselves, do each of Winifred's statements relate to Henry's three points? If so, then which one and how?

Let's start with Winifred's first statement: *"Not necessarily. Most animals have several ways of accomplishing critical tasks."*

Does this relate to any of the following? Is Winifred responding to either of Henry's three claims?

- Henry's First Claim: *Honeybees don't dance to communicate food location.*
- Henry's Second Claim: *Honeybees can leave scent trails to communicate food location.*
- Henry's Third Claim: *Honeybees must dance for another reason.*

It seems to me Winifred's first statement is a direct response to Henry's third claim, Winifred thinks that animals can have different ways to get the same job done. So they can leave scent trails AND dance. It's also indirectly rebutting Henry's first claim. But it doesn't appear to be related to Henry's second claim.

Winifred's Second Statement: *Bees of some species can navigate using either the position of the Sun or the memory of landmarks.*

Is this a rebuttal of Henry's three claims?

Henry never mentions bee navigation. This is one of Winifred's supporting claims and not directly related to Henry's claims.

Let's look at Winifred's last statement: *Similarly, for honeybees, scent trails are a supplementary not an exclusive means of communicating.*

Winifred is saying bees don't just use scent trails to communicate. What else did Winifred think that bees use to communicate food location? Dancing. This is again in direct opposition to Henry's first and third claim. Winifred is essentially saying, "bees can dance to communicate too."

Four Steps to Practice POD Questions

So, as we can see in our walkthrough above, the point of issue in Henry and Winifred's debate is centered on why bees dance. Henry thinks bees dance for another reason, Winifred thinks they do it to communicate food location. Henry thinks honeybees don't dance to communicate food location, Winifred thinks they can and they do.

So, if you are having trouble relating a wide array of seemingly discontinuous ideas between two speakers to each other, do the following:

> Read Speaker A's statements normally, summarize, take notes in bullet form if needed.
>
> Read Speaker B's first statement, summarize and take notes if needed.
>
> Ask yourself if and how does B's first statement relate to any of Speaker A's points? Do they share the same scope? Is there agreement or disagreement?
>
> Repeat the process for each of Speaker B's other statements.

By manually checking every claim made by Speaker B against the claims made by Speaker A, we are essentially training our mind to find connections, agreements, or disagreements between the two parties. It's a drill that I assigned to my students, especially those who had difficulties relating one speaker's claim to the other's.

Like the Solution to Difficult Trait 1, this difficulty can only be overcome through constant practice. There are **three main reasons** why students end up stuck in the 150s or 160s. One, we haven't looked hard enough at the questions we got wrong to locate our specific weak points in knowledge and habit. Two, we have not designed drills or exercises that can target our weaknesses. Three, even after realizing what we need to do, we don't go through with the execution.

Going from the low 170s to the high 170s requires even further finetuning of many of our micro habits, but we'll talk about that at the end of the book.

Reasons 1 and 2, at least for the LR section, are largely dealt with in this book, but it's really up to you to actually practice the drills we designed in this book, familiarize yourself with the habits we preached so they become second nature, and finally fill in whatever theoretical knowledge gaps you may have.

Following all these steps may seem tedious, but they are essential for training our reading habits and connection making skills. As you get better it will seem more natural to you, and perhaps you can even skip a few steps. But start slowly, follow the steps, and gradually build up your proficiency, that's extremely important!

For **comparative passages** in RC, we can follow a similar process, with the exception that we are reading the second passage more for its ideas conveyed rather than summarizing each sentence. Check out RC Perfection for more details.

***

Let's look at one more POD stimulus, list the claims made by the first speaker, and compare the second speaker's claims to those made by the first.

Tina: For centuries oceans and human eccentricity have been linked in the literary and artistic imagination. Such linkage is probably due to the European Renaissance practice of using ships as asylums for the socially undesirable.

Sergio: No. Oceans have always been viewed as mysterious and unpredictable – qualities that people have invariably associated with eccentricity.

Tina makes two claims in her statement:

- Tina's first claim: There is a long-time linkage between oceans and human eccentricity.
- Tina's second claim: This linkage is due to a social practice of using ships as asylums.

Note how Tina's second claim is causal. Using ships as asylums ⇒ Linkage between oceans and human eccentricity.

Sergio: No. Oceans have always been viewed as mysterious and unpredictable – qualities that people have invariably associated with eccentricity.

Now look at Sergio's claim. Sergio says "no." But is he disagreeing with Tina's first claim or second claim?

Is Sergio saying "no, there is NOT a long-time linkage?" or is he saying "no, the linkage is NOT due to a social practice?"

When we compare Sergio's claims *individually* with Tina's claims, the answer is fairly obvious. Sergio doesn't think the linkage between oceans and eccentricity is due to using ships as asylums, but rather, due to human views of the ocean.

If we strip the stimulus down to its causal logic barebones, it will look like this:

Tina: A ⇒ B

Sergio: No, C ⇒ B

Tina and Sergio disagree on the cause behind the linkage between oceans and human eccentricity.

Difficult Trait #3: I have trouble deciding on an answer choice

The third area where students trip up are the answer choices. POD answer choices can be especially difficult, in fact, they reminded me of both Role Question answer choices and MSS answer choices.

Harder POD answer choices are often worded in abstract terms, and we need to understand what they are referring to first before we can actually determine whether it's the correct answer or not. In this respect POD answers are similar to Role/Method answer choices, and the skillset of extracting keywords from answer choices and matching them up with the stimulus is something shared by all three question types.

POD answer choices can also be full of seemingly harmless details, but quite often, it's these details that make or break an answer choice.

It can also be hard to match up the correct answer with the stimulus as well. Because now the stimulus is divided into two parts (Speaker A and Speaker B), we need to match the answer choice not once, but twice with the information in the stimulus. (We need to check if Speaker A agrees/disagrees with the answer choice, then do the same thing for Speaker B.) This extra step can also present a challenge for some students.

Solution: Seek to understand the answer choices, and go back to the stimulus for support

In order to successfully navigate POD answer choices we follow a **three-step** process: we ask ourselves the following three questions in succession.

1. Do I fully understand the meaning of this answer choice? Are there details or keywords that I need to take into consideration?

2. What is Speaker A's position on this answer choice? Is there explicit textual support in the stimulus?

3. What is Speaker B's position on this answer choice? Is there explicit textual support in the stimulus?

For Disagreement Questions, the positions taken by Speaker A and Speaker B must be in opposition to each other: for the correct answer choice, if Speaker A is in agreement with the position described, Speaker B MUST be against it, and vice versa.

For Agreement Questions, both Speakers must share the same opinion. They can both disagree with the correct answer choice, or both agree with it, as long as they are in unison.

And just like MSS Questions, we need explicit support from the stimulus to back up our claim. For example, if we say that "Speaker A agrees with answer choice A," then we must be able to provide evidence from Speaker A's own words in the stimulus to back up that claim.

Let's go back to the question stimuli we have examined previously, but this time with the answer choices:

PT19 S4 Q16

Henry: Some scientists explain the dance of honeybees as the means by which honeybees communicate the location of whatever food source they have just visited to other members of the hive. But honeybees do not need so complicated a mechanism to communicate that information. Forager honeybees returning to their hive simply leave a scent trail from the food source they have just visited. There must therefore be some other explanation for the honeybees' dance.

Winifred: Not necessarily. Most animals have several ways of accomplishing critical tasks. Bees of some species can navigate using either the position of the Sun or the memory of landmarks. Similarly, for honeybees, scent trails are a supplementary not an exclusive means of communicating.

The point at issue between Henry and Winifred is whether

> A. Theories of animal behavior can be established on the basis of evidence about only one species of animal.
> B. There is more than one valid explanation for the dance of the honeybees.
> C. Honeybees communicate the location of food sources through their dance.
> D. The honeybee is the only species of bee that is capable of communicating navigational information to other hive members.
> E. The honeybee's sense of smell plays a role in its foraging strategies.

We have already looked at the stimulus in detail, so let's jump straight to the answer choices:

A. _Theories_ of animal behavior can be established on the basis of evidence about _only one_ species of animal.

What is this answer saying?

Can theories be based on only one species of animal? For example, can a theory about all birds be established on evidence based only on eagles?

What does Speaker A say? Remember, we need _explicit textual evidence._ Just because you think Speaker A might agree or disagree with this is not good enough.

Neither Speaker A nor B makes any statements confirming or denying this point.

B. There is more than one valid _explanation_ for the dance of the honeybees.

We know that "explanation" means "cause" on the LSAT. So Answer Choice B is saying that there is more than one cause for why honeybees dance.

In order for this answer to work, one person must say "honeybees dance for more than one reason," and the other person must say "no, honeybees dance for only one reason."

So why do honeybees dance?

We know Winifred thinks it's to communicate food location. Winifred thinks that there are _multiple ways_ to communicate food location (scent trail and dancing), but she doesn't say that there are _multiple explanations_ for dancing.

Henry says the explanation is not food communication, so it must be something else. But we still don't know if this "something else" is just one alternate explanation, or multiple alternate explanations.

Many students found this answer especially tricky, because the way it's worded is so close to the stimulus.

But by striving to understand this answer choice independent of the stimulus, and then going back to the stimulus for evidence of disagreement, we can avoid being pulled into its trap. (**Reverse Confirmation**)

C. Honeybees communicate the location of food sources through their dance.

So honeybees dance to communicate food location. Does one person say "yes," and the other person says "no?"

What does Henry say? "There must be some other explanation (not food communication)..."

What does Winifred say? "Scent trails are a supplementary not an exclusive means of communicating."

The disagreement here is implied, it's never explicitly stated, this is a common feature on the hardest POD Questions.

Ideally, I would still want an answer choice whose disagreement can be more explicitly backed up by claims in the stimulus. But we shall keep this answer choice for now, and let's see if D and E are better.

D. The honeybee is _the only_ species of bee that is capable of communicating navigational information to other hive members.

This answer choice is saying that the honeybee is the only bee that can communicate with others. In other words, no other species of bees can do this. In order for this answer to work, one person has to say that "other bees can also communicate," and the other person has to say, "no they can't, only honeybees can."

This doesn't happen in our stimulus.

> E. The honeybee's <u>sense of smell</u> plays a role in its foraging strategies.

What is this answer talking about?

The "sense of smell" is talking about the "scent trails" mentioned in the stimulus. So do honeybees use scent trails to communicate food location?

Henry says yes, scent trails are the only way to communicate food location.

Winifred also says yes, scent trails and dancing are both used to communicate food location.

This is an answer choice with which both parties *agree*. But since we are looking for a point of *disagreement*, <u>C</u> is the best available and correct answer.

***

<u>PT30 S4 Q21</u>

Tina: For centuries oceans and human eccentricity have been linked in the literary and artistic imagination. Such linkage is probably due to the European Renaissance practice of using ships as asylums for the socially undesirable.

Sergio: No. Oceans have always been viewed as mysterious and unpredictable – qualities that people have invariably associated with eccentricity.

Tina and Sergio's statements lend the most support to the claim that they disagree about which one of the following statements?

- A. Eccentric humans were considered socially undesirable during the European Renaissance.
- B. Oceans have always been viewed as mysterious and unpredictable.
- C. The linkage between oceans and eccentricity explains the European Renaissance custom of using ships as asylums.
- D. People have never attributed the same qualities to oceans and eccentrics.
- E. The linkage between oceans and eccentricity predates the European Renaissance.

We start by reading each person's statement separately. Let's start with Tina.

Tina: For centuries oceans and human eccentricity have been linked in the literary and artistic imagination. Such linkage is probably due to the European Renaissance practice of using ships as asylums for the socially undesirable.

Tina makes two points here: one, there is a linkage between oceans and human eccentricity; and two, this is due to the Renaissance practice of using ships to jail those with mental problems.

Remember earlier in the book when we studied the structure of causal arguments, a common way in which test makers present a causal argument is to first give the effect/phenomenon, and then offer up a cause for it. Essentially, in Tina's statement, the order in which the cause-and-effect relationship is presented is reversed. She gives us the effect first, then the cause.

So if we rearrange her statement in a more logically understandable way, it should look like this:

Because socially undesirable people were imprisoned on ships during the Renaissance, oceans and human eccentricity have been linked in our imagination.

As a causal relationship, Using Ships as Asylums ⇒ Linkage between Oceans and Human Eccentricity

Now for Sergio's statement:

Sergio: No. Oceans have always been viewed as mysterious and unpredictable – qualities that people have invariably associated with eccentricity.

We know, obviously, that Sergio disagrees with Tina on some certain issue. But what exactly does he disagree with Tina on?

Sergio *agrees* with Tina that oceans are associated with eccentricity, but he thinks that it's due to an alternate reason/cause. *It's because oceans have always been viewed as mysterious and unpredictable that people associate oceans and human eccentricity.* In other words, Tina and Sergio disagree on the cause of why we associate oceans with human eccentricity.

Herein lies the disagreement, a table could display it nicely.

	Tina	Sergio
We associate eccentricity with the ocean	Yes	Yes
Why	Renaissance Practice	We've always viewed the ocean as mysterious

Let's look at the answer choices. Remember to practice the skill of Keyword Extraction (K in SLAKR), as well as figuring out what each answer choice is really saying before making a decision.

Remember, Point of Disagreement Question Answer Choices can often be vague or abstract, just like Role/Method Question Answer Choices. Refer back to the exercise we did in the Role Questions chapter to refresh your memory on how to make sense of vague answer choices.

> A.   *Eccentric humans were considered socially undesirable during the European Renaissance.*

For Tina, there is definitely a connection between eccentric humans and the socially undesirable. Perhaps eccentricity was a quality possessed by undesirable people. But Sergio does not touch upon this topic.

If an answer choice was only mentioned by one of the speakers, it will not be correct.

> B.   *Oceans have always been viewed as mysterious and unpredictable.*

This is one of Sergio's views, Tina makes no explicit reference to whether views of the ocean have changed in the past.

> C.   *The linkage between oceans and eccentricity <u>explains</u> the European Renaissance custom of using ships as asylums.*

This answer gets a bit more tricky. Remember what the word "explains" means on the LSAT? It means "cause."

So here, what answer choice C is saying is that "the link between oceans and eccentricity caused Europeans used ships as asylums."

This reverses the causal relationship in Tina's argument, neither would agree with this.

> D.   *People <u>have never</u> attributed the same qualities to oceans and eccentrics.*

Both Tina and Sergio believe there to be a linkage between the ocean and eccentrics. Both would disagree with this answer. So Sergio and Tina would actually share the same position.

> E.   *The linkage between oceans and eccentricity <u>predates</u> the European Renaissance.*

What does this answer mean? "Predates" means "happened before." So did people link oceans and eccentricity prior to the Renaissance? Sergio would agree with this, as he thinks that "oceans have ALWAYS been viewed as mysterious." Tina, on the other hand, thinks it's the Renaissance practice of using ships as asylums that caused this link. So according to Tina, the linkage happened only after the European Renaissance.

<u>This answer is the correct answer</u>, and similar to the correct answer in PT19 S4 Q16, **it is not explicitly stated in the stimulus but must be inferred.**

Difficult Trait #4: The point of disagreement/agreement is not explicitly stated in one person's statement and must be inferred.

But wait, didn't we also say that the correct answer choice will have "explicit textual support?"

Yes, there is a distinction here. Take a look at the following example:

Assume in a hypothetical question there are two detectives, A and B, who are arguing about the identity of the criminal.

Let's say the correct answer choice is this: "John is the criminal."

So now we need one detective to agree with this statement, and the other detective to disagree.

We don't need detective A to explicitly state that "yes, John is definitely the criminal," nor do we need detective B to explicitly state that "no, John cannot be the criminal."

In order words, the stimulus doesn't have to have a word for word confirmation or negation of the answer choice.

But what we do need is explicit evidence that supports such a disagreement between A and B. For example, if B said in the stimulus that "John was in another city when the crime occurred," then that's good enough. That's enough evidence to show us that detective B doesn't think John to be the criminal.

Similarly, detective A doesn't have to state outright that it's John who committed the crime. But we do need evidence that would commit him to this position. For example, detective A could say something like "out of the three suspects, only John doesn't have an alibi." That's enough explicit evidence committing detective A to agreeing with the answer choice.

***

Remember what our anticipated answer was? After reading the stimulus, what did we think was the disagreement between Tina and Sergio?

Tina and Sergio disagreed on the cause behind the linkage between oceans and eccentricity.

Here, no answer matched our anticipated answer, but answer choice E was the only answer that had supporting evidence. We can infer from Tina's statement that she would say "no" to answer E, while Sergio would say "yes."

So while Tina never said something like "the linkage doesn't predate the Renaissance," and Sergio never said that "the linkage did predate the Renaissance." We nonetheless have enough evidence from their respective statements to infer what their exact reaction would be to answer E.

Let's look at one more question, this time in its entirety.

Remember to make a note of all the claims made by both speakers, think about Speaker B's claims in relation to Speaker A's claims, and finally, think about what each answer choice entails, and make sure the answer choice you chose has the best support from both sides in the stimulus.

PT63 S1 Q14

Waller: If there were really such a thing as extrasensory perception, it would generally be accepted by the public since anyone with extrasensory powers would be able to convince the general public of its existence by clearly demonstrating those powers. Indeed, anyone who was recognized to have such powers would achieve wealth and renown.

Chin: It's impossible to demonstrate anything to the satisfaction of all skeptics. So long as the cultural elite remains closed minded to the possibility of extrasensory perception, the popular media reports, and thus public opinion, will always be biased in favor of such skeptics.

Waller's and Chin's statements commit them to disagreeing on whether

    A.   Extrasensory perception is a real phenomenon.
    B.   Extrasensory perception, if it were a real phenomenon, could be demonstrated to the satisfaction of all skeptics.
    C.   Skeptics about extrasensory perception have a weak case.
    D.   The failure of the general public to believe in extrasensory perception is good evidence against its existence.
    E.   The general public believes that extrasensory perception is a real phenomenon.

Let's start with Waller's claims:

Waller: If there were really such a thing as extrasensory perception, it would generally be accepted by the public since anyone with extrasensory powers would be able to convince the general public of its existence by clearly demonstrating those powers. Indeed, anyone who was recognized to have such powers would achieve wealth and renown.

I was able to extract the following views from Waller's statements:

1. If extrasensory perception existed it would be generally accepted by the public.
2. If you have extrasensory powers you will be able to convince the public.
3. If you can convince the public/be recognized for these powers you will be rich and famous.

Let's look at Chin's claims:

It's impossible to demonstrate anything to the satisfaction of all skeptics.

Is this claim a direct response to any of Waller's claims above?

It seems like a partial rebuttal of Waller's second claim. Chin is saying that you can't convince everyone.

So long as the cultural elite remains closed minded to the possibility of extrasensory perception, the popular media reports, and thus public opinion, will always be biased in favor of such skeptics.

So Chin thinks the popular media and public opinion is biased. If the public is biased towards the skeptics, then where does that lead us?

I guess even if you do have extrasensory powers, you won't really be able to convince the public (they wouldn't believe you anyways).

It seems that Waller and Chin's most direct point of conflict is on whether the public will be convinced if extrasensory perception existed. Waller thinks the public will be convinced, but Chin thinks the public will be biased and not so easily convinced.

Let's look at the answer choices:

A. *Extrasensory perception is a real phenomenon.*

Does one person think ESP to be real, and the other person think it to be fake?

Maybe you can make the argument that Waller thinks it to be fake. Waller says that if it's real it would have been accepted by the public. The underlying assumption is that if it hasn't been accepted by the public, it can't be real.

But even if we make the argument that Waller thinks ESP is fake, we can't find any evidence to support the idea that Chin thinks it to be real. All Chin did was to point out the weakness in Waller's argument.

B. *Extrasensory perception, if it were a real phenomenon, could be demonstrated to the satisfaction of all skeptics.*

In order for this answer to work, one person must say that "if ESP is real, all skeptics could be convinced."

The person in disagreement would say that "if ESP is real, some skeptics could not be convinced."

We know that Chin argues the latter point: Chin thinks that not all skeptics could be convinced.

But does Waller think that all skeptics could be convinced?

Waller thinks that "it would generally be accepted by the public." Waller never said that "all" skeptics could be convinced.

Beware these subtle term shifts.

    C.   *Skeptics about extrasensory perception have a weak case.*

No one comments on whether the skeptics have a weak or strong case.

    D.   *The failure of the general public to believe in extrasensory perception is good evidence against its existence.*

Let's take a second to stop and think about what this answer choice means.

It's essentially saying that if the public doesn't believe in ESP, then it doesn't exist. Or by contrapositive, if ESP exists, then the public will believe in it.

What does Waller think? If ESP is real, then it would generally be accepted.

What does Chin think? Even if ESP is real, the public will still believe the skeptics.

Answer choice D is just a super indirect way describing our anticipated answer. That's why it's so crucial to try to understand what each answer choice is really saying. This is the correct answer.

    E.   *The general public believes that extrasensory perception is a real phenomenon.*

What does the public actually believe? According to Chin, the public would rather believe the skeptics (so they don't believe in ESP); Waller never states what he thinks, but as we mentioned earlier, there is the assumption that the public doesn't currently believe in ESP.

So both parties actually both would reject answer E. Both Waller and Chin would agree on that point.

Difficult Trait #5: I am stuck between two attractive answer choices and always pick the wrong one.

This happens quite often in POD Questions, especially when there are multiple answer choices that can be construed to match the stimulus. With harder questions, the advanced student can often quite easily eliminate three out of the five potential answer choices but end up stuck between the last two.

In the hardest questions, this is often the case. The correct answer might have something that we didn't quite like about it, while the other answer choice, while still problematic, is not so obviously wrong. This happens in a lot of difficult RC questions as well. We end up with two answers and pick the wrong one.

Solution 1: Pay more attention to keywords in answers

Whenever we are faced with two answer choices and we can't decide, we need to focus on one thing and one thing only: **Keyword Analysis** or Keyword Extraction (The K in the SLAKR Method)

Re-read each of the attractive answer choices again, one at a time, focusing on *every single word* in that answer choice. Pay special attention to the quantifier words (some, most, all, etc.) as well as the adjectives and adverbs. I usually underline these words in the answer choice first, and ask myself, "is there evidence in the stimulus supporting the existence of this word?"

Answer choices are written deliberately, no word appears in an answer choice out of random or by chance. If the test makers included a word, however inconspicuous it may seem, it must be for a reason. If it cannot be backed up by stimulus evidence, then it's a potential source of error.

After having carefully re-examined both answer choices and underlined/highlighted any word that stood out to you, then we need to compare the two. Ask yourself again, armed with a more detailed understanding of each answer choice and the stimulus, which answer is more supported by information in the stimulus?

Just like Strengthen/Weaken/MSS Questions, sometimes the correct answer is imperfect. So all we need to do is to find the answer that is *more* supported by the stimulus, even if it still contains a gap. We have included one question below, but also take a look at 32-4-20 and 66-4-23, both with very tricky answers, for additional practice.

PT68 S2 Q21

Justine: Pellman Inc. settled the lawsuit out of court by paying $1 million. That Pellman settled instead of going to trial indicates their corporate leaders expected to lose in court.

Simon: It is unclear whether Pellman's leaders expected to lose in court. But I think they expected that, whether they won or lost the case, the legal fees involved in going to trial would have been more costly than the settlement. So settling the lawsuit seemed the most cost-effective solution.

The dialogue provides the most support for the claim that Justine and Simon disagree with each other about which one of the following?

A. If the lawsuit against Pellman had gone to trial, it is likely that Pellman would have lost in court.
B. Pellman's corporate leaders were able to accurately estimate their chances of winning in court.
C. If Pellman's legal fees for going to trial would have been more costly than the settlement, then settling the lawsuit was the most cost-effective solution for the corporation.
D. If Pellman's corporate leaders had expected that the legal fees for going to trial would have been less costly than the settlement, they would have taken the lawsuit to trial.
E. If Pellman's corporate leaders had expected to win in court, then they would not have settled the lawsuit out of court for $1 million.

Let's look at Justine's claims first:

Pellman Inc. settled the lawsuit out of court by paying $1 million. That Pellman settled instead of going to trial indicates their corporate leaders expected to lose in court.

Three points can be extracted from Justine's claims:

1. Pellman settled.
2. Settling means that Pellman expected to lose in court.
3. So Pellman expected that they would lose in court.

What does Simon think?

It is unclear whether Pellman's leaders expected to lose in court.

Simon starts off by casting doubt on Justine's third claim.

But I think they expected that, whether they won or lost the case, the legal fees involved in going to trial would have been more costly than the settlement.

This is a new piece of information unmentioned by Justine. Simon thinks that the legal fees will be greater than $1 million.

So settling the lawsuit seemed the most cost-effective solution.

Here, Simon offers up an alternative reason as to why Pellman settled. Simon thinks it's because avoiding going to trial is more economical. This seems like a response to Justine's second claim. Simon would say that "settling doesn't mean Pellman expected to lose, they settled because it's the smart thing to do."

So the disagreement between Justine and Simon revolves around why Pellman settled:

Justine: Pellman settled because they knew they were gonna lose.
Simon: Pellman settled because it's the most cost effective thing to do.

Let's look at the answer choices:

A. *If the lawsuit against Pellman had gone to trial, it is likely that Pellman <u>would have lost</u> in court.*

Be careful of subtle **term shifts**! Justine thinks that the Pellman leadership *expected to lose in court*. Simon, on the other hand, thinks it's unclear what these leaders expected.

Answer choice A is saying that Pellman would actually have lost in court. If answer choice A had said that Pellman "would have expected to lose" in court, then this answer would probably be ok.

B. *Pellman's corporate leaders were able to <u>accurately</u> estimate their chances of winning in court.*

Again, we do not know if Pellman would actually have lost. Justine says that Pellman thinks they will lose, whereas Simon thinks it's unclear. So there is no way to know whether Pellman's estimation is accurate.

In order to select this answer, we need one speaker to say that the leaders are able to accurately estimate their chances; and the other speaker to say that they are not. We simply don't have this kind of evidence in the stimulus.

> C.   *If Pellman's legal fees for going to trial would have been more costly than the settlement, then settling the lawsuit was the <u>most cost-effective solution</u> for the corporation.*

Simon would agree with this, but what would Justine say? Justine never talks about cost-efficiency. So we do not have evidence that Justine would disagree with this statement.

> D.   *If Pellman's corporate leaders had expected that the <u>legal fees</u> for going to trial would have been <u>less costly</u> than the settlement, they would have taken the lawsuit to trial.*

Simon thinks that because going to trial is too costly, they chose to settle. I suppose he might agree that conversely, if going to trail is not costly, they would have chosen to go to trail. This is not a perfect inference but as we have seen in MSS Questions, "no cause, so no effect" is an acceptable inference in answer choices. So we'll let it slide.

But for Justine, the cost of legal fees didn't factor into her argument at all. She thinks that if Pellman expected to win, they might have a greater chance of taking the lawsuit to trial. We don't know how a change in costs would factor into Pellman's decision making process based on Justine's statements alone.

> E.   *If Pellman's corporate leaders had expected to win in court, then they would not have settled the lawsuit out of court for $1 million.*

So Expect Win → Not Settle.

Justine thinks that Pellman settling means that they expected to lose, that's the contrapositive of answer E. So Justine would agree with this.

What would Simon say? As usual with harder POD Questions, we have no explicit mention of how an expectation of trial success would influence whether Pellman settles in Simon's statements, but that doesn't automatically mean answer E is out of scope.

Simon thinks that Pellman settled because it's the most economical thing to do. If Pellman expected to win, would the legal fees still be exorbitant? Yes. So the most economical/cost effective thing to do would still be to settle. In other words, even if Pellman expected to win, they would still settle. Simon would disagree with this statement, so <u>Answer Choice E is the correct answer.</u>

 As we saw in this question and the previous question, test makers love to throw subtle term shifts into trap answer choices. Make sure you are reading each answer choice word for word!

Solution 2: Rank Answer Choices

We saw in the previous chapter as well as in Strengthen, Weaken, and MSS Questions that the habit of ranking your answer choices according to the requirements of the question type is something we must master in order to attain perfection on the LR section. This has only become more important in recent PTs.

Take a look at the question below, there are several attractive trap answers. Try to rank the answer choices from best to worst, and really think about the pros and cons of each one.

***

PT86 S1 Q17

Xavier: The new fast-food place on 10th Street is out of business already. I'm not surprised. It had no indoor seating, and few people want to sit outside and breathe exhaust fumes while they eat.

Miranda: The bank should have realized that with all the fast-food places on 10th Street, one lacking indoor seating was likely to fail. So it was irresponsible of them to lend the money for it.

It can be inferred from the dialogue that Xavier and Miranda agree that

A. few people want to sit outside while they eat.
B. banks should not finance restaurants lacking indoor seating.
C. if the new fast-food place had indoor seating, it probably would have been successful.
D. a fast-food place on 10th Street is likely to fail if it has any outdoor seating.
E. the new fast-food place on 10th Street was a risky venture.

Note how this question is asking us about something that both Xavier and Miranda would *agree* on. In other words, both speakers would say "yes, that is true" to the correct answer choice. How we approach the stimulus, extract information, and compare them is the same as in a Point of Disagreement Question.

Xavier: The new fast food place on 10th Street is out of business already. I'm not surprised. It had no indoor seating, and few people want to sit outside and breathe exhaust fumes while they eat.

These are the points that I've extracted from Xavier's statements.

1. Restaurant is out of business
2. Restaurant had no indoor seating
3. Few people want to sit outside/most people want to sit inside
4. It's not surprising that the restaurant failed

The advanced student will also notice that Xavier's reasoning is underlined by a causal assumption/belief. The cause for the restaurant's failure, according to Xavier, is due to it having no indoor seating. In other words, No Indoor Seating ⇒ Not Enough Customers ⇒ Restaurant Failed.

Let's look at Miranda's statement:

Miranda: The bank should have realized that with all the fast-food places on 10th Street, one lacking indoor seating was likely to fail. So it was irresponsible of them to lend the money for it.

On which points do Miranda and Xavier agree?

Well, the obvious one is that both agree that the restaurant failed. But other than this, is there anything else? Let's take apart Miranda's argument as well:

1. There are a lot of fast-food restaurants on 10th Street
2. Having no indoor seating increased the restaurant's chances of failure
3. The bank should have realized this
4. It was irresponsible for the bank to lend money to the restaurant

My initial anticipated answer after reading the stimulus was that both Miranda and Xavier *agreed* that the lack of indoor seating caused/increased the chances of the restaurant's failure.

***

But of course, sometimes the answer choices don't match up with our anticipated answer, let's look at the answer choices now in turn:

> A. *few people want to sit outside while they eat.*

Xavier explicitly mentions this, but does Miranda?

We know that Miranda thinks that lacking indoor seating is a cause for failure. In other words, in order to have a successful restaurant, you need at least some indoor seating.

But does that mean few people want to sit outside?

This is quite tricky. I suppose you can make the argument that since having no indoor seating is a bad idea, there's a bunch of people who want to sit inside.

But just because a bunch of people want to sit inside doesn't really mean that <u>few</u> people want to sit outside.

For example, Miranda can argue that both indoor and outdoor seating are crucial to a restaurant's success. You want indoor seating when the weather is cold, and outdoor seating on warm sunny days. Having no indoor seating means the restaurant is likely to fail, but that doesn't necessarily mean that few people want to sit outside.

   B.   *banks should not finance restaurants lacking indoor seating.*

What banks should or should not do is absent from Xavier's argument, nor can it be inferred.

   C.   *if the new fast-food place had indoor seating, it probably would have been successful.*

This is also quite tricky. We know that both Xavier and Miranda would agree that the lack of indoor seating caused the restaurant to fail.

Can you negate that causal relationship and infer that both would also agree that with indoor seating, the restaurant would succeed?

In other words, because Cause ⇒ Effect, can you infer that ~~Cause~~ ⇒ ~~Effect~~?

Remember Chapters 18 and 19, we saw that such an inference is acceptable, but *only when no better alternatives are available.* In certain question types where we need to rank the answer choices, answer choice C would be an acceptable answer if it's the best of the bunch. But it has its own issues as well. We just don't know if an alternative cause can achieve the same effect. Here, maybe even if the restaurant had indoor seating, its abysmal service or bland food would still have doomed it to failure.

Let's look and answer choices D and E to see if there's an alternative that is better than C.

   D.   *a fast-food place on 10th Street is likely to fail if it has <u>any</u> outdoor seating.*

Subtle shift in strength here. Both speakers are arguing that the lack of indoor seating is causing the restaurant to fail. This answer is saying that regardless of how many indoor tables you have, if you had one seat placed outside, the restaurant is likely to fail. I don't think there's evidence for that.

   E.   *the new fast-food place on 10th Street was a risky venture.*

Does Xavier think the restaurant a risky venture? He isn't surprised at its failure, risk is defined as the likelihood of failure, so Xavier's agreement can be inferred.

Does Miranda think the restaurant a risky venture? Just like Xavier, she never explicitly mentions this, but we know that she thought it likely to fail, and that the bank should also have realized this. In other words, there's significant risk involved with lending money to the restaurant, because it was a risky venture/likely to fail.

E is the correct answer.

This question is especially tricky because there are not just one, but two, attractive trap answers. Answer Choice E is correct because we can find indirect support from both speakers; while answer choice C and A have less support and require gaps in reasoning that must be hurdled.

So whenever you are stuck on several different answers, read the answers more carefully, look for relevant keywords. But also compare the answers to the information in the stimulus and ask yourself which answer choice has *the most support* from the stimulus.

One Final Note: Point of Agreement Questions

So far, we have mostly looked at Point of Disagreement (POD) questions, where the correct answer choice is a point that Speaker A and B *disagree about*.

But in the last question, we saw that our job was to find something that both speakers would *agree* on.

In more recent tests, we have seen growing instances of this variation, and we are instead asked to pick an answer choice that is a point *agreed* upon by both Speaker A and Speaker B.

So instead of Speaker A agreeing with the answer, and Speaker B disagreeing with it, we are now looking for an answer choice to which both people would share the same view. **Both speakers would agree or disagree with the correct answer choice in Point of Agreement Questions.**

The process of tackling these questions is still the same except for when we come to the answer choices. Make sure you read the question carefully, and don't confuse an Agreement Question with a Disagreement Question.

Take a look at 35-1-26 and 81-2-26 for additional practice.

21. Explain Questions

Explain Questions, or Explain a Result/Paradox Questions, however you like to call them, are unlike any question type that we have seen before. We are not analyzing the argument for gaps and leaps in reasoning, unlike Assumption Family Questions; nor are we extracting, linking, and inferring information, as we did in MBT/MSS Questions.

Explain Questions are primarily concerned with one issue: "Why? Why did things turn out the way they did?"

You see, within every Explain Stimulus is a description of something that happened, a situation or scenario. Our job is to find an answer choice that most plausibly tells us the reason for this.

Take a look at the following example:

John was late for work this morning.

Why was John late? There are many potential explanations for this. Maybe John was not feeling well, so he took more time than usual getting ready. Maybe John's alarm clock broke, maybe he had an emergency, or maybe his car broke down. Maybe he is just a tardy person in general. Maybe he was caught in a traffic jam.

Just like in this example, we can have a whole bunch of answer choices that offer a potentially valid reason as to why things turned out the way they did in the stimulus. If all we had to do is to explain the result, then a lot of answer choices can work.

But of course, Explain Question aren't that simple. In addition to knowing *what actually happened,* there is another question that we must be able to answer as well. We must also know *what should have happened.*

Let's develop our example a little further:

John is usually never late, but John was late for work this morning.

Now our example contains two pieces of information. We are still trying to explain what *actually happened,* or why was John late this morning? However, the example now contains additional information that would seemingly lead to a contradictory inference. If John is usually never late, *then what should have happened this morning?*

We now have the information we need to answer both our questions, *what should have happened,* and *what actually happened.*

What should have happened: We know that John is usually on time, so he probably should have been on time this morning as well.

What actually happened: John was late for work this morning.

Our job, when reading the Explain Stimulus, is to locate both the **Expectation** (what should have happened) and the **Reality** (what actually happened). There will be a conflict or contradiction between the two, and our job is to give a reason for how it came about.

Let's go back to one of the potential answers that we came up with earlier, "John is a tardy person in general."

Can this answer choice still work? Not anymore. Because the example has already told us that *John is usually never late.* This potential answer can be eliminated because it is contradictory to the information given to us.

Let's modify our example a little more to drive this point home:

John lives across the street from his office and walks to the office. He doesn't own a car. John is usually never late, but he was late this morning.

Now potential answer choices like "John's car broke down" can be eliminated as well. While it seems like a possible explanation if we only consider the actual result (John was late this morning), it wouldn't work because it directly contradicts other information given to us in the stimulus.

As a result, our job is to find not just any reason why things happened the way they did, but that reason must not contradict information already given to us in the stimulus.

So in summary, the *basic approach* to every Explain Question is twofold:

1. Identify Expectation and Reality
2. Find an answer choice that tells us why Reality occurred, without contradicting the stimulus

***

Now this is where things get interesting, would the answer "John was stuck in a traffic jam" work?

Maybe. We know that John walks to work and doesn't own a car. So it seems unlikely that being stuck in a traffic jam was the cause for his lateness. But perhaps he was coming to work from his friend's house or directly from the airport? Then it's possible that he was stuck in a traffic jam, even though he lives next to his office and walks to work.

Ultimately, this would not be my top choice, but it's still a possible answer. Because it doesn't really contradict our stimulus. This just shows that we have to really think about all the information presented to us, along with their nuances.

We will now take a look at a real question, one that you are probably familiar with, before tackling the more advanced aspects of Explain Questions.

PT18 S2 Q19

Oxygen-18 is a heavier than normal isotope of oxygen. In a rain cloud, water molecules containing oxygen 18 are rarer than water molecules containing normal oxygen. But in rainfall, a higher proportion of all water molecules containing oxygen-18 than of all water molecules containing ordinary oxygen descends to earth. Consequently, scientists were surprised when measurements along the entire route of rain clouds' passage from above the Atlantic Ocean, the site of their original formation, across the Amazon forests, where it rains almost daily, showed that the oxygen-18 content of each of the clouds remained fairly constant.

Which one of the following statements, if true, best helps to resolve the conflict between scientists' expectations, based on the known behavior of oxygen-18, and the result of their measurements of the rain clouds' oxygen 18 content?

    A.   Rain clouds above tropical rain forests are poorer in oxygen-18 than rain clouds above unforested regions.
    B.   Like the oceans, tropical rain forests can create or replenish rain clouds in the atmosphere above them.
    C.   The amount of rainfall over the Amazon rain forests is exactly the same as the amount of rain originally collected in the clouds formed above the Atlantic Ocean.
    D.   The amount of rain recycled back into the atmosphere from the leaves of forest vegetation is exactly the same as the amount of rain in river runoffs that is not recycled into the atmosphere.
    E.   Oxygen-18 is not a good indicator of the effect of tropical rain forests on the atmosphere above them.

We should have some familiarity with this stimulus, we have looked at it but for a different question in the MBT/MSS section. This time, instead of extracting information from the stimulus, we are trying to explain a **contradiction**.

So what is the contradiction? Explain Question stimuli will have two pieces of key information. One piece of information will lead to an **expectation**, but another piece of information will tell us what the **reality** actually is. Our job is to explain why reality turned out the way it did.

The conflict between expectations and reality is the contradiction that we are trying to locate in the stimulus. The correct answer choice to Explain Questions does exactly one thing, it tells us *why things turned out the way they did.*

***

There's a lot of information to unpack in this stimulus: we know that O-18 is rarer than normal Oxygen in rain clouds, we also know that a higher percentage of O-18 leaves the cloud during rainfall than regular oxygen. If there are 100 oxygen molecules in a cloud, then the number of O-18 is < than 50. The number of regular oxygen molecules is greater than 50.

Let's say that hypothetically, there are 40 O-18 molecules and 60 regular oxygen molecules in our cloud.

The percentage of O-18 that falls as rain is *greater* than the percentage of regular oxygen molecules. So that means if 50% of regular oxygen molecules falls in the rain (50% of 60, or 30), the number of O-18 molecules that falls to the earth must be greater than 50%. (> 50% of 40, or > 20)

So if 30 regular oxygen molecules fall as rain, the number of O-18 molecules that fall must be between 21 and 40.

Let's take the *least* number of O-18 molecules that needs to fall, or 21; so our cloud started with 40 O-18 and 60 O-16 (regular oxygen). 40 - 21 = 19, 60 - 30 = 30.

So now we have 19 O-18 vs. 30 O-16.

Previously, the ratio between O-18 and O-16 was 40:60, or 2:3. We now know if the rain falls, the ratio between O-18 and O-16 will be at a minimum 19:30, if not higher.

So what should be our **expectation**? If we started with a lower amount, but kept on losing a higher percentage, what would happen? We will run out faster. The expectation is that *O-18 will run out faster than O-16 with each successive rainfall, or that the proportion of O-18 will decrease at a faster rate than O-16.*

Is this what actually happens? No: according to the stimulus, from the beginning of the clouds' formation to when the rain falls, *O-18 content remained fairly constant.* What does that mean? Basically the amount of O-18 stayed the same.

Expectation: We will lose O-18 faster than O-16.
Reality: O-18 stayed the same.

Think of the following analogy:

John's income is lower than Peter's. John also spends a higher percentage of his income than Peter. But John's savings have stayed the same.

How do we explain this? Really, the only viable answer would be that John has other ways to replenish his bank account. He has to have other sources of income, maybe another job, maybe a side hustle, or maybe his family supports him financially.

It's the same case in this question. There must be another way to replenish the rain clouds' O-18 content. It has to come from elsewhere. Maybe it's drawn from the atmosphere, or maybe the clouds are able to synthesize it or transform O-16 into O-18 (highly unlikely but it's an explanation).

A. *Rain clouds above tropical rain forests are poorer in oxygen-18 than rain clouds above unforested regions.*

This doesn't really explain where the extra O-18 came from. All it tells us is that maybe there's a connection between forests and the amount of O-18 lost. But if we develop this idea further and say that perhaps it's because it rains more over forests, so more O-18 is lost, that still doesn't tell us why the O-18 content in the clouds has remained *constant*.

B. *Like the oceans, tropical rain forests can create or replenish rain clouds in the atmosphere above them.*

This answer is not as direct as we'd like. Remember that we are looking for an answer that says "O-18 is replenished regularly." It can be better, but it's along the same lines of reasoning as we had anticipated. I'd keep this answer and look at the rest of them.

C. *The amount of rainfall over the Amazon rain forests is exactly the same as the amount of rain originally collected in the clouds formed above the Atlantic Ocean.*

This could work if the percentage of O-18 lost is the same as O-16. Because if you gained 500 gallons of extra water and then dumped it all over the Amazon, then there's no change to your original O-18 content, right? But we know that in rainfall, a higher percentage of O-18 is lost than O-16.

The question we need to answer is *why has the O-18 content remained constant despite a faster rate of loss.*

This answer is tricky because it uses seemingly familiar language, but ultimately, it doesn't address our concern.

D. *The amount of rain recycled back into the atmosphere from the leaves of forest vegetation is exactly the same as the amount of rain in river runoffs that is not recycled into the atmosphere.*

What this answer is telling us is that of all the rain fall, 50% returns to the clouds. But does the recycled rain contain a higher proportion of O-18? That would be a good answer, but we don't know.

E. *Oxygen-18 is not a good indicator of the effect of tropical rain forests on the atmosphere above them.*

So if O-18 is not a good indicator, what is? What is the effect rain forests have on the atmosphere? Does it replenish O-18?

Ultimately, only answer choice B is *indirectly* giving us what we are looking for. Normally, correct Explain answer choices are direct and clear cut, but since B is the best answer available, it's what we will choose.

B is the correct answer.

***

Thus, with Explain Questions, we want to devote the majority of our attention and energy to isolating the **expectation** and **reality**. What did it seem like was going to happen? What really happened? Why didn't things go according to plan? Why did things happen the way they did? What has changed?

We now move to the more difficult aspects of Explain Questions:

***

Navigating Complex Stimuli: When there are multiple ways to explain a situation

Take a look at the following example:

Smoking in bed has long been the main cause of home fires. Despite a significant decline in cigarette smoking in the last two decades, however, there has been no comparable decline in the number of people killed in home fires.

What should have happened? What actually happened?

What are some of the ways to explain what actually happened?

Stop and actually think about this before turning to the next page.

Reality: *there has been no comparable decline in the number of people killed in home fires.*

So the number of people killed in home fires did not decrease. The word "comparable" is interesting, I think that means there is no corresponding decrease, perhaps there was a net decrease? But I am not sure how this word would impact our answer choice selection process just yet.

Expectation: *smoking in bed is the main cause of home fires…there is a significant decrease in cigarette smoking.*

There is a causal relationship here, Smoking $\Rightarrow$ Home Fires. There is a decrease in the cause, so *what should have happened?*

We can probably expect there to be a decrease in the number of home fires too. While we can't know for sure, as there can be other potential causes for home fires not taken into consideration, a decrease in the number of smokers leading to a decrease in the number of home fires is a reasonable expectation.

On a side note, we have considered both the logical element (causal) and the keyword element ("comparable") as we are reading through the stimulus. That's the L and K of SLAKR. These are things that should come naturally to you the more you practice.

Now back to the example.

Expectation: Less smoking, less home fires, less people killed in home fires?

Reality: People killed in home fires did not decrease.

What are some potential ways in which we can explain what actually happened?

Well, we can potentially suggest that even though less people smoke, the number of home fires has stayed constant. How can this be?

Perhaps the new main cause of home fires is charging your electric vehicle at home, or perhaps more and more houses are built out of flammable materials in order to save costs. The stimulus had stated that "smoking in bed *has long been* the main cause of home fires." We can potentially argue that was in the past, and smoking is *no longer* the main cause of home fires.

In other words, we can find an alternative cause for home fires. This wouldn't necessarily contradict the stimulus, so it should be ok.

Are there other ways to explain why the number of people killed in home fires did not decrease?

We can also suggest that even though less people are smoking and there are less home fires, the number of people killed in home fires has actually gone up. Perhaps due to budget cuts, the fire department is now underfunded, so they are unable to get to the fires on time. Perhaps more and more people live in apartment buildings, where it's harder to escape.

In other words, harder Explain Questions can have multiple potential explanations for why things turned out the way they did. **It really helps when practicing to slow down and try to brainstorm as many potential ways to explain the question as you can.** By forcing ourselves to explore the stimulus fully, with all its implications and nuances, we will have a much easier time with the answer choices.

On the contrary, if we are not coming up with potential answers or only coming up with one possible answer before moving on, the answer choice elimination process can be brutal for the hardest questions. You could easily eliminate something that would work but you didn't anticipate, or even eliminate a correct answer choice that's confusingly worded (as we saw in 18-2-19).

Let's now look at a real question, try to think if there are multiple ways to explain what actually happened:

PT19 S4 Q23

Construction contractors working on the cutting edge of technology nearly always work on a "cost-plus" basis only. One kind of cost-plus contract stipulates the contractor's profit as a fixed percentage of the contractor's costs; the other kind stipulates a fixed amount of profit over and above costs. Under the first kind of contract, higher costs yield higher profits for the contractor, so this is where one might expect final costs in excess of original cost estimates to be more common. Paradoxically, such cost overruns are actually more common if the contract is of the fixed profit kind.

Which one of the following, if true, most helps to resolve the apparent paradox in the situation described above?

    A. Clients are much less likely to agree to a fixed profit type of cost-plus contract when it is understood that under certain conditions the project will be scuttled than they are when there is no such understanding.

    B. On long term contracts, cost projections take future inflation into account, but since the figures used are provided by the government, they are usually underestimates.

    C. On any sizable construction project, the contractor bills the client monthly or quarterly, so any tendency for original cost estimates to be exceeded can be detected early.

    D. Clients billed under a cost-plus contract are free to review individual billings in order to uncover wasteful expenditures, but they do so only when the contractor's profits varies with cost.

    E. The practice of submitting deliberately exaggerated cost estimates is most common in the case of fixed-profit contracts, because it makes the profit, as a percentage of estimated cost, appear modest.

Let's break down the stimulus, what is our expectation and what is the reality?

There are two possible ways to calculate payment on a "cost plus" basis:

Profits as a fixed percentage of the contractor's costs

This means that if you construct something, the cost being 1 million dollars, the agreed upon profit is 20%, the contractor will receive 1.2 million dollars.

Similarly, if the cost ends up being 2 million dollars, you will receive 2.4 million as total compensation.

Profits as a fixed amount

This means that you will receive a fixed amount plus cost, so say the fixed amount is 500,000 and the cost is 1 million, you receive 1.5 million; if the cost is 2 million, you receive 2.5 million, etc.

Expectation: final cost overruns should be more common under the percentage profit scheme.

Why? Because the higher the cost, the higher the profits. If you had an extra 10 million dollars in cost overruns, then your profits would increase by an extra 2 million if the agreed upon percentage was 20%.

So the contractor will have a higher incentive to go over, so to speak.

Reality: cost overruns are more common when profits are fixed.

If we expected A to cost more, but instead B costs more (that's the essence of this stimulus), what are some ways to explain this?

I can think of two possible ways: either there is some reason why A costs much less than we expected (why cost overruns are actually really infrequent in percentage schemes), **or** there is some reason why B costs much more than we expected (why fixed fee schemes actually lead to frequent cost overruns). Or maybe both.

Perhaps under the percentage/pro rata payment scheme, going over cost by a lot will cause the contractor to be ineligible for future bids? So that's enough incentive for contractors to keep within cost?

Perhaps with fixed fee schemes, because the profit is guaranteed, contractors are more at ease and do a better job? Better job means higher costs perhaps?

There can be a myriad of possibilities, but they will fall into one of these two camps. Let's look at the answer choices.

A. *Clients are much less likely to agree to a fixed profit type of cost plus contract when it is understood that under certain conditions the project will be scuttled than they are when there is no such understanding.*

When do clients prefer fixed cost profits? When there is no understanding that causes the project to be abandoned.

If there is no understanding, and no mechanism for project abandonment, I suppose there is a higher chance of cost overruns. So this answer can potentially explain why fixed costs lead to more overruns I suppose.

But this version of the answer choice really depends on what the test makers mean by "*understanding that under certain conditions the project will be scuttled.*" I am interpreting it to mean that if the project is scuttled, then there won't be any cost overruns. But does this mean that when there is no such understanding, the project just keeps on going? Let's keep this answer for now.

> B. On long term contracts, cost projections take future inflation into account, but since the figures used are provided by the government, they are usually underestimates.

We want an answer that tells us why fixed amounts lead to more cost overruns, or why percentage leads to less. This answer doesn't even distinguish between the two.

> C. On any sizable construction project, the contractor bills the client monthly or quarterly, so any tendency for original cost estimates to be exceeded can be detected early.

This one also doesn't differentiate between the two methods, it can be eliminated right away.

> D. Clients billed under a cost-plus contract are free to review individual billings in order to uncover wasteful expenditures, but they do so only when the contractor's profits varies with cost.

When profits vary with cost, which method is that? It's the percentage profit method.

When do clients review costs to uncover waste? Under the percentage profit method. What happens when the bills are reviewed by clients? Less chance of cost overruns.

So there is less of a chance of cost overruns under the percentage method.

Are bills reviewed under the fixed method? No, they are only reviewed under the percentage method.

This answer perfectly explains why A costs less (client reviews) and B costs more (no client reviews)

Compared to answer choice A, this is a much clearer answer. It addresses both of our concerns, whereas answer A had to be interpreted in such a particular way in order to partially address the issues.

> E. The practice of submitting deliberately exaggerated <u>cost estimates</u> is most common in the case of fixed-profit contracts, because it makes the profit, as a percentage of estimated cost, appear modest.

This answer choice is so damned tricky. It's talking about *cost estimates*. We are talking about *cost overruns*. So according to E, exaggerated cost estimates are common in fixed profit contracts. Let's say that it costs a contractor 10 million to build a building, how much do they estimate the cost to be to the owner? Since they deliberately exaggerate cost estimates, they will tell the owner that it will cost 20 million.

When do cost overruns occur? When it goes over the cost estimate. So in order for cost overrun to cover, the actual cost will have to be more than 20 million.

Real Cost: 10 million
Cost Estimate: 20 million
Cost Overrun: >20 million (real cost has to more than double in order for cost overrun to occur)

So actually, according to E, cost overruns are *less likely* for fixed profit contracts.

The SLAKR method will cover more than 90% of your bases in the hardest LR questions

Keyword Extraction/Analysis in answer choices (K in SLAKR) saved me on this one. <u>D is the correct answer.</u>

Navigating Complex Stimuli: Isolating the Key Contradiction

Besides presenting us with a reality that can be explained in several different ways, a rarer trick that the test makers can throw at us is to hide the contradiction between expectation and reality deep within the stimulus.

Our response is to pay more attention to the stimulus, with harder Explain Questions, vocalizing or even writing out the Expectation vs. Reality dualism on paper will help us attain a clearer understanding.

Sometimes there are multiple unexpected results in one single stimulus, and when faced with such a dilemma, we need to decide which actual result it is that we are primarily concerned with explaining.

We will now look at one such question.

PT23 S2 Q22

Shortly after the Persian Gulf War, investigators reported that the area, which had been subjected to hundreds of smoky oil fires and deliberate oil spills when regular oil production slowed during the war, displayed less oil contamination than they had witnessed in prewar surveys of the same area. They also reported that the levels of polycyclic aromatic hydrocarbons (PAHs) – used as a marker of combustion products spewed from oil wells ignited during the war – were also relatively low, comparable to those recorded in the temperate oil-producing areas of the Baltic Sea.

Which one of the following, if true, does most to resolve the apparent discrepancy in the information above?

    A. Oil contaminants have greater environmental effects in temperate regions than in desert regions.
    B. Oil contamination and PAH pollution dissipate more rapidly in temperate regions than in desert regions.
    C. Oil contamination and PAH pollution dissipate more rapidly in desert regions than in temperate regions.
    D. Peacetime oil production and transport in the Persian Gulf result in high levels of PAHs and massive oil dumping.
    E. The Persian Gulf War ended before the oil fires and spills caused as much damage as originally expected.

The Iraqi Army had set fire to Kuwaiti oil fields following their retreat after defeat during Operation Desert Storm. Oil fields burned for months, creating massive amounts of smoke and soot.

Expectation: There should be massive amounts of pollution and contamination.

What is the reality?

Here is where things get a little confusing. Two unexpected things happen:

1. The level of oil contamination is actually lower than before the war.
2. The levels of PAH are comparable to the Baltic Sea.

What are we trying to explain here? Is it the low levels of PAH or that the level of oil contamination is actually lower than before the war?

Let's look at both in conjunction with our expectation, which one makes more sense?

There should have been massive amounts of contamination after the war, but instead the levels of contamination actually turned out to have actually decreased.

Or

There should have been massive amounts of contamination after the war, but instead the levels of PAH are comparable to the Baltic Sea.

You see, in our expected result, levels of PAH were not talked about. We don't know if and by how much PAH should have gone up due to the fires. Instead, it was about how contamination should have gone up due to the war. That is more directly related to our first expectation.

Furthermore, PAHs are a form of pollution as well, so that statement is supportive of the actual result that contamination was not as high as expected to be.

The **primary** discrepancy, or contradiction is between what we expected the levels of pollution to be, and how much pollution there actually was.

Again, we can think of two ways to explain this result. Why did the environment turn out to be cleaner? Either the Persian Gulf was really contaminated prior to the war, or the fires and spills did not cause as much damage as we thought they would.

For example, we can say that a lot of drilling companies worked in the area before the war, creating huge amounts of pollution. When the war happened they all left. So the pollution they caused was actually worse than the fires and spills.

Or we can suggest that maybe there was a hurricane or storm that swept away all the pollution after the war.

Either way, we need an answer choice that tells us why even though we thought it would be dirtier, it actually turned out to be cleaner.

A. *Oil contaminants have greater <u>environmental effects</u> in temperate regions than in desert regions.*

Can this explain why the oil spills and fires didn't cause more pollution? Not really. This answer is comparing *environmental effects* in temperate regions (such as the Baltic Sea) and in desert regions (Persian Gulf). This answer would tell us that the environmental effects of oil contaminants would have a worse effect on the flora and fauna in the Baltics than in the Gulf, but does nothing to explain why pollution actually lessened in the Gulf.

If the stimulus had talked about how there was a similar amount of contamination in the Baltics and the Gulf, but animals and plants suffered much more in the Baltics, then this answer would make sense.

B. *Oil contamination and PAH pollution dissipate more rapidly in temperate regions than in desert regions.*

This would explain why, given the same amount of pollution, temperate regions would return to normal sooner. The stimulus tells us that post war PAH levels were comparable between the Baltics and the Gulf. So if the pollution dissipates faster in temperate regions, this means that the Baltics were dirtier to begin with. It doesn't explain why the Gulf got cleaner.

C. *Oil contamination and PAH pollution dissipate more rapidly in desert regions than in temperate regions.*

This answer is the opposite of the previous one. If PAH dissipates more rapidly in the desert than in temperate regions, that would explain why even though contamination levels were comparable between the two post war, the Gulf was dirtier than the Baltics to begin with.

This might explain our second, and less important discrepancy, namely that even though there were fires and contamination due to the war, PAH levels were similar to the Baltics. I will keep this for now.

D. *Peacetime oil production and transport in the Persian Gulf result in high levels of PAHs and massive oil dumping.*

This would more directly address our first, and more important contradiction/discrepancy. Why wasn't the Gulf dirtier after the war? Because a significant source of pollutants has been removed. Before the war, there was a lot of pollution due to oil production. This was interrupted by the war, and the fires and spills related to pollution caused by the war were less severe than the pollution caused during peacetime oil production.

E. *The Persian Gulf War ended before the oil fires and spills caused as much damage as <u>originally expected.</u>*

So it's not as dirty as it could have been, but this doesn't really explain why it was cleaner than before the war.

I deliberated a long time between answer choices C and D. I ended up choosing D because the unexpected result it explains is the more significant of the two. There were two potential discrepancies/contradictions in this stimulus, and if we had made a decision on which is the more central contradiction to be addressed, then we should have gotten this question right. <u>D is the correct answer.</u>

Choosing the Right Answer

Picking the right answer can be especially difficult in Explain Questions because there are a myriad of ways in which what actually happened can be explained. Unlike a lot of the question types which we have considered previously, (SA, Parallel, etc.) where we have a general idea of the answer that we are looking for, correct Explain Question answers can come in all shapes and sizes. But this does not mean that we shouldn't try to **anticipate** what the correct answer will be. In trying to come up with potential solutions before we even look at the answer choices, we are training ourselves to really think about the stimulus and engage with it. Having a general idea of what a potentially correct answer would look like can also help us immensely during the answer choice selection process. If we are lucky, we will be able to match what we anticipated with one of the actual answers; and even when we can't, we are much more likely to avoid wrong answers that stray too far from our anticipated answers.

Take a look at the following stimulus, and see if you can come up with an explanation for what actually happened:

When a community opens a large shopping mall, it often expects a boost to the local economy, and in fact a large amount of economic activity goes on in these malls. Yet the increase in the local economy is typically much smaller than the total amount of economic activity that goes on in the mall.

Why did this happen? Can you think of any potential explanations? Try to brainstorm before turning to the next page.

In regard to our expectations of what should have happened, there are two pieces of information:

It often expects a boost to the local economy, and in fact a large amount of economic activity goes on in these malls.

A special note here: the mall forms a part of the local economy.

So if we construct a new mall and there's 50 million dollars of economic activities that goes on in there, we should expect a corresponding increase in the local economy.

But what actually happened?

The increase in the local economy is typically much smaller than the total amount of economic activity that goes on in the mall.

What does this mean? So if the mall generates 50 million dollars in GDP, how much did the local economy increase? It's much smaller than 50, so let's say that the increase in the local economy's GDP is only 10 million.

So before the mall was constructed, let's assume that the GDP was 200 million. A mall that generates 50 million in GDP was constructed, but the total is now 210 million. Why isn't it 250 million?

Where did the extra 40 million go?

Well, there must be something that caused a decrease of 40 million dollars in economic activities in the community but not in the mall. How can this happen? Perhaps the mall and its chain stores drove a lot of local businesses out? Perhaps the price of real estate shot up thanks to the mall and a lot of people got priced out of the market and had to leave?

We are essentially looking for an answer that tells us that either the mall, or another factor connected to the mall's constructor, led to a decrease in economic activity in the community outside of the mall.

***

PT28 S1 Q17

When a community opens a large shopping mall, it often expects a boost to the local economy, and in fact a large amount of economic activity goes on in these malls. Yet the increase in the local economy is typically much smaller than the total amount of economic activity that goes on in the mall.

Which one of the following, if true, most helps to explain the discrepancy described above?

    A. When large shopping malls are new they attract a lot of shoppers but once the novelty has worn off they usually attract fewer shoppers than does the traditional downtown shopping district.

    B. Most of the money spent in a large shopping mall is spent by tourists who are drawn specifically by the mall and who would not have visited the community had that mall not been built.

    C. Most of the jobs created by large shopping malls are filled by people who recently moved to the community and who would not have moved had there been no job offer in the community.

    D. Most of the money spent in a large shopping mall is money that would have been spent elsewhere in the same community had that mall not been built.

    E. Most of the jobs created by the construction of a large shopping mall are temporary, and most of the permanent jobs created are low paying.

Let's look at each answer choice:

> A. *When large shopping malls are new they attract a lot of shoppers but once the novelty has worn off they usually attract fewer shoppers than does the traditional downtown shopping district.*

So according to this answer, malls initially generate a lot of economic activity, but they gradually taper off. But that's not what was unexpected in the stimulus!

We are not surprised that GDP growth slowed down, but rather, we are surprised that while the mall generated a lot of economic activity, the local economy didn't enjoy a corresponding growth.

> B. *Most of the money spent in a large shopping mall is spent by tourists who are drawn specifically by the mall and who would not have visited the community had that mall not been built.*

So most of the income comes from the outside, that's good. The mall has helped the local economy receive an injection of tourist dollars. Money is coming in. But why is the local economy languishing?

> C. *Most of the jobs created by large shopping malls are filled by people who recently moved to the community and who would not have moved had there been no job offer in the community.*

So the new jobs created by the mall weren't taken by locals. Did the locals stay in their old jobs? Did they lose their jobs? The people who moved into the community to take up jobs, did they spend in the community or simply transfer all their money away? There are too many unknowns with this answer choice. We can potentially make it work, but in doing so we have to fill in so much extra untenable speculation.

> D. *Most of the money spent in a large shopping mall is money that would have been spent elsewhere in the same community had that mall not been built.*

This answer is saying that the mall siphoned off money that would have been spent elsewhere in the community. Instead of making purchases at your local grocery store, you now opt to go to Whole Foods at the mall. So the increase in money being spent at the mall is actually matched by a decrease elsewhere in the community.

This is not exactly what we anticipated, but it's similar. We were looking for an answer that told us the mall had taken away from the local community. This is the correct answer.

> E. *Most of the jobs created by the construction of a large shopping mall are temporary, and most of the permanent jobs created are low paying.*

This answer is similar to A. It's talking about a temporal relationship. So before the mall's construction finished, there was a boost to the GDP. This doesn't really matter as we know that the mall, even when it became operational, still generated a lot of economic activity.

So the jobs generated by permanent jobs are low paying. But these are new jobs, even if they are low paying, it should still represent a net increase in total economic activity. We need an answer that tells us *why* economic activity in the community outside the mall had in fact *decreased*.

***

If we didn't have a clear anticipatory answer in the previous question, we could have easily been led astray by any of the answers. **It is human nature to try to fit the answer choices to the stimulus as we are trying to understand its meaning, so with unclear answers, we can often subconsciously bring in our own assumptions and biases.** This is something even more evident in Reading Comprehension Questions than here, but one of the best ways to fight it is to have a more defined idea of what we are looking for. In order to do that we need to practice predicting answers whenever possible.

But sometimes even our best efforts at correct answer prediction falls short. The correct answer may be something that we totally didn't expect. Take a look at the following question:

PT71 S1 Q20

Adjusted for inflation, the income earned from wool sales by a certain family of Australian sheep farmers grew substantially during the period from 1840 to 1860. This is because the price of wool sold on the international market was higher than the price paid on domestic markets and the percentage and amount of its wool that this family sold internationally increased dramatically during that period. But even though the family generated more income from selling their wool, they failed to enjoy a commensurate increase in prosperity.

Which one of the following would, if true, help most to resolve the apparent paradox described above?

A. At the end of the 1800s, prices in general in Australia rose more rapidly than did the wholesale price of wool sold domestically.
B. The prices of wool sold to domestic markets by Australian sheep farmers decreased dramatically during the period in question.
C. The international and domestic prices for mutton, sheepskins, and certain other products produced by all Australian sheep farmers fell sharply during the period in question.
D. Competition in wool sales increased during the period in question, leaving Australian wool producers in a less favorable position than previously.
E. Among Australian sheep farmers, the percentage who made their living exclusively from international wool sales increased significantly during the period in question.

So the income earned from wool sales increased. The family should be making more money, right?

Wool prices internationally increased, and the family is selling more and more on the international market.

- Expectation: *the family's income from wool increased.*
- Reality: *they failed to enjoy a commensurate increase in prosperity.*

"Commensurate" just means "corresponding," so there was no similar increase in prosperity even though their income from wool sales increased.

"Prosperity" is a rather vague word, I assume it just means the family's standard of living didn't increase in step with their growing income.

How could that be? We can eliminate rising costs of living right off the bat. The stimulus stated that the increase in income was adjusted for inflation, so even if the cost of living was increasing, their income grew faster.

Perhaps their expenses are piling up? Perhaps they had to service a high interest debt that they took out to buy the sheep in the first place? Perhaps the family started drinking and gambling? We are looking for an answer that tells us *even though they are making more money from wool, their lives are not getting better.*

   A. At the <u>end</u> of the 1800s, <u>prices in general</u> in Australia rose more rapidly than did the wholesale price of wool sold <u>domestically.</u>

There's three things wrong with this answer choice. In the first place, the timing is wrong. The stimulus is talking about the mid-century, this is talking about the end of the nineteenth century.

Secondly, this answer is talking about an increase in prices in general (AKA inflation), but we already know that income grew even adjusted for inflation.

Lastly, inflation is compared to the price of wool sold domestically. But the family sold most of their wool on the international market.

So if we take this answer at face value, international price > inflation > domestic price. The family's main revenue stream is from international sales. This answer choice side-steps that issue.

   B. The prices of wool sold to <u>domestic</u> markets by Australian sheep farmers decreased dramatically during the period in question.

Again, this is irrelevant to the family in question. Their income increased, and they sold to the international market.

   C. The international and domestic prices for mutton, sheepskins, and certain other products produced by all Australian sheep farmers fell sharply during the period in question.

This was not the answer that we anticipated, but ask yourself, what would happen if the prices for other products decreased?

Well I suppose that depends on what proportion of the family's total income is derived from wool sales, and what percentage is derived from these other products.

But this *could* explain why even though income from wool went up, their living standards didn't go up: their other revenue streams dried up, so their total income either stagnated or even dropped.

Normally, we prefer answer choices that offer a definitive explanation of why things turned out the way they did. This answer, unfortunately, is open to interpretation. What if this family does not sell mutton, sheepskins and other sheep related products? **But then again, imperfect answer choices are okay as long as they are better than the rest.**

> D. *Competition in wool sales increased during the period in question, leaving Australian wool producers in a less favorable position than previously.*

This answer choice contradicts what we already know from the stimulus. Remember how at the very beginning of the chapter we explicitly mentioned that the correct answer will explain reality **without** contradicting the information already given to us?

Australian wool producers suffered due to competition, but not this family, their income from wool sales increased.

> E. *Among Australian sheep farmers, the percentage who made their living exclusively from international wool sales increased significantly during the period in question.*

So more people started focusing on the international market, but why did this family, which is making good money, not enjoying a better life?

The correct answer is C.

As we saw in this question, sometimes the actual correct answer doesn't fully match our anticipated answer. Whenever we come across an answer choice whose implication is unclear at first, it's crucial to try to make the connection between such an answer choice and the *exact result* we are trying to explain. If this answer is true, does it provide an explanation for our unexpected reality?

So again, the habit of RANKING answers comes into play. In more recent PTs, the difference between the correct answer choice and the wrong answers are not so black and white anymore.

Take a look at 78-3-16 and 83-1-10 for additional practice. When looking over the answer choices, think of your job as finding the best answer, rather than the one correct answer.

***

Tempting Wrong Answers

So far, we have stressed the importance of properly locating the Expectation and the Reality in the stimulus, to avoid the traps common in more complex stimuli, and to always try to anticipate the answer.

For me personally, the trickiest thing about Explain Questions after you have gained some familiarity with them are the wrong answer choices. There are **two** categories of wrong answer choices that can be especially tricky, some of which we have already seen.

Let's go back to our initial hypothetical:

John lives across the street from his office and walks to the office. He doesn't own a car. John is usually never late, but he was late this morning.

Take a look at the following answer choices, what's wrong with them?

John deliberately chose an apartment close to work because he knew how congested traffic is in the mornings.

John has been working two jobs since last year and as a result can't wake up on time in the mornings and misses work.

Common Trap Answer #1: Answers that explain something other than the actual result/reality, or out-of-scope answers

The first answer, "John deliberately chose an apartment close to work…" doesn't explain why he was late this morning. It is explaining something, namely why he lives across the street. Similarly, if an answer choice had said "John likes to be the first person in the office because he is more productive when it's all quiet" would explain why he is usually never late, but still wouldn't tell us why he was late this morning.

Answers choices that seem to explain something can be tempting. We are looking for explanations, and we automatically lean towards answers that offer a potential explanation. But we must also make sure the answer choice we are looking at is in fact explaining Reality, or what had actually happened. Know exactly what it is that we are trying to find a cause for.

Common Trap Answer #2: Answers that contradict pre-existing information given to us in the stimulus

The second answer, "John has to work two jobs…" is also explanatory, it seems to be explaining why he was late, but be careful! Our hypothetical tells us that John is usually on time. This answer tells us that he can't wake up on time. This is contradictory to the pre-existing information given to us in the stimulus. If John was always late, this answer would work, but we know that he isn't. John is usually never late, but this answer tells us that he sleeps in and misses work.

We have already seen this type of wrong answer choice several times.

If an answer choice brings in information that contradicts the stimulus, it will be wrong.

Let's look at a few more questions.

PT29 S4 Q19

In the decade from the mid 1980s to the mid 1990s, large corporations were rocked by mergers, reengineering, and downsizing. These events significantly undermined employees' job security. Surprisingly, however, employees' perception of their own job security hardly changed over that period. Fifty-eight percent of employees surveyed in 1984 and 55 percent surveyed in 1994 stated that their own jobs were very secure.

Each of the following contributes to an explanation of the surprising survey results described above EXCEPT:

    A. A large number of the people in both surveys work in small companies that were not affected by mergers, reengineering, and downsizing.
    B. Employees who feel secure in their jobs tend to think that the jobs of others are secure.
    C. The corporate downsizing that took place during this period had been widely anticipated for several years before the mid 1980s.
    D. Most of the major downsizing during this period was completed within a year after the survey.
    E. In the mid 1990s, people were generally more optimistic about their lives, even in the face of hardship, than they were a decade before.

This is an Except Question, meaning that out of the five answer choices, four answer choices will actually provide a valid explanation. One answer choice, on the other hand, will not. So we are actually looking for an "incorrect" answer.

What is our expectation in this stimulus? There were a lot of mergers, reengineering, and downsizing during the eighties and nineties. Employee job security was influenced.

- Expectation: *Employees should really be worried about their jobs.*
- Reality/What actually happened: A survey conducted in 1984 (just before the downsizing) was compared to a survey conducted in 1994 (after the downsizing), and *a similar percentage of employees felt secure in their own jobs.*

What are some of the ways we can explain this discrepancy?

Maybe the survey is flawed? Maybe the people being interviewed are two different groups of people? Maybe in 1984 no one expected to be fired, and in 1994 the people being surveyed were the people who escaped getting fired?

A. *A large number of the people in both surveys work in small companies that were not affected by mergers, reengineering, and downsizing.*

This would explain why the surveys didn't reflect the increased sense of insecurity. The surveys covered a lot of small businesses, whereas the firing and mergers occurred in larger companies.

B. *Employees who feel secure in their jobs tend to think that the jobs of others are secure.*

What is the unexpected reality that we are trying to explain? Why employees felt secure about *their own* job security.

Feeling secure about your own job makes you think others' jobs are secure too. But why are you feeling secure about your own job in the first place? The answer choice does not answer that.

This answer doesn't explain the reality we need, always be aware of the **exact issue** with which we are concerned.

C. *The corporate downsizing that took place during this period had been widely anticipated for several years before the mid 1980s.*

With wide anticipation, then perhaps the sense of job insecurity already started before 1984? So the 58% in 1984 already reflects a lower sense of job security. Perhaps it was 80% in 1979.

D. *Most of the major downsizing during this period was completed within a year after the survey.*

Which survey are we talking about? Since the two surveys were used to gauge the "before and after" effects of the downsizing, the actual downsizing itself must have happened after 1984 and before 1994.

So according to this answer, the downsizing happened in 1985. Which means that when the second survey happened, 9 years had passed. Any sense of insecurity has worn off by then, and that's why the sentiments reflected by the two surveys did not change significantly.

E. *In the mid 1990s, people were generally more optimistic about their lives, even in the face of hardship, than they were a decade before.*

So this would also explain why sentiments were relatively unaffected. People were more resilient in the mid 1990s. So even after having lost their jobs, they remained more optimistic.

The correct answer is B.

*****

PT53 S3 Q22

A recent survey indicates that the average number of books read annually per capita has declined in each of the last three years. However, it also found that most bookstores reported increased profits during the same period.

Each of the following, if true, helps to resolve the survey's apparently paradoxical results EXCEPT:

    A. Recent cutbacks in government spending have forced public libraries to purchase fewer popular contemporary novels.
    B. Due to the installation of sophisticated new antitheft equipment, the recent increase in shoplifting that has hit most retail businesses has left bookstores largely unaffected.
    C. Over the past few years many bookstores have capitalized on the lucrative coffee industry by installing coffee bars.
    D. Bookstore owners reported a general shift away from the sale of inexpensive paperback novels and toward the sale of lucrative hardback books.
    E. Citing a lack of free time, many survey respondents indicated that they had canceled magazine subscriptions in favor of purchasing individual issues at bookstores when time permits.

So the number of books read per capita (that means the number of books per person) has been in decline. But bookstores have posted increased profits.

- Expectation: people are reading less books so bookstores should be making less money.
- Reality: Bookstores have increased profits. (Either increased revenue, less cost, or both)

We can think of several ways to explain this: perhaps bookstores have reduced their physical footprint and closed down a lot of locations, selling more online and thereby saving money; perhaps bookstores are selling more magazines or videogames or other products that generate a lot of additional revenue stream. In other words, something that tells us that even though people are reading less books, bookstores are still making good money.

   A. *Recent cutbacks in government spending have forced* <u>public libraries</u> *to purchase fewer popular contemporary novels.*

What happens when public libraries purchase fewer popular novels? Readers have to turn to alternative places to get the books. They may be forced to buy these books. Even though people are reading fewer books, the really popular books are selling better than ever. This can explain why bookstores' profits have increased

   B. *Due to the installation of sophisticated new antitheft equipment, the recent increase in shoplifting that has hit most retail businesses has left bookstores largely unaffected.*

This is tricky. So if a lot of books were stolen, what would happen to the bookstores' bottom line? They would have to post losses which means a decrease in revenue and profits.

If books were not stolen, then their profits would not be affected. But it wouldn't necessarily rise. Think about it. If you started a business, and your computer was stolen, you would be losing money. But if your computer was not stolen, have you made extra money?

The only way this answer would work is if the losses have been continuous and long running, and with the installation of new equipment, they no longer have any losses. But this is not the case. The wave of shoplifting was a recent phenomenon.

This answer doesn't explain what we need explained. We need to explain why profits rose (why bookstores are making *more* money,) this answer would only tell us why they didn't *lose* money.

Be careful of answer choices that purport to explain, except that it is explaining something else.

   C. *Over the past few years many bookstores have capitalized on the lucrative coffee industry by installing coffee bars.*

Installing coffee bars can generate additional revenue for the bookstores.

   D. *Bookstore owners reported a general shift away from the sale of inexpensive paperback novels and toward the sale of lucrative hardback books.*

More lucrative books = more profits

   E. *Citing a lack of free time, many survey respondents indicated that they had canceled magazine subscriptions in favor of purchasing individual issues at bookstores when time permits.*

Canceling a magazine subscription means that more people are going to bookstores to buy magazines, increasing another source of revenue for the bookstores.

Answer choices A and E, while weak, can still explain why bookstores' profits have increased. B, on the other hand, is explaining a separate issue. <u>B is the correct answer.</u>

<u>PT1 S3 Q18</u>

In the United States proven oil reserves – the amount of oil considered extractable from known fields – are at the same level as they were ten years ago. Yet over this same period no new oil fields of any consequence have been discovered, and the annual consumption of domestically produced oil has increased.

Which one of the following, if true, best reconciles the discrepancy described above?

A. Over the past decade the annual consumption of imported oil has increased more rapidly than that of domestic oil in the United States.

B. Conservation measures have lowered the rate of growth of domestic oil consumption from what it was a decade ago.

C. Oil exploration in the United States has slowed due to increased concern over the environmental impact of such exploration.

D. The price of domestically produced oil has fallen substantially over the past decade.

E. Due to technological advances over the last decade, much oil previously considered unextractable is now considered extractable.

So no new oil fields have been discovered, and domestic oil consumption has increased.

If the total amount of oil available did not increase, and domestic consumption increased, the total amount of oil available should be decreasing, right?

So our Expectation should be that *oil reserves are decreasing.*

But what happens in reality?

In reality *there had been no change in oil reserves.*

How could this be? Normally we'd say that new oil fields were discovered, but this has been ruled out by the stimulus.

I found it rather difficult to come up with a potential explanation, so let's go straight to the answer choices.

A. *Over the past decade the annual consumption of imported oil has increased more rapidly than that of domestic oil in the United States.*

So there is a greater increase in international oil, ok. Some students read this answer and get misled into thinking that it's because we now use imported oil so domestic oil has been saved. But they forget that the stimulus also tells us domestic oil consumption has also been increasing as well!

This answer choice can't possibly explain why oil reserves stayed the same without **contradicting** the stimulus.

B. *Conservation measures have lowered the rate of growth of domestic oil consumption from what it was a decade ago.*

Again, domestic oil consumption has been lowered, but still increasing. It doesn't mean it has stopped. We know that it's growing still, albeit at a slower rate.

If we tried to follow this answer and argue that conservation measures have stopped domestic oil consumption, leading to oil reserves maintaining at the same level, it would **contradict** what we already know from the stimulus.

C. *Oil exploration in the United States has slowed due to increased concern over the environmental impact of such exploration.*

This answer is explaining why no new oil fields have been discovered. That's not what we are trying to explain.

D. *The price of domestically produced oil has fallen substantially over the past decade.*

If the price is falling, perhaps production and demand are down? We don't know for sure. But consumption is still increasing. So this answer doesn't have an effect.

E. *Due to technological advances over the last decade, much oil previously considered unextractable is now considered extractable.*

So we can extract more oil from shale, for example. So what does that mean? We know that "extractable" oil has stayed the same while domestic oil consumption has increased. This answer tells us that even though oil reserves have stayed the same and no new oil fields have been discovered, the consumption of this oil has been replenished by getting more oil from existing oil fields.

This would explain why there had been no change in oil reserves. <u>E is the correct answer.</u>

***

Let's look at one more question with a very attractive trap answer, think about whether each answer choice is out of scope, or contradicting given information?

<u>PT90 S3 Q12</u>

The only effective check on grass and brush fires is rain. If the level of rainfall is below normal for an extended period of time, then there are many more such fires. Yet grass and brush fires cause less financial damage overall during long periods of severe drought than during periods of relatively normal rainfall.

Which one of the following, if true, would most help to resolve the apparent paradox described above?

A. Fire departments tend to receive less funding during periods of severe drought than during periods of normal rainfall.
B. Areas subject to grass and brush fires tend to be less densely populated than areas where there are few such fires.
C. Unusually large, hard to control grass and brush fires typically occur only when there is a large amount of vegetation for them to consume.
D. Grass and brush fires that are not caused by human negligence or arson tend to be started by lightning.
E. When vegetation is destroyed in a grass or brush fire, it tends to be replaced naturally by vegetation that is equally if not more flammable.

In the stimulus, we are told that when there is less rain, there are more fires. Conversely, when there is more rain, there are less fires. All good and simple.

So we should expect that *less fires cause less damage, so when there is more rain, the level of damage should be less*, right?

Not quite. The reality is that fires cause more damage when there is more rain. In other words:

More Rain ~ Less Fires ~ MORE damage

Less Rain ~ More Fires ~ LESS damage

How is this possible? Why would fires cause more damage when their frequency is lower?

One thing that came to mind was the possibility that during the dry season, you get a whole bunch of small fires; whereas during normal weather, you can get one or two big fires, which causes significantly more damage.

It's like the case with earthquakes, if a place is constantly getting a whole bunch of small earthquakes, then the buildings and protocols are probably in place to prevent a lot of unnecessary damage. Tokyo, for instance, has really advanced earthquake proof buildings. But if the occurrence of earthquakes are rarer, then people might be more careless, and when "the big one" hits, there's going to be a lot more damage.

It's also important to note that in this question, we are comparing times when the rain is normal vs. when the rain is scarcer. So rather than comparing two different locations, it seems more likely that we are comparing the same locale but during different times. So a better explanation would be that during the dry season, the fire department is on higher alert for fires and have a faster response time; whereas during the normal season, perhaps the fire department becomes more careless or devotes its limited resources to other areas.

> A.   Fire departments tend to receive less funding during periods of severe drought than during periods of normal rainfall.

This doesn't explain our actual reality. According to this answer, during droughts fire departments have less funding, so the damage should be more severe during droughts, rather than during normal rainfall.

> B.   Areas subject to grass and brush fires tend to be less densely populated than areas where there are few such fires.

So areas with more fires (forests in California, for example) are less densely populated than areas with less fires (e.g. Manhattan).

So areas with more fires suffer less financial damage than areas with less fires.

This could potentially work. But remember the exact wording/scope of our actual reality? The stimulus tells us that less damage is caused during periods of drought than during periods of normal rainfall. In other words, more damage is caused in Californian forest during normal rainfall than during a drought.

This answer would explain the discrepancy between two different locations, but what we are really trying to explain is the discrepancy during two different seasons.

> C.   Unusually large, hard to control grass and brush fires typically occur only when there is a large amount of vegetation for them to consume.

When is there a large amount of vegetation? Probably during periods of normal rainfall. So in other words, during droughts you get a whole bunch of really small fires which are easily put out. But during the normal season, you don't get as many fires, but you end up with massive blazes which causes significant damage.

This answer is a more direct explanation for the scenario we are faced with.

> D. *Grass and brush fires that are not caused by human negligence or arson tend to be started by lightning.*

This answer is irrelevant. It tells us the three causes for grass and brush fires. But why would fires cause more damage when there is more rain?

> E. *When vegetation is destroyed in a grass or brush fire, it tends to be replaced naturally by vegetation that is equally if not more flammable.*

This answer tells us that after each fire, the likelihood of another fire increases. So during the dry season, the number of fires should increase exponentially, right? It doesn't really explain why less fires end up causing more damage.

The correct answer is C.

***

This question is a perfect illustration of the need not only to rank our answer choices, **but to also really focus on the wording/scope of the result that we are trying to explain.** Answer choices that seems to be explaining the paradox but are really explaining a different situation need to be avoided.

Whenever you are unsure, go back to the stimulus and carefully read the part describing what actually happened. Ask yourself if the answer choice selected really explain this exact situation, or merely something related.

Take a look at 78-1-17 and 83-1-19, really focus on the wording of the result that we are trying to explain, and eliminate the **out of scope** answer choices.

Finally, don't forget that answer choices that may seem to explain the result but actually **contradict** our stimulus can be eliminated as well. Take a look at 71-3-16 and find this trap answer.

How to Double-Check Your Answers

Throughout the book, we have consistently emphasized the importance of going back to the stimulus to check your answer. For SA Questions, we combined the chosen answer choice with the argument's premise to see if we can prove the conclusion; for NA Questions, we negated the chosen answer choice to see if it would damage the plausibility of the argument's conclusion. For MBT and MSS Questions, we went back to the stimulus to find explicit support for the answer we selected.

For Explain Questions, we also need to get into the habit of double-checking our answers. We combine the answer choice we have selected with the Expectation vs. Reality dualism found in the stimulus in the following format:

Even though, **Expectation**

Actually, **Answer Choice**

Therefore, **Reality**

I would mentally repeat these three pieces of key information back to myself, in the process making sure that the answer choice is not in conflict with our expectation, as well as actually explain why reality occurred.

21. Explain Questions

22. A Road Map to Perfection

22. A Road Map to Perfection

Revisiting the SLAKR method

By now, we have covered all the material needed to attain perfection in the Logical Reasoning section. Armed with the knowledge and habits needed to successfully navigate each question type, our goal is to practice until both our timing and accuracy have reached the desired level.

Throughout this book, we have stressed the importance of both **knowledge** and **habits**. Both can be further separated into knowledge/habits specifically relevant to a particular question type, and more generalized knowledge and habits that can be helpful across the board.

For example, ranking answers and accepting an imperfect answer when there are no better alternatives is a habit that would be helpful regardless of the question type; whereas knowing that Type I/Type II answer choices are preferable to Type III answer choices is only relevant to Strengthen/Weaken Questions.

Similarly, parsing the answer choices carefully for keywords should be a universal habit. But when we get to Necessary Assumption answer choices, we know that strong adjectives/adverbs should be something to be especially wary about.

As such, the SLAKR method offers a nearly exhaustive repertoire of tools that we can throw at the most difficult questions. Whenever you are stuck, go down the list and find what you are missing.

Structure: Does the stimulus contain an argument? If so, we will probably need to determine the author's premises and main conclusion. In regard to the question I am currently faced with, do I have to identify the premises and the conclusion; find the gap between the two; strengthen/weaken them; or match it up with an answer choice?

Logic: Does the author advance the argument via conditional or causal logic? What am I to do with this logic? Am I trying to strengthen/weaken it? Find flaws with it? Or deriving inferences from it?

Assumption: Does the author leave certain things unsaid? Are there gaps in the author's reasoning? Can I fill in the gaps with additional information to make it clearer? If we are faced with an Assumption Family question, we must focus on the main gap between the premises and the main conclusion.

Keywords: What do the nouns in the answer choices refer to? If they are abstract and vague, can we link them to an idea that appeared in the stimulus? Is the answer choice out of scope? What about the verbs, adjectives, and adverbs?

Ranking: Have I found grounds for eliminating four of the answer choices? Is the answer choice that you have chosen perfect? If there's something you still don't like about it, is it a deal breaker? Compared to the other answer choices, does it have the least number of problems? What kind of answer choices are preferred in my specific question? What kind of answer choices should I be suspicious of?

Timing and A Road Map to Perfection

Now it's time to put everything to practice. Attaining LR perfection can be achieved in three stages:

Stage I: By Type Practice

As we have seen time and time again, different question types require different things from us. How we analyze the stimulus and what kind of answer choice we prefer are drastically different for different question types.

So it's absolutely crucial that we have a clear and discrete understanding of what is asked of us for each of the seventeen question types. For example, for SA Questions, the correct answer can often be anticipated, and we have a preference for a strongly worded answer choice. For NA Questions, on the other hand, while we approach the stimulus in the same way, the correct answer is harder to anticipate, and we have a preference for weaker answer choices. To test the validity of a SA answer, we plug it back into the stimulus, and see if this answer choice, when combined with the premises, can prove the validity of the conclusion. While to test a NA answer choice, we negate it and see if it can weaken the validity of the conclusion.

If you are having trouble recalling the differences between each question type, **it helps to make a one-page outline of what our job is for different question types.** This was how I initially practiced. I would have this outline next to me as I practiced, constantly reminding myself of what I needed to do. When I have committed everything to memory, I threw away the outline.

In other words, just seeing the question in an LR question should **trigger a reaction** in us. When I see a Weaken Question, for example, my immediate reaction is this:

"Ok, Weaken Question. I will read for the argument in the stimulus, make sure I differentiate between the premises and the conclusion. Weaken answers can come in multiple forms. It's best that I find an answer choice that attacks the gap. Second best if the answer choice uses outside information to independently question the truthfulness of the conclusion. If all else fails I can accept a premise attacker as well."

"Harder Weaken Questions can also have multiple 'correct' answers, so I need to rank the answers too. Make sure I find the answer choice that is most on point and most directly attacks the author's reasoning."

Similarly, when I see a Flaw Question, even before I read the stimulus, my subconscious reaction is this:

"Hmmmm, Flaw Question. Again, read the stimulus for argument, does the author commit one of those classic fallacies? I will also need to look for causal or conditional reasoning, does it exist and is it flawed? Flaw Questions are much easier if you can figure out what the flaw is before going on to the answer choices, so let me be extra careful reading the stimulus."

When I get to the answer choices, my first thought is this:

"Flaw answers can be abstract, I gotta use the keywords here as clues as to what the heck they are saying. Also be careful of 'assumes without warrant' or 'overlook' type answer choices!"

In other words, I'm using the questions to mentally prepare myself for how to approach the stimulus and subsequent answer choices.

***

Detailed Progression of By-Type Practice:

Nearly all the high scoring students will have practiced LR questions by type. But it's not as simple as spending a few days on each question type and then moving on.

When I was tutoring students whose first language was not English, so many additional unknown variables were involved. I had to devise a more detailed, executable plan to get them to 170+. I had carefully recorded my by-type speed and accuracy rate by the time I was consistently scoring in the 175+ range. This was how I was performing on LR questions prior to my exam:

Difficulty	Time Goal	Accuracy goal before moving to the next difficulty
Level 1: Easiest	1:00	100%
Level 2: Easier	1:00	100%
Level 3: Normal	1:30	100%
Level 4: Harder	2:00	95%
Level 5: Hardest	2:00 - 3:00	90%

LR Questions can be divided into five levels of ascending difficulty. Some commercial LSAT prep websites already do this for you. I would have my students practice different question types in segments of 10, starting with the easiest level.

For example, if we are practicing Weaken Questions, I would have my students start with the easiest Weaken Questions. I would have them do 10 of these in a row. If they can get all of them correct, then we move to harder questions, so on and so forth. Once you can achieve a **winning streak** of 10 questions, it's time to move to the next difficulty!

This way of practicing will determine where your plateau is. For example, if you are unable to consistently get 10 level 3 questions right in a row, then that's where we stop and focus our efforts. The end goal is to get level 1-3 questions perfect, make one mistake every 20 questions or so in level 4 questions, and one mistake every ten questions in the hardest questions.

Of course, you should always aim for perfection, but this is a quantifiable and measurable goal that you should aim for if your goal is 170+ or even 175+.

***

By Type Timing:

The most important thing to remember is that accuracy comes before timing.

I'll say it again,

ACCURACY BEFORE TIMING

Only worry about speed when you are consistently getting questions right.

Many people have said that you cannot learn the LSAT, which is blatantly false. But the LSAT is not a content-based test. The actual material that you will see on the exam will contain information which you have never seen before. **So our job, when studying for the LSAT, is not to memorize and regurgitate information.**

This is where many students make a fatal mistake. I've had students come to me with hundreds of pages of notes. This doesn't help at all. Think about it. On the actual exam you have on average a minute or two per question, you are stressed and extremely nervous. Your brain will be foggy and you will automatically revert to whatever habits you developed during PTs. How much of those hundreds of pages of information are you going to remember?

Our job, instead, is to train our way of thinking by developing good habits. Regardless of who you are, you will fall back on old habits on the actual exam. So the only thing we can do is to make sure that we have in our repertoire only those habits that can help us get the question right.

For example, if we are consistently extracting abstract keywords from Role Question answer choices and asking ourselves what they are referring to during practice, then we will do the same thing on the exam. If we come up with the contrapositive of a conditional as soon as we find a conditional relationship in the stimulus, then we will do the same thing on the day of the test. The information contained in the stimulus and answer choices may be different, but our job is the same.

Developing good habits involve breaking old habits and brainwashing ourselves into doing things differently. This takes time and repetition. The mind is a stubborn animal. If we tried to speed things up without fully developing these good habits, we are just setting ourselves up for failure down the road. This is the single most important reason why students plateau in the 150s, 160s, or even low 170s.

So often we need to slow down in order to speed up.

But when do we know that we are ready to focus on the timing aspect? We let data do the talking. For each level of difficulty, if you are consistently getting 100% correct, or 10 out of 10, that's enough proof that you have what it takes to handle questions of this caliber.

In the table above, I have also listed my average timing for each level of difficulty when I was scoring in the 175+ range. We know that an LSAT section is 35 minutes long and will usually have 25 to 26 questions. So that's roughly 1:45 per question.

But not all LR questions are created equal. If you are spending 1:45 on the easiest question as well as the hardest question, something is seriously wrong.

Instead, we should devote the majority of our time and attention to the harder and hardest questions. There were sections where I spent 25 minutes on the first 20 questions, but there were one or two questions which took over three minutes each. Remember, we are in pursuit of perfection here.

Of course, if you attain this and there's still time left before your exam, you should keep on going. After finishing writing this book and having gone through each individual question half a dozen times on average in the past two years, either tutoring students or just analyzing the questions on my own, I'm probably averaging a minute each for levels 1-4 questions (100% accuracy rate), and 2:00 for level 5 questions (95% accuracy rate). Yes, the returns are diminishing, and I am still making mistakes and learning.

***

Differentiate Between Easier and Harder Questions

We have mentioned that commercial test prep websites will categorize LR questions in terms of difficulty for you, that makes our job a whole lot easier. But if for some reasons, you choose to go at it on your own, here is how to determine how to categorize a question in terms of its difficulty:

There are six ways in which the test makers can make an LR question harder, five of which we have already seen:

The five habits we have emphasized in this book, per our acronym SLAKR, are also five of the six areas of an LR question where the test makers can lay out traps to increase a question's difficulty. Structurally, the test makers can deliberately word the stimulus in a way so that the main conclusion is hard to differentiate from the intermediate conclusion; logically, the stimulus may contain complex conditionals or even hybrid causal/conditional reasoning. The argument may have a hard to spot gap that needs to be filled by an assumption that we must provide; answer choices may contain subtle term shifts or vague terms that must be solved by keyword analysis; and there may be multiple attractive answer choices that we must compare and contrast.

These are just some of the examples of how a difficult question may differ from an easier one. We have covered nearly all of the tricks and traps commonly seen in harder LR questions throughout the book.

One final mark of harder questions is the discussion of **esoteric topics and use of abstract language** in the stimulus. Stimuli discussing scientific or philosophical ideas can be especially challenging.

In my experience, level 4 questions usually have one or two of these traits, while level 5 (the hardest) questions usually have two or three of these. For instance, a level 4 Role Question may have a structural trap (conclusion placed in the middle of the stimulus, while the intermediate conclusion comes at the very end), as well as a correct answer choice that is stated in vague terms (2 out of 6). A level 5 Strengthen Question may have a really abstract stimulus topic, two answer choices that both strengthen the argument, and hidden causal logic. (3 out of 6)

Our goal is to be able to recognize a difficult question when it presents itself, and to treat it with the respect and attention it deserves.

Stage II: Section Practice

Once we have a deeper understanding of the traits and quirks of each question type, as well as attaining our desired accuracy and speed, it's time to move to practicing whole sections of LR questions.

There are two things to watch out for when moving from Stage I to Stage II:

***

Transitions

Because we have been only looking at one type of question at a time previously, we didn't really have to think about different types of questions in quick succession. Now that we are doing an entire section of LR questions, each question type is going to be different from the last one. So make sure to read the question and use this time to mentally prepare yourself for the question at hand. In other words, if you just finished a SA Question, stop thinking about SA Questions when you move to the next one. Start afresh with every question.

Use each question stem to mentally prepare ourselves for the question at hand. If you can't instinctively remember how to approach a certain type of question, then bringing back the **outline** can be helpful.

***

Timing

The second thing to focus on is timing. Instead of giving ourselves 10 minutes to do 10 easy questions in a row, or 20 minutes to do 10 harder questions in a row, we are now faced with about 25 questions of varying difficulty.

In general, the level of difficulty on LR questions progresses as we move through the section. Questions 1-10 are usually fairly simple and straightforward, levels 1 to 3 questions. The difficulty picks up a little around questions 12 or 13, there may be one or two level 4 or level 5 questions before question 15. From questions 16 to question 22 or 23 it's the most difficult. The majority of level 4 and level 5 questions will be in this sector. Finally, the difficulty will taper off for the last few questions, but this is not guaranteed.

22. A Road Map to Perfection

This is a general breakdown of my timing progression throughout a typical LR section:

Questions 1 - 10	Usually Fairly Easy	Aim to finish by 10-minute mark
Questions 11 - 15	Getting harder, may have one or two difficult questions	Aim to finish by 15-minute mark, but may take you 17-18 minutes
Questions 16-23	The hardest questions, proceed with caution!	Take your time with these, if you took the time to practice the hardest LR questions with two minutes per question, it shouldn't be too hard. Aim to get to question 23 when 30 minutes have passed
Questions 24-26	Varies, but can be slightly easier	Don't let your guard down, finish strong and review your work

A word of **warning**: it's been a general trend on the LSAT that the earlier questions are easier than the later ones. But as more students realize this, the test makers can just as easily switch up the difficulty. So take this with a grain of salt: the ultimate goal is still to be able to differentiate between easier and harder questions while we are doing them, and plan accordingly. Just take a look at PT94 S4 Q9 for an example of a difficult question that popped up early.

As you can see, for a high scorer, how successful you are is largely dependent on your speed and timing early on in the section. We want to power through the easier questions without too much deliberation, saving the majority of our time and energy for the hardest part of the section.

For myself, I will usually have a decent idea of how I will perform on the section by the time I get to the middle of the section. If by question 15 I have only used 15 or 16 minutes, then I will be mentally relaxed and prepared for the more difficult questions coming up.

But if I was stuck on an earlier question and by the time I reach question 15, almost 20 minutes or more have passed, then I know I will either be rushing through the hardest part in order to complete the section, probably committing careless mistakes, or I won't be able to finish the last question or two.

We want to save time early on so we can spend it later on.

Finally, there's also a subtle mental transition involved when doing an LR section. For the first half of the section, follow your instincts and habits and try not to overthink. Overthinking easier questions will lead to avoidable errors. For the second half of the section, it helps to analyze and think about each question with as much attention to detail as you can.

Stage III: PT

Two things to note when we are taking an entire Practice Test:

In the first place, make sure to mentally focus when you start an LR section. There were countless times when I came to an LR section after a LG or RC section, and my mind was still thinking about the game board or RC passage that I had struggled with. This is distracting and the worst thing you can possibly do. Before starting an LR section, mentally prepare yourself. Remind yourself that it's LR time now, remind yourself of the five key habits, and remind yourself to look at each question stem before anything else.

From there on it's no different from doing an LR section.

Secondly, because the whole test is four sections. We will be mentally drained by the end of it. When I did PTs, I focused on the endurance aspect of the test by doing 5 sections in a row. I would do an additional LR, LG, or RC section immediately after having completed the PT, depending on whichever section was my weakest link.

***

Blind Review

Perhaps the single most helpful thing we can do to improve is to blind review our work. Flag or make a note of every question that we are not 100% certain. Once we have completed the section/test, come back and re-examine these flagged questions without looking at the answers.

Blind review is helpful because it takes away the benefit of hindsight. Once we know the correct answer to a question, then we will subconsciously try to come up with ways to justify this answer, while simultaneously trying to find fault with every other answer. In other words, we cannot help but to apply a double standard to the question being reviewed.

But on the actual test itself, we do not have such a luxury. So by forcing ourselves to consider each answer choice on equal footing, without knowing which one is the correct answer, we are literally forcing ourselves to depend only on our knowledge and understanding of the question, and nothing else.

During blind review, we can spend a little more time to do a deep dive into the question itself. Slow down and conduct a thorough SLAKR analysis of the question, make a note of everything that you have missed or wasn't sure about previously.

If there are two answer choices you are stuck between. Write down the pros and cons of each answer, remind yourself of what this particular question type is asking for, and write down your rationale for picking one answer over the other.

In terms of timing, we want to gradually shorten the time we use for blind review, until ideally, you can finish blind review within the 35 minutes allotted per section.

***

Fighting Your Intuition

The social psychologist Jonathan Haidt, who developed the social intuition model in moral psychology, believes that people make moral judgments based on intuition and rationalize them afterwards. Whether or not you agree with his theory, it's something that we must avoid on the LSAT.

Too often students will pick an answer choice based on intuition. During blind review, all they try to do is to selectively look for evidence to back up their choice and eliminate the alternatives. Instead of using blind review to reaffirm our decision and feel good about ourselves, we need to re-examine each answer choice rationally and on equal footing. Using the criteria and techniques you have learned in this book, strive to compare each answer choice from a rational and holistic perspective.

***

Wrong Question Review

Finally, it's time to review the questions we have gotten wrong.

It is inevitable that we make mistakes. The important thing is to learn from our mistakes and to build up our repertoire of knowledge and habits so we won't make the same mistake again. Many students make the mistake of a localized approach to wrong question review. They will go online to look at discussions on the question, read the question again, and once they feel like they have understood this question, they move on and forget about it.

This is not enough.

Our goal, instead, should be to think about what this question can teach us. We need a takeaway from each wrong question that reveals a specific weakness in our understanding or habits.

Why did you get this question wrong? Is it because you didn't fully understand the complex conditional in the stimulus? Is it a specific flaw that you missed in a Flaw Question? Review the relevant **theoretical knowledge** that's available in this book.

Was the error committed due to a **bad habit**? Were you simply picking the first reasonable answer and then letting your guard down when examining the subsequent answer choices? Remind yourself to approach each answer choice with equal respect even if you already have a clear preference for one answer choice. Are you struggling with vague answer choices? Remind yourself to highlight or underline keywords in answer choices and really think about what they mean. Are you consistently picking probably true/could be true answers rather than must be true answers on MBT Questions? Remember to go back to the stimulus to find proof for the answer choice you had chosen.

Make a table like this and record your mistakes. But more importantly, try to find the source of your errors, whether it's an unclear understanding of the theoretical knowledge, or bad habits that need to be avoided.

PT-S-Q	Question Type	Pattern/Difficult Trait	Knowledge Insights	Bad Habits to Break

As we gather more and more wrong questions, we will see a pattern emerging. I, for example, saw that a majority of my Weaken mistakes were made when there were two or more answer choices that both 'weaken' the author's argument. I was regularly choosing Type III answer choices over Type II and Type I answer choices. This made me realize that I would need to consciously remind myself to truly compare multiple attractive answer choices, and I needed to show a clear preference for answer choices that target the gap in the author's reasoning, answers that are more direct, or answers that are worded more strongly.

Make a list of the habits that you need to develop. Print it out, keep it next to you as you practice more questions. Only when we have internalized these habits and practice them like second nature, are we truly on the path towards LR perfection.

Final Thoughts

Well, that's everything for now! I hope you have enjoyed the book and found it helpful in your LSAT journey. Analyze each question that you are unsure of, and especially the ones you get wrong. Think about the structure and logic of the argument, relevant keywords, and why one answer is better than the rest.

More importantly, learn from your mistakes. Think about the mistakes you have committed, is it due to incomplete knowledge or bad habits? Every mistake we make should be an opportunity to upgrade our understanding and habits, only then will we see continuous improvement.

My other LSAT book, **RC Perfection**, is also available on Amazon. A few chapters are available for free preview and download via my website. The book itself is divided into four sections:

- Part I: The Passage, which trains our active reading abilities and how to break down the passage structurally while noting the relevant details;

- Part II: The Questions, which looks at nearly twenty types of RC questions and how to approach them;

- Part III: The Answers, which goes over answer choice elimination and ranking; and

- Part IV: Topic Specific Strategies, which examines comparative passages and offers tactics for science, law, humanities, and arts themed passages.

My website, www.dragontest.org, offers additional resources and guides for the high-scoring student. My discord server (https://discord.com/invite/2khvCBBRbk or discord.io/lsatdragon) is a welcoming community of advanced students who regularly discuss LSAT and law school-related questions. Me and other high scoring former students will answer any LSAT related questions that you might have, free of charge. :)

I also offer LSAT tutoring in Mandarin. My Wechat Account is Lsatdragon (说中文的同学可加我微信)

Lastly, if you have any thoughts or advice on how to improve this book, or errors and mistakes that I haven't been able to detect, please send me an email. A review on Amazon would also help immensely: reviews are the only way for an aspiring author to get noticed and to sell more copies, both of which are necessary for me to continue writing.

I am currently offering a free 30 minute tutoring session via Zoom to all my readers. **After finishing the book**, simply email me a screenshot of your Amazon order and we can set up a time. If you have also finished RC Perfection, that's 60 minutes in total. I ask that you finish the book first because its more efficient this way. There will be many questions that can be answered simply by reading the rest of the material, and we can use the time to work on more niche problems.

Thank you again and very gratefully,

Joshua

LR Perfection - Appendix I

Flaw Questions Fallacies Cheat Sheet

Make sure you are aware of not just the basic tenets of each of these fallacies, but how they may manifest themselves in more difficult LR questions. (See Chapter 8 for additional information)

Also, beware of misdirection when reading the stimulus. For example, a flaw stimulus that starts off talking about a survey is not necessarily going to contain a sample flaw. It may very well be something else. Practice by trying to ID as many potential flaws in an argument as you can.

<table>
<tr><td colspan="3" align="center"><h1>21 Fallacies</h1></td></tr>
<tr>
<td>Sampling Flaw: Sample representative of the population? Flawed methodology?</td>
<td>Percentage vs. Amount: three variables (total sum, change in percentage, change in amount); you need two to derive the third.</td>
<td>Inducing future from past events: Inferring the future from the past.</td>
</tr>
<tr>
<td>Ad Hominem: Attacking source's practice, history, or motives instead of addressing their argument</td>
<td>Circular Reasoning: Premise = Conclusion; because of A, therefore A.</td>
<td>Selective Attention Fallacy: Presented with two options, arbitrarily picks one without justification.</td>
</tr>
<tr>
<td>Appeal to Authority: Does the expert bring support to their argument? Is the expert qualified on the topic discussed?</td>
<td>Self Contradiction: The author explicitly contradicts themselves, ignores contradictory evidence, or present information that leads to an inferred contradiction.</td>
<td>Relative/Absolute Confusion: Being better is not the same as good, being healthier is not the same as healthy. Beware usages of "more" and "most."</td>
</tr>
<tr>
<td>Appeal to Ignorance: Can't prove X, so X is false; or X's argument is weak, so let's automatically reject it.</td>
<td>Gambler's Fallacy: Mistakenly inferring individual occurrences from general probability. Do not confuse with Law of Large Numbers</td>
<td>False Conversion: Some, Most, All relationships and associated extrapolations. Beware of S/M/A relationships dressed up like percentages/proportions.</td>
</tr>
<tr>
<td>False Dichotomy: Choosing one out of two options when it's unknown if there are more possibilities</td>
<td>Non Sequitur: Falsely inferring a belief/view on to someone.</td>
<td>Appeal to Extremes or Slippery Slope: using unlikely cases as justification.</td>
</tr>
<tr>
<td>Fallacy of Division or Composition: Part vs. Whole, not automatically fallacious, consider on case by case basis.</td>
<td>Conditional vs. Causation: Confusing one form of logic for the other.</td>
<td>Appeal to Belief: because people believe A, A is true.</td>
</tr>
<tr>
<td>Equivocation: Using the same word in two different senses. Beware of instances where the second use is implied</td>
<td>Appeal to Probability or Possibility: Because something is probable or possible, it is true.</td>
<td>False Analogy: A and B similar in one respect, they are similar in another; or A and B dissimilar in one aspect, they are dissimilar in another.</td>
</tr>
</table>

LR Perfection - Appendix II

Recent trends in LR and traits to pay attention to (Since PT70)

Many students have complained about the sudden "rise" in difficulty in LR questions in more recent PTs. If you have read the book thoroughly, you will have realized that many of the more difficult questions have been concentrated in the 70s, and especially the 80s PTs. This is no coincidence. Correct answer choices have grown vaguer, and the certainty that once accompanied the answer choice selection process has significantly receded. The correct answer being an imperfect choice that is slightly better than the other four alternatives is a trend increasingly seen on the hardest questions, especially among the Strengthen/Weaken and MSS types.

There are subtle trends I see happening in other question types as well. Below, I've listed some of the newer difficult traits that you might encounter, categorized based on question type. Take a look at the following and go back to the relevant chapters for additional information.

Find the Conclusion Questions: Finding the answer choice that actually has support rather than going by feeling or tone of the stimulus. (Chapter 3 - Difficult Trait #1)

Role/Method Questions: Growing prevalence of the Intermediate Conclusion Trap (Chapter 4 - Difficult Trait #1), and more abstract answer choices (Chapter 6 - Difficult Trait #5).

Flaw Questions: Return of the circular and self-contradiction fallacies, false conversions, appeal to extremes, selective attention, and possible/probable fallacies. (See Chapter 8, 21 Fallacies)

Sufficient Assumption Questions: The correct answer needs to be re-combined with information from the stimulus to make sense (Chapter 10 - Difficult Trait #7); more complicated conditional linkage diagramming (Chapter 10 - Difficult Trait #4).

Necessary Assumption Questions: Conditional/strongly worded answer choices (Chapter 11 - Difficult Trait #2), multiple NAs can be derived from the stimulus (Chapter 11 - Difficult Trait #4).

Strengthen/Weaken Questions: Imperfect right answers (Chapter 13), practice ranking answers (Chapters 13, 14, 20), return of the premise boosters (Chapter 13 – III).

Principle Questions: Advanced conditionals (15 - Difficult Trait #1).

Parallel Questions: Advanced conditionals, subtle shift in conclusion language (Chapter 16 - Difficult Trait #1), order variation of statements.

MBT: Synthesis and inference type answer choices (Chapter 17 – Correct Answer Choices).

MSS: Ranking of answer choices, tricky keywords in answer choices. (Chapters 18, 19)

Point of Disagreement: Inferred disagreements (Chapter 20 – Difficult Trait #4)

Explain: Multiple contradictions in stimulus, isolate key contradiction (Chapter 21).

Made in United States
Orlando, FL
22 August 2024

50645318R20315